The Collected Essays of Arthur Miller

Arthur Miller was born in New York City in 1915. After graduating from the University of Michigan, he began work with the Federal Theatre Project. His first Broadway hit was *All My Sons*, closely followed by *Death of a Salesman*, *The Crucible* and *A View from the Bridge*. His other writing include *Focus*, a novel; *The Misfits*, first published as a short story, then as a cinema novel; *In Russia*, *In the Country*, *Chinese Encounters* (all in collaboration with his wife, photographer Inge Morath) and *'Salesman' in Beijing*, non-fiction; and his autobiography, *Timebends*, published in 1987. Among his other plays are: *Incident At Vichy*, *The Creation of the World and Other Business*, *The American Clock*, *The Last Yankee*, *Resurrection Blues* and *Finishing the Picture*. His novella, *Plain Girl*, was published in 1995 and his second collection of short stories, Presence, in 2007. He died in February 2005 aged eighty-nine.

Matthew Roudané is Regents' Professor of English at Georgia State University. He specializes in American drama, modern drama and American literature.

The Collected Essays of Arthur Miller

Introduction by Matthew Roudané

Bloomsbury Methuen Drama
An imprint of Bloomsbury Publishing Plc

BLOOMSBURY

LONDON · OXFORD · NEW YORK · NEW DELHI · SYDNEY

Bloomsbury Methuen Drama
An imprint of Bloomsbury Publishing Plc

Imprint previously known as Methuen Drama

50 Bedford Square
London
WC1B 3DP
UK

1385 Broadway
New York
NY 10018
USA

www.bloomsbury.com

THE COLLECTED ESSAYS OF ARTHUR MILLER comprising:

ECHOES DOWN TIIE CORRIDOR
Edited by Steven R. Centola
First published in 2000 by Methuen Publishing Ltd

First published in the United States by Viking Penguin, a member of Penguin Putnam Inc.

THE THEATER ESSAYS OF ARTHUR MILLER
Edited by Robert A. Martin and Steven R. Centola
First published in the United States in 1978 by The Viking Press
Published in a revised edition by Da Capo Press in 1996

Interviews by Matthew Roudané, Christopher Bigsby and Janet Balakian are
reprinted with the kind permission of the interviewers

Published by Bloomsbury Methuen Drama as
THE COLLECTED ESSAYS OF ARTHUR MILLER 2015

British Library Cataloguing-in-Publication Data
A catalogue record for this book is available from the British Library.

ISBN: HB: 978-1-4725-9174-6
        ePDF: 978-1-4725-9176-0
        ePub: 978-1-4725-9175-3

Typeset by RefineCatch Limited, Bungay, Suffolk
Printed and bound in Great Britain

Contents

Essays: 1962–1970

Essays: 1972–1980

Essays: 1982–1990

Acknowledgements

Thanks to the following colleagues and friends who gave me valuable advice while developing this project: Susan Abboston, Susan Ashely, Anna Barattin, Christopher Bigsby, Jane Dominick, William Long, Randy Malamud, Stephen Marino, Brenda Murphy, June Schlueter and Carol Winkler. A special thanks to my editor in London who worked with me on every step of this project, Anna Brewer. Thanks, too, to the late Robert A. Martin and Steven R. Centola, both of whom I knew and whose earlier work on Miller paved the way for this volume. And, finally, thanks to the late Arthur Miller, who first welcomed me into his home in 1983 and whose conversations I enjoyed over the years.

Matthew C. Roudané

Introduction

Arthur Miller remains one of the greatest playwrights of the contemporary stage. Indeed, from *All My Sons* (1947), *Death of a Salesman* (1949), and *The Crucible* (1953) through *Broken Glass* (1994), *Resurrection Blues* (2002), and the last play of an illustrious career, *Finishing the Picture* (2004), Miller's plays spotlight selected public issues of a nation as reflected through the private anxieties of the individual. This public/private dialectic informs his entire oeuvre. His work continues to attract global audiences, for his plays have been staged in such countries as the United States, Canada, Great Britain, Spain, France, Italy, the former Soviet Union, India, Germany, Greece, Japan, Chile, China, Israel, and, among many others, South Korea. In honor of the 2015 Miller centennial, there is a year-long celebration of his work—in Costa Rica. *Death of a Salesman*, alone, "has been produced on six continents, in every country that has a Western theatrical tradition, and in some that have not."[1] Plays first staged decades ago remain as fresh today as when *Death of a Salesman* made its epochal debut on February 10, 1949, at the Morosco Theatre in New York City. And ten years after his death, in April 2015, The Library of America published *Arthur Miller: Collected Plays 1987-2004 with Stage and Radio Plays of the 1930s & 40s*, a volume that contains what Tony Kushner calls the "Early Plays" and "Radio Plays" that have been previously unpublished.[2] An indefatigable artist, Miller wrote dozens of plays, radio plays, screenplays, works of fiction, an autobiography, and non-fiction.

Included among those works of non-fiction are an astonishing number of essays. These essays, a significant number of which are included in this volume, reveal much about the playwright's dramatic theory and practise, his political stance, and his moral optimism. Like his plays, these essays provide a clear idea of Miller's world view. In a sense these essays give readers a portrait of two Arthur Millers: the Arthur Miller as a playwright of genuine originality and immense theatrical power, and the Arthur Miller as an engaged and engaging public intellectual. Miller is nowhere better seen as that public intellectual than in his remarkable essays spanning nearly seven decades. As Robert A. Martin wrote in *The Theater Essays of Arthur Miller*, it is through his "essays that Miller speaks most directly of his social and dramatic convictions, and of his craftsmanship as a playwright; they comprise a body of critical commentary that is both distinguished and significant in the history of American drama and culture. Collectively, Arthur Miller's essays on drama and the theater may well represent the single most important statement of critical principles to appear in England and America by a major playwright since the Prefaces of George Bernard Shaw."[3] Although Martin registered these observations in 1977, such remarks remain accurate as we celebrate the centennial of Arthur Miller.

And so the title of this book suggests its scope and emphasis: *The Collected Essays of Arthur Miller* is a selected gathering of Miller's essays—and a few of the many interviews he granted over the years—drawn from two sources: *The Theater Essays of Arthur Miller* (1996), edited by Robert A. Martin and Steven R. Centola in their revised and expanded version of Martin's origin volume of the same title published in 1978; and *Echoes Down the Corridor: Collected Essays, 1944-2000* (2000), edited by Steven R. Centola. Within these two volumes, we see, Miller wrote nearly 90 essays totaling nearly 900 pages. To be sure, Miller wrote other essays not included in Martin and Centola's collection, but the ones included are representative of some of his best, and at times most provocative, pieces of non-fiction. The essays included also complement many of the key themes found in the plays. Those essays from Martin and Centola's *Theater Essays* and Centola's *Echoes Down the Corridor*, combined in one new volume and arranged chronologically, constitute *The Collected Essays of Arthur Miller*. My hope is this collection will make it easier to read the theater essays in a single volume—for both theatergoers long familiar with Miller's work and a new generation of theatergoers perhaps discovering Miller for the first time.

Impressive as the sheer quantity of all this work may be, however, the quality of thought and vigorous yet clear style within Miller's reflections stand out. His essays reveal his passionate commitment to social justice and human rights, his life-long civic engagement with national and international politics, and his unwavering commitment to the various ways in which his theater and essays capture something of the sweep and play of a nation thinking, or not thinking, in front of itself. His essays cover a wide range of subjects, from defending a famous dissident writer from abroad, a local teenager falsely accused of murder, to a President of the United States. As Tony Kushner remarked at Miller's memorial service held at the Majestic Theater on May 9, 2005 in New York City, "If Arthur's Emersonian temperament saved him from the terrible mistakes of the doctrinaire left of his time, if his habits of scrupulousness and independence carried him into a healthy, immensely vital skepticism, if he refused partisanship, he also never ceased in reminding us of his indebtedness to, indeed affinity with, the left, with progressive thought. He never became a cynic, or a nihilist, or an ego-anarchist, or a despoiler of humanist utopian dreams, or a neocon. His great personal courage and his graceful confidence in his stature and talents made it unnecessary for him to cuddle up to power elites, allowed him to retain his sympathy, his affinity for the disinherited, the marginal and the powerless. He never wanted us to forget that without economic justice, the concept of social justice is an absurdity and, worse, a lie."[4]

Miller began writing essays while a student at the University of Michigan in the 1930s. However, it was his "Tragedy and the Common Man" (1949) article in *The New York Times* that signaled the beginning of the playwright's commitment to composing essays about the theater, politics, world affairs, and what it means to be a citizen in a post-World War II cosmos. The moral seriousness embedded in his plays, we see, reveals itself in the collected essays as well: "Now, if it is true that tragedy is the consequence of a man's total compulsion to evaluate himself justly, his destruction in the attempt posits a wrong or an evil in his environment. And this is precisely the morality of tragedy and its lesson. The discovery of the moral law, which is what the enlightenment of tragedy consists of, is not the discovery of some abstract or metaphysical quantity."[5] This from a 34-year-old whose Willy Loman first graced the stage but 17 days earlier. Miller would continue to write passionately about the theater and world affairs into the twenty-first century, the last essay in this volume, "Subsidized Theatre" (2000), appearing when the playwright was the same age as Dave Singleman from *Death of a Salesman*—84-years-old.

An essayist of great range, Miller sometimes writes deeply personal works, such as "A Boy Grew in Brooklyn," (1955) and "Thoughts on a Burned House" (1984). "Burned House," for instance, provides readers with a better sense of the man behind the art, as when his daughter called Miller and Inge Morath in China with the shocking news that their home partially went up in flames. At other times he becomes a literary critic of sorts, as in "Tennessee Williams's Legacy: An Eloquence and Amplitude of Feeling" (1984) and "On Mark Twain's Chapters from *My Autobiography*" (1996). Miller displays an impressive command of his fellow literary artists, the modernist temper, and in a prose style that is most accessible. A versatile writer, he sometimes displays humor, wit, and satire, as in "A Modest Proposal for the Pacification of the Public Temper" (1954), "Get It Right: Privatize Executions" (1992), and "Let's Privatize Congress" (1995).

His sense of the comedic informs these particular essays, even as he tackles serious subjects. At other times Miller emerges as an insightful political observer, as evident in "The Battle of Chicago: From the Delegates' Side" (1968), "The Limited Hang-Out: The Dialogues of Richard Nixon as a Drama of the Antihero" (1974), and "Clinton in Salem" (1998). These overtly political essays show a writer committed to democratic principles and ideals in a world fraught with opportunistic partisanship. As Steven R. Centola notes, "Nothing escapes Miller's piercing scrutiny as he discusses such subjects as the Holocaust, the Nazi War Crimes Trials, the Great Depression, the Cold War, McCarthyism, the Vietnam War, anti-Semitism, censorship, juvenile delinquency, the Watergate scandal, capital punishment, and the oppression of dissident writers in foreign countries, in an effort to understand the sources of human misery and conflict in the twentieth century. In one memorable essay after another, he captures the frenzied spirit of a schizophrenic age and records poignant observations on the political unrest and moral decline rampant in this century."[6]

Indeed, reading Miller's essays in this volume is, in a sense, reading an ongoing narrative history of modern America and, indeed, the modern world. This was a person who, after all, was born in1915 during World War I, as a teenager watched as his parents—and the vast majority of Americans—lost most of their savings during the 1929 stock market crash, endured as a young man the Great Depression in the 1930s and lived through the unprecedented horrors of the Holocaust and the advent of the nuclear age in the 1940s. A writer who eschewed the lure of Hollywood in the 1950s, he found himself at the very epicenter of that glamorous world when he married Marilyn Monroe in 1956, the very year he was brought before the House Un-American Activities Committee, refused to name names, and was convicted of contempt of Congress and sentenced to a one-month suspended jail time and fined $500.

By the time Miller returned to Broadway with his play *After the Fall*, in 1964, the Beatles, the Rolling Stones, and Bob Dylan mesmerized Great Britain and the United States. Four years later, in 1968, he campaigned for Democratic presidential candidate Eugene McCarthy and, as a delegate from Roxbury, CT, traveled to Chicago to witness the Democratic Party convention. In 1968 Miller visited the Soviet Union and Czechoslovakia while his play *The Price,* which had premiered on Broadway in February, opened in Tel Aviv, Israel. Miller lived through, and protested against, the Vietnam War, lived through the Watergate scandal and watched a President resign in August of 1974. In the 1980s he directed *Death of a Salesman* in Beijing, China, and in the 1990s, while staging several new plays, he read and wrote about the Bill Clinton/ Monica Lewinsky scandal. A major voice in contemporary theater and politics, he remained a significant force well into the earlier twenty-first century. During the last decades of his long life, he emerged as the elder statesman of the American stage, and by the time he died on February 10, 2005, in Roxbury, Connecticut, Arthur Miller was rightfully regarded as one of America's and, indeed, the world's most inventive and exemplary literary figures.

Many of the essays contained in this volume dovetail with key themes long associated with the plays. The playwright seems entranced by the primal family unit and its combative yet loving members. In his exploration of the family, Miller dramatizes questions of heredity and genetics, biology and spirituality, social responsibility and individual duty—and the various ways in which family members psychologically spar with love and each other. This also allows Miller, as seen in "On Social Plays" (1955), to explore the tragic: "It is a world in which the human being can live as a naturally political, naturally private, naturally engaged person, a world in which once again a true tragic victory may be scored." [7] Miller consistently explores such subjects, although, as in his play *After the Fall* (1964), for instance, they often take shape in the more personal quests on which his protagonists embark. Debates between the Self and the Other, often set in a social world of diminished possibilities, animate the stage.

The myth of the American Dream, too, emerges as a central force in his work. This myth is implicit in the "Introduction to the *Collected Plays*" (1957) essay and in all of his plays. As Miller explained in one of the interviews in this volume:

The American Dream is the largely unacknowledged screen in front of which all American writing plays itself out—the screen of the perfectibility of man. Whoever is writing in the United State is using the American Dream as an ironical pole of his story. Early on we all drink up certain claims to self-perfection that are absent in a large part of the world. People elsewhere tend to accept, to a far greater degree anyway, that the conditions of life are hostile to man's pretensions. The American idea is different in the sense that we think that if we could only touch it, and live by it, there's a natural order in favor of us; and that the object of a good life is to get connected with that live and abundant order. And this forms a context of irony for the kinds of stories we generally tell each other. After all, the stories of most significant literary works are of one or another kind of failure. And it's a failure in relation to that screen, that backdrop. I think it pervades American writing, including my own. It's there in *The Crucible,* in *All My Sons,* in *After the Fall*—an aspiration to an innocence that when defeated or frustrated can turn quite murderous, and we don't know what to do with this perversity; it never seems to "fit" us. [8]

Beyond the myth of the America Dream are many other issues, such as free will, the truth, choice, betrayal, illusions, tragedy, and ethical accountability that come into play as his characters' decisions affect both the public and private worlds they inhabit. Such issues often reveal themselves in Miller's theater essays and prefaces as well. In both the plays and in essays questions of justice—social, economic, legal, moral—underpin his works. In nearly all of the essays addressing his plays directly, Miller discusses these issues, as in "Guilt and *Incident at Vichy*," to cite but one example. Christopher Bigsby suggests "that he has charted so accurately the shifting mood of his times has, indeed, made him a kind of moral historian to whom we can look for understanding of the chaos that so often seems to confront us."[9]

In reading his theater essays, prefaces, and interviews in this volume, then, we get a revealing sense of the man and his theatrical and political ideals. For decades, Miller's non-fiction contributions outline many of the public issues of a nation as reflected through the private anxieties of the individual. The essays, in retrospect, stand as historical markers of a nation that prides itself on its exceptionalism while often overlooking its tragic flaws. The essays—vigorous in their plain style and perspicuity—are statements of Miller's fundamental belief that the theater may promote social change within the polis and may promote a new found self-awareness that so often eludes his fated heroes. And it is evident throughout this volume that Miller relished, above all, the civic dimension of the theater. As Miller explains:

> Another element in a great theater is that it tried to place aesthetics at the service of its civic function. See how the plays that we call great have made us somehow more civilized. The great Greek plays taught the western mind the law. They taught the western mind how to settle tribal conflicts without murdering each other. The great Shakespearean plays set up structures of order which became parts of our mental equipment. In the immense love stories, the wonderful comedies, there's all sorts of color. But back of these great plays is a civic function. The author was really a poet-philosopher. A forty dollar ticket [1983 Broadway price] brooks no philosophies, tends toward triviality. I believe that if we had some means of expanding our audience it would take awhile but playwrights would respond to that challenge. They'd smell *blood* out there![10]

While Miller refers to many writers from the distant past as poet-philosophers, it is not too fanciful to suggest that he himself was one of the most influential poet-philosophers whose essays speak directly and gracefully to readers around the world.

A note on the final contents of the present book. Due to the sheer amount of essay material that Miller wrote over his career, it is not possible to include it all in this volume. Similarly, in a few cases, copyright to material Miller has written or been involved in has been held elsewhere. However, I am confident that the final contents of *The Collected Essays of Arthur Miller* stand as an impressive and balanced selection of some of Arthur Miller's very best writings, which is exactly what the volume set out to do.

Matthew Roudané

Notes

1   Brenda Murphy, *Miller: 'Death of a Salesman'* (Cambridge: Cambridge University Press, 1995), p. 106.

2   Tony Kushner, "Note on the Texts," in Tony Kushner, ed., *Arthur Miller: Collected Plays 1987-2004 with Stage and Radio Plays of the 1930s & 40s* (New York: The Library of America, 2015), p. 888.

3   Robert A. Martin, "Introduction to the Original Edition," in *The Theater Essays of Arthur Miller*, eds Robert A. Martin and Steven R. Centola (New York: Da Capo Press, 1996), p. xx.

4   Tony Kushner, "Arthur Miller: An Appreciation," (New York: The Library of America, 2015), pp. 5-6.

5   Arthur Miller, "Tragedy and the Common Man," in Martin and Centola, p. 5.

6   Steven R. Centola, "A Note on the Selection," in Steven R. Centola, ed., *Echoes Down the Corridor* (Viking, 2000), xiii-xiv.

7   Arthur Miller, "On Social Plays," in Martin and Centola, pp. 57-8.

8   Matthew Roudané, "An Interview with Arthur Miller," in Roudané, ed., *Conversations with Arthur Miller* (Jackson and London: University Press of Mississippi, 1987), pp. 361-62. 'Interview conducted in 1983; first published in 1985 in the *Michigan Quarterly Review* and republished in 1987 in *Conversations With Arthur Miller* by the University of Mississippi Press.

9   Christopher Bigsby, "Introduction to the Revised Edition," in *The Portable Arthur Miller*, ed. Christopher Bigsby (New York: Penguin, 1995), p. xxxiv.

10 Roudané, "An Interview with Arthur Miller," p. 374.

Author's Foreword to the First Edition of
The Theater Essays of Arthur Miller:
Sorting Things Out

I find it hard to read through these essays without wanting to make changes on each page and often in each sentence. Nothing written about the theater ever comes out right, the thing is forever escaping its commentators.

I am a little surprised that I have written so much on the subject in the past thirty years, and it is hard now to remember what drove me to it. I think it may have been the feeling that it was being trivialized in most published commentary at a time when I thought it the most important thing in the world. It could be of some great importance, I still think, if we ever get it beyond the childish delights of the commercial hit-flop situation.

I have not so much changed my opinions about certain issues as added to what I believed, but I have often wished that I had never written a word on the subject of tragedy. I am not a scholar, not a critic, and my interest in the phenomenon was and is purely practical, so that having delivered myself of certain views I only unwittingly entered an arena of near-theological devoutness which I had not known existed. The damage having been done, however, there is no further reason to withhold new thoughts, which may or may not line up with those of the ancients and their modern heirs.

I have not yet seen a convincing explanation of why the tragic mode seems anachronistic now, nor am I about to attempt one. But it has often seemed to me that what tragedy requires—of the artist first and of the audience thereafter—is a kind of grief without which the tragic area somehow cannot be approached. Instead of grief we have come to substitute irony and even comedy, black or otherwise. I am too lazy to go back to Aristotle, but I do not recall his mentioning grief; most probably because he took for granted that his hero's catastrophe would entail that emotion all by itself.

It is probably not that we have lost the capacity to grieve, but that we have misplaced the ritual through which grief can be shown to others and shared. Of course the waning of organized religion is a factor, but I wonder if it is not more a result than a cause. And I wonder, too, if we are awkward about grieving because the loss of one person evokes in us only the paradoxical fact of death without the straightforward and clear image of a sacred identity that has vanished. Rather, we know that nothing and no one is truly sacred, but that a biological set of forces have been used up so that there is something faintly fatuous, something perhaps operatic, in the kind of grief-outbreak which underlies the real tragedies as they approach their moments of terror and death.

If we are this way—rationalized and beyond the reach of public grief—it is interesting to wonder why it has happened. And inevitably there arise the images of the carnage of two world wars, the many revolutions and counter-revolutions, the Nazi

Holocaust—this, after all, has been the most spendthrift of all centuries with human lives. Perhaps the public psyche has simply been overloaded and, like an electrical circuit, has blown its fuse and gone cold under the weight of too many impulses. So that the tragic proposal is simply presumptuous—this making so much out of one death when we know it is meaningless. In other words, in an important respect we have ceased to feel.

I would agree, except that we can still respond to the old tragedies as much as people apparently did in early times. Is this merely nostalgia? It doesn't seem so in the theater.

My own view, or at least my leaning, is toward a less alarming explanation. Clearly, however tragedy is defined or explained, it must allow the hero to speak for himself. This may sound so rudimentary as not to be worth discussing, but in contemporary drama few major characters are allowed this privilege, it being assumed that something like naturalism is one thing we can't have. What we have instead are forms of authorial ironical comment or directorial interpretation of the character's situation total enough to wipe out his autonomy entirely. We are being spared the incoherence of the character's feeling for the coherence of our own interpretation, which allows us to observe the outlines of suffering without very much participation in it. Thus, it is absurd to attempt the kind of protest that tragedy always has entailed, a cry against heaven, fate, or what you will. That cry may still be implicit, but it has been stylized into a glance upwards or even a grin and a cough. From one or another philosophical points of view this makes lots of sense, but is it really the viewpoint of the sufferer or of the one observing him? If we could get this sorted out, we might well see tragic emotions forming again.

What I think has been forgotten is that the objectivity of a Shakespeare is expressed through his form—the balancing of responsibility between various persons, interests, and forces—but that the sufferings that result are not at all objectified, dried up, or gentled. It may be we have lost the art of tragedy for want of a certain level of self-respect, finally, and are in disgrace with ourselves. Compared to the tragic emotion, the others are covered with a certain embarrassment, even shame, as though suffering were a sign of one's failure or a loss of dignity, like being caught with a hole in one's stocking at an affair of state. People not free enough to weep or cry out are not fit subjects for tragedy, at least not on the stage, and weeping without self-respect is mere self-pity.

As for the sociology in these pieces, I still support its main point, the need to subsidize the American theater. I have had far more experience with such theaters abroad than I had decades ago, and I would add now that a mixed private and public theater would be the most useful rather than a monopoly by either type. A subsidy is a form of power that always tends toward bureaucratization and needs challenging from outside the organization. We are still, at this writing, paying less for the upkeep of theater art than any other viable nation.

Finally, there is a question of tone in these pieces—an overemphasis here and there on what has already been proved. I would ask the reader to remember that an unspoken gentleman's agreement was prevalent in the 1940s and 50s, if not earlier, under which every playwright had to present himself to critics and the public as a pure entertainer, a man in an aesthetic daze who barely knew the name of the president or how to negotiate a subway turnstile. This image was good for business, conforming to the

Anglo-Saxon tradition of the separation of church and state, poesy and instruction, form and meaning. A play, needless to say, could not teach without exploding into its several parts, so that the most authentically aesthetic of experiences was necessarily the one without any perceptible reference to society or life as it was lived. The exception was George Bernard Shaw, but only because he was funny, and funny in a definitely aristocratic manner that gave him license to preach the virtues of a socialism of wits and a capitalism whose horrors were familiar, somehow warm, and somehow bearable after all.

Thus, the lessons of a play, its meaning and theme, had to spread out like a contagion if they were to be aesthetic, in which case few would be aware they were even infected. In a word, what I was trying to do was to objectify the social situation of our theater, and even of some of the creative procedures that produced one style of playwriting or another, rather than leaving these matters—as our critics normally did—to temperament and taste without deeper reason or cause.

Nevertheless and notwithstanding, the theater is first of all imitation, mimickry. If anything contrary is found in these pieces, it was not intended to be there. We need food, sex, and an image. The rest is commentary on these.

Arthur Miller
1977

Author's Foreword to the Second Edition of
The Theater Essays of Arthur Miller

Great changes have taken place in American theatre since these essays were written. There was always a reason to complain about the super-commercialization of Broadway theatre (read O'Neill's letters or Odets') but at the same time it was paradoxically undeniable that Broadway producers were the only ones who took risks with new plays, the regional theatres normally picking up last year's hits for local audiences. The opposite is true now; only musicals originate on Broadway any more. The few straight plays produced in the so-called professional theatre, namely on Broadway, are gleaned from regional and off-Broadway theatres and abroad, mostly England.

No one can be certain that this dire condition is permanent but it does look that way now.

For most actors the theatre as a whole in the United States, not excluding the regional theatre which in many places is partially subsidized by city or state, has devolved into a mere stepping stone to films and television. It was only yesterday, historically speaking, that one could confidently imagine a lifelong career as an actor or writer for the stage, and could regard oneself as part of an unbroken line of such artists stretching back into history. I doubt that even the most talented and accepted of our young today thinks of the future in anything like so permanent a way.

The air is filled with the fog of unwelcome. It is a rare writer who attempts more than one or two plays after his initial success, if indeed he has one. The actors cannot wait to escape to film or television where there may at least be a living to be made. A theatre culture, a continuum of work and of artists and passionately interested audiences, has seemingly scattered. It may be that the former New York audience, with its more or less coherent views, prejudices and outlook, has fragmented while the Hispanic, the African-American, and other previously unheard-from minorities have not yet formed a new coherency. Nowhere has drama thrived where it has had to shout into a roaring crowd of turbulent groups struggling with one another for a place in the cultural sun.

In New York the theatre is terrified, there is no other word for it. The measure is total success or total obliteration; with a single newspaper swamping the reviewing field by its over-whelming influence, the pretty good, flawed play, condemned as something less than a must-see masterpiece, is no more, for the idea of a countervailing critical consensus has eroded away. Either the *Times* likes it or it begins its slide into nothingness, and the *Times*, worse yet, may be more right than wrong about a show's public acceptability if not its real worth. The problem is the absence of a meaningful critical consensus that would lend at least sufficient support to a less than masterful play to keep it going. Must every play, if it is not to close in a week, cause hysterical joy in the *Times* man's breast? If such a view were taken retroactively and all but certified masterpieces were eliminated from human consciousness, something like five or six American plays would be allowed onto Parnassus from the whole century-long repertoire of productions.

Yet not-great plays, like the same quality of movies, paintings, novels or anything else man makes, were the norm not many years ago. Indeed, they kept the audience in being until the very rare fine play made its appearance. The fine play today shows up amid a general denial that the theatre can create anything decent any more so that even with a good *Times* review people don't come, at least not the way they used to when a year's run for a praised play was not at all extraordinary and a two years' stay was merely a proper hit. There is such a thing as audience morale and ours is at the bottom.

It may be that the twenties and thirties—decades which we generally use as base lines—were actually unique in theatre history. After all, Ibsen's plays ran a matter of weeks in his own time and he made his living from his published works and not basically from the stage. Perhaps we are merely returning to where we were, and where maybe we belong as a minority art geared to a relative handful of interested communicants. It may also be wise to remember that as the arts go relatively few plays seem to survive their time, and even fewer playwrights. Maybe we have made too much of the whole business of theater when in fact it matters little to by far the vast majority and will probably continue meaning little until our educational system begins to work.

That said, it is still hard to watch—not just the theater's decline but the immense social pressures on it to disappear. In more and more cities there is only one newspaper now, and in New York only one whose reviews mean much to the public, so that people who call themselves producers are not ashamed to openly calculate whether so-and-so, the reigning *Times* critic at the moment, is likely to go for it, failing which, a play is simply not going to be produced. The lone critic in a large Eastern city is actually consulted before a revival is cast as to which actors he would prefer among a list of possibles, and he blithely gives his strong opinion. I can't claim to be in on the latest news on the Rialto but it is hard to imagine such abjectness in people calling themselves producers. London has its grave problems, but with a dozen main papers and critics, plus influential TV and magazine reviews, something like a consensus is still possible. This variety of view helps create a far less hysterical atmosphere and from time to time a season of greatly varied styles of play will still appear.

Of course, it is the subsidized British theaters that keep London alive at all. Despite terrific pressure for a time by Conservative governments hostile to any publicly underwritten social activity, government support has been regained, probably because it is too obvious that without the National, the Young Vic, the Court, the Royal Shakespeare Company, and others, London theater would be just about where New York is now. It is the productions of the British subsidized theaters that have kept alive the reach and breadth of embrace of real theater. Total privatization, whatever its virtues in industry and business, means the end of symphony orchestras, ballet, public libraries, art galleries, most hospitals and medical schools and many other services we customarily think of as necessities for a civilized life. The theater, unfortunately, can very occasionally make a lot of money and this periodic golden glow has distracted many from the underlying truth, a truth which is now plain to everyone: left solely to market forces the New York theater is gasping and desperate.

For one thing, the confluence of a single critical opinion with rising costs and high ticket prices has proved lethal in New York, but the blame does not belong to critics. When it takes forty, fifty or sometimes a hundred dollars to see a show and another hundred for dinner and parking you are going to study the *Times* review very carefully before you lay out the equivalent of a couple of pairs of shoes or a new suit. And if the show is not described as a near-masterpiece you just might decide on a seven-dollar movie or a night at home with TV. Thus the coinage of critical vocabularies is inevitably corrupted; the excessive price enhances excessive praise and excessive condemnation, for the play simply will not get an audience if it is what nine times out of ten it really is— pretty good to fair.

Everything about theater has been twisted out of recognition, including the kind of play likely to be written and produced. I recently saw the new National Actors Theatre's revival of *The Crucible* and was shocked when the cast lined up across the stage for curtain calls and filled it from one side to the other. Who would ever think to write such a large-cast play today? Would I? I doubted it. Yet the heroically conceived play, while always doubtful as a producer's risk, was once not quite an utterly insane project, although to be sure the reigning opinion back in the thirties and forties was that any play with more than perhaps eight or ten actors was bound to lose money and quickly die. Still, to have written such a play I must have thought it reasonably possible to find a producer for it and even to have expected a commercial success. New York now is being entertained by one-man or woman shows, or tidy little scenes with four or five actors at most. The big casts, the full-throated stories—and the big themes—are in the movies when they are anywhere.

The sight of that big cast, however, brought back memories of the late forties and early fifties and a tiny band of producers on Broadway willing and able to take big risks. Their kind is gone now. It is not only that costs are so much greater now but that the negative odds are simply too overwhelming and a certain faith, as unjustified as it mostly proved to be, is dead. Faith in the importance of theater itself. That handful of crazy men thought of themselves as artists *manqué*, absolutely essential helpmates for the production of theater as art, meaning theater that would most likely meet resistance in critics and audiences. The object now, it seems to me, is to avoid resistance by producing works that are not too objectionable either in form or content. The New York theater exists almost purely to entertain and divert; theater's ancient burden, and sometimes its glory, the moral illumination of society and the human condition, is too heavy to bear in an unmitigatedly commercialized system. Inevitably, there are counter currents from time to time, in Lincoln Center, LaMama, the numerous off-Broadway attempts to overleap the system or bypass it. These deserve all the praise that can be mustered but they cannot resolve certain dilemmas, whatever their dedication to high aims.

One of these dilemmas is the casting idiocy. With extraordinarily few exceptions, the New York theater cannot hold its actors into their maturity and this makes it very difficult to cast plays that are not about adolescent or very young people. The top-class ripened actor is in the movies; the theater gets him when he is starting out or over the hill, or simply too odd for films. In sports terms, it is like trying to field a first class team when only beginners or over-age players are available, those at their peak performance having left for a movie or TV show.

Economics, a notoriously boring subject, is surreal in the theater and need only detain us long enough to note that while high production expense is usually attributed to actors' salaries and authors' royalties, and rarely to advertising and publicity, these, in fact, eat up about one third of the usual budget. Thus, when *The New York Times* charges more for theatrical ads than for department stores' under the rationale that theaters cannot project advertising budgets far into the future as stores usually can, it leaves the mind agape. I am probably alone in not being able to understand this reasoning at all, but there it is, functioning unquestioningly year in year out, decade after decade.

It would be wrong to think that any of these problems are new but neither is the usual cancer. So secondary has stage work become for actors that a stage director nowadays has to be constantly recasting even a successful play, what with half the cast rushing off within weeks of opening to do a film or TV show. Theater is the stepchild now, beloved only when the real children are away.

But again, its defeat in the public's esteem is an old story. It was more than forty years ago that I hired a local farmhand to help me dig a new vegetable garden, and who asked me as we worked, "Is it true? They say you write moving pictures."

"No, stage plays."

He looked blank, and I explained, "You know, with actors and a curtain that goes up and down?"

"Oh!" he exclaimed, with an amused recognition, "them old-fashioned shows!"

And as for Broadway commercialization, it was before World War II that the producer, Robert Whitehead (just about the last of the old producer-idealists left now), approached Lee Shubert with an idea for a new theater with a two-dollar ticket. "Mister Lee", as he was called, listened to Whitehead's explication of this marvellous new low-priced theater which would draw in the impecunious young, the schoolteachers, the ordinary folk who make the freshest and most impressionable audiences, promising that they in turn would inspire new playwrights and create a terrific excitement in the theater.

Shubert, his shrewd little face browned to parchment by the Florida sun, listened intently. Whitehead finished and waited for the reaction of this fabled man who owned most of the Broadway theaters, not to mention dozens of others across the country. Finally Mr Lee spoke. "That's a great idea, Mr Whitehead. Marvellous. But why the two dollars?"

In short, if they were going to come they would come whatever the price. I hated Mr Lee when I heard this story but even I had to admit that as box office prices began to rise for my plays in the fifties it was the cheaper balcony seats that were the first to go unsold. And yet, I still believe that if prices were lower across the board more people would get the habit again.

To compound all the difficulties the city centres—where theaters have been traditionally located—are precisely where a lot of people dread going, especially at night. Old line department stores have either moved away altogether or rely more and more on shopping mall branches in the suburbs. There is no reason to put down suburban theatres but the cultural atmosphere of the suburb is a sterilized one compared to the culture of cities. Suburban culture is more likely to be conservative, defensively centered on family and a homogeneous society inhospitable to disturbing new ideas and party conflict. On the other hand, anonymity cloaks the patron of the city theater, freeing him to experience unsettling patterns of belief. The cutting edge has always been in the city.

One well-known consequence of this shift to the suburbs is the growing predominance of familiar classics in the repertoire of regional theaters, especially when times are as tough as at this writing and subsidy harder and harder to obtain; theatres operating in a sequestered, self-protective community cannot risk alienating too many of their clientele.

If the situation is tough in New York, it is more or less so everywhere in the Western world. Except perhaps in Stockholm, Helsinki and sometimes London one is forced to wonder whether theater as a form has finally lost the race for the public's attention and film has won it. Surely the stage cannot come close to the physical attractiveness and visceral excitement of the film form, the swift evocation of nature, of storm and flood, of light's miracles, of facial expressions, of tempo born of cross-cutting and montage and all the rest. Compared to all this flash and bang the theater is covered with dust.

And one has to confess that there is a more profound sign of the movies' triumph in the art of stage acting. Word-proud, demonstrative, projective, it has not only no influence on movie acting but is itself being transformed by movies, the contemporary stage actor miming the abject naturalism of film performance, with its barely audible volume, its underplayed gestures, its petite glances and often impenetrable mumbled internalizing. And as for subject matter, in a reversal of the past, the movies in recent times have surely tackled more significant themes than the contemporary stage which has inverted its gaze to more and more hermetic and private experience, pursuing prized irony into the luxurious bizarre, while more and more films attempt confrontations with social contradictions like corruption in the courts, the police, the financial leadership, not to mention the hysterical meaninglessness of television, our political depravities and the dark interior of life in our cities. From my no doubt skewed viewpoint the stage since the mid-fifties or thereabouts has, far more than movies, largely reflected a cosseted middle-class society where self-doubt lies down with abundance and anything seriously threatening to an unjust social structure is thought gauche and unaesthetic.

At all costs indirection; the howl of the outraged heart is a bore. Why? One can only turn to our non-theatrical experience; in a world filled with daily examples of the futility of ideas along with the endless variety of human perversity and cruelty on each evening's news, our minds have all but ceased to register. And so we turn with relief to value-shorn style; not to the hangman but the way he so elegantly ties his knot.

Has the range and size, the very aspiration of plays diminished, shrunk perhaps? But hasn't the same diminution, the same absence of urgency afflicted our political and social life? It is all one thing—the well-known and academically celebrated demise of story and character in plays reflects the victory of the improbable in life and the dulling of the ancient impulse to reach out to all manner of men with a physically useful, restoring image, even a saving one. If I have for many years advocated a certain amount of subsidy for theater it is not to increase the prosperity of artists but to bring down ticket prices and give entry to a far more mixed and representative audience, an audience that will bring its suffering into the theater and thus its urgent demands for useful questions to be raised.

Many years ago I gave a talk at a university to a largely non-academic, general audience and advocated publicly subsidized theater in more or less the German and British fashion. I recognized the inevitability of a new bureaucracy and new conflicts between a plebian public taste and an avant garde spending public money for its shenanigans, but we should at least have a focus for our lamentations. (As one German businessman said to me, "I love theatre and I approve of public support for it, but for a decade or more now all our state theaters show is nakedness and depravity and contempt for the audience. I am sick of it and I don't bother going any more.") Subsidy, in a word, simply creates new problems, but they may be the right ones, the creative ones, as I think the British have proved more often than not, with their responsible theater leadership which at the same time is not closed to new and imaginative work.

At the end of my speech a man asked a question: "I manufacture shoes. If my shoes don't sell I go out of business. If theater is giving the public what it wants it will thrive, if not, why should we tax ourselves to support it?"

A hard question. I couldn't find an answer, at least not a just one. All I could do was ask another question. "I see your point, but can you name one classical Greek or Elizabethan shoemaker?"

Embarrassing as it may be to remind ourselves, the theater does reflect the spirit of a people, and when it lives up to its potential it may even carry them closer to their aspirations. It is the most vulgar of the arts but it is really the simplest too. No cameras, no miles of cable, no crews, no multi-million-dollar budgets. All you need is a human and a board to stand on and something fascinating for him to say and do. With a few right words, sometimes, he can clarify the minds of thousands, still the whirling compass needle of their souls and point it once more toward the stars. You can't ask a shoemaker, vital as his work may be, to do that. Nor can you ask artists to be shoemakers, steadily turning out a saleable product every day. Theater is not going to die, it is as immortal as our dreaming, but history has shown that it can wither away for generations if there is not a decent respect for its nature and its minimal needs.

Arthur Miller
1992

Author's Preface to
Echoes Down The Corridor

Looking through the score of essays I have published over the past half century, I find myself surprised at how many were involved with the political life of the times. I hadn't quite realized. By political I don't mean the question of who should be elected to office but rather the life of the community and its apparent direction. This preoccupation, brought back to mind by this collection, reminds me once again of how the "givens" of any generation change and how the dominant literary tradition of one time loses relevance in another.

To one growing up in the Thirties, the new force in one's awareness, as in so much of the cultural comment, was, of course, the failure of capitalism and the promise of socialism. The depth of that failure is all but incommunicable any more, and the redolence of the cure even less so. The notion of the artist as activist was new and initially thrilling. One looked back with envy not only at the social realist Zola and his historic pamphlets that changed French political consciousness, but also at Tolstoy's and Dostoyevsky's pamphleteering, and even at Chekhov, seemingly a most private recorder of sensibility and quiet longing, who still found time to make a trip across the breadth of Russia, in an open carriage no less, to report on conditions of political prisoners on Sakhalin Island. And of course there was the long, illustrious line of British-Irish artist-politicos, most recently Shaw, who was still writing plays and trying to make sense of Britain's society. In contrast—at least it seemed so to me—American writers were far less involved in the nation's political life; and indeed for many critics the political itself was irreconcilable in principle with esthetic feeling or art in general. Or so it seemed.

So the young in the Thirties were self-consciously raising the banners of social protest and commitment, a prideful distinction challenging the ivory tower in which most writers seemed to have lived in the glamorous and rather silly Twenties. Very little of the writing of that exciting new dispensation has survived, having died with the issues with which it was so tightly bound up. The few surviving works of high art, like Henry Roth's *Call It Sleep*, while powerfully depicting the poverty and squalor of the city life of working-class people, were essentially aimed elsewhere, at the subjective experiences of the author, in fact, and his personal sensations of life in a certain time and place.

But one took it for granted, and without really giving it much thought, that the very idea of "writer" had less to do with the entertainer (which he has fundamentally become) and everything to do with remaking humanity in one way or another (and of course winning fame at the same time). And this meant politics and social commitment and indeed embodied a rather short view. But this was inevitable when one lived as though in a permanent emergency, as it were, a time-passage which would end with either the triumph or defeat of fascism, including the fascism of the heart which was all around us. Germany and Italy, two of the great cultures of Europe, had already been taken over by that plague. And at home it was a time, after all, when lynching was not uncommon in the South, when the Ford plant had tear gas in its sprinkler systems in case workers pulled a sit-down strike, and the private Ford police had the right to enter any employee's house to see if he was living as Ford thought he should; when there were discreet signs in front of New Jersey summer hotels reading, "No dogs or Jews"; when a boatload of Jews allowed by Hitler to leave Germany was not allowed to land in an American port and was forced to return to Germany to deliver its cargo to the ovens. It was a time when autoworkers, newly organized and freshly aware of the idea of social justice, would still insist on separate white and black picket lines. I cannot recall seeing a black New York policeman then, and of course the armed forces were tightly segregated.

The point of remarking on all this now is that Americans and Europeans, Jews and non-Jews alike, had silenced themselves, declining to protest what they knew was happening in Germany; non-Jews, because they no doubt feared that their concern—if they felt any—would open the country to a flood of refugees; Jews, lest drawing attention to themselves would make them even better targets at home than they already were. But then, not very many people thought it particularly odd that the new reformist labor movement, with all its newly born social idealism, was also thoroughly racist.

It seems to me that all this has wildly changed now, that people on every side are easily given to protest loudly at what they see as injustice to themselves or others. The "givens" of this new century are of an entirely different order from those that existed in most of the last. But the "givens" have shifted back and forth in several directions in the sixty years since the Thirties.

There was a kind of implicit cease-fire on social criticism during World War II after the explosively contentious years of the Depression. (I wrote *All My Sons* during the war, expecting much trouble, but the war ended just as I was completing the play, leaving some room for the un-sayable, which everyone knew—that the war had made some people illicit, sometimes criminal fortunes.) The Fifties began the Cold War's religiously imposed silencing of any sharp criticism, lest the Communists benefit therefrom, and the cap was blown off again in the Sixties with the drug culture and the anti–Vietnam War movement. I can't recall anything at all happening in the Seventies, and by the Eighties the Reagan trance was in place and writers—so it seems to me now—felt surrounded by an ever expanding suburbia of the mind, which, as I write in the new century, has flowered into a culture of entertainment that absorbs whatever is dropped on it like a sponge, mixing everything into a general dampness beyond all definition. In a word, more dramatic work in movies especially (far less in theater) is built around themes of social importance than ever in memory, but none of it seems able to resist the public's transformation of all information—even the most alarming kind—into something like a good time. There was a time when a novel, John Steinbeck's *Grapes of Wrath*, would rouse Congress to pass legislation to ameliorate conditions in the transient labor camps in the West, an inconceivable event now when congressmen are unlikely even to be aware of a novel, let alone to take it seriously as a picture of real people's lives rather than the lives of entertainment people.

But to a greater or lesser extent through the decades the popular culture, where my plays existed, has always made it difficult to get at all serious about life. Nor was this a purely American phenomenon. It took many long years for Bernard Shaw, as great an agitator as he was, to get Ibsen produced in Britain, where he was assumed to be a madman; and I can say from personal experience that even into the Fifties there was an overwhelming resistance to serious considerations of contemporary life in the British theater. Indeed, it was the American play that the avant-garde looked to as an example of what they should be doing in England, few and far apart as those plays were on Broadway.

In any case, I have been spouting off over the years away from the stage as well as on it, and this collection is part of the record of the things that interested me enough to write about over the past half century.

Essays: 1944–1950

Belief in America
(from *Situation Normal*)

Riding away from the camp it became clear for the first time why I had looked so hard for a sign of Belief in the Army. It was, I saw, a personal reason. I had an instinctive fear that millions of men could not be put through the hell of battle and be expected to return to American life as whole men unless they had some basic elementary understanding of why they had had to go through their battle. I had been, I saw now, afraid of what such men would do to America and what their returning to America would do to them. My fear had not been, as I thought all along, that they would not fight well without the Belief, for everything I saw convinced me that our soldiers, for many different and sometimes totally irrelevant reasons, have sufficient faith in their leaders to follow them into battle. Now I saw that the danger lay in the return of the warriors, in the time when they were no longer webbed into the Army organization, no longer under their military leaders commanding them in the pressure of battle and war. Riding away from the camp I wondered for the first time whether I ought not be wandering through St. Paul and Kansas City, New York and Los Angeles, instead of through the camps. For as far as Watson was concerned it was in America as much as in the island where he fought that his wholeness had been wrecked and his mind distracted. It was not only the Japanese who had shaken his wits. We here did our part in that, and with terrible effect.

It is wrong to use a single man as the basis of a statement about all soldiers, but from what I have been able to learn since speaking to him I have come to the conclusion that he represents a nearly classic extreme of a state of mind found in all men who have been in actual battle, hard battle.

For want of a better word—this one has certain sneering connotations—Watson was in love, in love with his comrades in arms. I sensed it as he spoke to me, and I was sure of it when I had left him. Probably his whole conflict consists of his fear of returning to battle, set against his love for his unit. The feeling of guilt that such a dilemma would generate in a man needs no defining. He was not merely letting "the Army" down or his "unit." He was being forced by fear to forsake a group of men whom he had loved. His avowal that he would die for any of them was even truer than I had imagined.

Now what happens to a Watson when he returns to America? It must be remembered that as far as anyone could tell he returned whole, sane, and fit for further training. What happened to him here? What did he see or fail to see here that so shook him?

I can only guess at that. But I am not trying to solve Watson's problem. In the present state of American affairs I do not know how his problem can be solved. But Watson is an extreme. Many hundreds of thousands of men are going to return from terrible battles, and in some degree they will have shared Watson's feeling of love and identity with their particular comrades and units. And in differing degrees they are going to have to transfer that love to other—civilian—"units" or be forever in that restless, aimless state of emotional thirst which in other countries at other times has made veterans the anxious and willing collaborators of any demagogue who joins them together under a common color of shirt, for a common and often violent social purpose. We will dispense with the argument against those who still say it can't happen here. It has begun to happen here too many times for us to argue about it at this late date. But what about Watson, about the millions of Watsons who are even now coming down the gangplanks in American ports . . .

They have fought their battle. Carried forward by faith in an officer, by a feeling of love for their comrades, by an innate sense of honor, by a plain love of adventure and danger, by whatever drive obtained in them at the time of battle, they fought their battle, and now they are home. No man has ever felt identity with a group more deeply and intimately than a soldier in battle. But now their uniforms are off. They walk out of the circle of the imperative order, out of the unity of feeling they had known in the Army. They go home.

Home is many things. Home can be a family well loved or a wife longed for whose love is all-sufficing. Home may be the feverish joy of resuming projects left half finished. Home may give Watson—many of them—a satisfying substitute for the close comradeship of the battlefield. The battlefield and its emotions may quickly fade once the fighter is really home.

But maybe not. Home, to many, perhaps to most, means a town or a city cut into a thousand little disjointed pieces, each one an exclusive class in itself. If on returning home, the veteran should find the town in immediate danger of being inundated by a flood, with every sort of person in it working together toward a common goal, the problem might hardly exist for him. With each citizen protecting his neighbor, as he does in time of danger, and all divisions of race, economic and social position melted away in the face of the peril, the veteran would find himself strangely at home among his people. But a flood is a rare thing. The usual veteran returning to his city or town on the usual day finds no common goal at all. He finds every group in town excluding the proximate group. It is rich and poor again, it is white and black again, it is Jew and Gentile again, it is, above all, a mass of little groups each of whose apparent goals in life conflict with the goals of the next group. Watson must return to his former group. He must reassume its little prejudices, its hates, its tiny aims. He must lop off at once that onetime feeling of exhilaration he got from the knowledge that whatever the insignificance of his job, it was helping an enormous mass of men toward a great and worthy goal. Now he must forget that. Now he must live unto himself, for his own selfish welfare. Half of him, in a sense, must die, and with it must pass away half the thrill he knew in being alive. He must, in short, become a civilian again.

There is a great and deep sense of loss in that. A man who has known the thrill of giving himself does not soon forget it. It leaves him with a thirst. A thirst for a wider life, a more exciting life, a life that demands all he can give. Civilian life in America is private, it is always striving for exclusiveness. Our lifelong boast is that we got ahead of the next guy, excluded him. We have always believed in the fiction—and often damned our own belief—that if every man privately takes care of his own interests, the community and the nation will prosper and be safe. Unless your Watson's attachment to his family or his wife or his girl is so overwhelming that nothing can distract him from it, he is going to feel the loss of a social unit, a group to which he can give himself, a social goal worth his sacrifice. He may find that unit and that goal in his trade union, his club. But most Americans do not belong to unions, and the goals of most American clubs will never make up in vitality and largeness for the goal he left behind. Watson, then, if he has the average social connections which are slight, is going to wander around his American town, and he is going to find himself severely lonely a great and growing part of the time. America, to him, is not moving in any direction. His life is standing still. And he is alone and dissatisfied.

What could civilian America possibly give Watson that it did not give? There is only one answer to that. The Belief. America tried everything else imaginable, and nothing satisfied your Watson. It tried giving him medals, it tried giving him a parade, it tried big publicity for him, it tried to give him everything within reach of its well-meaning heart. When people met him they tried being sympathetic, and that did not help. They tried being sorry for him and they tried being proud, and he did not seem to react fully to any of it. What did he want from them? They would give him anything he wanted if only he could tell them what it was that would make him feel at home in America.

Knowing it or not Watson wanted to find the Belief in America. It is a very hard concept to nail down; Belief so often means a dogma of some kind to be memorized and bowed down to, and that is not a thing that could satisfy Watson. But say it this way. If when he returned to this shore he walked in the cities and the towns and all about him he sensed and heard evidence that the people were unified in one concept—that he, Watson, had gone forth to rescue something very very precious and that had he not gone forth, and had that thing been lost, the people would have been left in mourning for it the rest of their lives. What Watson wanted in America is equivalent to what the Russian or British soldier must find when he returns home. In Russia or Britain the broken cities and the maimed children and the many civilian dead and missing say in so many words nearly everything the returning soldier needs to hear. It is very clear, there, why he went; it is superlatively clear what a unity of feeling lay behind him while he was gone, and it is bloody well apparent and understood what it was that he accomplished by going. The force of bombs and the horror of rape and destruction has spawned the quantities of a unified Belief there, and when Tommy and Ivan come marching home their people *know* them through the very arterial link of that commonly held Belief, that rock-like understanding. But here the marks of war are different. Watson found a people without scars and without any commonly held understanding of why he had to go and what he accomplished by going. True, his comrades too were not sure of what, in the end, they were accomplishing by their battles, but for them that kind of understanding, that kind of political Belief was compensated for by an emotional unity born of the common danger and the common military goal—they *knew* each other through that and they were one with each other because of it. What links Watson with the civilians at home though? A parade? Sympathy? Pride in him based on the same kind of understanding required for pride in the hometown football team? The only means by which Watson can rejoin himself with America is by sharing with civilian America a well-understood Belief in the rightness, the justness, the necessity of his fight. That is how he will be made to feel at home. It will by no means dissolve his memories and solve all his problems, but without it nothing can be solved in Watson. He will be wondering why he went and why he is alive for the rest of his days. And what could that Belief be?

Since the war began our most brilliant statesmen and writers have been trying—only in America, as far as I know—to frame a statement, a "name" for this war. They have not found it, and they will not find it, because they are looking for something new. It is pretty late now for this kind of talk, but not too late. From the first day of this war we should have understood that the kind of thing we fight for is a very old thing. We fought for it in 1776 and in 1865, and we found the words for it then, and they are perfectly good words, easy to understand and not at all old-fashioned. They are good words because they recur more times in our ordinary conversation and in the historic conversations of our long tradition than any other words. They represent a concept which, to the vast majority of Americans, must not be offended. The words are not "free enterprise," as the well-known ads of our big industries maintain. Nor are the words, "Keep America the Same," as a certain automobile company insists nearly every week in the national magazines. Neither the people of America nor those of any other nation ever fought a war in order to keep everything the same and certainly never for free enterprise or jobs. No man in his right mind would risk his life to get a job. But we did fight two wars for our Belief. And that Belief says, simply, that we believe all men are equal. We really believe it, most of us, and because a powerful force has arisen in the world dedicated to making the people of the world—us included—unequal, we have therefore decided to fight. We insist upon a state of affairs in which all men will be regarded as equal. There is no nonsense about it. We believe that everything will rot and decline and go backwards if we are forced to live under laws that hold certain nations and peoples to be inferior and without rights. We are thinking primarily of ourselves and our own rights, naturally, but that is perfectly all right, for once our right to be equal is assured we will want nothing better than to see every nation on our level. I believe the majority of Americans agree to this.

Now, if the implications of "all men are equal" were drilled into our men and women, in the Army and out, with at least the assiduousness that the brand names of certain toothpastes are, we would have, I maintain, many fewer Watsons with us now and after the war is over. The concept of equality of man is very easy for a soldier, especially, to take. It is in our tradition quite as firmly as is blueberry pie, for which our radio programs seem to feel most adult Americans are fighting, and sheds considerably more light on the meaning of this war. Its ramifications could be explained in the five-minute orientation periods in the camps quite as easily as the nature of the millimeter. And finally, it happens to be the one idea which Hitler and the Japanese deny most completely and with the heaviest use of force. They, at bottom, demand that this world be fixed into a pattern of inequality of man against man. As Americans we were marked for a secondary status in that world. We refuse to accept it. We are as good as they are, and in time, perhaps, we will help them to be as good as we are. But first we must beat hell out of them until they no longer can dictate our status. Then we will go about making them understand about equality. Again, if this concept of the war, oversimplified as it is, lacking in economic factors as it is, were "sold" across America on even half the advertising budget of our best-selling mouthwash, perhaps—I too am willing to wait and see, but perhaps—the chaos of mind that is America today would be put somewhat in order and many of our returning soldiers made to feel at home.

Watson—the real Watson, the Watson whose story you have just read—is alone in America today. He in particular is alone and lonely because his comrades are not with him, the men he loves. But he is alone and misfitted here also—and more tragically— because America offers him no great social goal. Were we conscious of our Belief, were we *here in America* acting and working and fighting as civilians for the attainment of that goal, Watson would feel it, he would have a place fighting for it, and it would demand of him that part of his character which requires sharing. As it is, the company is gone and all that the company meant. He must wall himself in from his fellow man, he must live only his own little life and do his own unimportant, unsatisfying job when he gets out of the Army. He must begin again the stale and deadly competition with his fellow men for rewards that now seem colorless, even if necessary to his survival. He is alone. Cut off from mankind and that great movement of mankind he once was part of. And the world is alien, and battle . . . It keeps coming back to me with what apparent suddenness Watson came to fear returning to battle. Is it not possible, as Watson's captain implied, that battle is ten thousand times more horrible to him now than it actually was when he was in it, because he is looking at it now as a man cut off, as a man alone with a lonely man's fears, while at the front he saw it as a joined and united part of the race, as a man who is fighting with and for those he loved? Danger breeds understanding, it breeds a growth of common unity among men. And so does Belief. Not as suddenly, perhaps, and without the bottomless emotional depths that danger plumbs, but understanding and love are bred by a commonality of Belief. We have the Belief. We have always had it, but we have stowed it away like a relic, an heirloom to be taken down from the attic on a Sunday afternoon when visitors come and then hidden away. We need it every day now. For Belief is not a bullet, as has been said. Belief is a shield. When will we start the mills that roll such armament? And who will wither away because he went and returned, unarmed?

1944

Tragedy and the Common Man

In this age few tragedies are written. It has often been held that the lack is due to a paucity of heroes among us, or else that modern man has had the blood drawn out of his organs of belief by the skepticism of science, and the heroic attack on life cannot feed on an attitude of reserve and circumspection. For one reason or another, we are often held to be below tragedy—or tragedy above us. The inevitable conclusion is, of course, that the tragic mode is archaic, fit only for the very highly placed, the kings or the kingly, and where this admission is not made in so many words it is most often implied.

I believe that the common man is as apt a subject for tragedy in its highest sense as kings were. On the face of it this ought to be obvious in the light of modern psychiatry, which bases its analysis upon classic formulations, such as the Oedipus and Orestes complexes, for instances, which were enacted by royal beings, but which apply to everyone in similar emotional situations.

More simply, when the question of tragedy in art is not at issue, we never hesitate to attribute to the well-placed and the exalted the very same mental processes as the lowly. And finally, if the exaltation of tragic action were truly a property of the high-bred character alone, it is inconceivable that the mass of mankind should cherish tragedy above all other forms, let alone be capable of understanding it.

As a general rule, to which there may be exceptions unknown to me, I think the tragic feeling is evoked in us when we are in the presence of a character who is ready to lay down his life, if need be, to secure one thing—his sense of personal dignity. From Orestes to Hamlet, Medea to Macbeth, the underlying struggle is that of the individual attempting to gain his "rightful" position in his society.

Sometimes he is one who has been displaced from it, sometimes one who seeks to attain it for the first time, but the fateful wound from which the inevitable events spiral is the wound of indignity, and its dominant force is indignation. Tragedy, then, is the consequence of a man's total compulsion to evaluate himself justly.

In the sense of having been initiated by the hero himself, the tale always reveals what has been called his "tragic flaw," a failing that is not peculiar to grand or elevated characters. Nor is it necessarily a weakness. The flaw, or crack in the character, is really nothing—and need be nothing—but his inherent unwillingness to remain passive in the face of what he conceives to be a challenge to his dignity, his image of his rightful status. Only the passive, only those who accept their lot without active retaliation, are "flawless." Most of us are in that category.

But there are among us today, as there always have been, those who act against the scheme of things that degrades them, and in the process of action everything we have accepted out of fear or insensitivity or ignorance is shaken before us and examined, and from this total onslaught by an individual against the seemingly stable cosmos surrounding us—from this total examination of the "unchangeable" environment—comes the terror and the fear that is classically associated with tragedy.

More important, from this total questioning of what has previously been unquestioned, we learn. And such a process is not beyond the common man. In revolutions around the world, these past thirty years, he has demonstrated again and again this inner dynamic of all tragedy.

Insistence upon the rank of the tragic hero, or the so-called nobility of his character, is really but a clinging to the outward forms of tragedy. If rank or nobility of character was indispensable, then it would follow that the problems of those with rank were the particular problems of tragedy. But surely the right of one monarch to capture the domain from another no longer raises our passions, nor are our concepts of justice what they were to the mind of an Elizabethan king.

The quality in such plays that does shake us, however, derives from the underlying fear of being displaced, the disaster inherent in being torn away from our chosen image of what and who we are in this world. Among us today this fear is as strong, and perhaps stronger, than it ever was. In fact, it is the common man who knows this fear best.

Now, if it is true that tragedy is the consequence of a man's total compulsion to evaluate himself justly, his destruction in the attempt posits a wrong or an evil in his environment. And this is precisely the morality of tragedy and its lesson. The discovery of the moral law, which is what the enlightenment of tragedy consists of, is not the discovery of some abstract or metaphysical quantity.

The tragic right is a condition of life, a condition in which the human personality is able to flower and realize itself. The wrong is the condition which suppresses man, perverts the flowing out of his love and creative instinct. Tragedy enlightens—and it must, in that it points the heroic finger at the enemy of man's freedom. The thrust for freedom is the quality in tragedy which exalts. The revolutionary questioning of the stable environment is what terrifies. In no way is the common man debarred from such thoughts or such actions.

Seen in this light, our lack of tragedy may be partially accounted for by the turn which modern literature has taken toward the purely psychiatric view of life, or the purely sociological. If all our miseries, our indignities, are born and bred within our minds, then all action, let alone the heroic action, is obviously impossible.

And if society alone is responsible for the cramping of our lives, then the protagonist must needs be so pure and faultless as to force us to deny his validity as a character. From neither of these views can tragedy derive, simply because neither represents a balanced concept of life. Above all else, tragedy requires the finest appreciation by the writer of cause and effect.

No tragedy can therefore come about when its author fears to question absolutely everything, when he regards any institution, habit or custom as being either everlasting, immutable or inevitable. In the tragic view the need of man to wholly realize himself is the only fixed star, and whatever it is that hedges his nature and lowers it is ripe for attack and examination. Which is not to say that tragedy must preach revolution.

The Greeks could probe the very heavenly origin of their ways and return to confirm the rightness of laws. And Job could face God in anger, demanding his right and end in submission. But for a moment everything is in suspension, nothing is accepted, and in this stretching and tearing apart of the cosmos, in the very action of so doing, the character gains "size," the tragic stature which is spuriously attached to the royal or the highborn in our minds. The commonest of men may take on that stature to the extent of his willingness to throw all he has into the contest, the battle to secure his rightful place in his world.

There is a misconception of tragedy with which I have been struck in review after review, and in many conversations with writers and readers alike. It is the idea that tragedy is of necessity allied to pessimism. Even the dictionary says nothing more about the word than that it means a story with a sad or unhappy ending. This impression is so firmly fixed that I almost hesitate to claim that in truth tragedy implies more optimism in its author than does comedy, and that its final result ought to be the reinforcement of the onlooker's brightest opinions of the human animal.

For, if it is true to say that in essence the tragic hero is intent upon claiming his whole due as a personality, and if this struggle must be total and without reservation, then it automatically demonstrates the indestructible will of man to achieve his humanity.

The possibility of victory must be there in tragedy. Where pathos rules, where pathos is finally derived, a character has fought a battle he could not possibly have won. The pathetic is achieved when the protagonist is, by virtue of his witlessness, his insensitivity or the very air he gives off, incapable of grappling with a much superior force.

Pathos truly is the mode for the pessimist. But tragedy requires a nicer balance between what is possible and what is impossible. And it is curious, although edifying, that the plays we revere, century after century, are the tragedies. In them, and in them alone, lies the belief—optimistic, if you will, in the perfectibility of man.

It is time, I think, that we who are without kings, took up this bright thread of our history and followed it to the only place it can possibly lead in our time—the heart and spirit of the average man.

1949

The Nature of Tragedy

There are whole libraries of books dealing with the nature of tragedy. That the subject is capable of interesting so many writers over the centuries is part proof that the idea of tragedy is constantly changing, and more, that it will never be finally defined.

In our day, however, when there seems so little time or inclination to theorize at all, certain elemental misconceptions have taken hold of both critics and readers to a point where the word has often been reduced to an epithet. A more exact appreciation of what tragedy entails can lead us all to a finer understanding of plays in general, which in turn may raise the level of our theater.

The most common confusion is that which fails to discriminate between the tragic and the pathetic. Any story, to have validity on the stage, must entail conflict. Obviously the conflict must be between people. But such a conflict is of the lowest, most elementary order; this conflict purely *between* people is all that is needed for melodrama and naturally reaches its apogee in physical violence. In fact, this kind of conflict defines melodrama.

The next rung up the ladder is the story which is not only a conflict between people, but at the same time within the minds of the combatants. When I show you why a man does what he does, I may do so melodramatically; but when I show why he almost did not do it, I am making drama.

Why is this higher? Because it more closely reflects the actual process of human action. It is quite possible to write a good melodrama without creating a single living character; in fact, melodrama becomes diffused wherever the vagaries and contradictions of real characterizations come into play. But without a living character it is not possible to create drama or tragedy. For as soon as one investigates not only why a man is acting, but what is trying to prevent him from acting—assuming one does so honestly—it becomes extremely difficult to contain the action in the forced and arbitrary form of melodrama.

Now, standing upon this element of drama we can try to reach toward tragedy. Tragedy, first of all, creates a certain order of feeling in the audience. The pathetic creates another order of feeling. Again, as with drama and melodrama, one is higher than the other. But while drama may be differentiated psychologically from melodrama—the higher entailing a conflict *within* each character—to separate tragedy from the mere pathetic is much more difficult. It is difficult because here society enters in.

Let me put it this way. When Mr. B., while walking down the street, is struck on the head by a falling piano, the newspapers call this a tragedy. In fact, of course, this is only the pathetic end of Mr. B. Not only because of the accidental nature of his death; that is elementary. It is pathetic because it merely arouses our feelings of sympathy, sadness, and possibly of identification. What the death of Mr. B. does not arouse is the tragic feeling.

To my mind the essential difference, and the precise difference, between tragedy and pathos is that tragedy brings us not only sadness, sympathy, identification and even fear; it also, unlike pathos, brings us knowledge or enlightenment.

But what sort of knowledge? In the largest sense, it is knowledge pertaining to the right way of living in the world. The manner of Mr. B.'s death was not such as to illustrate any principle of living. In short, there was no illumination of the ethical in it. And to put it all in the same breath, the reason we confuse the tragic with the pathetic, as well as why we create so few tragedies, is twofold: in the first place many of our writers have given up trying to search out the right way of living, and secondly, there is not among us any commonly accepted faith in a way of life that will give us not only material gain but satisfaction.

Our modern literature has filled itself with an attitude which implies that despite suffering, nothing important can really be learned by man that might raise him to a happier condition. The probing of the soul has taken the path of behaviorism. By this method it is sufficient for an artist simply to spell out the anatomy of disaster. Man is regarded as essentially a dumb animal moving through a pre-constructed maze toward his inevitable sleep.

Such a concept of man can never reach beyond pathos, for enlightenment is impossible within it, life being regarded as an immutably disastrous fact. Tragedy, called a more exalted kind of consciousness, is so called because it makes us aware of what the character might have been. But to say or strongly imply what a man might have been requires of the author a soundly based, completely believed vision of man's great possibilities. As Aristotle said, the poet is greater than the historian because he presents not only things as they were, but foreshadows what they might have been. We forsake literature when we are content to chronicle disaster.

Tragedy, therefore, is inseparable from a certain modest hope regarding the human animal. And it is the glimpse of this brighter possibility that raises sadness out of the pathetic toward the tragic.

But, again, to take up a sad story and discover the hope that may lie buried in it, requires a most complete grasp of the characters involved. For nothing is so destructive of reality in literature as thinly motivated optimism. It is my view—or my prejudice—that when a man is seen whole and round and so characterized, when he is allowed his life on the stage over and beyond the mould and purpose of the story, hope will show its face in his, just as it does, even so dimly, in life. As the old saying has it, there is some good in the worst of us. I think that the tragedian, supposedly the saddest of citizens, can never forget this fact, and must strive always to posit a world in which that good might have been allowed to express itself instead of succumbing to the evil. I began by saying that tragedy would probably never be wholly defined. I end by offering you a definition. It is not final for me, but at least it has the virtue of keeping mere pathos out.

You are witnessing a tragedy when the characters before you are wholly and intensely realized, to the degree that your belief in their reality is all but complete. The story in which they are involved is such as to force their complete personalities to be brought to bear upon the problem, to the degree that you are able to understand not only why they are ending in sadness, but how they might have avoided their end. The demeanor, so to speak, of the story is most serious—so serious that you have been brought to the state of outright fear for the people involved, as though for yourself.

And all this, not merely so that your senses shall have been stretched and your glands stimulated, but that you may come away with the knowledge that man, by reason of his intense effort and desire, which you have just seen demonstrated, is capable of flowering on this earth.

Tragedy arises when we are in the presence of a man who has missed accomplishing his joy. But the joy must be there, the promise of the right way of life must be there. Otherwise pathos reigns, and an endless, meaningless, and essentially untrue picture of man is created—man helpless under the falling piano, man wholly lost in a universe which by its very nature is too hostile to be mastered.

In a word, tragedy is the most accurately balanced portrayal of the human being in his struggle for happiness. That is why we revere our tragedies in the highest, because they most truly portray us. And that is why tragedy must not be diminished through confusion with other modes, for it is the most perfect means we have of showing us who and what we are, and what we must be—or should strive to become.

1949

The Salesman Has a Birthday

Experience tells me that I will probably know better next year what I feel right now about the first anniversary of *Death of a Salesman*—it usually takes that long to understand anything. I suppose I ought to try to open some insights into the play. Frankly, however, it comes very fuzzily to mind at this date. I have not sat through it since dress rehearsal and haven't read it since the proofs went to the publisher. In fact, it may well be that from the moment I read it to my wife and two friends one evening in the country a year ago last fall, the play cut itself off from me in a way that is incomprehensible.

I remember that night clearly, best of all. The feeling of disaster when, glancing up at the audience of three, I saw nothing but glazed looks in their eyes. And at the end, when they said nothing, the script suddenly seemed a record of a madness I had passed through, something I ought not admit to at all, let alone read aloud or have produced on the stage.

I don't remember what they said, exactly, excepting that it had taken them deeply. But I can see my wife's eyes as I read a—to me—hilarious scene, which I prefer not to identify. She was weeping. I confess that I laughed more during the writing of this play than I have ever done, when alone, in my life. I laughed because moment after moment came when I felt I had rapped it right on the head—the non sequitur, the aberrant but meaningful idea racing through Willy's head, the turn of story that kept surprising me every morning. And most of all the form, for which I have been searching since the beginning of my writing life.

Writing in that form was like moving through a corridor in a dream, knowing instinctively that one would find every wriggle of it and, best of all, where the exit lay. There is something like a dream's quality in my memory of the writing and the day or two that followed its completion.

I remember the rehearsal when we had our first audience. Six or seven friends. The play working itself out under the single bulb overhead. I think that was the first and only time I saw it as others see it. Then it seemed to me that we must be a terribly lonely people, cut off from each other by such massive pretense of self-sufficiency, machined down so fine we hardly touch any more. We are trying to save ourselves separately, and that is immoral, that is the corrosive among us.

On that afternoon, more than any time before or since, the marvel of the actor was all new to me. How utterly they believed what they were saying to each other!

To watch fine actors creating their roles is to see revealed the innocence, the naïve imagination of man liberated from the prisons of the past. They were like children wanting to show that they could turn themselves into anybody, thus opening their lives to limitless possibilities.

And Elia Kazan, with his marvelous wiles, tripping the latches of the secret little doors that lead into the always different personalities of each actor. That is his secret; not merely to know what must be done, to know the way to implement the doing for actors trained in diametrically opposite schools, or not trained at all. He does not "direct," he creates a center point, and then goes to each actor and creates the desire to move toward it. And they all meet, but for different reasons, and seem to have arrived there by themselves.

Was there ever a production of so serious a play that was carried through with so much exhilarating laughter? I doubt it. We were always on the way, and I suppose we always knew it.

There are things learned—I think, by many people—from this production. Things which, if applied, can bring much vitality to our theater.

There is no limit to the expansion of the audience's imagination so long as the play's internal logic is kept inviolate. It is not true that conventionalism is demanded. They will move with you anywhere; they will believe right into the moon so long as you believe who tell them this tale. We are at the beginning of many explosions of form. They are waiting for wonders.

A serious theme is entertaining to the extent that it is not trifled with, not cleverly angled, but met in head-on collision. They will not consent to suffer while the creators stand by with tongue in cheek. They have a way of knowing. Nobody can blame them.

And there have been certain disappointments, one above all. I am sorry the self-realization of the older son, Biff, is not a weightier counterbalance to Willy's disaster in the audience's mind.

And certain things are more clearly known, or so it seems now. We want to give of ourselves, and yet all we train for is to take, as though nothing less will keep the world at a safe distance. Every day we contradict our will to create, which is to give. The end of man is not security, but without security we are without the elementary condition of humaneness.

A time will come when they will look back at us astonished that we saw something holy in the competition for the means of existence. But already we are beginning to ask of the great man, not what has he got, but what has he done for the world. We ought to be struggling for a world in which it will be possible to lay blame. Only then will the great tragedies be written, for where no order is believed in, no order can be breached, and thus all disasters of man will strive vainly for moral meaning.

And what have such thoughts to do with this sort of reminiscence? Only that to me the tragedy of Willy Loman is that he gave his life, or sold it, in order to justify the waste of it. It is the tragedy of a man who did believe that he alone was not meeting the qualifications laid down for mankind by those clean-shaven frontiersmen who inhabit the peaks of broadcasting and advertising offices. From those forests of canned goods high up near the sky, he heard the thundering command to succeed as it ricocheted down the newspaper-lined canyons of his city, heard not a human voice, but a wind of a voice to which no human can reply in kind, except to stare into the mirror at a failure.

So what is there to feel on this anniversary? Hope, for I know now that the people want to listen. A little fear that they want to listen so badly. And an old insistence—sometimes difficult to summon, but there nonetheless—that we will find a way beyond fear of each other, beyond bellicosity, a way into our humanity.

1950

Essays: 1951–1960

Preface to
an Adaptation of Ibsen's
An Enemy of the People

At the outset it ought to be said that the word "adaptation" is very distasteful to me. It seems to mean that one writer has ventured into another's chickencoop, or worse, into the sacred chamber of another's personal creations and rearranged things without permission. Most of the time an adaptation is a playwright's excuse for not writing his own plays, and since I am not yet with my back against that particular wall, I think it wise to set down what I have tried to do with *An Enemy of the People,* and why I did it.

There is one quality in Ibsen that no serious writer can afford to overlook. It lies at the very center of his force, and I found in it—as I hope others will—a profound source of strength. It is his insistence, his utter conviction, that he is going to say what he has to say, and that the audience, by God, is going to listen. It is the very same quality that makes a star actor, a great public speaker, and a lunatic. Every Ibsen play begins with the unwritten words: "Now listen here!" And these words have shown me a path through the wall of "entertainment," a path that leads beyond the formulas and dried-up precepts, the pretense and fraud, of the business of the stage. Whatever else Ibsen has to teach, this is his first and greatest contribution.

In recent years Ibsen has fallen into a kind of respectful obscurity that is not only undeserved but really quite disrespectful of culture—and a disservice to the theater besides. I decided to work on *An Enemy of the People* because I had a private wish to demonstrate that Ibsen is really pertinent today, that he is not "old-fashioned," and, implicitly, that those who condemn him are themselves misleading our theater and our playwrights into a blind alley of senseless sensibility, triviality, and the inevitable waste of our dramatic talents; for it has become the fashion for plays to reduce the "thickness" of life to a fragile facsimile, to avoid portraying the complexities of life, the contradictions of character, the fascinating interplay of cause and effect that have long been part of the novel. And I wished also to buttress the idea that the dramatic writer has, and must again demonstrate, the right to entertain with his brains as well as his heart. It is necessary that the public understand again that the stage is *the* place for ideas, for philosophies, for the most intense discussion of man's fate. One of the masters of such a discussion is Henrik Ibsen, and I have presumed to point this out once again.

I have attempted to make *An Enemy of the People* as alive to Americans as it undoubtedly was to Norwegians, while keeping it intact. I had no interest in exhuming anything, in asking people to sit respectfully before the work of a celebrated but neglected writer. There are museums for such activities; the theater has no truck with them, and ought not to have.

And I believe this play could be alive for us because its central theme is, in my opinion, the central theme of our social life today. Simply, it is the question of whether the democratic guarantees protecting political minorities ought to be set aside in time of crisis. More personally, it is the question of whether one's vision of the truth ought to be a source of guilt at a time when the mass of men condemn it as a dangerous and devilish lie. It is an enduring theme—in fact, possibly the most enduring of all Ibsen's themes—because there never was, nor will there ever be, an organized society able to countenance calmly the individual who insists that he is right while the vast majority is absolutely wrong.

The play is the story of a scientist who discovers an evil and, innocently believing that he has done a service to humanity, expects that he will at least be thanked. However, the town has a vested interest in the perpetuation of that evil, and his "truth," when confronted with that interest, must be made to conform. The scientist cannot change the truth for any reason disconnected with the evil. He clings to the truth and suffers the social consequences. At rock bottom, then, the play is concerned with the inviolability of objective truth. Or, put more dynamically, that those who attempt to warp the truth for ulterior purposes must inevitably become warped and corrupted themselves. This theme is valid today, just as it will always be, but some of the examples given by Ibsen to prove it may no longer be.

I am told that Ibsen wrote this play as a result of his being practically stoned off the stage for daring to present *Ghosts*. The plot is supposed to have come from a news item which told of a Hungarian scientist who had discovered poisoned water in the town's water supply and had been pilloried for his discovery. If this was the case, my interpretation of the theme is doubly justified, for it then seems beyond doubt that Ibsen meant above and beyond all else to defend his right to stand "at the outpost of society," alone with the truth, and to speak from there to his fellow men.

However, there are a few speeches, and one scene in particular, which have been taken to mean that Ibsen was a fascist. In the original meeting scene in which Dr. Stockmann sets forth his—and Ibsen's—point of view most completely and angrily, Dr. Stockmann makes a speech in which he turns to biology to prove that there are indeed certain individuals "bred" to a superior apprehension of truths and who have the natural right to lead, if not to govern, the mass.

If the entire play is to be understood as the working-out of this speech, then one has no justification for contending that it is other than racist and fascist—certainly it could not be thought of as a defense of any democratic idea. But, structurally speaking, the theme is not wholly contained in the meeting scene alone. In fact, this speech is in some important respects in contradiction to the actual dramatic working-out of the play. But that Ibsen never really believed that idea in the first place is amply proved by a speech he delivered to a workers' club after the production of *An Enemy of the People*. He said then: "Of course I do not mean the aristocracy of birth, or of the purse, or even the aristocracy of the intellect. I mean the aristocracy of character, of will, of mind—that alone can free us."

I have taken as justification for removing those examples which no longer prove the theme—examples I believe Ibsen would have removed were he alive today—the line in the original manuscript that reads: "There is no established truth that can remain true for more than seventeen, eighteen, at most twenty years." In light of genocide, the holocaust that has swept our world on the wings of the black ideology of racism, it is inconceivable that Ibsen would insist today that certain individuals are by breeding, or race, or "innate" qualities superior to others or possessed of the right to dictate to others. The man who wrote *A Doll's House,* the clarion call for the equality of women, cannot be equated with a fascist. The whole cast of his thinking was such that he could not have lived a day under an authoritarian regime of any kind. He was an individualist sometimes to the point of anarchism, and in such a man there is too explosive a need for self-expression to permit him to conform to any rigid ideology. It is impossible, therefore, to set him beside Hitler.

On reading the standard translation of Ibsen's work it quickly became obvious that the false impressions that have been connected with the man would seem to be justified were he to be produced in "translated" form. For one thing, his language in English sounds impossibly pedantic. Combine this with the fact that he wore a beard and half-lenses in his eyeglasses, and that his plays have always been set forth with yards of fringe on every tablecloth and drapery, and it was guaranteed that a new production on the traditional basis would truly bury the man for good.

I set out to transform his language into contemporary English. Working from a pidgin-English, word-for-word rendering of the Norwegian, done by Mr. Lars Nordenson, I was able to gather the meaning of each speech and scene without the obstruction of any kind of English construction.

For instance, Mr. Nordenson, working from the original Norwegian manuscript, set before me speeches such as: "But, dear Thomas, what have you then done to him again?" Or: "The Mayor being your brother, I would not wish to touch it, but you are as convinced as I am that truth goes ahead of all other considerations." Or: "Well, what do you say, Doctor? Don't you think it is high time that we stir a little life into the slackness and sloppiness of half-heartedness and cowardliness?" This last speech now reads: "Well, what do you say to a little hypodermic for these fence-sitting deadheads?"

It was possible to peer into the original play with as clear an eye as one could who knew no Norwegian. There were no English sentences to correct and rewrite, only the bare literalness of the original. This version of the play, then, is really in the nature of a new translation into spoken English.*

But it is more too. The original has a tendency to indulge in transitions between scenes that are themselves uninteresting, and although as little as possible of the original construction has been changed and the play is exactly as it was, scene for scene, I have made each act seem of one piec e, instead of separate scenes. And my reason

---

* It might be added, however, that I did not "use" Ibsen as an easy way to make contemporary points, as more than one critic has complained. The glaring example is my alleged invention of the idea that Dr. Stockmann emigrate to America where tolerance and liberality will make his life easier, which was taken as my jab at our own anti-radicalism. In fact, emigration to liberal America is in the original, and is not at all an ironical suggestion but seriously intended as a contrast with Norwegian narrowness. (A.M., 1977.)

for doing this is simply that the tradition of Ibsen's theater allowed the opera-like separation of scenes, while ours demands that the audience never be conscious that a "scene" has taken place at all.

Structurally the largest change is in the third act—Ibsen's fifth. In the original the actual dramatic end comes a little past the middle of the act, but it is followed by a wind-up that keeps winding endlessly to the curtain. I think this overwriting was the result of Ibsen's insistence that his meaning be driven home—and from the front door right through to the back, lest the audience fail to understand him. Generally, in this act, I have brought out the meaning of the play in terms of dramatic action, action which was already there and didn't need to be newly invented, but which was separated by tendentious speeches spoken into the blue.

Throughout the play I have tried to peel away its trappings of the moment, its relatively accidental details which ring the dull green tones of Victorianism, and to show that beneath them there still lives the terrible wrath of Henrik Ibsen, who could make a play as men make watches, precisely, intelligently, and telling not merely the minute and the hour but the age.

1951

Many Writers: Few Plays

It is impossible for anyone living in the midst of a cultural period to say with certainty why it is languishing in its produce and general vitality. This is especially true of the theater, where we tend to compare our usually vapid present with "Chekhov's period," or "Ibsen's," or our own previous decades, much to our disadvantage, forgetting that the giants usually stood alone in their time. Nevertheless, even optimists now confess that our theater has struck a seemingly endless low by any standard. I cannot hope to try to explain the reasons for this but certain clues keep recurring to me when thinking on the matter.

We can find no solace in the fact that there never have been more than a handful of first-class playwrights in any one country at any one time, for we have more than the usual number in America now, but few plays from them, and fewer still of any weight. A lizardic dormancy seems to be upon us; the creative mind seems to have lost its heat. Why?

I think the answers will be found in the nature of the creative act. A good play is a good thought; a great play is a great thought. A great thought is a thrust outward, a daring act. Daring is of the essence. Its very nature is incompatible with an undue affection for moderation, respectability, even fairness and responsibleness. Those qualities are proper for the inside of the telephone company, not for creative art.

I may be wrong, but I sense that the playwrights have become more timid with experience and maturity, timid in ethical and social idea, theatrical method, and stylistic means. Because they are unproduced, no firm generalization can be made about the younger playwrights, but from my personal impressions of scripts sent me from time to time, as well as from talks I have had with a few groups of them, I have been struck and dismayed by the strangely high place they give to inoffensiveness.

I find them old without having been young. Like young executives, they seem proudest of their sensibleness—what they call being practical. Illusion is out; it is foolish. What illusion? The illusion that the writer can save the world. The fashion is that the world cannot be saved. Between the determinism of economics and the iron laws of psychiatrics they can only appear ridiculous, they think, by roaring out a credo, a cry of pain, a point of view. Perhaps they really have no point of view, or pain either. It is incomprehensible to me.

Recently a young Chilean director, who has put on more than thirty plays in his own country, and spent the past three years studying theater on a fellowship in France, in Britain, and in two of our leading universities, told me this: "Your students and teachers seem to have no interest at all in the meanings of the ideas in the plays they study. Everything is technique. Your productions and physical apparatus are the best in the world, but among all the university people I came to know, as well as the professionals, scarcely any want to talk about the authors' ethical, moral, or philosophical intentions. They seem to see the theater almost as an engineering project, the purpose being to study successful models of form in order, somehow, to reproduce them with other words."

All this means to me, if true, is that this generation is turning Japanese. The Japanese are said to admire infinite repetitions of time-hallowed stories, characters, and themes. It is the triumph of the practical in art. The most practical thing to do is to repeat what has been done and thought before. But the very liquor of our art has always been originality, uniqueness. The East is older. Perhaps this sterile lull is therefore the sign of our aging. Perhaps we are observing several seasons of hush and silence to mark the passage through our youth. Our youth that was Shaw and Ibsen and O'Neill and all the great ones who kept turning and turning the central question of all great art—how may man govern himself so that he may live more humanly, more alive?

Japanism, so to speak, took over Hollywood long ago, and now the movie is ritual thinly veiled. The practical took command. The "showman" won. High finance took sterility by the hand, and together they rolled the product smooth, stripped off all its offensive edges, its individuality, and created the perfect circle—namely, zero.

I think the same grinding mill is at work in the theater, but more deceptively because we have no big companies enforcing compliance to any stated rules. But we have an atmosphere of dread just the same, an unconsciously—or consciously—accepted party line, a sanctified complex of moods and attitudes, proper and improper. If nothing else comes of it, one thing surely has: it has made it dangerous to dare, and, worse still, impractical. I am not speaking merely of political thought. Journalists have recently made studies of college students now in school and have been struck by the absence among them of any ferment, either religious, political, literary, or whatever. Wealthy, powerful, envied all about, it seems the American people stand mute.

We always had with us the "showman," but we also had a group of rebels insisting on thrusting their private view of the world on others. Where are they? Or is everybody really happy now? Do Americans really believe they have solved the problems of living for all time? If not, where are the plays that reflect the soul-racking, deeply unseating questions that are being inwardly asked on the street, in the living room, on the subways?

Either the playwrights are deaf to them, which I cannot believe, or they are somehow shy of bringing them onto the stage. If the last is true we are unlikely to have even the "straight" theater again—the melodramas, the farces, the "small" plays. It is hard to convince you of this, perhaps, but little thoughts feed off big thoughts; an exciting theater cannot come without there being a ferment, a ferment in the colleges, in the press, in the air. For years now I seem to have heard not expressions of thought from people but a sort of oblong blur, a reflection in distance of the newspapers' opinions.

Is the knuckleheadedness of McCarthyism behind it all? The Congressional investigations of political unorthodoxy? Yes. But is that all? Can an artist be paralyzed except he be somewhat willing? You may pardon me for quoting from myself, but must one always be not merely liked but well liked? Is it not honorable to have powerful enemies? Guardedness, suspicion, aloof circumspection—these are the strongest traits I see around me, and what have they ever had to do with the creative act?

Is it quixotic to say that a time comes for an artist—and for all those who want and love theater—when the world must be left behind? When, like some pilgrim, he must consult only his own heart and cleave to the truth it utters? For out of the hectoring of columnists, the compulsions of patriotic gangs, the suspicions of the honest and the corrupt alike, art never will and never has found soil.

I think of a night last week when a storm knocked out my lights in the country, and it being only nine o'clock it was unthinkable to go to bed. I sat a long time in the blacked-out living room, wide awake, a manuscript unfinished on the table. The idea of lying in bed with one's eyes open, one's brain alive, seemed improper, even degrading. And so, like some primitive man discovering the blessings of fire, I lit two candles and experimentally set them beside my papers. Lo! I could read and work again.

Let a storm come, even from God, and yet it leaves a choice with the man in the dark. He may sit eyeless, waiting for some unknown force to return him his light, or he may seek his private flame. But the choice, the choice is there. We cannot yet be tired. There is work to be done. This is no time to go to sleep.

1952

University of Michigan

My first affection for the University of Michigan was due, simply, to their accepting me. They had already turned me down twice because my academic record (I had flunked algebra three times in my Brooklyn high school) was so low as to be practically invisible, but the dean reversed himself after two letters in which I wrote that since working for two years—in a warehouse at fifteen dollars a week—I had turned into a much more serious fellow. He said he would give me a try, but I had better make some grades. I could not conceive of a dean at Columbia or Harvard doing that.

When I arrived in 1934, at the bottom of the Depression, I fell in love with the place, groggy as I was from the bus ride, because I was out of the warehouse at last and at least formally a part of a beautiful town, the college town of Ann Arbor. I resolved to make good for the dean and studied so hard my first semester that in the history exam my mind went completely blank and the professor led me out of the class and told me to go to sleep and to come back and take the exam again.

I loved it also because of the surprises. Elmo Hamm, the son of a potato farmer in Upper Michigan, turned out to be as sharp a student as any of the myopic drudges who got the best grades in New York. I loved it because Harmon Remmel, the son of an Arkansas banker, lived in the room next to mine, and from him I got a first glimpse of what the South meant to a Southerner, a Southerner who kept five rifles racked on the wall, and two. 38's in his valise, and poured himself bullets in a little mold he kept on his desk. (In his sophomore year he disappeared, and I found out he had been unable to bear it any longer once duck-hunting time had rolled around again.)

I loved the idea of being separated from the nation, because the spirit of the nation, like its soil, was being blown by crazy winds. Friends of mine in New York, one of them a cum laude from Columbia, were aspiring to the city fireman's exam, but in Ann Arbor I saw that if it came to the worst a man could live on nothing for a long time. I earned fifteen dollars a month for feeding a building full of mice—the National Youth Administration footing the bill—and out of it I paid $1.75 a week for my room and squeezed the rest for my Granger tobacco (two packs for thirteen cents), my books, laundry, and movies. For my meals I washed dishes in the coop cafeteria. My eyeglasses were supplied by the health service, and my teeth were fixed for the cost of materials. The girls paid for themselves, including the one I married.

I think I sent more students to Michigan than anybody else who ever went there.

It was a great place for anybody who wanted to write. The Hopwood Awards, with prizes ranging from $250 to $1500, were an incentive, but there was something more. The English Department had, and still has, a serious respect for undergraduate writing efforts. Professor Kenneth Rowe, who teaches playwriting, may not have created a playwright (no teacher ever did), but he surely read what we wrote with the urgency of one who actually had the power to produce the play. I loved the place, too, because it was just big enough to give one the feeling that his relative excellence or mediocrity had real meaning, and yet not so big as to drown one in numbers.

I remember the June of each year when the Hopwood Awards were announced, and the crowds would form to hear the featured speaker—some literary light from the book world—after which the presentations were made. How I hated those speakers for holding up the awards! And those prizes meant more than recognition. In my case at least, they meant the end of mouse-feeding and room-sharing and the beginning of a serious plan to become a playwright. Avery Hopwood made millions by writing bedroom farces like *Getting Gertie's Garter* and *Up in Mabel's Room*; if my sense of it is correct, never was so much hope created in so many people by so modest an accomplishment. I have never sweated on an opening night the way I did at Hopwood time.

I do not know whether the same thing happened at Harvard or Columbia or Yale, but when I was at Ann Arbor I felt I was at home. It was a little world, and it was man-sized. My friends were the sons of diemakers, farmers, ranchers, bankers, lawyers, doctors, clothing workers and unemployed relief recipients. They came from every part of the country and brought all their prejudices and special wisdoms. It was always so wonderful to get up in the morning. There was a lot learned every day. I recall going to hear Kagawa, the Japanese philosopher, and how, suddenly, half the audience stood up and walked out because he had used the word Manchukuo, which is Japanese, for the Chinese province of Manchuria. As I watched the Chinese students excitedly talking outside on the steps of Hill Auditorium, I felt something about the Japanese attack on China that I had not felt before.

It was a time when the fraternities, like the football team, were losing their glamour. Life was too earnest. But I remember glancing with sadness at the photographs of Newman, Oosterbaan, and the other gridiron heroes and secretly wishing that the gladiatorial age had not so completely disappeared. Instead, my generation thirsted for another kind of action, and we took great pleasure in the sit-down strikes that burst loose in Flint and Detroit, and we gasped when Roosevelt went over the line with the TVA, and we saw a new world coming every third morning, and some of the old residents thought we had gone stark raving mad.

I tell you true, when I think of the library I think of the sound of a stump speaker on the lawn outside, because so many times I looked up from what I was reading to try to hear what issue they were debating now. The place was full of speeches, meetings, and leaflets. It was jumping with Issues.

But political facts of life were not all I learned. I learned that under certain atmospheric conditions you could ice-skate up and down all the streets in Ann Arbor at night. I learned that toward June you could swim in a certain place without a suit on and that the Arboretum, a tract of land where the botanists studied plants and trees, was also good for anatomical studies, especially in spring under a moon. I had come to school believing that professors were objective repositories of factual knowledge; I found that they were not only fallible but some of them were damn fools and enough of them seekers and questioners to make talking with them a long-lasting memory.

I left Ann Arbor in the spring of 1938 and in two months was on relief. But, whether the measurement was false or not, I felt I had accomplished something there. I knew at least how much I did not know. I had found many friends and had the respect of the ones that mattered to me. It had been a small world, gentler than the real one but tough enough. It was my idea of what a university ought to be.

What is it now? You can see at once, I hope, that my judgment is not objective, if only because my memories of the place are sweet and so many things that formed those memories have been altered. There are buildings now where I remembered lawn and trees. And yet, I told myself as I resented these intrusions, in the Thirties we were all the time calling for these dormitories and they are finally built. In my day bequests were used for erecting less useful things—the carillon tower whose bells woke us up in the morning, the Rackham Building, a grand mausoleum which seemed to have been designed for sitting around in a wide space.

There are certain facts about the university today that can be disposed of right off. In almost every field of study, a student will probably find no better training anywhere than at Michigan. Some say that in forestry, medicine, creative writing, and many other fields it is really the top. I wouldn't know, I never went to any other school.

The student will need about a thousand dollars a year, which is cheaper than a lot of places. He will get free medical care and hospitalization; he will be able to borrow money from the university if he needs it and may take nearly forever to pay it back; he will use modern laboratories in the sciences and an excellent library in the humanities; as a freshman he will live in new dormitories, and the girls will have to be in bed at ten-thirty; if he flies to school he will land at the Willow Run Airport, the safest in the country, owned now by the university; he will have a radio station and a television station to try his scripts, if he writes, and if he is more literary than that he can try for a Hopwood Award in poetry, drama, the essay and the novel.

He will meet students of many backgrounds. Two thirds will be from Michigan and a large proportion of those from small towns. About nine hundred will be foreign, including Japanese, Turks, Chinese and Europeans. If he is Negro he will find little discrimination, except in a few Greek-letter fraternities. Most of his classes will be large in the first years, but his teachers have regular visiting hours, and with a little push he can get to know them. He will not be permitted to drive a car or to keep liquor in his room.

On many winter mornings he will wake to find great snows, and there will be a serene hush upon the campus and the creaking of branches overhead as he walks to his class. In spring he will glance outside at a blossoming world and resolve to keep his eye away from the girl sitting beside him. By June, the heat of the prairies will threaten to kill him and he will leave just in time.

If he has the talent, he may join the *Michigan Daily* staff, and the *Daily* is as close to a real newspaper as he will find in any school. On its own press, it prints about 7500 copies a day, has the Associated Press wire service and syndicated columnists, and its student staff is paid twelve dollars a month and up. The university athletic plant includes a stadium seating nearly 100,000 people, indoor and outdoor tennis courts, swimming pools, and so on.

If a figure can convey an idea of complexity and size, it costs about $40 million a year to keep the place going. There are now better than 18,000 students and nearly 1200 faculty, and the figures will rise next year and the year after. The school has just bought 347 acres for new buildings. More facts may be had for the asking; but in any case, you couldn't do better for facilities.

Things seem to be getting *done* now. For instance, on the north side of the campus the Phoenix Project is going up, the only thing of its kind in the country. It was conceived by an alumnus in the advertising business who discovered, while traveling through Europe, that we were being accused of using the atom for war only. Returning here, he began a campaign for alumni contributions to create an institute which will accept no government money, do no war work, and instead of operating in secrecy will attempt to discover and disperse the knowledge of the atom that will, some say, revolutionize human life. Research projects are under way, although the scientists are not yet housed in one building, and already a method has been found by which the dreaded trichina, often found in pork, is destroyed. One of the men in charge of the project told me that the implications of Phoenix will reach into every science, that it has already moved into botany, medicine, dentistry, and eventually will span them all.

There is an enormous growth in all kinds of theater since I was at Michigan. Somewhere, sometime this year on campus, you could have seen *Brigadoon,* Gilbert and Sullivan, a German play, a French play, Aristophanes, Pirandello, *Deep Are the Roots, Faust, Madame Butterfly, Mister Roberts*, and more, all acted by students. A professional theater has done Camus, Bridie, Shakespeare, Saroyan, Yeats, Gertrude Stein, Sophocles, Synge and the Norwegian Krog. A symphony orchestra and a jazz band play student compositions frequently; there is a practically continuous art show going on, with both traveling and local exhibitions on view; the best foreign and art films are shown once a week, and the joint is jumping with concerts. All this is proof that a considerable number of people in Ann Arbor are looking for more than technology and are eager to feed their souls—a fact sometimes doubted by many in and out of the university.

The increase in students goes far to explain the impression of great activity, of building, of research, the scores of research projects, and of course the great increases in the faculty, especially in the English and Psychology Departments. But the changes are also qualitative. As one small sign, the music school has a few teachers who actually compose. The old idea of the university is not passing away, it is being worked away, it seems; the study of phenomena is giving way to the creation of useful things. *Generation*, the literary magazine, does not merely publish essays on music but new scores, as well as poetry, photographs and stories.

The university has the feel of a practical workshop these days. In my time a great deal of research and thesis writing was carried on by people who were simply hiding from the Depression. When you asked undergraduates what they intended to major in, and what career they meant to follow, you saw an oblong blur float across their eyes. These days nearly everybody seems to be quite sure. I knew graduate students who lived in an abandoned house with no electricity or heat and never took the boardings off the windows for fear of discovery, and one of them had been around so long he had gone through every course in the lit school but Roman Band instruments. The lucky ones got an assistantship at $600 a year and even so looked like they had dropped out of a novel by Dostoyevski. Now, in some departments, a man doing his dissertation hooks into a research project and earns $2400 a year and sometimes gets secretarial help in the bargain.

The Psychology Department, for instance, which used to have about a half-dozen members, and was year in year out trying to discover the learning processes of rats put through an enormous maze, now spreads out over a whole floor of offices, and spends tens of thousands investigating mass behavior of *people*, of all things, problems of industrial psychology, and in the words of one troubled researcher, "how to make people do what you want them to while thinking they are doing it because *they* want to."

From the physical, quantitative point of view, it seems to me that if by some magic this university of 1953 had suddenly materialized on a morning in 1935, let's say, we would have decided that the millennium had arrived. The mere fact that every morning the Michigan *Daily* displays two columns of invitations from corporations and government bureaus to students to apply for positions would have been enough.

The millennium is here, and yet it isn't here. What's wrong, then? I have no proof for this, but I felt it many times in my stay and I'll say it: I did not feel any love around the place. I suspect that I resent the Detroit Modern architecture of the new administration building and the new Haven and Mason Halls, and the fluorescent lighting and the gray steel furniture in the teachers' office cubicles. Can steel furniture ever belong to anybody, or can anybody ever belong to steel furniture? Is it all right to need so much administration that you have to put up an office building with nothing but administrators in it? Maybe it's all right, but God, it's not a university, is it? Why not? I don't know why not, it just feels like an insurance company, that's all. And yet, with eighteen to twenty thousand students, I suppose you've got to have it. Somebody's got to count them. But there is no love in it.

There is a certain propriety around the place that I found quite strange. Or was it always that way and I didn't notice? I do not remember teachers lowering their voices when they spoke to you in the corridors, but they do that now. At first I thought it was my imagination, and I asked a few men about it, but they denied that they do it. Still, they are doing it. The place is full of comportment. Maybe I have been around theatrical folk too long but it seemed to me that everybody had turned into engineers—in my day all engineers wore black suits and short, antiseptic haircuts. The curious thing is that now the engineers affect buckskin shoes and dungarees or tan chino work pants.

The lists of help-wanted notices alone would have solved the problem of my generation. And yet in talking with a certain high administrative official, it quickly became evident that the millennium had not yet arrived. I found it hard to believe that this gentleman had been elevated to administration, because when he was my teacher several hundred years ago he used to drop his coat on the floor sometimes and forget about tying his tie correctly, and his suits were usually rumpled. He just wasn't executive. Now his suits are pressed and finished worsted not tweed, but the smile is still warm and the eyes crinkle with a great love for humanity. He is very proud of the school, but there is a cloud. There is a cloud over the whole place which is hard to define, and here is part of it. I do not quote him but summarize what he said:

There is less hanging around the lamppost than there used to be. The student now is very young and he has little background. He generally comes with high respect for Michigan's academic standards. The school takes the top half of the in-state students and the top twenty percent of the out-staters. Fear of the competition is one reason why they absorb themselves in the pursuit of grades. Another is that they do not want to lose their Army deferments. Finally, in the old days a corporation would interview a C student because he might have other valuable qualities, while today the selections are almost statistical—they see the very top of the class and no others. The students know this and are more methodical about grades to the neglect of other interests.

The implication seemed to be that they are more machinelike and perhaps even duller. Or perhaps he meant only that some spirit had departed.

What spirit was he referring to? I think I know. The word university used to imply a place of gentle inquiry, an absorbing waste of time from the money point of view, a place where one "broadened" oneself. And I think he meant that everything is being *defined* now, it is all becoming so purposeful in the narrow sense of the trade school that some of the old separation between university and commerce, university and vocation, university and practicality in the narrow sense, is disappearing.

One symptom of this is the growing and dangerous rivalry with Michigan State College. In my day State was an agricultural college, and the University of Michigan was "The Harvard of the West." Today State is challenging the university for supremacy in all departments, even threatening to rename itself Michigan State *University*. Dr. John A. Hannah, State's vigorous president, has been able to raise enough funds to build a row of impressive dormitories along the main road. The public can see and count the things it is getting for its money. The university cannot compete for the public's appreciation—and support—on the basis of invisible accomplishments like culture and broadening. Consequently, a new and in my time unheard-of slogan is going around the faculty gatherings. Service to the state is the idea. Do things they can *see*. My friend spoke with startlingly serious irritation, real misgivings, about State's victories over Michigan in football. It has come even to that.

As in everything else, therefore, the competition must be carried through on the level of the lowest bidder. Michigan State has always been able to show that where one blade of corn had grown now there were two because of its new insecticides, and the cows were happier for its vaccines. Michigan State went on television, got its own station, so the university decided to win friends and acquire *its* station.

A professor of English was speaking to me in his office. I must note the incongruity of this particular man sitting in this particular office. In my time this man was, how shall I say, dusty. We were all afraid of him because in his classes you either knew your stuff or you didn't. His subject had made him pale and austerely exact. A great poem was a structure that had to be turned and turned until you understood its time, its place, its rhythms, and the telling reference in every line. Only a powerful love for the poem itself could have generated his kind of energy in teaching it. He is the kind of man who just does not go with fluorescent lighting and long hallways with little cubicles opening off them, and rivalry toward Michigan State. Or so it seemed long ago.

I asked if he noticed any difference between the present student and school, and the student and school of fifteen years ago. A repressed anger crackled in his eyes.

"It's *all* different. Take the study of literature. Who are its judges? The psychologist is looked to for an analysis of motivations. But even that isn't as bad as looking at a book or a play to discover what kind of Oedipus complex the author had. The sociologists are deferred to as the only men who can really say how typical the situation is in society, and the anthropologist also has a few words handy. Now, I am only an amateur in these disciplines. They are the experts. And what about the literary people? They are becoming experts in their own way. We have what are called The New Critics. The poem to them is a thing in itself. If the diction is exact, the imagery consistent, the writing original and the form consonant with the breadth of the matter, that's the end of it. It is as though the values of humanity——"

The Values. A certain few themes kept coming up wherever I went, and The Values were in the center. The impression gained from certain quarters is that, in 1953, it is thought sufficient to have described a piece of existence, whether it is a book or an isotope. The conflict is being played around certain connected themes. One is The Values. Another is Apathy.

Another English teacher told me: "The student today has no spine. He thinks he is here to receive something that is wrapped up, easily digestible and complete. He is not really working anything *out*."

The *Michigan Daily* keeps bewailing "apathy" among the students. One reason is that it cannot find enough men to man its positions. The Values and Apathy.

I went back to the *Daily* building and looked up the papers of my day, '34 to '38. I was surprised and amused to read that the Michigan student was a lizard, apathetic, uninterested in campus affairs.

So it gets more complicated. The student is apathetic, but the *Daily* thought he was apathetic in 1936. In those days we laughed at research-for-its-own-sake and now people are disturbed because everything has got so practical, provable and dangerously unvague.

A psychology professor told me: "The student *is* different. The back-talk is feeble. They *are* passive. Imagine a graduate student asking me to tell him what his dissertation subject should be. I couldn't believe my ears at first, but it is happening regularly now. And more than that, they expect me to lay out the lines of their research, and when I try not to do it, they are astonished. They regard themselves as instruments. It is as though they thought it a waste of time to speculate, to move into unknown territory, which is just what they should be doing."

Another psychologist said: "The most embarrassing question you can ask a researcher is, 'Why are you doing this?' He can tell you its immediate application, but whether it is good or bad to apply it or whether it could be a disastrous power to put in the wrong hands either is not his business or else he is just hoping for the best."

I began to feel after a while that something was chasing everybody here. The Necessity to Keep Doing. A fantastic number of discoveries being made and a gnawing worry about What it is All For. I think the Phoenix Project is one answer, a statement of the university's conscience.

One example of this atmosphere of pursuit is the television question.

A professor of English: "Now we are going on television. Why? Allegedly to spread education among the people. But is that really why? It is not. It is because Michigan

State is winning friends and influencing people, so we must. Did you know that they send out calendars reading, 'Come to Michigan State, The Friendly College'? We are now going to be 'friendly'! Can you really teach people on a university level through TV? My subject is hard. It requires that a student work to understand it. Isn't it inevitable that we will have to make it easier and easier and lower our standards in order to compete? The TV audience is profoundly passive. It is looking for a massage, not a message. And in addition my subject has 'controversial' aspects. Can a teacher maintain the courage to speak his heart in the face of the pressure groups and the mass ignorance they can arouse against him? I don't believe it. We are being asked to become entertainers, and the time will come when a professor will be cast for voice, looks and camera manners. Oh, you can laugh, but it is absolutely in the cards. We are going to have to put ourselves over, we are going to have to sell Michigan. The neon age of education is upon us. And don't confuse this with democracy. It is the triumph of the leveler, and the man in charge is an advertising man."

I could go on endlessly because in nearly every conversation these themes kept cropping up. But there are many who deny their validity.

A physicist: "I know they are all beefing about passivity, but I don't find it in my field. They are as hep and alive as they ever were. Some of this 'apathy' is really a kind of maturity. Kids don't join things so much now, because they are more serious. There is, of course, the problem of values. The atomic boys found that out with a jolt. It is not enough to discover something, one must work on the problem of its use. And you can be sure that a scientist who has the brains to work in nuclear physics is intelligent enough to worry about values. So much so that some people risked a great deal and went to the government to implore them to understand what the atom implied. Don't think for a minute that we are automatons without conscience. Nothing is farther from the truth."

Another English professor: "I can't tell any great difference between these kids and any peacetime class. I think what some of the others are complaining about is really based on our experience with the veterans who left here about 1948. It's true, they were thrilling people to teach. They were serious but inquisitive, they were after the facts, but they knew that a philosophy, a standard of values, was of first importance. But the pre-war classes didn't measure up to the veterans either."

I met students in the restaurants, in dormitories, classrooms, hall-ways, and in the union, the center for nonfraternity students. If there were no two alike, they nevertheless had certain common feelings that came up to the surface very quickly. Michigan means freedom to them. It has nothing to do with academic freedom but a release from home and the neighborhood or town they came from. This is as it always was, but I had forgotten what an adventure it was to leave home. One afternoon I sat with the girls on the veranda of the Martha Cook dormitory. Martha Cook is brick and ivy, lawns and old trees, and windows you remember as leaded but which are not, mellow wood, and an outline of Tudor-out-of-Yale.

The Girl From Massachusetts: "Oh, gosh, yes. I would never dare do at home what I think nothing of doing here. What, exactly? Well, I don't know, but I go out with fellows my parents wouldn't approve of. You couldn't be friendly, really, with a Chinese or a Negro in my town. Not really, you couldn't. You can here."

The Girl From New York (the intellectual): "Well, that's not quite true. It's very complicated."

The Girl From Ohio (who will marry a law student after graduation and settle in Rio, where he will practice): "I think it's enormously freer. It's like, well, it's an explosion, almost. I started in literature, then I went to botany, and now I'm in music." And brother, she was. As they used to say, she was bursting with life, sitting there in blue jeans, her heels tucked against her buttocks, her knees up around her cheeks, and a sunburned face sucking in everything that was said and ever would be said. But the others thought she was hasty in planning to settle outside the country. I was surprised. I had thought they would all be thrilled at the prospect of foreign lands. It took a minute for them to say exactly why they thought her hasty.

"There might be a revolution there," they finally agreed. It would be better to stay home.

Maybe they were just envious. But they weren't apathetic, if that means dull, without thought. The Depression means to them what World War I meant to us; that is, an old-fashioned thing. Time after time I got the same image—"It couldn't happen that way again. The government wouldn't let it, I don't think." They seem to feel that society is under control; it is so enormous, and it *is* operating, that there is just nothing to think about in that department. They feel there is enormous opportunity for anybody; that men are rewarded pretty much according to their abilities, and time and time again said the same line, "It's up to me."

The famous panty raids that swept the country started at Michigan last year and these girls had witnessed that strange crusade. It seems that some guy was blowing a trumpet in one of the men's dorms, and somebody else yelled at him to stop, and the trumpet player dared the other guy to make him stop, but instead of fighting they decided to invade the women's dormitories and steal panties. A crowd gathered and kept getting bigger all night as one dormitory after another was entered. Martha Cook was among those that "fell." The girls were quite gay about it and told the story as though they kind of wished more of the same would happen now and then.

The story sounded as though it might well have happened at any time, the Thirties included, but to my ear there was nevertheless a strange note in it. It did not sound like a simple sexual outburst. As the girls spoke, I had the feeling that the panty raids were one of those phenomena which are only superficially sexual and were directed more as a challenge to the atmosphere of paternal repression which is, and always was, quite strong at Michigan.

An administrative official arranged a luncheon for me with a dozen or so student leaders. I feared this would be a polite waste of time and it is no reflection on the man to say that they were under wraps in his presence. As they themselves told me later, the paternalism of the administration is not conducive to student expression. It was always a rather heavily administration-dominated school, but in the old days they had a fight for their money. I remember one hell of a racket when Fred Warner Neal, probably the most prolific reporter the paper ever had, resigned from the *Daily*—which gave him a full column on Page 1 to write his resignation—because the administration had forbidden him to write some story or other. And I remember he was reinstated.

I remember committees demanding to see the president whenever they didn't like something, and I remember a few times when they won the argument, or half won it.

These dozen, being interested enough to head up the student legislature, the interfraternity council and so on, were the contemporary equivalents of the people who made the noise in my time. While the official was with us they weren't very noisy; it might have been a meeting of young bankers. But he had to leave soon and we were alone and it started coming.

"People are afraid to say anything."

Afraid of what?

"Well, for instance, a lot of people are tired of paying high prices for books. We want a university bookstore, but we know we'll never get one because the bookstores will raise hell and, besides, the administration won't pay any attention to us."

But you're evidently not afraid to make the demand.

"No, not exactly afraid——"

What do you think would happen if you tried to rally support on campus for a demand like that?

"You mean, like to have a meeting or demonstrate?"

They all looked uncomfortable. Some laughed nervously.

One boy said, "We'd be called communists."

You mean that truly?

"Sure. But the worst thing would be that back home the papers would pick up our names and there might be trouble."

You mean they'd think you'd been turned into Reds here?

"Some people would think so, but it's not exactly being called communists, it's different."

What exactly is it?

"Well, it's that when you went to, let's say, the local plant for a job, and if they found out about it they would—well, they wouldn't like you."

Oh.

A girl: "I live in a cooperative house." And really, she blushed. "I'm getting ashamed to mention it because people on campus ask me why do you live with those collectivists? But it's cheaper, and anyway they're not collectivists." They all laughed but they knew that what she was saying was true.

A boy hitherto silent: "I know for a fact that everything you do is being written down and sent to the authorities."

Like what?

"Never mind, I just know it."

I had, the day before, been sitting in the *Daily* building going through the 1934–38 papers. A middle-aged man with eyeglasses and a thick neck took out a file and after a while began noting things down. A reporter came over to me and whispered that this man was a state policeman, and his job was to check up on subversives in the school. The reporter said that he and the others on the paper were always trying to tell the man that the people he was listing were not Reds, but he went right on, in a very affable way, listing anyone who was connected with anything "controversial."

It is necessary to add that at the luncheon, the very broaching of this subject reddened some faces. They were bravely willing to discuss it, and really quite eager to, but if they were not in fear I do not understand anything.

"That's why everybody wants to get into Intelligence."

What's that?

"I'm telling you the facts."

"Oh, go on, they just feel they won't get shot in Intelligence."

"There's a lot of jobs in the Army where you don't get shot. I swear, they all want to get into Intelligence."

So that they can investigate other people?

"No, they don't want to investigate other people, but they feel once they get in there they won't be bothered any more."

Would you like to get into Intelligence?

Laughter. "Sure, I'd take it."

And he blushes. That is, he blushes, but he would take it although he's against it.

There are more evidences of gumshoeing around the campus, but it would be false to picture the place as being in fear of any specific thing. The important fact to me is that the gumshoeing is disliked, sometimes scorned, but accepted as perfectly natural. Sometimes the old liberalism will crop up, however. Not long ago the university prohibited a communist from speaking on campus, and Professor Slosson went to the hall where the man had to make his address, debated with him, and from all accounts slaughtered him.

Compared to my years at Michigan there does seem to be a blanket over the place now. The tone is more subdued, if one measures tone by the amount of discussion, argument and protest openly indulged in. In my day we were more likely to believe that what we thought and did would have an effect upon events, while the present student sees himself separated from the great engine that is manufacturing his and the country's fate.

But it would be inaccurate to think that these boys and girls are inert. I sat in on a graduate seminar in political science one afternoon at which five students and a professor were discussing the subtlest relationships between political ideologies over a span of three centuries. It is a long time since I witnessed such complete concentration upon essentials, sharpness of mind, and freedom from cant and sloganeering. In the Thirties such a discussion would have verged on partisanship after an hour, but it never did here, and that is a big change, I think.

They know now that the old easy solutions are suspect, and they are examining rather than exhorting each other. In this sense they are more mature than we were, yet they are also more separated and removed from the idea of action. But action is immensely more complicated than it was and more difficult to conceive; for instance, one of the heaviest loads they bear is the Army draft. In my day we could rally and vote against conscription because it was only a threat, while today there is nothing to be done about it, and it makes futile many of their plans and weakens as well the very idea of controlling their own destinies.

I do not know how things will work out at Michigan any more than the next man does. It may be the faculty men are correct who see a profound shift of values which will make of Michigan a place not unintelligent, not overtly browbeaten, but a school of obedient pragmatists where each individual walks in blinders toward his niche in government or giant corporation, his soul unswept by the hot blasts of new ideas and vast social concepts. The very bigness of Michigan, the size of the investment in it, and the mutual suspicion that is gripping so many people are forces that would help such a process along. And there is a deeper, less-noticed frame of mind which goes even farther to create such an atmosphere, and I think of the faculty man-of-goodwill, in this context, who was talking to me about a certain administrator who paid no attention to the students' ideas or complaints or suggestions. "It's a pity," said this faculty man, "that X's public relations are not better." Whether X might in fact have *been* authoritarian and unheeding was evidently beside the point. The fault to remedy was X's inability to put himself over. It is in such remarks and attitudes that one sees the absence of an idealism I clearly remember at Michigan and in its place a kind of pragmatism that threatens to create a race of salesmen in the tawdry sense of that word.

I cannot promise that it will not end this way: a chromium-plated silence, a highly organized, smoothly running factory for the production of conformism. I only know that in my time it was supposed to be a training ground for leftists or, from the opposite viewpoint, a cave of vigilantism, and it turned out to be neither. I know that when I recently sat with individual students they spoke like seekers, their clean, washed faces as avid for truth as I suppose we were so long ago. I know that they do not think of themselves as a "silent generation" or as a generation at all but simply as "me." I know that in their rooming houses and dormitories the old bull sessions go on into the mornings, but I also know that what so many of them really feel—and here, I think, lies the difference between the generations—they are not saying in public nowadays, if it seems to question that this is the best of all possible worlds. It is simply not done in 1953.

When I stood waiting for the plane at Willow Run I tried to summon up the memory of the other time I had left Ann Arbor, in the fall of 1938. I had had a ride to New York with a young salesman of saddles and riding equipment who had just passed through Ann Arbor. He had been in contact only with the upper echelons of the community— certain high officials, industrialists, a regent or two who owned horses. He had sold a lot of saddles in Ann Arbor. He was leaving with the impression of a fairly ritzy school. For myself, I had not known a single soul in four years who had mounted a horse.

As he started the engine I waved to a girl who was standing in front of the Women's League, a girl that I dared not dream I would ever have money enough, or security of soul enough, to marry. As we drove east, through Toledo, Ashtabula, the red-brick roads through the Ohio farmlands, I tried to tell him what Michigan really was. It was the professor who, with selected members of his class, held séances during which the spirits of Erasmus, Luther and other historical figures were summoned and listened to. It was the fraternity boys sitting on the porches of their mansions, singing nostalgic Michigan songs as in a movie, and it was three radicals being expelled. It was, in short, the testing ground for all my prejudices, my beliefs and my ignorance, and it helped to lay out the boundaries of my life. For me it had, above everything else, variety and freedom. It is probably the same today. If it is not, a tragedy is in the making.

1953

Journey to *The Crucible*

The Crucible is taken from history. No character is in the play who did not take a similar role in Salem, 1692. The basic story is recorded, if briefly, in certain documents of the time. It will be a long time before I shall be able to shake Rebecca Nurse, John Proctor, Giles Corey and the others out of my mind. But there are strange, even weird memories that have connected themselves to this play, and these have to do with the present, and it has all got mixed up together.

I went to Salem for the first time early last spring. I already knew the story, and had thought about it for a long time. I had never been to Salem before and, driving alone up the brand-new superhighway, I felt a shock at seeing the perfectly ordinary, steel sign reading, "Salem 3 mi." I confess it—some part of my mind had expected to see the old wooden village, not the railroad tracks, the factories, the trucks. These things were not real, suddenly, but intruders, as tourists are in the halls of Versailles. Underneath, in the earth, was the reality. I drove into the town.

I asked the courthouse clerk for the town records for 1692. A lawyer-looking man in an overcoat asked for 1941. A lady, who looked like she was planning to sue somebody, asked for 1913. The clerk handed over a volume to each of us and we sat at separate tables, the three of us, turning pages.

The lawyer began copying—possibly from a deed. The woman read perhaps a will—and got angrier. I looked into 1692. Here were wills, too, and deeds, and warrants sworn out, and the usual debris a town leaves behind it for the legal record.

And then . . . dialogue! Prosecutor Hathorne is examining Rebecca Nurse. The court is full of people weeping for the young girls who sit before them strangling because Rebecca's spirit is out tormenting them. And Hathorne says, "It is awful to see your eye dry when so many are wet." And Rebecca replies, "You do not know my heart. I never afflicted no child, never in my life. I am as clear as the child unborn."

They hanged her. She was in her seventies. They had hesitated to go and arrest her because of her high reputation; but they took her from her sickbed, they took her from her lovely house that stands in the countryside yet, and they hanged her by the neck over the long Salem Bay.

The lawyer in the overcoat was copying his deed; the lady was back at the counter, asking the clerk for 1912. Did they know what had happened here?

In the museum all is silent. An old man, looking like a retired professor, is reading a document. Two middle-aged couples come in from their automobile outside and ask to see the pins: the pins the spirits stuck the children with. The pins are in the courthouse, they are told. They look about at the books, the faded fragments of paper that once meant Proctor must hang tomorrow, paper that came through the farmhouse door in the hand of a friend who had a half-determined, half-ashamed look in his eyes.

The tourists pass the books, the exhibits, and no hint of danger reaches them from the quaint relics. I have a desire to tell them the significance of those relics. It is the desire to write.

Day after day in the courthouse, until the evenings begin to arrive with forebodings in the night breeze. The locations of the old farmhouses are in my mind, their directions from the spot on which I stand; on Essex Street was a house, perhaps a few yards from here, where Reverend Parris lived and at night discussed with certain others who in the town was acting suspiciously, who might have shown signs of the Devil's touch. Salem was taken from the Hebrew, Sholom, meaning peace, but now in my mind and in the streets it is a dark word.

The stroll down Essex Street I remember, and the empty spaces between the parking meters, the dark storefronts—but further down a lighted store, and noise. I take a look. A candy store. A mob of girls and boys in their teens running in and out, ganging around on the vacant street; a jalopy pulls up with two wet-haired boys, and a whispered consultation with a girl on the running board; she runs into the store, comes out with a friend, and off they go into the night, the proud raccoon tail straightening from the radiator cap. And suddenly, from around a corner, two girls hopping with a broomstick between their legs, and a general laughter going up at the special joke. A broomstick. And riding it. And I remember the girls of Salem, the only Salem there ever was for me—the 1692 Salem—and how they purged their sins by embracing God and pointing out His enemies in the town.

And a feeling of love at seeing Rebecca Nurse's house on its gentle knoll; the house she lay in, ill, when they came, shuffling their feet, ashamed to have to ask her to come to court because the children said she had sent her spirit out.

And the great rock, standing mum over the bay, the splintered precipice on which the gibbet was built. The highway traffic endlessly, mindlessly humming at its foot, but up here the barrenness, the clinkers of broken stones, and the vast view of the bay; here hung Rebecca, John Proctor, George Jacobs—people more real to me than the living can ever be. The sense of a terrible marvel again; that people could have such a belief in themselves and in the rightness of their consciences as to give their lives rather than say what they thought was false. Or, perhaps, they only feared Hell so much? Yet, Rebecca said, and it is written in the record, "I cannot belie myself." And she knew it would kill her. They knew who they were.

My friends return, the men of my own life—in the hotel taproom a circle of salesmen sitting around, waiting for bedtime. I listen. They are comparing the sizes of their television screens. Which one is the big-earner? Yep, that one. He says less, but they listen more when he says it. They are all wishing they were him. And all a little lost in the eyes, and nice fellas, so damned eager, and men-among-men, and around the eyes ever so faintly lost; laughing a little more than they want to, listening longer than they want to, sorry without sorrow, laughing with less than joy, until up in the hotel room alone there is only one certainty—tomorrow will come. Another day, another chance to find out—who they are. How they got there. Where they're going.

The rock stands forever in Salem. They knew who they were. Nineteen.

1953

A Modest Proposal for the Pacification of
the Public Temper

There being in existence at the present time a universally held belief in the probability of treasonous actions;

And at the same time no certain method of obtaining final assurance in the faithfulness of any citizen toward his country, now that outright Treason, dallying with the Enemy, and other forms of public and private perfidy have been abundantly demonstrated in and among persons even of the highest office;

I herewith submit a Proposal for the Pacification of the Public Temper, and the Institution among the People of Mutual Faith and Confidence;

Having clearly in mind the Damages, both financial and Spiritual, which have already accrued due to the spread of Suspicion among Citizens, the said Proposal follows, namely:

The Proposal

1. That upon arriving at his eighteenth (18th) birthday, and every second year thereafter so long as he lives, providing said day does not fall upon a Sunday or nationally proclaimed Legal Holiday; in which case performance shall take place on the first regular day of business following, every Citizen of the United States of America shall present himself at the office of the United States Marshal nearest his place of residence;

Duties of Marshal

1. That said Marshal shall immediately place the Citizen under what is hereby officially described and determined as Patriotic Arrest or National Detention, which shall in every way conform to regular and ordinary incarceration in the prison, jail, or other Federal Detention Facility normally used in that locality;

Duties of Incarcerated Citizen

1. That without undue delay the citizen shall be informed that he may avail himself of all subpoena powers of the Government in order to secure for himself all documents, papers, manifolds, records, recorded tapes or discs, witnesses and/or other paraphernalia which he requires to prove his Absolute and steady Allegiance

to this Country, its Government, Army and Navy, Congress, and the Structure, Aims, and History of its Institutions;

2. That upon assembling such documents and/or witnesses in support, he shall be brought before a Judge of the United States Court of Clearance, which Court to be established herewith;

Duties of Judge in Court of Clearance

1. That said Judge shall hear all of the defendant's witnesses and examine faithfully all evidence submitted;
2. That said Judge shall, if he deems it necessary, call upon the Federal Bureau of Investigation to refute or corroborate any or all claims submitted by the Citizen in defense of his Loyalty;
3. That if said proofs then be found invalid, untruthful, immaterial, irrelevant, or inconclusive, the Citizen shall be so notified and may thereupon at his option demand a Second Hearing meanwhile being consigned by Warrant and Seal of said Judge within one of the three Classifications hereunder described as Class CT, Class AT, or Class U.

Classifications

Classification CT (Class CT)

1. Classification or Class CT shall be deemed to signify Conceptual Traitor;

Classification CT (Class CT) Defined

1. Class CT signifying Conceptual Traitor is herewith defined as including, but not exclusively,

   a. Any person otherwise of good character, without police record of felony, who has been adjudged at his or her Clearance Trial and/or Second Hearing as having engaged in Conversations, talks, public or private meetings, lectures, visits, or communications the nature of which is not illegal but on the other hand not Positively Conducive to the Defense of the Nation against the Enemy;

   b. Any person who, on evidence submitted by the FBI, or in the Absence of Evidence to the Contrary, has shown himself to have actually expressed concepts, parts of concepts, or complete ideas or sentiments Inimical to the Defense of the Nation against the Enemy;

   c. Persons who have not actually expressed such concepts in whole or part, but have demonstrated a receptivity to such concepts as expressed by others;

   d. Persons who have neither expressed themselves, nor shown a receptivity to expressions by others of concepts or sentiments Inimical to the Defense of the

Nation against the Enemy, but on the other hand have failed to demonstrate a lively, visible, or audible resentment against such concepts or sentiments as orally expressed or written by others;

All the above described, but not exclusively, shall be classified Conceptual Traitors by the duly constituted Court of Clearance.

Classification AT (Class AT)

1. Classification or Class AT shall be deemed to signify Action Traitor;

Classification AT (Class AT) Defined

1. Class AT signifying Action Traitor is herewith defined as including, but not exclusively,

    a. Any person who has been proved to have actually attended meetings of any group, organization, incorporated or unincorporated body, secretly or publicly, whose title is to be found upon the Attorney General's list of proscribed organizations;

    b. Any person who has committed any of the acts attributable to Conceptual Traitor as above defined, but in addition, and within hearing of at least one witness, has spoken in praise of such groups or affiliates or members thereof, or of non-members who have themselves spoken in praise of said groups or organizations so listed;

    c. Any and all persons not falling under the categories above described who nevertheless have been summoned to testify before any Committee of Congress and have failed to testify to the Expressed Satisfaction of said Committee or any two members thereof in quorum constituted;

Penalties

1. Penalties shall be laid upon those classified as Conceptual Traitors, as follows, namely:

    a. The Judge of the Court of Clearance shall cause to be issued Identity Card CT. Upon all correspondence written by said Class CT Citizen the words Conceptual Traitor or the letters CT shall be prominently displayed in print or in ink; as well upon any and all books, articles, pamphlets or announcements whatsoever written by said Citizen; as well any appearance on radio, television, theatrical or other public medium by said Citizen shall be preceded by the clearly spoken announcement of his Classification; and in addition his calling or business cards shall be so marked as well as any other cards, (Christmas, birthday, New Year's, etc., but not exclusively), which he may mail to anyone beyond his own family so connected by blood;

    b. Any organization or person employing said citizen with or without remuneration in money or kind, shall, upon agreeing to such employment, apply to the Federal Bureau of Clearance, to be established herewith, for a Conceptual Traitor Employment Permit;

c. It shall be an infraction of this Act to refuse employment to a citizen Classified as Conceptual Traitor, or to discriminate against said Citizen for having been so Classified, and the employer, upon receiving his Conceptual Traitor's Employment Permit, shall cause to be imprinted upon all his stationery, vouchers, public circulars, and advertisements, the following words or legend— "We Employ A Conceptual Traitor"—or the initials, "WECT."

Release of Incarcerated CT's

1. Conceptual Traitors, upon being duly classified by the Court of Clearance, shall be instantly released and guaranteed all the rights and privileges of American Citizenship as defined in the Constitution of the United States.

   a. No Conceptual Traitor duly classified shall be detained in jail or prison more than forty-eight hours (48) beyond the time of his Classification;

   b. No person awaiting Classification shall be detained more than one year (1 year).

Penalties for Action Traitors

1. Persons classified Action Traitors shall be fined two thousand dollars and sentenced to serve not more than eight (8) years in a Federal House of Detention, nor less than five years (5 years).

Unclassified Persons

1. Persons who are neither Classified as Action Traitor nor Conceptual Traitor shall be classified as Unclassified, or "U."

Unclassified Persons Defined

1. Unclassified persons, (U), shall be defined, although not exclusively, as those persons who are:

   a. Unable to speak or understand the English language or any language for which an accredited Interpreter can be found, or can be reasonably thought to exist within the Continental United States or its Territories, Possessions, or Territories held in Trust;

   b. Able to speak the English language or any of the languages for which an Interpreter may be found, but unable to understand the English language or any of the languages for which an Interpreter may be found;

   c. Committed to institutions for the Insane or Homes for the Aged and Infirm;

   d. Accredited members of the Federal Bureau of Investigation;

e. Accredited members of any Investigating Committee of the Congress of the United States;
f. Officers of the United States Chamber of Commerce;
g. Persons who are able to read, write, and understand the English language but have not registered their names in any Public Library as Lenders or Borrowers; and persons who have been registered as Borrowers in Public Libraries, but whose cards have never been stamped;
h. Listless persons, or persons who cannot keep their minds attentive to the questions asked by the Judge of the Court of Clearance;
i. All Veterans of the War Between the States;
j. All citizens who have Contributed to the Walter Winchell Damon Runyon Cancer Fund or who have been favorably mentioned in the newspaper column written by Ed Sullivan;
k. Most children, providing;

That none of the entities above mentioned be constituted as exclusive; and that no abridgment is made of the right of Congress to lengthen or shorten any of the defining qualifications of any of the above categories.

Release of Unclassified Persons (Class U)

1. All Unclassified Persons shall be instantly released, but with the proviso that any and all Unclassified Persons may be recalled for Classification.

Possible Objections to This Proposal

The author of the above proposal, or Act, is well aware of certain objections which are bound to be made. All argument will inevitably reduce itself to the question of Civil Liberties.

The author wishes to state that, as will soon become apparent, it is only his devotion to Civil Liberties which has prompted creation of this Proposal, and in order to Enlighten those who on these grounds feel a reservation about this Proposal, he states quite simply the most vital argument against it which is that it sends absolutely everybody to jail.

This, unfortunately, is true. However, the corollary to this objection, namely, that this is exactly what the Russians do, is emphatically not true. I insist that no Russian goes to jail excepting under duress, force, and unwillingly; hence, he loses his liberty. But under this Act the American Presents himself to the prison officials, which is a different thing entirely. Moreover, he Presents himself without loss of liberty, his most precious possession, because he Presents himself with Love in his Heart, with the burning desire to Prove to all his fellow-citizens that he Is an American and is eager to let everybody know every action of his Life and its Patriotic Significance. It may as well be said that if an American boy is good enough to fight he is good enough to go to jail for the peace of mind of his Country.

The author can easily Visualize that going to the local Marshal for his Patriotic Arrest will soon become a kind of Proud Initiation for the Young American. He can Visualize the growth among the Citizens of Coming Out Parties when the young member of the family is released, and there is no doubt that the national Radio and Television Networks will do their best to popularize this form of Patriotic Thanksgiving, and the entire process of Waiting, Classification, and ultimate Deliverance will eventually become a hallowed Ritual without which no young man or woman would feel Complete and At Ease. It is, after all, nothing more than the Winning of Citizenship, something we who were given the blessing of American Birth have come to take for granted.

I would go even farther and say that the psychological significance of Arrest is beneficial. At the age of eighteen, or thereabouts, a person is just getting out of his adolescence, a period marked by strong feelings of guilt due to Pimples and so forth. This guilt, or Pimples, leads many an individual of that age to feelings of high idealism at which point he is amazed to discover the presence of Evil in the world. In turn, the recognition of Evil is likely to cause him to scoff at the Pretensions of the Older Generation, his parents and teachers, who in his new and emotional opinion have Failed to make a decent world for him. He is then wide open to the Propaganda of the Enemy.

It is at this very moment, when his spiritual pores, so to speak, are open, that under this Act he is sent immediately to Jail, and then through a Court of Clearance, to which institution he may Open his Heart. Under this Act, in short, every American over the age of eighteen (18) is automatically regarded as technically and momentarily Guilty. This, of course, represents no profound novelty, but instead of making it possible for only Traitors to Be Discovered, as at present, under this Act everyone will have the opportunity of being, so to speak, Discovered, but as a Patriot, which after all is what most Americans are.

The simple and pervasive Logic of this proposal will be completely evident if one reflects on the fact that in almost every other sphere of human activity the Society does in fact "clear" and give its stamp of Approval beforehand rather than afterwards; in most states we have to renew our dog licenses every year, and no dog with, for instance, rabies, is entitled to a license; we inspect cattle, motorists, buildings, railroads, elevators, sprinkler systems, teachers, and fish markets, for instance; nor do we wait until any of these have caused damage to the community. On the contrary, you have no need of suspecting an elevator, for instance, upon entering it because you know that it has been cleared, in effect, Before you arrived and you may therefore repose in it your utmost Confidence, nor do you take a Driver's Test after you have killed a pedestrian, you take it Before.

It is necessary to imagine, or Project, as the psychologists say, the National Situation as it will be after this Act is operative.

When walking down the street, buying in a store, waiting for a street car or bus, getting gas, buying stocks, Meeting Someone hitherto unknown, answering the doorbell, listening to a lecture, seeing a movie or Television Show, the Citizen will automatically know where everybody around him Stands. A sense of Confidence and Mutual Trust will once more flow into the Land. The Citizen will need have no fear of reading anything, attending any meeting, or being introduced to anyone; instead of an atmosphere of innuendo, suspicion, aborted conversations and low vocal tones, we shall have a situation in which you know and I know that you were in jail and I was in jail and that we are therefore good Americans, and if there was anything Wrong one of us, or both of us, would not be out here talking like this. That is, by and large.

Aside from avowed enemies there are, unfortunately, Patriotic people who will unquestionably be found in opposition to this Act. Mothers, for instance, may shudder at the idea of sending their boys to Jail. But they will quickly see that a short stay in Jail will be the Hallmark of every Good American.

To sum up, then, it can be said that the current sensations of Confusion, Ferment, Distrust, and Suspicion are obviously not being dissolved by any present methods of Investigation and Exposure. A Permanent, Regular, and Uniform Clearance Procedure is vitally necessary, therefore. Everyone knows that a Man is Innocent until proved Guilty. All this Act is meant to provide is a means for securing that proof. God Forbid the day when in America a man is guilty without Proof. Once it was a Land that millions of Americans were trekking thousands of miles to find; later it was Gold; recently Uranium has been sought for at great effort and expense. But it is fair to say that with our characteristic energy we are devoting more time, more concentrated effort, and more Patriotic Concern with discovering Proof than any other material in our Nation's History. Now, in a dignified manner, in a Regularized and profoundly American manner, we shall all have it.

1954

The American Theater

The American theater occupies five side streets, Forty-fourth to Forty-ninth, between Eighth Avenue and Broadway, with a few additional theaters to the north and south and across Broadway. In these thirty-two buildings every new play in the United States starts its life and ends it. There will undoubtedly be many objections to this statement—you cannot say anything about our theater without fear of contradiction—and demurrers will come from professors of drama, stock-company directors, and little-theater people in New York, Texas, California, and elsewhere who will claim that Broadway is not the United States and that much theatrical production is going on in other places. I agree, and repeat only that with practically no exceptions, the *new* American plays originate on Broadway. I would add that I wish they didn't, but they do. The American theater is five blocks long, by about one and a half blocks wide.

It would seem a simple matter to characterize so limited an area, but I write this with the certainty that whatever I say will appear not only new and strange to many theater people but utterly untrue. And this is because the man or woman whose tapping shoes you hear from the second-story dance studio over the delicatessen on Forty-Sixth Street is in the theater, the ballet girl hurrying to rehearsal in her polo coat with a copy of Rimbaud in her pocket is in the theater, the peasant-faced Irish stagehand sunning himself on the sidewalk with a *Racing Form* in his hand is in the theater, the slow-staring, bald-headed ticket broker blinking out through his agency window is in the theater, the wealthy, Park-Avenue-born producer is in the theater, and his cigar-smoking colleague from the West Bronx is in the theater.

In the audience itself, though the bulk of it is of the middle class, there is no uniformity either. There will be the businessman in town from Duluth sitting beside Marlene Dietrich, whom he will probably not recognize, and behind them two esthetes from Harvard. The word theater means different things to different groups. To some its very pinnacle is *South Pacific,* which is despised by the esthetes, who in turn cherish a wispy fantasy whose meaning escapes the Duluth man. There is a vast group of people for whom the theater means nothing but amusement, and amusement means a musical or light comedy; and there are others who reserve their greatest enthusiasm for heavy dramas that they can chew on.

The actors, directors, and writers themselves are just as varied. There are playwrights who are as illiterate as high-school boys, and there are playwrights like Maxwell Anderson, who have spent a good deal of their lives studying the Elizabethan drama and attempting to recreate its mood and luxuriance on Broadway. There are fine actors who are universally admired but who have absolutely no theory of acting and there are other actors, equally good or equally bad, who have spent years studying the history of acting, taking voice lessons, and learning how to dance in order to walk more gracefully.

The theater, obviously, is an entirely different animal to each of these groups. As for myself, I cannot pretend to any Olympian viewpoint about it either. I believe there is a confusion in many minds between Show Business and the Theater. I belong to the Theater, which happens at the moment to be in a bad way, but since this word, when capitalized, usually implies something uplifting and boring, I must add that the rarely seen but very real Theater is the most engrossing theater of all; and when it isn't it is nothing. I make the distinction so that the reader will be warned where my prejudice lies and discount accordingly.

The "glamour of the theater," which is and always will be its most powerful attraction, is a subject of daily reporting by almost every newspaper, gossip columnist, and radio station. Every year, around the first cool days of fall, the illustrated sections of the press and the picture magazines and newsreels run the familiar photographs of the limousines gliding up to the lighted marquees, the taxis and cars pressing into Forty-fourth Street for the opening of some musical or drama, the inevitable montage of Sardi's restaurant at dinner time, and so on. For anyone who has made the slightest mark in this occupation there is a line of type waiting when he so much as pays his rent on time. Soon after *Death of a Salesman* opened, it was reported that I was a millionaire, which was pleasant news, if not true, and that despite my new affluence I still rode the subways. I keep wondering who was watching me going through the turnstiles. And the importance of this news still escapes me.

In fact, while everybody in the business is worried about its future—and if there is a heart of uncertainty in the country its loudest beat may be heard on these five blocks—to read the columns and the usual sources of theatrical information you would think it was all a continuous carnival of divorce, practical jokes, hilarious wit, elopements, and sudden acquisition of enormous wealth.

But there is evidently no way of glamourizing the often inspiring and heart-lifting experiences of the work itself, a kind of labor that began in the Western world about three thousand years ago, and which has provided some of the most powerful insights we possess into the way men think and feel.

The net result of this image of our theater, the carnival image, is that the out-of-towner strolling these streets may quickly sense that he has been bilked. He will discover, especially if he arrives in midday, that the theater buildings themselves are tawdry-looking, and may well be disillusioned when he sees that some of the marquees do not have even the electrically lit signs of his home movie house—only temporary cardboards painted with the title of the show within. When he ventures into the outer lobby he will perhaps be shocked to discover that a seat costs six—or even eight—dollars and, if the show is a hit, that he won't get a ticket for six months or a year unless he pays a scalper twenty-five to a hundred dollars. If it is not a hit, and he buys a ticket legitimately, he may learn that he could have bought two for the price of one; and by the time he gets inside for the performance, some of the glamour of it all may have worn a bit thin.

Once inside, however, our visitor may find certain compensations. He may recognize very important people, from statesmen to movie stars, sitting nearby, whom he would not see in the home-town movie house. He will notice a certain dressed-up air about people, a few even wearing evening clothes. There are ushers to show him to his seat, and there is a program, and possibly a little more surprising is the coat-check man waiting as he passes through the outer door. There is still a vestigial ceremony about play-going from which one may derive a sense of self-importance if not careful, and it all may lead our visitor to feel that he is, indeed, among ladies and gentlemen.

Then, as the lights go down and the curtain rises, our visitor may feel a certain strange tension, an expectancy, and an intense curiosity that he never knew in a theater before. Instead of the enormity of the movie image before which he could sit back and relax, he is confronted by human beings in life-size, and since their voices do not roar out at him from a single point to which his ear may tune in once and then relax, he must pay more attention, his eyes must rove over a thirty-foot expanse; he must, in other words, *discover*. And if there happens to be something real up there, something human, something true, our visitor may come away with a new feeling in his heart, a sense of having been a part of something quite extraordinary and even beautiful. Unlike the movies, unlike television, he may feel he has been present at an *occasion*. For outside this theater, no one in the world heard what he heard or saw what he saw this night. I know that, for myself, there is nothing so immediate, so actual, as an excellent performance of an excellent play. I have never known the smell of sweat in a movie house. I have known it in the theater— and they are also air-conditioned. Nor have I known in a movie house the kind of audience unity that occasionally is created in the theater, an air of oneness among strangers that is possible in only one other gathering place—a church.

Nevertheless, by every account our theater is a vanishing institution. We have some thirty-two houses going today in New York as against forty or more ten years ago, and between seventy and eighty in the twenties. I could weave you such a tapestry of evil omens as to make it a closed case that we will have no theater in America in two decades. What I should like to do instead, however, is wonder aloud, as it were, why it is that each year thousands of aspiring actors, directors, and playwrights continue to press into these five blocks from every corner of the country when they know, or learn very quickly, that ninety percent of the professional actors are normally unemployed, that most of the producers are dead broke or within three cigars of being broke, and that to become a director of a Broadway show one must be prepared to gamble five to ten to fifteen years of one's life. And yet, on all the trains they keep coming, aspiring actors and eager audiences both.

As for the aspiring actors, I will not pretend to hunt for an answer, because I know it. It is simply that there are always certain persons who are born without all their marbles. Even so, the full-blown actors are merely the completed types of the secret actors who are called producers, backers, directors, yes, and playwrights. The rest of us would have been actors had we had the talent, or a left and right foot instead of two left ones, or straight teeth, or self-assurance. The actor himself is the lunacy in full profusion—the lunacy which in the others is partially concealed.

All over the country there are nine-year-old girls, for instance, who are walking around the house as my daughter is at this very moment, in high-heeled shoes with the lace tablecloth trailing from their shoulders. If mine doesn't recover before she is sixteen she will wake up one morning and something will click inside her head and she will go and hang around some producer's office, and if he talks to her, or just asks her what time it is, she may well be doomed for life.

The five blocks, therefore, are unlike any other five blocks in the United States, if only because here so many grown people are walking around trailing the old lace tablecloth from their shoulders.

If you know how to look you will find them waiting on you in Schrafft's, or behind the orange-drink counter at Nedick's. As a matter of fact, I have got so attuned to a certain look in their eyes that I can sometimes spot them on Sixth Avenue, which is not in the theater district. I was passing a truck being loaded there one day when I noticed a boy, unshaven, his hair uncombed, wearing paratroop boots; he was pitching boxes into the truck. And he looked at me, just a glance, and I thought to myself that he must be an actor. And about three days later I was sitting in my producer's office interviewing actors for *The Crucible,* when in he walked. Characteristically, he did not remember seeing me before—actors rarely do, since they are not looking at anyone but rather are being looked *at.* When asked the usual questions about his experience he just shrugged, and when asked if he wanted to read for us he shrugged again, quite as though the questions were impertinent when addressed to a great artist, and I knew then why I had tabbed him for an actor. It was the time when all the young actors were being Marlon Brando. He was being Marlon Brando even when loading the truck, for a real truck driver would never show up for work looking so unkempt.

The blessed blindness of actors to everything around them, their intense preoccupation with themselves, is the basic characteristic of all Broadway, and underlies most of its troubles, which, in another industry, would have been solved long ago. But since it is glamour which brings the young to Broadway, as well as the audience, it cannot be so quickly dismissed. The fact is, it exists. But it is not the glamour you are probably thinking of.

The time is gone when the Great Producer kept four or five Great Stars in ten-room apartments on Park Avenue, and they waited in their gilded cages for days and weeks for the Impresario to call for them—for without him they were forbidden to be seen in public lest they lose their "distance," their altitude above the common things of life. The time is gone when the leading lady dared not arrive at the theater in anything but a limousine with chauffeur and lap robe, while a line of stove-pipe-hatted men waited in the stage-door alley with flowers in their manicured hands. There are a few hangovers, of course, and I remember a show in Boston a few years ago whose leading lady, an hour before curtain time, phoned the producer to say she was ill and could not play. The poor man was desperate, but there was an old-time doorman in that theater who happened to be near the phone and he said, "Get a limousine and a chauffeur." The producer, a contemporary type who was as familiar with gallantry as any other businessman, mastered his uncertainty and hired a car and chauffeur and sent a mass of roses to the lady's hotel room. Her fever vanished in roughly four minutes and she played better than she ever had, and I must confess I couldn't blame her for wanting the glamour even if she had had to make it herself.

But leading ladies, nowadays, arrive in a taxi, and a lot of them come in by bus or subway.

I have been around only ten years or so and I never knew the kind of glamour that evidently existed. But a few years ago I had occasion to visit John Golden in his office, and I saw then that there was, in fact, a kind of bravado about being in the theater, a declaration of war against all ordinariness that I can find no more.

The average theatrical producer's office today consists mainly of a telephone, a girl to answer it, an outer room for actors to wait in, and an inner room with a window for the producer to stare out of when he has nothing to produce.

John Golden's office is different. It rests on top of the St. James Theatre; you rise in a private elevator, and come out in a dark, paper-cluttered reception room where an elderly and very wise lady bars you—with the help of a little gate—from entry. You know at once that behind her is not merely a man, but a Presence.

In his office the walls are painted with smoke. They are very dark and covered with hundreds of photographs, plaques, statuettes, hanging things, and jutting things of gold, silver, and shiny brass. There is an Oriental rug on the floor, an ornate desk at the distant end of the room, and there sits John Golden, who is now eighty years old. Behind him stands an imposing ascent of bookshelves filled with leather-bound plays he has produced. In a smaller adjoining room is a barber chair where his hair is cut, his beard shaved, and, I presume, his shoes shined. The windows are covered with drapes and obstructing statuary, because when this office was created, the man who worked in it had no time to look out into the street.

It was a time when the railroads were freighting out one after another of his productions, winter and summer, to all sections of the country. It was a time when, unlike now, important performers and even playwrights were kept on long-term contracts, when a producer owned his own theater and used his own money and was therefore not an accountant, nor even a businessman, but an impresario. In short, it was the time before the masses had left the theater for the new movies, and the theater was the main source of American popular entertainment. This office is now a kind of museum. There were once many like it, and many men like John Golden.

Their counterparts, the reflected images of Ziegfeld, Frohman, Belasco, and the others, appeared only later in Hollywood, for the masses are needed to create impresarios, or more precisely, a lucrative mass market. In Golden's office I saw the genesis of so much we have come to associate with Hollywood: the stars under long-term contract, the planning of one production after another instead of the present one-shot Broadway practice, the sense of permanence and even security. None of these are part of Broadway now, and they appear in their afterglow above the St. James; for it is not the masses we serve any more, not the "American People," but a fraction of one class—the more or less better-educated people, or the people aspiring to culture.

Golden's eyes blazed with pleasure as he talked of plays long since gone, like *Turn to the Right* and *Lightnin'* and others I remember my father raving about when I was a boy, and finally he sat back and mused about playwriting.

"You fellows have a much harder time," he said, "much harder than in the old days; nowadays every show has to seem new and original. But in the old days, you know, we had what you might call favorite scenes. There was the scene where the mother puts a candle on the window sill while she waits for her long-lost boy to come home. They loved that scene. We put that scene in one play after another. You can't do things like that anymore. The audience is too smart now. They're more educated, I suppose, and sophisticated. Of course it was all sentimental, I guess, but they were good shows."

He was right, of course, except you *can* do that now; the movies have been doing it for thirty or forty years and now television is doing it all over again. I remember a friend who had worked in Hollywood writing a picture. The producer called him in with a bright new idea for a scene to be inserted in the script. My friend listened and was amazed. "But just last month you released a picture with that same scene in it," he reminded the producer.

"Sure," said the producer, "and didn't it go great?"

The Golden species of glamour is gone with the masses; it went with the big money to Hollywood, and now it is creating itself all over again in television. The present-day actors and directors would probably seem tame and dull to their counterparts of thirty and forty years ago. David Belasco, for instance, had even convinced himself that his was a glamorous profession, and took to dressing in black like a priest—the high priest of the theater—and turned his collar around to prove it. He carried on as no contemporary director would dare to do. Toward the last days of rehearsal, when he wanted some wooden but very beautiful leading lady to break down and weep, he would take out a watch, the watch he had been displaying for weeks as the one his mother gave him on her deathbed, and smash it on the floor in a high dudgeon, thus frightening the actress to tears and making her putty in his hands. It need hardly be added that he kept a large supply of these watches, each worth one dollar.

The traditional idea of the actor with his haughty stance, his peaked eyebrows, elegant speech, artistic temperament, and a necessary disdain for all that was common and plain, has long since disappeared. Now they are all trying to appear as ordinary as your Uncle Max. A group of actors sitting at a bar these days could easily be mistaken for delegates to a convention of white-collar people. They are more likely, upon landing in a hit show, to hurry over to the offices of a tax consultant than to rush out and buy a new Jaguar. For a few years after the war a certain amount or effort was put into aging their dungarees and wearing turtle-neck sweaters, and some of them stopped combing their hair, like the boy I noticed loading the truck. But you don't get Marlon Brando's talent by avoiding a bath, and gradually this fad has vanished. There are more "colorful" personalities up here in the tiny Connecticut village where I spend summers than you will find on all Broadway. The only real showman I know of is Joshua Logan, who can throw a party for a hundred people in his Park Avenue apartment and make it appear a normal evening. Logan is the only director I can name who would dare to knock a stage apart and build into it a real swimming pool, as he did for the musical *Wish You Were Here,* and can still talk about the theater with the open, full-blown excitement of one who has no reservations about it. The other directors, at least the half-dozen I know—and there are not many more—are more likely to be as deadly serious as any atomic physicist, and equally worried.

There is a special aura about the theater, nevertheless, a glamour, too, but it has little connection with the publicity that seeks to create it. There is undoubtedly as much sexual fooling around as there is in the refrigerator business, but I doubt if there is much more. The notion of theatrical immorality began when actors were socially inferior by common consent; but now a Winnifred Cushing (of the Boston Cushings), the loose woman in *Death of a Salesman,* hurries home to her mother after each show.

Not that it is an ordinary life. There is still nothing quite like it, if only because of the fanaticism with which so many respond to its lure. One cannot sit in a producer's office day after day interviewing actors for a play without being struck by their insistence that they belong in the theater and intend to make their lives in it. In the outer reception rooms of any producer's office at casting time is a cross section of a hundred small towns and big cities, the sons and daughters of the rich families and of the middle-class families and of families from the wrong side of the tracks. One feels, on meeting a youngster from a way-station town or a New Mexico ranch, that the spores of this poor theater must still possess vitality to have flown so far and rooted so deep. It is pathetic, it is saddening, but a thing is dead only when nobody wants it, and they do want it desperately. It is nothing unusual to tell a girl who has come to a casting office that she looks too respectable for the part, and to be greeted by her an hour later dressed in a slinky black dress, spike heels, outlandishly overdone make-up, and blond dye in her hair that has hardly had time to dry. One of our best-known actresses had her bowlegs broken in order to appear as she thought she must on the stage, and there is an actor who did the same to his knees in order to play Hamlet in tights.

There is, it must be admitted, an egotism in this that can be neither measured nor sometimes even stomached, but at casting time, when one spends hour after hour in the presence of human beings with so powerful a conviction and so great a desire to be heard and seen and judged as artists, the thing begins to surpass mere egotism and assumes the proportion of a cause, a belief, a mission. And when such sacrifices are made in its name one must begin to wonder at the circumstances that have reduced it to its present chaos. It might be helpful to take a look at how the whole thing is organized—or disorganized.

Everything begins with a script. I must add right off that in the old mass theater that came to an end somewhere in the late twenties, when the movies took over, the script was as often as not a botch of stolen scenes, off-the-cuff inventions of the producer or director, or simply pasted-together situations designed for some leading player. The audience today, however, demands more, and so the script has become the Holy Grail for which a producer dreams, prays, and lives every day of his life. Being so valuable, and so difficult to write, it is leased by the author on a royalty basis and never sold outright. He receives, I am happy to report, roughly ten percent of the gross receipts, or between two and three thousand dollars a week if he has a hit. (I would add that he resolves not to change his standard of living but he has a wife, and that is that.)

Three or four times a year the playwrights have a meeting of the Dramatists Guild, their union, in a private dining room of the St. Regis Hotel. Moss Hart, the author of *The Climate of Eden* and, with George Kaufman, of a string of successes like *The Man Who Came to Dinner* and *You Can't Take It With You*, is the current president of the Guild. There is probably more money represented here than at most union luncheons, the only trouble being that with a few exceptions none of the playwrights has any assets; that is, you can't write a hit every time so the three thousand a week begins to look smaller and smaller when it is averaged out over a period of unfruitful years. Oscar Hammerstein, another Guild member, put an ad in *Variety* after his *South Pacific* opened, listing a dozen or so of his failures that everyone had forgotten, and at the bottom of the page repeated the legend of show business, "I did it before and I can do it again."

Between the turtle soup and the veal scaloppine, various issues are discussed, all of which are usually impossible to solve, and the luncheons roll by and we know that our profession is on the edge of an abyss because the theater is contracting; and we all go home to write our plays. Occasionally we meet with a group of producers, and Max Gordon can usually be relied on to demand the floor; and red in the face, full of his wonderful fight, he will cut to the heart of the problem by shouting at the playwrights, "The producers are starving, you hear me? Starving!" Leland Hayward, who has scraped by on *South Pacific, Mister Roberts,* and other such titbits, will accuse me of making too much money, and Herman Shumlin, the producer of *The Little Foxes, The Children's Hour, Watch on the Rhine,* will solemnly avow that he is leaving the business forever unless we writers cut our royalties; and then we all go home. Once the late Lee Shubert came with the others to discuss the problems of the theater, and when he was asked if he would reduce the rentals of his many theaters, since the playwrights were willing to reduce their royalties, he looked as though the butter was, indeed, melting in his mouth, so he didn't open it. And we all went home again.

There are seemingly hundreds of producers, but actually only fifteen or twenty go on year after year. Few are wealthy, and money is usually promoted or lured out of any crack where it can be found. It is a common, although not universal, practice to hold a gathering of potential backers before whom either the playwright or the director reads the script. Established producers regard this as beneath their dignity, but some don't, or can't afford to. These readings usually take place either on Park Avenue or on swank Beekman Place, for some reason, and while I never attended one, I have known many playwrights who have, but never heard of one dollar being raised in that way.

Script in hand, then, and money either raised or on its way—usually in amounts under five hundred dollars per backer—the producer hires a director, also on a percentage with a fee in advance, and a scene designer; the set is sketched, approved, and ordered built. Casting begins. While the author sits home revising his script—for some reason no script can be produced as the author wrote it—agents are apprised of the kinds of parts to be filled, and in the producer's reception room next morning all hell breaks loose.

The basis upon which actors are hired or not hired is sometimes quite sound; for example, they may have been seen recently in a part which leads the director to believe they are right for the new role; but quite as often a horde of applicants is waiting beyond the door of the producer's private office and neither he nor the director nor the author has the slightest knowledge of any of them. It is at this point that things become painful, for the strange actor sits before them, so nervous and frightened that he either starts talking and can't stop, and sometimes *says* he can't stop, or is unable to say anything at all and says *that.* During the casting of one of my plays there entered a middle-aged woman who was so frightened she suddenly started to sing. The play being no musical, this was slightly beside the point, but the producer, the director, and myself, feeling so guilty ourselves, sat there and heard her through.

To further complicate matters there is each year the actor or actress who suddenly becomes what they call "hot." A hot performer is one not yet well-known, but who, for some mysterious reason, is generally conceded to be a coming star. It is possible, naturally, that a hot performer really has talent, but it is equally possible, and much more likely, that she or he is not a whit more attractive or more talented than a hundred others. Nevertheless, there comes a morning when every producer in these five blocks—some of them with parts the performer could never play —simply has to have him or her. Next season, of course, nobody hears about the new star and it starts all over again with somebody else.

All that is chancy in life, all that is fortuitous, is magnified to the bursting point at casting time; and that, I suspect, is one of the attractions of this whole affair, for it makes the ultimate winning of a part so much more zesty. It is also, to many actors, a most degrading process and more and more of them refuse to submit to these interviews until after the most delicate advances of friendship and hospitality are made to them. And their use of agents as intermediaries is often an attempt to soften the awkwardness of their applying for work.

The theatrical agents, in keeping with the unpredictable lunacy of the business, may be great corporations like the Music Corporation of America, which has an entire building on Madison Avenue, and will sell you anything from a tap dancer to a movie star, a symphony orchestra, saxophonists, crooners, scene designers, actors, and playwrights, to a movie script complete with cast; or they may be like Jane Broder, who works alone and can spread out her arms and touch both walls of her office. They may even be like Carl Cowl, who lives around the corner from me in Brooklyn. Carl is an ex-seaman who still ships out when he has no likely scripts on hand to sell, and when things get too nerve-racking he stays up all night playing Mozart on his flute. MCA has antique desks, English eighteenth-century prints, old broken clocks and inoperative antique barometers hanging on its paneled walls, but Carl Cowl had a hole in his floor that the cat got into, and when he finally got the landlord to repair it he was happy and sat down to play his flute again; but he heard meowing, and they had to rip the floor open again to let out the cat. Still, Carl is not incapable of landing a hit play and neither more nor less likely than MCA to get it produced, and that is another handicraft aspect of this much publicized small business, a quality of opportunity which keeps people coming into it. The fact is that theatrical agents do not sell anyone or anything in the way one sells merchandise. Their existence is mainly due to the need theater people have for a home, some semblance of order in their lives, some sense of being wanted during the long periods when they have nothing to do. To have an agent is to have a kind of reassurance that you exist. The actor is hired, however, mainly because he is wanted for the role.

By intuition, then, by rumor, on the recommendation of an agent—usually heartfelt; out of sheer exhaustion, and upsurge of sudden hope or what not, several candidates for each role are selected in the office of the producer, and are called for readings on the stage of a theater.

It is here that the still unsolved mystery begins, the mystery of what makes a stage performer. There are persons who, in an office, seem exciting candidates for a role, but as soon as they step onto a stage the observers out front—if they are experienced—know that the blessing was not given them. For myself, I know it when, regardless of how well the actor is reading, my eyes begin to wander up to the brick wall back of the stage. Conversely, there are many who make little impression in an office, but once on the stage it is impossible to take one's attention from them. It is a question neither of technique nor of ability, I think, but some quality of surprise inherent in the person.

For instance, when we were searching for a woman to play Linda, the mother in *Death of a Salesman,* a lady came in whom we all knew but could never imagine in the part. We needed a woman who looked as though she had lived in a house dress all her life, even somewhat coarse and certainly less than brilliant. Mildred Dunnock insisted she was that woman, but she was frail, delicate, not long ago a teacher in a girl's college, and a cultivated citizen who probably would not be out of place in a cabinet post. We told her this, in effect, and she understood, and left.

And the next day the line of women formed again in the wings, and suddenly there was Milly again. Now she had padded herself from neck to hem line to look a bit bigger, and for a moment none of us recognized her, and she read again. As soon as she spoke we started to laugh at her ruse; but we saw, too, that she *was* a little more worn now, and seemed less well-maintained, and while she was not quite ordinary, she reminded you of women who were. But we all agreed, when she was finished reading, that she was not right, and she left.

Next day she was there again in another getup, and the next and the next, and each day she agreed with us that she was wrong; and to make a long story short when it came time to make the final selection it had to be Milly, and she turned out to be magnificent. But in this case we had known her work; there was no doubt that she was an excellent actress. The number of talented applicants who are turned down because they are unknown is very large. Such is the crap-shooting chanciness of the business, its chaos, and part of its charm. In a world where one's fate so often seems machined and standardized, and unlikely to suddenly change, these five blocks are like a stockade inside which are people who insist that the unexpected, the sudden chance, must survive. And to experience it they keep coming on all the trains.

But to understand its apparently deathless lure for so many it is necessary, finally, to have participated in the first production of a new play. When a director takes his place at the beaten-up wooden table placed at the edge of the stage, and the cast for the first time sit before him in a semicircle, and he gives the nod to the actor who has the opening lines, the world seems to be filling with a kind of hope, a kind of regeneration that, at the time, anyway, makes all the sacrifices worthwhile.

The production of a new play, I have often thought, is like another chance in life, a chance to emerge cleansed of one's imperfections. Here, as when one was very young, it seems possible again to attain even greatness, or happiness, or some otherwise unattainable joy. And when production never loses that air of hope through all its three-and-a-half-week rehearsal period, one feels alive as at no other imaginable occasion. At such a time, it seems to all concerned that the very heart of life's mystery is what must be penetrated. They watch the director and each other and they listen with the avid attention of deaf mutes who have suddenly learned to speak and hear. Above their heads there begins to form a tantalizing sort of cloud, a question, a challenge to penetrate the mystery of why men move and speak and act.

It is a kind of glamour that can never be reported in a newspaper column, and yet it is the center of all the lure theater has. It is a kind of soul-testing that ordinary people rarely experience except in the greatest emergencies. The actor who has always regarded himself as a strong spirit discovers now that his vaunted power somehow sounds querulous, and he must look within himself to find his strength. The actress who has made her way on her charm discovers that she appears not charming so much as shallow now, and must evaluate herself all over again, and create anew what she always took for granted. And the great performers are merely those who have been able to face themselves without remorse.

In the production of a good play with a good cast and a knowing director a kind of banding together occurs; there is formed a fraternity whose members share a mutual sense of destiny. In these five blocks, where the rapping of the tap-dancer's feet and the bawling of the phonographs in the record-shop doorways mix with the roar of the Broadway traffic; where the lonely, the perverted, and the lost wander like the souls in Dante's hell and the life of the spirit seems impossible, there are still little circles of actors in the dead silence of empty theaters, with a director in their center, and a new creation of life taking place.

There are always certain moments in such rehearsals, moments of such wonder that the memory of them serves to further entrap all who witness them into this most insecure of all professions. Remembering such moments the resolution to leave and get a "real" job vanishes, and they are hooked again.

I think of Lee Cobb, the greatest dramatic actor I ever saw, when he was creating the role of Willy Loman in *Death of a Salesman*. When I hear people scoffing at actors as mere exhibitionists, when I hear them ask why there must be a theater if it cannot support itself as any business must, when I myself grow sick and weary of the endless waste and the many travesties of this most abused of all arts, I think then of Lee Cobb making that role and I know that the theater can yet be one of the chief glories of mankind.

He sat for days on the stage like a great lump, a sick seal, a mourning walrus. When it came his time to speak lines, he whispered meaninglessly. Kazan, the director, pretended certainty, but from where I sat he looked like an ant trying to prod an elephant off his haunches. Ten days went by. The other actors were by now much further advanced: Milly Dunnock, playing Linda, was already creating a role; Arthur Kennedy as Biff had long since begun to reach for his high notes; Cameron Mitchell had many scenes already perfected; but Cobb stared at them, heavy-eyed, morose, even persecuted, it seemed.

And then, one afternoon, there on the stage of the New Amsterdam way up on top of a movie theater on Forty-second Street (this roof theater had once been Ziegfeld's private playhouse in the gilded times, and now was barely heated and misty with dust), Lee rose from his chair and looked at Milly Dunnock and there was a silence. And then he said, "I was driving along, you understand, and then all of a sudden I'm going off the road. . . ."

And the theater vanished. The stage vanished. The chill of an age-old recognition shuddered my spine; a voice was sounding in the dimly lit air up front, a created spirit, an incarnation, a Godlike creation was taking place; a new human being was being formed before all our eyes, born for the first time on this earth, made real by an act of will, by an artist's summoning up of all his memories and his intelligence; a birth was taking place above the meaningless traffic below; a man was here transcending the limits of his body and his own history. Through the complete concentration of his mind he had even altered the stance of his body, which now was strangely not the body of Lee Cobb (he was thirty-seven then) but of a sixty-year-old salesman; a mere glance of his eye created a window beside him, with the gentle touch of his hand on this empty stage a bed appeared, and when he glanced up at the emptiness above him a ceiling was there, and there was even a crack in it where his stare rested.

I knew then that something astounding was being made here. It would have been almost enough for me without even opening the play. The actors, like myself and Kazan and the producer, were happy, of course, that we might have a hit; but there was a good deal more. There was a new fact of life, there was an alteration of history for all of us that afternoon.

There is a certain immortality involved in theater, not created by monuments and books, but through the knowledge the actor keeps to his dying day that on a certain afternoon, in an empty and dusty theater, he cast a shadow of a being that was not himself but the distillation of all he had ever observed; all the un-singable heartsong the ordinary man may feel but never utter, he gave voice to. And by that he somehow joins the ages.

And that is the glamour that remains, but it will not be found in the gossip columns. And it is enough, once discovered, to make people stay with the theater, and others to come seeking it.

I think also that people keep coming into these five blocks because the theater is still so simple, so old-fashioned. And that is why, however often its obsequies are intoned, it somehow never really dies. Because underneath our shiny fronts of stone, our fascination with gadgets, and our new toys that can blow the earth into a million stars, we are still outside the doorway through which the great answers wait. Not all the cameras in Christendom nor all the tricky lights will move us one step closer to a better understanding of ourselves, but only, as it always was, the truly written word, the profoundly felt gesture, the naked and direct contemplation of man which is the enduring glamour of the stage.

1954

A Boy Grew in Brooklyn

Nobody can know Brooklyn, because Brooklyn is the world, and besides it is filled with cemeteries, and who can say he knows those people? But even aside from the cemeteries it is impossible to say that one knows Brooklyn. Three blocks from my present house live two hundred Mohawk Indians. A few blocks from them are a group of Arabs living in tenements in one of which is published an Arabic newspaper. When I lived on Schermerhorn Street I used to sit and watch the Muslims holding services in a tenement back yard outside my window, and they had a real Moorish garden, symmetrically planted with curving lines of white stones laid out in the earth, and they would sit in white robes—twenty or thirty of them, eating at a long table, and served by their women who wore the flowing purple and rose togas of the East. All these people, plus the Germans, Swedes, Jews, Italians, Lebanese, Irish, Hungarians and more, created the legend of Brooklyn's patriotism, and it has often seemed to me that their having been thrown together in such abrupt proximity is what gave the place such a Balkanized need to proclaim its never-achieved oneness.

But this is not the Brooklyn I know or was brought up in. Mine was what is called the Midwood section, which now has no distinguishing marks, but thirty years ago was a flat forest of great elms through which ran the elevated Culver Line to Coney Island, two and a half miles distant. My Brooklyn consisted of Jews, some Italians, a few Irish— and a Mr. Dunham, whom I remember only because he was reputed to carry a gun as part of his duties as a bank guard.

Children going to school in those days could be watched from the back porch and kept in view for nearly a mile. There were streets, of course, but the few houses had well-trodden trails running out of their back doors which connected with each other and must have looked from the air like a cross section of a mole run; these trails were much more used than the streets, which were as unpaved as any in the Wild West and just as muddy. Today everything is paved and your bedroom window is just far enough away from your neighbor's to leave room to swing the screens out when fall comes.

My aunts and uncles, who moved there right after World War I, could go to Manhattan on the Culver Line for a nickel (although my cousins always climbed around the turnstile, which was easy, so long as you didn't mind hanging from iron railings a hundred feet or so above the street), but they had to buy potatoes in hundred-pound sacks because there was no grocery store within four miles. And they planted tomatoes, and they canned fruits and vegetables, and kept rabbits and chickens and hunted squirrels and other small game. The Culver Line cars were made of wood, like trolleys hooked together, and clattered above the cemeteries and the elms, and I must say there was something sweet about it when you got aboard in the morning and there was always the same conductor who knew you and even said good morning.

I don't precisely know why, but Brooklyn in my memory has always been full of characters and practical jokers. I suppose it is really a collection of villages which all seem the same to the stranger's eye, but are not; and characters thrive and express their special ways in a village atmosphere. My father was one, and is the last of those Mohicans as he sits in front of his frame house on a Sunday afternoon, remembering, as he glances down the tree-lined block, the old friends and screwballs who lived in each of the houses and are now resting peacefully in the cemetery that spreads out two blocks away, their pinochle decks laid down forever, their battles done.

My father, a large, square-headed man who looks like a retired police captain, and has that kind of steady severity, is likely to feel the need, from time to time, to "start something." Years ago, he sat down on the Culver Line one morning, and seeing a neighbor whom he regarded as particularly gullible, moved over to him and in his weightiest manner, began:

"You hear my brother-in-law got back from Florida?"

"Yes, I heard," said the neighbor. "What does he do down there? Just fish and like that?"

"Oh, no," my father said, "haven't you heard about his new business?"

"No. What?"

"He raises cockroaches there."

"Cockroaches! What does he do with the cockroaches?"

"What does he do with the cockroaches? Sells them!"

"Who wants cockroaches?"

"Who wants cockroaches! There's a bigger demand for cockroaches than for mink. Of course they gotta be of a certain breed. He breeds them down there. But they're all purebred."

"But what good are they?"

"Listen," my father confided, lowering his voice. "Don't say I even mentioned it, but if you happen to see any cockroaches around, in your house, or anywhere like that, my brother-in-law would appreciate it if you brought them all to him. Because I tell you why, see—he's raising them up here now, right in his house, but in Brooklyn it's against the law, you understand?—but once in a while a couple of them escape, and he's bashful to ask people, but you'd be doing him a big favor if you happen to catch any, bring them to him. But be very careful. Don't hurt them. He'll pay five dollars for any purebred cockroach anybody brings him."

"Five dollars!"

"Well, listen, that's his business. But don't tell anybody I told you because it's against the law, you know?"

Having planted this seed, my father left the neighbor. A week or so later my uncle's doorbell rang, and there was the man, considerably insecure in his mind, but there nevertheless, with a matchbox full of cockroaches. For three whole days my uncle refused to play casino with my father.

There is Ike Samuels, who runs—or rather sits outside—the hardware store. Ike's way with women who come in not knowing precisely what they want is something not easily described. I have watched him double-talking a *Hausfrau* for better than ten minutes; but when they come in with complaints he rises to a height of idiotic evasion that is positively lyrical. I was myself a victim of his for years, as a boy. We lived three blocks from his store, and often as I passed he would open his eyes against the sunlight where he sat in his rocker beside the door, and say, "Raining on Ocean Parkway?"

For years I answered him seriously because he has a remorseless poker face and thick lenses on his eyeglasses that make a clear view of his eyes impossible. Out of respect, at first. I described the weather three blocks away; but later I began to doubt myself and came to wonder, now and then, whether it *had* been raining there while the sun shone here.

But that was the least of Ike Samuels. I happened to be in his store one morning when a woman entered. Like so many of them at eleven A.M., she had a coat on top of her nightgown—and in her hands was an electric broiler which Ike had repaired only a week before. She strode in, a large woman with lumpy hair that, in her anger at the broiler, she had neglected to comb, and she plunked the broiler down on the counter.

"You said you fixed it!" she began.

"What is the trouble?" Ike said.

"It don't heat! My husband came home last night, I put four lamb chops in, we could've dropped dead from hunger, it was like an ice box in there!"

Ike took the top off the broiler and made as though to examine its works. There was a silence. He peered this way and that inside it, and I could tell that he was winding up for a stroke that would resound through his whole day. Looking up at her like a detective on the scent, he asked, "What did you say you put in here?"

Suspecting, perhaps, that she had in fact done something wrong, she parried: "What do you mean what did I put in here?"

Like a prosecutor, Ike leaned in toward her: "Answer my question, madam; what did you put in this broiler?"

Her voice smaller now, off balance, she replied, "I said—lamb chops."

"Lamb chops!" Ike rolled his eyes at the ceiling, where the mops and pails hung. "Lamb chops she puts in!"

Close to tears now, the woman began to plead, "Well, what's the matter with lamb chops?"

"What's the matter with lamb chops!" Ike roared indignantly. "Can't you read, lady? What night school did you go to? Look!" With which he turned the broiler upside down and pointed to the brass plate riveted to the bottom, on which were embossed the long serial numbers of the manufacturer's patents, and the Underwriters' Laboratory seal.

She bent over to peer at the tiny numbers and the few words. And before she could fix her eyes Ike was on her. "It's plain as day. 'No Lamb Chops,' it says; this is written by naval architects, graduate engineers from the Massachusetts Institute of Technology—'No lamb chops'—and you throw lamb chops in there. What do you want from me, lady? I fixed it for steak!"

Her eyes were distraught now, utterly bewildered. "But he likes lamb chops," she pleaded.

And now, having won the initiative, he came around the counter and escorted her to the door. "Now look, don't be discouraged. I'll do my best, and I'll fix it for lamb chops. I got a license for that, but you gotta have a double affixative on the forspice."

"Could you put one on?" she asked, exhausted.

"For you anything, darling," he said, and sent her on her way.

It was a village, even down to the feeble-minded Danny, who hung around Ike's store, and when you came by he would point at you and say, "Navarre 8-7135," because his pride lay in remembering everybody's phone number. If he overheard Ike talking about somebody's aunt, he would interject, "Dewey 9-0518," which, in his mind, identified the aunt. "Ulster 5-8009 is getting married, Ike," he announced one morning. Asked who the bride was, he answered, "Navarre 8-6661." But he had his dignity, which he enforced. If they started kidding him, he would get off the barrel and leave, saying, "I gotta see a party."

It was a village, and while to the stranger's eye one street was no different from another, we all knew where our "neighborhood" somehow ended, and the line of demarcation was never more than three blocks away. Beyond that, a person was somehow a stranger.

It was a village with village crimes. I don't recall any time when the cops had to be called. Everyone was so well and thoroughly known that the frown of his neighbors was enough law to keep things in line. When we stole from the candy store, when we played handball against the druggist's window and broke it, it was enough for the offended proprietor to let it be known to the parents. Although I must add that Mr. Dozik, the pharmacist, had it a little harder. The wall of his building was perfect for handball, and poor Dozik had to be all the time giving us water from his soda fountain. He tried putting up billboards that projected from the wall, but we played around them, until finally he had his soda fountain removed. Mr. Dozik is the first man in history to discover that boys cannot play handball where there is no cold drinking water.

He's still there as he was then—a kind of doctor who knows what ails everybody; a man who sewed up the arms, hands and ears of all my cousins and remembers every stitch.

It was a village with no stream, however, so my cousins and I would get up at four in the morning and climb around the turnstile of the Culver Line, and go rickety-rackety down the two-mile track to Coney Island and fish off the rocks and bring home flounder or sea bass—even in winter, when the wind was raw off the ocean.

I got to know those village winters especially well because I delivered rolls and bread every morning for the bakery before I went to school. There were no gloves warm enough to keep the icy cold of the handlebars away from my fingers, so I wore long woolen plaid stockings that came up to my elbows, and with the basket over the front wheel piled high with bags of bread, rolls and bagels, I would ride forth through the streets at four-thirty in the morning.

In the spring and fall it was lovely and one could sing out loud for the beauty of it, but when the snow fell, or worse yet, when the streets were covered with ice, a special kind of hell broke loose. Bread means something very special to these people. A man rising to breakfast in those houses *expects* his bagel, or his rye bread, or his onion roll or whatever it is he craves most. Give a bagel man an onion roll and his whole day is ruined, while for a rye-bread man a bagel is beneath contempt, especially for breakfast when one's taste buds are fresh and quivering and so very delicately attuned to flavors.

So it used to be with a somewhat trembling care that I would guide the bike down the streets when there was ice, because each bag was filled with its special order, and each one marked in crayon with its proper address. I would slowly ride down the center of the street, carefully holding to the crown of the road, and the cold cats would follow me, meowing and pleading for warmth and food, and the dark sky of winter was merciless over my head. And there came a time, once, when the bike suddenly slid out from under me, and the bags tumbled out of the wire basket, and many broke, and others just opened because they were overstuffed, and as I sat there on the ice, I could see bagels, onion rolls, whole rye breads, sliding out over the sheet ice in all directions. Few people can imagine how far a bagel will slide on clean ice. I know.

And besides, the baker had gallstones. I hadn't the heart to return and tell him of this catastrophe. So I went about on the empty street, gathering up the cargo, some of which had come to a stop three quarters of a block away. I then sat on the ice, flashlight gleaming, trying to put things back into the proper bags. Some were easy, because the bags had been packed so tightly that the impressions made by the hump of a rye bread's back and the circle of a bagel were unmistakable. But most were simply bags, like any other bags, and I finally just stuffed them as best I could, spreading the bagels through the lot, and offering, in short, what I thought was a nice variety to each customer. I had, as amateur mechanics do when they try to assemble a machine that has been taken apart, several pieces left over, which I simply ate before delivering the bags.

I returned to the bakery to leave the bike, and already the phone was ringing, or more accurately, burning. The baker looked ghastly. In his whole life nothing like this had happened. Utterly baffled, he listened to Mrs. 1690 screaming in his ear for her onion rolls, her husband is going to be shaved in five minutes! And Mrs. 1277 asking when in her nine years of dealing with him she had ever ordered rye bread! And the poor man turned to me, his two overcoats making him look like a mountain of horrification, and I explained at last. But it remained a tragedy from which, as far as I could tell, he never fully recovered.

I do not think I am painting it more serene than it was. There was a rhythm and a flowing to the days that began with the men trekking to Avenue M from all the side streets in the early morning, and like a column of ants climbing up the long steep stairs to the Culver Line, and it ended toward nightfall when they trekked down again and dispersed into their houses. We walked three miles to James Madison High School, and the ambitious track men among us trotted all the way, stopping only to look at the girl setting out the blackberry tarts in the window of the Ebinger Bakery. I do not think there were any intellectuals among us and as far as I can remember the greatest thing anybody could do was to get on the football team, or run like hell, or swim a couple of miles in the ocean in the summer. I know that in later years, when I began to publish, my old high-school teachers looked through their records in an attempt to remember me, but not one of them could. I was, in fact, thoroughly invisible during the entire four years, and this is by all odds my most successful accomplishment so far. Because the idea all of us subscribed to, was to get out onto the football field with the least possible scholastic interference, and I can fairly say we were none of us encumbered by anything resembling a thought.

The first ripple of what may properly be called the Outside World was felt one day when a crowd of people formed at the doors of The Bank of the United States—which was not even in our neighborhood, being five blocks away. To be succinct about it, the thing had closed. This in itself did not bother me particularly because, while I had been a depositor to the tune of twelve dollars, I had withdrawn the entire amount the very day before to buy Joey Backus's Columbia racer. What did bother me was that the day after the bank closed I got hungry, left the bike in front of our house, went inside for some bread and jam, and came out to find no bike, and a block can never look as empty as it does to a boy whose bike should be on it and isn't. In that emptiness lay the new reality.

With this incident I was introduced to the Depression Age. Suddenly, overnight, in fact, the postman became an envied character because he could not lose his job and even had a paid vacation. Our postman, unlike some others, did not flaunt his new superiority but went right on opening our front door, coming into the living room and calling up to my mother to read her the mail: "Nothing important, Mrs. Miller. Gas bill, electric bill, and a card from your sister. She says she's enjoying the hotel and will be home next Friday," with which he simply went out, just as he always had.

But other things had begun to change, sometimes in a weird way. The government soon took over practically every mortgage on the block, and the result was that all the housewives started making more and better coffee. When the man came to our house to collect the payments, my mother, for one, got out the coffeepot and her wonderful coffeecake, and he would sit down and before he could say a number she was stuffing him, and for about a year or so this collector always left our block bloated, and not with money either. It got so he would never mention the mortgage, but just sit there and wait to be served.

There was a lot of tension, though, in that time, and in a little while you could see grown men sitting on the porches in the middle of a weekday afternoon, and the trotters to Madison High were thinned out as one after another had to go looking for work. And the line of breadwinners coming down the stairs of the Culver Line had the slump of humiliation and bewilderment in their shoulders, and there were stores empty now, and when you ripped your shirt it was a minor tragedy, and every now and then, toward midnight, there were voices raised in loud argument within the houses. It got so bad that one night, after dinner, my grandfather put down his paper—he who had been a Republican all his life and believed, if you pressed him hard enough, that what America needed was a king like they had in Austria—my grandfather turned to me with his great bald head and the bags under his eyes like von Hindenburg's, and said, "You know what you ought to do? You ought to go to Russia."

The silence that fell is better described as a vacuum so powerful it threatened to suck the walls in. Even my father woke up on the couch. I asked why I should go to Russia.

"Because in Russia they haven't got anything. Here they got too much. You can't sell anything here any more. You go to Russia and open a chain of clothing stores; you could do a big business. That's a new country, Russia."

"But," I said, "you can't do that there."

"Why not?" he said, disbelieving.

"The government owns the stores there."

His face would have put fear into Karl Marx himself. "Them bastards," he said, and went back to his paper.

By this time, of course, inevitable changes had helped to destroy so much that was human and lovely in my neighborhood (although much remains even today)—changes that had nothing to do with the Depression. The woods were gone now and there were houses everywhere, and even the last lot left to play football on was turned into a fenced-in junkyard. Bars had begun to sprout along Gravesend Avenue, and the whole idea of drinking, which the old neighborhood had never known, became quite normal.

An invisible vise seemed to be forever closing tighter and tighter, and the worst, most unimaginable fates became ordinary. The star football player became a shipping clerk, and was glad to have the job; I, who had planned to go to Cornell because they offered a free course in biology—although I had not the slightest interest in the subject—waited around until the fall term began, and seeing that nobody in the house was in possession of the fare, I went to the employment offices for a couple of months and ended up in a warehouse. It was the time Nick appeared on the scene and the time my grandfather decided to die.

About Nick in a moment. One hot afternoon, while the neighborhood and the nation slumbered in the tortured sleep of the Depression and a fiery heat wave in the bargain, my grandfather began to pant. He rarely sat outside his bedroom without his jacket, stiff collar and tie, but that day he gradually took off all but his shirt, and even went for his wire-frame glasses, which were cooler, he believed, than the tortoise-shell ones. Then he lay down on the couch and heaved his chest and looked terrible, and my mother called the doctor and her two sisters and several sisters-in-law, and in half an hour they were all wailing around him and trying to prevent him from speaking, but at last his right arm raised up imperiously, palm out, and they fell silent.

He had been a blunt sort of Germanic businessman all his life; had had a factory of importance for many years, and it is enough to say of his physique that whenever there was a strike in his plant he would pick up two workers and knock their heads together. This was as far as his ideas of labor relations went.

With the Depression his income was gone, and he had been shunted from one daughter's house to another's, and while no one dared cross him, they did manage to palm him off on the next one every six months or so "for his sake." Unfortunately, he could not get sick. He drank gallons of mineral water, panted, and I had often seen him striding down Avenue M with his cane flashing and hardly touching the pavement, but when he turned into our block, he would slow down, pant, lean heavily on the cane and barely make it to the door. Then he would eat the equivalent of a wash basin of thick soup, as many chops as there were, and sit down to listen to Lowell Thomas, and if some fool forgot and asked him how he was feeling, he would shake his head like an ailing emperor and could barely be heard complaining. He was so neat he folded his socks before putting them in the laundry hamper, and it took him five minutes to get his two pillows set exactly where he wanted them on the bed before he lay down, or rather half sat up, to go to sleep. Once a week he went to the barber to have his little Vandyke trimmed, and insisted on being sprayed with toilet water of a certain brand. Even his rubber heels he wore out evenly, and his four hats were kept in their original boxes. Once every week he smoked a cigar.

And now he lay dying. Slowly the last words issued from his lips. Like Lear parceling out the nation he told each daughter what she was to have of his possessions. The trouble was that he only had twenty-six dollars left, and his hats. But it made no difference, each one burst into thankful tears as her bequest was mentioned. And finally, he said, "And don't bury me in the old plot. It's too crowded there. I want a little room. And I don't want to be where people are going to be walking over me all the time." He always liked room and plenty of air. "Put me on the aisle," he concluded, probably feeling at the moment that it would be cooler there.

Having gotten their agreement, he groaned and sat up. After a while they tried to make him lie down but he said he felt better now. The conversation turned to other things, and pretty soon the women were playing rummy and forgot all about him. The next they knew he was coming down the stairs, cane, jacket, felt hat, stiff collar and tie. "Where you going, Papa?" his daughters screamed.

He turned in the doorway, his brows drawn together as though in preparation for a mission of importance. "I gotta go for a fitting," he said.

"A fitting!" they called. "You can't go out in this weather!"

"I'm having a suit made downtown. Beautiful material. Two pairs of pants." With which he walked out and lived ten years longer. The whole thing was just due to the general discouragement, I guess.

Equally unforeseeable, but a sign of the times and the nature of the neighborhood, was the way Nick made out. One day, in the year of especially long bread lines, a man knocked on my aunt's door and asked if he could wash the windows for her. He was built low to the ground, lisped, and was neatly combed and obviously quite poor. In those days strange men were constantly appearing in the neighborhood looking for work or a piece of bread, and we had more than a few who fainted from hunger on our steps and only my mother's chicken soup could revive them. My father, slightly more cynical than some others, said, "Sure, they smell the chicken soup and decide it's a good place to faint," and we spent one whole Sunday morning looking all over the house for any mark or secret sign that seemed to lead these fellows directly to our door.

But my aunt hired Nick and he worked carefully, and when night came she let him sleep in the cellar. Next morning, when the family came down, the dining-room table was set with a tablecloth and napkins standing up stiffly. The breakfast he cooked and the way he served it swept them all away, as well it might, since Nick had been a steward on three great ocean liners for fifteen years. To make a long story short, Nick lived to bury my uncle and my aunt, painted the house three or four times in the nearly twenty years he lived there, and was periodically thrown out never to return because he would wait until my uncle had squeezed all the grapes and made the wine, and then drank it up down in the cellar, gallon after gallon, and had to have his stomach pumped by the ambulance driver, who, after a while, got out the stomach pump the minute he pulled up in front of the house.

It was a village, and the people died like the elms did, and I do not know those who live in their houses now. I go back there now and then, but whether it is I that am no longer young or the people who have changed, I know only that things are alien to me there and I am as strange to the place as if I had never known it. The cars, for one thing, jam bumper to bumper along the curbs on streets where there was so much clear space we could have bumping matches with our first jalopies, and ride backwards and forwards and up on the sidewalks and never find an obstruction anywhere. And people seem to move in and out more often than they did, and there are many who have lived there five or six years now and the people next door still don't know what they do for a living, or anything more than their names. The drugstore has a chromium front now and fluorescent lighting, and young Mr. Dozik is a gray-haired man. A lot of picture windows are being put in to get a better view of the wall of the next house a driveway's width away. And when anyone looks out the picture window all the people next door are there watching television anyway.

But there is still the smell of the leaves being burned in the fall, and I imagine some boy is delivering the rolls, and all these strangers must be close to somebody, although I would swear they are more formal toward each other than we used to be, and there is an indifference in their eyes, even the ones who sit out in front of their houses in the cool of the evening. My father sits out there waiting for a friendly conversation, and usually ends up, after an hour or so, going up to bed without having talked to anyone. There has been a scandal or two and amorous conflicts the like of which were rare before, but the children still wonder if my father is really the mayor, as he claims to be in such dead earnest, and now and again a few who have not yet caught on will come to the house leading a cat by a rope because, in a sudden fit of ennui, a few weeks ago, he said to a little boy passing by, "I buy all kinds of cats," or a child will stop a stranger to ask what his business might be because my father, what with all the casino games dead and gone, has persuaded the five-year-olds to "stand guard and watch the block."

But I think, as I watch him sitting there, that the smell of the burning leaves and autumn will never be enough to make those few, once space-filled blocks the center of the world again, the way they used to seem. Instead of the pies and cakes being trafficked back and forth across the street, and much visiting from house to house and the late card games and a certain energetic noisiness that was full of heat, there is now an order, and more politeness, and even when people do live there a long time now, they always have the feeling that someday they might not, and that changes things.

Still, as my father said the other night, "It's a different kind of people, but so is the world. They'll make out all right." And he stared down the street at the unbroken line of cars, at the old houses ludicrously changed to look more ranchy, at the tall apartment houses beyond the corner, and the metallic sound such buildings seem to make, and he got up and folded his chair and carried it into the house.

Brooklyn is a lot of villages. And this was one of them.

1955

On Social Plays

A Greek living in the classical period would be bewildered by the dichotomy implied in the very term "social play." Especially for the Greek, a drama created for public performance had to be "social." A play to him was by definition a dramatic consideration of the way men ought to live. But in this day of extreme individualism even that phrase must be further defined. When we say "how men ought to live," we are likely to be thinking of psychological therapy, of ridding ourselves individually of neurotic compulsions and destructive inner tendencies, of "learning how to love" and thereby gaining "happiness."

It need hardly be said that the Greek dramatist had more than a passing interest in psychology and character on the stage. But for him these were means to a larger end, and the end was what we isolate today as social. That is, the relations of man as a social animal, rather than his definition as a separated entity, was the dramatic goal. Why this should have come to be is a large historical question which others are more competent to explain, as several already have. For our purposes it will be sufficient to indicate one element in the life of classical Greece that differs so radically from anything existing in the modern world as to throw a bright light on certain of our attitudes which we take for granted and toward which we therefore are without a proper perspective.

The Greek citizen of that time thought of himself as belonging not to a "nation" or a "state" but to a *polis*. The polis were small units, apparently deriving from an earlier tribal social organization, whose members probably knew one another personally because they were relatively few in number and occupied a small territory. In war or peace the whole people made the vital decisions, there being no profession of politics as we know it; any man could be elected magistrate, judge, even a general in the armed forces. It was an amateur world compared to our stratified and specialized one, a world in which everyone knew enough about almost any profession to practice it, because most things were simple to know. The thing of importance for us is that these people were *engaged,* they could not imagine the good life excepting as it brought each person into close contact with civic matters. They were avid argufiers. Achilles was blessed by the gods with the power to fight well and make good speeches. The people had a special sense of pride in the polis and thought that it in itself distinguished them from the barbarians outside who lived under tyrannies.

The preoccupation of the Greek drama with ultimate law, with the Grand Design, so to speak, was therefore an expression of a basic assumption of the people, who could not yet conceive, luckily, that any man could long prosper unless his polis prospered. The individual was at one with his society; his conflicts with it were, in our terms, like family conflicts the opposing sides of which nevertheless shared a mutuality of feeling and responsibility. Thus the drama written for them, while for us it appears wholly religious, was religious for them in a more than mystical way. Religion is the only way we have any more of expressing our genuinely social feelings and concerns, for in our bones we as a people do not otherwise believe in our oneness with a larger group. But the religiousness of the Greek drama of the classical time was more worldly; it expressed a social concern, to be sure, but it did so on the part of a people already unified on earth rather than the drive of a single individual toward personal salvation. The great gap we feel between religious or "high" emotion and the emotions of daily life was not present in their mass affairs. The religious expression was not many degrees higher for them than many other social expressions, of which their drama is the most complete example.

It is necessary to add that as the polis withered under the impact of war and historical change, as commerce grew and a differentiation of interest separated man from man, the Greek drama found it more and more difficult to stand as a kind of universal mass statement or prayer. It turned its eye inward, created more elaborated characterizations, and slowly gave up some of its former loftiness. Men, as H. D. F. Kitto has said in *The Greeks,* replaced Man in the plays. Nevertheless, to the end the Greek drama clearly conceived its right function as something far wider than a purely private examination of individuality for the sake of the examination or for art's sake. In every dramatic hero there is the idea of the Greek people, their fate, their will, and their destiny.

In today's America the term "social play" brings up images which are historically conditioned, very recent, and, I believe, only incidentally pertinent to a fruitful conception of the drama. The term indicates to us an attack, an arraignment of society's evils such as Ibsen allegedly invented and was later taken up by left-wing playwrights whose primary interest was the exposure of capitalism for the implied benefit of socialism or communism. The concept is tired and narrow, but its worst effect has been to confuse a whole generation of playwrights, audiences, and theater workers.

If one can look at the idea of "social drama" from the Greek viewpoint for one moment, it will be clear that there can be only either a genuinely social drama or, if it abdicates altogether, its true opposite, the antisocial and ultimately anti-dramatic drama.

To put it simply, even over-simply, a drama rises in stature and intensity in proportion to the weight of its application to all manner of men. It gains its weight as it deals with more and more of the whole man, not either his subjective or his social life alone, and the Greek was unable to conceive of man or anything else except as a whole. The modern playwright, at least in America, on the one hand is importuned by his most demanding audience to write importantly, while on the other he is asked not to bring onto the stage images of social function, lest he seem like a special pleader and therefore inartistic. I am not attempting a defense of the social dramas of the thirties, most of which were in fact special pleadings and further from a consideration of the whole man than much of the antisocial drama is. I am trying only to project a right conception of what social drama was and what it ought to be. It is, I think, the widest concept of drama available to us thus far.

When, however, a contemporary dramatist is drawn for but a moment toward a concept of form even remotely Greek, certain lacks become evident—a certain abyss even begins to appear around him. When you are writing in the name of a people unified in a self-conscious and rather small band, when you yourself as a writer are not an individual entrepreneur offering wares to a hostile marketplace but a member of a group who is in other ways no different from the rest—when, in short, the dramatic form itself is regarded as inevitably a social expression of the deepest concerns of all your fellow men—your work is bound to be liberated, freed of even the hypothesis of partisanship, if only because partisanship cannot thrive where the idea of wholeness is accepted. Thus in such a situation what we call social matters become inseparable from subjective psychological matters, and the drama is once again whole and capable of the highest reach.

If one considers our own drama of the past forty years in comparison with that of classical Greece, one elemental difference—the difference which seems to me to be our crippling hobble—will emerge. The single theme to which our most ambitious plays can be reduced is frustration. In all of them, from O'Neill's through the best of Anderson, Sidney Howard, and the rest, the underlying log jam, so to speak, the unresolvable paradox, is that, try as he will, the individual is doomed to frustration when once he gains a consciousness of his own identity. The image is that of the individual scratching away at a wall beyond which stands society, his fellow men. Sometimes he pounds at the wall, sometimes he tries to scale it or even blow it up, but at the end the wall is always there, and the man himself is dead or doomed to defeat in his attempt to live a human life.

The tragic victory is always denied us because, I believe, the plays cannot project with any conviction what the society, in the playwrights' views at any rate, has failed to prove. In Greece the tragic victory consisted in demonstrating that the polis—the whole people—had discovered some aspect of the Grand Design which also was the right way to live *together.* If the American playwrights of serious intent are in any way the subconscience of the country, our claims to have found that way are less than proved. For when the Greek thought of the right way to live it was a whole concept; it meant a way to live that would create citizens who were brave in war, had a sense of responsibility to the polis in peace, and were also developed as individual personalities.

It has often seemed to me that the Soviet Russians have studied classical Greece and have tried to bridge with phraseology profound differences between their social organization and that of Greece, while demanding of their writers what in effect is a Greek social drama. The word "cosmopolitan," as Kitto points out, was invented in Greece when the small polis were disintegrating, and when the drama itself was beginning to turn inward, away from the largest questions of social fate to the fate of individuals alone. It was invented to describe a new kind of man, a man whose allegiance was not primarily to his society, his polis, but to others of like mind anywhere in the world. With it goes an intimation—or more—of skepticism, of self-removal, that presages the radical separation of man from society which the American drama expresses ultimately through themes of frustration. To supplant the polis and allegiance to it, the Soviets have a thousand kinds of social organizations, and, for all one knows, the individual Russian might well feel a sense of connection with civic affairs which the West does not afford its citizens. The crucial difference, however, is that only the most theoretical Russian can trace the effects, if any, of his personality upon the policies of his country, while the Greek could literally see what he had done when he made his speech and swayed or failed to sway his fellow men.

Thus the Russian drama after the Revolution, much as ours, is a drama of frustration, the inability of industrialized men to see themselves spiritually completed through the social organization. But in the Soviet case the frustration is not admitted; it is talked away in large phrases having to do with a victory of the people through tragic sacrifice. The fact remains, however, that nowhere in the world where industrialized economy rules—where specialization in work, politics, and social life is the norm—nowhere has man discovered a means of connecting himself to society except in the form of a truce with it. The best we have been able to do is to speak of a "duty" to society, and this implies sacrifice or self-deprivation. To think of an individual fulfilling his subjective needs through social action, to think of him as living most completely when he lives most socially, to think of him as doing this, not as a social worker acting out of conscientious motives, but naturally, without guilt or sense of oddness—this is difficult for us to imagine, and when we can, we know at the same time that only a few, perhaps a blessed few, are so constructed as to manage it.

As with Greece, so with us—each great war has turned men further and further away from preoccupation with Man and drawn them back into the family, the home, the private life and the preoccupation with sexuality. It has happened, however, that at the same time our theater has exhausted the one form that was made to express the private life—prose realism. We are bored with it; we demand something more, something "higher," on the stage, while at the same time we refuse, or do not know how, to live our private lives excepting as ego-centers. I believe it is this paradox that underlies the kind of struggle taking place in the drama today—a struggle at one and the same time to write of private persons privately and yet lift up their means of expression to a poetic—that is, a social—level. You cannot speak in verse of picayune matters—at least not on the stage—without sounding overblown and ridiculous, and so it should be. Verse reaches always toward the general statement, the wide image, the universal moment, and it must be based upon wide concepts—it must speak not merely of men but of Man. The language of dramatic verse is the language of a people profoundly at one with itself; it is the most public of public speech. The language of prose is the language of the private life, the kind of private life men retreat to when they are at odds with the world they have made or been heirs to.

The social drama, then—at least as I have always conceived it—is the drama of the whole man. It seeks to deal with his differences from others not *per se,* but toward the end that, if only through drama, we may know how much the same we are, for if we lose that knowledge we shall have nothing left at all. The social drama to me is only incidentally an arraignment of society. *A Streetcar Named Desire* is a social drama; so is *The Hairy Ape,* and so are practically all O'Neill's other plays. For they ultimately make moot, either weakly or with full power, the ancient question, how are we to live? And that question is in its Greek sense, its best and most humane sense, not merely a private query.

The social drama, as I see it, is the main stream and the antisocial drama a bypass. I can no longer take with ultimate seriousness a drama of individual psychology written for its own sake, however full it may be of insight and precise observation. Time is moving; there is a world to make, a civilization to create that will move toward the only goal the humanistic, democratic mind can ever accept with honor. It is a world in which the human being can live as a naturally political, naturally private, naturally engaged person, a world in which once again a true tragic victory may be scored.

But that victory is not really possible unless the individual is more than theoretically capable of being recognized by the powers that lead society. Specifically, when men live, as they do under any industrialized system, as integers who have no weight, no *person*, excepting as either customers, draftees, machine tenders, ideologists, or whatever, it is unlikely (and in my opinion impossible) that a dramatic picture of them can really overcome the public knowledge of their nature in real life. In such a society, be it communistic or capitalistic, man is not tragic, he is pathetic. The tragic figure must have certain innate powers which he uses to pass over the boundaries of the known social law—the accepted mores of his people—in order to test and discover necessity. Such a quest implies that the individual who has moved onto that course must be somehow recognized by the law, by the mores, by the powers that design—be they anthropomorphic gods or economic and political laws—as having the worth, the innate value, of a whole people asking a basic question and demanding its answer. We are so atomized socially that no character in a play can conceivably stand as our vanguard, as our heroic questioner. Our society—and I am speaking of every industrialized society in the world—is so complex, each person being so specialized an integer, that the moment any individual is dramatically characterized and set forth as a hero, our common sense reduces him to the size of a complainer, a misfit. For deep down we no longer believe in the rules of the tragic contest; we no longer believe that some ultimate sense can in fact be made of social causation, or in the possibility that any individual can, by a heroic effort, make sense of it. Thus the man that is driven to question the moral chaos in which we live ends up in our estimate as a possibly commendable but definitely odd fellow, and probably as a compulsively driven neurotic. In place of a social aim which called an all-around excellence—physical, intellectual, and moral—the ultimate good, we have set up a goal which can best be characterized as "happiness"—namely, staying out of trouble. This concept is the end result of the truce which all of us have made with society. And a truce implies two enemies. When the truce is broken it means either that the individual has broken out of his ordained place as an integer, or that the society has broken the law by harming him unjustly—that is, it has not left him alone to be a peaceful integer. In the heroic and tragic time the act of questioning the-way-things-are implied that a quest was being carried on to discover an ultimate law or way of life which would yield excellence; in the present time the quest is that of a man made unhappy by rootlessness and, in every important modern play, by a man who is essentially a victim. We have abstracted from the Greek drama its air of doom, its physical destruction of the hero, but its victory escapes us. Thus it has even become difficult to separate in our minds the ideas of the pathetic and of the tragic. And behind this melting of the two lies the overwhelming power of the modern industrial state, the ignorance of each person in it of anything but his own technique as an economic integer, and the elevation of that state to a holy, quite religious sphere.

What, after all, are our basic social aims as applied to the individual? Americans are often accused of worshiping financial success, but this is, first of all, not an American monopoly, and, second, it does not as a concept make clear what is causing so much uneasiness and moral pain. My own belief, at any rate, is that America has merely arrived first at the condition that awaits every country that takes her economic road without enforcing upon every development of industrial technique certain quite arbitrary standards of value.

The deep moral uneasiness among us, the vast sense of being only tenuously joined to the rest of our fellows, is caused, in my view, by the fact that the person has value as he fits into the pattern of efficiency, and for that alone. The reason *Death of a Salesman*, for instance, left such a strong impression was that it set forth unremittingly the picture of a man who was not even especially "good" but whose situation made clear that at bottom we are alone, valueless, without even the elements of a human person, when once we fail to fit the patterns of efficiency. Under the black shadow of that gigantic necessity, even the drift of some psychoanalytic practice is toward the fitting-in, the training of the individual whose soul has revolted, so that he may once again "take his place" in society—that is, do his "work," "function," in other words, accommodate himself to a scheme of things that is not at all ancient but very new in the world. In short, the absolute value of the individual human being is believed in only as a secondary value; it stands well below the needs of efficient production. We have finally come to serve the machine. The machine must not be stopped, marred, left dirty, or outmoded. Only men can be left marred, stopped, dirty, and alone. Our pity for the victim is mixed, I think. It is mixed with an air of self-preserving superiority—we, thank God, know how to fit in, therefore this victim, however pitiful, has himself to thank for his fate. We believe, in other words, that to fit into the patterns of efficiency is the ultimate good, and at the same time we know in our bones that a crueler concept is not easy to arrive at.

Nor may the exponents of socialism take heart from this. There is no such thing as a capitalist assembly line or dry goods counter. The disciplines required by machines are the same everywhere and will not be truly mitigated by old-age pensions and social-security payments. So long as modern man conceives of himself as valuable only because he fits into some niche in the machine-tending pattern, he will never know anything more than a pathetic doom.

The implications of this fact spread throughout our culture, indeed, throughout the culture of the industrialized parts of the world. Be it in music, literature, drama, or whatever, the value of a work is, willy-nilly, equated with its mass "acceptance," i.e., its efficiency. All the engines of economic law are, like the mills of the gods, working toward that same end. The novel of excellence that could once be published without financial loss if it sold two or three thousand copies can no longer be published, because the costs of production require that every book sell at least ten, twelve, or fifteen thousand copies. The play that might have been produced at a decent profit if it could fill half a house for a few months can no longer be produced, for the costs of production require a play to draw packed houses from the first night.

When one has the temerity to suggest that the Greek theater was subsidized, that so much of the world's great music, art, and literature was stubbornly patronized by people who found honor in helping to bring beauty onto the earth, one is not quite suspect, to be sure, but the suggestion nevertheless has an unreal air, an air of being essentially at odds and possibly in dangerous conflict with some unspoken sense of values. For we do believe that a "good" thing, be it art or toothpaste, proves its goodness by its public acceptance. And at the same time we know, too, that something dark and dreadful lies within this concept.

The problem, then, of the social drama in this generation is not the same as it was for Ibsen, Chekhov, or Shaw. They, and the left-wing playwrights of the thirties who amplified their findings and repeated their forms, were oriented either toward an arraignment of some of the symptoms of efficiency men or toward the ultimate cure by socialism. With the proliferation of machine techniques in the world, and the relative perfection of distributing techniques, in America first and the rest of the world soon, the time will shortly be upon us when the truth will dawn. We shall come to see, I think, that Production for Profit and Production for Use (whatever their relative advantages— and each has its own) leave untouched the problem which the Greek drama put so powerfully before mankind. How are we to live? From what fiat, from what ultimate source are we to derive a standard of values that will create in man a respect for himself, a real voice in the fate of his society, and, above all, an aim for his life which is neither a private aim for a private life nor one which sets him below the machine that was made to serve him?

The social drama in this generation must do more than analyze and arraign the social network of relationships. It must delve into the nature of man as he exists to discover what his needs are, so that those needs may be amplified and exteriorized in terms of social concepts. Thus, the new social dramatist, if he is to do his work, must be an even deeper psychologist than those of the past, and he must be conscious at least of the futility of isolating the psychological life of man lest he fall always short of tragedy, and return, again and again and again, to the pathetic swampland where the waters are old tears and not the generative seas from which new kinds of life arise.

It is a good time to be writing because the audience is sick of the old formulations. It is no longer believed—and we may be thankful for it—that the poor are necessarily virtuous or the rich necessarily decayed. Nor is it believed that, as some writers would put it, the rich are necessarily not decayed and the poor necessarily the carriers of vulgarity. We have developed so democratic a culture that in America neither the speech of a man nor his way of dressing nor even his ambitions for himself inevitably mark his social class. On the stage social rank tells next to nothing about the man any more. The decks are cleared. There is a kind of perverse unity forming among us, born, I think, of the discontent of all classes of people with the endless frustration of life. It is possible now to speak of a search for values, not solely from the position of bitterness, but with a warm embrace of mankind, with a sense that at bottom every one of us is a victim of this misplacement of aims.

The debilitation of the tragic drama, I believe, is commensurate with the fracturing and the aborting of the need of man to maintain a fruitful kind of union with his society. Everything we learn, everything we know or deem valuable for a man to know, has been thrown into the creation of a machine technology. The nuclear bomb, as a way of waging war, is questioned only now—because we have it, because we have invented it: not before both sides knew how to make it. Both sides have the bomb and both sides have the machine. Some day the whole world will have both and the only force that will keep them from destructive use will be a force strange to machine psychology, a force born of will—the will of man to survive and to reach his ultimate, most conscious, most knowing, most fulfilled condition, his fated excellence.

History has given the social drama its new chance. Ibsen and Shaw had to work through three acts to prove in the fourth that, even if we are not completely formed by society, there is little left that society does not affect. The tremendous growth in our consciousness of social causation has won for these writers their victory in this sense: it has given to us a wider consciousness of the causes that form character. What the middle of the twentieth century has taught us is that theirs was not the whole answer. It is not enough anymore to know that one is at the mercy of social pressures; it is necessary to understand that such a sealed fate cannot be accepted. Nor is courage alone required now to question this complex, although without courage nothing is possible, including real dramatic writing. It is necessary to know that the values of commerce, values which were despised as necessary but less than noble in the long past, are now not merely perversely dominant everywhere but claimed as positive moral goodness itself. The question must begin to be asked; not whether a new thing will work or pay, not whether it is more efficient than its predecessor, more popular, and more easily accepted; but what it will do to human beings. The first invention of man to create that response in all nations was the atomic bomb. It is the first "improvement" to have dramatized for even the numbest mind the question of value. Over the past decade this nation and this world have been gripped by an inner debate on many levels, a debate raised to consciousness by this all-destroying "improvement." Alongside it is the "improvement" called automation, which will soon displace workers who mass-produce in industry. The conquest of poverty and hunger is the order of the day; the refusal of the dark peoples to live in subjection to the white is already a fact. The world, I think, is moving toward a unity, a unity won not alone by the necessities of the physical developments themselves, but by the painful and confused re-assertion of man's inherited will to survive. When the peace is made, and it will be made, the question Greece asked will once again be a question not reserved for philosophers and dramatists; it will be asked by the man who can live out his life without fear of hunger, joblessness, disease, the man working a few hours a day with a life-span probability of eighty, ninety, or perhaps a hundred years. Hard as it is for most people, the sheer struggle to exist and to prosper affords a haven from thought. Complain as they may that they have no time to think, to cultivate themselves, to ask the big questions, most men are terrified at the thought of not having to spend most of their days fighting for existence. In every sphere, and for a hundred hard reasons, the ultimate questions are once again becoming moot, some because without the right answers we will destroy the earth, others because the peace we win may leave us without the fruits of civilized life. The new social drama will be Greek in that it will face man as a social animal and yet without the petty partisanship of so much of past drama. It will be Greek in that the "men" dealt with in its scenes—the psychology and characterizations—will be more than ends in themselves and once again parts of a whole, a whole that is social, a whole that is Man. The world, in a word, is moving into the same boat. For a time, their greatest time, the Greek people were in the same boat—their polis. Our drama, like theirs, will, as it must, ask the same questions, the largest ones. Where are we going now that we are together? For, like every act man commits, the drama is a struggle against his mortality, and meaning is the ultimate reward for having lived.

A Note on These Plays

A Memory of Two Mondays is about several things. It is about mortality, first, in that the young man caught in the warehouse cannot understand what point there can be, beyond habit and necessity, for men to live this way. He is too young to find out, but it is hoped that the audience will glimpse one answer. It is that men live this way because they must serve an industrial apparatus which feeds them in body and leaves them to find sustenance for their souls as they may.

This play is a mortal romance. It expresses a preoccupation with the facts that everything we do in this fragmented world is so quickly wiped away and the goals, when won, are so disappointing. It is also the beginning of a further search and it lays the basis for a search. For it points the different roads people do take who are caught in warehouses, and in this play the warehouse is our world—a world in which things are endlessly sent and endlessly received; only time never comes back.

It is an abstract realism in form. It is in one act because I have chosen to say precisely enough about each character to form the image which drove me to write the play—enough and no more.

It is in one act, also, because I have for a long time wished I could turn my back on the "demands" of the Broadway theater in this regard. There are perfectly wonderful things one can say in one sentence, in one letter, one look, or one act. On Broadway this whole attitude has been suspect, regarded as the means taken by fledglings to try their wings. My ambition is to write shorter and shorter plays. It is harder to hit a target with one bullet—perhaps that is why.

A View from the Bridge is in one act because, quite simply, I did not know how to pull a curtain down anywhere before its end. While writing it, I kept looking for an act curtain, a point of pause, but none ever developed. Actually it is practically a full-length play in number of pages, needing only the addition of a little material to make it obvious as such.

That little material, that further elaboration, is what seemed to me, however, exactly what it ought not to have. Like *A Memory of Two Mondays,* this play has been in the back of my head for many years. And, as with the former, I have been asking of it why it would not get any longer. The answer occurred finally that one ought to say on the stage as much as one knows, and this, quite simply, is what I know about these subjects.

This is not to say that there is nothing more I could tell about any of the people involved. On the contrary, there is a great deal—several plays' worth, in fact. Furthermore, all the cues to great length of treatment are there in *A View from the Bridge.* It is wide open for a totally subjective treatment, involving, as it does, several elements which fashion has permitted us to consider down to the last detail. There are, after all, an incestuous motif, homosexuality, and, as I shall no doubt soon discover, eleven other neurotic patterns hidden within it, as well as the question of codes. It would be ripe for a slowly evolving drama through which the hero's antecedent life forces might, one by one, be brought to light until we know his relationships to his parents, his uncles, his grandmother, and the incident in his life which, when revealed toward the end of the second act, is clearly what drove him inevitably to his disaster.

But as many times as I have been led backward into Eddie's life, "deeper" into the subjective forces that made him what he evidently is, a counter-impulse drew me back. It was a sense of form, the shape of this work which I saw first sparely, as one sees a naked mast on the sea, or a barren cliff. What struck me first about this tale when I heard it one night in my neighborhood was how directly, with what breathtaking simplicity, it did evolve. It seemed to me, finally, that its very bareness, its absolutely unswerving path, its exposed skeleton, so to speak, was its wisdom and even its charm and must not be tampered with. In this instance to cleave to his story was to cleave to the man, for the naïveté with which Eddie Carbone attacked his apparent enemy, its very directness and suddenness, the kind of blatant confession he could make to a near-stranger, the clarity with which he saw a wrong course of action—these *qualities* of the events themselves, their texture, seemed to me more psychologically telling than a conventional investigation in width which would necessarily relax that clear, clean line of his catastrophe.

This play falls into a single act, also, because I saw the characters purely in terms of their action and because they are a kind of people who, when inactive, have no new significant definition as people. I use the word "significant" because I am tired of documentation which, while perfectly apt and evidently reasonable, does not add anything to our comprehension of the tale's essence. In so writing, I have made the assumption that the audience is like me and would like to see, for once, a fine, high, always visible are of forces moving in full view to a single explosion.

There was, as well, another consideration that held ornamentation back. When I heard this tale first it seemed to me that I had heard it before, very long ago. After a time I thought that it must be some re-enactment of a Greek myth which was ringing a long-buried bell in my own subconscious mind. I have not been able to find such a myth and yet the conviction persists, and for that reason I wished not to interfere with the myth-like march of the tale. The thought has often occurred to me that the two "submarines," the immigrants who come to Eddie from Italy, set out, as it were, two thousand years ago. There was such an iron-bound purity in the autonomic egocentricity of the aims of each of the persons involved that the weaving together of their lives seemed almost the work of a fate. I have tried to press as far as my reason can go toward defining the objective and subjective elements that made that fate, but I must confess that in the end a mystery remains for me and I have not attempted to conceal that fact. I know a good many ways to explain this story, but none of them fills its outline completely. I wrote it in order to discover its meanings completely, and I have not got them all yet, for there is a wonder remaining for me even now, a kind of expectation that derives, I think, from a sense of having somehow stumbled upon a hallowed tale.

The form of this play, finally, had a special attraction for me because once the decision was made to tell it without an excess line, the play took a harder, more objective shape. In effect, the form announces in the first moments of the play that only that will be told which is cogent, and that this story is the only part of Eddie Carbone's life worth our notice and therefore no effort will be made to draw in elements of his life that are beneath these, the most tense and meaningful of his hours. The form is what it is because its aim is to recreate my own feeling toward this tale—namely, wonderment. It is not designed primarily to draw tears or laughter from an audience but to strike a particular note of astonishment at the way in which, and the reasons for which, a man will endanger and risk and lose his very life.

1955

1956 and All This*

I obviously can have no special competence in the field of foreign policy. I only know what I read in the papers, and the fact that I am a creative writer does not make my opinions either wiser or more persuasive than those of any other man. But it seems to me that there might be some good purpose in one of my profession expressing himself on this kind of problem. A certain awareness of attitudes outside our borders has been forced on me over the past ten years. My plays are regularly produced on the stages of Europe, Asia, Australia, and other areas. I have not traveled extensively abroad for some seven years now, but I do receive a steady mail from artists, producers, and audiences in foreign countries; there are visits and a steady correspondence with them and frequent newspaper reviews and articles concerning my work.

From all these sources I have a certain group of impressions, especially of Europe, which have at least one rather unusual basis, namely, the comparative foreign reaction to works written for the American audience.

Through these varying reactions to the same object, national attitudes can be examined in a perspective less turbulent and possibly of more lasting truth than purely political studies will elicit. In a theater, people are themselves; they come of their own volition; they accept or reject, are moved or left cold not by virtue of reason alone or of emotion alone, but as whole human beings.

A communion through art is therefore unusually complete; it can be a most reliable indication of a fundamental unity; and an inability to commune through art is, I think, a stern indication that cultures have not yet arrived at a genuine common ground. Had there been no Flaubert, no Zola, no Proust, de Maupassant, Stendhal, Balzac, Dumas; had there been no Mark Twain, or Poe, Hawthorne, Emerson, Hemingway, Steinbeck, Faulkner, or the numerous other American artists of the first rank, our conviction of essential union with France and of France with us would rest upon the assurances of the two Departments of State and the impressions of tourists. I think that had there been no Tolstoy, no Gogol, no Turgenev, no Chekhov or Dostoyevsky, we should have no assurance at all nor any faint hope that the Russian heart was even ultimately comprehensible to us. Just recently the new government of Ceylon, which has just replaced the avowedly pro-British, pro-American regime, was and is still thought to be anti-American. The program is to nationalize foreign-owned plantations, and for the first time in history they will exchange Ambassadors with Moscow and Peking. The Prime Minister, an Oxford graduate, took pains to correct the idea he was anti-Western. He said, "How could I be against a country that produced Mark Twain?"

---

* Originally published as "The Playwright and the Atomic World".

There is more than a literary appreciation behind this remark, I think. Literature of the first rank is a kind of international signaling service, telling all who can read that wherever that distant blinker is shining live men of a common civilization.

Now, at the outset, I want to make clear that I disagree with those who believe the United States has entirely failed in its foreign policy since the close of World War II. But I think that the values this country has stood for in the past, more than in the present, have helped to keep alive a promise of a democratic future for the world. I do not believe, however, that our policy has stopped communism. I think that our armament has been a deterrent. But that is all. A policy of merely deterring anything is negative. I believe the time is upon us, and has been for some time now, when an entirely new approach has to be taken to the whole problem of what the future is to be. I base this upon the assumption that the atomic and armament statement is a historic fact which will remain for an indefinite period. In short, the policy was justified, if it was at all, on the basis of an imminence of war. I am proceeding on the ground that there will not be a war and cannot be. I summarize these conclusions at the outset so that the criticisms I may level now will be taken as they are intended—as guides to a positive foreign policy, and not an exercise in sarcasm. For good or ill, what the government has done in the world we have done; equally, what it will do in the future must represent, more than ever before, the real feelings and the judgments of the people. My quarrel, in fact, is that our policy has ceased to reflect the positive quality of the American people, and rests basically on their fears, both real and imaginary. We are much more than our fears, but the world does not often know that. And now to certain observations from my experience as a dramatist.

To begin with, I have often been struck, in foreign reviews of my plays, by the distinct difference in the foreign critic's attitudes toward meaning in a play, toward the theater as an institution. Here, our critics and most of the people in our audiences are pragmatists. As in our scientific tradition, our industrial tradition, in most of the things we do, we are almost wholly absorbed by the immediate impact of an idea or an invention. A thing is judged almost exclusively by whether it works, or pays, or is popular. In the scientific fields, my understanding is that this has been both an advantage and a liability, because our traditionally meager interest in theoretical, pure science has held back our scientific advance. At the same time, of course, our concentration upon practical, applied science has helped to give us a highly developed industry and a profusion of consumers' goods. The roster of those scientists who developed the atomic bomb is, as we know, very heavily weighted with foreign names, for this was a child of pure research. The opposing emphasis here and abroad is probably accounted for by the smallness of the European market for the products of applied science, for one thing. From this lack they have in this case made a virtue. But the irony remains that despite our enormous scientific establishment and our admitted superiority in many applied fields, there is evidently an impression abroad, founded until recently on fact, that we have little intellectual interest in science. I believe there is now a consciousness here of that need which is long past due.

In the field of the drama the same sort of irony prevails, and I think its operating principle has a certain effect upon a rather wide sector of European opinion. On the one hand, one feels the European writer, the critic, and from my mail the audience too are more interested in the philosophic, moral and principled values of the play than we are. One senses that they rather look askance at our lack of interest in these matters, and I often think that for this among other reasons they so often regard us as essentially a people without seriousness. The truth is that while our plays move much more rapidly than theirs do, are less likely to dwell on long conversations woven around piquant paradox and observation for its own sake, and while they strive more to be actions than thoughts, it is often admitted that if there is a leadership in the contemporary play since the Second World War, at least in terms of international public appeal, America has it. Put simply, we write plays for people and not for professors or philosophers; the people abroad accept and love many of our plays, and in some cases, even the philosophers do too. The point I would make here is that without any special consciousness of the attempt, we have created in the past few decades a kind of American dramatic style. We have also created an American movie style, an American style of dress, and probably architecture, and a style of shopping, and a style of comic books, and a style of novel writing and popular music—in a word, we have spontaneously created methods of reaching the great mass of the people whose effectiveness and exportability, if one may use an ugly word, are not equaled anywhere else.

This has had a multiple effect and it is not easy to separate the good from the bad. But I know, for instance, that there is great resentment among thinking people in Europe at the inroads made by *Reader's Digest* and comic books. One finds Dick Tracy all over the place. As a result of this particular kind of export, we are unwittingly feeding the idea that we incline ever so slightly to the moronic. The idea, for instance, of publishing an abridged novel is barbaric to them, and I'm not sure they're wrong. At the same time, however, our best writers are in many cases their secret or admitted models.

It is time to interject here some word about the importance of what is vaguely called culture in our foreign relations, a matter to which our government, to put it gently, is stupendously indifferent. In 1950, I was interviewed by the press in Copenhagen. It was an entirely literary interview. But when the reporters had left, one man stayed behind. Unlike the others who were of an intellectual sort, he wanted to know where I lived, what sort of a house, whether I played with my children, owned a car, dressed for dinner, and so forth. He turned out to have been from a tabloid paper which was read mainly by what he termed shopgirls. Now, I have yet to be interviewed by the New York *Daily News,* for instance, so I asked him what interest his readers could have in a person who wrote such morose and dreary plays. "It is very important for them to know that there are writers in America," he said. I could hardly believe they doubted that. "Oh yes," he said, "they will be very surprised to read about you, that you exist." But if they were that ignorant, I said, what difference would it make to them whether writers exist in America? What importance could the whole question have for them? "Very important," he said. "They are not intellectuals, but they think anyway that it is necessary for a country to have intellectuals. It will make them more sympathetic to America."

This is but one of many similar incidents which have made me wonder whether we are struggling, unknowingly, with a difference in cultural attitudes which may even warp and change purely political communication at any particular moment.

It is not that we are a people without seriousness. It is that we measure seriousness in an entirely different way than they do. They are the inheritors of a culture which was established, and I believe still exists, on an essentially aristocratic concept, which is to say, out of societies whose majority was nearly illiterate, education was for the few and the artist a kind of adornment to the political state, a measure of its glory and its worth. The artist for us, even as we may pay him much better than they do and cheat him much less, is more of an odd duck, and even among his fellow artists here he does not really exist except when he gains a great popular following. Again, our pragmatism is at work. I think that more Americans than not concede an artist his importance in proportion to his ability to make money with what he creates, for our measure of value is closely attuned to its acceptance by the majority. The artistic product has traditionally had little if any intrinsic justification for most of us. And this has presented our artists with a very lonely and frustrating life on the one hand, but on the other with a worthy if nearly impossible challenge. We regard it as our plain duty to make high art, if we are able, but to make it for all the people. More often than not, however, the art that *is* made sacrifices art for popularity partly because popularity pays fabulously among us. But the challenge is the right one anyway, I believe. The thing of importance now, however, is that even as we have produced some of the best works of literature of this era, we yet stand accused with perfect sobriety of being a mindless country. In this area the Russians have an inherited advantage over us. Despite all their differences from the Western tradition, their inherited attitude toward the artist and the intellectual has essentially the same sort of consciousness as that of the European. I think, for instance, of the time Dostoyevsky died. The entire Russian nation went into mourning for a novelist. I think of the endless lines of people who came to sit at Tolstoy's feet in his later years. I think too of the time a few years ago when I visited the Royal Dramatic Theater in Stockholm and saw an announcement of a forthcoming cycle of Strindberg's plays. I asked the director whether Strindberg was a popular writer in his native Sweden, and the director said he was not. Still for at least one period in each season, Strindberg's plays are regularly produced. "But why do you do this if he is not very popular?" I asked. "That isn't the point," he said. "He was our greatest dramatist and one of the best in the world; it is up to us to keep his plays alive and before the public." Later, we walked through the vast dressing room area of the theater, and there was one which, he said, is not often used. It belonged to a great actor who was now too aged to play. Yet they kept his dressing room solely for his use just in case he might drop in to rest of an afternoon. They needed dressing rooms badly, but it was inconceivable to take this once-great actor's name off his door until he had died.

This is not the occasion to examine the right and wrong of that system; I only wish to say that there is in Europe at least the strong remnant of the idea that the artist is the vessel of his country's selfhood, the speaker who has arisen among his countrymen to articulate if not to immortalize their age. I believe, as well, that because this reverence remains, it leads them to believe that they care more for art than we do, and that it follows we have no real life of the spirit but only a preoccupation with commodities. I would go even further and say that often our immense material wealth is the cue for them to believe that we care less for people than for things. I will not comment here on how much we care for people or how little; I am trying to avoid the question of the civilizing value of this kind of reverence for art. I will only say that at least in one country, Germany, its alleged pride in its artists did not seem to mitigate its ferocity in two world wars. But this is not the whole story either, and I leave it to go on with my observations.

In the different attitudes toward art can be detected attitudes which may be of significance politically. The reviews and comments upon my own play, *Death of a Salesman,* are of interest in this connection. When the play opened in New York it was taken for granted that its hero, the Salesman, and the story itself, were so American as to be quite strange if not incomprehensible to people of other nations; in some countries there is, for instance, no word that really conveys the idea of the salesman in our sense. Yet, wherever it has been shown there seems to have been no difficulty at all in understanding and identifying with the characters, nor was there any particular notice taken of the hero's unusual occupation. It seems to me that if this instantaneous familiarity is any guide, we have made too much of our superficial differences from other peoples. In Catholic Spain, where feudalism is still not a closed era; among fishermen in Norway at the edge of the Arctic Circle; in Rome, Athens, Tokyo—there has been an almost disappointing similarity of reaction to this and other plays of mine in one respect at least. They all seem to feel the anxieties we do; they are none of them certain of how to dissolve the questions put by the play, questions like—what ultimate point can there be for a human life? What satisfaction really exists in the ideal of a comfortable life surrounded by the gadgets we strive so hard to buy? What ought to be the aim for a man in this kind of a world? How can he achieve for himself a sense of genuine fulfillment and an identity? Where, in all the profusion of materiality we have created around us, is the cup where the spirit may reside? In short, what is the most human way to live?

I have put these questions because the commentators around the world have put them, but also because they do inform the play and I meant them to. Yet, no American reviewer actually brought up any of these questions. A play is rarely discussed here as to its philosophic meanings, excepting in a most cursory way; yet the basic effect upon us and the effect upon foreign audiences is evidently very similar. What I am trying to point out, again, is that it is less often the fact itself, the object itself about which we differ, than our unwillingness to rationalize how we feel. I sense that even as we do create the things of the spirit it seems to them rather an accident, rather a contradiction of our real character. I would add that had my plays not worked in Europe, which is to say that had they really been only philosophical works and not infused with the American pragmatic need for scenes to move with a pace and with characters made clear and familiar, the European would not be likely to be interested in them either.

I think it is true to say that for the most part as a nation we do not understand, we do not see that art, our culture itself, is a very sinew of the life we lead. Truly, we have no consciousness of art even as it has changed our tastes in furniture, in the houses we buy, in the cars we want. Only as it is transformed into things of daily use have we the least awareness of its vital functioning among us, and then it is only as its by-products appear in the most plain aspects of usefulness. As an example, even while abstract art is gazed at without comprehension, if not with hatred, its impact upon our linoleum designs, our upholsteries, our drapes, our women's dresses, our buildings, our packages, our advertising—these uses or misuses are quickly accepted without a thought. We have made in real life a most modern environment in many cases and have little conscious awareness of modernity; they have kept an outmoded environment in many cases and have a heightened awareness of what is modern.

This whole antipathy for theorizing, of knowing intellectually what we are doing, has very often crippled our ability to appraise reality. We so often become drowned in our own actions. For instance, it seems to me that this government has acted time and again as, though its reasons would be automatically accepted without question or suspicion. In recent months we have armed Pakistan, a nation imbedded in the Indian nation, and one with which India has some potentially explosive disagreements. The reason given for arming Pakistan was security against Russia and China. For the Indian government, however, there could only be one result of this arming and it would be to strengthen Pakistan against India. To defend our act by claiming naïveté will simply not do under the circumstances. We intended the arms for defense against Russia and China, therefore that is all they will be used for. To rise above our immediate action and interest, to see beyond the moment and through the eyes of another country—this requires a kind of imagination which, to be sure, is not very difficult to achieve, but one must be accustomed to using it. In general, it seems to me, speaking as an artist and not a politician, this government has proceeded at times quite as though individual actions could have no larger meaning; quite as though, in dramatic terms, each moment of the play we are writing were to be judged for itself and separately from the play as a whole.

This evident inability to see a context behind an action does not stop at Politics. I think it is part of our method of seeing life. Again, I will use the theater as an example. Our critics will be inclined to see the hero of a play as a psychological figure, as an individual, a special case always, and their interest flags beyond that point. It is even said that, strictly speaking, it is not their business as to the larger significance of a character portrayed on the stage. They are present to discern whether he is interesting, logically formed, persuasive as a fiction, and so forth. The European, however, while interested in the character's manifest surface, is equally intent upon discovering what generality he represents. It is not the business of our critics to decide or most often to even discuss whether a play is built upon a tattered and outworn idea; if an old and worn idea is made to work on the stage once again in terms of effects and suspense and so forth, it is enough. In the European review one will inevitably find some estimate of the value of the concept behind the play. In other words, it is assumed to begin with that a thing is always made with an intention and that the intention is as important to evaluate as the effects it manages to create.

Thus it is that we find ourselves unable to meet the suspicions of Europeans in many situations, and find ourselves puzzled and even angered as a result. For instance, it is no secret to anyone in Europe that our borders are, in effect, sealed. And when, as happened recently, a writer of the eminence of Graham Greene is denied entry here for a visit in transit to the Far East, I am sure that most Americans cannot find the slightest patriotic interest in the situation. It happens that for a short time some decades ago, Mr. Greene, a converted Catholic, belonged to the Communist Party and has been an anti-Communist ever since. More importantly, his works are known around the world, and they are regarded by tens of thousands of people as sincere attempts to wrestle with some of the most serious moral and religious and ethical problems of this age. I can only ascribe his exclusion to a complete unwillingness, perhaps even an inability, to admit that Mr. Greene is not any Greene but a very particular Greene existing in a definite Red context; that being a writer of his stature is not a fact of any consequence but a politically important consideration; that for millions of people in the world his profession and the high seriousness with which he has practiced it lend him a certain dispensation, the dispensation of the truth-seeker; and finally, that to refuse him entry into this country implied that this country feared what he might see here. I am sure that given these considerations, our officials would reply that the law is the law; that a writer is only another name to them. Yet it is impossible not to conclude that the real interests of the United States, to say nothing of its dignity, are transgressed by such an action.

I believe that this attitude toward culture is a disservice to us all because it lays us open to extremely dangerous suspicions which can spread out to stain our whole effort to preserve the democratic idea in the world, especially when we have had to create so large a military machine. A display of force is always a generator of fear in others, whether it be in private or public, local or international affairs. We consent to the policeman's carrying a gun not because we have lost our fear of the bullet but because we have agreed to suspend that fear on the assurance that the policeman carrying it is acculturated with us, that he shares our values, that he holds high what we hold high. But at the same time he must be willing to use that gun, he must be psychologically able to commit violence if we are to believe in his protection, and his willingness to slay, if it is not securely hedged about by his very clearly displayed respect for our values, quickly becomes a fearful thing. It is no different with a nation which would convince the world of its peaceful intentions even as it is heavily armed and its troops are stationed around the world. In the final analysis a reliance on force is always a confession of moral defeat, but in the affairs of nations it is tragically necessary sometimes to confess that defeat and to gather and rely on force. But to forget even for a moment that only the most persuasively demonstrated belief in civilized values can keep the image of force from being distorted into a menacing image—to forget this is to invite the easy demolition of our efforts for peace.

To prove an assertion whose implications are so vast is impossible, yet I must say that in a very profound way the differences I have indicated in our attitudes toward culture itself have often made it possible for Russian propaganda to raise fear of us in foreign peoples.

In passing, I should like to touch for a moment on a minor but I think indicative paradox inherent here. A recent article in *The New York Times Magazine* on Russian education and another group of photographs in *Life* described the high seriousness of the Russian college students, their evident dedication to their work, a picture so intense as to throw up in the mind the counter-image of so many American students for whom college is quite another thing. Unless I am entirely mistaken, the same article and the same photographs would not appear extraordinary to the European. What would be strange to him and cause him to wonder on his community with us, would be pictures of some of the shenanigans indulged in by some of our students. What I am trying to indicate here again is that there are superficial differences in our attitudes to culture in this particular area which show us to be less intimately connected to the European than the Russian is. The same is true of our kind of theater as contrasted with the German, let us say, and the Russian. I emphasize that the official attitude toward these manifestations of culture is extremely weighty outside this country. Yet the fact remains, and I believe it to be a demonstrable fact, that with all our absence of apparent awe, we have produced more than a decent quota of cultural works in the past two decades. The crucial importance of the image we cast in the world is not appreciated among us and, in my opinion, is one of the wounds through which the blood of our influence and our dignity is constantly seeping out. I go back once again to the image of our force. If our enormous power to destroy—and whatever else it is, military force is a destructive force—if we are content to allow it to appear in the hands of a people who make nothing of culture, who are content to appear solely as businessmen, technicians, and money-makers, we are handing to the Russian, who appears to make so much of culture, an advantage of regiments. And the further irony is that the serious Russian, both student and artist, has been so hamstrung by the tyrannical strictures on thought in his country, that his intellectual production has in recent years been brought to nearly a standstill, excepting in those scientific pursuits connected with militarily valuable science. It is, in their case, an irony which does not escape the notice of the world, in fact, it is precisely their tyranny that has kept nations out of their grasp. I believe, in short, that if we could only recognize and admit to our successes in culture, if the policy of our government and our people toward the things of the mind and the spirit were especially conscious and made serious, we have at hand a means of coming into closer harmony with other peoples who at bottom share our basic values.

But lest I seem to advocate a new advertising campaign, let me quickly correct the impression. To be sure, the object of a business or a nation in its relations with the world outside is to show its best qualities. More precisely, the obvious thing to do is to exhibit to the world whatever the world will most easily take to its heart for its own, those things which will make other peoples fear us less and love us more, those things with which they can identify themselves. For it is easier to misunderstand and hate that which seems alien and strange.

Our most popular, most widely seen cultural export is the American movie. It is a powerful convincer because hardly anybody in the world doesn't like to go to the movies. More important, however, it is spontaneously made, it appears without an ulterior political motive. So the man who sees it does so voluntarily and with his resistance down.

The trouble with the movies, however, is the same sort of trouble which Americans themselves often create when they go to Europe. Our movies draw the affections of people, their admiration, and envy for the opulence they generally portray, and also their disgust—as for instance, when a woman douses a cigarette in a perfectly good, uneaten, fried egg. At the same time, the movie star is beloved, his private life is followed with the interest long ago reserved for the minor gods. As such, we can only be glad so many foreigners like to see our pictures.

But even as we gain by them, we lose something of tremendous importance. Most movies are admittedly and even proudly brainless. When you have as much destructive power as we do, it is of the first importance that the world be continuously made aware not merely of how silly we can be, and at times how vulgar, but of how deep an attachment the American people have for the nicest cultivation of humane values.

It is in our novels, our poems, our dance, our music, and some of our plays, primarily, that we can and do reveal a better preoccupation. Yet, I can say from personal experience and from the experiences of other writers, that the work of art in which we really examine ourselves, or which is critical of society, is not what this government regards as good propaganda. I am not aware, for instance, that the export of any comic book has been interfered with, but only recently a nonfiction book was refused a congressional appropriation for inclusion in our overseas libraries because it showed a dust storm and a picture of an old-time country schoolhouse. In my opinion, it is not only not bad to show such things, nor bad to send our critical works around the world, but a necessity. For it is clearly one of our handicaps that we somehow insist, at least officially, that we have no inkling of a tragic sense of life. We posture before the world at times as though we had broken with the entire human race and had hold of a solution to the enigma of existence that was beyond questioning. As a dramatist I know that until the audience can identify itself with the people and the situations presented on the stage, it cannot be convinced of anything at all; it sits before an utterly uncomprehensible play of shadows against an unseeable wall. Thus, when a work or an action or a speech or a declaration of the world is presented without a trace of decent humility before the unsolved problems of life, it is not only that we do not really reflect our real selves, but that we must inevitably alienate others. For the truth is that we have not discovered how to be happy and at one with ourselves, we have only gone far in abolishing physical poverty, which is but one single element in the solution. And by harping only on that, we in effect declare a want of spirituality, a want of human feeling, a want of sympathy in the end. I believe we have solutions for poverty which the world must eventually come to adopt or adapt to other conditions, and we are obligated to demonstrate always what we have accomplished, obligated not only to ourselves but to humanity, which hungers for ways to organize production and create material wealth. But along with our success we have created a body of art, a body of literature which is markedly critical, which persists in asking certain human questions of the patterns we have created, and they are questions whose ultimate answers will prove or disprove our claims to having built a genuine civilization and not merely a collection of dominating inventions and bodily comforts. We are too often known abroad as dangerous children with toys that can explode the planet for us to go on pretending that we are not conscious of our underlying ethical and moral dilemmas.

It is no disgrace to search one's soul, nor the sign of fear. It is rather the first mark of honesty and the pool from which all righteousness flows. The strength of a Lincoln as he appeared in the eye of the world was not compounded of a time-bound mastery of military force alone, nor of an image monolithic and beyond the long reach of doubt. That man could lead and in our best moments leads us yet because he seemed to harbor in his soul an ever-renewing tear for his enemies and an indestructible desire to embrace them all. He commanded armies in the cruelest kind of war between brothers, yet his image is of a peaceful man. For even as history cast him as a destroyer of men, as every leader in war must always be, he seemed never to have lost that far-off gaze which cannot obliterate the tragic incompleteness of all wisdom and must fill with sympathy the space between what we know and what we have to do. For me, it is a reassuring thing that so much attention and appreciation is shown our novels and plays of high seriousness, for it signifies, I think, that others wish to see us more humanly and that the world is not as satisfied as we sometimes wish to appear that we have come to the end of all philosophy and wonderment about the meaning of life. It is dangerous to be rich in a world full of poverty. It is dangerous in obvious ways and in ways not so obvious.

During the war I worked for some time in the Brooklyn Navy Yard repairing and building ships for our fleet. The ships of many allied nations were often repaired there and we got to know many of the foreign crews. I remember one afternoon standing on the deck of a British destroyer with a British sailor at my side, when alongside us an American destroyer was passing out into the harbor. It was a boiling hot summer day. As the American ship moved slowly beside us a sailor appeared on her deck and walked over to a water cooler on the deck and drank. On British destroyers a thirsty man went below to a tap and drank lukewarm water; when he bathed it was out of a portable basin, the same one he washed his clothes in. I glanced at the British seaman sweating on the deck beside me and I said, "That's what you guys ought to have, eh?" "Oh," he said, with an attempt at a sneer, "your ships are built for comfort." It was not that he couldn't bear the idea of ice water on a hot day. I feel reasonably sure he would not have joined a demonstration against the British Admiralty had a water cooler been installed on his deck. But the mere fact that we had coolers on our decks did not at once overwhelm him with a reverence for our superiority. The essential emotion in his mind was a defense of his own dignity and the dignity of his country in the face of what ought to have been a promising hope for himself but was taken as a challenge, if not a kind of injury to his own pride. I am not saying we ought not to have water coolers, either in our ideas or on our ships, but a foreign policy based solely on water coolers and water coolers alone may create as much envy, distrust, and even hatred as anything else. As a matter of fact, his deprivation he made into a positive virtue. It was common to hear Britishers say that their fleet was made to fight, unlike ours, that they had no comforts, no shower baths, plenty of cockroaches, and what to us would be miserable food, because they had no time and ought to have no time for anything but their guns, and because a ship of the fleet had no right to be anything but a floating gun platform. And finally, they convinced themselves that we couldn't hit anything anyway.

It is important for us to recall that there was a time not long ago when the positions were almost exactly reversed. It was the time of our frontier, the time when for the European, America was an uncomfortable place, without the amenities of his civilization. And at that time a stock situation in our plays and novels and our folklore was the conflict between the elegant but effete European or Englishman being outwitted or mocked or in some other way overcome morally by the inelegant, poor, roughhewn Yankee the mark of whose superiority was his relative poverty, an inability to spell, and a rugged, even primitive jealousy of his own independence. I was reminded of this irony by the latest novel of the aforementioned Graham Greene called *The Quiet American*. This is the story of an American working in Asia for a cloak and dagger bureau in Washington, and his friendship and conflict with a British newspaperman. One is struck time and again by the Britisher's resentment of the American's precautions again disease or dirt—a veritable phobia of contamination—quite like the old literature in which the Englishman appears in tweeds and cap to shoot buffalo in the West, his sandwich hamper neat and ready, the napkin included. It is not merely the resentment which is important, but Greene's evident conviction that the American's relative wealth insulates him from any interest or insight into the realities around him, particularly the stubborn problem of the meanings of existence, meanings which transcend the victory over material want. And Greene reflects as well a kind of grudging admiration for the Asiatic Communists compared to the smooth-faced, naïve American, for the Communist, he says, knows how to talk to his fellow poor. In contrast, the Americans are prosperous and spiritually blank-eyed; they walk with the best of intentions in the impenetrable delusion that theirs is the only civilized way to live; in this book they walk in a closed circle outside of which the alien millions of the world, especially the poor, lead a life unknown and unknowable to them, and they are forced, the Americans are in this book, finally to rely upon devious policies of political opportunism and terroristic force. I will add that there is a pronounced quality of the caricature in this book, a caricature which quite astounded me coming from the pen of Graham Greene. It is easy to cast a stone at him and walk away, but there it is, a book which evidently appears quite accurate to the British and presumably to the European, whose reviewers took no note of the caricature in it; the work of a man who has not shown himself to be a fool in the past and is surely not against democracy.

It is time, I think, for us to step back and with open eyes, and a dignified humility, to look at where we are. How does it come to pass that so successful a system and so free should so steadily lose its hold upon the hearts of men over a single decade, when its competition is a tyranny whose people live in comparative poverty and under the rule of men instead of law? Is it truly possible that everything can be laid to the success of Communist propaganda? If that is true, then I think the jig is up, for then history is truly made of words, and words that lie. But it is demonstrably untrue, for there has never been a Communist revolution in a country with parliamentary government, except for Czechoslovakia, which was a revolution under Russian bayonets. Nevertheless, there is a sense in the world that somehow we are helpless, except for our armament, against a positive ideology which moves forward as we stand still or move backward. The conviction grows, it seems, that we have nothing really to say that we haven't said, and nothing to do except to stand by our guns.

I would make certain simple and self-evident observations and leave the largest conclusions to you. There is a revolution going on every single day in this era. Sometimes it erupts only in North Africa, sometimes in Iran, sometimes in a less obvious way in Greece, sometimes in the heart of Africa itself. By and large the foreign policy of the United States has gone on the assumption that things ought to remain as they are. By and large we have adopted a posture of resistance to change and have linked our fate and our dignity and our idea of safety to those regimes and forces which are holding things down. It is as though the misery of most of the world would not exist had the Communists not given it a name. We have, in more ways than one, made them into magicians. We had a Point Four program. We were going to buy the friendship of peoples with a few hundred million dollars. But the basic conditions of misery, the basic setup under which this misery is perpetuated and will continue to be perpetuated—for this we have no official word. The deepest hope, and we must come to admit it, was that they would take our aid and stop shouting. As a consequence, even by our own admission, enormous amounts of our aid have made the rich richer, as in Greece, and the poor no better off. Nor is this entirely our fault in a technical sense. It is not our fault that thieves steal for themselves, but there is a possibility which lies in another direction, a possibility which costs money to realize, but in my view presents our one great hope. One, but only one element in it, involves our resolution as a people and as a government that abject poverty and human freedom cannot coexist in the world. It is the desperation born of poverty that makes freedom a luxury in men's minds. Were this country to place as the first object in its foreign policy a resolution, a call, a new dedication to the war on poverty, a new wind would, I think, begin to blow through the stifled atmosphere of international relations.

I believe such a program set at the very forefront of our work in the world would have not economic consequences alone, but ultimately political and institutional changes would occur. There ought to be in training here technicians and experts for loan wherever they are needed, an army of them ready to move into any land asking for them. We ought to be building as many atomic power reactors as we can build, and we ought to be offering them to any nation asking for them. And above all, we ought to make clear that there are no strings attached.

The objection will be that we have already tried this and what have we got in return? I say that we have not tried it unpolitically. In India, in Italy, in Greece and other places, we have given aid on conditions of political fealty, and there is no blinking that fact. We have said, in effect, your misery does not move our hearts if you do not believe as we do. I say that it is the peoples of the world more than their governments who must be reached and raised up, and if that is the aim, if the love of the American people and their sympathy is permitted to surround this aid, instead of the fear of the American people turning all help into a species of bribery, we shall have reason for hope. Nehru is not suspicious of America because we have given India help in the past but because we have withheld it at times and threatened to at others when he says something we don't like. We ought to make it absolutely clear to the world that we are precisely what has never been before, a nation devoting itself now to the international onslaught on poverty, a nation eager for change, not in fear of it. Certainly we shall be greeted with cynicism, but if we adopt cynicism we are falling into the trap set for us, as we so often have over the past ten years.

But along with economic and technical aid on a scale far beyond that of the past, our entire attitude toward cultural matters must be revolutionized. There ought to be an army of teachers in training here for foreign service, people who can teach languages, mathematics, science, and literature. We ought to appear in the world as the source and pool from which the nations may draw for the new age that is to come. Our own gates must be thrown open to the musicians, the players, the writers, the literature of these countries, and our own artists must be invited to perform wherever there is an audience for them. And what do we get in return? Nothing. Nothing but the slow, but I believe inevitable, understanding of the peoples of the world, nothing but the gradual awakening to the fact that we are not a fearful country, nor a country that knows all the answers, but a country with an understanding for the poor, a country which has such an abundance of materials and talents that it wishes to reach out its hand to others less favored.

But whatever the technical aspects of this approach, however difficult they may be to put into force, they are simple compared to the change in spirit required of us.

I think the single most important alteration that has occurred among us since the Second World War is an insidious infusion of cynicism. No more were we going to be naïve, not again taken in by large visions and giveaways and the whole social-worker, Rooseveltian panorama of idealism. We were dealing now with sharks, and we must know how.

Yet, when was it that we held our undisputed moral leadership in the world? When did we start to lose it? It is simply no good laying the blame on communist propaganda because it was no more wily after the war than before. We have lost sight of the context in which we are living. We have come to imagine that because there are two major powers there can only be one of two ways the social and economic organization of the world can materialize. But already there are three. There is Tito's Yugoslavia, striving to remain independent, trying to establish a kind of socialism and at the same time to put forth at least a root from which may grow a tradition of civil liberty. And there are four. There is India, insistent upon social planning and a high degree of government supervision of economic life, yet tolerant of private property and private business, but rejecting the American system of unrestricted private enterprise. And there are five, with Israel mixing completely socialized villages and farms with a private economy developing in the cities. And there will probably be six, seven, eight, or a dozen different combinations of social and economic forces in as many areas before the next decade is finished. Only one rule can guide us if we are to be wise, and it is, again, that misery does not breed freedom but tyranny.

We have long since departed from any attempt to befriend only democratic nations and not others. The police states included by us in what we call the Free World are too numerous to mention. The Middle East and certain states in South America are not noteworthy for their respect for civil rights, nor is Franco Spain or the Union of South Africa. All these states promise only one thing in common—an allegiance to the West. But if we are not to be taken in by our own propaganda we shall have to see that they have other less amiable traits in common. They are economically backward and their regimes have vested interests in backwardness. Why then do we include them in the Free World? Because they claim in common a hatred of socialism and a willingness to fight with our side in case of war. But what if there is not to be war in our generation? Then we have only collected deserts that might have been watered but were not.

This brings me to my final point and it is the most vital and the most debatable of all. I believe that the world has now arrived, not at a moment of decision, but two minutes later. When Russia exploded her atom bomb the decision of history was made, and it was that diplomacy based either on the fear or the confidence that the final decision would be made by war, is no longer feasible. I believe the arms stalemate is with us for an indefinite time to come, and that to base a foreign policy upon an ingathering of states willing to side with us in war is to defeat ourselves in the other contest, the main contest, the crucial contest. I believe that the recent shift of Russian emphasis to economic, social, and cultural penetration rather than revolutionary tactics issuing in ultimate war, is based on this new situation. I believe that literally the hands, or more precisely, the fists, of the nations are tied if they only knew it, and that it is their hearts and minds which are left with the struggle. I believe that in its own devious way history has placed the nations squarely in a moral arena from which there is no escape.

But the implications go even further. The whole concept of Russian-type socialism and American capitalism competing for the allegiance of mankind is going to fall apart. There will be no pure issue from this struggle. There will be so many mutations and permutations of both systems, that it will be impossible to untangle them and call them one or the other.

The danger, I believe, is that the Communist idea will, in fact, be able to accommodate itself to the new complexity, but that we shall not, because we shall have refused to see that great social changes can be anything but threats to us. The danger is that without our participation in the reorganization of the backward sections of the world, our central value, the dignity of the human being based upon a rule of law and civil liberty, will never become part of the movement of peoples striving to live better at any cost.

For that and that alone ought to be our mission in this world. There are many mansions not only in heaven but on earth. We have or ought to have but one interest, if only for our safety's sake, and it is to preserve the rights of man. That ought to be our star and none other. Our sole aim in the past ten years was the gathering in of states allied against the Soviet Union, preparing for an attack from that source. As from some fortress town of the Middle Ages, we have seen the world. But now as then history is making fortresses ridiculous, for the movement of man is outside and his fate is being made outside. It is being made on his farm, in his hut, in the streets of his cities, and in his factories.

In the period of her so-called naïveté, America held the allegiance of people precisely because she was not cynical, because her name implied love and faith in people, and because she was the common man's country. In later years we have gone about forgetting our simplicity while a new ideology has risen to call for justice, however cynically, and imparting the idea that Russia stood for the working man. Meanwhile in a small voice we have spoken of justice and in a big voice of arms and armaments, wars and the rumors of wars. Now we must face ourselves and ask—what if there is to be no more war? What is in us that the world must know of? When we find this, the essence of America, we shall be able to forge a foreign policy capable of arousing the hopes and the love of the only force that matters any more, the force that is neither in governments nor armies nor banks nor institutions, the force that rests in the heart of man. When we come to address ourselves to this vessel of eternal unrest and eternal hope, we shall once again be on our way.

1956

The Family in Modern Drama

Most people, including the daily theater reviewers, have come to assume that the forms in which plays are written spring either from nowhere or from the temperamental choice of the playwrights. I am not maintaining that the selection of a form is as objective a matter as the choice of let us say a raincoat instead of a linen suit for a walk on a rainy day; on the contrary, most playwrights, including myself, reach rather instinctively for that form, that way of telling a play, which seems inevitably right for the subject at hand. Yet I wonder whether it is all as accidental, as "free" a choice, as it appears to be at a superficial glance. I wonder whether there may not be within the ideas of family on the one hand, and society on the other, primary pressures which govern our notions of the right form for a particular kind of subject matter.

It has gradually come to appear to me over the years that the spectrum of dramatic forms, from Realism over to the Verse Drama, the Expressionistic techniques, and what we call vaguely the Poetic Play, consists of forms which express human relationships of a particular kind, each of them suited to express either a primarily familial relation at one extreme, or a primarily social relation at the other.

When we think of Realism we think of Ibsen—and if we don't we ought to, because in his social plays he not only used the form but pressed it very close to its ultimate limits. What are the main characteristics of this form? We know it by heart, of course, since most of the plays we see are realistic plays. It is written in prose; it makes believe it is taking place independently of an audience which views it through a "fourth wall," the grand objective being to make everything seem true to life in life's most evident and apparent sense. In contrast, think of any play by Aeschylus. You are never under an illusion in his plays that you are watching "life"; you are watching a play, an art work.

Now at the risk of being obvious I must remind you that Realism is a style, an artful convention, and not a piece of reportage. What, after all, is real about having all the furniture in a living room facing the footlights? What is real about people sticking to the same subject for three consecutive hours? Realism is a style, an invention quite as consciously created as Expressionism, Symbolism, or any of the other less familiar forms. In fact, it has held the stage for a shorter period of time than the more poetic forms and styles which dominate the great bulk of the world repertoire, and when it first came into being it was obvious to all as a style, a poet's invention. I say this in order to make clear that Realism is neither more nor less "artistic" than any other form. The only trouble is that it more easily lends itself in our age to hack work, for one thing because more people can write passable prose than verse. In other ages, however, as for instance in the lesser Elizabethan playwrights, hack work could also make of the verse play a pedestrian and uninspired form.

As with any artist, Ibsen was writing not simply to photograph scenes from life. After all, at the time he wrote *A Doll's House* how many Norwegian or European women had slammed the door upon their hypocritical relations with their husbands? Very few. So there was nothing, really, for him to photograph. What he was doing, however, was projecting through his personal interpretation of common events what he saw as their concealed significance for society. In other words, in a perfectly "realistic" way he did not report so much as project or even prophesy a meaning. Put in playwriting terms, he created a symbol on the stage.

We are not ordinarily accustomed to juxtaposing the idea of a symbol with the idea of Realism. The symbolic action, symbolic speech, have come to be reserved in our minds for the more poetic forms. Yet Realism shares equally with all other ways of telling a play this single mission. It must finally arrive at a meaning symbolic of the underlying action it has set forth. The difference lies in its method of creating its symbol as opposed to the way the poetic forms create theirs.

Now then, the question arises: Why, if Ibsen and several other playwrights could use Realism so well to make plays about modern life, and if in addition the modern American audience is so quickly at home with the form—why should playwrights over the past thirty years be so impatient with it? Why has it been assaulted from every side? Why do so many people turn their backs on it and revere instead any kind of play which is fanciful or poetic? At the same time, why does Realism always seem to be drawing us all back to its arms? We have not yet created in this country a succinct form to take its place. Yet it seems that Realism has become a familiar bore; and by means of cutout sets, revolving stages, musical backgrounds, new and more imaginative lighting schemes, our stage is striving to break up the old living room. However, the perceiving eye knows that many of these allegedly poetic plays are Realism underneath, tricked up to look otherwise. I am criticizing nobody, only stating that the question of form is a deeper one, perhaps, than we have been willing to admit.

As I have indicated, I have come to wonder whether the force or pressure that makes for Realism, that even requires it, is the magnetic force of the family relationship within the play, and the pressure which evokes in a genuine, unforced way the un-realistic modes is the social relationship within the play. In a generalized way we commonly recognize that forms do have some extra-theatrical, common-sense criteria; for instance, one of the prime difficulties in writing modern opera, which after all is lyric drama, is that you cannot rightly sing so many of the common thoughts of common life. A line like "Be sure to take your bath, Gloria," is difficult to musicalize, and impossible to take seriously as a sung concept. But we normally stop short at recognition of the ridiculous in this problem. Clearly, a poetic drama must be built upon a poetic idea, but I wonder if that is the whole problem. It is striking to me, for instance, that Ibsen, the master of Realism, while writing his realistic plays in quite as serious a frame of mind as in his social plays, suddenly burst out of the realistic frame, out of the living room, when he wrote *Peer Gynt*. I think that it is not primarily the living room he left behind, in the sense that this factor had made a poetic play impossible for him, but rather the family context. For Peer Gynt is first of all a man seen alone; equally, he is a man confronting non-familial, openly social relationships and forces.

I warn you not to try to apply this rule too mechanically. A play, like any human relationship, has a predominant quality, but it also contains powerful elements which, although secondary, may not be overlooked, and may in fact be crucial in the development of that relationship. I offer this concept, therefore, as a possible tool and not as a magic key to the writing or understanding of plays and their forms.

I have used Ibsen as an example because he wrote in several forms; another equally experimental dramatist was O'Neill. It ought to be noted that O'Neill himself described his preoccupation as being not with the relations between man and man, but with those between man and God. What has this remark to do with dramatic form? Everything, I think. It is obvious, to begin with, that Ibsen's mission was to create not merely characters, but a context in which they were formed and functioned as people. That context, heavily and often profoundly delineated, was his society. His very idea of fate, for instance, was the inevitability residing in the conflict between the life force of his characters struggling with the hypocrisies, the strangling and abortive effects of society upon them. Thus, if only to create a climax, Ibsen had to draw society in his plays as a realistic force embodied in money, in social mores, in taboos, and so on, as well as an internal, subjective force within his characters.

O'Neill, however, seems to have been seeking for some fate-making power behind the social force itself. He went to ancient Greece for some definition of that force; he reached toward modern religion and toward many other possible sources of the poetic modes. My point here, however, is that so long as the family and family relations are at the center of his plays his form remains—indeed, it is held prisoner by—Realism. When, however, as for instance in *The Hairy Ape* and *Emperor Jones,* he deals with men out in society, away from the family context, his forms become alien to Realism, more openly and self-consciously symbolic, poetic, and finally heroic.

Up to this point I have been avoiding any question of content except that of the family relation as opposed to relations out in the world—social relations. Now I should like to make the bald statement that all plays we call great, let alone those we call serious, are ultimately involved with some aspect of a single problem. It is this: How may a man make of the outside world a home? How and in what ways must he struggle, what must he strive to change and overcome within himself and outside himself if he is to find the safety, the surroundings of love, the ease of soul, the sense of identity and honor which, evidently, all men have connected in their memories with the idea of family?

One ought to be suspicious of any attempt to boil down all the great themes to a single sentence, but this one—"How may a man make of the outside world a home?"— does bear watching as a clue to the inner life of the great plays. Its aptness is most evident in the modern repertoire; in fact, where it is not the very principle of the play at hand we do not take the play quite seriously. If, for instance, the struggle in *Death of a Salesman* were simply between father and son for recognition and forgiveness it would diminish in importance. But when it extends itself out of the family circle and into society, it broaches those questions of social status, social honor and recognition, which expand its vision and lift it out of the merely particular toward the fate of the generality of men.

The same is true—although achieved in different ways—of a play like *A Streetcar Named Desire,* which could quite easily have been limited to a study of psychopathology were it not that it is placed clearly within the wider bounds of the question I am discussing. Here Blanche Dubois and the sensitivity she represents has been crushed by her moving out of the shelter of the home and the family into the uncaring, anti-human world outside it. In a word, we begin to partake of the guilt for her destruction, and for Willy's, because the blow struck against them was struck outside the home rather than within it—which is to say that it affects us more because it is a social fact we are witnessing.

The crucial question has an obverse side. If we look at the great plays—at *Hamlet, Oedipus, Lear*—we must be impressed with one fact perhaps above all others. These plays are all examining the concept of loss, of man's deprivation of a once-extant state of bliss unjustly shattered—a bliss, a state of equilibrium, which the hero (and his audience) is attempting to reconstruct or to recreate with new, latter-day life materials. It has been said often that the central theme of the modern repertoire is the alienation of man, but the idea usually halts at the social alienation—he cannot find a satisfying role in society. What I am suggesting here is that while this is true of our plays, the more or less hidden impulse antedating social alienation, the unsaid premise of the very idea of "satisfaction," is the memory of both playwright and audience of an enfolding family and of childhood. It is as though both playwright and audience believed that they had once had an identity, a *being*, somewhere in the past which in the present has lost its completeness, its definitiveness, so that the central force making for pathos in these large and thrusting plays is the paradox which Time bequeaths to us all: we cannot go home again, and the world we live in is an alien place.

One of the forms most clearly in contrast to Realism is Expressionism. I should like now to have a look at its relevancy to the family-social complex.

The technical arsenal of Expressionism goes back to Aeschylus. It is a form of play which manifestly seeks to dramatize the conflict of either social, religious, ethical, or moral forces *per se*, and in their own naked roles, rather than to present psychologically realistic human characters in a more or less realistic environment. There is, for instance, no attempt by Aeschylus to create the psychology of a violent "character" in *Prometheus Bound*, or of a powerful one; rather he brings on two figures whose names are Power and Violence, and they behave as the *idea* of Power and the *idea* of Violence ought to behave, according to the laws of Power and Violence. In Germany after the First World War, playwrights sought to dramatize and unveil the social condition of man with similar means. For instance, in *Gas I* and *Gas II* Georg Kaiser placed the figure of man against an image of industrial society but without the slightest attempt to characterize the man except as a representative of one or the other of the social classes vying for control of the machine. There are, of course, numerous other examples of the same kind of elimination of psychological characterization in favor of what one might call the presentation of forces. In *The Great God Brown*, for instance, as well as in *The Hairy Ape*, O'Neill reached toward this very ancient means of dramatization without psychology—without, one might say, behavior as we normally know it. *Everyman* is another work in that long line.

In passing, I must ask you to note that expressionist plays—which is to say plays preoccupied with the open confrontation of moral, ethical, or social forces—seem inevitably to cast a particular kind of shadow. The moment realistic behavior and psychology disappear from the play all the other appurtenances of Realism vanish too. The stage is stripped of knickknacks; instead it reveals symbolic *designs,* which function as overt pointers toward the moral to be drawn from the action. We are no longer under quite the illusion of watching through a transparent fourth wall. Instead we are constantly reminded, in effect, that we are watching a theater piece. In short, we are not bidden to lose our consciousness of time and place, the consciousness of ourselves, but are appealed to through our intelligence, our faculties of knowing rather than of feeling.

This difference in the area of appeal is the difference between our familial emotions and our social emotions. The two forms not only spring from different sectors of human experience but end up by appealing to different areas of receptivity within the audience. Nor is this phenomenon confined to the play.

When one is speaking to one's family, for example, one uses a certain level of speech, a certain plain diction perhaps, a tone of voice, an inflection suited to the intimacy of the occasion. But when one faces an audience of strangers, as a politician does, for instance—and he is the most social of men—it seems right and proper for him to reach for the well-turned phrase, even the poetic word, the aphorism, the metaphor. And his gestures, his stance, his tone of voice, all become larger than life; moreover, his character is not what gives him these prerogatives, but his role. In other words, a confrontation with society permits us, or even enforces upon us, a certain reliance upon ritual. Similarly with the play.

The implications of this natural wedding of form with inner relationships are many, and some of them are complex. It is true to say, I think, that the language of the family is the language of the private life—prose. The language of society, the language of the public life, is verse. According to the degree to which the play partakes of either relationship, it achieves the right to move closer or further away from either pole. I repeat that this "right" is given by some common consent which in turn is based upon our common experience in life.

It is interesting to look at a couple of modern plays from this viewpoint and to see whether critical sense can be made of them. T. S. Eliot's *The Cocktail Party,* for instance, drew from most intelligent auditors a puzzled admiration. In general, one was aware of a struggle going on between the apparencies of the behavior of the people and what evidently was the preoccupation of the playwright. There were a Husband and a Wife whom we were evidently expected to accept in that commonly known relationship, especially since the setting and the mode of speech and much of its diction were perfectly real if inordinately cultivated for a plebeian American audience. Even the theme of the play was, or should have been, of importance to most of us. Here we were faced with the alternative ways of giving meaning to domestic existence, one of them being through the cultivation of self, partly by means of the psychoanalytic ritual; the other and victorious method being the martyrization of the self, not for the sake of another, or as a rebuke to another, as martyrdom is usually indulged in in family life, but for the sake of martyrdom, of the disinterested action whose ultimate model was, according to the author, Jesus Christ. The heroine is celebrated for having been eaten alive by ants while on a missionary work among savages, and the very point is that there was no point—she converted nobody at all. Thus she gained her self by losing self or giving it away. Beyond the Meaningless she found Meaning at last.

To say the least, Eliot is manifestly an apt writer of verse. The inability of this play to achieve a genuine poetic level cannot therefore be laid to the usual cause—the unpoetic nature of the playwright's talent. Indeed, *Murder in the Cathedral* is a genuine poetic play, so he had already proved that he could achieve a wholeness of poetic form. I believe that the puzzlement created by *The Cocktail Party,* the sense of its being drawn in two opposite directions, is the result of the natural unwillingness of our minds to give to the Husband-Wife relation—a family relation—the prerogatives of the poetic mode, especially when the relationship is originally broached, as it is in this play, through any means approaching Realism.

Whether consciously or not, Eliot himself was aware of this dichotomy and wrote, and has said that he wrote, a kind of line which would not seem obtrusively formal and poetic to the listening ear. The injunction to keep it somehow unpoetic was issued by the central family situation, in my opinion. There was no need to mask his poetry at all in *Murder in the Cathedral,* because the situation is social, the conflict of a human being with the world. That earlier play had the unquestioned right to the poetic because it dealt with man as a public figure and could use the public man's style and diction.

We recognize now that a play can be poetic without verse, and it is in this middle area that the complexities of tracing the influence of the family and social elements upon the form become more troublesome. *Our Town* by Thornton Wilder is such a play, and it is important not only for itself but because it is the progenitor of many other works.

This is a family play which deals with the traditional family figures, the father, mother, brother, sister. At the same time it uses this particular family as a prism through which is reflected the author's basic idea, his informing principle—which can be stated as the indestructibility, the everlastingness, of the family and the community, its rhythm of life, its rootedness in the essentially safe cosmos despite troubles, wracks, and seemingly disastrous, but essentially temporary, dislocations.

Technically, it is not arbitrary in any detail. Instead of a family living room or a house, we are shown a bare stage on which actors set chairs, a table, a ladder to represent a staircase or an upper floor, and so on. A narrator is kept in the foreground as though to remind us that this is not so much "real life" as an abstraction of it—in other words, a stage. It is clearly a poetic rather than a realistic play. What makes it that? Well, let us first imagine what would make it more realistic.

Would a real set make it realistic? Not likely. A real set would only discomfit us by drawing attention to what would then appear to be a slightly unearthly quality about the characterizations. We should probably say, "People don't really act like that." In addition, the characterization of the whole town could not be accomplished with anything like its present vividness if the narrator were removed, as he would have to be from a realistic set, and if the entrances and exits of the environmental people, the townspeople, had to be justified with the usual motives and machinery of Realism.

The preoccupation of the entire play is quite what the title implies—the town, the society, and not primarily this particular family—and every stylistic means used is to the end that the family foreground be kept in its place, merely as a foreground for the larger context behind and around it. In my opinion, it is this larger context, the town and its enlarging, widening significance, that is the bridge to the poetic for this play. Cut out the town and you will cut out the poetry.

The play is worth examining further against the Ibsen form of Realism to which it is inevitably related if only in contrast. Unlike Ibsen, Wilder sees his characters in this play not primarily as personalities, as individuals, but as forces, and he individualizes them only enough to carry the freight, so to speak, of their roles as forces. I do not believe, for instance, that we can think of the brother in this play, or the sister or the mother, as having names other than Brother, Sister, Mother. They are not given that kind of particularity or interior life. They are characterized rather as social factors, in their roles of Brother, Sister, Mother, in Our Town. They are drawn, in other words, as forces to enliven and illuminate the author's symbolic vision and his theme, which is that of the family as a timeless, stable quantity which has not only survived all the turmoil of time but is, in addition, beyond the possibility of genuine destruction.

The play is important to any discussion of form because it has achieved a largeness of meaning and an abstraction of style that created that meaning, while at the same time it has moved its audiences subjectively—it has made them laugh and weep as abstract plays rarely if ever do. But it would seem to contradict my contention here. If it is true that the presentation of the family on the stage inevitably forces Realism upon the play, how did this family play manage to transcend Realism to achieve its symbolistic style?

Every form, every style, pays its price for its special advantages. The price paid by *Our Town* is psychological characterization forfeited in the cause of the symbol. I do not believe, as I have said, that the characters are identifiable in a psychological way, but only as figures in the family and social constellation, and this is not meant in criticism, but as a statement of the limits of this form. I would go further and say that it is not *necessary* for every kind of play to do every kind of thing. But if we are after ultimate reality we must make ultimate demands.

I think that had Wilder drawn his characters with a deeper configuration of detail and with a more remorseless quest for private motive and self-interest, for instance, the story as it stands now would have appeared oversentimental and even sweet. I think that if the play tested its own theme more remorselessly, the world it creates of a timeless family and a rhythm of existence beyond the disturbance of social wracks would not remain unshaken. The fact is that the juvenile delinquent is quite directly traced to the breakup of family life and, indeed, to the break in that ongoing, steady rhythm of community life which the play celebrates as indestructible.

I think, further, that the close contact which the play established with its audience was the result of its coincidence with the deep longing of the audience for such stability, a stability which in daylight out on the street does not truly exist. The great plays pursue the idea of loss and deprivation of an earlier state of bliss which the characters feel compelled to return to or to recreate. I think this play forgoes the loss and suffers thereby in its quest for reality, but that the audience supplies the sense of deprivation in its own life experience as it faces what in effect is an idyl of the past. To me, therefore, the play falls short of a form that will press into reality to the limits of reality, if only because it could not plumb the psychological interior lives of its characters and still keep its present form. It is a triumph in that it does open a way toward the dramatization of the larger truths of existence while using the common materials of life. It is a truly poetic play.

Were there space, I should like to go into certain contemporary works with a view to the application in them of the forces of society and family—works by Clifford Odets, Tennessee Williams, Lillian Hellman, William Saroyan, and others. But I will jump to the final question I have in mind. If there is any truth in the idea of a natural union of the family and Realism as opposed to society and the poetic, what are the reasons for it?

First, let us remind ourselves of an obvious situation, but one which is often overlooked. The man or woman who sits down to write a play, or who enters a theater to watch one, brings with him in each case a common life experience which is not suspended merely because he has turned writer or become part of an audience. We—all of us—have a role anteceding all others: we are first sons, daughters, sisters, brothers. No play can possibly alter this given role.

The concepts of Father, Mother, and so on were received by us unawares before the time we were conscious of ourselves as selves. In contrast, the concepts of Friend, Teacher, Employee, Boss, Colleague, Supervisor, and the many other social relations came to us long after we gained consciousness of ourselves, and are therefore outside ourselves. They are thus in an objective rather than a subjective category. In any case, what we feel is always more "real" to us than what we know, and we feel the family relation while we only know the social one. Thus the former is the very apotheosis of the real and has an inevitability and a foundation indisputably actual, while the social relation is always relatively mutable, accidental, and consequently of a profoundly arbitrary nature to us.

Today the difficulty in creating a form that will unite both elements in a full rather than partial onslaught on reality is the reflection of the deep split between the private life of man and his social life. Nor is this the first time in history that such a separation has occurred. Many critics have remarked upon it, for instance, as a probable reason for the onset of Realism in the later Greek plays, for it is like a rule of society that, as its time of troubles arrives, its citizens revert to a kind of privacy of life that excludes society, as though man at such times would like to banish society from his mind. When this happens, man excludes poetry too.

All of which, while it may provide a solution, or at least indicate the mansion where the solution lives, only serves to point to the ultimate problem more succinctly. Obviously, the playwright cannot create a society, let alone one so unified as to allow him to portray man in art as a monolithic creature. The playwright is not a reporter, but in a serious work of art he cannot set up an image of man's condition so distant from reality as to violate the common sense of what reality is. But a serious work, to say nothing of a tragic one, cannot hope to achieve truly high excellence short of an investigation into the whole gamut of causation of which society is a manifest and crucial part. Thus it is that the common Realism of the past forty or fifty years has been assaulted—because it could not, with ease and beauty, bridge the widening gap between the private life and the social life. Thus it is that the problem was left unsolved by Expressionism, which evaded it by forgoing psychological realism altogether and leaping over to a portrayal of social forces alone. Thus it is that there is now a certain decadence about many of our plays; in the past ten years they have come more and more to dwell solely upon psychology, with little or no attempt to locate and dramatize the social roles and conflicts of their characters. For it is proper to ascribe decay to that which turns its back upon society when, as is obvious to any intelligence, the fate of mankind is social.

Finally, I should say that the current quest after the poetic as poetic is fruitless. It is the attempt to make apples without growing trees. It is seeking poetry precisely where poetry is not: in the private life viewed entirely within the bounds of the subjective, the area of sensation, or the bizarre and the erotic. From these areas of the private life have sprung the mood plays, the plotless plays for which there is much admiration as there is much relief when one turns from a problem to a ramble in the woods. I do not ask you to disdain such plays, for they are within the realm of art; I say only that the high work, the tragic work, cannot be forged waywardly, while playing by ear. There is a charm in improvisation, in letting one chord suggest the other and ending when the moment wanes. But the high order of art to which drama is fated will come only when it seeks to account for the total condition of man, and this cannot be improvised.

Whatever is said to describe a mood play, one point must be made: such plays all have in common an air of self-effacement—which is to say that they wish to seem as though they had not only no plot but no writer. They would convince us that they "just happen," that no directing hand has arranged matters—contrary to the Ibsen plays, for instance, or, for that matter, the Shakespearean play or the Greek.

Furthermore, the entire operation is most moody when the characters involved have the least consciousness of their own existence. The mood play is a play in hiding. A true plot is an assertion of meaning. The mood play is not, as it has been mistaken for, a rebellion of any kind against the so-called well-made play, especially when Ibsen is widely held to be a writer of well-made plays. For there is as much subjectivity and inner poetry in *Hedda Gabler*—I daresay a lot more—as in any of these mood plays. What is really repulsive in Ibsen to one kind of contemporary mind is not openly mentioned: it is his persistent search for an organizing principle behind the "moods" of existence and not the absence of mood in his work.

An art form, like a person, can achieve greatness only as it accepts great challenges. Over the past few decades the American theater, in its best moments, has moved courageously and often beautifully into the interior life of man, an area that had most often been neglected in the past. But now, I think, we are in danger of settling for tears, as it were—for any play that "moves" us, quite as though the ultimate criterion of the art were lachrymosity. For myself, I find that there is an increasing reliance upon what pass for realistic, even tough, analytical picturizations of existence, which are really quite sentimental underneath; and the sentiment is getting thicker, I think, and an end in itself. Sentimentalism is perfectly all right, but it is nowhere near a great challenge, and to pursue it, even under the guise of the exotic atmosphere and the celebration of the sensuous, is not going to bring us closer to the fated mission of the drama.

What, after all, is that mission? I may as well end with such a question because it underlies and informs every word I have written. I think of it so: Man has created so many specialized means of unveiling the truth of the world around him and the world within him—the physical sciences, the psychological sciences, the disciplines of economic and historical research and theory. In effect, each of these attacks on the truth is partial. It is within the rightful sphere of the drama—it is, so to speak, its truly just employment and its ultimate design—to embrace the many-sidedness of man. It is as close to being a total art as the race has invented. It can tell, like science, what is—but more, it can tell what ought to be. It can depict, like painting, in designs and portraits, in the colors of the day or night; like the novel it can spread out its arms and tell the story of a life, or a city, in a few hours—but more, it is dynamic, it is always on the move as life is, and it is perceived like life through the motions, the gestures, the tones of voice, and the gait and nuance of living people. It is the singer's art and the painter's art and the dancer's art, yet it may hew to fact no less tenaciously than does the economist or the physician. In a word, there lies within the dramatic form the ultimate possibility of raising the truth-consciousness of mankind to a level of such intensity as to transform those who observe it.

The problem, therefore, is not simply an aesthetic one. As people, as a society, we thirst for clues to the past and the future; least of all, perhaps, do we know about the present, about what *is*. It is the present that is always most evasive and slippery, for the present always threatens most directly our defenses against seeing what we are, and it is the present, always the present, to which the dramatic form must apply or it is without interest and a dead thing, and forms do die when they lose their capacity to open up the present. So it is its very nature to bring us closer to ourselves if only it can grow and change with the changing world.

In the deepest sense, I think, to sophisticated and unsophisticated alike, nothing is quite so real to us, so extant, as that which has been made real by art. Nor is this ironical and comic. For the fact is that art is a function of the civilizing act quite as much as is the building of the water supply. American civilization is only recently coming to a conscious awareness of art not as a luxury but as a necessity of life. Without the right dramatic form a genuine onslaught upon the veils that cloak the present is not possible. In the profoundest sense I cannot create that form unless, somewhere in you, there is a wish to know the present and a demand upon me that I give it to you.

For at bottom what is that form? It is the everlastingly sought balance between order and the need of our souls for freedom; the relatedness between our vaguest longings, our inner questions, and private lives and the life of the generality of men which is our society and our world. How may man make for himself a home in that vastness of strangers and how may he transform that vastness into a home? This, as I have repeated, is the question a form must solve anew in every age. This, I may say, is the problem before you too.

1956

Concerning the Boom

I read in the papers that this 1956 Broadway season has been the most exciting in many years, as well as the most successful financially. The pressure for theaters has been so heavy that even the Lunts were forced to hover in the hinterland with *The Great Sebastians* until a show should close (in this case one of mine, as it turned out). We are, in other words, within yards of the millennium for commercial theater.

As always, there are the vehicles, like *The Desk Set* for Shirley Booth, *Janus* for Margaret Sullavan and Claude Dauphin, and the aforementioned Lunts' play. At least one exceptional musical is with us in the shape of *My Fair Lady* with Rex Harrison, and there are several others which, like most musicals, go on and on whether they are any good or not. There are the realistic plays written in deadly earnest just as they could have been twenty years ago, an improvisation called *A Hatful of Rain,* and even what one could call a social documentary with Paul Muni—*Inherit the Wind.*

In a word, it is the usual trendless jumble. Why such a large percentage of the shows that open should be judged by the critics as hits, I certainly cannot say. I am not a first-nighter, and when I go to the theater at all it is because there seems to be promise of something new, some exciting acting or a novel invention of form. Musicals aside, the three plays which seemed to me to possess a genuine creative vitality were Wilder's *The Matchmaker*, Norman Rosten's adaptation of Joyce Cary's novel, *Mister Johnson*, and *The Chalk Garden* by Enid Bagnold.

My private opinion is that the Wilder play would not have found its audience without the astounding performance of Ruth Gordon. I say this not to denigrate the play, although it is not, in my opinion, his best-organized work, but because Miss Gordon translates its metaphysic in sufficiently broad emotional language for it to appear within the realm of the familiar. Without her filling in the spaces between its always threatening—or promising—passages of abstractness, it might well have been gravely saluted and allowed to die by the critics. Yet, the fact remains as a tribute to the eagerness of this audience that it is a rather successful Broadway show in Broadway's terms. It ought not to be overlooked, however, that the problem of survival for the truly serious work remains unsolved here.

I say this because Wilder's play is not turning them away, nor is *Tiger At The Gates* nor *The Lark* (Lillian Hellman's adaptation from Anouilh), nor *Mister Johnson*. In some cases, as with *Tiger* and *The Lark*, more impetus could not have been asked from the critics, yet the pressure of a real hit never developed around these plays. *Will Success Spoil Rock Hunter?*, a much criticized farcical sex-play, is a hit and will probably run on a long time.

I saw *Chalk Garden* on its closing night and was quite astonished, recalling dimly the carping reviews I had read of it. It is the most steadily interesting, deeply felt, and civilized piece of work I have seen in a very long time. Its final audience, as a matter of fact, behaved as though it were the remnant of a dispersed army rallying to a fallen flag. They were mostly young people, I noticed, and like the audience that came to cheer O'Casey's *Red Roses For Me*, which also failed to gain either critical or audience celebration, the stalwarts who came to bury this work with at least a fond gesture of appreciation were obviously a small minority of those who buy tickets on Broadway.

I have been in this work a long time now, and I cannot yet understand the code under which our critics operate. *A Hatful of Rain*, for instance, was slapped together as an exercise in class at the Actors' Studio, taken onto Broadway by Shelley Winters and Ben Gazzara, who play the leads, and greeted with roars of critical approval. Yet, it is so full of illogical behavior, so evasive in its confrontation with its theme, so unevenly finished in almost every department, that had I seen it before its opening I should have thought it hadn't a chance. Perhaps its appearance of unpretentiousness gratified the critics who saw none of its really serious inner contradictions.

At the same time, *Mister Johnson*, which is at times a genuine lyric thrust, and is always a meaningful dramatic and ethical struggle, if theatrically loose-boned, is for the most part decisively defeated by the critics' cautious praise. But perhaps it is not they who are to blame. The majority of the audience is still essentially a party-going, amusement-seeking throng. Confronted with anything that is not directly linked to some aspect of sexuality it cannot be deeply engaged by a serious work excepting in extremely rare instances.

When I say "serious" I do not mean merely that the author has a message or the play some social or ethical significance. I am speaking mainly of a theatrical seriousness which is made of an ethical preoccupation in the first place but must express itself in new terms and forms. *Inherit the Wind* is a sociological drama without any great exploration of interior human forces; it is a big hit, to be sure, but when Paul Muni had to leave the show temporarily the line leading to the Refunds window stretched to the end of the block.

In one way, perhaps, people like myself have been spoiled. It is true our work has to compete with the lowest of the low or we cannot exist, and that was always the case among us; but despite this we have succeeded often enough in achieving runs of a year or even two, so that when we merely go on for three months it comes as a shock. Yet there aren't many places in the world where any play can run that long, let alone a genuinely serious one. My feeling, however, is that when we do make a real hit out of a serious play it is not because it is serious but in some way sensational. *Cat on a Hot Tin Roof*, Tennessee Williams's work of last season, which is still running well, is, I think, one of these. I venture this undermining thought not only because it has occurred to me but because the critics never seem willing or even interested in discussing the real preoccupation of the writers of these plays but only their most evident effects. I doubt that many people in the audience realize what *Cat* is really saying, for if they did they might not "enjoy" it with such self-assurance. For it is really an attack, I think, on nearly everyone who watches it.

Ibsen's *When We Dead Awaken* comes to mind in this context. Recall the leading character, the world-famous, highly successful and admired sculptor who in his old age points to the many heads in his studio and reveals that they were meant not as flattering portraits of his famous clients but as the images of beasts, of wolves, and dogs, and bears. Papa Ibsen was voicing, I think, the complaint of so many artists who succeed with the public—that they knew not what they saw, and the effects which he labored so hard to achieve were only too successful in concealing what lay behind them.

In the case of *Chalk Garden* the woven surface was perhaps too involved for us; perhaps its admirably hard and even brittle shell demanded too much attention of us. We are not yet ready to follow psychology into a higher atmosphere where its aesthetic reflection glows and spits and then grows cool. Our theater is still essentially the theater of realism. There have been more and more assaults upon it—or, more precisely, some attempts at stretching its bonds, but it is still empathy we want to feel, and the simplest sort of identification still carries a play further than any style or magnification of life can hope to do.

What the sudden boom of hits signifies for the future I can't say. I do not believe that anything has been really changed. No acting company has been put together, no genuine new approach to anything has been developed, and it goes without saying that the theaters still take about forty percent of the gross, and one chain is demanding fifty. The price of seats is still astronomical by my standards, and unless people have adopted an entirely new idea of the value of money, which is not impossible, the audience must still be composed of a very small segment of the population. I doubt that anyone else can account for our sudden prosperity, and if they can't it means that we are building nothing for the future but a fond memory of how good it was in 1956. The fact, nevertheless, is that more people than ever seem eager to come to the theater, and that is at least a good beginning, although toward exactly what end I have not the slightest notion. The thing remains, as always, a chaos of a business having only the most incidental tangency with aesthetic preoccupations.

Another reason for my suspicion of the health of this boom is the remarkable consistency with which the authors of our plays are not mentioned in advertising. Even Wilder's name is off the ad for *Matchmaker*, and the only author mentioned at all is Tennessee Williams. It has gone as far as the elimination of authors' names on the theater marquees themselves. I hope I am not speaking merely as a member of the Dramatists Guild when I say that this, among other things, points to the revival of the star's and director's theater, than which, in my opinion, nothing could promise less for the future, not only the future of the author but of the actors and the directors and finally the audience. For when the power to draw the public is too confined to the actors, as it is coming to be if it is not already a fact, the choice of plays to be produced is inevitably weighted toward the individual part. To put it as quickly and as simply as I can, life is not reflected in plays of that kind.

With all my doubts, however, I must confess that a lot of activity, however dubious its purport, is better than too little. I talk occasionally before groups of yet unknown playwrights, and I get a certain amount of mail from some I have never seen, and it does seem to me that lately there is a kind of dramatic questioning which is deeper and less easily satisfied with opportune answers than once was the case. There seems to be a genuine dissatisfaction with the uncourageous play or the ill-made, meandering work whose only justification is its spontaneity and its departure from living room realism. There is an as yet half-conscious but nevertheless growing awareness of the larger social mission of theater among these people which was not there even two years ago, in my estimation. Form is no longer spoken of as though it were a free choice of the writer, but its roots in the play's forces are being investigated. And despite the preoccupation of the daily critics with questions of effect, and effect at almost any cost, I sense in these writers a need to come to an agreement with themselves as to the value and the meaning for man of these effects. Thus, it is possible that two opposing lines of force are burgeoning at the same time. Our theater is striving at any cost for effect, and its new writers who are as yet unknown are casting a suspicious eye on this kind of pragmatism.

I can hardly end this ramble without mentioning the most enthralling dramatic experience I have had since I first read Ibsen. It is Eugene O'Neill's recently published play, *Long Day's Journey Into Night.* I think it his most moving work. It is as true as an oak board, a remorselessly just play, a drama from which all his other plays seem to have sprung. Excepting for a very few passages, when once again the dramatic strategy threatens to leave his people alone with their self-consciousness, or the author's, the work is written on an exactly hewn plane of awareness which is only rarely violated— for his great previous fault, to my mind, was a mawkishness in voicing his themes. It is his most modern play, his most fluidly written. It is as though here his symbol and his action came up out of him intertwined and at one with each other. His pity here, and his justice, lift him as a writer to a genuinely philosophic height. Its only production took place recently in Sweden. I have not heard that there is a line of producers clamoring for it here, but it will surely be done and it must be for all our sakes. It will be good once again to watch a play which holds on to its prey with the teeth of a bulldog.

1956

Introduction to the *Collected Plays*

I

As a writer of plays I share with all specialists a suspicion of generalities about the art and technique of my craft, and I lack both the scholarly patience and the zeal to define terms in such a way as to satisfy everyone. The only other course, therefore, is to stop along the way to say what *I* mean by the terms I use, quite certain as I do so that I will be taken to task by no small number of people, but hopeful at the same time that something useful may be said about this art, a form of writing which generates more opinions and fewer instructive critical statements than any other. To be useful it seems impossible not to risk the obvious by returning always to the fundamental nature of theater, its historic human function, so to speak. For it seems odd, when one thinks of it, that an art which has always been so expensive to produce and so difficult to do well should have survived in much the same general form that it possessed when it began. This is especially striking now, when almost alone among the arts the theater has managed to live despite the devouring mechanization of the age, and, in some places and instances, even to thrive and grow. Under these circumstances of a very long if frequently interrupted history, one may make the assumption that the drama and its production must represent a well-defined expression of profound social needs, needs which transcend any particular form of society or any particular historic moment. It is therefore possible to speak of fundamentals of the form too when its only tools of importance never change, there being no possibility of drama without mimicry, conflict, tale, or speech.

My approach to playwriting and the drama itself is organic; and to make this glaringly evident at once it is necessary to separate drama from what we think of today as literature. A drama ought not be looked at first and foremost from literary perspectives merely because it uses words, verbal rhythm, and poetic image. These can be its most memorable parts, it is true, but they are not its inevitable accompaniments. Nor is it only convention which from Aristotle onward decreed that the play must be dramatic rather than narrative in concept and execution. A Greek's seat was harder than an American's and even he had to call a halt to a dramatic presentation after a couple of hours. The physiological limits of attention in a seated position enforce upon this art an interconnected group of laws, in turn expressed by aesthetic criteria, which no other writing art requires. But it is not my intention here to vivisect dramatic form or the techniques of playwriting. I only want to take advantage of this rare opportunity—a collected edition—to speak for myself as to my own aims; not to give my estimates of what can portentously be called the dramatic problem in this time, but simply to talk in workaday language about the problem of how to write so that one's changing vision of people in the world is more accurately represented in each succeeding work.

A few of the inevitable materials of the art dictate to me certain aesthetic commitments which may as well be mentioned at the outset, for they move silently but nevertheless with potent influence through the plays in this book as well as in my thoughts about them. These plays were written on the assumption that they would be acted before audiences. The "actor" is a person, and he no sooner appears than certain elementary questions are broached. Who is he? What is he doing here? How does he live or make his living? Who is he related to? Is he rich or poor? What does he think of himself? What do other people think of him, and why? What are his hopes and fears; and what does he say they are? What does he claim to want, and what does he really want?

The actor brings questions onto the stage just as any person does when we first meet him in our ordinary lives. Which of them a play chooses to answer, and how they are answered, are the ruling and highly consequential imperatives which create the style of the play, and control what are later called the stylistic levels of its writing. If, for instance, the actor is masked as he appears and his body movements are constricted and highly ordered, we instantly expect that the common surfaces of life will also be breached by the kinds of questions he or the play will respond to. He will very probably speak about the theme or essential preoccupation of the play directly and without getting to it by circuitous routes of naturalistic detail. If he appears in the costume of his trade, class, or profession, however, we expect that he or the play will give us the answers to his common identity, and if they do not they risk our dissatisfaction and frustration. In a word, the actor's appearance on the stage in normal human guise leads us to expect a realistic treatment. The play will either be intent upon rounding out the characters by virtue of its complete answers to the common questions, or will substitute answers to a more limited group of questions which, instead of being "human," are thematic and are designed to form a symbol of meaning rather than an apparency of the "real." It is the nature of the questions asked and answered, rather than the language used—whether verse, ordinary slang, or colorless prose—that determines whether the style is realistic or non-realistic. When I speak of style, therefore, this is one of the relationships I intend to convey. In this sense the tragedies of Shakespeare are species of realism, and those of Aeschylus and Sophocles are not. We know a great deal more about Macbeth and Hamlet, apart from their functions as characters in their particular given dramas, than we can ever surmise about Oedipus the king, or the heroes and heroines of Strindberg's plays. To put it another way, when the career of a person rather than the detail of his motives stands at the forefront of the play, we move closer to non-realistic styles, and vice versa. I regard this as the one immovable and irremediable quality which goes to create one style or another. And there is always an organic connection rather than a temperamental choice involved in the style in which a play is written and must be performed. The first two plays in this book were written and performed with the intention of answering as many of the common questions as was possible. *The Crucible, A Memory of Two Mondays,* and *A View from the Bridge* were not so designed, and to this extent they are a departure from realism.

Another decisive influence upon style is the conception and manipulation of time in a play. Broadly speaking, where it is conceived and used so as to convey a natural passage of hours, days, or months, the style it enforces is pressed toward realism. Where action is quite openly freed so that things mature in a moment, for instance, which would take a year in life, a true license for non-realistic styles is thereby won. As is obvious, the destruction of temporal necessity occurs in every play if only to a rudimentary degree; it is impossible that in life people should behave and speak in reference to a single thematic point for so continuous a time. Events, therefore, are always collapsed and drawn together in any drama. But as the collapsing process becomes more self-evident, and as the selection of events becomes less and less dominated by the question of their natural maturation, the style of the play moves further and further away from realism. *All My Sons* attempts to account for time in terms of months, days, and hours. *Death of a Salesman* explodes the watch and the calendar. *The Crucible* is bound by natural time—or strives to appear so.

The compacting of time destroys the realistic style not only because it violates our sense of reality, but because collapsing time inevitably emphasizes an element of existence which in life is not visible or ordinarily felt with equivalent power, and this is its symbolic meaning. When a criminal is arraigned, for instance, it is the prosecutor's job to symbolize his behavior for the jury so that the man's entire life can be characterized in one way and not in another. The prosecutor does not mention the accused as a dog lover, a good husband and father, a sufferer from eczema, or a man with the habit of chewing tobacco on the left and not the right side of his mouth. Nor does he strive to account for the long intervals of time when the accused was behaving in a way quite contrary to that symbolic characterization. The prosecutor is collapsing time—and destroying realism—by fastening only on those actions germane to the construction of his symbol. To one degree or another every play must do this or we should have to sit in a theater for years in order to appreciate a character and his story. But where the play does pretend to give us details of hours, months, and years which are not clearly and avowedly germane to the symbolic meaning, we come closer and closer to what is called a realistic style. In passing, I should say that the Greek "unity" of time imposed on the drama was not arbitrary but a concomitant of the preponderant Greek interest in the fate and career of the hero rather than his private characteristics, or, to put it another way, his social and symbolic side rather than his family role.

Another material, so to speak, of drama is not describable in a word, and has a less direct influence on style. I mention it, however, because it is probably the single most powerful influence on my way of writing and enforces on me a kind of taste and approach to the art which marks these plays. It is necessary, if one is to reflect reality, not only to depict why a man does what he does, or why he nearly didn't do it, but why he cannot simply walk away and say to hell with it. To ask this last question of a play is a cruel thing, for evasion is probably the most developed technique most men have, and in truth there is an extraordinarily small number of conflicts which we must, at any cost, live out to their conclusions. To ask this question is immediately to impose on oneself not, perhaps, a style of writing but at least a kind of dramatic construction. For I understand the symbolic meaning of a character and his career to consist of the kind of commitment he makes to life or refuses to make, the kind of challenge he accepts and the kind he can pass by. I take it that if one could know enough about a human being one could discover some conflict, some value, some challenge, however minor or major, which he cannot find it in himself to walk away from or turn his back on. The structure of these plays, in this respect, is to the end that such a conflict be discovered and clarified. Idea, in these plays, is the generalized meaning of that discovery applied to men other than the hero. Time, characterizations, and other elements are treated differently from play to play, but all to the end that that moment of commitment be brought forth, that moment when, in my eyes, a man differentiates himself from every other man, that moment when out of a sky full of stars he fixes on one star. I take it, as well, that the less capable a man is of walking away from the central conflict of the play, the closer he approaches a tragic existence. In turn, this implies that the closer a man approaches tragedy the more intense is his concentration of emotion upon the fixed point of his commitment, which is to say the closer he approaches what in life we call fanaticism. From this flows the necessity for scenes of high and open emotion, and plays constructed toward climax rather than the evocation of a mood alone or of bizarre spectacle. (The one exception among these plays is *A Memory of Two Mondays*—as will be seen later.)

From such considerations it ought to be clear that the common tokens of realism and non-realism are in themselves not acceptable as criteria. That a play is written prosaically does not make it a realistic play, and that the speech is heightened and intensified by imagery does not set it to one side of realism necessarily. The underlying poem of a play I take to be the organic necessity of its parts. I find in the arbitrary not poetry but indulgence. (The novel is another matter entirely.) A very great play can be mimed and still issue forth its essential actions and their rudiments of symbolic meaning; the word, in drama, is the transformation into speech of what is *happening*, and the fiat for intense language is intensity of happening. We have had more than one extraordinary dramatist who was a cripple as a writer, and this is lamentable but not ruinous. Which is to say that I prize the poetic above else in the theater, and because I do I insist that the poem truly be there.

II

The assumption—or presumption—behind these plays is that life has meaning. I would now add, as their momentary commentator, that what they meant to me at the time of writing is not in each instance the same as what they mean to me now in the light of further experience. Plato, by banning artists from citizenship in his ideal republic, expressed at least a partial truth; the intention behind a work of art and its effects upon the public are not always the same. Worse yet, in his conscious intention the artist often conceals from himself an aim which can be quite opposed to his fondest beliefs and ideas. Those more tempted by an evil, for instance, are more likely to feel deeply about it than those who have only known the good. From this, two ironic propositions logically flow. The first is that a play's "idea" may be useful as a unifying force empowering the artist to evoke a cogent emotional life on the stage, but that in itself it has no aesthetic value, since, after all, it is only a means to an end. The second is that since every play means something—even the play which denies all meaning to existence—the "idea" of a play is its measure of value and importance and beauty, and that a play which appears merely to exist to one side of "ideas" is an aesthetic nullity.

Idea is very important to me as a dramatist, but I think it is time someone said that playwrights, including the greatest, have not been noted for the new ideas they have broached in their plays. By new I mean an original idea invented by the playwright, quite as such things are created, if infrequently, by scientists, and occasionally by philosophers. Surely there is no known philosophy which was first announced through a play, nor any ethical idea. No social concept in Shaw's plays could have been much of a surprise to the Webbs and thousands of other Socialists of the time; nor can Ibsen, Chekhov, Strindberg, or O'Neill be credited with inventing any new thoughts. As a matter of fact, it is highly unlikely that a new idea could be successfully launched through a play at all, and this for several good reasons.

A genuine invention in the realm of ideas must first emerge as an abstruse and even partial concept. Be it Christianity, Darwinism, Marxism, or any other that can with reason be called original it has always been the product of proofs which, before they go to form a complete and new concept, require years and often generations of testing, research, and polemic. At first blush a new idea appears to be very close to insanity because to be new it must reverse important basic beliefs and assumptions which, in turn, have been institutionalized and are administered by one or another kind of priesthood with a vested interest in the old idea. Nor would the old idea be an idea at all, strictly speaking, if some goodly section of the population did not believe in it. If only because no dramatic structure can bear the brunt of the incredulity with which any really new idea is greeted, the play form would collapse under the burdens of having to deliver up the mountain of proof required for a new idea to be believed. And this would be true even if the audience were all philosophers—perhaps even truer, for the philosopher requires proofs even more exact than the layman does.

The dramatic form is a dynamic thing. It is not possible to dally in it for reflection. The polemical method, as well as the scientific exposition, the parable, or the ethical teaching, all depend upon a process which, in effect, says, "What you believe is wrong for these reasons; what the truth is is as follows." Tremendous energy must go into destroying the validity of the ancient proposition, and destroying it from an absolutely opposite viewpoint. An idea, if it is really new, is a genuine humiliation for the majority of the people; it is an affront not only to their sensibilities but to their deepest convictions. It offends against the things they worship, whether God or science or money.

The conflict between a new idea and the very notion of drama is remorseless and not resolvable because, among other things, plays are always performed before people sitting en masse and not alone. To a very large degree, much greater than is generally realized, we react *with* a surrounding crowd rather than against it; our individual criteria of truth are set to one side and we are no longer at the mercy of a performance alone, but of the surrounding reaction to it. A man walking down a deserted street sees another man beating a horse; he does not like this, he is possibly revolted by it, even angered. Perhaps he walks on, or perhaps he stops to remonstrate with the horsewhipper, who then perhaps threatens *him* with the same whip. Depending on the character of the man, he either fights or decides it is none of his business, really, and goes on about his life. The same man on the same street, but this time a busy street with many people, sees the same scene of cruelty. He is now behaving in public; he cries out and hears his cries echoed; he is encouraged; he moves in to stop the cruelty and when he himself is threatened the conflict in him over whether to back off or to fight is much higher and more intense, for now he is surrounded by the administrators of shame or the bestowers of honor—his fellow men. He is no longer looking at the same scene in the same way; the very significance of the experience is changed and more likely than not his own actions. So it is in the theater. Inevitably, to one degree or another, we see what we see on the stage not only with our own eyes but with the eyes of others. Our standards of right and wrong, good taste and bad, must in some way come into either conflict or agreement with social standards, and a truth, however true, is no longer merely itself, but itself plus the conventional reaction to it; and in the case of a genuinely new idea the conventional reaction, by definition, will come down on it like a ton of bricks, and it is finished, however beautifully written.

If plays have not broached new ideas, they have enunciated not-yet-popular ideas which are already in the air, ideas for which there has already been a preparation by non-dramatic media. Which is to say that once an idea is "in the air" it is no longer an idea but a feeling, a sensation, an emotion, and with these the drama can deal. For one thing, where no doubt exists in the hearts of the people, a play cannot create doubt: where no desire to believe exists, a play cannot create a belief. And again, this springs from the nature of dramatic form and its inevitable dynamism; it must communicate as it proceeds and it literally has no existence if it must wait until the audience goes home to think before it can be appreciated. It is the art of the present tense par excellence.

Thus it is that the forms, the accents, the intentions of the plays in this book are not the same from play to play. I could say that my awareness of life was not the same and leave it at that, but the truth is wider, for good or for ill. It is also that the society to which I responded in the past decade was constantly changing, as it is changing while I write this sentence. These plays, in one sense, are my response to what was "in the air," they are one man's way of saying to his fellow men, "This is what you see every day, or think or feel; now I will show you what you really know but have not had the time, or the disinterestedness, or the insight, or the information to understand consciously." Each of these plays, in varying degrees, was begun in the belief that it was unveiling a truth already known but unrecognized as such. My concept of the audience is of a public each member of which is carrying about with him what he thinks is an anxiety, or a hope, or a preoccupation which is his alone and isolates him from mankind; and in this respect at least the function of a play is to reveal him to himself so that he may touch others by virtue of the revelation of his mutuality with them. If only for this reason I regard the theater as a serious business, one that makes or should make man more human, which is to say, less alone.

III

When *All My Sons* opened on Broadway, it was called an "Ibsenesque" play. Some people liked it for this reason and others did not. Ibsen is relevant to this play but what he means to me is not always what he means to others, either his advocates or his detractors. More often than not, these days, he is thought of as a stage carpenter with a flair for ideas of importance. The whole aim of shaping a dramatic work on strict lines which will elicit a distinct meaning reducible to a sentence is now suspect. "Life" is now more complicated than such a mechanical contrasting of forces can hope to reflect. Instead, the aim is a "poetic" drama, preferably one whose ultimate thought or meaning is elusive, a drama which appears not to have been composed or constructed, but which somehow comes to life on a stage and then flickers away. To come quickly to the point, our theater inclines toward the forms of adolescence rather than analytical adulthood. It is not my place to deal in praise or blame, but it seems to me that a fair judge would be compelled to conclude, as a minimum, that the run of serious works of the past decade have been written and played under an intellectually—as well as electrically—diffused light. It is believed that any attempt to "prove" something in a play is somehow unfair and certainly inartistic, if not gauche, more particularly if what is being proved happens to be in any overt way of social moment. Indeed, one American critic believes that the narrowness of the theater audience—as compared with that for the movies and television—is the result of the masses' having been driven away from the theater by plays that preached.

This is not, of course, a new attitude in the world. Every major playwright has had to make his way against it, for there is and always will be a certain amount of resentfulness toward the presumption of any playwright to teach. And there will never be a satisfactory way of explaining that no playwright can be praised for his high seriousness and at the same time be praised for not trying to teach; the very conception of a dramatic theme inevitably means that certain aspects of life are selected and others left out, and to imagine that a play can be written disinterestedly is to believe that one can make love disinterestedly.

The debatable question is never whether a play ought to teach but whether it is art, and in this connection the basic criterion—purely technical considerations to one side—is the passion with which the teaching is made. I hasten to add the obvious—that a work cannot be judged by the validity of its teaching. But it is entirely misleading to state that there is some profound conflict between art and the philosophically or socially meaningful theme. I say this not out of a preference for plays that teach but in deference to the nature of the creative act. A work of art is not handed down from Olympus from a creature with a vision as wide as the world. If that could be done a play would never end, just as history has no end. A play must end, and end with a climax, and to forge a climax the forces in life, which are of infinite complexity, must be made finite and capable of a more or less succinct culmination. Thus, all dramas are to that extent arbitrary—in comparison with life itself—and embody a viewpoint if not an obsession on the author's part. So that when I am told that a play is beautiful and (or because) it does not try to teach anything, I can only wonder which of two things is true about it: either what it teaches is so obvious, so inconsiderable as to appear to the critic to be "natural," or its teaching has been embedded and articulated so thoroughly in the action itself as not to appear as an objective but only a subjective fact.

All My Sons was not my first play but the eighth or ninth I had written up to the mid-forties. But for the one immediately preceding it, none of the others were produced in the professional theater, and since the reader can have little knowledge of this one—which lasted less than a week on Broadway—and no knowledge at all of the others, a word is in order about these desk-drawer plays, particularly the failure called *The Man Who Had All the Luck.*

This play was an investigation to discover what exact part a man played in his own fate. It deals with a young man in a small town who, by the time he is in his mid-twenties, owns several growing businesses, has married the girl he loves, is the father of a child he has always wanted, and is daily becoming convinced that as his desires are gratified he is causing to accumulate around his own head an invisible but nearly palpable fund, so to speak, of retribution. The law of life, as he observes life around him, is that people are always frustrated in some important regard; and he conceives that he must be too, and the play is built around his conviction of impending disaster. The disaster never comes, even when, in effect, he tries to bring it on in order to survive it and find peace. Instead, he comes to believe in his own superiority, and in his remarkable ability to succeed.

Now, more than a decade later, it is possible for me to see that far from being a waste and a failure this play was a preparation, and possibly a necessary one, for those that followed, especially *All My Sons* and *Death of a Salesman,* and this for many reasons. In the more than half-dozen plays before it I had picked themes at random—which is to say that I had had no awareness of any inner continuity running from one of these plays to the next, and I did not perceive myself in what I had written. I had begun with a play about a family, then a play about two brothers caught on either side of radicalism in a university, then a play about a psychologist's dilemma in a prison where the sane were inexorably moving over to join the mad, a play about a bizarre ship's officer whose desire for death led him to piracy on the seas, a tragedy on the Cortes-Montezuma conflict, and others. Once again, as I worked on *The Man Who Had All the Luck,* I was writing, I would have said, about what lay outside me. I had heard the story of a young man in a midwestern town who had earned the respect and love of his town and great personal prosperity as well, and who, suddenly and for no known reason, took to suspecting everyone of wanting to rob him, and within a year of his obsession's onset had taken his own life.

In the past I had rarely spent more than three months on a play. Now the months went by with the end never in sight. After nearly ten years of writing, I had struck upon what seemed a bottomless pit of mutually canceling meanings and implications. In the past I had had less difficulty with forming a "story" and more with the exploration of its meanings. Now, in contrast, I was working with an overwhelming sense of meaning, but however I tried I could not make the drama continuous and of a piece; it persisted, with the beginning of each scene, in starting afresh as though each scene were the beginning of a new play. Then one day, while I was lying on a beach, a simple shift of relationships came to mind, a shift which did not and could not solve the problem of writing *The Man Who Had All the Luck,* but, I think now, made at least two of the plays that followed possible, and a great deal else besides.

What I saw, without laboring the details, was that two of the characters, who had been friends in the previous drafts, were logically brothers and had the same father. Had I known then what I know now I could have saved myself a lot of trouble. The play was impossible to fix because the overt story was only tangential to the secret drama its author was quite unconsciously trying to write. But in writing of the father-son relationship and of the son's search for his relatedness there was a fullness of feeling I had never known before; a crescendo was struck with a force I could almost touch. The crux of *All My Sons,* which would not be written until nearly three years later, was formed; and the roots of *Death of a Salesman* were sprouted.

The form of *All My Sons* is a reflection and an expression of several forces, of only some of which I was conscious. I desired above all to write rationally, to write so that I could tell the story of the play to even an unlettered person and spark a look of recognition on his face. The accusation I harbored against the earlier play was that it could not make sense to common-sense people. I have always been in love with wonder, the wonder of how things and people got to be what they are, and in *The Man Who Had All the Luck* I had tried to grasp wonder, I had tried to make it on the stage, by writing wonder. But wonder had betrayed me and the only other course I had was the one I took—to seek cause and effect, hard actions, facts, the geometry of relationships, and to hold back any tendency to express an idea in itself unless it was literally forced out of a character's mouth; in other words, to let wonder rise up like a mist, a gas, a vapor from the gradual and remorseless crush of factual and psychological conflict. I went back to the great book of wonder, *The Brothers Karamazov,* and I found what suddenly I felt must be true of it: that if one reads its most colorful, breathtaking, wonderful pages, one finds the thickest concentration of hard facts. Facts about the biographies of the characters, about the kind of bark on the moonlit trees, the way a window is hinged, the exact position of Dmitri as he peers through the window at his father, the precise description of his father's dress. Above all, the precise collision of inner themes during, not before or after, the high dramatic scenes. And quite as suddenly I noticed in Beethoven the holding back of climax until it was ready, the grasp of the rising line and the unwillingness to divert to an easy climax until the true one was ready. If there is one word to name the mood I felt it was *Forgo.* Let nothing interfere with the shape, the direction, the intention. I believed that I had felt too much in the previous play and understood too little.

I was turning thirty then, the author of perhaps a dozen plays, none of which I could truly believe were finished. I had written many scenes, but not a play. A play, I saw then, was an organism of which I had fashioned only certain parts. The decision formed to write one more, and if again it turned out to be unrealizable, I would go into another line of work. I have never loved the brick and mortar of the theater, and only once in my life had I been truly engrossed in a production—when Ruth Gordon played in the Jed Harris production of *A Doll's House.* The sole sense of connection with theater came when I saw the productions of the Group Theatre. It was not only the brilliance of ensemble acting, which in my opinion has never been equaled since in America, but the air of union created between actors and the audience. Here was the promise of prophetic theater which suggested to my mind the Greek situation when religion and belief were the heart of drama. I watched the Group Theatre from fifty-five-cent seats in the balcony, and at intermission time it was possible to feel the heat and the passion of people moved not only in their bellies but in their thoughts. If I say that my own writer's ego found fault with the plays, it does not detract from the fact that the performances were almost all inspiring to me, and when I heard that the Group was falling apart it seemed incredible that a society of saints—which they were to me, artistically, even as I had never met one of them—should be made up of people with less than absolute dedication to their cause.

All My Sons was begun several years after the Group had ceased to be, but it was what I can only call now a play written for a prophetic theater. I am aware of the vagueness of the term but I cannot do very well at defining what I mean. Perhaps it signifies a theater, a play, which is meant to become part of the lives of its audience—a play seriously meant for people of common sense, and relevant to both their domestic lives and their daily work, but an experience which widens their awareness of connection—the filaments to the past and the future which lie concealed in "life."

My intention in this play was to be as untheatrical as possible. To that end any metaphor, any image, any figure of speech, however creditable to me, was removed if it even slightly brought to consciousness the hand of a writer. So far as was possible nothing was to be permitted to interfere with its artlessness.

It seems to me now that I had the attitude of one laying siege to a fortress in this form. The sapping operation was to take place without a sound beneath a clear landscape in the broad light of a peaceful day. Nor was this approach arbitrary. It grew out of a determination to reverse my past playwriting errors, and from the kind of story I happened to have discovered.

During an idle chat in my living room, a pious lady from the Middle West told of a family in her neighborhood which had been destroyed when the daughter turned the father into the authorities on discovering that he had been selling faulty machinery to the Army. The war was then in full blast. By the time she had finished the tale I had transformed the daughter into a son and the climax of the second act was full and clear in my mind.

I knew my informant's neighborhood, I knew its middle-class ordinariness, and I knew how rarely the great issues penetrate such environments. But the fact that a girl had not only wanted to, but had actually moved against an erring father transformed into fact and common reality what in my previous play I had only begun to hint at. I had no awareness of the slightest connection between the two plays. All I knew was that somehow a hard thing had entered into me, a crux toward which it seemed possible to move in strong and straight lines. Something was crystal clear to me for the first time since I had begun to write plays, and it was the crisis of the second act, the revelation of the full loathsomeness of an anti-social action.

With this sense of dealing with an existing objective fact, I began to feel a difference in my role as a writer. It occurred to me that I must write this play so that even the actual criminal, on reading it, would have to say that it was true and sensible and as real as his life. It began to seem to me that what I had written until then, as well as almost all the plays I had ever seen, had been written for a theatrical performance, when they should have been written as a kind of testimony whose relevance far surpassed theatrics.

For these reasons the play begins in an atmosphere of undisturbed normality. Its first act was later called slow, but it was designed to be slow. It was made so that even boredom might threaten, so that when the first intimation of the crime is dropped a genuine horror might begin to move into the heart of the audience, a horror born of the contrast between the placidity of the civilization on view and the threat to it that a rage of conscience could create.

It took some two years to fashion this play, chiefly, I think now, because of a difficulty not unconnected with a similar one in the previous play. It was the question of relatedness. The crime in *All My Sons* is not one that is about to be committed but one that has long since been committed. There is no question of its consequences' being ameliorated by anything Chris Keller or his father can do; the damage has been done irreparably. The stakes remaining are purely the conscience of Joe Keller and its awakening to the evil he has done, and the conscience of his son in the face of what he has discovered about his father. One could say that the problem was to make a fact of morality, but it is more precise, I think, to say that the structure of the play is designed to bring a man into the direct path of the consequences he has wrought. In one sense, it was the same problem of writing about David Beeves in the earlier play, for he too could not relate himself to what he had done. In both plays the dramatic obsession, so to speak, was with the twofold nature of the individual—his own concept of his deeds, and what turns out to be the "real" description of them. *All My Sons* has often been called a moral play, and it is that, but the concept of morality is not quite as purely ethical as it has been made to appear, nor is it so in the plays that follow. That the deed of Joe Keller at issue in *All My Sons* is his having been the cause of the death of pilots in war obscures the other kind of morality in which the play is primarily interested. Morality is probably a faulty word to use in the connection, but what I was after was the wonder in the fact that consequences of actions are as real as the actions themselves, yet we rarely take them into consideration as we perform actions, and we cannot hope to do so fully when we must always act with only partial knowledge of consequences. Joe Keller's trouble, in a word, is not that he cannot tell right from wrong but that his cast of mind cannot admit that he, personally, has any viable connection with his world, his universe, or his society. He is not a partner in society, but an incorporated member, so to speak, and you cannot sue personally the officers of a corporation. I hasten to make clear here that I am not merely speaking of a literal corporation but the concept of a man's becoming a function of production or distribution to the point where his personality becomes divorced from the actions it propels.

The fortress which *All My Sons* lays siege to is the fortress of unrelatedness. It is an assertion not so much of a morality in terms of right and wrong, but of a moral world's being such because men cannot walk away from certain of their deeds. In this sense Joe Keller is a threat to society and in this sense the play is a social play. Its "socialness" does not reside in its having dealt with the crime of selling defective materials to a nation at war—the same crime could easily be the basis of a thriller which would have no place in social dramaturgy. It is that the crime is seen as having roots in a certain relationship of the individual to society, and to a certain indoctrination he embodies, which, if dominant, can mean a jungle existence for all of us no matter how high our buildings soar. And it is in this sense that loneliness is socially meaningful in these plays.

To return to Ibsen's influence upon this play, I should have to split the question in order to make sense of it. First, there was the real impact of his work upon me at the time: this consisted mainly in what I then saw as his ability to forge a play upon a factual bedrock. A situation in his plays is never stated but revealed in terms of hard actions, irrevocable deeds; and sentiment is never confused with the action it conceals. Having for so long written in terms of what people felt rather than what they did, I turned to his works at the time with a sense of homecoming. As I have said, I wanted then to write so that people of common sense would mistake my play for life itself and not be required to lend it some poetic license before it could be believed. I wanted to make the moral world as real and evident as the immoral one so splendidly is.

But my own belief is that the shadow of Ibsen was seen on this play for another reason, and it is that *All My Sons* begins very late in its story. Thus, as in Ibsen's best-known work, a great amount of time is taken up with bringing the past into the present. In passing, I ought to add that this view of action is presently antipathetic to our commonly held feeling about the drama. More than any other quality of realism, or, to be more exact, of "Ibsenism" as a technique, this creates a sense of artificiality which we now tend to reject, for in other respects realism is still our reigning style. But it is no longer acceptable that characters should sit about discussing events of a year ago, or ten years ago, when in "life" they would be busy with the present. In truth, the effort to eliminate antecedent material has threatened to eliminate the past entirely from any plays. We are impatient to get on with it—so much so that anyone making a study of some highly creditable plays of the moment would be hard put to imagine what their characters were like a month before their actions and stories begin. *All My Sons* takes its time with the past, not in deference to Ibsen's method as I saw it then, but because its theme is the question of actions and consequences, and a way had to be found to throw a long line into the past in order to make that kind of connection viable.

That the idea of connection was central to me is indicated again in the kind of revision the play underwent. In its earlier versions the mother, Kate Keller, was in a dominating position; more precisely, her astrological beliefs were given great prominence. (The play's original title was *The Sign of the Archer.*) And this, because I sought in every sphere to give body and life to connection. But as the play progressed the conflict between Joe and his son Chris pressed astrology to the wall until its mysticism gave way to psychology. There was also the impulse to regard the mystical with suspicion, since it had, in the past, given me only turgid works that could never develop a true climax based upon revealed psychological truths. In short, where in previous plays I might well have been satisfied to create only an astrologically obsessed woman, the obsession now had to be opened up to reveal its core of self-interest and intention on the character's part. Wonder must have feet with which to walk the earth.

But before I leave this play it seems wise to say a few more words about the kind of dramatic impulse it represents, and one aspect of "Ibsenism" as a technique is the quickest path into that discussion. I have no vested interest in any one form—as the variety of forms I have used attests—but there is one element in Ibsen's method which I do not think ought to be overlooked, let alone dismissed as it so often is nowadays. If his plays, and his method, do nothing else they reveal the evolutionary quality of life. One is constantly aware, in watching his plays, of process, change, development. I think too many modern plays assume, so to speak, that their duty is merely to show the present countenance rather than to account for what happens. It is therefore wrong to imagine that because his first and sometimes his second acts devote so much time to a studied revelation of antecedent material, his view is static compared to our own. In truth, it is profoundly dynamic, for that enormous past was always heavily documented to the end that the present be comprehended with wholeness, as a moment in a flow of time, and not—as with so many modern plays—as a situation without roots. Indeed, even though I can myself reject other aspects of his work, it nevertheless presents barely and unadorned what I believe is the biggest single dramatic problem, namely, how to dramatize what has gone before. I say this not merely out of technical interest, but because dramatic characters, and the drama itself, can never hope to attain a maximum degree of consciousness unless they contain a viable unveiling of the contrast between past and present, and an awareness of the process by which the present has become what it is. And I say this, finally, because I take it as a truth that the end of drama is the creation of a higher consciousness and not merely a subjective attack upon the audience's nerves and feelings. What is precious in the Ibsen method is its insistence upon valid causation, and this cannot be dismissed as a wooden notion.

This is the "real" in Ibsen's realism for me, for he was, after all, as much a mystic as a realist. Which is simply to say that while there are mysteries in life which no amount of analyzing will reduce to reason, it is perfectly realistic to admit and even to proclaim that hiatus as a truth. But the problem is not to make complex what is essentially explainable; it is to make understandable what is complex without distorting and oversimplifying what cannot be explained. I think many of his devices are, in fact, quite arbitrary; that he betrays a Germanic ponderousness at times and a tendency to over-prove what is quite clear in the first place. But we could do with more of his basic intention, which was to assert nothing he had not proved, and to cling always to the marvelous spectacle of life forcing one event out of the jaws of the preceding one and to reveal its elemental consistencies with surprise. In other words, I contrast his realism not with the lyrical, which I prize, but with sentimentality, which is always a leak in the dramatic dike. He sought to make a play as weighty and living a fact as the discovery of the steam engine or algebra. This can be scoffed away only at a price, and the price is a living drama.

IV

I think now that the straightforwardness of the *All My Sons* form was in some part due to the relatively sharp definition of the social aspects of the problem it dealt with. It was conceived in wartime and begun in wartime; the spectacle of human sacrifice in contrast with aggrandizement is a sharp and heartbreaking one. At a time when all public voices were announcing the arrival of that great day when industry and labor were one, my personal experience was daily demonstrating that beneath the slogans very little had changed. In this sense the play was a response to what I felt "in the air." It was an unveiling of what I believed everybody knew and nobody publicly said. At the same time, however, I believed I was bringing news, and it was news which I half expected would be denied as truth.

When, in effect, it was accepted, I was gratified, but a little surprised. The success of a play, especially one's first success, is somewhat like pushing against a door which is suddenly opened from the other side. One may fall on one's face or not, but certainly a new room is opened that was always securely shut until then. For myself, the experience was invigorating. It suddenly seemed that the audience was a mass of blood relations, and I sensed a warmth in the world that had not been there before. It made it possible to dream of daring more and risking more. The Wonderful was no longer something that would inevitably trap me into disastrously confusing works, for the audience sat in silence before the unwinding of *All My Sons* and gasped when they should have, and I tasted that power which is reserved, I imagine, for playwrights, which is to know that by one's invention a mass of strangers has been publicly transfixed.

As well, the production of the play was an introduction to the acting art and its awesome potentials. I wanted to use more of what lay in actors to be used. To me, the most incredible spectacle of this first successful production was the silence it enforced. It seemed then that the stage was as wide and free and towering and laughingly inventive as the human mind itself, and I wanted to press closer toward its distant edges. A success places one among friends. The world is friendly, the audience is friendly, and that is good. It also reveals, even more starkly than a failure—for a failure is always ill-defined—what remains undone.

The wonder in *All My Sons* lay in its revelation of process, and it was made a stitch at a time, so to speak, in order to weave a tapestry before our eyes. What it wanted, however, was a kind of moment-to-moment wildness in addition to its organic wholeness. The form of the play, I felt, was not sensuous enough in itself. Which means that its conception of time came to appear at odds with my own experience.

The first image that occurred to me, which was to result in *Death of a Salesman,* was of an enormous face the height of the proscenium arch which would appear and then open up, and we would see the inside of a man's head. In fact, *The Inside of His Head* was the first title. It was conceived half in laughter, for the inside of his head was a mass of contradictions. The image was in direct opposition to the method of *All My Sons*—a method one might call linear or eventual in that one fact or incident creates the necessity for the next. The *Salesman* image was from the beginning absorbed with the concept that nothing in life comes "next" but that everything exists together and at the same time within us; that there is no past to be "brought forward" in a human being, but that he is his past at every moment and that the present is merely that which his past is capable of noticing and smelling and reacting to.

I wished to create a form which, in itself as a form, would literally be the process of Willy Loman's way of mind. But to say "wished" is not accurate. Any dramatic form is an artifice, a way of transforming a subjective feeling into something that can be comprehended through public symbols. Its efficiency as a form is to be judged—at least by the writer—by how much of the original vision and feeling is lost or distorted by this transformation. I wished to speak of the salesman most precisely as I felt about him, to give no part of that feeling away for the sake of any effect or any dramatic necessity. What was wanted now was not a mounting line of tension, nor a gradually narrowing cone of intensifying suspense, but a bloc, a single chord presented as such at the outset, within which all the strains and melodies would already be contained. The strategy, as with *All My Sons,* was to appear entirely unstrategic but with a difference. This time, if I could, I would have told the whole story and set forth all the characters in one unbroken speech or even one sentence or a single flash of light. As I look at the play now its form seems the form of a confession, for that is how it is told, now speaking of what happened yesterday, then suddenly following some connection to a time twenty years ago, then leaping even further back and then returning to the present and even speculating about the future.

Where in *All My Sons* it had seemed necessary to prove the connections between the present and the past, between events and moral consequences, between the manifest and the hidden, in this play all was assumed as proven to begin with. All I was doing was bringing things to mind. The assumption, also, was that everyone knew Willy Loman. I can realize this only now, it is true, but it is equally apparent to me that I took it somehow for granted then. There was still the attitude of the unveiler, but no bringing together of hitherto unrelated things; only pre-existing images, events, confrontations, moods, and pieces of knowledge. So there was a kind of confidence underlying this play which the form itself expresses, even a naïveté, a self-disarming quality that was in part born of my belief in the audience as being essentially the same as myself. If I had wanted, then, to put the audience reaction into words, it would not have been "What happens next and why?" so much as "Oh, God, of course!"

In one sense a play is a species of jurisprudence, and some part of it must take the advocate's role, something else must act in defense, and the entirety must engage the Law. Against my will, *All My Sons* states, and even proclaims, that it is a form and that a writer wrote it and organized it. In *Death of a Salesman* the original impulse was to make that same proclamation in an immeasurably more violent, abrupt, and openly conscious way. Willy Loman does not merely suggest or hint that he is at the end of his strength and of his justifications, he is hardly on the stage for five minutes when he says so; he does not gradually imply a deadly conflict with his son, an implication dropped into the midst of serenity and surface calm, he is avowedly grappling with that conflict at the outset. The ultimate matter with which the play will close is announced at the outset and is the matter of its every moment from the first. There is enough revealed in the first scene of *Death of a Salesman* to fill another kind of play which, in service to another dramatic form, would hold back and only gradually release it. I wanted to proclaim that an artist had made this play, but the nature of the proclamation was to be entirely "inartistic" and avowedly unstrategic; it was to hold back nothing, at any moment, which life would have revealed, even at the cost of suspense and climax. It was to forgo the usual preparations for scenes and to permit—and even seek—whatever in each character contradicted his position in the advocate-defense scheme of its jurisprudence. The play was begun with only one firm piece of knowledge and this was that Loman was to destroy himself. How it would wander before it got to that point I did not know and resolved not to care. I was convinced only that if I could make him remember enough he would kill himself, and the structure of the play was determined by what was needed to draw up his memories like a mass of tangled roots without end or beginning.

As I have said, the structure of events and the nature of its form are also the direct reflection of Willy Loman's way of thinking at this moment of his life. He was the kind of man you see muttering to himself on a subway, decently dressed, on his way home or to the office, perfectly integrated with his surroundings excepting that unlike other people he can no longer restrain the power of his experience from disrupting the superficial sociality of his behavior. Consequently he is working on two logics which often collide. For instance, if he meets his son Happy while in the midst of some memory in which Happy disappointed him, he is instantly furious at Happy, despite the fact that Happy at this particular moment deeply desires to be of use to him. He is literally at that terrible moment when the voice of the past is no longer distant but quite as loud as the voice of the present. In dramatic terms the form, therefore, *is* this process, instead of being a once-removed summation or indication of it.

The way of telling the tale, in this sense, is as mad as Willy and as abrupt and as suddenly lyrical. And it is difficult not to add that the subsequent imitations of the form had to collapse for this particular reason. It is not possible, in my opinion, to graft it onto a character whose psychology it does not reflect, and I have not used it since because it would be false to a more integrated—or less disintegrating—personality to pretend that the past and the present are so openly and vocally intertwined in his mind. The ability of people to down their past is normal, and without it we could have no comprehensible communication among men. In the hands of writers who see it as an easy way to elicit anterior information in a play it becomes merely a flashback. There are no flashbacks in this play but only a mobile concurrency of past and present, and this, again, because in his desperation to justify his life Willy Loman has destroyed the boundaries between now and then, just as anyone would do who, on picking up his telephone, discovered that this perfectly harmless act had somehow set off an explosion in his basement. The previously assumed and believed-in results of ordinary and accepted actions, and their abrupt and unforeseen—but apparently logical—effects, form the basic collision in this play, and, I suppose, its ultimate irony.

It may be in place to remark, in this connection, that while the play was sometimes called cinematographic in its structure, it failed as a motion picture. I believe that the basic reason—aside from the gross insensitivity permeating its film production—was that the dramatic tension of Willy's memories was destroyed by transferring him, literally, to the locales he had only imagined in the play. There is an inevitable horror in the spectacle of a man losing consciousness of his immediate surroundings to the point where he engages in conversations with unseen persons. The horror is lost—and drama becomes narrative—when the context actually becomes his imagined world. And the dream evaporates because psychological truth has been amended, a truth which depends not only on what images we recall but in what connections and contexts we recall them. The setting on the stage was never shifted, despite the many changes in locale, for the precise reason that, quite simply, the mere fact that a man forgets where he is does not mean that he has really moved. Indeed, his terror springs from his never-lost awareness of time and place. It did not need this play to teach me that the screen is time-bound and earth-bound compared to the stage, if only because its preponderant emphasis is on the visual image, which, however rapidly it may be changed before our eyes, still displaces its predecessor, while scene-changing with words is instantaneous; and because of the flexibility of language, especially of English, a preceding image can be kept alive through the image that succeeds it. The movie's tendency is always to wipe out what has gone before, and it is thus in constant danger of transforming the dramatic into narrative. There is no swifter method of telling a "story" but neither is there a more difficult medium in which to keep a pattern of relationships constantly in being. Even in those sequences which retained the real backgrounds for Willy's imaginary confrontations the tension between now and then was lost. I suspect this loss was due to the necessity of shooting the actors close-up—effectively eliminating awareness of their surroundings. The basic failure of the picture was a formal one. It did not solve, nor really attempt to find, a resolution for the problem of keeping the past constantly alive, and that friction, collision, and tension between past and present was the heart of the play's particular construction.

A great deal has been said and written about what *Death of a Salesman* is supposed to signify, both psychologically and from the socio-political viewpoints. For instance, in one periodical of the far Right it was called a "time bomb expertly placed under the edifice of Americanism," while the *Daily Worker* reviewer thought it entirely decadent. In Catholic Spain it ran longer than any modern play and it has been refused production in Russia but not, from time to time, in certain satellite countries, depending on the direction and velocity of the wind. The Spanish press, thoroughly controlled by Catholic orthodoxy, regarded the play as commendable proof of the spirit's death where there is no God. In America, even as it was being cannonaded as a piece of Communist propaganda, two of the largest manufacturing corporations in the country invited me to address their sales organizations in conventions assembled, while the road company was here and there picketed by the Catholic War Veterans and the American Legion. It made only a fair impression in London, but in the area of the Norwegian Arctic Circle fishermen whose only contact with civilization was the radio and the occasional visit of the government boat insisted on seeing it night after night—the same few people— believing it to be some kind of religious rite. One organization of salesmen raised me up nearly to patron-sainthood, and another, a national sales managers' group, complained that the difficulty of recruiting salesmen was directly traceable to the play. When the movie was made, the producing company got so frightened it produced a sort of trailer to be shown before the picture, a documentary short film which demonstrated how exceptional Willy Loman was; how necessary selling is to the economy; how secure the salesman's life really is; how idiotic, in short, was the feature film they had just spent more than a million dollars to produce. Fright does odd things to people.

On the psychological front the play spawned a small hill of doctoral theses explaining its Freudian symbolism, and there were innumerable letters asking if I was aware that the fountain pen which Biff steals is a phallic symbol. Some, on the other hand, felt it was merely a fountain pen and dismissed the whole play. I received visits from men over sixty from as far away as California who had come across the country to have me write the stories of their lives, because the story of Willy Loman was exactly like theirs. The letters from women made it clear that the central character of the play was Linda; sons saw the entire action revolving around Biff or Happy, and fathers wanted advice, in effect, on how to avoid parricide. Probably the most succinct reaction to the play was voiced by a man who, on leaving the theater, said, "I always said that New England territory was no damned good." This, at least, was a fact.

That I have and had not the slightest interest in the selling profession is probably unbelievable to most people, and I very early gave up trying even to say so. And when asked what Willy was selling, what was in his bags, I could only reply, "Himself." I was trying neither to condemn a profession nor particularly to improve it, and, I will admit,

I was little better than ignorant of Freud's teachings when I wrote it. There was no attempt to bring down the American edifice nor to raise it higher, to show up family relations or to cure the ills afflicting that inevitable institution. The truth, at least of my aim—which is all I can speak of authoritatively—is much simpler and more complex.

The play grew from simple images. From a little frame house on a street of little frame houses, which had once been loud with the noise of growing boys, and then was empty and silent and finally occupied by strangers. Strangers who could not know with what conquistadorial joy Willy and his boys had once re-shingled the roof. Now it was quiet in the house, and the wrong people in the beds.

It grew from images of futility—the cavernous Sunday afternoons polishing the car. Where is that car now? And the chamois cloths carefully washed and put up to dry, where are the chamois cloths?

And the endless, convoluted discussions, wonderments, arguments, belittlements, encouragements, fiery resolutions, abdications, returns, partings, voyages out and voyages back, tremendous opportunities and small, squeaking denouements—and all in the kitchen now occupied by strangers who cannot hear what the walls are saying.

The image of aging and so many of your friends already gone and strangers in the seats of the mighty who do not know you or your triumphs or your incredible value.

The image of the son's hard, public eye upon you, no longer swept by your myth, no longer rousable from his separateness, no longer knowing you have lived for him and have wept for him.

The image of ferocity when love has turned to something else and yet is there, is somewhere in the room if one could only find it.

The image of people turning into strangers who only evaluate one another.

Above all, perhaps, the image of a need greater than hunger or sex or thirst, a need to leave a thumbprint somewhere on the world. A need for immortality, and by admitting it, the knowing that one has carefully inscribed one's name on a cake of ice on a hot July day.

I sought the relatedness of all things by isolating their unrelatedness, a man superbly alone with his sense of not having touched, and finally knowing in his last extremity that the love which had always been in the room unlocated was now found.

The image of a suicide so mixed in motive as to be unfathomable and yet demanding statement. Revenge was in it and a power of love, a victory in that it would bequeath a fortune to the living and a flight from emptiness. With it an image of peace at the final curtain, the peace that is between wars, the peace leaving the issues above ground and viable yet.

And always, throughout, the image of private man in a world full of strangers, a world that is not home nor even an open battleground but only galaxies of high promise over a fear of falling.

And the image of a man making something with his hands being a rock to touch and return to. "He was always so wonderful with his hands," says his wife over his grave, and I laughed when the line came, laughed with the artist-devil's laugh, for it had all come together in this line, she having been made by him though he did not know it or believe in it or receive it into himself. Only rank, height of power, the sense of having won he believed was real—the galaxy thrust up into the sky by projectors on the rooftops of the city he believed were real stars.

It came from structural images. The play's eye was to revolve from within Willy's head, sweeping endlessly in all directions like a light on the sea, and nothing that formed in the distant mist was to be left uninvestigated. It was thought of as having the density of the novel form in its interchange of viewpoints, so that while all roads led to Willy the other characters were to feel it was their play, a story about them and not him.

There were two undulating lines in mind, one above the other, the past webbed to the present moving on together in him and sometimes openly joined and once, finally, colliding in the showdown which defined him in his eyes at least—and so to sleep.

Above all, in the structural sense, I aimed to make a play with the veritable countenance of life. To make one the many, as in life, so that "society" is a power and a mystery of custom and inside the man and surrounding him, as the fish is in the sea and the sea inside the fish, his birthplace and burial ground, promise and threat. To speak commonsensically of social facts which every businessman knows and talks about but which are too prosaic to mention or are usually fancied up on the stage as philosophical problems. When a man gets old you fire him, you have to, he can't do the work. To speak and even to celebrate the common sense of businessmen, who love the personality that wins the day but know that you've got to have the right goods at the right price, handsome and well-spoken as you are. (To some, these were scandalous and infamous arraignments of society when uttered in the context of art. But not to the businessmen themselves; they knew it was all true and I cherished their clear-eyed talk.)

The image of a play without transitional scenes was there in the beginning. There was too much to say to waste precious stage time with feints and preparations, in themselves agonizing "structural" bridges for a writer to work out since they are not why he is writing. There was a resolution, as in *All My Sons,* not to waste motion or moments, but in this case to shear through everything up to the meat of a scene; a resolution not to write an unmeant word for the sake of the form but to make the form give and stretch and contract for the sake of the thing to be said. To cling to the process of Willy's mind as the form the story would take.

The play was always heroic to me, and in later years the academy's charge that Willy lacked the "stature" for the tragic hero seemed incredible to me. I had not understood that these matters are measured by Greco-Elizabethan paragraphs which hold no mention of insurance payments, front porches, refrigerator fan belts, steering knuckles, Chevrolets, and visions seen not through the portals of Delphi but in the blue flame of the hot-water heater. How could "Tragedy" make people weep, of all things?

I set out not to "write a tragedy" in this play, but to show the truth as I saw it. However, some of the attacks upon it as a pseudo-tragedy contain ideas so misleading, and in some cases so laughable, that it might be in place here to deal with a few of them.

Aristotle having spoken of a fall from the heights, it goes without saying that someone of the common mould cannot be a fit tragic hero. It is now many centuries since Aristotle lived. There is no more reason for falling down in a faint before his *Poetics* than before Euclid's geometry, which has been amended numerous times by men with new insights; nor, for that matter, would I choose to have my illnesses diagnosed by Hippocrates rather than the most ordinary graduate of an American medical school, despite the Greek's genius. Things do change, and even a genius is limited by his time and the nature of his society.

I would deny, on grounds of simple logic, this one of Aristotle's contentions if only because he lived in a slave society. When a vast number of people are divested of alternatives, as slaves are, it is rather inevitable that one will not be able to imagine drama, let alone tragedy, as being possible for any but the higher ranks of society. There is a legitimate question of stature here, but none of rank, which is so often confused with it. So long as the hero may be said to have had alternatives of a magnitude to have materially changed the course of his life, it seems to me that in this respect at least, he cannot be debarred from the heroic role.

The question of rank is significant to me only as it reflects the question of the social application of the hero's career. There is no doubt that if a character is shown on the stage who goes through the most ordinary actions, and is suddenly revealed to be the President of the United States, his actions immediately assume a much greater magnitude, and pose the possibilities of much greater meaning, than if he is the corner grocer. But at the same time, his stature as a hero is not so utterly dependent upon his rank that the corner grocer cannot outdistance him as a tragic figure—providing, of course, that the grocer's career engages the issues of, for instance, the survival of the race, the relationships of man to God—the questions, in short, whose answers define humanity and the right way to live so that the world is a home, instead of a battleground or a fog in which disembodied spirits pass each other in an endless twilight.

In this respect *Death of a Salesman* is a slippery play to categorize because nobody in it stops to make a speech objectively stating the great issues which I believe it embodies. If it were a worse play, less closely articulating its meanings with its actions, I think it would have more quickly satisfied a certain kind of criticism. But it was meant to be less a play than a fact; it refused admission to its author's opinions and opened itself to a revelation of process and the operations of an ethic, of social laws of action no less powerful in their effects upon individuals than any tribal law administered by gods with names. I need not claim that this play is a genuine solid-gold tragedy for my opinions on tragedy to be held valid. My purpose here is simply to point out a historical fact which must be taken into account in any consideration of tragedy, and it is the sharp alteration in the meaning of rank in society between the present time and the distant past. More important to me is the fact that this particular kind of argument obscures much more relevant considerations.

One of these is the question of intensity. It matters not at all whether a modern play concerns itself with a grocer or a president if the intensity of the hero's commitment to his course is less than the maximum possible. It matters not at all whether the hero falls from a great height or a small one, whether he is highly conscious or only dimly aware of what is happening, whether his pride brings the fall or an unseen pattern written behind clouds; if the intensity, the human passion to surpass his given bounds, the fanatic insistence upon his self-conceived role—if these are not present there can only be an outline of tragedy but no living thing. I believe, for myself, that the lasting appeal of tragedy is due to our need to face the fact of death in order to strengthen ourselves for life, and that over and above this function of the tragic viewpoint there are and will be a great number of formal variations which no single definition will ever embrace.

Another issue worth considering is the so-called tragic victory, a question closely related to the consciousness of the hero. One makes nonsense of this if a "victory" means that the hero makes us feel some certain joy when, for instance, he sacrifices himself for a "cause," and unhappy and morose because he dies without one. To begin at the bottom, a man's death is and ought to be an essentially terrifying thing and ought to make nobody happy. But in a great variety of ways even death, the ultimate negative, can be, and appear to be, an assertion of bravery, and can serve to separate the death of man from the death of animals; and I think it is this distinction which underlies any conception of a victory in death. For a society of faith, the nature of the death can prove the existence of the spirit, and posit its immortality. For a secular society it is perhaps more difficult for such a victory to document itself and to make itself felt, but, conversely, the need to offer greater proofs of the humanity of man can make that victory more real. It goes without saying that in a society where there is basic disagreement as to the right way to live, there can hardly be agreement as to the right way to die, and both life and death must be heavily weighted with meaningless futility.

It was not out of any deference to a tragic definition that Willy Loman is filled with a joy, however broken-hearted, as he approaches his end, but simply that my sense of his character dictated his joy, and even what I felt was an exultation. In terms of his character, he has achieved a very powerful piece of knowledge, which is that he is loved by his son and has been embraced by him and forgiven. In this he is given his existence, so to speak—his fatherhood, for which he has always striven and which until now he could not achieve. That he is unable to take this victory thoroughly to his heart, that it closes the circle for him and propels him to his death, is the wage of his sin, which was to have committed himself so completely to the counterfeits of dignity and the false coinage embodied in his idea of success that he can prove his existence only by bestowing "power" on his posterity, a power deriving from the sale of his last asset, himself, for the price of his insurance policy.

I must confess here to a miscalculation, however. I did not realize while writing the play that so many people in the world do not see as clearly, or would not admit, as I thought they must, how futile most lives are; so there could be no hope of consoling the audience for the death of this man. I did not realize either how few would be impressed by the fact that this man is actually a very brave spirit who cannot settle for half but must pursue his dream of himself to the end. Finally, I thought it must be clear, even obvious, that this was no dumb brute heading mindlessly to his catastrophe.

I have no need to be Willy's advocate before the jury which decides who is and who is not a tragic hero. I am merely noting that the lingering ponderousness of so many ancient definitions has blinded students and critics to the facts before them, and not only in regard to this play. Had Willy been unaware of his separation from values that endure he would have died contentedly while polishing his car, probably on a Sunday afternoon with the ball game coming over the radio. But he was agonized by his awareness of being in a false position, so constantly haunted by the hollowness of all he had placed his faith in, so aware, in short, that he must somehow be filled in his spirit or fly apart, that he staked his very life on the ultimate assertion. That he had not the intellectual fluency to verbalize his situation is not the same thing as saying that he lacked awareness, even an overly intensified consciousness that the life he had made was without form and inner meaning.

To be sure, had he been able to know that he was as much the victim of his beliefs as their defeated exemplar, had he known how much of guilt he ought to bear and how much to shed from his soul, he would be more conscious. But it seems to me that there is of necessity a severe limitation of self-awareness in any character, even the most knowing, which serves to define him as a character, and more, that this very limit serves to complete the tragedy and, indeed, to make it at all possible. Complete consciousness is possible only in a play about forces, like *Prometheus,* but not in a play about people. I think that the point is whether there is a sufficient awareness in the hero's career to make the audience supply the rest. Had Oedipus, for instance, been more conscious and more aware of the forces at work upon him he must surely have said that he was not really to blame for having cohabited with his mother since neither he nor anyone else knew she was his mother. He must surely decide to divorce her, provide for their children, firmly resolve to investigate the family background of his next wife, and thus deprive us of a very fine play and the name for a famous neurosis. But he is conscious only up to a point, the point at which guilt begins. Now he is inconsolable and must tear out his eyes. What is tragic about this? Why is it not even ridiculous? How can we respect a man who goes to such extremities over something he could in no way help or prevent? The answer, I think, is not that we respect the man, but that we respect the Law he has so completely broken, wittingly or not, for it is that Law which, we believe, defines us as men. The confusion of some critics viewing *Death of a Salesman* in this regard is that they do not see that Willy Loman has broken a law without whose protection life is insupportable if not incomprehensible to him and to many others; it is the law which says that a failure in society and in business has no right to live. Unlike the law against incest, the law of success is not administered by statute or church, but it is very nearly as powerful in its grip upon men. The confusion increases because, while it is a law, it is by no means a wholly agreeable one even as it is slavishly obeyed, for to fail is no longer to belong to society, in his estimate. Therefore, the path is opened for those who wish to call Willy merely a foolish man even as they themselves are living in obedience to the same law that killed him. Equally, the fact that Willy's law—the belief, in other words, which administers guilt to him—is not a civilizing statute whose destruction menaces us all; it is, rather, a deeply believed and deeply suspect "good" which, when questioned as to its value, as it is in this play, serves more to raise our anxieties than to reassure us of the existence of an unseen but humane metaphysical system in the world. My attempt in the play was to counter this anxiety with an opposing system which, so to speak, is in a race for Willy's faith, and it is the system of love which is the opposite of the law of success. It is embodied in Biff Loman, but by the time Willy can perceive his love it can serve only as an ironic comment upon the life he sacrificed for power and for success and its tokens.

V

A play cannot be equated with a political philosophy, at least not in the way a smaller number, by simple multiplication, can be assimilated into a larger. I do not believe that any work of art can help but be diminished by its adherence at any cost to a political program, including its author's, and not for any other reason than that there is no political program—any more than there is a theory of tragedy—which can encompass the complexities of real life. Doubtless an author's politics must be one element, and even an important one, in the germination of his art, but if it is art he has created it must by definition bend itself to his observation rather than to his opinions or even his hopes. If I have shown a preference for plays which seek causation not only in psychology but in society, I may also believe in the autonomy of art, and I believe this because my experience with *All My Sons* and *Death of a Salesman* forces the belief upon me. If the earlier play was Marxist, it was a Marxism of a strange hue. Joe Keller is arraigned by his son for a willfully unethical use of his economic position; and this, as the Russians said when they removed the play from their stages, bespeaks an assumption that the norm of capitalist behavior is ethical or at least can be, an assumption no Marxist can hold. Nor does Chris propose to liquidate the business built in part on soldiers' blood; he will run it himself, but cleanly.

The most decent man in *Death of a Salesman* is a capitalist (Charley) whose aims are not different from Willy Loman's. The great difference between them is that Charley is not a fanatic. Equally, however, he has learned how to live without that frenzy, that ecstasy of spirit which Willy chases to his end. And even as Willy's sons are unhappy men, Charley's boy, Bernard, works hard, attends to his studies, and attains a worthwhile objective. These people are all of the same class, the same background, the same neighborhood. What theory lies behind this double view? None whatever. It is simply that I knew and know that I feel better when my work is reflecting a balance of the truth as it exists. A muffled debate arose with the success of *Death of a Salesman* in which attempts were made to justify or dismiss the play as a Left-Wing piece, or as a Right-Wing manifestation of decadence. The presumption underlying both views is that a work of art is the sum of its author's political outlook, real or alleged, and more, that its political implications are valid elements in its aesthetic evaluation. I do not believe this, either for my own or other writers' works.

The most radical play I ever saw was not *Waiting for Lefty* but *The Madwoman of Chaillot*. I know nothing of Giradoux's political alignment, and it is of no moment to me; I am able to read this play, which is the most open indictment of private exploitation of the earth I know about. By the evidence of his plays, Shaw, the socialist, was in love not with the working class, whose characters he could only caricature, but with the middle of the economic aristocracy, those men who, in his estimate, lived without social and economic illusions. There is a strain of mystic fatalism in Ibsen so powerful as to throw all his scientific tenets into doubt, and a good measure besides of contempt—in this radical—for the men who are usually called the public. The list is long and the contradictions are embarrassing until one concedes a perfectly simple proposition. It is merely that a writer of any worth creates out of his total perception, the vaster part of which is subjective and not within his intellectual control. For myself, it has never been possible to generate the energy to write and complete a play if I know in advance everything it signifies and all it will contain. The very impulse to write, I think, springs from an inner chaos crying for order, for meaning, and that meaning must be discovered in the process of writing or the work lies dead as it is finished. To speak, therefore, of a play as though it were the objective work of a propagandist is an almost biological kind of nonsense, provided, of course, that it is a play, which is to say a work of art.

VI

In the writing of *Death of a Salesman* I tried, of course, to achieve a maximum power of effect. But when I saw the devastating force with which it struck its audiences, something within me was shocked and put off. I had thought of myself as rather an optimistic man. I looked at what I had wrought and was forced to wonder whether I knew myself at all if this play, which I had written half in laughter and joy, was as morose and as utterly sad as its audiences found it. Either I was much tougher than they, and could stare at calamity with fewer terrors, or I was harboring within myself another man who was only tangentially connected with what I would have called my rather bright viewpoint about mankind. As I watched and saw tears in the eyes of the audience I felt a certain embarrassment at having, as I thought then, convinced so many people that life was not worth living—for so the play was widely interpreted. I hasten to add now that I ought not have been embarrassed, and that I am convinced the play is not a document of pessimism, a philosophy in which I do not believe.

Nevertheless, the emotionalism with which the play was received helped to generate an opposite impulse and an altered dramatic aim. This ultimately took shape in *The Crucible*, but before it became quite so definite and formed into idea, it was taking hold of my thoughts in a purely dramatic and theatrical context. Perhaps I can indicate its basic elements by saying that *Salesman* moves with its arms open wide, sweeping into itself by means of a subjective process of thought-connection a multitude of observations, feelings, suggestions, and shadings much as the mind does in its ordinary daily functions. Its author chose its path, of course, but, once chosen, that path could meander as it pleased through a world that was well recognized by the audience. From the theatrical viewpoint that play desired the audience to forget it was in a theater even as it broke the bounds, I believe, of a long convention of realism. Its expressionistic elements were consciously used as such, but since the approach to Willy Loman's characterization was consistently and rigorously subjective, the audience would not ever be aware—if I could help it—that they were witnessing the use of a technique which had until then created only coldness, objectivity, and a highly styled sort of play. I had willingly employed expressionism but always to create a subjective truth, and this play, which was so manifestly "written," seemed as though nobody had written it at all but that it had simply "happened." I had always been attracted and repelled by the brilliance of German expressionism after World War I, and one aim in *Salesman* was to employ its quite marvelous shorthand for humane, "felt" characterizations rather than for purposes of demonstration for which the Germans had used it.

These and other technical and theatrical considerations were a preparation for what turned out to be *The Crucible,* but "what was in the air" provided the actual locus of the tale. If the reception of *All My Sons* and *Death of a Salesman* had made the world a friendly place for me, events of the early fifties quickly turned that warmth into an illusion. It was not only the rise of "McCarthyism" that moved me, but something which seemed much more weird and mysterious. It was the fact that a political, objective, knowledgeable campaign from the far Right was capable of creating not only a terror, but a new subjective reality, a veritable mystique which was gradually assuming even a holy resonance. The wonder of it all struck me that so practical and picayune a cause, carried forward by such manifestly ridiculous men, should be capable of paralyzing thought itself, and worse, causing to billow up such persuasive clouds of "mysterious" feelings within people. It was as though the whole country had been born anew, without a memory even of certain elemental decencies which a year or two earlier no one would have imagined could be altered, let alone forgotten. Astounded, I watched men pass me by without a nod whom I had known rather well for years; and again, the astonishment was produced by my knowledge, which I could not give up, that the terror in these people was being knowingly planned and consciously engineered, and yet that all they knew was terror. That so interior and subjective an emotion could have been so manifestly created from without was a marvel to me. It underlies every word in *The Crucible*.

I wondered, at first, whether it must be that self-preservation and the need to hold on to opportunity, the thought of being exiled and "put out," was what the fear was feeding on, for there were people who had had only the remotest connections with the Left who were quite as terrified as those who had been closer. I knew of one man who had been summoned to the office of a network executive and, on explaining that he had had no Left connections at all, despite the then current attacks upon him, was told that this was precisely the trouble; "You have nothing to give them," he was told, meaning he had no confession to make, and so he was fired from his job and for more than a year could not recover the will to leave his house.

It seemed to me after a time that this, as well as other kinds of social compliance, is the result of the sense of guilt which individuals strive to conceal by complying. Generally it was guilt, in this historic instance, resulting from their awareness that they were not as Rightist as people were supposed to be; that the tenor of public pronouncements was alien to them and that they must be somehow discoverable as enemies of the power overhead. There was a new religiosity in the air, not merely the kind expressed by the spurt in church construction and church attendance, but an official piety which my reading of American history could not reconcile with the free-wheeling iconoclasm of the country's past. I saw forming a kind of interior mechanism of confession and forgiveness of sins which until now had not been rightly categorized as sins. New sins were being created monthly. It was very odd how quickly these were accepted into the new orthodoxy, quite as though they had been there since the beginning of time. Above all, above all horrors, I saw accepted the notion that conscience was no longer a private matter but one of state administration. I saw men handing conscience to other men and thanking other men for the opportunity of doing so.

I wished for a way to write a play that would be sharp, that would lift out of the morass of subjectivism the squirming, single, defined process which would show that the sin of public terror is that it divests man of conscience, of himself. It was a theme not unrelated to those that had invested the previous plays. In *The Crucible*, however, there was an attempt to move beyond the discovery and unveiling of the hero's guilt, a guilt that kills the personality. I had grown increasingly conscious of this theme in my past work, and aware too that it was no longer enough for me to build a play, as it were, upon the revelation of guilt, and to rely solely upon a fate which exacts payment from the culpable man. Now guilt appeared to me no longer the bedrock beneath which the probe could not penetrate. I saw it now as a betrayer, as possibly the most real of our illusions, but nevertheless a quality of mind capable of being overthrown.

I had known of the Salem witch hunt for many years before "McCarthyism" had arrived, and it had always remained an inexplicable darkness to me. When I looked into it now, however, it was with the contemporary situation at my back, particularly the mystery of the handing over of conscience which seemed to me the central and informing fact of the time. One finds, I suppose, what one seeks. I doubt I should ever have tempted agony by actually writing a play on the subject had I not come upon a single fact. It was that Abigail Williams, the prime mover of the Salem hysteria, so far as the hysterical children were concerned, had a short time earlier been the house servant of the Proctors and now was crying out Elizabeth Proctor as a witch; but more—it was clear from the record that with entirely uncharacteristic fastidiousness she was refusing to include John Proctor, Elizabeth's husband, in her accusations despite the urgings of the prosecutors. Why? I searched the records of the trials in the courthouse at Salem but in no other instance could I find such a careful avoidance of the implicating stutter, the murderous, ambivalent answer to the sharp questions of the prosecutors. Only here, in Proctor's case, was there so clear an attempt to differentiate between a wife's culpability and a husband's.

The testimony of Proctor himself is one of the least elaborate in the records, and Elizabeth is not one of the major cases either. There could have been numerous reasons for his having been ultimately apprehended and hanged which are nowhere to be found. After the play opened, several of his descendants wrote to me; and one of them believes that Proctor fell under suspicion because, according to family tradition, he had for years been an amateur inventor whose machines appeared to some people as devilish in their ingenuity, and—again according to tradition—he had had to conceal them and work on them privately long before the witch hunt had started, for fear of censure if not worse. The explanation does not account for everything, but it does fall in with his evidently liberated cast of mind as revealed in the record; he was one of the few who not only refused to admit consorting with evil spirits, but who persisted in calling the entire business a ruse and a fake. Most, if not all, of the other victims were of their time in conceding the existence of the immemorial plot by the Devil to take over the visible world, their only reservation being that they happened not to have taken part in it themselves.

It was the fact that Abigail, their former servant, was their accuser, and her apparent desire to convict Elizabeth and save John, that made the play conceivable for me.

As in any such mass phenomenon, the number of characters of vital, if not decisive, importance is so great as to make the dramatic problem excessively difficult. For a time it seemed best to approach the town impressionistically, and, by a mosaic of seemingly disconnected scenes, gradually to form a context of cause and effect. This I believe I might well have done had it not been that the central impulse for writing at all was not the social but the interior psychological question, which was the question of that guilt residing in Salem which the hysteria merely unleashed, but did not create. Consequently, the structure reflects that understanding, and it centers in John, Elizabeth, and Abigail.

In reading the record, which was taken down verbatim at the trial, I found one recurring note which had a growing effect upon my concept, not only of the phenomenon itself, but of our modern way of thinking about people, and especially of the treatment of evil in contemporary drama. Some critics have taken exception, for instance, to the unrelieved badness of the prosecution in my play. I understand how this is possible, and I plead no mitigation, but I was up against historical facts which were immutable. I do not think that either the record itself or the numerous commentaries upon it reveal any mitigation of the unrelieved, straightforward, and absolute dedication to evil displayed by the judges of these trials and the prosecutors. After days of study it became quite incredible how perfect they were in this respect. I recall, almost as in a dream, how Rebecca Nurse, a pious and universally respected woman of great age, was literally taken by force from her sickbed and ferociously cross-examined. No human weakness could be displayed without the prosecution's stabbing into it with greater fury. The most patent contradictions, almost laughable even in that day, were overridden with warnings not to repeat their mention. There was a sadism here that was breathtaking.

So much so, that I sought but could not at the time take hold of a concept of man which might really begin to account for such evil. For instance, it seems beyond doubt that members of the Putnam family consciously, coldly, and with malice aforethought conferred in private with some of the girls, and told them whom it was desirable to cry out upon next. There is and will always be in my mind the spectacle of the great minister, and ideological authority behind the prosecution, Cotton Mather, galloping up to the scaffold to beat back a crowd of villagers so moved by the towering dignity of the victims as to want to free them.

It was not difficult to foresee the objections to such absolute evil in men; we are committed, after all, to the belief that it does not and cannot exist. Had I this play to write now, however, I might proceed on an altered concept. I should say that my own—and the critics'—unbelief in this depth of evil is concomitant with our unbelief in good, too. I should now examine this fact of evil as such. Instead, I sought to make Danforth, for instance, perceptible as a human being by showing him somewhat put off by Mary Warren's turnabout at the height of the trials, which caused no little confusion. In my play, Danforth seems about to conceive of the truth, and surely there is a disposition in him at least to listen to arguments that go counter to the line of the prosecution. There is no such swerving in the record, and I think now, almost four years after the writing of it, that I was wrong in mitigating the evil of this man and the judges he represents. Instead, I would perfect his evil to its utmost and make an open issue, a thematic consideration of it in the play. I believe now, as I did not conceive then, that there are people dedicated to evil in the world; that without their perverse example we should not know the good. Evil is not a mistake but a fact in itself. I have never proceeded psychoanalytically in my thought, but neither have I been separated from that humane if not humanistic conception of man as being essentially innocent while the evil in him represents but a perversion of his frustrated love. I posit no metaphysical force of evil which totally possesses certain individuals, nor do I even deny that given infinite wisdom and patience and knowledge any human being can be saved from himself. I believe merely that, from whatever cause, a dedication to evil, not mistaking it for good, but knowing it as evil and loving it as evil, is possible in human beings who appear agreeable and normal. I think now that one of the hidden weaknesses of our whole approach to dramatic psychology is our inability to face this fact—to conceive, in effect, of Iago.

The Crucible is a "tough" play. My criticism of it now would be that it is not tough enough. I say this not merely out of deference to the record of these trials, but out of a consideration for drama. We are so intent upon getting sympathy for our characters that the consequences of evil are being muddied by sentimentality under the guise of a temperate weighing of causes. The tranquility of the bad man lies at the heart of not only moral philosophy but dramaturgy as well. But my central intention in this play was to one side of this idea, which was realized only as the play was in production. All I sought here was to take a step not only beyond the realization of guilt, but beyond the helpless victimization of the hero.

The society of Salem was "morally" vocal. People then avowed principles, sought to live by them and die by them. Issues of faith, conduct, society, pervaded their private lives in a conscious way. They needed but to disapprove to act. I was drawn to this subject because the historical moment seemed to give me the poetic right to create people of higher self-awareness than the contemporary scene affords. I had explored the subjective world in *Salesman* and I wanted now to move closer to a conscious hero.

The decidedly mixed reception to the play was not easily traceable, but I believe there are causes for it which are of moment to more than this play alone. I believe that the very moral awareness of the play and its characters—which are historically correct—was repulsive to the audience. For a variety of reasons I think that the Anglo-Saxon audience cannot believe the reality of characters who live by principles and know very much about their own characters and situations, and who say what they know. Our drama, for this among other reasons, is condemned, so to speak, to the emotions of subjectivism, which, as they approach knowledge and self-awareness, become less and less actual and real to us. In retrospect I think that my course in *The Crucible* should have been toward greater self-awareness and not, as my critics have implied, toward an enlarged and more pervasive subjectivism. The realistic form and style of the play would then have had to give way. What new form might have evolved I cannot now say, but certainly the passion of knowing is as powerful as the passion of feeling alone, and the writing of the play broached the question of that new form for me.

The work of Bertolt Brecht inevitably rises up in any such quest. It seems to me that, while I cannot agree with his concept of the human situation, his solution of the problem of consciousness is admirably honest and theatrically powerful. One cannot watch his productions without knowing that he is at work not on the periphery of the contemporary dramatic problem, but directly upon its center—which is again the problem of consciousness.

VII

The Crucible, then, opened up a new prospect, and, like every work when completed, it left behind it unfinished business. It made a new freedom possible, and it also threw a certain light upon the difference between the modern playwriting problem of meaning and that of the age preceding the secularization of society. It is impossible to study the trial record without feeling the immanence of a veritable pantheon of life values in whose name both prosecution and defense could speak. The testimony is thick with reference to Biblical examples, and even as religious belief did nothing to temper cruelty—and in fact might be shown to have made the cruel crueler—it often served to raise this swirling and ludicrous mysticism to a level of high moral debate; and it did this despite the fact that most of the participants were unlettered, simple folk. They lived and would die more in the shadow of the other world than in the light of this one (and it is no mean irony that the theocratic prosecution should seek out the most religious people for its victims).

The longer I dwelt on the whole spectacle, the more clear became the failure of the present age to find a universal moral sanction, and the power of realism's hold on our theater was an aspect of this vacuum. For it began to appear that our inability to break more than the surfaces of realism reflected our inability—playwrights and audiences— to agree upon the pantheon of forces and values which must lie behind the realistic surfaces of life. In this light, realism, as a style, could seem to be a defense against the assertion of meaning. How strange a conclusion this is when one realizes that the same style seventy years ago was the prime instrument of those who sought to illuminate meaning in the theater, who divested their plays of fancy talk and improbable locales and bizarre characters in order to bring "life" onto the stage. And I wondered then what was true. Was it that we had come to fear the hard glare of life on the stage and under the guise of an aesthetic surfeited with realism were merely expressing our flight from reality? Or was our condemned realism only the counterfeit of the original, whose most powerful single impetus was to deal with man as a social animal? Any form can be drained of its informing purpose, can be used to convey, like the Tudor façades of college dormitories, the now vanished dignity and necessity of a former age in order to lend specious justification for a present hollowness. Was it realism that stood in the way of meaning or was it the counterfeit of realism?

Increasingly over the past five years and more the poetic plays, so-called, some of them much admired by all sorts of critics, were surprisingly full of what in the university years ago was called "fine" writing. If one heard less of the creak of plot machinery there was more of the squeak of self-pity, the humming of the poetic poseur, the new romance of the arbitrary and the uncompleted. For one, I had seen enough of the "borrowings" of the set, the plot, the time-shifting methods, and the lighting of *Death of a Salesman* to have an intimate understanding of how a vessel could be emptied and still purveyed to the public as new wine. Was realism called futile now because it needed to illuminate an exact meaning behind it, a conviction that was no more with us? Confusion, the inability to describe one's sense of a thing, often issues in a genuine poetry of feeling, and feeling was now raised up as the highest good and the ultimate attainment in drama. I had known that kind of victory myself with *Salesman;* but was there not another realm even higher, where feeling took awareness more openly by the hand and both equally ruled and were illuminated? I had found a kind of self-awareness in the bloody book of Salem and had thought that since the natural, realistic surface of that society was one already immersed in the questions of meaning and the relations of men to God, to write a realistic play of that world was already to write in a style beyond contemporary realism. That more than one critic had found the play "cold" when I had never written more passionately was by this time an acceptable and inevitable detail of my fate, for, while it will never confess to it, our theater is trained—actors, directors, audience, and critics—to take to its heart anything that does not prick the mind and to suspect everything that does not supinely reassure.

If *Salesman* was written in a mood of friendly partnership with the audience, *The Crucible* reminded me that we had not yet come to terms. The latter play has been produced more often than any of the others, and more successfully the more time elapses from the headline "McCarthyism" which it was supposed to be "about." I believe that on the night of its opening, a time when the gale from the Right was blowing at its fullest fury, it inspired a part of its audience with an unsettling fear and partisanship which deflected the sight of the real and inner theme, which, again, was the handing over of conscience to another, be it woman, the state, or a terror, and the realization that with conscience goes the person, the soul immortal, and the "name." That there was not one mention of this process in any review, favorable or not, was the measure of my sense of defeat, and the impulse to separate, openly and without concealment, the action of the next play, *A View from the Bridge*, from its generalized significance. The engaged narrator, in short, appeared.

I had heard its story years before, quite as it appears in the play, and quite as complete, and from time to time there were efforts to break up its arc, to reshuffle its action so that I might be able to find what there was in it which drew me back to it again and again—until it became like a fact in my mind, an unbreakable series of actions that went to create a closed circle impervious to all interpretation. It was written experimentally not only as a form, but as an exercise in interpretation. I found in myself a passionate detachment toward its story as one does toward a spectacle in which one is not engaged but which holds a fascination deriving from its monolithic perfection. If this had happened, and if I could not forget it after so many years, there must be some meaning in it for me, and I could write what had happened, why it had happened, and to one side, as it were, express as much as I knew of my sense of its meaning for me. Yet I wished to leave the action intact so that the onlooker could seize the right to interpret it entirely for himself and to accept or reject my reading of its significance.

That reading was the awesomeness of a passion which, despite its contradicting the self-interest of the individual it inhabits, despite every kind of warning, despite even its destruction of the moral beliefs of the individual, proceeds to magnify its power over him until it destroys him.

I have not dealt with the business of production until now because it is a subject large enough for separate treatment, but at this point it is unavoidable. *A View from the Bridge* was relatively a failure in New York when it was first produced; a revised version, published in this volume, became a great success in London not long afterward. The present version is a better play, I think, but not that much better; and the sharp difference between the impressions each of the productions created has a bearing on many themes that have been treated here.

Certain objective factors ought to be mentioned first. In New York, the play was preceded by *A Memory of Two Mondays*. That one of its leading performers on opening night completely lost his bearings and played in a state bordering on terror destroyed at the outset any hope that something human might be communicated by this evening in the theater. *A Memory of Two Mondays* was dismissed so thoroughly that in one of the reviews, and one of the most important, it was not even mentioned as having been played. By the time *A View from the Bridge* came on, I suppose the critics were certain that they were witnessing an aberration, for there had been no suggestion of any theatrical authority in the first play's performance. It was too much to hope that the second play could retrieve what had been so completely dissipated by the first.

A Memory of Two Mondays is a pathetic comedy; a boy works among people for a couple of years, shares their troubles, their victories, their hopes, and when it is time for him to be on his way he expects some memorable moment, some sign from them that he has been among them, that he has touched them and been touched by them. In the sea of routine that swells around them they barely note his departure. It is a kind of letter to that subculture where the sinews of the economy are rooted, that darkest Africa of our society from whose interior only the sketchiest messages ever reach our literature or our stage. I wrote it, I suppose, in part out of a desire to relive a sort of reality where necessity was open and bare; I hoped to define for myself the value of hope, why it must arise, as well as the heroism of those who know, at least, how to endure its absence. Nothing in this book was written with greater love, and for myself I love nothing printed here better than this play.

Nevertheless, the fact that it was seen as something utterly sad and hopeless as a comment on life quite astonishes me still. After all, from this endless, timeless, will-less environment, a boy emerges who will not accept its defeat or its mood as final, and literally takes himself off on a quest for a higher gratification. I suppose we simply do not want to see how empty the lives of so many of us are even when the depiction is made hopefully and not at all in despair. The play speaks not of obsession but of rent and hunger and the need for a little poetry in life and is entirely out of date in those respects—so much so that many took it for granted it had been written a long time ago and exhumed.

It shares with *A View from the Bridge* the impulse to present rather than to represent an interpretation of reality. Incident and character are set forth with the barest naïveté, and action is stopped abruptly while commentary takes its place. The organic impulse behind *Salesman,* for instance, and *All My Sons* is avowedly split apart; for a moment I was striving not to make people forget they were in a theater, not to obliterate an awareness of form, not to forge a pretense of life, but to be abrupt, clear, and explicit in setting forth fact as fact and art as art so that the sea of theatrical sentiment, which is so easily let in to drown all shape, meaning, and perspective, might be held back and some hard outline of a human dilemma be allowed to rise and stand. *A Memory of Two Mondays* has a story but not a plot, because the life it reflects appears to me to strip people of alternatives and will beyond a close and tight periphery in which they may exercise a meager choice.

The contradiction in my attitude toward these two plays and what was hoped for them is indicated by the experience of the two productions of *A View from the Bridge,* the one a failure and "cold," the other quite the opposite. In writing this play originally I obeyed the impulse to indicate, to telegraph, so to speak, rather than to explore and exploit what at first had seemed to me the inevitable and therefore unnecessary emotional implications of the conflict. The Broadway production's setting followed the same impulse, as it should have, and revealed nothing more than a platform to contain the living room, the sea behind the house, and a Grecian-style pediment overhanging the abstract doorway to the house. The austerity of the production, in a word, expressed the reticence of the writing.

This version was in one act because it had seemed to me that the essentials of the dilemma were all that was required, for I wished it to be kept distant from the empathic flood which a realistic portrayal of the same tale and characters might unloose.

On seeing the production played several times I came to understand that, like the plays written previously, this one was expressing a very personal preoccupation and that it was not at all apart from my own psychological life. I discovered my own relationships to what quite suddenly appeared as, in some part, an analogy to situations in my life, a distant analogy but a heartening proof that under the reticence of its original method my own spirit was attempting to speak. So that when a new production was planned for London it was not possible to let the original go on as it was. Now there were additional things to be said which it became necessary to say because I had come to the awareness that this play had not, as I had almost believed before, been "given" to me from without, but that my life had created it.

Therefore, many decisive alterations, small in themselves but nonetheless great in their over-all consequences, began to flow into the conception of the play. Perhaps the two most important were an altered attitude toward Eddie Carbone, the hero, and toward the two women in his life. I had originally conceived Eddie as a phenomenon, a rather awesome fact of existence, and I had kept a certain distance from involvement in his self-justifications. Consequently, he had appeared as a kind of biological sport, and to a degree a repelling figure not quite admissible into the human family. In revising the play it became possible to accept for myself the implication I had sought to make clear in the original version, which was that however one might dislike this man, who does all sorts of frightful things, he possesses or exemplifies the wondrous and humane fact that he too can be driven to what in the last analysis is a sacrifice of himself for his conception, however misguided, of right, dignity, and justice. In revising it I found it possible to move beyond contemplation of the man as a phenomenon into an acceptance for dramatic purposes of his aims themselves. Once this occurred the autonomous viewpoints of his wife and niece could be expressed more fully and, instead of remaining muted counterpoints to the march of Eddie's career, became involved forces pressing him forward or holding him back and eventually forming, in part, the nature of his disaster. The discovery of my own involvement in what I had written modified its original frieze-like character and the play moved closer toward realism and called up the emphatic response of its audience.

The conception of the new production was in accordance with this new perspective. Peter Brook, the London director, designed a set which was more realistically detailed than the rather bare, if beautiful, New York background, and at the same time emphasized the environment of the neighborhood. Its central idea was to bring the people of the neighborhood into the foreground of the action. Two high wings closed to form the face of the house where Eddie lived, a brick tenement, and when opened revealed a basement living room. Overhead and at the sides and across the back were stairways, fire escapes, passages, quite like a whole neighborhood constructed vertically. The easier economics of the London theater made it possible to use many more neighbors than the three or four extras we could hire in New York, and there was a temperate but nevertheless full flow of strangers across the stage and up and down its stairways and passages. The maturing of Eddie's need to destroy Rodolpho was consequently seen in the context which could make it of real moment, for the betrayal achieves its true proportions as it flies in the face of the mores administered by Eddie's conscience—which is also the conscience of his friends, co-workers, and neighbors and not just his own autonomous creation. Thus his "oddness" came to disappear as he was seen in context, as a creature of his environment as well as an exception to it; and where originally there had been only a removed sense of terror at the oncoming catastrophe, now there was pity and, I think, the kind of wonder which it had been my aim to create in the first place. It was finally possible to mourn this man.

Perhaps more than any other production experience, this helped to resolve for me one important question of form and meaning. I warn, however, that like everything else said here this is highly personal, and even as I avow it I know that there are other paths and other standards which can issue in a worthwhile kind of dramatic experience. For myself, the theater is above all else an instrument of passion. However important considerations of style and form have been to me, they are only means, tools to pry up the well-worn, "inevitable" surfaces of experience behind which swarm the living thoughts and feelings whose expression is the essential purpose of art. I have stood squarely in conventional realism; I have tried to expand it with an imposition of various forms in order to speak more directly, even more abruptly and nakedly of what has moved me behind the visible facades of life. Critics have given me more praise than a writer can reasonably hope for, and more condemnation than one dares believe one has the power to survive. There are certain distillations which remain after the dross rises to the top and boils away, certain old and new commitments which, despite the heat applied to them and the turmoil that has threatened to sweep them away, nevertheless remain, some of them purified.

A play, I think, ought to make sense to common-sense people. I know what it is to have been rejected by them, even unfairly so, but the only challenge worth the effort is the widest one and the tallest one, which is the people themselves. It is their innate conservatism which, I think, is and ought to be the barrier to excess in experiment and the exploitation of the bizarre, even as it is the proper aim of drama to break down the limits of conventional unawareness and acceptance of outmoded and banal forms.

By whatever means it is accomplished, the prime business of a play is to arouse the passions of its audience so that by the route of passion may be opened up new relationships between a man and men, and between men and Man. Drama is akin to the other inventions of man in that it ought to help us to know more, and not merely to spend our feelings.

The ultimate justification for a genuine new form is the new and heightened consciousness it creates and makes possible—a consciousness of causation in the light of known but hitherto inexplicable effects.

Not only in the drama, but in sociology, psychology, psychiatry, and religion, the past half century has created an almost overwhelming documentation of man as a nearly passive creation of environment and family-created psychological drives. If only from the dramatic point of view, this dictum cannot be accepted as final and "realistic" any more than man's ultimate position can be accepted as his efficient use by state or corporate apparatus. It is more "real," however, for drama to "liberate" itself from this vise by the route of romance and the spectacle of free will and a new heroic formula than it is "real" now to represent man's defeat as the ultimate implication of an overwhelming determinism.

Realism, heightened or conventional, is neither more nor less an artifice, a species of poetic symbolization, than any other form. It is merely more familiar in this age. If it is used as a covering of safety against the evaluation of life it must be overthrown, and for that reason above all the rest. But neither poetry nor liberation can come merely from a rearrangement of the lights or from leaving the skeletons of the flats exposed instead of covered by painted cloths; nor can it come merely from the masking of the human face or the transformation of speech into rhythmic verse, or from the expunging of common details of life's apparencies. A new poem on the stage is a new concept of relationships between the one and the many and the many and history, and to create it requires greater attention, not less, to the inexorable, common, pervasive conditions of existence in this time and this hour. Otherwise only a new self-indulgence is created, and it will be left behind, however poetic its surface.

A drama worthy of its time must first, knowingly or by instinctive means, recognize its major and most valuable traditions and where it has departed from them. Determinism, whether it is based on the iron necessities of economics or on psychoanalytic theory seen as a closed circle, is a contradiction of the idea of drama itself as drama has come down to us in its fullest developments. The idea of the hero, let alone the mere protagonist, is incompatible with a drama whose bounds are set in advance by the concept of an unbreakable trap. Nor is it merely that one wants arbitrarily to find a hero and a victory. The history of man is a ceaseless process of overthrowing one determinism to make way for another more faithful to life's changing relationships. And it is a process inconceivable without the existence of the will of man. His will is as much a fact as his defeat. Any determinism, even the most scientific, is only that stasis, that seemingly endless pause, before the application of man's will administering a new insight into causation.

The analogy to physics may not be out of place. The once-irreducible elements of matter, whose behavior was seen as fixed and remorseless, disintegrated under the controlled bombardment of atomic particles until so fine a perception as the scale of atomic weights appears as a relatively gross concept on the road to man's manipulation of the material world. More to the point: even as the paths, the powers, and the behavior of smaller and smaller elements and forces in nature are brought into the fields of measurement, we are faced with the dialectical irony that the act of measurement itself changes the particle being measured, so that we can know only what it is at the moment when it receives the impact of our rays, not what it was before it was struck. The idea of realism has become wedded to the idea that man is at best the sum of forces working upon him and of given psychological forces within him. Yet an innate value, an innate will, does in fact posit itself as real not alone because it is devoutly to be wished, but because, however closely he is measured and systematically accounted for, he is more than the sum of his stimuli and is unpredictable beyond a certain point. A drama, like a history, which stops at this point, the point of conditioning, is not reflecting reality. What is wanted, therefore, is not a poetry of escape from process and determinism, like that mood play which stops where feeling ends or that inverted romanticism which would mirror all the world in the sado-masochistic relationship. Nor will the heightening of the intensity of language alone yield the prize. A new poem will appear because a new balance has been struck which embraces both determinism and the paradox of will. If there is one unseen goal toward which every play in this book strives, it is that very discovery and its proof—that we are made and yet are more than what made us.

1957

Brewed in *The Crucible*

One afternoon last week I attended a rehearsal of the imminent Off-Broadway production of *The Crucible*. For the first time in the five years since its opening on Broadway, I heard its dialogue, and the experience awakened not merely memories but the desire to fire a discussion among us of certain questions a play like this ought to have raised.

Notoriously, there is what is called a chemistry in the theater, a fusion of play, performance, and audience temper which, if it does not take place, leaves the elements of an explosion cold and to one side of art. For the critics, this seems to be what happened with *The Crucible*. It was not condemned; it was set aside. A cold thing, mainly, it lay to one side of entertainment, to say nothing of art. In a word, I was told that I had not written another *Death of a Salesman*.

It is perhaps beyond my powers to make clear, but I had no desire to write another *Salesman*, and not because I lack love for that play but for some wider, less easily defined reasons that have to do with this whole question of cold and heat and, indeed, with the future of our drama altogether. It is the question of whether we—playwrights and audiences and critics—are to declare that we have reached the end, the last development of dramatic form. More specifically, the play designed to draw a tear; the play designed to "identify" the audience with its characters in the usual sense; the play that takes as its highest challenge the emotional relations of the family, for that, as it turns out, is what it comes to.

I was disappointed in the reaction to *The Crucible* not only for the obvious reasons but because no critic seemed to sense what I was after. In 1953 McCarthyism probably helped to make it appear that the play was bounded on all sides by its arraignment of the witch hunt. The political trajectory was so clear—a fact of which I am a little proud—that what to me were equally if not more important elements were totally ignored. The new production, appearing in a warmer climate, may, I hope, flower, and these inner petals may make their appropriate appearance.

What I say now may appear more technical than a writer has any business talking about in public. But I do not think it merely a question of technique to say that with all its excellences the kind of play we have come to accept without effort or question is standing at a dead end. What "moves" us is coming to be a narrower and narrower aesthetic fragment of life. I have shown, I think, that I am not unaware of psychology or immune to the fascinations of the neurotic hero, but I believe that it is no longer possible to contain the truth of the human situation so totally within a single man's guts as the bulk of our plays presuppose. The documentation of man's loneliness is not in itself and for itself ultimate wisdom, and the form this documentation inevitably assumes in playwriting is not the ultimate dramatic form.

I was drawn to write *The Crucible* not merely as a response to McCarthyism. It is not any more an attempt to cure witch hunts than *Salesman* is a plea for the improvement of conditions for traveling men, *All My Sons* a plea for better inspection of airplane parts, or *A View from the Bridge* an attack upon the Immigration Bureau. *The Crucible* is, internally, *Salesman*'s blood brother. It is examining the questions I was absorbed with before—the conflict between a man's raw deeds and his conception of himself; the question of whether conscience is in fact an organic part of the human being, and what happens when it is handed over not merely to the state or the mores of the time but to one's friend or wife. The big difference, I think, is that *The Crucible* sought to include a higher degree of consciousness than the earlier plays.

I believe that the wider the awareness, the felt knowledge, evoked by a play, the higher it must stand as art. I think our drama is far behind our lives in this respect. There is a lot wrong with the twentieth century, but one thing is right with it—we are aware as no generation was before of the larger units that help make us and destroy us. The city, the nation, the world, and now the universe are never far beyond our most intimate sense of life. The vast majority of us know now—not merely as knowledge but as feeling, feeling capable of expression in art—that we are being formed, that our alternatives in life are not absolutely our own, as the romantic play inevitably must presuppose. But the response of our plays, of our dramatic form itself, is to faint, so to speak, before the intricacies of man's wider relationships and to define him further and redefine him as essentially alone in a world he never made.

The form, the shape, the meaning of *The Crucible* were all compounded out of the faith of those who were hanged. They were asked to be lonely and they refused. They were asked to deny their belief in a God of all men, not merely a god each individual could manipulate to his interests. They were asked to call a phantom real and to deny their touch with reality. It was not good to cast this play, to form it so that the psyche of the hero should emerge so "commonly" as to wipe out of mind the process itself, the spectacle of that faith and the knowing will which these people paid for with their lives.

The "heat" infusing this play is therefore of a different order from that which draws tears and the common identifications. And it was designed to be of a different order. In a sense, I felt, our situation had thrown us willy-nilly into a new classical period. Classical in the sense that the social scheme, as of old, had reached the point of rigidity where it had become implacable as a consciously known force working in us and upon us. Analytical psychology, when so intensely exploited as to reduce the world to the size of a man's abdomen and equate his fate with his neurosis, is a re-emergence of romanticism. It is inclined to deny all outer forces until man is only his complex. It presupposes an autonomy in the human character that, in a word, is false. A neurosis is not a fate but an effect. There is a higher wisdom, and if truly there is not, there is still no aesthetic point in repeating something so utterly known, or in doing better what has been done so well before.

For me *The Crucible* was a new beginning, the beginning of an attempt to embrace a wider field of vision, a field wide enough to contain the whole of our current awareness. It was not so much to move ahead of the audience but to catch up with what it commonly knows about the way things are and how they get that way. In a word, we commonly know so much more than our plays let on. When we can put together what we do know with what we feel, we shall find a new kind of theater in our hands. *The Crucible* was written as it was in order to bring me, and the audience, closer to that theater and what I imagine can be an art more ample than any of us has dared to strive for, the art of Man among men, Man amid his works.

1958

The Shadows of the Gods

I see by the papers that I am going to talk today on the subject of the literary influences on my work. It is probably a good subject, but it isn't what Harold Clurman and I discussed when he asked if I would speak here. What he had in mind was something else. I am supposed to widen your horizons by telling something about the frame of reference I used when I started to write, and that included books I read, or music I heard, or whatnot.

I doubt whether anybody can widen horizons by making a speech. It is possible, perhaps, by writing a play. Still, I may be able to suggest an approach to our theater which—even if it is not valid for everyone—will not be quite the same as that of the various critics; and if nothing else is accomplished here maybe it will at least appear that there is another way of looking at drama.

Tolstoy wrote a book called *What Is Art?* The substance of it is that almost all the novels, plays, operas, and paintings were not art but vanity, and that the rhythm with which a Russian peasant swung a scythe was more artful than all the dance on Moscow stages, and the paintings of peasants on the sides of their wagons more genuine than all the paintings in the museums. The thing that disheartened him most, I believe, was that inevitably artistic creation became a profession, and the artist who may have originated as a natural quickly became self-conscious and exploited his own gifts for money, prestige, or just for want of an honest profession.

Yet, Tolstoy went on writing. The truth, I suppose, is that soon or late we are doomed to know what we are doing, and we may as well accept it as a fact when it comes. But the self-knowledge of professionalism develops only as a result of having repeated the same themes in different plays. And for a whole theater the time for self-appraisal comes in the same way. We are, I believe, at the end of a period. Certain things have been repeated sufficiently for one to speak of limitations which have to be recognized if our theater is not to become absurd, repetitious, and decayed.

Now one can no sooner speak of limitations than the question of standards arises. What seems like a limitation to one man may be an area as wide as the world to another. My standard, my viewpoint, whether it appears arbitrary, or true and inevitable, did not spring out of my head unshaped by any outside force. I began writing plays in the midst of what Allan Seager, an English teacher friend of mine at Michigan, calls one of the two genuinely national catastrophes in American history—the Great Depression of the thirties. The other was the Civil War. It is almost bad manners to talk about depression these days, but through no fault or effort of mine it was the ground upon which I learned to stand.

There are a thousand things to say about that time but maybe one will be evocative enough. Until 1929 I thought things were pretty solid. Specifically, I thought—like most

Americans—that somebody was in charge. I didn't know exactly who it was, but it was probably a businessman, and he was a realist, a no-nonsense fellow, practical, honest, responsible. In 1929 he jumped out of the window. It was bewildering. His banks closed and refused to open again, and I had twelve dollars in one of them. More precisely, I happened to have withdrawn my twelve dollars to buy a racing bike a friend of mine was bored with, and the next day the Bank of the United States closed. I rode by and saw the crowds of people standing at the brass gates. Their money was inside! And they couldn't get it. And they would never get it. As for me, I felt I had the thing licked.

But about a week later I went into the house to get a glass of milk and when I came out my bike was gone. Stolen. It must have taught me a lesson. Nobody could escape that disaster.

I did not read many books in those days. The depression was my book. Years later I could put together what in those days were only feelings, sensations, impressions. There was the sense that everything had dried up. Some plague of invisible grasshoppers was eating money before you could get your hands on it. You had to be a Ph.D. to get a job in Macy's. Lawyers were selling ties. Everybody was trying to sell something to everybody else. A past president of the Stock Exchange was sent to jail for misappropriating trust funds. They were looking for runaway financiers all over Europe and South America. Practically everything that had been said and done up to 1929 turned out to be a fake. It turns out that there had never been anybody in charge.

What the time gave me, I think now, was a sense of an invisible world. A reality had been secretly accumulating its climax according to its hidden laws to explode illusion at the proper time. In that sense 1929 was our Greek year. The gods had spoken, the gods, whose wisdom had been set aside or distorted by a civilization that was to go onward and upward on speculation, gambling, graft, and the dog eating the dog. Before the crash I thought "Society" meant the rich people in the Social Register. After the crash it meant the constant visits of strange men who knocked on our door pleading for a chance to wash the windows, and some of them fainted on the back porch from hunger. In Brooklyn, New York. In the light of weekday afternoons.

I read books after I was seventeen, but already, for good or ill, I was not patient with every kind of literature. I did not believe, even then, that you could tell about a man without telling about the world he was living in, what he did for a living, what he was like not only at home or in bed but on the job. I remember now reading novels and wondering, What do these people do for a living? When do they work? I remember asking the same questions about the few plays I saw. The hidden laws of fate lurked not only in the characters of people, but equally if not more imperiously in the world beyond the family parlor. Out there were the big gods, the ones whose disfavor could turn a proud and prosperous and dignified man into a frightened shell of a man whatever he thought of himself, and whatever he decided or didn't decide to do.

So that by force of circumstance I came early and unawares to be fascinated by sheer process itself. How things connected. How the native personality of a man was changed by his world, and the harder question, how he could in turn change his world. It was not academic. It was not even a literary or a dramatic question at first. It was the practical problem of what to believe in order to proceed with life. For instance, should one admire success—for there were successful people even then. Or should one always see through it as an illusion which only existed to be blown up, and its owner destroyed and humiliated? Was success immoral?—when everybody else in the neighborhood not only had no Buick but no breakfast? What to believe?

An adolescent must feel he is on the side of justice. That is how human indignation is constantly renewed. But how hard it was to feel justly, let alone to think justly. There were people in the neighborhood saying that it had all happened because the workers had not gotten paid enough to buy what they had produced, and that the solution was to have Socialism, which would not steal their wages any more the way the bosses did and brought on this depression. It was a wonderful thought with which I nearly drove my grandfather crazy. The trouble with it was that he and my father and most of the men I loved would have to be destroyed.

Enough of that. I am getting at only one thought. You can't understand anything unless you understand its relations to its context. It was necessary to feel beyond the edges of things. That much, for good or ill, the Great Depression taught me. It made me impatient with anything, including art, which pretends that it can exist for its own sake and still be of any prophetic importance. A thing becomes beautiful to me as it becomes internally and externally organic. It becomes beautiful because it promises to remove some of my helplessness before the chaos of experience. I think one of the reasons I became a playwright was that in dramatic form everything must be openly organic, deeply organized, articulated from a living center. I used long ago to keep a book in which I would talk to myself. One of the aphorisms I wrote was, "The structure of a play is always the story of how the birds came home to roost." The hidden will be unveiled; the inner laws of reality will announce themselves; I was defining my impression of 1929 as well as dramatic structure.

When I was still in high school and ignorant, a book came into my hands, God knows how, *The Brothers Karamazov*. It must have been too rainy that day to play ball. I began reading it, thinking it was a detective story. I have always blessed Dostoevsky for writing in a way that any fool could understand. The book, of course, has no connection with the depression. Yet it became closer, more intimate to me, despite the Russian names, than the papers I read every day. I never thought to ask why, then. I think now it was because of the father and son conflict, but something more. It is always probing beyond its particular scenes and characters for the hidden laws, for the place where the gods ruminate and decide, for the rock upon which one may stand without illusion, a free man. Yet the characters appear liberated from any systematic causation.

The same yearning I felt all day for some connection with a hidden logic was the yearning in this book. It gave me no answers but it showed that I was not the only one who was full of this kind of questioning, for I did not believe—and could not after 1929—in the reality I saw with my eyes. There was an invisible world of cause and effect, mysterious, full of surprises, implacable in its course. The book said to me:

"There is a hidden order in the world. There is only one reason to live. It is to discover its nature. The good are those who do this. The evil say that there is nothing beyond the face of the world, the surface of reality. Man will only find peace when he learns to live humanly, in conformity to those laws which decree his human nature."

Only slightly less ignorant, I read Ibsen in college. Later I heard that I had been reading problem plays. I didn't know what that meant. I was told they were about social problems, like the inequality of women. The women I knew about had not been even slightly unequal; I saw no such problem in *A Doll's House*. I connected with Ibsen not because he wrote about problems, but because he was illuminating process. Nothing in his plays exists for itself, not a smart line, not a gesture that can be isolated. It was breath-taking.

From his work—read again and again with new wonders cropping up each time—as well as through Dostoevsky's, I came to an idea of what a writer was supposed to be. These two issued the license, so to speak, the only legitimate one I could conceive, for presuming to write at all. One had the right to write because other people needed news of the inner world, and if they went too long without such news they would go mad with the chaos of their lives. With the greatest of presumption I conceived that the great writer was the destroyer of chaos, a man privy to the councils of the hidden gods who administer the hidden laws that bind us all and destroy us if we do not know them. And chaos, for one thing, was life lived oblivious of history.

As time went on, a lot of time, it became clear to me that I was not only reporting to others but to myself first and foremost. I wrote not only to find a way into the world but to hold it away from me so that sheer, senseless events would not devour me.

I read the Greeks and the German Expressionists at the same time and quite by accident. I was struck by the similarity of their dramatic means in one respect—they are designed to present the hidden forces, not the characteristics of the human beings playing out those forces on the stage. I was told that the plays of Aeschylus must be read primarily on a religious level, that they are only lay dramas to us now because we no longer believe. I could not understand this because one did not have to be religious to see in our own disaster the black outlines of a fate that was not human, nor of the heavens either, but something in between. Like the howling of a mob, for instance, which is not a human sound but is nevertheless composed of human voices combining until a metaphysical force of sound is created.

I read O'Neill in those days as I read everything else—looking to see how meaning was achieved. He said something in a press conference which in the context of those years seemed to be a challenge to the social preoccupations of the thirties. He said, "I am not interested in the relations of man to man, but of man to God." I thought that very reactionary. Until, after repeated and repeated forays into one play of my own after another, I understood that he meant what I meant, not ideologically but dramatically speaking. I too had a religion, however unwilling I was to be so backward. A religion with no gods but with godlike powers. The powers of economic crisis and political imperatives which had twisted, torn, eroded, and marked everything and everyone I laid eyes on.

I read for a year in economics, discovered my professors dispensing their prejudices which were no better founded than my own; worse yet, an economics that could measure the giant's footsteps but could not look into his eyes.

I read for a year in history, and lost my last illusion on a certain afternoon at two-thirty. In a lecture class a student at question time rose to ask the professor if he thought Hitler would invade Austria. For fifteen minutes the professor, by no means a closet historian but a man of liberal and human interests, proved why it was impossible for Hitler to invade Austria. It seems there were treaties forbidding this which went back to the Congress of Vienna, side agreements older than that, codicils, memoranda, guarantees—and to make a long story short, when we got out at three o'clock there was an extra being hawked. Hitler had invaded Austria. I gave up history. I knew damned well Hitler was going to invade Austria.

In that sense it was a good time to be growing up because nobody else knew anything either. All the rules were nothing but continuations of older rules. The old plays create new plays, and the old histories create new histories. The best you could say of the academic disciplines was that they were breathlessly running after the world. It is when life creates a new play that the theater moves its limbs and wakens from its mesmerized fixation on ordinary reality; when the present is caught and made historic.

I began by speaking of standards. I have labored the point long enough to state it openly. My standard is, to be sure, derived from my life in the thirties, but I believe that it is as old as the drama itself and was merely articulated to me in the accent of the thirties. I ask of a play, first, the dramatic question, the carpenter-builder's question—What is its ultimate force? How can that force be released? Second, the human question—What is its ultimate relevancy to the survival of the race?

Before proceeding with these two queries I want to jump ahead to say that my object remains to throw some light on our dramatic situation today, the challenge, so to speak, which I think lies before us. I will pause for a moment or two in order to say a few things about a writer who has been, along with Ibsen, an enormous influence upon our theater whether we know it or not.

It is hard to imagine any playwright reading Chekhov without envying one quality of his plays. It is his balance. In this, I think he is closer to Shakespeare than any dramatist I know. There is less distortion by the exigencies of the telescoping of time in the theater, there is less stacking of the cards, there is less fear of the ridiculous, there is less fear of the heroic. His touch is tender, his eye is warm, so warm that the Chekhovian legend in our theater has become that of an almost sentimental man and writer whose plays are elegies, postscripts to a dying age. In passing, it must be said that he was not the only Russian writer who seemed to be dealing with all his characters as though he were related to them. It is a quality not of Chekhov alone but of much Russian literature, and I mention it both to relate him to this mood and to separate him from it.

Chekhov is important to us because he has been used as a club against two opposing views of drama. Sometimes he seems—as he evidently does to Walter Kerr—to have encouraged dramatists to an overly emphasized introspection if not self-pity. To this kind of viewpoint, he is the playwright of inaction, of perverse self-analysis, of the dark blue mood. In the thirties he was condemned by many on the Left as lacking in militancy, and he was confused with the people he was writing about.

His plays, I think, will endure, but in one sense he is as useless as a model as the frock coat and the horse and carriage. Our civilization is immeasurably more strident than his and to try to recreate his mood would be to distort our own. But more important, I think, is that—whatever the miseries of his characters—their careers are played out against a tradition of which they are quite conscious, a tradition whose destruction is regarded by them as the setting of their woes. Whether or not it was ever objectively true is beside the point, of course; the point is that they can look back to a time when the coachman was young and happy to be a coachman, when there was a large, firmly entrenched family evenly maturing over the slow-passing years, when, in a word, there was an order dominated by human relations. Now—to put it much more briefly than its complexity warrants—the Cherry Orchard is cut down by a real estate man, who, nice fellow that he may be, simply has to clear land for a development.

The closest we have ever gotten to this kind of relation to a tradition is in Tennessee Williams, when a disorganized refugee from a plantation arrives in our civilization some eighty years after the plantation itself has been destroyed. We cannot reproduce Chekhov if only because we are long past the time when we believe in the primacy of human relations over economic necessity. We have given up what was still in his time a live struggle. We believe—or at least take it completely for granted—that wherever there is a conflict between human relations and necessity, the outcome is not only inevitable but even progressive when necessity wins, as it evidently must.

The main point I would make here in relation to our theater, however, is that while Chekhov's psychological insight is given full play, and while his greatest interest is overwhelmingly in the spiritual life of his characters, his farthest vision does not end with their individual psychology. Here is a speech to remind you—and it is only one of a great many which do not at all fit with the conventional characterization of these allegedly wispy plays —concerned with nothing more than realistic character drawing and introspection. In *Three Sisters* Vershinin speaks:

> What else am I to say to you at parting? What am I to theorize about? (Laughs) Life is hard. It seems to many of us blank and hopeless; but yet we must admit that it goes on getting clearer and easier, and it looks as though the time were not far off when it will be full of happiness. (Looks at his watch.) It's time for me to go! In old days men were absorbed in wars, filling all their existence with marches, raids, victories, but now all that is a thing of the past, leaving behind it a great void which there is so far nothing to fill; humanity is searching for it passionately, and of course will find it. Ah, if only it could be quickly. If, don't you know, industry were united with culture and culture with industry.... (Looks at his watch.) But, I say, it's time for me to go....

In other words, these plays are not mere exercises in psychology. They are woven around a very critical point of view, a point of view not only toward the characters, but toward the social context in which they live, a point of view which—far from being some arbitrary angle, as we have come to call such things—is their informing principle. I haven't the time here to investigate the plays one by one and it is not the business of the moment. All I have said comes down to this: that with all our technical dexterity, with all our lighting effects, sets, and a theater more solvent than any I know about, yes, with all our freedom to say what we will—our theater is narrowing its vision year by year, it is repeating well what it has done well before.

I can hear already my critics complaining that I am asking for a return to what they call problem plays. That criticism is important only because it tells something important about the critic. It means that he can only conceive of man as a private entity, and his social relations as something thrown at him, something "affecting" him only when he is conscious of society. I hope I have made one thing clear to this point—and it is that society is inside of man and man is inside society, and you cannot even create a truthfully drawn psychological entity on the stage until you understand his social relations and their power to make him what he is and to prevent him from being what he is not. The fish is in the water and the water is in the fish.

I believe we have arrived in America at the end of a period because we are repeating ourselves season after season, despite the fact that nobody seems to be aware of it. In almost every success there is a striking similarity of mood and of mode. There is one play after another in which a young person, usually male, usually sensitive, is driven either to self-destructive revolt or impotency by the insensitivity of his parents, usually the father. A quick and by no means exhaustive look brings to mind, *Look Homeward Angel, Dark at the Top of the Stairs, Cat on a Hot Tin Roof, A Hatful of Rain*. I wish to emphasize at once that I am not here as a critic of these plays as plays, nor do I intend to equate their worth one with the other. I am rather looking at them as a stranger, a man from Mars, who would surely have to wonder at so pervasive a phenomenon.

Now I am not saying there is anything "wrong" with this theme, if only because I have written more than once on it myself. It lies at the heart of all human development, and its echoes go to *Hamlet,* to *Romeo and Juliet,* to *Oedipus Rex.* What I am critical of is that our theater is dealing almost exclusively with affects. Where the parent stands the world ends, and where the son stands is where the world should begin but cannot because he is either made impotent, or he revolts, or more often runs away. What is there wrong with this? Does it not happen all the time? It must, or so many playwrights would not be repeating the theme, and it would not have the fascination it evidently does for so many audiences.

What is wrong is not the theme but its failure to extend itself so as to open up ultimate causes. The fact, for one thing, is not merely the frustration of the children, or even the bankruptcy of moral authority in the parents, but also their common awareness in our time of some hidden, ulterior causation for this. If only because this theme is so recurrent, the phenomenon has the right to be called a generalized social one. Therefore, it is proper in this instance to say that the potential vision of these plays is not fulfilled and their potential aesthetic size and perfection is left unrealized. And perhaps even more important, there is implicit in this cut-down vision a decay of nerve, a withering of power to grasp the whole world on the stage and shake it to its foundations as it is the historic job of high drama to do. The mystery of our condition remains, but we know much more about it than appears on our stage.

I am not asking for anything new, but something as old as the Greek drama. When Chekhov, that almost legendary subjectivist, has Vershinin—and many others in his plays—objectifying the social questions which his play has raised, he is merely placing himself within the great tradition which set its art works fully in view of the question of the survival of the race. It is we who are the innovators, or more precisely, the sports, when we refuse to reflect on our stage a level of objective awareness at least as great as exists commonly in our lives outside.

I am asking for the world to be brought into the stage family, to be sure, but I begin and I end from the viewpoint of the dramatist, the dramatist seeking to intensify the power of his plays and his theater. There is something dramatically wrong, for instance, when an audience can see a play about the Nazi treatment of a group of Jews hiding in an attic, and come away feeling the kind of—I can only call it gratification—which the audiences felt after seeing *The Diary of Anne Frank*. Seeing this play I was not only an audience or even a Jew, but a dramatist, and it puzzled me why it was all so basically reassuring to watch what must have been the most harrowing kind of suffering in real life.

As a constructor of plays I had nothing technical of consequence to add. And I found myself putting to this play the question I have put to you—what is its relevancy to the survival of the race? Not the American race, or the Jewish race, or the German race, but the human race. And I believe the beginning of an answer has emerged. It is that with all its truth the play lacks the kind of spread vision, the over-vision beyond its characters and their problems, which could have illuminated not merely the cruelty of Nazism but something even more terrible. We see no Nazis in this play. Again, as with the plays I have mentioned, it is seen from the viewpoint of the adolescent, a poignant and human viewpoint to be sure, but surely a limited one. The approach of the Nazi is akin to the approach of a childhood Demon.

What was necessary in this play to break the hold of reassurance upon the audience, and to make it match the truth of life, was that we should see the bestiality in our own hearts, so that we should know how we are brothers not only to these victims but to the Nazis, so that the ultimate terror of our lives should be faced—namely our own sadism, our own ability to obey orders from above, our own fear of standing firm on humane principle against the obscene power of the mass organization. Another dimension was waiting to be opened up behind this play, a dimension covered with our own sores, a dimension revealing us to ourselves.

Once this dimension had been unveiled we could not have watched in the subtly perverse comfort of pathos; our terror would no longer be for these others but for ourselves, once that part of ourselves which covertly conspires with destruction was made known. Then, for one thing, even tragedy would have been possible, for the issue would not have been why the Nazis were so cruel, but why human beings—ourselves, us—are so cruel. The pathetic is the refusal or inability to discover and face ultimate relevancy for the race; it is therefore a shield against ultimate dramatic effect.

In this instance the objection will be raised that I am demanding a different kind of play than *Diary* was intended to be. I am. I make this demand, if one can presume so far, even though I believe that the original book was very faithfully followed by the dramatists who adapted it. Who am I to argue with the martyred girl who wrote the original document? Her right to her point of view is irreproachable. I agree that it is irreproachable. I repeat, as a matter of fact, what I said earlier—that the adolescent viewpoint is and should be precious to us. In this instance, first of all, I am treating the play as a separate work, as another play opening in New York. Secondly, I am using it to show that even when the adolescent viewpoint is most perfectly announced and movingly dramatized, it nevertheless has a nature, an inner dynamic which prevents it from seeing what it cannot see and still be itself.

It is necessary, in short, to be able to appreciate a thing for what it is, and to see what it is not and what it might be. Our present failure to distinguish between low and high altitude, between amplitude and relative narrowness, leaves us—as it leaves the critics for the most part—at the mercy of "affects"; which is to say that if a small play of minor proportions achieves its affects well, it is as good as a large play of greater proportions.

One consequence of this inability to distinguish between the sizes of things, so to speak, is to condemn ourselves ultimately to minor art. For it is always more likely that small things of shallow breath will show fewer defects than the large, and if the perfecting of affects, regardless of their larger relevancies or irrelevancies, is to be our criterion, as it threatens now to be, we shall turn the theater into a kind of brooding conceit, a show-place for our tricks, a proving ground for our expertise, a shallows protected from the oceans.

I repeat that I am not here as a critic of individual plays but of the dramatic viewpoint which I believe imposes by no means unbreakable limitations upon them. They are limitations which tend to force repetitions of mood, mode, style, yes, and even the lighting and setting of one play after another, even as they are written by writers in their individual isolation. While on the one hand we prize the original work, the new creation, we are surprisingly unconscious of the sameness of so much that passes for new. But the new, the truly new dramatic poem will be, as it has always been, a new organization of the meaning, the generalized significance of the action.

A moment ago I threw together several plays for the purposes of this discussion, one of which I should like now to set apart. In every way but one *Cat on a Hot Tin Roof* differs from *Diary of Anne Frank,* as well as from the others mentioned. Williams has a long reach and a genuinely dramatic imagination. To me, however, his greatest value, his aesthetic valor, so to speak, lies in his very evident determination to unveil and engage the widest range of causation conceivable to him. He is constantly pressing his own limit. He creates shows, as all of us must, but he possesses the restless inconsolability with his solutions which is inevitable in a genuine writer. In my opinion, he is properly discontented with the total image some of his plays have created. And it is better that way, for when the image is complete and self-contained it is usually arbitrary and false.

It is no profound thing to say that a genuine work of art creates not completion, but a sustained image of things in tentative balance. What I say now is not to describe that balance as a false or illusory one, but one whose weighing containers, so to speak, are larger and greater than what has been put into them. I think, in fact, that in *Cat on a Hot Tin Roof,* Williams in one vital respect made an assault upon his own viewpoint in an attempt to break it up and reform it on a wider circumference.

Essentially it is a play seen from the viewpoint of Brick, the son. He is a lonely young man sensitized to injustice. Around him is a world whose human figures partake in various ways of grossness, Philistinism, greed, money-lust, power-lust. And—with his mean-spirited brother as an example—it is a world senselessly reproducing itself through ugly children conceived without the grace of genuine affection, and delivered not so much as children but as inheritors of great wealth and power, the new perpetuators of inequity.

In contrast, Brick conceives of his friendship with his dead friend as an idealistic, even gallant and valorous and somehow morally elevated one, a relationship in which nothing was demanded, but what was given was given unasked, beyond the realm of price, of value, even of materiality. He clings to this image as to a banner of purity to flaunt against the world, and more precisely, against the decree of nature to reproduce himself, to become in turn the father, the master of the earth, the administrator of the tainted and impure world. It is a world in whose relations—especially between the sexes—there is always the element of the transaction, of materiality.

If the play confined itself to the psychiatry of impotence, it could be admired or dismissed as such. Williams's plays are never really that, but here in addition, unlike his other plays, there is a father. Not only is he the head of a family, but the very image of power, of materiality, of authority. And the problem this father is given is how he can infuse his own personality into the prostrated spirit of his son so that a hand as strong as his own will guide his fortune when he is gone—more particularly, so that his own immortality, his civilization will be carried on.

As the play was produced, without the surface realism of living-room, bedroom, walls, conventional light—in an atmosphere, instead, of poetic conflict, in a world that is eternal and not merely this world—it provided more evidence that Williams's preoccupation extends beyond the surface realities of the relationships, and beyond the psychiatric connotations of homosexuality and impotence. In every conceivable fashion there was established a goal beyond sheer behavior. We were made to see, I believe, an ulterior pantheon of forces and a play of symbols as well as of characters.

It is well known that there was difficulty in ending this play, and I am certainly of no mind to try it. I believe I am not alone in saying that the resolutions wherein Brick finally regains potency was not understandable on the stage. But my feeling is that even if this were more comprehensively motivated so that the psychiatric development of the hero were persuasively completed, it in itself could not embrace the other questions raised in the play.

We are persuaded as we watch this play that the world around Brick is in fact an unworthy collection of unworthy motives and greedy actions. Brick refuses to participate in this world, but he cannot destroy it either or reform it and he turns against himself. The question here, it seems to me, the ultimate question is the right of society to renew itself when it is, in fact, unworthy. There is, after all, a highly articulated struggle for material power going on here. There is literally and symbolically a world to win or a world to forsake and damn. A viewpoint is necessary, if one is to raise such a tremendous issue, a viewpoint capable of encompassing it. This is not a study in cynicism where the writer merely exposes the paradoxes of all sides and is content to end with a joke. Nor, again, is it mere psychiatry, aiming to show us how a young man reclaims his sexuality. There is a moral judgment hanging over this play which never quite comes down. A tempting analogy would be that of a Hamlet who takes up his sword and neither fights nor refuses to fight but marries an Ophelia who does not die.

Brick, despite his resignation from the race, has thrown a challenge to it which informs the whole play, a challenge which the father and the play both recognize and ignore. But if it is the central challenge of the play—as the play seems to me to emphasize—then the world must either prove its worthiness to survive, or its unworthiness must lie dramatically proved, to justify Brick's refusal to renew it—or, like a Hamlet who will neither do battle nor put down his sword, it must condemn Brick to inaction and perhaps indifference to its fate.

Because of Williams's marvelous ability, I for one would be willing to listen—and perhaps to him alone—even as he pronounced ultimate doom upon the race—a race exemplified in his play by the meanest of motives. This is a foundation grand enough, deep enough, and worthy of being examined remorselessly and perhaps even shaken and smashed. Again, as with *The Diary of Anne Frank,* had the implicit challenge ripened, we should no longer be held by our curiosity or our pity for someone else, but by that terror which comes when we must in truth justify our most basic assumptions. The father in this play, I think, must be forced to the wall in justification of his world, and Brick must be forced to his wall in justification of his condemning that world to the ultimate biological degree. The question of society's right to insist upon its renewal when it is unworthy is a question of tragic grandeur, and those who have asked this question of the world know full well the lash of its retaliation.

Quite simply, what I am asking is that the play pursue the ultimate development of the very questions it asks. But for such a pursuit, the viewpoint of the adolescent is not enough. The father, with the best will in the world, *is* faced with the problem of a son he loves best refusing to accept him and his spirit. Worse yet, it is to the least worthy son that that spirit must be handed if all else fails. Above the father's and the son's individual viewpoints the third must emerge, the viewpoint, in fact, of the audience, the society, and the race. It is a viewpoint that must weigh, as I have said, the question of its own right to biological survival—and one thing more, the question of the fate of the sensitive and the just in an impure world of power. After all, ultimately someone must take charge; this is the tragic dilemma, but it is beyond the viewpoint of adolescence. Someone must administer inequity or himself destroy that world by refusing to renew it, or by doing battle against its injustice, or by declaring his indifference or his cynicism. The terms upon which Brick's potency returns are left waiting to be defined and the play is thus torn from its climax.

Again, I am not criticizing this play, but attempting to mark the outlines of its viewpoint—which is an extension of our theater's viewpoint to its present limits. Nor is this an entirely new and unheralded idea. Be it Tolstoy, Dostoevsky, Hemingway, you, or I, we are formed in this world when we are sons and daughters and the first truths we know throw us into conflict with our fathers and mothers. The struggle for mastery—for the freedom of manhood or womanhood as opposed to the servility of childhood—is the struggle not only to overthrow authority but to reconstitute it anew. The viewpoint of the adolescent is precious because it is revolutionary and insists upon justice. But in truth the parent, powerful as he appears, is not the source of injustice but its deputy.

A drama which refuses or is unable to reach beyond this facade is denying itself its inherited chance for greatness. The best of our theater is standing tiptoe, striving to see over the shoulders of father and mother. The worst is exploiting and wallowing in the self-pity of adolescence and obsessive keyhole sexuality. The way out, as the poet has said, is always *through.* We will not find it by huddling closer to the center of the charmed circle, by developing more and more naturalism in our dialogue and our acting, that "slice-of-life" reportage which is to life what an overheard rumor is to truth; nor by setting up an artificial poetic style, nor by once again shocking the householders with yet other unveilings of domestic relations and their hypocrisies. Nor will we break out by writing problem plays. There is an organic aesthetic, a tracking of impulse and causation from the individual to the world and back again which must be reconstituted. We are exhausting the realm of affects, which is the world of adolescence taken pure.

The shadow of a cornstalk on the ground is lovely, but it is no denial of its loveliness to see as one looks on it that it is telling the time of the day, the position of the earth and the sun, the size of our planet and its shape, and perhaps even the length of its life and ours among the stars. A viewpoint bounded by affects cannot engage the wider balance of our fates where the great climaxes are found.

In my opinion, if our stage does not come to pierce through affects to an evaluation of the world it will contract to a lesser psychiatry and an inexpert one at that. We shall be confined to writing an *Oedipus* without the pestilence, an *Oedipus* whose catastrophe is private and unrelated to the survival of his people, an *Oedipus* who cannot tear out his eyes because there will be no standard by which he can judge himself; an *Oedipus*, in a word, who on learning of his incestuous marriage, instead of tearing out his eyes, will merely wipe away his tears thus to declare his loneliness. Again, where a drama will not engage its relevancy for the race, it will halt at pathos, that tempting shield against ultimate dramatic effect, that counterfeit of meaning.

Symbolically, as though sensing that we are confined, we have removed the doors and walls and ceilings from our sets. But the knowing eye still sees them there. They may truly disappear and the stage will open to that symbolic stature, that realm where the father is after all not the final authority, that area where he is the son too, that area where religions are made and the giants live, only when we see beyond parents, who are, after all, but the shadows of the gods.

A great drama is a great jurisprudence. Balance is all. It will evade us until we can once again see man as whole, until sensitivity and power, justice and necessity are utterly face to face, until authority's justifications and rebellion's too are tracked even to those heights where the breath fails, where—because the largest point of view as well as the smaller has spoken—truly the rest is silence.

1958

On Adaptations

The presentation in the same week of television adaptations of *Don Quixote* and *A Doll's House* raises questions concerning the propriety of laying hands on classic works without investigating the full depth of responsibility entailed.

The vast majority of viewers has not read or seen these works in their original forms. Therefore, television must face the fact that it is really presenting not adaptations of them but, in reality, the works themselves—so far as the public knows.

In its original form *A Doll's House* would need close to three hours of playing time, or thereabouts. You cannot cut it in half without cutting in half its emotional, philosophical and human value. Specifically, a profound work, the orchestration of whose themes is quite marvelous, becomes a superficial "story" at worst, and a hint of something more at best, when it is told by leaping from one high point to another.

The adapters of these classics are neither guilty nor innocent, nor are the sponsors. The illusion is overpowering among us that it is possible to reduce everything to a painless capsule without losing its meaning. Nor is television alone in this. I happened on a paperback edition of Tolstoy's *War and Peace,* which the publishers proudly declared was shorn of all its political and social speculation, leaving its "human" story uncluttered by the author's thought. There are digests of novels published with their authors' consent, and the movies have for years purveyed adaptations of great books and plays.

Only one thing is lost by "digesting" great works, and it is possibly the main thing, namely, the depth of experience one might find in the originals. However skillfully one "cuts to the story," eliminating the gradual development of motive and meaning, one is of necessity cutting the reason for the story to a greater or lesser extent. Literature is reduced to what E. M. Forster has called the cave man element—the "what happens next?" Why it happened; why it had to happen, what significance the happenings might have—these questions are the crucial ones for the creator and for mankind, and we are being deprived of them by digesting them out of the great works we see.

However well they are played and directed, these truncated versions must inevitably confirm the opinion of those who cannot tell why they should bother with real literature or drama, for they are being given basically the plots at best, the skeletons of living organisms. The person who has always heard of *Don Quixote* and *A Doll's House* but never got around to reading them, has now "seen them." Worse than utter ignorance is the knowledge that is not knowledge but its shadow.

We are breaking the continuity of culture by passing on its masterpieces through mutilated distortions. This is not "better than nothing." The wholeness of viewpoint, the completeness of the human beings in certain masterpieces is being fragmented so that the marvel of a complete experience—which a great work is—is denied millions of people who, worse yet, go forth under the illusion that they have actually had it.

The fault seems to be the question of adequate time. Do you imagine you have heard the Fifth Symphony of Beethoven, let us say, when the orchestra has eliminated everything but its main and most thunderous themes? A fine work is wedded to the time it takes to perform or read it.

Perhaps it might be excusable if, instead of using the titles of *Don Quixote* and *A Doll's House*, we were told that what we are about to see are themes from these works, and warned before and after their presentations that only the broad outlines have been suggested, and that the originals are far more challenging and interesting. As it is, nothing less than a deception is being carried on, a positive act of misinformation and miseducation.

I said above that the adapters and sponsors are neither guilty nor innocent, given the power of the tendency to digest everything. I take it back. After all, those who are knowledgeable enough to adapt classics are to that degree in charge of them for the moment, so to speak, and are as responsible as a librarian who tears out half the pages of a work in order to get more busy people to read it. The justification that half is better than nothing does not hold when one knows the humanizing power of the originals. You cannot digest a real work of art because it is digested in the first place; it is the ultimate distillation of the author's vision by definition.

When television spends all day and all night purveying junk, is it really too much to ask that two, two and a half, or three hours be set aside once in a while for the full-length presentation of a masterpiece?

Failing this, the digests of such works ought not bear their original titles any more than diluted beer or perfume can be sold with the brand name of the manufacturer who makes the real thing. The integrity of a masterpiece is at least equal to that of a can of beans.

1959

Introduction to
A View from the Bridge
(Two-act Version)

A play is rarely given a second chance. Unlike a novel, which may be received initially with less than enthusiasm, and then as time goes by hailed by a large public, a play usually makes its mark right off or it vanishes into oblivion. Two of mine, *The Crucible* and *A View from the Bridge,* failed to find large audiences with their original Broadway productions. Both were regarded as rather cold plays at first. However, after a couple of years *The Crucible* was produced again Off-Broadway and ran two years, without a line being changed from the original. With McCarthy dead it was once again possible to feel warmly toward the play, whereas during his time of power it was suspected of being a special plea, a concoction and unaesthetic. On its second time around its humanity emerged and it could be enjoyed as drama.

At this writing I have not yet permitted a second New York production of *A View from the Bridge* principally because I have not had the desire to see it through the mill a second time. However, a year or so after its first production it was done with great success in London and then in Paris, where it ran two years. It is done everywhere in this country without any apparent difficulty in reaching the emotions of the audience. This play, however, unlike *The Crucible,* I have revised, and it was the revision which London and Paris saw. The nature of the revisions bears directly upon the questions of form and style which interest students and theater workers.

The original play produced on Broadway (Viking, 1955) was in one act. It was a hard, telegraphic, unadorned drama. Nothing was permitted which did not advance the progress of Eddie's catastrophe in a most direct way. In a Note to the published play, I wrote:

> What struck me first about this tale when I heard it one night in my neighborhood was how directly, with what breathtaking simplicity, it did evolve. It seemed to me, finally, that its very bareness, its absolutely unswerving path, its exposed skeleton, so to speak, was its wisdom and even its charm and must not be tampered with....
> These *qualities* of the events themselves, their texture, seemed to me more psychologically telling than a conventional investigation in width which would necessarily relax that clear, clean line of his catastrophe.

The explanation for this point of view lies in great part in the atmosphere of the time in which the play was written. It seemed to me then that the theater was retreating into an area of psycho-sexual romanticism, and this at the very moment when great events both at home and abroad cried out for recognition and analytic inspection. In a word, I was tired of mere sympathy in the theater. The spectacle of still another misunderstood victim left me impatient. The tender emotions, I felt, were being overworked. I wanted to write in a way that would call up the faculties of knowing as well as feeling. To bathe the audience in tears, to grip people by the age-old methods of suspense, to theatricalize life, in a word, seemed faintly absurd to me if not disgusting.

In *The Crucible* I had taken a step, I felt, toward a more self-aware drama. The Puritan not only felt, but constantly referred his feelings to concepts, to codes and ideas of social and ethical importance. Feeling, it seemed to me, had to be made of importance; the dramatic victory had to be more than a triumph over the audience's indifference. It must call up a concept, a new awareness.

I had known the story of *A View from the Bridge* for a long time. A waterfront worker who had known Eddie's prototype told it to me. I had never thought to make a play of it because it was too complete, there was nothing I could add. And then a time came when its very completeness became appealing. It suddenly seemed to me that I ought to deliver it onto the stage as fact; that interpretation was inherent in the very existence of the tale in the first place. I saw that the reason I had not written it was that as a whole its meaning escaped me. I could not fit it into myself. It existed apart from me and seemed not to express anything within me. Yet it refused to disappear.

I wrote it in a mood of experiment—to see what it might mean. I kept to the *tale,* trying not to change its original shape. I wanted the audience to feel toward it as I had on hearing it for the first time—not so much with heart-wringing sympathy as with wonder. For when it was told to me I knew its ending a few minutes after the teller had begun to speak. I wanted to create suspense but not by withholding information. It must be suspenseful because one knew too well how it would come out, so that the basic feeling would be the desire to stop this man and tell him what he was really doing to his life. Thus, by knowing more than the hero, the audience would rather automatically see his life through conceptualized feelings.

As a consequence of this viewpoint, the characters were not permitted to talk about this and that before getting down to their functions in the tale; when a character entered he proceeded directly to serve the catastrophe. Thus, normal naturalistic acting techniques had to be modified. Excessive and arbitrary gestures were eliminated; the set itself was shorn of every adornment. An atmosphere was attempted in which nothing existed but the purpose of the tale.

The trouble was that neither the director, the actors, nor I had had any experience with this kind of staging. It was difficult to know how far to go. We were all aware that a strange style was called for which we were unsure how to provide.

About a year later in London new conditions created new solutions. Seemingly inconsequential details suggested these solutions at times. For one, the British actors could not reproduce the Brooklyn argot and had to create one that was never heard on heaven or earth. Already naturalism was evaporated by this much: the characters were slightly strange beings in a world of their own. Also, the pay scales of the London theater made it possible to do what I could not do in New York—hire a crowd.

These seemingly mundane facts had important consequences. The mind of Eddie Carbone is not comprehensible apart from its relation to his neighborhood, his fellow workers, his social situation. His self-esteem depends upon their estimate of him, and his value is created largely by his fidelity to the code of his culture. In New York we could have only four strategically placed actors to represent the community. In London there were at least twenty men and women surrounding the main action. Peter Brook, the British director, could then proceed to design a set which soared to the roof with fire escapes, passageways, suggested apartments, so that one sensed that Eddie was living out his horror in the midst of a certain normality, and that, invisibly and without having to speak of it, he was getting ready to invoke upon himself the wrath of his tribe. A certain size accrued to him as a result. The importance of his interior psychological dilemma was magnified to the size it would have in life. What had seemed like a mere aberration had now risen to a fatal violation of an ancient law. By the presence of his neighbors alone the play and Eddie were made more humanly understandable and moving. There was also the fact that the British cast, accustomed to playing Shakespeare, could incorporate into a seemingly realistic style the conception of the play—they moved easily into the larger-than-life attitude which the play demanded, and without the self-conscious awkwardness, the uncertain stylishness which hounds many actors without classic training.

As a consequence of not having to work at making the play seem as factual, as bare as I had conceived it, I felt now that it could afford to include elements of simple human motivation which I had rigorously excluded before—specifically, the viewpoint of Eddie's wife, and *her* dilemma in relation to him. This, in fact, accounts for almost all the added material which made it necessary to break the play in the middle for an intermission. In other words, once Eddie had been placed squarely in his social context, among his people, the myth-like feeling of the story emerged of itself, and he could be made more human and less a figure, a force. It thus seemed quite in keeping that certain details of realism should be allowed; a Christmas tree and decorations in the living room, for one, and a realistic make-up, which had been avoided in New York, where the actor was always much cleaner than a longshoreman ever is. In a word, the nature of the British actor and of the production there made it possible to concentrate more upon realistic characterization while the universality of Eddie's type was strengthened at the same time.

But it was not only external additions, such as a new kind of actor, sets, and so forth, which led to the expansion of the play. As I have said, the original was written in the hope that I would understand what it meant to me. It was only during the latter part of its run in New York that, while watching a performance one afternoon, I saw my own involvement in this story. Quite suddenly the play seemed to be "mine" and not merely a story I had heard. The revisions subsequently made were in part the result of that new awareness.

In general, then, I think it can be said that by the addition of significant psychological and behavioral detail the play became not only more human, warmer and less remote, but also a clearer statement. Eddie is still not a man to weep over; the play does not attempt to swamp an audience in tears. But it is more possible now to relate his actions to our own and thus to understand ourselves a little better not only as isolated psychological entities, but as we connect to our fellows and our long past together.

1960

Essays: 1962–1970

The Bored and the Violent

If my own small experience is any guide, the main difficulty in approaching the problem of juvenile delinquency is that there is very little evidence about it and very many opinions as to how to deal with it. By evidence I do not mean the news stories telling of gang fights and teenage murders—there are plenty of those. But it is unknown, for instance, what the actual effects are on the delinquent of prison sentences, psychotherapy, slum-clearance projects, settlement-house programs, tougher or more lenient police attitudes, the general employment situation, and so on. Statistics are few and not generally reliable. The narcotics problem alone is an almost closed mystery.

Not that statistical information in itself can solve anything, but it might at least outline the extent of the disease. I have it, for instance, from an old and deservedly respected official—it is his opinion anyway—that there is really no great increase in delinquent acts but a very great intensification of our awareness of them. He feels we are more nervous now about infractions of the social mores than our ancestors, and he likes to point out that Shakespeare, Boccaccio, and other writers never brought on stage a man of wealth or station without his bravos, who were simply his private police force, necessary to him when he ventured out of his house, especially at night. He would have us read *Great Expectations, Oliver Twist, Huckleberry Finn*, and other classics, not in a romantic mood but in the way we read about our own abandoned kids and their depredations. The difference lies mainly in the way we look at the same behavior.

The experts have only a little more to go on than we have. Like the surgeon whose hands are bloody a good part of the day, the social worker is likely to come to accept the permanent existence of the delinquency disease without the shock of the amateur who first encounters it.

A new book on the subject [by Vincent Riccio and Bill Slocum], *All the Way Down*, reports the experience of a social worker—of sorts—who never got used to the experience, and does not accept its inevitability. It is an easy book to attack on superficial grounds because it has no evident sociological method, it rambles and jumps and shouts and curses. But it has a virtue, a very great and rare one, I think, in that it does convey the endless, leaden, mind-destroying boredom of the delinquent life. Its sex is without romance or sexuality, its violence is without release or gratification—exactly like the streets—movies and plays about delinquency notwithstanding.

Unlike most problems which sociology takes up, delinquency seems to be immune to the usual sociological analyses or cures. For instance, it appears in all technological societies, whether Latin or Anglo-Saxon or Russian or Japanese. It has a very slippery correlation with unemployment and the presence or absence of housing projects. It exists among the rich in Westchester and the poor in Brooklyn and Chicago. It has spread quickly into the rural areas and the small towns. Now, according to Harrison

Salisbury, it is the big problem in the Soviet Union. So that any single key to its causation is nowhere visible. If one wants to believe it to be essentially a symptom of unequal opportunity—and certainly this factor operates—one must wonder about the Russian problem, for the Soviet youngster can, in fact, go right up through the whole school system on his ability alone, as many of ours cannot. Yet the gangs are roaming the Russian streets, just as they do in our relatively permissive society.

So no one knows what "causes" delinquency. Having spent some months in the streets with boys of an American gang, I came away with certain impressions, all of which stemmed from a single, overwhelming conviction—that the problem underneath is boredom. And it is not strange, after all, that this should be so. It is the theme of so many of our novels, our plays, and especially our movies in the past twenty years and is the hallmark of society as a whole. The outcry of Britain's so-called Angry Young Men was against precisely this seemingly universal sense of life's pointlessness, the absence of any apparent aim to it all. So many American books and articles attest to the same awareness here. The stereotype of the man coming home from work and staring dumbly at a television set is an expression of it, and the "New Wave" of movies in France and Italy propound the same fundamental theme. People no longer seem to know why they are alive; existence is simply a string of near experiences marked off by periods of stupefying spiritual and psychological stasis, and the good life is basically an amused one.

Among the delinquents the same kind of mindlessness prevails, but without the style—or stylishness—which art in our time has attempted to give it. The boredom of the delinquent is remarkable mainly because it is so little compensated for, as it may be among the middle classes and the rich who can fly down to the Caribbean or to Europe, or refurnish the house, or have an affair, or at least go shopping. The delinquent is stuck with his boredom, stuck inside it, stuck to it, until for two or three minutes he "lives"; he goes on a raid around the corner and feels the thrill of risking his skin or his life as he smashes a bottle filled with gasoline on some other kid's head. In a sense, it is his trip to Miami. It makes his day. It is his shopping tour. It gives him something to talk about for a week. It is *life*. Standing around with nothing coming up is as close to dying as you can get. Unless one grasps the power of boredom, the threat of it to one's existence, it is impossible to "place" the delinquent as a member of the human race.

With boredom in the forefront, one may find some perspective in the mélange of views which are repeated endlessly about the delinquent. He is a rebel without a cause, or a victim of poverty, or a victim of undue privilege, or an unloved child, or an overloved child, or a child looking for a father, or a child trying to avenge himself on an uncaring society, or whatnot. But face to face with one of them, one finds these criteria useless, if only because no two delinquents are any more alike than other people are. They do share one mood, however. They are drowning in boredom. School bores them, preaching bores them, even television bores them. The word rebel is inexact for them because it must inevitably imply a purpose, an end.

Other people, of course, have known boredom. To get out of it, they go to the movies, or to a bar, or read a book, or go to sleep, or turn on TV or a girl, or make a resolution, or quit a job. Younger persons who are not delinquents may go to their room and weep, or write a poem, or call up a friend until they get tired talking. But note that each of these escapes can only work if the victim is sure somewhere in his mind, or reasonably hopeful, that by so doing he will overthrow his boredom and with luck may come out on the other side where something hopeful or interesting waits. But the delinquent has no such sense of an imminent improvement. Most of the kids in the Riccio and Slocum book have never known a single good day. How can they be expected to project one and restrain themselves in order to experience such joy once more?

The word rebel is wrong, too, in that it implies some sort of social criticism in the delinquent. But that would confuse him with the bourgeois beatnik. The delinquent has only respect, even reverence, for certain allegedly bourgeois values. He implicitly believes that there are good girls and bad girls, for instance. Sex and marriage are two entirely separate things. He is, in my experience anyway, deeply patriotic. Which is simply to say that he respects those values he never experienced, like money and good girls and the Army and Navy. What he has experienced has left him with absolute contempt, or more accurately, an active indifference. Once he does experience decency—as he does sometimes in a wife—he reacts decently to it. For to this date the only known cure for delinquency is marriage.

The delinquent, far from being the rebel, is the conformist par excellence. He is actually incapable of doing anything alone, and a story may indicate how incapable he is. I went along with Riccio and the gang in his book to a YMCA camp outside New York City for an overnight outing. In the afternoon we started a baseball game, and everything proceeded normally until somebody hit a ball to the outfield. I turned to watch the play and saw ten or twelve kids running for the catch. It turned out that not one of them was willing to play the outfield by himself, insisting that the entire group hang around out there together. The reason was that a boy alone might drop a catch and would not be able to bear the humiliation. So they ran around out there in a drove all afternoon, creating a stampede every time a ball was hit.

They are frightened kids, and that is why they are so dangerous. But again, it will not do to say—it is simply not true—that they are therefore unrelated to the rest of the population's frame of mind. Like most of us, the delinquent is simply doing as he was taught. This is often said but rarely understood. Only recently a boy was about to be executed for murder in New York state. Only after he had been in jail for more than a year after sentencing did a campaign develop to persuade the governor to commute his sentence to life imprisonment, for only then was it discovered that he had been deserted by his father in Puerto Rico, left behind when his mother went to New York, wandered about homeless throughout his childhood, and so on. The sentencing judge learned his background only a week or two before he was to be officially murdered. And then what shock, what pity! I have to ask why the simple facts of his deprivation were not brought out in court, if not before. I am afraid I know the answer. Like most people, it was probably beyond the judge's imagination that small children sometimes can be treated much worse than kittens or puppies in our cities.

It is only in theory that the solution seems purely physical—better housing, enlightened institutions for deserted kids, psychotherapy, and the rest. The visible surfaces of the problem are easy to survey—although we have hardly begun even to do that.

More difficult is the subterranean moral question which every kind of delinquency poses. Not long ago a gang was arrested in a middle-class section of Brooklyn, whose tack was to rob homes and sell the stuff to professional fences. Many of these boys were top students, and all of them were from good, middle-class backgrounds. Their parents were floored by the news of their secret depredations, and their common cry was that they had always given their sons plenty of money, that the boys were secure at home, that there was no conceivable reason for this kind of aberration. The boys were remorseful and evidently as bewildered as their parents.

Greenwich, Connecticut, is said to be the wealthiest community in the United States. A friend of mine who lives there let his sons throw a party for their friends. In the middle of the festivities a gang of boys arrived—their own acquaintances, who attend the same high school. They tore the house apart, destroyed the furniture, pulled parts off the automobile and left them on the lawn, and split the skulls of two of the guests with beer cans.

Now if it is true that the slum delinquent does as he is taught, it must be true that the Greenwich delinquent does the same. But obviously the lines of force from example to imitation are subtler and less easily traced here. It is doubtful that the parents of this marauding gang rip up the furniture in the homes to which they have been invited. So that once again it is necessary to withhold one's cherished theories. Rich delinquency is delinquency, but it is not the same as slum delinquency. But there is one clear common denominator, I think. They do not know how to live when alone. Most boys in Greenwich do not roam in gangs, but a significant fraction in both places find that counterfeit sense of existence which the gang life provides.

Again, I think it necessary to raise and reject the idea of rebellion, if one means by that word a thrust of any sort. For perspective's sake it may be wise to remember another kind of youthful reaction to a failed society in a different era. In the Thirties, for instance, we were also contemptuous of the given order. We had been brought up to believe that if you worked hard, saved your money, studied, kept your nose clean, you would end up made. We found ourselves in the Depression, when you could not get a job, when all the studying you might do would get you a chance, at best, to sell ties in Macy's. Our delinquency consisted in joining demonstrations of the unemployed, pouring onto campuses to scream against some injustice by college administrations, and adopting to one degree or another a socialist ideology. This, in fact, was a more dangerous kind of delinquency than the gangs imply, for it was directed against the social structure of capitalism itself. But, curiously, it was at the same time immeasurably more constructive, for the radical youth of the Thirties, contemptuous as he was of the social values he had rejected, was still bent upon instituting human values in their place. He was therefore a conserver, he believed in *some* society.

Gide wrote a story about a man who wanted to get on a train and shoot a passenger. Any train, any passenger. It would be a totally gratuitous act, an act devoid of any purpose whatever, an act of "freedom" from purpose. To kill an unknown man without even anger, without unrequited love, without love at all, with nothing in his heart but the sheerly physical contemplation of the gun barrel and the target. In doing this one would partake of death's irreproachable identity and commit an act in revolt against meaning itself, just as death is, in the last analysis, beyond analysis.

To think of contemporary delinquency in the vein of the Thirties, as a rebellion toward something, is to add a value to it which it does not have. To give it even the dignity of cynicism run rampant is also overelaborate. For the essence is not the individual at all; it is the gang, the herd, and we should be able to understand its attractions ourselves. It is not the thrust toward individual expression but a flight from self in any defined form. Therefore, to see it simply as a protest against conformism is to stand it on its head; it is profoundly conformist but without the mottoes, the entablature of recognizable, "safe" conformism and its liturgy of religious, patriotic, socially conservative credos.

The Greenwich gang, therefore, is also doing as it was taught, just as the slum gang does, but more subtly. The Greenwich gang is conforming to the hidden inhumanity of conformism, to the herd quality in conformism; it is acting out the terror-fury that lies hidden under Father's acceptable conformism. It is simply conformity sincere, conformity revealing its true content, which is hatred of others, a stunted wish for omnipotence, and the conformist's secret belief that nothing outside his skin is real or true. For which reason he must redouble his obeisance to institutions lest, if the acts of obeisance be withheld, the whole external world will vanish, leaving him alone. And to be left alone when you do not sense any existence in yourself is the ultimate terror. But this loneliness is not the poet's, not the thinker's, not the loneliness that is filled with incommunicable feeling, insufficiently formed thought. It is nonexistence and must not be romanticized, as it has been in movies and some of the wishful Beat literature. It is a withdrawal not from the world but from oneself. It is boredom, the subsidence of inner impulse, and it threatens true death unless it is overthrown.

All of which is said in order to indicate that delinquency is not the kind of "social problem" it is generally thought to be. That is, it transcends even as it includes the need for better housing, medical care, and the rest. It is our most notable and violent manifestation of social nihilism. In saying this, however, it is necessary to short-circuit any notion that it is an attempt by the youth to live "sincerely." The air of "sincerity" which so many writers have given the delinquent is not to be mistaken as his "purpose." This is romanticism and solves nothing except to sentimentalize brutality. The gang kid can be sincere; he can extend himself for a buddy and risk himself for others; but he is just as liable, if not more so than others, to desert his buddies in need and to treat his friends disloyally. Gang boys rarely go to visit a buddy in jail excepting in the movies. They forget about him. The cult of sincerity, of true human relations uncontaminated by money and the social rat race, is not the hallmark of the gang. The only moment of truth comes when the war starts. Then the brave show themselves, but few of these boys know how to fight alone and hardly any without a knife or a gun. They are not to be equated with matadors or boxers or Hemingway heroes. They are dangerous pack hounds who will not even expose themselves singly in the outfield.

If, then, one begins to put together all the elements, this "social problem" takes on not merely its superficial welfare aspects but its philosophical depths, which I think are the controlling ones. It is not a problem of big cities alone but of rural areas too; not of capitalism alone but of socialism as well; not restricted to the physically deprived but shared by the affluent; not a racial problem alone or a problem of recent immigrants, or a purely American problem. I believe it is in its present form the product of technology destroying the very concept of man as a value in himself.

I hesitate to say what I think the cure might be, if only because I cannot prove it. But I have heard most of the solutions men have offered, and they are spiritless, they do not assume that the wrong is deep and terrible and general among us all. There is, in a word, a spirit gone. Perhaps two world wars, brutality immeasurable, have blown it off the earth; perhaps the very processes of technology have sucked it out of man's soul; but it is gone. Many men rarely relate to one another excepting as customer to seller, worker to boss, the affluent to the deprived and vice versa—in short, as factors to be somehow manipulated and not as intrinsically valuable persons.

Power was always in the world, to be sure, and its evils, but with us now it is strangely, surrealistically masked and distorted. Time was, for example, when the wealthy and the politically powerful flaunted themselves, used power openly as power, and were often cruel. But this openness had the advantage for man of clarity; it created a certain reality in the world, an environment that was defined, with hard but touchable barriers. Today power would have us believe—everywhere—that it is purely beneficent. The bank is not a place which makes more money with your deposits than it returns to you in the form of interest; it is not a sheer economic necessity, it is not a business at all. It is "Your Friendly Bank," a kind of welfare institution whose one prayer, day and night, is to serve your whims or needs. A school is no longer a place of mental discipline but a kind of daycare center, a social gathering where you go through a ritual of games and entertainments which insinuate knowledge and the crafts of the outside world. Business is not the practice of buying low and selling high, it is a species of public service. The good life itself is not the life of struggle for meaning, not the quest for union with the past, with God, with man that it traditionally was. The good life is the life of ceaseless entertainment, effortless joys, the air-conditioned, dust-free languor beyond the Mussulman's most supine dream. Freedom is, after all, comfort; sexuality is a photograph. The enemy of it all is the real. The enemy is conflict. The enemy, in a word, is life.

My own view is that delinquency is related to this dreamworld from two opposing sides. There are the deprived who cannot take part in the dream; poverty bars them. There are the oversated who are caught in its indefiniteness, its unreality, its boring hum, and strike for the real now and then—they rob, they hurt, they kill. In flight from the nothingness of this comfort they have inherited, they butt against its rubber walls in order to feel a real pain, a genuine consequence. For the world in which comfort rules is a delusion, whether one is within it or deprived of it.

There are a few social theorists who look beyond poverty and wealth, beyond the time when men will orient themselves to the world as breadwinners, as accruers of money-power. They look to the triumph of technology, when at least in some countries the physical struggle to survive will no longer be the spine of existence. Then, they say, men will define themselves through varying "styles of life." With struggles solved, nature tamed and abundant, all that will be left to do will be the adornment of existence, a novel-shaped swimming pool, I take it, or an outburst of artistic work.

It is not impossible, I suppose. Certainly a lot of people are already living that way—when they are not at their psychiatrists. But there is still a distance to go before life's style matters very much to most of humanity in comparison with next month's rent. I do not know how we ought to reach for the spirit again, but it seems to me we must flounder without it. It is the spirit which does not accept injustice complacently and yet does not betray the poor with sentimentality. It is the spirit which seeks not to flee the tragedy which life must always be but seeks to enter into it, thereby to be strengthened by the fullest awareness of its pain, its ultimate non sequitur. It is the spirit which does not mask but unmasks the true function of a thing, be it business, unionism, architecture, or love.

Riccio and Slocum's book, with all its ugliness, its crudeness, its lack of polish and design, is good because it delivers up the real. It is only as hopeless as the situation is. Its implied solutions are good ones: reform of idiotic narcotics laws, a real attempt to put trained people at the service of bewildered, desperate families, job-training programs, medical care, reading clinics—all of it is necessary, and none of it would so much as strain this economy. But none of it will matter, none of it will reach further than the spirit in which it is done. Not the spirit of fear with which so many face delinquency, nor the spirit of sentimentality which sees in it some virtue of rebellion against a false and lying society. The spirit has to be that of those people who know that delinquents are a living expression of our universal ignorance of what life ought to be, even of what it is, and of what it truly means to live. Bad pupils they surely are. But who from his own life, from his personal thought, has come up with the good teaching, the way of life that is joy? This book shows how difficult it is to reach these boys; what the country has to decide is what it is going to say if these kids should decide to listen.

1962

The Nazi Trials and the German Heart

There is an unanswerable question hovering over the courtroom at Frankfurt, where twenty-two Hitler SS men are on trial for murdering inmates in the Auschwitz concentration camp during World War II. Can the kind of movement which gave life-and-death power to such men ever again rise in Germany?

It seemed to me, sitting at one side of the courtroom one day last week, that as in all murder trials the accused here were becoming more and more abstract. Once the jackbooted masters of a barbed-wire world, they are now middle-aged Germans in business suits, nearsighted some of them, laboriously taking notes, facing the high tribunal with a blue-uniformed policeman at each one's elbow. The two exceptions are indeed extraordinary. One has an imbecile stupidity written on his face, the other shifts constantly in his chair, a free-floating violence so clear in his eyes that one would find him frightening if met on a train, let alone on trial for murder.

But the others could pass for anybody's German uncle. In fact, the lives most of them have lived since they scooted into oblivion before the allied advance show them entirely capable of staying out of trouble. Some have turned into successful business men, professionals and ordinary workers. They have reared families and even became civic leaders in their communities. When arrested they were not picked up drunk or disorderly, but at work or at rest in the bosom of their families.

For example, the one whose violence seemed to show in his quick roving eyes was, in fact, a real sadist. He was almost constantly drunk in the camp and liked to walk into a barracks and fire his pistol at random into the sleeping prisoners. If he didn't like the look of a passing inmate he would blow his head off.

But after the war this man got a job in a hospital as a nurse, and his patients have written to the court saying that he was an especially tender helper, an unusually warm person. "Papa Kaduk," they called him. No one knows anymore exactly how many defenseless people Papa Kaduk murdered in his four years at Auschwitz. A massive man, overweight now, his small eyes blaze with mocking victory whenever a witness sounds uncertain of a date or a fact, and he reaches over to nudge his black-robed lawyer who then rises to protest hearsay evidence. He seems, in short, to be quite convinced that he is indeed Papa Kaduk and not at all the monster being painfully described from the witness chair.

Another is a pharmacist who helped select prisoners for the gas chambers. He has become an important man in his town; the arresting officer had had to wait for him to return from a hunting expedition in Africa, and the local gentry showed real surprise on learning of the charges against him. Especially since it had been he who suggested that whenever the town leaders met to discuss civic affairs they wear tuxedos. How, it was actually asked, could a gentleman of such sensibility have done such awful things?

Yet, the doctor testifying hour after hour this day leaves no doubt about the facts. He was himself an inmate, but since he did get more food than the others he is here to tell the tale. And as he describes babies ripped from their mothers' arms, bed linen changed twice a year, the almost total absence of medicine, Red Cross trucks being used to transport prisoners to their deaths, tortures and beatings, and names one of the defendants after the other as the actual perpetrators, the German housewives who comprise most of the jury burst into tears or sit with open horror in their faces. And they are of an age which indicates they lived in Nazi Germany while this was happening: they were shopping, putting their children to bed, going on picnics on sunny days, worrying about a daughter's wedding dress or a son's well-being in the army while mothers like themselves and children no different from their own were forced to undress, to walk into a barren hall, and breathe the gas which some of the defendants now sitting here carefully administered.

Yet, lawyers on the tiny prosecution staff believe that ninety percent of the German people are opposed to this and other trials like it. They base their judgment on the mail they receive and on their own difficulties in getting local cooperation for some of the arrests they have made, and finally, on the absence of any clear voice or movement from among the Germans demanding that the country's honor be cleared by bringing such murderers to justice.

On the contrary, it is widely felt, according to these lawyers, that trials like this only give Germany a bad name; that it all happened so long ago why pluck men out of their lives at this late date, and so on. Time and again these lawyers have had to escort arrested men across Germany to the Frankfurt jail because they could not find a police officer to help. And the government has given them twenty-five marks a day for expenses on these trips; the most common lodging for a night costs eleven marks. This handful of Germans nevertheless intends to go on searching for every last man down to the truck drivers who drove prisoners to the gas chambers, until justice is done.

But is there really any long-range point in all this? They do not know. Some of them have been on these cases since 1959 when the first arrests were made in this particular group of cases. They have read through millions of words of testimony, stared at photographs of the camps taken by an SS man with a penchant for photography, showing the defendants actually at work separating the doomed from those temporarily spared for labor in the camp. By this they have lost any sensitivity about what others might think and are doggedly pursuing the goal.

And what is the goal? These lawyers are in their middle thirties, veterans of the Wehrmacht themselves, German through and through. They know their people and they know that even if every last SS man were convicted for his particular crime, it would not in itself prevent a new recrudescence of brutal nationalism which could once again confront the world with a German problem. It is something else they are after.

Imbedded in every word of testimony, and in the very existence of this trial, is a dilemma which is first of all a German dilemma, given the history of concentration camps, but is actually an unresolved problem for all mankind. For the final defense of these accused is that they acted under government orders.

When so many Germans oppose this trial, it is not simply an insensitivity to suffering, or even an immunity to the question of justice. Germans too weep for their dead and help the sick and care very much about their children. As for a respect for law, they have that even to an inordinate degree. What scares some Germans, however, and makes the German to this day an enigma to many foreigners, is his capacity for moral and psychological collapse in the face of a higher command.

Several times during the course of this trial, newsmen covering it were ordered to leave, for one reason or another, and the dozen or so police who sit below the judges' tribunal are in charge of carrying out such orders. Not long ago three policemen were asked what they would do if ordered to shoot a newsman who disobeyed the court's command. One replied that he could not do that; the other two said they would carry out orders.

The point which the prosecution is trying to open up first to Germany, and then to the world, is individual conscience and responsibility in the face of inhuman orders. A judge (who has no connection with this trial) told me that his fears for Germany stemmed from precisely this profound tendency to abjure freedom of choice, to fall into line on orders from above. Another man of the law, a high official in this court, feels that the day is far off, but that his duty is to work for its coming when the Germans would question authority. He sees the root of the difficulty in the especially authoritarian role of the father in the German family, which is the microcosm reflected in the authoritarian state. The underlying point of these trials is that there can be no mitigating excuse for the conscious and planned murder of six million men, women and children, orders or no orders. Some six thousand SS men did duty in Auschwitz during its four years of operation, and not one is known to have refused to do what he was told. And it is no mean irony that the Jew, whose skepticism once leavened the authoritarian character of German culture, is not around any more to help humanize the pompous general with a little healthy doubt as to his real importance.

All of which sounds hopeless and dangerous, and perhaps that is all that should be said. But there are a few unknowns which some Germans would point to with some small and uncertain hopefulness. The young, they say, are less hermetically sealed in the old German ways than any younger generation of the past. Movies, television, books and plays from abroad flood Germany. Germans travel more than they used to, and tourists from abroad come in greater numbers than ever, and there are over one million foreign workers employed in the country now.

So that a German youth is perhaps more internationally minded than his parents and not as contemptuous of strangers and ways of life that are not German. Finally there is the more impressive fact that Germany for the first time in modern history is not flanked by a line of backward peasant countries whose defenselessness was all too tempting in the past. The equalization of industrial and hence military strength through the whole of Europe makes expansion by force a good deal less possible than before.

It is in this context, a context of much distrust and some hopefulness, that the prosecution presses for a German verdict of guilty upon members of the German armed forces. Thus far none of the accused has suggested he may have done something wrong; there is no sign of remorse, and they appear to maintain a certain unity among themselves even now. Some have been in jail two, three and four years awaiting trial and have undoubtedly read what the world press has had to say about their deeds, but no sign shows of any change of attitude toward the past.

In fact, one defendant carries out his familial duties from prison, and his authority and racial ideas are still so powerful (he dropped the gas cartridges into the gas chambers full of people) that his daughter broke off with her betrothed because he, the defendant, believes that no good German girl can possibly marry an Italian.

This trial will go on for about a year, during which time some three hundred psychologically and physically scarred survivors will face the high tribunal in Frankfurt, living evidence of how one of the most educated, technically developed, and artistic nations in the world gave itself over to the absolute will of beings it is difficult to call human. And while that testimony fills the silent courtroom, and the world press prints its highlights, German industry will pour out its excellent automobiles, machine tools, electronic equipment, German theaters will excellently produce operas and plays, German publishers will put out beautifully designed books—all the visible signs and tokens of civilization will multiply and make even more abstract, more bewildering the answer to the riddle which the impassive faces of the accused must surely present to any one who looks at them. How was it possible in a civilized country?

It is the same question to which Cain gave his endlessly echoed answer, and I have often thought that this is why it is the first drama in the Bible, for it provides the threat, the energy for all that comes after. If man can murder his fellows, not in passion but calmly, even as an "honorable" duty leading to a "higher" end—can any civilization be called safe from the ravages of what lies waiting in the heart of man? The German government which Hitler destroyed had some of the most intelligent and advanced legislation in the world. The present republic also is buttressed by excellent laws.

What is in the German heart, though? Does the rule of law reach into that heart or the rule of conformity and absolute obedience? Surely, if the German police had picked up a twenty-two-man gang that had tortured and killed merely for money, or even for kicks, an outcry would go up from the Germans, a demand that justice be done. Why is there this uneasy silence at best, and this resentment at worst, excepting that in the Frankfurt cases these accused worked for a state under its orders? Perhaps the problem becomes clearer now, and not only for the Germans.

The disquieting, nagging truth which I think dilutes the otherwise clear line this trial is taking is that the human mind does in fact accept one kind of murder. It is the murder done under the guise of social necessity. War is one example of this, and all peoples reject the idea of calling soldiers murderers. In fact, the entire nation so deeply shares in this kind of killing that it must reject any condemnation of the individuals who actually do the killing, lest they have to condemn themselves.

The problem for the Germans is that they are being called upon to identify themselves with the victims when their every instinct would lead them to identify with the uniformed, disciplined, killers. In short, they are being called on to be free, to rebel in their spirit against the age-old respect for authority which has plagued their history.

This, I think, is why it is perfectly logical for the German housewife on the jury to weep as any human being would at the horrors she hears, even as she and her millions of counterparts have, for at least a decade now, heard just such evidence a hundred times with no sign of public protest against Nazism. It is why the officers who tried to assassinate Hitler in 1944 have never been celebrated in Germany either: for they did the unthinkable, they took a moral decision against their obedience to authority.

So that the German looking at these twenty-two men may well be revolted by their crimes and yet feel paralyzed at the thought of truly taking sides against them. For part of his soul is caught in the same airtight room with theirs—the part that finds honor and goodness and decency in obedience.

But who, in what country, has not heard men say, "If I did not do this someone else would, so I might as well go along?"

So the question in the Frankfurt courtroom spreads out beyond the defendants and spirals around the world and into the heart of every man. It is his own complicity with murder, even the murders he did not perform himself with his own hands. The murders, however, from which he profited if only by having survived.

It is this profound complicity which the Frankfurt prosecution is trying to open up by sticking to its seemingly simple contention that all murder is murder. With the atomic bomb in so many different hands now it might be well to take a good look at the ordinariness of most of the defendants in Frankfurt. The thought is hateful, to be sure, and no one would willingly think it, but we do, after all, live in the century when more people have been killed by other people than at any other period. Perhaps the deepest respect we can pay the millions of innocent dead is to examine what we believe about murder, and our responsibility as survivors for the future.

1964

Foreword to *After the Fall*

This play is not "about" something; hopefully, it is something. And primarily it is a way of looking at man and his human nature as the only source of the violence which has come closer and closer to destroying the race. It is a view which does not look toward social or political ideas as the creators of violence, but into the nature of the human being himself. It should be clear now that no people or political system has a monopoly on violence. It is also clear that the one common denominator in all violent acts is the human being.

The first real "story" in the Bible is the murder of Abel. Before this drama there is only a featureless Paradise. But in that Eden there was peace because man had no consciousness of himself nor any knowledge of sex or his separateness from plants or other animals. Presumably we are being told that the human being becomes "himself" in the act of becoming aware of his sinfulness. He "is" what he is ashamed of.

After all, the infraction of Eve is that she opened up the knowledge of good and evil. She presented Adam with a choice. So that where choice begins, Paradise ends, Innocence ends, for what is Paradise but the absence of any need to choose this action? And two alternatives open out of Eden. One is Cain's alternative—or, if you will, Oswald's; to express without limit one's unbridled inner compulsion, in this case to murder, and to plead unawareness as a virtue and a defense. The other course is what roars through the rest of the Bible and all history—the struggle of the human race through the millennia to pacify the destructive impulses of man, to express his wishes for greatness, for wealth, for accomplishment, for love, but without turning law and peace into chaos.

The question which finally comes into the open in this play is, how is that pacification to be attained? Quentin, the central character, arrives on the scene weighed down with a sense of his own pointlessness and the world's. His success as an attorney has crumbled in his hands as he sees only his own egotism in it and no wider goal beyond himself. He has lived through two wrecked marriages. His desperation is too serious, too deadly to permit him to blame others for it. He is desperate for a clear view of his own responsibility for his life, and this because he has recently found a woman he feels he can love, and who loves him; he cannot take another life into his hands hounded as he is by self-doubt. He is faced, in short, with what Eve brought to Adam—the terrifying fact of choice. And to choose, one must know oneself, but no man knows himself who cannot face the murder in him, the sly and everlasting complicity with the forces of destruction. The apple cannot be stuck back on the Tree of Knowledge; once we begin to see, we are doomed and challenged to seek the strength to see more, not less. When Cain was questioned, he stood amazed and asked, "Am I my brother's keeper?" Oswald's first words on being taken were, "I didn't do anything." And what country has ever gone into war proclaiming anything but injured innocence? Murder and violence require Innocence, whether real or cultivated. And through Quentin's agony in this play there runs the everlasting temptation of Innocence, that deep desire to return to when, it seems, he was in fact without blame. To that elusive time, which persists in all our minds, when somehow everything was part of us and we so pleasurably at one with others, and everything merely "happened" to us. But the closer he examines those seemingly unified years the clearer it becomes that his Paradise keeps slipping back and back. For there was always his awareness, always the choice, always the conflict between his own needs and desires and the impediments others put in his way. Always, and from the beginning, the panorama of human beings raising up in him and in each other the temptation of the final solution to the problem of being a self at all—the solution of obliterating whatever stands in the way, thus destroying what is loved as well.

This play, then, is a trial; the trial of a man by his own conscience, his own values, his own deeds. The "Listener," who to some will be a psychoanalyst, to others God, is Quentin himself turned at the edge of the abyss to look at his experience, his nature and his time in order to bring to light, to seize and—innocent no more—to forever guard against his own complicity with Cain, and the world's.

But a work of fiction, like an accident witnessed in the street, inevitably gives rise to many differing accounts. Some will call it a play "about" Puritanism, or "about" incest, or "about" the transformation of guilt into responsibility, or whatever. For me it is as much a fact in itself as a new bridge. And in saying this I only dare to express what so many American writers are trying to bring to pass—the day when our novels, plays, pictures and poems will indeed enter into the business of the day, the mindless flight from our own actual experience, a flight which empties out the soul.

1964

Guilt and *Incident at Vichy*

About ten years ago a European friend of mine told me a story. In 1942, said he, a man he knew was picked up on the street in Vichy, France, during a sudden roundup of Jews, taken to a police station, and simply told to wait. Refugees of all sorts had been living in Vichy since the invasion of France because the relatively milder regime of Marshal Pétain had fended off some of the more brutal aspects of German occupation. With false papers, which were not hard to buy, a Jew or a politically suspect person could stay alive in the so-called Unoccupied Zone, which covered the southern half of the country. The racial laws, for one thing, had not been applied by Pétain.

In the police station the arrested man found others waiting to be questioned, and he took his place on line. A door at the front of the line would open, a Vichy policeman would beckon, a suspect would go in. Some soon came out again and walked free into the street. Most did not reappear. The rumor moved down the line that this was a Gestapo operation and that the circumcised would have to produce immaculate proof of their Gentileness, while the uncircumcised would of course go free.

The friend of my friend was a Jew. As he got closer and closer to the fatal door he became more and more certain that his death was near. Finally, there was only one man between him and that door. Presently, this last man was ordered into the office. Nothing stood between the Jew and a meaningless, abrupt slaughter.

The door opened. The man who had been the last to go in came out. My friend's friend stood paralyzed, waiting for the policeman to appear and beckon him into the office. But instead of walking past him with his pass to freedom, the Gentile who had just come out stopped in front of my friend's friend, thrust his pass into his hand, and whispered for him to go. He went.

He had never before laid eyes on his saviour. He never saw him again.

In the ten years after hearing it, the story kept changing its meaning for me. It never occurred to me that it could be a play until this spring when *Incident at Vichy* suddenly burst open complete in almost all its details. Before that it had been simply a fact, a feature of existence which sometimes brought exhilaration with it, sometimes a vacant wonder, and sometimes even resentment. In any case, I realize that it was a counterpoint to many happenings around me in this past decade.

That faceless, unknown man would pop up in my mind when I read about the people in Queens refusing to call the police while a woman was being stabbed to death on the street outside their windows. He would form himself in the air when I listened to delinquent boys whose many different distortions of character seemed to spring from a common want of human solidarity. Friends troubled by having to do things they disapproved of brought him to mind, people for whom the very concept of choosing their actions was a long forgotten thing. Wherever I felt the seemingly implacable tide of human drift and the withering of will in myself and in others, this faceless person came to mind. And he appears most clearly and imperatively amid the jumble of emotions surrounding the Negro in this country and the whole unsettled moral problem of the destruction of the Jews in Europe.

At this point I must say that I think most people seeing this play are quite aware it is not "about Nazism" or a wartime horror tale; they do understand that the underlying issue concerns us now and that it has to do with our individual relationships with injustice and violence. But since a few critics persist in their inability to differentiate between a play's story and its theme, it is just as well to make those differences plain.

The story as I heard it never presented a "problem": everyone believes that there are some few heroes among us at all times. In the words of Hermann Broch, "And even if all that is created in this world were to be annihilated, if all its aesthetic values were abolished ... dissolved in skepticism of all law ... there would yet survive untouched the unity of thought, the ethical postulate." In short, the birth of each man is the rebirth of a claim to justice and requires neither drama nor proof to make it known to us.

What is dark if not unknown is the relationship between those who side with justice and their implication in the evils they oppose. So unknown is it that today in Germany it is still truly incomprehensible to many people how the crude horrors of the Nazi regime could have come to pass, let alone have been tolerated by what had for generations been regarded as one of the genuinely cultured nations of the world. So unknown that here in America, where violent crime rises at incredible rates—and, for example, the United Nations has to provide escorts for people leaving the building after dark in the world's greatest city—few people even begin to imagine that they might have some symbolic or even personal connection with this violence.

Without for an instant intending to lift the weight of condemnation Nazism must bear, does its power not become more comprehensible when we see our own helplessness toward the violence in our own streets? How many of us have looked into ourselves for even a grain of its cause? Is it not for us—as it is for the Germans—the others who are doing evil?

The other day on a news broadcast I heard that Edward R. Murrow had been operated on for lung cancer. The fact was hardly announced when the commercial came on—"Kent satisfies best!" We smile, even laugh; we must, lest we scream. And in the laughter, in the smile, we dissolve by that much. Is it possible to say convincingly that this destruction of an ethic also destroys my will to oppose violence in the streets? We do not have many wills, but only one: it cannot be continuously compromised without atrophy setting in altogether.

The first problem is not what to do about it but to discover our own relationship to evil, its reflection of ourselves. Is it too much to say that those who do not suffer injustice have a vested interest in injustice?

Does any of us know how much of his savings-bank interest is coming from investments in Harlem and Bedford-Stuyvesant real estate, those hovels from which super profits are made by jamming human beings together as no brute animals could be jammed without their dying? Does anyone know how much of his church's income is derived from such sources?

Let the South alone for a moment—who among us has asked himself how much of his own sense of personal value, how much of his pride in himself is there by virtue of his not being black? And how much of our fear of the Negro comes from the subterranean knowledge that his lowliness has found our consent and that he is demanding from us what we have taken from him and keep taking from him through our pride?

It was not to set forth a hero, either as a fact of history or as an example for us now, that I wrote this play but to throw some light on evil. The good and the evil are not compartments but two elements of a transaction. The hero of the play, Prince Von Berg, is mistakenly arrested by a Nazi race "expert." He comes into the detention room with his pride of being on the humane side, the right side, for he has fled his Austria and his rank and privilege rather than be part of a class which oppresses people.

None of the horrors he witnesses are really surprising to him here, nothing is forbidden any more, as he has long known. What he discovers in this place is his own complicity with the force he despises, his own inherited love for a cousin who, in fact, is a Nazi and an oppressor, the material cause, in short, for what before was a general sense of guilt, namely, his own secret joy and relief that, after all, he is not a Jew and will not be destroyed.

Much is made of guilt these days, even some good jokes. Liberalism is seen now as a response to guilt; much of psychiatry has made a business of evaporating guilt; the churches are no longer sure if their age-old insistence on man's guilt is not an unwitting spur to neurosis and even the acting-out of violence; the Roman Catholic church has only recently decided to lift the Crucifixion guilt from the Jews alone and to spread it evenly over mankind.

I have no "solution" to human guilt in this play, only a kind of remark, no more. I cannot conceive of guilt as having an existence without the existence of injustice. And injustice, like death itself, creates two opposing interests—one more or less profits from it, the other more or less is diminished by it. Those who profit, either psychically or materially, seek to even out the scales by the weight of guilt. A "moral" ounce is taken up to weigh down the otherwise too-light heart which contemplates uneasily its relative freedom from injustice's penalty, the guilt of having been spared.

In my play, the hero is that man whose guilt is no longer general but suddenly a clear transaction—he has been, he sees, not so much an opponent of Nazism but a vessel of guilt for its brutalities. As a man of intense sympathy for others he will survive but at a price too great for him to pay—the authenticity of his own self-image and his pride. And here I stop; I do not know why any man actually sacrifices himself any more than I know why people commit suicide. The explanation will always be on the other side of the grave, and even that is doubtful.

If they could speak, could the three boys who were murdered in Mississippi really explain why they had to go to the end? More—if each of them could discover for us in his personal history his motives and the last and most obscure corner of his psychology, would we really be any closer to the mystery of why we first require human sacrifices before our guilt can be transformed into responsibility? Is it not an absurdity that the deaths of three young men should make any difference when hundreds have been lynched and beaten to death before them, and tens of thousands humiliated?

The difference, I think, is that these, including Chaney, the young Negro, were not inevitable victims of Mississippi but volunteers. They had transformed guilt into responsibility and in so doing opened the way to a vision that leaped the pit of remorse and helplessness. And it is no accident that the people of Mississippi at first refused to concede they had been murdered, for they have done everything in their power to deny responsibility for the "character" of the Negro they paternalistically "protect," and here in these three young bodies was the return with interest for their investment in the guilt that does not act.

At the end of *Incident at Vichy*, the Prince suddenly hands his pass to a Jew, a psychiatrist, who accepts it in astonishment, in awe and wonder, and walks out to freedom. With that freedom he must accept the guilt of surviving his benefactor. Is he a "good" man for accepting his life this way or a "bad" one? That will depend on what he makes of his guilt, of his having survived.

In any case, death, when it takes those we have loved, always hands us a pass. From this transaction with the earth the living take this survivor's reproach; consoling it and at turns denying its existence in us, we constantly regenerate Broch's "unity of thought, the ethical postulate"—the debt, in short, which we owe for living, the debt to the wronged.

It is necessary to say something more about Germany in this context of guilt. I cannot read anyone's mind, let alone a nation's, but one can read the drift of things. About a year ago I wrote some thoughts about the current Frankfurt trials of Nazi war criminals, which were published in Germany, among other countries. There was much German mail in response and a good lot of it furious, in part because I asked the question whether a recrudescence of Nazism was possible again in the future. The significant thing in many letters was a resentment based on the idea that the Nazis and the regime were something apart from the German people. In general, I was giving Germany a "bad name."

Apart from the unintended humor, I think this reaction is to be faced by the world and especially by the Germans. It is, in fact, no good telling people they are guilty. A nation, any more than an individual, helps nobody by going about beating its chest. I believe, in truth, that blame and emotional charges of a generalized guilt can only help to energize new frustrations in the Germans and send them striving for dignity through a new, strident, and dangerous nationalism. Again, guilt can become a "morality" in itself if no active path is opened before it, if it is not transformed into responsibility. The fact, unfortunately, is that for too many the destruction of the Jews by Germans has become one of Orwell's nonactions, an event self-propelled and therefore incomprehensible.

But if the darkness that persists over human guilt were to be examined not as an exceptional condition or as illness but as a concomitant of human nature, perhaps some practical good could come of it instead of endless polemic. If the hostility and aggression which lie hidden in every human being could be accepted as a fact rather than as reprehensible sin, perhaps the race could begin to guard against its ravages, which always take us "unawares," as something from "outside," from the hands of "others."

The reader has probably been nodding in agreement with what I have just said about Germany, but who among us knew enough to be shocked, let alone to protest, at the photographs of the Vietnamese torturing Vietcong prisoners, which our press has published? The Vietnamese are wearing United States equipment, are paid by us, and could not torture without us. There is no way around this—the prisoner crying out in agony is *our prisoner.*

It is simply no good saying that the other side probably does the same thing; it is the German's frequent answer when you raise the subject of Nazi atrocities—he begins talking about Mississippi. And more, if he is intelligent he will remind you that the schoolbooks sent to Germany by the United States immediately after the war included the truth about Nazism, but that they were withdrawn soon after when the Cold War began, so that a generation has grown up which has been taught nothing about the bloodiest decade in its country's history.

What is the lesson? It is immensely difficult to be human precisely because we cannot detect our own hostility in our own actions. It is tragic, fatal blindness, so old in us, so ingrained, that it underlies the first story in the Bible, the first personage in that book who can be called human. The rabbis who collected the Old Testament set Cain at its beginning not out of some interest in criminology but because they understood that the sight of his own crimes is the highest agony a man can know and the hardest to relate himself to.

Incident at Vichy has been called a play whose theme is "Am I my brother's keeper?" Not so. "Am I my own keeper?" is more correct.

Guilt, then, is not a featureless mist but the soul's remorse for its own hostility. We punish ourselves to keep from being punished and to keep from having to take part in regenerating that "unity of thought, that ethical postulate," which nevertheless is reborn with every child, again and again forever.

1965

What Makes Plays Endure?

More than any other art, theater asks for relevance. A play that convinces us that "this is the way it is now" can be excused many shortcomings. At any one moment there is a particular quality of feeling which dominates in human intercourse, a tonality which marks the present from the past, and when this tone is struck on the stage, the theater seems necessary again, like self-knowledge. Lacking this real or apparent contemporaneity, many well-written plays pass quickly into oblivion, their other virtues powerless to convince us of their importance.

Before a play is art it is a kind of psychic journalism, a mirror of its hour, and this reflection of contemporary feeling is exactly what makes so many plays irrelevant to later times. For the last generation was always naïve to this one; all strong feelings tend finally to form into squares as time goes by. For nearly a decade O'Neill had little appeal. When life seemed enslaved to Economics, it was old-fashioned and pointless to stare so at Fate.

But "conditions" change rather swiftly and nothing is harder to remember, let alone convey to a later generation, than the quality of an earlier period. What finally survives, when anything does, are archetypal characters and relationships which can be transferred to the new period.

Ibsen's focal point of attack, his contemporaneity, was rebellion against small-town narrowness, smugness, the sealed morality whose real fruit was spiritual death. But we cannot bring *his* context to *Hedda Gabler* anymore. Society, conditions, have melted away and she lives autonomously now, a recognizable neurotic who transcends her historical moment. The journalistic shell of a play—its reflective mirror surface—is its mortal part without which it could not be born. But its transcendency springs from the author's blindness rather than his sight, from his having identified himself with a character or a situation rather than from his criticism of it.

Thus, history unveils the painful irony, the irony without which no play continues to live: that without a certain love for what he hates, without a touch of hands with his adversary, his work will not outlive its necessary journalism, its mortal frame. Perhaps this is why the seeing of old works is always underscored by a kind of consolation, a conciliation at least. It is like reading of old wars in which the heroism of the enemy is finally conceded and something like Truth seems to appear.

The relations of a particular play to its time are therefore shifting and complicated. Consciously or not, a writer is addressing not only his audience, his own past or his present agonies, but also other plays, his wife's mood, an item in the paper, a lost lover, a face he saw in a crowd. "Why" a play was written is really unanswerable, the more so as it survives its first moment at all. But some things can be said about the genesis of *A View from the Bridge*, which, at least, throw some light on theatrical conditions and one man's reaction to them ten years ago, and possibly on the play itself.

The first condition that ought to be mentioned is that the play was not written for Broadway or the commercial theater. A man I hardly knew then—Martin Ritt—was acting in *The Flowering Peach* by Clifford Odets; the play was losing business and the cast wanted to use the theater, which was closed on Sundays, to put on one-act plays for invited audiences free of charge. I had never written one-acters, but I said I would think about it.

Within the next three or four weeks I wrote *A Memory of Two Mondays* and *A View from the Bridge*. By the time they were finished *The Flowering Peach* had closed, and the project ended up on Broadway as a regular commercial production. I mention this genesis only to indicate why both plays, for different and even opposite reasons, were to one side of the then reigning ideas in the theater.

Memory is a plotless and leisurely play, an exploration of a mood, the mood of the thirties and the pathos of people forever locked into the working day. Some people paid me the inverse compliment of saying it had been written twenty years earlier and dredged out of the drawer, but, in fact, it was a reaching toward some kind of bedrock reality at a time, in 1954, when it seemed to me that the very notion of human relatedness had come apart.

It was McCarthy's time, when even the most remote conception of human solidarity was either under terrific attack or forgotten altogether. *A Memory of Two Mondays,* however lyrical and even nostalgic, was the evocation of a countervailing idea, the idea, quite simply, of "other people," of sympathy for others, and finally of what I believed must come again lest we lose our humanity—a sense of sharing a common fate even as one escaped from it.

Bridge, written in the same month, was the other side of the same coin. What kills Eddie Carbone is nothing visible or heard, but the built-in conscience of the community whose existence he has menaced by betraying it. Whatever both plays are, they are at bottom reassertions of the existence of the community. A solidarity that may be primitive but which finally administers a self-preserving blow against its violators. In both plays there is a search for some fundamental fiat, not moral in itself but ultimately so, which keeps a certain order among us, enough to keep us from barbarism.

It was still a time when Absurdity had a pejorative connotation, and was a kind of moral insanity; for when a senator, waving empty file cards in his hand, could strike terror into the highest government officials, how could one relish Absurdity, how could one simply stop there and merely report, in a play, that life had turned out to be utterly senseless? The Absurd was something one had to be able to afford. The abrogation of cause and effect was entertaining so long as one had never felt the effects.

This pressure of the time's madness is reflected in the strict and orderly cause-and-effect structure of *A View from the Bridge*. Apart from its meaning, the manner in which the story itself is told was a rejection of that enervated "acceptance" of illogic which was the new wisdom of the age. Here, actions had consequences again, betrayal was not greeted with a fashionably lobotomized smile.

To be sure, any such considerations lie to one side of an evaluation of any play as a play, but they are not entirely personal either. A few nights before the play's opening in London, for example, I asked Peter Brook, who was directing it, whether its locale and characters would be comprehensible to the British. "They may find it bizarre, but they like that sort of thing," he said. "What may put them off, though, is its logical inevitability. The British are terribly disturbed by any suggestion that the future is so closely determined by the present. If that were so, you see, we should have to blow our brains out. Of course, this is all happening in Brooklyn, and they may allow it there."

In France, where he also directed the play, its logic was of course taken for granted and, with Raf Vallone as Eddie, it became a tale of sexual passion. *Cavalleria Rusticana* cropped up in the Italian reviews. In Russia last winter I saw it and was astounded to hear Eddie, in the first ten minutes of the play, facing Catherine in the presence of his wife, and announcing that he was in love with the girl—they had simply eliminated anything subconscious from the whole story.

A phone call from an actor in a failing play, the temper of the American fifties, my own relationships to the time—none of it matters, excepting that it all went into the writing of the play whose present relevance or irrelevance stems from God knows what shifting forces of the hour. *Death of a Salesman* was hardly noticed when it opened in Paris some fifteen years ago. A new production now is a great success. In 1950, Willy was a man from Mars. Today, the French are up to their necks in time payments, broken washing machines, dreams of fantastic success, new apartment houses shading out the vegetables in the backyard, and the chromed anxiety of a society where nothing deserves existence that doesn't pay.

Recently, as I watched Ulu Grosbard's production of *A View from the Bridge* downtown, it was striking how the passage of time, the shifting of social context and even the theatrical context, both reinforces the original impulse behind the writing of a play and distorts it. Ironically, the play written for a Sunday night and an informal group of actors rather than a Broadway production, was finally being done more or less that way and it was simpler than the original, authentic and plain.

The audience that night was very young, sprawled in the current attitudes of the cool. Characters get excited at the prospect of buying a rug, making forty dollars a week, a girl is un-touched at the age of seventeen.

The laughter, at first, seems to come at the wrong moments, full of strange surprise. And Eddie enters the play not like a tragic character but a longshoreman scratching himself after a long day on the ships. The audience seems to be watching it from a British distance, an exotic workers' world where people do get caught in a dilemma and not stylishly but for real, and as the plot unfolds and the silence deepens in the little theater, the cool goes, the sprawls tighten up, and one knows that even though Catherine and Rodolpho now do the frug to the rock 'n' roll phonograph record instead of the original, sedate-seeming dance, and the question of informers no longer means very much, something human is working all by itself, sprung free of the original context, perhaps even purified of any of its author's preoccupations at the time of writing.

And yet one knows that, while this purely human spectacle is the ultimate fruit of any work, one will, nevertheless, sit down to write again at a particular hour pressed by the unique weight of a particular day, addressing that day and that hour whose consequences will not even appear to the audience a year or two hence, to say nothing of a decade or in another country. It is the kind of lesson one must remember and forget at the same time.

1965

It Could Happen Here—And Did

I keep no file of reviews, but if memory serves, *The Crucible* was generally dismissed as a cold, anti-McCarthy tract, more an outburst than a play. A relatively small band of rooters kept it on the Broadway stage for six months or so.

It is certain that a reading now of those reviews would leave unexplained, to say the least, why the play has continued to be produced here and around the world these fifteen years, or why it should have run through several seasons in France and remains in many permanent repertories, including Olivier's National Theatre in Britain. There have been years when it was more often performed than *Death of a Salesman*. Something living must thrive in the play which, I was told on its opening, was a dead husk.

Perhaps its victory over adversities has made me prouder of it than of anything else I have written, and perhaps it is permissible to say why I think it has refused to be dismissed.

The prime point at issue in 1953 when it opened was whether the analogy was a sound one between the Massachusetts witch hunt and the then-current hysteria about Communists boring from within the government, labor, education, entertainment and the intellectual community. After all, there never were any witches while there certainly were Communists, so that *The Crucible* appeared to some as a misreading of the problem at best—a "naïveté," or at worst a specious and even sinister attempt to whitewash the guilt of the Communists with the noble heroism of those in 1692 who had rather be hanged than confess to nonexistent crimes. Indeed, the critic Eric Bentley wrote that one never knew what a Miller play was about.

I believe that life does provide some sound analogies now and again, but I don't think they are any good on the stage. Before a play can be "about" something else, it has to be about itself. If *The Crucible* is still alive, it can hardly be due to any analogy with McCarthyism. It is received in the same way in countries that have never known such a wave of terror as those that have. The bulk of the audiences, for example, in the British National Theatre, are too young to have known McCarthyism, and England is not a hysterical country. Nor, quite rightly, is it for them a play about a "problem" to be "solved."

The truth is that as caught up as I was in opposition to McCarthyism, the playwriting part of me was drawn to what I felt was a tragic process underlying the political manifestation. It is a process as much a part of humanity as walls and food and death, and no play will make it go away. When irrational terror takes to itself the fiat of moral goodness, somebody has to die. I thought then that in terms of this process the witch hunts had something to say to the anti-Communist hysteria. No man lives who has not got a panic button and when it is pressed by the clean white hand of moral duty, a certain murderous train is set in motion. Socially speaking this is what the play is and was "about," and it is this which I believe makes it survive long after the political circumstances of its birth have evaporated in the public mind.

Is it a political play? It is, I think, but in a particular sense. It is very often done in Latin America just before a dictatorship is about to take over—as a warning—and just after one has been overthrown, as a reminder. It was one of the first foreign works to be done after Stalin's death, and I will wager that it will be done soon after Franco goes to his reward. As I say, it is very popular in England, where hysteria is not one of the national vices. I think it is a political play but not in terms of Left and Right. Its underlying reference is to political paranoia, whichever side makes use of that source of power.

But paranoid politics is not easy to discuss for the reason that *our* fears are always based on something quite palpable and real, while *theirs* are illusory. I realize now that it was probably impossible to have expected an audience and critics in 1953 to feel the heat of a play which so much as implied that a state of deep fear was not entirely new in the world, let alone that the evil plotters might just be worth some dispassionate examination. On top of this, to have treated this fear as a tragic thing rather than a necessary and realistic and highly moral sort of patriotism, was more than could be borne by liberals and conservatives alike.

We customarily think of paranoia as a craziness, a diseased delusionary state in which fears are obviously out of proportion to any conceivable stimulus. But if this were all, we should never be endangered by it. Paranoia has a power and it rises not basically from ravings about plots and hidden conspiracies, but from the grain of recognizable fact around which the fantasies are woven.

The paranoid feels endangered by some person or group mysteriously controlling his actions despite his will. His violence is therefore always defensive, trained against oppressors who mean to kill him before he can kill them. His job is therefore to unmask and disarm, to find the seemingly innocent traces of the pervading malevolence, and he comes to recognize hostility even in the way a person folds his hands or turns his head. His only hope is power, power to neutralize the dangers around him. Naturally, since those dangers can be anywhere, his power must also be total in order to work.

And of course it is true that to one degree or another we are, in fact, hostile to each other, and when we are accused of holding that hostility, we do indeed hate the accusation and the accuser. So that the paranoid creates the reality which proves him right. And this is why the paranoid, who in normal times might merely end in an institution, can rise to the leadership of a society which is really insecure and at a loss as to the causes of its spiritual debility. Nothing is as frightening as to not know why one is frightened. Given the "cause" we can act, and thus keep ourselves from flying apart altogether.

Paranoid politics is seductive, too, because all politics requires that we symbolize people, until individuals cease to exist and there are only compliant supporters or the opposition. The paranoid discovers the murderous potential in the opposition, which it therefore must destroy. When, during World War II, for example, we ripped 100,000 Japanese-Americans out of their California farms and shops and confined them to Midwestern camps, we were indulging the paranoid side of our realistic fears of Japan.

But was it really probable that *all* these men, women and children were secret agents? The grain of truth was that some, or perhaps one of them, was. Their non-"whiteness" enhanced our irrationality; we never rounded up German-Americans even though crowds of them, unlike the Japanese, had been marching around with Nazi flags in Jersey right up to the day we declared war.

A few years after its original production, *The Crucible* opened again in New York, Off-Broadway, and the script was now judged by many of the same critics as an impassioned play rather than a cold tract, and it ran two years. It is true that the original production was formalized and rather ballet-like, but not by that much. It was simply that in 1958 nobody was afraid any more. Nor do I imagine that I can convince many people that this is basically what was changed and for good reason. Great fear, like great pain, is not easily recalled, it is self-healing, and the more of it we have felt the less of it we can really get ourselves to remember. And this forgetfulness is part of the tragedy.

But no amount of paranoids walking around has very great political significance unless a partner appears who, naturally, is Interest. Hitler without the support of German big business would have merged with the legions of the mentally lost. Stalin in his last years slept in a different bed every night, employed food-tasters, and ordered the executions of people whose names he merely heard in conversation, but if the Revolution had created a healthy, ongoing society, it could not have tolerated such a chief. Had the witch-crying girls started their shenanigans in a stable community certain of itself and its future, they would have been soaked in cold water and put to bed.

But land titles were in dispute in Salem due to edicts from Boston and London; the repressions of the Puritan code no longer seemed holy to people born after the early deprivations of the militant pioneers. A host of socially disruptive pressures were upon Salem which seemed to threaten a disorder beyond the power of the mind to analyze. The girls lifted up a cause for it all out of the morass. Americans in the late forties and fifties felt paralyzed before a power of darkness expanding its reign; we had "lost" China (which we had never "had") and Eastern Europe. Enormous Communist parties existed in France and Italy. McCarthy solved the problem of our helplessness with a stroke— we were infiltrated by the enemy. Twenty years of conservative frustration with contemporary America was unleashed until, like the girls, McCarthy was in a position of such incredible authority that the greatest people in the land shuddered at the thought that their names might fall from his sniggering lips.

The fantasy of the fifties has rich documentation, but the Rosenberg case, because it ended in death, provides one insight which may throw some light on paranoid fear. In the final speech of the presiding judge is the statement that the defendants committed one of the gravest crimes in all history in giving the atom-bomb secret to Russia. Yet, no expert competent to make such a judgment had been called, and even more instructive—the defense attorney was so eager to prove *his* adherence to the reigning fear that he moved to impound the diagram of the bomb lens allegedly transmitted by the Rosenbergs, so that nobody in the future could steal it again—or, by the way, examine its validity. Recently, however, it was examined by a group of physicists who had actually worked on the lens, and their verdict was that it was scientifically a farce. I am reasonably sure that the passion of the judge's speech was real, and certainly he was not crazy. He was, however, afraid.

Can it all happen again? I believe it can. Will it?

The opposite of paranoid politics is Law and good faith. An example, the best I know, is the American Constitution, and the Bill of Rights, which de-symbolize the individual and consider him as the sum of his acts rather than his hidden thoughts and propensities for plotting evil.

And there are signs that somehow, someway, people in responsible positions have learned at least part of the lesson. Despite our being in a war, despite the immense opposition to it, the draft-card burning and demonstrations, the President and the leadership of the country as a whole have not rallied the unwashed to go hunting for people whose bad thoughts are cheating us of victory.

But what will happen if the American becomes more desperately frustrated, if this war goes on for years, if a sense of national powerlessness prepares the ground for cries of "Betrayal!"—the old paranoid cry to which the highly moral mad respond by seeing where others are blind?

Laws, as we know, are made of bendable stuff; panic systematized around a grain of fact waits forever in the human brain. The tragic reply, John Proctor's, is unfortunately no defense against this kind of social dissolution, but spoken in good time it is perhaps our only safety: "A fire, a fire is burning. I hear the boot of Lucifer, I see his filthy face. And it is my face, and yours, Danforth. For them that quail to bring men out of ignorance as I have quailed, and as you do now when you know in all your black hearts that this be fraud—God damns our kind especially...." A foisted analogy? Only if we are certain that the slide into darkness is far, far behind us. As things stand, Proctor's passion has its own life intact and will until Power is guaranteed against the temptations of the irrational. The surgeons say they work to make their job unnecessary. *The Crucible* was written in that spirit—that the coiled thing in the public heart might die of light. A reasonable thought, but an unreasonable hope which against all reason never disappears.

1967

The Battle of Chicago:
From the Delegates' Side

There was violence inside the International Amphitheater before violence broke out in the Chicago streets. One knew from the sight of the barbed wire topping the cyclone fence around the vast parking lot, from the emanations of hostility in the credential-inspecting police that something had to happen, but once inside the hall it was not the hippies one thought about any more, it was the delegates.

Violence in a social system is the sure sign of its incapacity to express formally certain irrepressible needs. The violent have sprung loose from the norms available for that expression. The hippies, the police, the delegates themselves were all sharers in the common breakdown of the form which traditionally has been flexible enough to allow conflicting interests to intermingle and stage meaningful debates and victories. The violence inside the amphitheater, which everyone knew was there and quickly showed itself in the arrests of delegates, the beatings of newsmen on the floor, was the result of the suppression, planned and executed, of any person or viewpoint which conflicted with the president's.

There had to be violence for many reasons, but one fundamental cause was the two opposite ideas of politics in this Democratic party. The professionals—the ordinary senator, congressman, state committeeman, mayor, officeholder—see politics as a sort of game in which you win sometimes and sometimes you lose. Issues are not something you feel, like morality, like good and evil, but something you succeed or fail to make use of. To these men an issue is a segment of public opinion which you either capitalize on or attempt to assuage according to the present interests of the party. To the amateurs— the McCarthy people and some of the Kennedy adherents—an issue is first of all moral and embodies a vision of the country, even of man, and is not a counter in a game. The great majority of the men and women at the convention were delegates from the party to the party.

Nothing else can explain their docility during the speeches of the first two days, speeches of a skull-flattening boredom impossible to endure except by people whose purpose is to demonstrate team spirit. "Vision" is always "forward," "freedom" is always a "burning flame," and "our inheritance," "freedom," "progress," "sacrifices," "long line of great Democratic presidents" fall like drops of water on the head of a tortured Chinese. And nobody listens; few even know who the speaker is. Every once in a while a cheer goes up from some quarter of the hall, and everyone asks his neighbor what was said. For most delegates just to be here is enough, to see Mayor Daley in the life even as the TV cameras are showing him to the folks back home. Just being here is the high point, the honor their fealty has earned them. They are among the chosen, and the boredom of the speeches is in itself a reassurance, their deepening insensibility is proof of their faithfulness and a token of their common suffering and sacrifice for the team. Dinner has been a frankfurter, the hotels are expensive, and on top of everything they have had to chip in around a hundred dollars per man for their delegation's hospitality room.

The tingling sense of aggressive hostility was in the hall from the first moment. There were no Chicago plainclothes men around the Connecticut delegation; we sat freely under the benign smile of John Bailey, the Democratic National Chairman and our own state chairman, who glanced down at us from the platform from time to time. But around the New York delegation there was always a squad of huskies ready to keep order—and indeed they arrested New Yorkers and even got in a couple of shoves against Paul O'Dwyer when he tried to keep them from slugging one of the members. Connecticut, of course, was safely machine, but New York had great McCarthy strength.

The McCarthy people had been warned not to bring posters into the hall, but at the first mention from the platform of Hubert Humphrey's name hundreds of three-by-five-foot Humphrey color photos broke out all over the place. By the third day I could not converse with anybody except by sitting down; a standing conversation would bring inspectors, sometimes every fifteen seconds, asking for my credentials and those of anyone talking to me. We were forbidden to hand out any propaganda on the resolutions, but a nicely printed brochure selling the Administration's majority Vietnam report was on every seat. And the ultimate mockery of the credentials themselves was the flooding of the balconies by Daley ward heelers who carried press passes. On the morning before the convention began, John Bailey had held up twenty-two visitors' tickets, the maximum, he said, allowed any delegation, as precious as gold.

The old-time humor of it all began to sour when one realized that of 7.5 million Democrats who voted in the primaries, eighty percent preferred McCarthy's and/or Robert Kennedy's Vietnam positions. The violence in the hall, let alone on the streets, was the result of this mockery of a vast majority who had so little representation on the floor and on the platform of the great convention. Had there never been a riot on Michigan Avenue the meeting in the amphitheater would still have been the closest thing to a session of the All-Union Soviet that ever took place outside of Russia. And it was not merely the heavy-handed discipline imposed from above but the passionate consent from below that makes the comparison apt.

On the record, some six hundred of these men were selected by state machines and another six hundred elected two years ago, long before the American people had turned against the Vietnam war. If they represent anything it is the America of two years past or the party machine's everlasting resolve to perpetuate the organization. As one professional said to me, "I used to be an idealist, but I learned fast. If you want to play ball you got to come into the park." Still, another of them came over to me during the speech of Senator Pell, who was favoring the bombing halt, and said, "I'd love to vote for that but I can't. I just want to tell you." And he walked away.

Connecticut caucused before casting its vote for the administration plank. We all, forty-four of us, sat in a caucus room outside the great hall itself and listened to Senator Benton defending the bombing position and Paul Newman and Joseph Duffey attacking it. The debate was subdued, routine. The nine McCarthy people and the thirty-five machine people were merely being patient with one another. One McCarthy man, a teacher, stood up and with a cry of outrage in his voice called the war immoral and promised revolution on the campuses if the majority plank was passed. Angels may have nodded, but the caucus remained immovable. Perhaps a few were angry at being called immoral, in effect, but they said nothing to this nut.

But when the roll was called, one machine man voted for the minority plank. I exchanged an astonished look with Joe Duffey. Another followed. Was the incredible about to happen?

We next began voting on the majority plank, the Johnson position. The machine people who had voted "Yes" on the minority plank also voted "Yes" on the majority plank. The greatness of the Democratic party is its ability to embrace conflicting viewpoints, even in the same individuals.

Having disposed of Vietnam, Mr. Bailey then suggested the delegation take this opportunity to poll itself on its preference for a presidential candidate, although nominations had not yet been made on the floor of the convention. This, I said, was premature since President Johnson, for one, might be nominated by some enthusiast and we would then have to poll ourselves all over again. In fact, I knew privately that William vanden Heuvel, among others, was seriously considering putting up the president's name on the grounds that the Vietnam plank was really a rephrasing of his program and that he should be given full credit as its author rather than Humphrey, who was merely standing in for him. But Mr. Bailey merely smiled at me in the rather witty way he has when his opponent is being harmlessly stupid, and Governor Dempsey, standing beside him behind the long table at the front of the room, assured all that as head of the delegation he would see to it that in the event of a nomination on the floor of any candidate other than Humphrey, McCarthy, and McGovern, we would certainly be allowed to change our votes. Immediately a small man leaped to his feet and shouted, "I nominate Governor Dempsey!" The governor instantly pointed at him and yelled, "Good morning, Judge!" This automatic reward of a seat on the bench, especially to a man obviously of no distinction, exploded most of the delegation—excepting the indignant teacher—into a burst of laughter and the governor and his nominator swatted at each other in locker-room style for a moment. Then seriousness returned, and resuming his official mien of gravity, the governor ordered the polling to begin. The nine McCarthy delegates voted for McCarthy and the rest for Humphrey, and there was no doubt of an honest count. It may be a measure of the tragedy in which both factions were caught that when, later on, the governor was handed teletyped reports of the Michigan Avenue riots, his face went white, and he sat with his head in his hands even as it became clearer by the minute that Humphrey and the administration would be victorious.

After two nights on the floor, whatever trends and tides the TV commentators might have been reporting, one felt like a fish floating about in still water. Nothing had been said on either side that aroused the slightest enthusiasm. The water above was dark, and whatever winds might be raising waves on the surface did not disturb the formless chaos, really the interior leaderlessness of the individual delegates. We were the crowd in an opera waiting for our cue to shout in unison when the time for it came. First depression and then anger began moving into the faces of the McCarthy people as the speeches ground on. Some of us had campaigned all over the state and the nation to rouse people to the issues of the war, and in many places we had succeeded. There was no trace of it here and clearly there never could have been. The machine had nailed down the nomination months before. We had not been able even to temper the administration's Vietnam plank, not in the slightest. The team belonged to the president, and the team owned the Democratic party.

As I sat there on the gray steel chair, it was obvious that we could hardly have expected to win. Behind Connecticut sat two rows of Hawaiians. Middle-aged, kindly looking, very polite, eager to return a friendly glance, they never spoke at all. When it came time for any vote, their aisle man picked up his phone, listened, hung up, stood, and turned thumbs up or down. The brown faces watched his hands. So much for deliberation. It was not quite that crude among the others, except for Illinois, but Illinois did not need thumbs. Illinois had somehow located the fact that we McCarthy people of Connecticut were occupying nine seats in the same row, and Illinois stared at us from time to time with open, almost comical, ferocity. Every time I turned to my left, I found the face of a man who might have been a retired hockey player. He sat staring at me through close-set eyes over a strong, broken nose, his powerful hands drooping between his knees, his pointy shoes worn at the heels, his immense neck bound to bursting by a tiny knot in his striped tie. Once I tried to give him a smile of greeting, a recognition of his interest. He gave nothing, like a watchdog trained to move only on signal.

There was this discipline but there was no leadership. None of the Humphrey people ever argued with me when I said they were sinking the party by hanging the Johnson position on the war around Humphrey's neck. None ever had a positive word to say about Humphrey himself. They were beyond—or beneath—discourse, and if by some miracle Humphrey had let it be known he was now in favor of an unconditional halt in the bombing they would have been as perfectly happy to applaud that stand as the opposite. They were lemming-like, clinging to one another in a mass that was moving toward where the leaders had pointed. And then, suddenly, there was a passion.

Representative Wayne Hays of Ohio got to the podium and began, like the others, in a rhetorical vein. Something to the effect that his teacher in school had taught him that history was a revelation of the past, a guide to the present, and a warning of the future. The delegates resumed their private conversations. But suddenly he was talking about hippies in paired contraries. Not long hair, he said, but long thought; not screaming in the streets but cleaning the streets; not . . .

Leadership, quite unannounced, had arrived. All around me men were turning to this clear voice on the platform. His list of mockeries of the errant generation mounted and grew more pointed, more vicious, more mocking, and applause was breaking out all over the floor, men were getting to their feet and yelling encouragement, and for the first time in two days there was electricity in the crowd, a vibrant union of mind, a will to act, a yea-saying from the heart. Men were hitting each other on the back with elation, fists were raised in encouragement, bull roars sounded out, and an ovation swept over Hays as he closed his papers and walked off. It was a congregation of the aged, men locked into a kind of political senility that was roaring its challenge across the six miles of superhighway to the ten thousand children just then gathering for the slaughter opposite the Conrad Hilton Hotel. The old bulls against the young bulls under the overhanging branches of the forest.

Then it struck me that there was no issue cleaving the convention; there was only a split in the attitude toward power, two mutually hostile ways of being human. The Humphrey men were supporting him not basically because he was right but because he was vice president and the candidate of the president. In any ten of them there will only be two or three at most who are themselves convinced that we should be in Vietnam, that if necessary we must fight on for years, that lamentable as the civilian casualties are they are justified by the need to protect democracy and the Thieu–Ky Government, and so on. This minority is passionate, it is deeply afraid that the communist powers, if they win in Vietnam, will flood over into Hawaii and ultimately California. But the others are supporting authority which happens at the moment to be fighting the war. Congressman Don Irwin of Norwalk, for example, is a principled supporter of the war and for him it is righteous, to the point where he openly says his position will probably defeat him the next time he runs. He is a man in his forties who smiles constantly and in a group quickly loses his voice from laughing so much, a common vocal problem with professionals, the accepted social greeting being laughter. They shake hands and laugh. It is not unnecessary, it is not merely a tic but a working out of conflict, for many of them have had terrible political battles against one another and have come close to insulting one another in various log jams, and the quick laugh is a signal of mutual disarmament, a warding-off of violence, for many are physical men quick to take umbrage, like their forefathers who more than once beat each other senseless in the halls of Congress.

There were two Americas in Chicago, but there always are. One is passionately loyal to the present, whatever the present happens to be; the other is in love with what is not yet. Oppressed by the team spirit all around me, I thought of a morning in Moscow when I was passing under the walls of the Kremlin with a young interpreter. I said that there must have been some terrific battles in those offices the day they decided to get rid of Khrushchev. The young man refused to join this idle speculation: "We don't think about what goes on in there. It is not our business. They know what they are doing."

But everywhere I went I also met young—and not so young—Russians who knew it was up to them to make the future of the country, men and women who wanted a hand on the tiller. But there they have no legal means of putting new ideas forward; here we do. Or did. The underlying fright in the Democratic convention, and the basic reason for the violence on Michigan Avenue, was that perhaps the social compact had fallen apart. As one TV correspondent said to me as we stood watching the line of troops facing the hippies across the boulevard from the Hilton, "It lasted two hundred years. What law says it may not be over? Maybe we've come to the end of the string. Those kids," he went on, "are not bohemians. Most of them aren't what you'd call hippies, even. There are a lot of graduate students in that crowd, medical students, too. They haven't dropped out at all. Somebody upstairs had better start asking himself what they're trying to tell the country."

To me, standing there at four in the morning with the arc lights blasting the street and no one knowing when the police and the troops would again go berserk, the strangest irony was that the leader they had come to hate, the president, had months ago removed himself as being too divisive. And yet all the force of the state was in play to give that president what he wanted in the convention. The whole thing might have been understandable if the country were in love with its leader. What, I wondered, was being so stoutly defended on this avenue?

The question itself only added to the general surrealism. In the main CBS workroom behind the auditorium, I watched a row of five TV sets. NBC was showing the attack by the club-swinging police, the swarming squads of helmeted cops, and one heard the appalling screaming. Next to it, CBS was showing the platform speaker inside the auditorium and the applauding delegates. Next to CBS was ABC, with close-ups of bleeding demonstrators being bandaged. Then a local station showing a commercial, Mister Clean having his moustache rubbed off. The last was another local station whose screen showed some sort of ballet.

In one of the corridors a young man stopped me, holding the microphone of a portable tape recorder up to my mouth. He came from the University of Chicago's radio station. We quickly agreed the whole spectacle was a horror. "How can you have anything to do with this?" he asked. My answer, which I found embarrassing at that moment, was that I had hoped to change it and that it might be changed if people like me tried to move into the party in a serious way rather than only during presidential campaigns.

"But how can you have any faith now in this kind of democratic politics?"

He was intelligent and eager and angry, and I thought I had misunderstood him. "What would you put in its place?" I asked.

"Well, I don't know. But not this."

"But what, then? One way or another people have to delegate powers to run the country, don't they? This is one way of delegating them. Right?"

"You mean you believe in this?" he asked, incredulously.

"Not this. Not this gang, no. But. . . ." I broke off, aware now that it was not merely the antics of the convention we were talking about. "Do you mean that the more intelligent should rule? The more idealistic? Is that it?"

"Well, not this," he repeated, his anger mounting.

"But what are you going to substitute for this?" The crowds were pushing us to one side and then another. The announcer on a nearby TV set was yelling a description of the battle on Michigan Avenue. "Are you just going to substitute intelligent people telling the others what to do instead of the others telling the intelligent? Isn't that the same kind of violence we're going through right here? What are you going to put in place of this?"

The look in his eyes amazed me. He seemed never to have considered the problem. It was unbelievable. He was ready, it seemed, for some kind of benevolent dictatorship. If this, this hall full of middle-aged men who had yelled their pleasure at the condemnation of the young—if this was democracy, he hated it, and that hatred was enough for him. We were being torn apart now by the crowd. I called to him as he moved away, "That's the problem, don't you see? What do you want? It's not enough to hate all this!" But he was gone.

Life is always more perfect than art. The endings and codas it provides to experience always tell more of the truth than any construction on the stage or in a book. At about two in the morning, after the fighting on Michigan Avenue had quieted, about five hundred delegates under the impromptu chairmanship of New York's Paul O'Dwyer decided to hold a march past the scene of the carnage. We gathered a few blocks from the Hilton, many of us holding lighted candles, and moved in near silence, some singing softly, toward the battleground. Police, who had been alerted to our plan, sat in squad cars on the avenue, none getting out, for we were official delegates and not to be pushed around, or not yet anyway. The night was lovely; all the stars were out. Chicago looked beautiful. A block from the Hilton we were stopped by a police captain. He was six-and-a-half-feet tall, wearing the blue crash helmet whose edges were lined with gray rubber, a hinged Plexiglas face shield pushed up. I have never seen such eyes or a smile so fixed and hard. The procession halted, and O'Dwyer stepped forward to parley.

"Now, what is it you want to do, gentlemen?" the officer asked.

O'Dwyer said that we intended to walk past the hippies, who were still congregated in the little park across the street from the hotel, past them and the line of soldiers and police facing them.

"I see," said the officer. "All right, then. Just keep it orderly and quiet. We are here to protect lives and property. Keep it orderly and keep moving."

We moved, and as we approached the hippies who had crowded to the edge of the park to see this strange, apparitional procession, they began whistling, and some said, "It's a wake, a funeral for the Democratic party." We kept coming, and some of them began to get the point. Cheers went up. We exchanged the V-for-victory sign. There was laughter and someone began to sing "We Shall Overcome." The line of soldiers stood expressionless, holding their rifles up to bar us from the hotel across the street, some of them looking at our candles as though they were in a hallucination. Nothing happened. In a while, the silence returned to the avenue again. The conversation between us and these kids was neither more nor less interesting than any such conversation on any street anywhere.

Next afternoon, I went to a TV studio to join a telecast being beamed by Telstar to England. I had been told to get there no later than three o'clock because the program was being sent live and the Telstar time was open only from 3:30 to 4. I had had to commandeer a taxi with a Time-Life sticker on the windshield, there being no free taxis or buses because of strikes. Breathless, I ran in at 3:10 to find that the other participants had not arrived. But the moderator, Byran Magee, told me to take it easy. "We are going to tape it and send it by plane to London, so there's time now. You see," he said, raising one eyebrow, "the United States Government has preempted the Telstar, due to the Czech crisis. No one believes it, of course."

In a few minutes, Pierre Salinger and former ambassador to Poland John Gronouski arrived. They knew nothing of the preemption. Once again Byran Magee said he did not believe the excuse for the preemption. Gronouski had no opinion, but he did not look happy. We proceeded to discuss the convention, the riots and Chicago, but someone had turned out our star just as someone had made it impossible for the TV people to shoot outside the International Amphitheater on simultaneous hookups.

Checking into this scandalous censorship, this heavenly blackout, I discovered later that it was not true. According to BBC in London, there had been no interruption in Telstar's availability. How and why Byran Magee had been misinformed I do not know, but the interesting fact remains that he, Salinger, Ambassador Gronouski and I never questioned that the government had indeed tried to block this telecast. The point is, that I remember quite clearly a time when something like this would not have been credible. Now everything is possible, anything at all, and that is where we're at.

I left Chicago while the final session was going on. What the new candidate might or might not say seemed the last thing in the world to concern oneself about. And this, because the authority, the leadership was not in him. It was not in anyone whose face was visible in Chicago. It was in the president, and he was only an unseen presence whom no majority man on that platform dared contradict or too openly obey. I wondered who would eat the president's birthday cake, now that he had decided it was too dangerous to appear—in one of his own cities, and in his own convention. I stood in the airport with thirty or so other passengers waiting to board the plane, which, quite symbolically, had had to be replaced with another because of a faulty oil warning light. We waited an hour.

A long line of draftees appeared, kids in shirtsleeves, carrying valises, chattering like campers, walking five abreast down the corridor. A few Negro boys were scattered in among them, and as one Negro passed he turned to the watching passengers and called out, "We're off to defend your country. Your country!" And another Negro boy just behind him held out his hand: "Got some pennies, anybody?" The passengers said nothing, their faces registered nothing.

During our telecast, Ambassador Gronouski had said that Hubert Humphrey could not be blamed for what had happened in Chicago. Pierre Salinger said he could be, that he was the leader and could at least have dissociated himself from a riot of police. Ambassador Gronouski said Hubert Humphrey had a good rapport with youngsters. I said it was time to stop talking like this. Mrs. Humphrey had announced she was going to visit all the new youth-aid projects, including the Junior Chamber of Commerce. Where had these people been living? What had to happen before the powers realized they were not living in this time and in this place?

On the wide lawn behind my house at five o'clock in the morning the stars hung as bright and orderly as they had over Michigan Avenue. The sun rose on time. The morning paper said that a poll showed that the majority of Americans sympathized with the police. It was not a surprise. Not in the least. The voice that might have spoken both with authority, respectability, and confidence about the honest despair of a generation of Americans had never been heard in Chicago. Within a day I was being asked from London to organize a protest against the jailing of writers by the Russians in Prague. Prague, perhaps the freest city, the most hopeful and experimental in Eastern Europe, was being cleansed of the enemies of the people.

1968

On the Theater in Russia

Russia is the only country I know of where one writer will passionately extol the works of a competitor. This is rather a shock at first and nearly unbelievable—and indeed, in some cases it is merely politic, but it happens genuinely often enough to force one to think about it. Of course in my presence they are talking to a foreigner, but that is just the point: in any other country the ignorant foreigner is usually sold on the unique excellence of the writer he happens to be speaking to at the moment—there is never much else of value. And in Russia it is also true that the more acclaim the writer has earned, the more he is at pains to draw one's attention to others less renowned but equally talented.

It is otherwise in France, England, Germany, or the United States, and it seems at first like a pure generosity of spirit, which it may well be, but it is also mildly tactical as well. There is a deep division among Soviet writers which reflects two conflicting attitudes toward power itself. As in any other country, the majority is not about to get in the way of the powerful. Most writers, like most other people, know where their bread is buttered. But there is also a minority in league with the future, the growing tip of the tree, and a certain amount of danger is always at their side. This is one of the reasons why both kinds of writer—although the vanguard is more likely to do this— will direct attention to colleagues of the same persuasion. It is a kind of politicking, a way of strengthening the side.

But what exactly are both factions after, what—beyond the obvious advantages of supporting the regime—are the so-called conservatives aiming at in their works, and what in the vanguard enrages them so?

The obvious answers are ideological, but they are not altogether explanatory. The conservative writer sees himself in the tradition of the realistic work of Tolstoy, for example—although he will disassociate himself from the master's mysticism and religiosity. Art, he would say, is basically the higher consciousness of the people, immediately comprehensible to them, and an enhancement of the values of socialism. Socialism is the Soviet system, whose fundamental objectives are humane, progressive, and generally directed toward the welfare of all. In a word, art is like science, a servant of the community. In fact, the whole concept is Platonic and by no means uniquely Russian or even Communist.

The Puritan fathers of the Massachusetts Bay Colony, for instance, would not have countenanced novels and poems which unearthed the sexual repressions enforced by their semi-military discipline, let alone advocated freer sexuality. The colony was always in danger and a man who kept himself apart from its spiritual defense, a man who deeply questioned the underlying propositions of the society, would not and did not last very long. The famed Roger Williams objected too strongly to the theocratic suppression of variant religious ideas and on top of that preached the equality in spirit of the Indians whom the white men were deceiving and robbing—and was promptly put out in the dead of winter to die. It was the Indians who saved him, and in Rhode Island he set up the first society on the American continent where the freedom to think was guaranteed.

The conservative Russian writer—the honest one anyway—is moved by the fear that the high communal aims of the Communist state will be atomized, diluted, and ultimately destroyed by the individualistic vanguard. But the writer who feels this way also has attitudes, apparently little connected with ideology, which also place him firmly in this ideological camp. He is more than likely, for example, to enjoy the feeling of solidarity with the party, with workers, and with other non-writers whose reality he shares. He is another kind of worker and takes pride in it, a worker in literature or art. It is not onerous but a matter of duty and goodness to accept party revisions of his work. He is likely to emphasize the virtues of craftsmanship, solid construction, and thoroughness in a work of art. He wants, in short, to be part of what-is. He is rationalist in his explanation of man.

It needs to be said that many of these men, like their counterparts everywhere, have been neither suborned nor corrupted by superior force. Accepting the fundamental bases of Soviet society, they honestly regard what injustice they see as temporary error or at worst a lamentable necessity which does not prove the rule. They are men who desire authority and fear chaos. For them life can never be tragic because the individual who comes to a bad end has simply separated himself from the victorious path of the society. Stalin stated their viewpoint most aptly—the writer is the engineer of the soul. Rather than speaking truth to power, he justifies power to the people. His greatest justification is quite probably the career and works of Mikhail Sholokhov, whose trilogy of the Russian Civil War in the Don Cossack area seems to demonstrate that art and absolute fealty to the state can be combined without damage.

There are those, on the other hand, who point out that Sholokhov revised his masterwork to minimize the values of those Cossacks who opposed the Red Army, and so weakened his achievement. Some even suggest that Sholokhov did not write these works but stood in as the author while the real author was liquidated. This last, however, seems unlikely as new Sholokhov stories have recently appeared and their style is the same as the works of thirty years ago. But the imputation indicates the depth of bitterness between the two factions. Sholokhov is a rauchy old Cossack now, advocating that the whipper-snappers be fed to the sharks if they don't like the way things are in the Soviet Union. His identification, in all likelihood, is with those first heroic revolutionaries who stood up like men before the Czar's agents and firing squads, and despite unimaginable deprivation, betrayals, and hardships, dragged Russia out of feudalism and into the age of science and modernity. To a Sholokhov, the power he respects and upholds is the power that fends off the decadence of the West—the pornography, the effeminacy, the rootless, nationless, cryptic, private art whose supremacy anywhere means the end of community itself. There are millions of Sholokhovs everywhere, needless to say, the difference being that in the Soviet Union a writer is far more than an individual facing a piece of blank paper alone in a room; he is state property and accountable for his attitudes. But as revolutionary ideas move into the streets in the West, much the same sort of conflict is rising among writers there. A LeRoi Jones, committed to black militancy, has no patience with Negro writers whose work does not forward the cause, and he would surely regard as an enemy and betrayer a talented Negro who spent his time dealing with matters irrelevant to that cause. Any claim to the autonomy of art must collapse when a people is in danger or struggling to preserve itself, and the single theme of Soviet political and social discourse for half a century has been its imminent peril before foreign and domestic enemies. Actually, much the same emotions work inside us. Until very recently it was a rare Hollywood movie that ventured to question any basic American social premise, and the studio heads exercised an ironbound censorship of any such story. They were avowedly providing "wholesome" entertainment in which fundamental conservative American ideas always emerged victorious—or at a minimum were awarded a metaphoric justification. School boards all over the country screen out material from textbooks they deem subversive of national values, whatever the validity of that material, and on the most blatant level the House Un-American Activities Committee for more than thirty years has arraigned writers and others whom it regards as dangerous to accepted thinking. Among other questions asked me by the chairman of that committee was, "Why do you write so sadly about this country?" It is a truly Stalinist question, if you will, and there are millions of Americans who share the chairman's feelings. Given the right political atmosphere, the kind we had in the 1950s, these deeply angry people will come out on the streets to picket movies and plays by authors they regard as hostile to American values, and given the legal power would unquestionably clean up our production in a matter of weeks.

The difference, therefore, is not in the uniqueness of Russian feelings toward such matters but in the legal systems; all Russian literature is published by the state and must meet the requirements of the Communist Party. That a certain number of works have been published which criticize or imply that all is not on the right track, indicates that within the party are men who have come to recognize that the role of the writer may not be quite as simple as Stalin thought. Obviously some of them see that the writer's criticisms might even strengthen the state by bringing to light real shortcomings which ought not be continually rationalized away. There are even a few who understand that the heavy censorship has bled much of Soviet writing of its individuality and sheer interest.

It is not possible to begin to understand anything about the feelings of either young or old Soviet artists without keeping in mind Ehrenburg's admission— "The thought came to me that I should have to remain silent for a very long time . . . I should have no one with whom to share my experiences."

Nothing is easier than to read a bad conscience into this, and little more; he should have fled when he could, or spoken out against what he knew was wrong, and so forth. But there is something much more. It is a little like a man trying to explain how he fell in love with a perfect woman who turned out to be murderous, vain, even insane, and cared nothing for him, a woman to whom he had dedicated his works, his life, and his highest idealistic feelings. How can you explain that, when the truth is now so obvious to your listener? It is impossible spiritually to tear oneself apart from a beloved without leaving a part of yourself behind, and the Soviet scene is still under the tension of this same paradox, even in the hearts of those too young to have been touched by Stalinism. For the power of the Communist ideal is on the level of the religious one, of any belief in sacrifice to a higher and worthier ideal than one's own selfish interests.

And that is why so many of the Ehrenburg generation, any of those who once felt the totality of belief, seem so saddened now regardless of the fact that some, at least, of the truth of Stalinism has been revealed and its excesses curbed—most of the time, anyway.

Konstantin Simonov is in his fifties now. He is the author of good, workable plays, poems, and novels, and during the war was a front-line correspondent who saw more action than a great many soldiers. His line of communication to the highest levels of the party is still open. He lives very well, sometimes in a spacious Moscow apartment, sometimes in a country house where the shelves are littered with icons, sculpture, and paintings from Russia and from the many other countries he has visited. The sentencing of Yuri Daniel to prison he does not agree with; Daniel was a soldier and wounded at that. Sinyavsky is another story, for he never served in the war, and worse, perhaps, knowingly had his manuscripts published abroad rather than standing up for them at home and struggling to get them accepted. Still, Simonov can swallow his resentment of Sinyavsky too, knowing that it was not intelligent, by even putting him on trial, to give the world a club with which to beat the Soviet Union. Simonov is caught, it seems, between a certain sense of honor, which to him Sinyavsky violated, and the hard-learned lesson that imprisonment is no longer the answer to literary dissidence.

At the same time Simonov will not forgo any chance to put down bad writers, whatever their loyalty, or foreign partisans of the Soviet whose works are empty. In short, he seems to have arrived at substantive rather than relative values. And inevitably, his journals of the war, a work he regards as perhaps the most important of his career, have been refused publication for several years now. But apparently he is determined to think and work within the slowly changing system and to fight the battle as he can.

Simonov may still be *persona grata* with the regime, but he is at bottom a working writer and knows that censorship finally means an instruction to writers to lie. A patriot, as Russian as you can get and still stay sober, he has that double vision of his country which the awakened live with; he often seems nearly ashamed of what is still done in the name of national security and socialist truth. But he is not an official, and I wanted to hear the official attitude toward writers and censorship.

Madame Ekaterina Furtseva is the nominal chief of all cultural work in the Soviet Union. We met in her office, a long and impressive room with a green felt-covered table in the center surrounded by armchairs, and a working desk at one end beneath two tall windows. Behind the chair was a ten-foot-long table piled high with possibly two hundred manuscripts and books. Slips of paper stuck out of those books and manuscripts—indicating, I assumed, marked passages.

Madame Furtseva was then in her sixties, a sensitive and still handsome woman, attentive and intelligent. Suffering had carved deeply into her face. Indeed, one day a few years ago, in the midst of a business meeting, a man in working clothes had entered her office and with a pair of clippers cut the wire of the phone that connected her office directly with Khrushchev's. She went home and slashed her wrists. Having been raised under Stalin, she knew what this gesture must mean. She was saved, however, and

Khrushchev ordered her restored to her position, for she had been a favorite of his. When it is said that Russia has not really changed much, one must keep in mind that "much" can sometimes mean everything. But what such an incident still leaves in the mind of the foreigner is that the restoration is still quite as arbitrary and unpredictable as the condemnation, resting on a leader's temperament rather than on legally secured rights.

I knew that writers rather liked her—all sorts of writers, conservative and vanguard alike, more or less. The general feeling was that she cared about literature and was basically humane, and was not simply a police agent in disguise. Four or five officials sat around the table, she at the head. These were chiefs of various departments, one in charge of theater, another of children's books, and so on. They said nothing and were clearly of a lower but still considerable rank. They wore dark, well-pressed suits, starched collars, and subdued ties. We might well have been in a bank, discussing a mortgage.

Madame Furtseva, arranging her long shawl over her shoulders, talked of the weather, of all our children, of plays she had seen—including my own. *A View from the Bridge* had been playing for a long time and I told her I had seen it the night before. She was immediately curious about my reaction to the production. I said that I thought some of the actors superb, but that certain excisions and changes in the script disturbed me. She was genuinely surprised at this—and as her office was in charge of translations, her responsibility was now on the agenda.

I went on to say that all the psychological motivation had been carefully removed from the play. Eddie Carbone, the hero, must *slowly* reveal an illicit attachment to his niece, a love which helps to move him toward a betrayal of his two brothers-in-law, who are illegal Sicilian immigrants. But in the Soviet version he has hardly entered the scene when he speaks of his love for his niece and whenever she appears he puts on an agony of frustration which makes any later revelation immaterial and foolish. One wondered why his wife remained in the house at all.

There were many other changes of the same sort—nothing is left to be developed and discovered, everything is stated at the outset, and rather crudely at that. I could not understand why the play was such a success.

Madame Furtseva was obviously appalled. She wanted to know from her assistants who had translated the play and why this had been allowed to happen. The matter would be looked into. Her sincerity emboldened me and I asked what the procedure was for selecting translators. To my astonishment she was quite vague about it. Not secretive, but genuinely vague, and even asked her assistants to help out with an explanation. The embarrassment now spread down the table. It turned out that translators in effect selected themselves; someone with a bit of English might hear of a foreign hit, get hold of a manuscript or a book, rush through a Russian version, and be the first to get to one of the Moscow or Leningrad theaters with a script. This, I said, sounded like arrant free enterprise, the rewards going not to the most able but to the most aggressive. We all had a good hollow laugh at this, but the problem remained.

After about an hour it seemed time to break up, and I said I did not want to keep her from her work any longer. She glanced behind her at the massive piles of books and manuscripts which awaited her perusal. Yes, she said, there was a vast amount of work to do. I asked if she had to read all those manuscripts and she said yes, she did have to; unfortunately it was necessary. What do you suppose would happen, I asked, if she just chucked it and didn't read them? Just let them go through. Would it really rock the country?

She laughed then, and I thought I detected a certain understanding in her laugh—as though the relaxation of censorship, even its abolition, had been discussed by her before this. I persisted; I had met some writers who were suspect to one degree or another, but their complaint was that the current system was not Communist enough rather than too Communist. As for Russia itself, their eyes melted at the mention of it. She nodded. She understood perfectly well. She knew it better than I did, I thought then.

Perhaps I was too taken with her and let myself read too much into that laugh—a certain recognition of at least a grain of absurdity in her exhausting attempts to keep the national mind loyal and clean and unquestioning. More, I thought at that moment that somewhere in her was the wish that the gates could open and that mistaken literature could be condemned by the people in their wisdom. But I could be wrong. I could also be right, however.

Two days later at a cocktail party one of her assistants sought me out. He handed me an envelope. It contained a chit for royalties due me on a story of mine which had been published in Moscow years before. I asked what this amount represented—was it all I was owed? He asked if I wanted more, the way you ask a guest if he wants more pickles. I said no, I wasn't here to dun them for royalties but was merely curious, although anything would be gratefully received. He then gave me the message which was obviously his chief business. Madame Furtseva had not spoken idly during our meeting; she wanted to assure me that she would personally see to it that from now on my translators would be the best that could be found. I thanked him. Then I asked, what about the translators for the other Americans they published and produced? He seemed taken aback, surprised; there had been no discussion of the others, or of the whole procedure of selecting translators. In short, this was irrelevant.

Perhaps I read too much into his reaction, but it seemed rather a harking back to the royal past. Rules applied to everyone excepting to those especially favored from on high, and his total and naïve acceptance of such a benign procedure was noteworthy, I thought—he saw nothing whatever unjust about it. I had earned a favor and would receive it. What could be better than that?

And yet—don't politicians do favors in Washington? Of course they do, but one imagines they are remotely ashamed. Perhaps one ought not imagine too much. Or is the moral simply that we are still laboring under some fringe of the old illusion which the great October Revolution raised before the world—that a government of and by the insulted and injured had finally risen on the earth, a society which had somehow abolished the motivations for immorality, the incarnation at long last of the human community. So that infractions here, any appearance of the Old Adam, are doubly scandalous, immensely more meaningful than anywhere else.

After the performance of *A View from the Bridge*, backstage talking to the actors, I kept looking around for the actor who had played Eddie, the hero of the play, and since he was not present I referred to his performance several times, saying, "The man who played Eddie . . ." until I noticed a certain shifting, an embarrassment among the actors, and it was pointed out finally that their Eddie was standing next to me. He was totally unrecognizable. For the characterization on stage he had built up a different nose.

At the Sovremennik (Contemporary) Theater the troupe is very young, but several characters in Efremov's dazzling production of Schwartz's *The Emperor's Clothes* are aged men. The oldest, a prime minister who trembles with senility, turned out to be a twenty-four-year-old actor, and on another night I watched him for two hours in a different role and never realized it was the same fellow. It is all in the nose, and the changes are not always gross. A widening of the bridge, a slight tilting of the tip, a new flare for the nostrils and the actor is catapulted into another age bracket and a new personality. Gogol, of course, was fascinated with noses, and physical description in Russian literature has traditionally been of great importance. People, whatever their psychological nature may be, are first of all bodies, and this fascination with the way people look is, I think, the foundation for the vividness of so much Russian acting.

A great deal has been made in the past twenty years of the staleness of Russian theater. Certainly it has kept out Ionesco, Beckett, the whole absurdist mode. But there is very little in the West that can match the vitality of the best Russian productions. Directors like Efremov and Lubimov would be of first importance anywhere. Their productions are highly finished and complete, yet imaginative and sometimes wild. Their actors are mostly young, full of enthusiasm and curiosity, and far better trained than the majority of Americans.

Even in plays with little distinction or novelty of form there is always some startling acting. *Uncle's Dream,* a dramatization of a Dostoevsky story, is a case in point. A great nobleman is passing through a provincial Russian town and his carriage breaks down. He must spend the night. The ladies of the best families vie with one another for the honor of sheltering him. The nobleman is unmarried, so naturally the mothers of eligible daughters are desperate to receive him. These are "the best people," and the nobleman is the incarnation of state authority and aristocratic distinction. The ladies meet in the living room of an important matron to decide who among them will have the honor. They have all agreed, however, not to invite Madame X (I have forgotten the character's name), who is universally regarded as a viper and a pest. Ten or twelve of them in satin and embossed velour dresses move about the stage, plotting, sweeping from couch to piano to the bust of Byron to the French doors opening on the garden, like a flock of excited geese, their words lengthening out into a kind of whining, half-sung chorale which nevertheless remains this side of reality. Comic as it is, it is somehow hair-raising. They sit down at last, sipping the drink of the cultivated—chocolate. In comes Madame X, who has gotten wind of this meeting to which she was denied admission.

Serafina Birman, the actress, as I later found out, was the age of the character—in her mid-seventies. She enters. The company falls silent in a hush of horror. The offended socialite stands center stage, surveying her betrayers. She begins to take them apart one by one, their private bad habits drawn upon their foreheads by her mocking, searing voice. For three minutes she continues without pause or mercy. Then four, then five, then six, then seven. Her breath begins to come hard, but she will not relent. She is unsteady on her feet now and takes a faltering step to the side as though about to collapse, but she goes right on. Suddenly—she goes down on one knee. Her brown satin gown, a veritable drapery, catches on her heel, her hair is falling into her eyes, but her bitterness flows on. She is losing her breath altogether, it seems, she is shaking in every bone, and she lies down on one side, propped up by her elbow, her free arm extended as she points from hated face to hated face. However collapsed, she never loses her nobility, her stertorous frightfulness, her righteous wrathfulness. She continues gasping out her curses, and now she lowers her free hand to the floor, turns over on her stomach, and points at the hostess, the arch culprit. "And as for you—I spit in your chocolate!" With which she sits upright, gets her feet under herself, and stands, swaying with exhaustion and a certain profound pleasure, and staggers out of the house. It is beyond acting, it is apocalypse, and backstage later I found for the first time in my life that I was pleased that someone had been given the Order of Lenin. She has been acting for over fifty years.

The physicalness of Russian acting, its mortal quality, was apparent also in what can only be called the disembodying of the nobleman. He appears at first as a caricature of an upper-class dandy. Obviously made-up to look young enough to attract women, he can barely move about in his patent-leather shoes, the lace pouring out from under his sleeves, the high stiff collar manacling his neck. Alone, finally, in a bedroom with his valet, he is being undressed for the night. The wide-chested jacket is removed, revealing a skinny torso; his gloves off show veined and aged hands. His fine head of hair goes into the wig box leaving him bald, his teeth go into a jar and his lips pucker up, and finally one eye comes out and there he sits, the mummy of the ruling class still chattering on about his possibilities as a lover. Of course the idea is not new, but the detail is so deftly etched that it still frightens and illusions the onlooker, who can only marvel at it.

No one who goes to the theater in Russia can fail to be struck by the audience. It is not bored and it is not uncritical, but it is passionately open to what it has come to see. Outside on the street there are always dozens of people pleading with each arrival for an extra seat. Young people make up the majority of the audiences, and particularly if the production offers something new and contemporary there is almost an atmosphere of adoration in the house, and open gratitude to the author, the actors, the director. It is as though there were still a sort of community in this country, for the feeling transcends mere admiration for professionals doing their work well. It is as though art were a communal utterance, a kind of speech which everyone present is delivering together.

The earthiness, the bodiliness, so to speak, of Russian acting even extends into its stylizations. Yuri Lubimov's production of *Ten Days That Shook the World* in his Taganka Theater is a sort of visualization of the atmosphere of the Revolution, rather than a play. From time to time a white screen is lowered over the whole stage, and, lit from behind, it shows the silhouettes of the actors, the people of the city caught up in the chaos. The detail of each silhouette instantly conveys not only that one is a prostitute, another a bourgeois, another a worker, another an old querulous gentleman, but somehow their attitudes toward the Revolution, and the impression comes from body postures, particularly of gestures, the way a head is held or a finger points. And as the light is moved back and more distant from the actor, his silhouette grows on the screen, so that at the end the figures of the new Red Army men, the defenders of the Revolution, move like giants as tall as the proscenium, dominating the whole theater.

Much of this production is sheer choreography and neither better nor worse than its counterparts elsewhere, but there is always some explosive conception. which instantly speaks of this particular Russian genius for physicalizing. A young man is being held before a firing squad. He is let go to face his death. The rifles rise to sight him. There is no explosion of bullets, but the young man rises onto his toes, then comes down on his heels. Then he rises again, a little higher this time, and comes down harder. Now he jumps up a few inches off the floor and comes down; then he jumps up about a foot off the floor and comes down; now he is springing, higher and higher, his hands behind his back, until he is flying upward in a movement of both escape and pride, of death's agony and life's unbelievable end, until one imagines he will succeed in simply flying upward and away—and then he comes down and crumples to the earth, and no sound is heard.

It is wordless and physical, the diametric opposite of the poets' avant-garde theater which Yevtushenko and Voznesensky, among others, are attempting to create. Neither is primarily a dramatist but, as in most countries now, the theater has attracted poets as a public forum where contact with wide audiences can make poetry stretch itself toward its classic applicability to public discourse. By the accident of their appearance as spokesmen for the youth their names are usually coupled, but their talents and traditions are not at all the same.

It is impossible for a foreigner really to appraise Yevtushenko's *Bratsk Station* or *The Triangular Pear* by Voznesensky because they both depend almost totally on language. One can, however, speak of two different kinds of feeling that are quite apparent and distinctive in each. Voznesensky's is a first-person work, a series of stylized scenes allowing actors to speak broken-up sections of his poems as individual speeches. It is rather a staged recitative than a dialogue, but the power of his verse over the audience is unmistakable. The near-surrealism of the staging is sophisticated and charming, but it would probably seem rather tame in some far-out Western theaters. Immersed as one inevitably is in mass theater in Russia, which is basically realistic theater, this performance reminds one that there is an "in" culture and an "out," a split in the sensibilities of the country. *The Triangular Pear* celebrates personal emotions and an individual's singular reaction to his time rather than any group or public destiny and if it has a moral purpose it is to raise up to view the response of one individual to the world he has found. Its beauty of language apart, perhaps it is this quality of individuation which attracts the young to it and to Voznesensky's verse. He pretends to speak for no one but himself, his own nature. It is also probable that this is what unnerves the authorities about him.

Bratsk Station is of another order, a sort of cantata embracing the sacrifices, the endurance, the heroism of the Russian people as well as hints of the injustices they suffered in the gigantic construction of modern Russia. With a cast of perhaps thirty young actors, using Egyptian slavery as a symbol of Stalinism, the work strives toward a Whitmanesque celebration of the people's victory over their history, their betrayers, and those who would enslave them. The work opens with a movie projected over the entire back of the stage, showing on grainy 1920 film stock a long line of workers with arms linked around each other's waists, rhythmically tramping their immense felt boots on soft concrete into the forms of the Bratsk Dam. Moving en masse from side to side over the cement, they perform a kind of massive Hora of brute human power driving a twentieth-century structure into the ancient Russian earth. The film appears again at the end, after we have seen how this very discipline and faith was taken advantage of by slave-driving betrayers, but this time it is interrupted by a rush onstage of a line of well-dressed, shiny-faced young couples who break into an arm-linked dance to the same rhythm as the old Bratsk workers use in the film—now, however, with a rock musical accompaniment which joins both generations together in the present. The new young people throw off an air of free and joyous energy which inevitably seems to taunt any who would do to them what was done to their fathers. And the one refrain of *Bratsk Station* is, indeed, "Russians never will be slaves."

Seeing these plays it is difficult to understand why they should have met with such opposition from the party if it were not still torn between rather primitive Stalinist and liberative factions. There surely seems to be no split in the audience's enthusiasm, nor does there appear to be any sense of scandal or exposé in the audience reception. That Russians never will be slaves is hardly a revolutionary slogan, and a regime which permits such sentiments on its official stage would merely seem to be feeling rather secure about its passage through a dark time. But the fact is that *Bratsk Station* went through many party-imposed revisions and line-changes. Only recently it was even taken out of production for a time and then allowed back again.

Ultimately there is an absurdity about this alternation between repression and freedom, and beyond the absurdity a question as to whether the leadership is, or dares to be, in touch with the people at all. If the invasion of Czechoslovakia is any guide, it is not. Justifying the invasion on the need to rescue the Czech Communist Party from counterrevolutionaries, the Russian government was unable to find a single Czech Communist leader of any repute who would come forward as a representative of the rescued. The Russians found themselves forced to treat with the very leadership against whose betrayals of Communism they had come to save the country. This bespeaks either total cynicism or a hermetic, self-induced illusion of such proportions as to astound the foreigner—and doubtless many Russians too. (The problem came up in conversations with Czech intellectuals in Prague in March 1969. With Soviet soldiers occupying their city, they were under the gun, yet they were not entirely able to dismiss the possibility that the invasion was to some degree the result of self-delusion on the part of the Soviet party, a sign of its incapacity to recognize realities which its a priori theories denied existed. Russian officers and soldiers stopped people on the streets in the early days of the occupation, asking to be led to the "counterrevolutionaries," and were shocked by the hostility of the Czechs. Others believed they had landed in West Germany, because the people were so antagonistic, and as well because the shops were so full of gadgets unseen in Russia; the mini-skirted girls and the general absence of fraternal sentiments helped this impression, too. The Czech intellectuals, however, filled with indignation and apprehension for their own futures, did not overlook the implicit naïveté, let alone the blind stupidity, of Russian pronouncements on the invasion. One lesson they seemed to draw from the experience was that in their own country—and, it is to be hoped, one day in the Soviet Union too—a legalized opposition must be allowed; not only to hedge power with law and law with the free-spoken opinions of the people, but also to prevent the party from atrophying. And finally—although they are neighbors, fellow Slavs, and fellow Communists—these Czechs find the atmosphere of religiosity surrounding the Soviet government as odd as it is to us. They did not, for example, admire the all but total silence of Russian intellectuals toward the fate of Czechoslovakia, but at the same time agreed when I said that for Russians to stand openly against their government is akin to heresy, with all its implications of guilt and sinfulness. Indeed, one could almost say that the rock on which Soviet moral presumptions broke apart in Czechoslovakia was that Czech socialism in its two liberalizing years had become anti-ritualistic, practical, and humane. In this view the purpose of the collective is the flowering of the individual; for the Soviets the collective is its own end and justification, the individual remaining a theoretically unaccounted-for, free-floating object whose real nature has never been fitted into the system.)

There is not supposed to be any anti-Semitism in the Soviet Union. It is all the more vehemently denied, especially as being part of state policy, because it was so blatantly a part of the Nazi ideology. A short time ago, however, a respected Soviet writer submitted for publication a series of memoirs of Russian writers of the twenties. The work was accepted with enthusiasm by the board of the publishing house, but, as always, there were a few editorial problems which needed talking about. One of the poets discussed in the work, a man who died in the early thirties, had been a Latvian German, and naturally had a German family name. His middle name, however—this, the editors felt, was an interesting variation of any German name they had ever heard of. In fact, they wondered aloud, it seemed to sound like a Jewish name.

The memoirist, a Russian of course, had never considered this at all. It was a name. He did not know if the middle name was Jewish, but if it was—did this represent a problem?

Not at all, the editors replied. But why must it be included? Why not call the man by his first and last names and simply leave out the middle name? The poems themselves were thoroughly Russian; why throw some sort of pall of misunderstanding over them? The poet's middle name was dropped.

Another Soviet writer—who shall also be nameless—wrote the story of the Bible for children. His rendition was also enthusiastically read by his editors. But, again, there were certain problems of a minor sort which required a conference, and one afternoon the author and his editors sat down to iron them out.

First of all, said the editors, there was this question of God. As we all know, God is a mythological construction, and in any strict sense mentioning God is really unnecessary.

But, replied the author, in the Bible . . .

Secondly, the editors went on, there is the whole business of "the Jewish People" cropping up again and again in your work, which is otherwise quite admirable. Why is that necessary?

Well, replied the author, the Bible, you see is . . .

Why not simply call them "the People"? After all, it comes to the same thing, and in fact it generalizes and enhances the significance of the whole story. Call them "the People." And there is one final question.

The author waited for the final question.

It is the title. "The Story of the Bible" is not a very exact title.

What would you suggest? the author asked.

How about, "Myths of the People"?

And that was that.

The Opera House in Tashkent looked so inviting, and they were playing *Leila and Mezhdu,* based on the national epic. We must go. Some difficulty in arranging tickets on such short notice. We arrive promptly at seven for a seven-thirty curtain, in order to see what the crowd looks like.

The building is some combination of Moorish, Spanish, City-Center-type architecture, but nevertheless very white and imposing, with wide-open concrete aprons around it and a nice flat stairway rising up from the street level. A strange quiet, however, as we pass beneath the outer archways, and in fact there is nobody in the lobby. Did we misunderstand the curtain time? It appears not, for the large lady usher takes our ticket and bids us follow her inside. Perhaps Uzbeks do not speak before the curtain goes up?

In the auditorium there is not one soul. Immaculately clean, the seat-arms polished, the carpet soft and well-vacuumed—but not a soul. We sit in the third row center. It is a vast house, with perhaps four thousand seats. Endless balconies, galleries, boxes. All empty.

Ten minutes pass like an hour and a half. Another couple comes down the aisle. Action! They are English. One can tell after a few minutes because they don't speak to one another but sit at polite attention quite as though the seats around them were full. Nothing whatever is odd, remarkable, wrong. If water started rising above their ankles they would not move or take note. One loves them, their truly *interested* attention as they stare at the empty orchestra pit. England will never die.

Movement behind us. Turning around I spy a customer. An Uzbek worker, he wears a cap sideways, a red bandanna around his neck, no shirt, his black wrinkled jacket and pants and shoes caked with white cement. He is alone, lounging in his seat, staring at the curtain up ahead. Things are moving. Soon we may have the ushers outnumbered and could force a performance.

A disturbance in the orchestra pit. A musician enters from under the stage. A man of sixty, his eyeglasses badly bent, he has no tie, wears a sweater. He sits and opens his violin case. Something wrong with the bridge. He adjusts it for ten minutes.

More action behind us. For some reason about eight people have entered the second balcony. Five or six now spread out behind us in the orchestra, one man sits alone in a side box.

Two more musicians enter the pit. One of them tests his clarinet, the other reads a newspaper. How forlorn. Three or four more come into the pit now. They tune up, but only barely take any notice of one another. Perhaps they have been exiled here? One, for some reason, is wearing a tuxedo. Probably a recent arrival from Moscow, still unaccustomed to frontier mores.

The tuning-up is getting louder and is much better than nothing. Suddenly, as though on cue, they all stop, pack up their instruments, and walk out under the stage! Can it all be over?

Inge is now weeping with laughter, a certain hysteria having entered our relationship. Neither one of us can say anything that is not funny.

A small note of revolt—the audience begins to clap in unison. It is now a quarter past eight. The English couple remains fascinated by the curtain, takes no note of the demonstration. The clapping dies away. Begins all over again.

The house lights go down as the musicians hurry back in. A full orchestra, the members glance out over the gala audience. A kind of utter exhaustion emanates from the conductor, who makes a play at a rapid, sprightly entrance. Somebody up in the gallery claps once.

The curtain rises. An Arab-type chieftain sits before a cardboard tent surrounded by his court. He seems angry as he sings baritone. The others try to placate him. He is stubborn, refusing comfort. Moussorgsky weaves through Tchaikovsky through intermittent Rimsky-Korsakov. Ignorant of the story, one still knows that the chieftain's daughter must soon appear. She sure as hell does. Beautiful girl, but can't sing. Which is the hero? Two or three young bravos appear and one knows which is the hero because he is the shortest and stands at the center, and whenever he points at something he also takes a gliding step in the same direction, while the others only point without taking a step. Very gradually one's sympathy begins to go out to all of them knocking themselves out for the empty house. What dreams of glory they must have had once! It is terribly hard work, this opera. Queen Victoria would have adored the purity of its emotions, the sweep of the music. It is all Cultural. Somewhere in this city must be some guys and girls hiding in a cellar playing some stringed instrument and singing to each other without a committee. The public has vetoed this opera, is all one can say. It has definitely decided to risk everything and not come. There is something heartening and universal, finally. As the box-office man on Broadway once said to me, "There is no power on earth that can keep the public from staying home."

Intermission. The audience rises. The combined sound is like eleven chickens scratching in Madison Square Garden. We stroll idly, politely, toward the lobby. The English couple, still *interested,* appears a few yards away. I confide to Inge that we are not remaining for the second act, although there is no doubt the English couple will do their national duty. We stroll out the front door rather as though wanting a breath of the night air. We keep on strolling at a sort of trot. Glancing behind, we see the English couple also strolling, looking about at the nonexistent native audience, but disappearing nevertheless into the bowels of Tashkent. And yet—what's the opera situation on a weekday night in Duluth, Minnesota?

There is an almost universal conviction that all hotel rooms are tapped, as well as many apartments. Visitors sometimes arrive with paper and pencil, communicating by writing while they carry on banter directed toward the bug, or at home play loud Beethoven passages while discussing anything of importance. The odd thing is that after a while one gets used to it oneself. Transistorized cartridge tape recordings are also good masking devices. One sits down to discuss some ordinary matter, and the host turns on a loud rock-and-roll number in his lap. Pretty soon, though, a sort of surrealistic mood develops, especially if the conversation is a sad one, or if both parties to it lapse into silent thought for a few moments while hillbilly music squeals on. When the recorder is turned off it is time to eat, or speak of happy or inconsequential things. But should the serious mood return again, on goes the tape recorder and the rock-and-roll. Ultimately it is an incredibly pleasurable thing simply to go to bed and think freely to oneself. Maybe this is why so many Russians seem so deep, and despite their gregariousness so solitary—perforce, they have done so much communing with themselves.

It may also be part of the explanation for the special importance of literature to them. So much that is ordinarily unsayable is given by the nuances of good writing, by its capacity to imply far more than its syntax, transmitting by definition a climactic social application. Thus the pressures on the writer and artist are compounded, and the contradictions too. Nowhere else are writers so close to being worshiped by their readers, nowhere does a regime go to such extremes to honor or hound them. The paradox is built into the writing craft itself, for on one hand nobody, not even the commissar, denies that writing to be any good must be personal, must be an individual's own thought and style. On the other, by expressing his individuality the writer takes hold of a certain power, a power which he must not use beyond the point where the regime feels comfortable with his use of it. Thus, periodically he must be humbled. It is as though there were an arena where the talented may venture at risk, and the seer or prophet at the risk of his life. The importance of literature stems, finally, from the penalties hanging over the practice of it. Thus a writer is always a step away from dread heroism and is worshiped like a sacrifice. After all, writing is almost the only act one cannot in Russia commit anonymously; even the great physicists and inventors are rarely credited by name, so that whatever power might accrue to individual scientists is waylaid. But a novel or play or poem cannot very well come into the world by itself, or as the result of a committee's resolution, and the power of authorship is thus unique; only the leaders can be so well known, and therefore in danger of such idolatry—or such humiliation, should conditions change.

Perhaps it is also why they so detest frivolous or fragmentary or self-indulgent writing. It is like telling bad jokes at a funeral or in a church. In a very real sense the national fate is in the writer's hands, the immortal fire of the race. And so the wrath is terrible when he appears to have some secret allegiance to foreign ideas, and it is very probable that that anger is not confined to the bureaucracy alone. Whatever the repressions it may use to perpetuate itself, there must surely be a deep strain of apathetic consent in the people or they could not possibly continue.

One could, and one ought to go even further, and face the fact that there is such a thing as working-class taste, or more precisely, an unalienated taste of whatever class. So many attempts have been made in England, America, and France, for example, to establish trade-union theater movements and thus to break through the ring of bourgeois audiences and middle-class prejudices and tastes. They have never come to anything. It seems as though people who are deeply immersed in the production process, people who spend their lives trying to make things work, and have, so to speak, invested themselves in sustaining and elaborating the productive process, are not going to enjoy a spectacle which lacks materiality, reality, purpose, and logic of an everyday kind. Every machine process moves from less to more, from nothing to something, from the imminent to the accomplished. Conflicts of thought, abstract symbolizations, much of the arsenal of what is called modern art, lack point for these people because, while these qualities may *be* something, they do not apparently *do* anything either to move such people, to educate them, or to give them an idea about themselves. The

Soviet hierarchy may well be basing itself upon the innate conservatism of all producers, and especially those who have no reason to be revolutionary. After all, the fame and impact of a Brecht was created with and among the alienated bourgeoisie and not among the working class. Finally, Solzhenitsyn, the one writer in Russia who is universally regarded as a classic, a genius, precisely fits the ultimate categories. He is a seer, an absolute truth-teller, and he writes simply, realistically, in a style untouched by the past fifty or even seventy-five years of literary experiment, a style which any literate worker, engineer, or schoolteacher can bite into and find nourishing. His latest books circulate in typewritten drafts, but they are not published. Yet he is known everywhere. He alone has had the audacity openly to call not for a relaxation of censorship but for its total abolition. He has entered the arena of the saints. And it needs to be added that there are not many writers anywhere in the world with this kind of insight, to say nothing of his courage, a courage which is not only expressed in the political implications of what he is saying, but in a style which dares be comprehensible to the alienated and the unalienated alike.

Our last night in Russia, inevitably, brought all the incipient chaos of feelings and unanswered questions to a head. Andrei Voznesensky and his wife, Zoya, good friends of Maya Plisetskaya, prima ballerina of the Bolshoi Ballet, had arranged for us to see her performance. Yevtushenko's wife, Galia, insisted we could not leave the country without seeing a certain painter's work in his apartment far from the center of town. Inge had meanwhile misplaced her passport. A Russian journalist who had broken his back in an Army plane (he crashed in Siberia in an attempt to machine-gun a bear) had insisted I take home a jar of special honey for my cold and would meet us anywhere. Appointments we had been postponing with three other people now had to be met. And through all these meetings and conversations and gift-giving Inge had to try to get through the telephone system to all the places we had been in the last twenty-four hours to try to locate her passport—a difficulty, when a lot of Russians do not answer their phones unless they have been notified ahead of time as to who is calling.

On top of it all there was a curious mood of uncertainty because a writer-friend of the Voznesenskys had just turned up; he had recently come under attack by the Writers' Union, which had gone so far as to publish an article against him in the press. The man some weeks before had gotten so apprehensive that he had gone off to a small town in Siberia to get away from the mutterings against him in Moscow. Now, just back, he was wondering if it had been wise to return. Then again, maybe he should issue some intransigent statement which might rally support for him; on the other hand, *would* others support him? Should he perhaps return again to Siberia? Should he go back to his own Moscow room? On the other hand, maybe he was overreacting altogether, and the whole business was unnerving him more than it should.

Meanwhile we were all moving into the immense crowd pressing into the Bolshoi Theater. To strange eyes it seemed as though the crowd had never before seen a ballet, the eagerness was so intense. We said good-by to the pale, uncertain writer at the stage entrance. He also knew Plisetskaya well and would love to go up to her dressing room and say hello with us, but maybe it was better he did not. We wound our way through the back corridors of the great theater; the public-address-system loudspeakers connected with the auditorium were alive with the powerful rumbling of people excitedly greeting each other as they took their seats out there. We climbed stairs, wound through other corridors, opened doors through sitting rooms, and the Bill of Rights seemed unutterably precious then, the sheer ignobility of hounding the man we had left in the street was a choking, enraging thing. Nothing, no progress could be worth the fear in that writer's face.

A gentleman in frock coat led us into a sitting room to wait until Plisetskaya had dressed. The walls were red velour, the Louis Something furniture covered with white sheeting as though waiting to be unveiled on some occasion of state, the mirror frames gilt, deeply carved—the very flower of the great age of the cataclysmic Czars. Here too the sound of the auditorium could be heard through the speakers, like a sea waiting to be calmed by the holy power of this dancer dressing on the other side of the paneled door. We waited, talked of the decor and its playful silliness, which now, however, seemed so innocent and naive. Perhaps a Czar had sat here, made to wait a few minutes by some primping ballerina, for it all smelled of Power and therein lay its impressiveness and fatuousness. The frock-coated gentleman, the impresario actually, passed through with a nod to Voznesensky sitting there in his pea jacket and sweater, and opened the paneled door, closing it behind him. In a moment the door opened again—she was ready now.

We filed into Plisetskaya's dressing room. A hall of mirrors. She kissed Andrei. Some time ago he had written one of his best poems about her. They were in league with a spirit that shone in their eyes. She bade us sit down. I had never seen a human being move like this. A racehorse, her muscles swathing the bones. The costume was deceptively casual and peasantlike; in fact, it was an athlete's, like a fighter's gloves, a runner's trunks, and she shifted the waistband of the skirt a quarter-inch as though that infinitesimal adjustment would in a few minutes release her from the pull of earth. She was working now as we talked, turning her feet, ever so slightly stretching her shoulders inside her skin, and the sound of the packed house flowed over her from the loudspeakers, the adoring and menacing sea-rumble of Moscow.

A separate balcony about thirty feet wide hangs over the orchestra of the Bolshoi, in it two high-backed thronelike chairs flanked by lower ones for the noble retainers, the great red drapes framing it all with immense loops and flowings of cloth. The Czar was not in either of the thrones. The stage is very brightly lighted, the faces of the audience await the magic. The curtain lumbers up and *Don Quixote* begins. As a non-fan of classical ballet I decided to sit back in our box just over the footlights and interest myself in the sociology of it all, but as soon as the Knight's soliloquy was over and the girls came on, sociology finished. Each seemed six feet tall, full-bodied, and light as air. What woman could dance more beautifully than these? And Plisetskaya materialized, her body arched forward, it seemed, and her legs and arms shot backward, like a speeding bow freed of the laws of physics. The audience seems to be under her feet, behind her back, over her head, watching every flicker of movement she makes as an infant watches its mother move.

The act is ending. The music stops. She turns to our box, and suddenly I remember that she will be dancing a special cadenza for us. She glances up and begins. The audience knows something unusual is on. A hum, a subdued roar of an oncoming cavalry shudders the house. Wild, noble, unbelievably concentrated inside herself and yet abandoned to a love of air and space, she greets all poets, and perhaps America, with a freed body.

The pleasure of the audience now is like a statement, and the seeming paradox of the Bolshoi is straightened out; there is a mood here different from that in any other place I saw in Russia: the archaism of the house and the classicism of the repertoire are really the forms in which people can simply face beauty, beauty without the measure of utility, cant, or rationalized social significance. Here you are Russian and here you are free, and all the rutted roads, the toilets that don't work, the moralizing posters, all progress and all decay are far, far away as this woman transcends the dialectic and the mortality of thought itself.

We cannot stay for the second act and in Plisetskaya's dressing room we are all, for some reason, kissing each other. And we are off in Galia's little car—from the Bolshoi, as it turns out, to the Bronx, a housing project where her painter friend lives—but it is necessary first to accept the jar of honey from the bear-hunting ex-pilot at the stage door and then to drop Voznesensky at his apartment because he is tired and needs sleep. And where has the pale writer gone to spend the night?

1969

Broadway, From O'Neill to Now

As anything approaching a mass entertainment, theater in America ceased to exist in the twenties when the talking picture drew off the unsophisticated. Then O'Neill introduced the audience that remained—the somewhat better-educated urban bourgeoisie—to a new, alienated content, announcing the hollowness of the standard American credo and the doom of a civilization based on optimism, materialism-as-salvation and the superiority of appearances over perverse, underlying reality.

O'Neill was not alone, of course. Babbitt-baiting, the spoofing of the Booboisie, the contempt for booming America's cultural barbarism, were the stock-in-trade of many writers of the twenties. The point, however, is that while plays and authors regarded as important were to one degree or another alienated, the bulk of Broadway's merchandise still remained well this side of controversy. Thus an incipient inner split in the theater audience already existed even if it lacked self-consciousness. Proponents of an "Art" theater had to struggle against the conservatism of audience and critics who joyfully declared, "When philosophy comes in, I go out," or, "If you have a message, send it by Western Union." These aphorisms were the pride of what can be called the majority theater that wanted entertainment, not agony, although it could tip its hat to "culture" if it had to. The only weapons O'Neill or any other American playwright had against them were superior showmanship and the sheer force of talent.

In short, there have been two audiences in the American theater for forty years or more. These audiences merge around certain plays at certain moments, their edges obscured by the universal appeal of particular productions (*The Great White Hope* is a current example). However, the crisis now is more obvious than before because the ground has nearly disappeared upon which the alienated and the unalienated can appreciate the same kind of art.

Looking back now, I believe that the late forties and early fifties—in fact, just before the Cold War froze what had been the tolerance of the Broadway theater—saw the last moments when both kinds of sensibility could share the same theater. It was then that Tennessee Williams and I, each from different vantage points, sought to speak to both kinds of people. For myself, it was never possible again after *The Crucible*. For Williams, quite obviously, the only audience left is the one that has nothing in common with the majority.

What movements or ideas gave vitality to the theater in the years after the twenties?

In the thirties, the Left theater groups, inspired by Marxist militancy, gave the alienated theater a new self-awareness as a theater apart and opposed to the majority theater. Still, even *their* aim was to succeed in the big time, to capture "Broadway." If "Broadway" ultimately captured most of their artists, it also absorbed their social consciousness, stripping the Left theater of its more arrant Marxist coloration and transforming it into a Liberal theater. For the audience, like society as a whole, had to adopt progressive revisions of the old American credo, and it did the same within the theater.

But not only a social attitude was involved in this process. The Group Theatre, for example, even though it failed to survive after a few years, injected a new method of actor-training, new ideals of ensemble performance, new extra-theatrical social references for stage reality which still rule in many diluted forms. It in turn was the heir of the old Provincetown experiments, and of Eva Le Gallienne, whose Civic Repertory on Fourteenth Street for many years brought Ibsen, Strindberg, Chekhov and the alienated European theater to an audience which would not find them on the commercial stage.

The greatest and most successful drive to expand the audience beyond the small, compact class represented on Broadway was the WPA Federal Theater Project. Government-supported and aimed primarily at giving employment to actors and other theater people hit by the Depression, it also hoped to reclaim the audience the talkies had drawn away. It played in ghettos, slums, churches, stores and small towns to people who had never before seen theater. However, a certain portion of its repertory was alienated theater, and the project was annulled in 1939 by congressmen who saw it as un-American. Indeed, the WPA Living Newspaper created perhaps the only new form invented in America, holding up the social system as such to inspection. When WPA died, the threat of the masses entering the theater receded.

In the past twenty years or so, alienation in society at large has become a highly self-conscious life-view, particularly with the youth but not only with them by any means. From being the property of the intellectual minority, alienated attitudes toward America-as-advertised have become the dominant code of communication among a very wide class of people. Alienation has thrown up its own critics, newspapers, radio stations, and new conventions of expressing faith, disbelief, idealism and nihilism. Its modes and styles, if not its moral and political content, have spilled over into those of the majority. In its myriad variations it still focuses on the old enemy, the unalienated American Credist.

There is no space here to evaluate the art of this insurgency or that of "Broadway," and that is not at issue here in any case. What needs to be recognized, I believe, is that an audience, and a large one, does exist for live theater, that it has an intense spiritual vitality, and that several forces within the presently constituted Broadway theater set-up actively repel this audience. At the same time, Broadway does not any longer attract a large enough part of that majority on which its life always depended. (I should add that I do not think that movies have somehow made live actors on a stage outmoded.)

I do not know that it will be possible for any but a few musical spectacles to support the price of midtown real estate over the next few years. This is the underlying competition of values which, if no other pathology entered, would destroy any professional theater in New York. The rock bottom process is that a play must earn enough income to ward off the physical removal of the theater and its replacement by buildings that can earn more.

It is now quite evident that marketplace laws, if allowed to continue operating without interference, will by themselves destroy what remains of the New York theater.

The only interference imaginable is public subsidy of some kind. I take this to be basic, and no conversation about the question of theater survival can proceed until the economic dilemma is faced and resolved. One admonition: government, being sworn to power, is always artistically reactionary and must not in itself be the direct source of funds, but only indirectly. What purity remains to government-supported science is there because scientists sometimes are able to dispense the money. Control must remain within the theater itself in principle.

But whether private producers end up as the managers of a reconstituted New York theater, or WPA-like public officers do the job of administration, the question of minority-majority theater will have to be faced as well. There is no reason why, for example, we cannot support two kinds of theater, providing we recognize them for what they are. At present, both suffer for lack of such recognition. For example, critics have for a long time been pulled and stretched and distorted in their attempts to bridge the gap, when reviewing certain plays, between the two sets of values implied in alienated and unalienated theater. They have by and large taken it upon themselves to keep alive the fiction that there is only one audience. Thus, when in effect they tell "you" whether the work at hand is worth the price of admission, the "you" is really two different people whose values are quite strange to each other, and a work which one group would admire is forced out of existence because it does not meet the standards of the other.

All this would do would be to recognize existing reality, which is being masked by such concepts as "Broadway" and "Off-Broadway," "professional" and "revolutionary," and so forth. There are shows Off-Broadway which should be "on," and shows which briefly appear "on" which belong "off." That is, if their ideas, attitudes, quality of performance and sophistication are any guide.

The most obvious gain in placing productions in their real relationships to either of the two audiences is that a play of either kind will not be wiped out critically because it fails to meet standards it never sought to meet, or to attract an audience it had no thought of entertaining or instructing. But beyond that, a subsidized theater, a theater no longer competing with industry for the right to occupy land, would be relieved at least of the particular kinds of pressure which this unacknowledged competition generates. If it were recognized by every element in the theater that two audiences had a right to exist, rather than one fictive monolith, each kind of theater could then reach its real level with the audience for which it was designed.

One might then hope to see the day when productions which are not striving to innovate could be judged for what they are, rather than for what they are not and have no wish to be. It is even possible that the strident anxiety in so much of the acting, writing and direction on Broadway would at least lessen, and the sheer mawkishness of so many insurgent productions would begin to vanish as their confidence grew that they were, indeed, playing to their rightful peers and not to enemies.

There is no particular aesthetic dividend, no incremental virtue for artists in facing audiences which in principle are hostile or even indifferent to everything those artists stand for. Nor is there any sign of self-indulgence in addressing like-minded communities which share the artists' aims and spirit.

The open recognition that there are two Americas—at least two—and two theatrical communities would perhaps break up the current race to see who can be further "out" and begin integrating the inventions of the last few years into a form or forms that would support more than the anecdotal short play. Similarly, the majority theater, relieved of its terror of being outmoded, could perhaps concentrate on its own strengths rather than try to imitate watered-down avant-garde ideas and theatrical propositions.

Ultimately, perhaps, a new synthesis will develop. The open recognition of a split theater in the institutional sense, and critically as well, can only be a way station. The biggest possible loss entailed in such a situation would be that both theaters would be indulging themselves in code communication solely with their respective cliques. Inconceivable as it may be at the moment, one ought still to recall that the two most fully articulated theaters were the ancient Greek and the Elizabethan, and both were forced—or had the blessed opportunity—to face relatively unfragmented, whole communities. For us now, however, it is better to face the split, to exploit it aesthetically as far as possible, and hope that, as the possibilities of each audience and each theater are run to earth, the need for a universally applicable theater will once again make itself felt, and a new theater will rise that can both address the majority and speak the truth of the time for every sort of man to understand.

Whether there will ever again be a "Broadway," a collection of expensive buildings housing a theatrical profession where actors, playwrights and the other artists will start young and practice the art through maturity, no one can say. At least one new office building, on the site of the Astor Hotel, will house a new theater and this bodes well, but the unacknowledged problem of the audience lies hidden here too—the thing will have 1,800 seats. That spells majority theater, a musical house, probably. What about the other audience? When the minority and majority one day combine, perhaps it will be useful, but now?

Broadway was originally the arena, so to speak, for the entertainment of the masses. Its whole structure—financing, labor arrangements, land-use practices—is still based on that mass-based enterprise, which no longer reflects reality. If it is going to continue to pretend, in effect, that the nature of its business is the same as it was before the talking picture was invented, it must of course disappear, as it has been doing at an escalating rate. But if it faces the changed content of its two audiences, it could conceivably make room for both. The time, it seems, has come for all concerned—the theater owner, the commercial producer, the unions, the artists, the Off-Broadway producers and groups—yes, and the audience—to sit down together and face the facts. I forgot the critics. They can come too.

1969

Kidnapped?

Even as I walked toward the turnstiles the light inside the massive airport building was rapidly turning blue, and through the tall columns of the portico outside the orange sunset sky was swiftly transforming to violet, and the surprising silence in such a place gave off a sudden sensation of a ruin. It must have been one of those statistically odd hours when for a few minutes no passengers were arriving for takeoffs and no planes discharging. My Caravelle from Paris had been two-thirds empty and the other passengers had somehow vanished by this time. I looked in every direction, out onto the portico and behind me toward the interior of the building, and to right and left down the block-long marble entrance hall, but the chauffeur was not there, only two women soundlessly mopping in the distance.

Outside on the stone steps, perhaps. I walked out under the portico and saw the sea of parked cars, but even here nothing moved. The soft Los Angeles air of Rome, the sexual damp. In the dusk, silver flecks of light flashed in the sky. The continuing silence—in an airport—was incredible, like a hole in all the schedules. I was caught in a vacuum and longed for a sound that would show the world had not died. Baldo's failure to send someone to meet me was angering; I had a good mind to catch the next plane back to Paris. Then there was someone running between the cars, toward me surely. A short man in a black suit. Yes, it could be a chauffeur's suit, although he had no cap. His arm was rising, his finger pointing at me. An embarrassed way of running, and quite properly so, I thought, since Baldo must be a tough boss to work for, rich as he was and in the line of spoiled princes.

"Signor Miller!" the man declared and asked, nearly skidding to a halt before me. I nodded down to him. He lowered his finger, and his eyes filled with excited relief. Had my plane been late, and he on the verge of returning to a furious Baldo with an empty car? As though to make up for the indignity of my few minutes' uncertainty, he held up a beseeching palm. *"Aspett', aspett'."* He already knew I could not speak Italian. Baldo had briefed him, no doubt. He turned and ran sideways, still holding up his palm. I followed his form as it entered the ranks of cars, my eyes alert for the Rolls, the Mercedes, the Ferrari, perhaps. The man disappeared. Then I could see an ordinary black Fiat sedan threading through the aisles of cars.

The man drove fast and in silence as though trying to make up for his failure to meet me promptly. Night had fallen but the headlights flashed among the old trees beside the highway. Twenty *(twenty?)* years ago there had been sunshine. The old green taxi had had a meter one ignored because it was still on the Fascist money scale, and I had paid seventeen dollars to get into Rome, the price of not being able to bargain in Italian. The driver then was thin, like most Italians, and his taxi a slope-nosed Fiat built in the Twenties. This Fiat now was tight and quiet; this driver had a filled-out face. I had not known a soul in Rome then. I soon met Emilio, an anarchist novelist just freed after fourteen years in jail. We met on the face of a cliff in front of one of the hundreds of holes bored into the earth where families lived. A ring of caves around Rome smelling of sewage. Emilio's hair grew straight out sideways from his temples, and he wore a brown overcoat, shoes and trousers but no socks, underwear or shirt. He was round and jolly, like a friar, but he had shot and killed two *Fascisti* the day of his release. He lived in a *palazzo* on a kind of balcony open to the air. On it he had a bed and a desk. Six or seven families shared the balcony, but the children never touched his papers because he was The Poet. I gave him razor blades and a shirt, but he gave them to "the poor." In the afternoons he went to a bordello and wrote at a marble table in a vast ballroom where a dozen women stood on display against a wall facing him, and customers sat on long padded benches, playing chess or reading newspapers or answering mail while their senses awoke. It was one of the few warm buildings in Rome then. Occasionally one would finish a letter or fold up his newspaper and go to the line of women and make a selection and disappear upstairs. Emilio died in the bordello one February afternoon.

The driver turned his head toward me and said something. I said, *"Non capisco."* He looked ahead again. After a moment he turned back and said simply, "Hotel?"

I had a flush of confusion. Surely Baldo had told him where to take me. He was holding a business conference in his home which would last into the late evening, and I had not wanted to hang around waiting for it to finish, so he had reserved a room for me at the Hotel d'Inghilterra. We would meet next morning and discuss my play, and I would return to Paris around noon. I said, "Hotel d'Inghilterra," and the driver nodded and said, "Ah, *sì, sì,*" and seemed more content now as he drove.

It was time to say something. I formed an Italian sentence in my mind and corrected it two or three times, then said, "How is Mr. di Castello?"

"Di Castello?"

"Yes." Possibly I was not pronouncing the name correctly, and I repeated it.

The driver shook his head. He did not know a Mr. di Castello, and it obviously was an embarrassment to him.

"The director of plays and films. Baldo di Castello," I reminded him.

Quite as though it were not of any importance, the driver shook his head again— then suddenly recalled. "Oh yes, the film director. I have heard of him. Baldo di Castello. Yes." Again his contentment returned, and he drove on in silence.

I stared out at the darkness. What was the word for "who"? And "sent"? And "meet"? Anger was breaking apart my attempt to translate French and Latin equivalents into Italian. I leaned forward and touched the driver's shoulder. He slowed the car. In the segment of his right eye that I could see there was undoubtedly an abnormal excitement. For the first time I noticed he had a wide, thick jaw. *"Qui,"* I said, hoping it was the same in Italian as in French, but then there was nothing. I sat back in the seat again. Possibly Baldo had hired the car through a secretary—he had a Mafia of boys and girls around him—and no one at the garage had bothered to tell this driver in whose name the car had been sent.

"Agenzia" sounded good for a car-rental place. I leaned forward again, touched the driver's shoulder and pointed at him. *"Auto agenzia?"*

He glanced at me with sweat shining on his forehead. "No, no," he said. A denial. The sting of accusation was in the air between us. Clearly now there was a commercial proposition somewhere in the car with us. I pointed beside him at the front seat. "Taxi?"

"No taxi. No, no. No taxi," he said.

I sat back again. In other words, I had been captured; he was just a private gangster preying on foreigners who looked as though they didn't know where they were going. I leaned forward again. *"Quanto"*—thank God for "quanto"—and then, *"per . . ."*

He looked at me again but this time real shock exploded on his face. He had met his match. This was not the Forties, not this time. This was the Sixties and the sentimental game was over. He would get exactly what such a trip was normally worth, and no tip. Christ's sake, Baldo's chauffeur was probably looking for me back at the airport this minute. *"Signor, il chauffeur—capisco?—il auto di Signor di Castello es* (*es?* Spanish?) *aspettar* (possible?) *por me a aeroporto."*

The driver, from the rear, seemed stabbed. It was unlooked for, his sinking into his suit like this, an encouragingly introverted sensitivity. Or was it that he knew he had been caught red-handed? But would a man with all these emotions be carrying on this kind of work?

What kind of work? Suddenly, as though it had been sitting inside my brain all the while, I saw the idea of being kidnapped. It had been happening in Italy—quite recently, in fact, some industrialist had been held for ransom. For all I knew, one of Baldo's journalist buddies may have put in the paper that I was arriving this afternoon. I dug in against dismissing it as ridiculous. The image of Luciano hung in the darkness before me.

The docks of Palermo, just after the war, still lay in pieces in the harbor. The Hôtel des Palmes, a vast Victorian architectural embrace, was nearly empty. The bandit Giuliano was still in the mountains. Vittorio and I were the only tourists in Palermo then, and after unpacking, we walked around the chaotic city, got hungry, and saw a restaurant in a store, a newly rebuilt place that seemed confident of itself. (The two or three others that were open were so evidently apologetic that we had retreated at the doorways.)

Inside, all the tables were empty, but along the right-hand wall a dozen or so had been put together, and about twenty men and women sat in absolute silence, with full plates and wineglasses, staring at us as we sat down. In one sweep of the eye it was possible to see how strange a collection they were. Two men in their forties, dressed in business suits, sat at the center, flanked by a pair of bleached-blond, heavy-breasted girls; then a few men with thick jackets and broad Sicilian country faces and some immense peasant women in shawls and one man who was peaked and thin and wore bent eyeglasses and might have been a journalist or a school-teacher. It was like a cross section of a society assembled for a sociological interview, except that their common silence implied some association, some secret meeting that we had interrupted.

Vittorio and I sat at a table, he facing the banquet, I with my back to it. There was already an awkwardness in the air. I could hear no knife touching a plate, no word spoken behind me, no shuffle of feet. Sunshine poured in through the window. The place was very clean, our tablecloth starched. Presently the owner appeared, a stout man, bald, with a warm look, and a white apron wrapped around his middle. He too was very clean and brought two new menus, nicely typed. He suggested some items, we discussed wines, and he left quite satisfied.

Now Vittorio looked at me with a grin of fear and challenge and whispered, "Don't look now, but there's somebody behind you."

"Who?"

"Lucky Luciano."

"Is that good or bad?"

"Don't laugh."

Then, too, I had to force myself to dig in against the ridiculous but true. Vittorio, who understood gangsters, was clearly wishing we had not come in here, and I tried to share his concern, but all I could feel was the absurdity. Vittorio pretended to go on studying the menu. A fine sweat was glistening on his face, and a fixed smile gave him a masklike look. I put one arm over the back of my chair and turned around.

The banquet table was empty! I had heard no sound of people getting up or leaving. Two men were approaching us from the rear of the restaurant. They came to our table and sat down, one on my right, one on my left. The one on my right was six feet tall or more, and as he sat down I could see the handle of a revolver protruding under the lapel of his well-pressed striped black jacket. The one on my left was undoubtedly Luciano. He had no revolver. His jacket clung beautifully to his chest, his fingers spread out on the tablecloth were manicured and small. He wore a black knitted tie and a steel-gray silk suit. He looked at me and then at Vittorio, who was obviously Italian, and then he looked at the black box containing my movie camera, which I had placed on the table.

He studied the black box quite openly. He was telling us that he wanted to know what was in the black box, which was rectangular and unshaped, unlike most camera boxes. And he kept only a faint smile going, enough to indicate that in principle he had not drawn any conclusions yet. "Where ya from?" he asked.

Then, too, I had found myself in an unwanted relationship in Italy, a pull and tug that had nothing to do with me, and danger inexplicable and absurd. When Vittorio answered, "Brooklyn," I could see Luciano's electricity turn on.

"Where 'bouts?"

Vittorio had an ambivalent attitude toward gangsters. As a lawyer to the underdog he fought against the rackets in unions, made speeches on the waterfront, and was even dabbling with the idea of running for Congress. But at the same time gangsters had a glamour for him, like actors—which is what he would rather have been. They played with power, were an elite, and above all, he thought, they walked in the glory of the courageous. He hated what they stood for but adored what they were; he could not help it. And now he was talking of "Biggie Cassalino," of "Fingers Levine," of "Marty Wholesome," his face close to Luciano's and his skin flushed with pride. He wanted to make good with Lucky, incredibly enough, and in a few minutes of their acquaintance it was clear where Luciano's power came from—himself.

On the right side of his face he looked like a small-town pharmacist. His left eye, however, had died. It blinked and moved normally, but it saw differently, and made judgments unobstructed by the warmth of the other eye. He heard with his right eye but he saw with his left. And it was with his left that he kept glancing at the black box on the table.

It took a long time for me to realize that the black camera box was the issue. Vittorio was now talking about the "boys" as though he hung with them every night. The bodyguard, with the box in front of him, simply stared at it and at me. The owner brought our food, and Luciano made him take back the olives and bring the better ones. He either owned the place or terrorized it. He ordered a glass of milk. They talked of Tom Dewey, who had helped to deport Luciano to Italy a year or two earlier, having convicted him of white-slavery charges. Dewey, then running against Truman, was Luciano's hopeful winner, the heavy implication being that Dewey as president would let him return to the United States because of his services to the Army during the war—he claimed to have fed inside information about the Fascist armies to American intelligence. But his mind was still strung to the black box on the table, and finally he turned to me fully for the first time.

"You lawyer too?"

"No, I'm a writer."

"What paper?"

"No, not papers. I write plays. For the stage."

"Uh huh." He did not believe it, but he did not *not* believe it. He looked at the black box. I reached over and opened it and took out the camera. He nodded. Obviously he wanted the camera opened too. I opened it, and he took it and examined the insides. Then he gave it back to me. I was as relieved as he was.

"So what the hell you doin' in Palermo?" he asked, leaning back now with his hands in his lap.

"Just tourists," Vittorio said.

Luciano had been exiled by the Italian government to Sicily, and it was hard for him to understand why anybody would come here willingly, let alone for pleasure.

"What's there to tour?" he asked, and I could see that the reassurance of the camera was fast wearing thin.

I said, "I have an idea for a play about Sicilians. I wanted to see what it was like here. I know a lot of Sicilians in New York."

He nodded. The left eye, dead as glass, estimated me. I felt I must be blushing. In fact, my whole story suddenly seemed a lie. The bodyguard, a balding man, very strong in the shoulders, said, "You know people here?"

"No," I said, "I don't know anybody here. We were walking around." I thought it might help to add, "And we just happened to see this place." The bodyguard, imitating Luciano, nodded. I thought we might get friendlier. "You come from New York?"

"No, I'm from here. I never been in New York." This obvious lie—obvious because he spoke like every New York Sicilian I had ever known—was said in order to register his conclusion that I had lied. Just as well, probably, because he was either wanted in New York or not wanted. I turned to Luciano, who was again talking to Vittorio, and when I turned back to the bodyguard I found his empty chair. They all moved like cats. And now we had finished eating, and I called for the bill.

Luciano would not hear of it—he took out a round coil of lire and tossed chunks of paper on the table. Vittorio and I both resisted and then gave up and let him pay, but our jab at independence told Luciano our wish to have nothing more to do with him, now that this accidental collision was past, and I felt I had to smooth things over, and I said of the lire—"They're beautiful."

"Funny money," he said. "Gimme one ugly American buck, you can have this crap."

The table was cleared now. There seemed nothing more to say. I made a move of my chair away from the table.

"Lemme drop you, where you going?" Luciano said.

"Just walking around," Vittorio said.

"Where to? I'll drop you. I got my car outside."

"No, we don't want to ride," I said. "We like to walk. We've never seen this place before."

"Well, what do you wanna see?"

Clearly we were not leaving. Not yet. And now I remembered that soon after the bodyguard had vanished I had heard a phone being dialed from the rear of the restaurant. And now the bodyguard returned and stood behind his chair and exchanged a quite open look with Luciano, who then turned to us and said, "Let's go," and we all got up. Some check had been made; another stage had been passed in our clearance.

He would not let us walk. Outside he had a new Lancia, which I openly admired. "Gimme any Chevy," he said in reply. We drove to the Hôtel des Palmes, where, curiously enough, he was also staying. We had had no intention of going to our room, but it seemed the best way to shake Luciano, so when he asked for his key, we asked for ours. The rooms turned out to be adjoining. Luciano looked at the number on the key in my hand, moving my finger open to see it better, then at the number on his. He did not speak at all then. The four of us walked to the elevator. I indicated for him to enter first, but he stood back and silently gestured us in before him. He and the bodyguard stood with their backs against the elevator walls. No one spoke. The fact of our adjoining rooms evidently was disturbing. He walked behind us down the hall and waited until I had unlocked our door. He watched as we went in and barely nodded as we said good-bye.

I closed our door and started to laugh. Vittorio threw himself onto the bed and held his head. Incredibly, he was seriously afraid. "But why?" I asked.

"God, we end up in the next room. He's not going to take this."

"Take what, for Christ's sake?"

"Baby, nobody tours Sicily now. Either we're the FBI or somebody else who doesn't mean him good. Don't laugh. We've got to get out of here."

"Well, let's get out then."

"No, wait. Let's wait half an hour. We don't want him to think we just came up because he wanted us to."

"Well, why the hell else did we come up? I didn't come to Sicily to sit with you in a hotel room."

"Wait a few minutes," Vittorio said.

And we sat there, at least a half an hour—why, neither of us knew exactly, except that it was no more absurd than anything else we might be doing. Suddenly, for no reason, we were in some kind of relationship with a killer. I sat at the long French window, looking down at the sunny street where hardly anything moved.

Now I sat in the Fiat looking out at the darkness with the same sort of feeling, not of being in danger but of not understanding what I should be feeling. Anything, I said to myself, is possible. This is the world now. Unoffending people are found dead every day behind a bush in the park where they went to feed a squirrel. Still, I was bigger than the driver, and he did not frighten me. Unless he had a gun. There my mind slowed to a halt. The choice of optimism or pessimism. Inevitably, the other part of the Luciano episode formed in the air.

To buttress our claim to being tourists, we had told Luciano that we had tried to rent a car and driver to tour the whole island, but we had been informed that it was impossible to buy gas outside Palermo. It had been a passing remark in Luciano's Lancia. Having waited a half hour or so in our hotel room, we opened the door quietly and tiptoed down the hall past Luciano's door. In the lobby a short man in a cape and a wide gray moustache and blue beret came up and hit Vittorio hard on the upper arm. They then embraced. The man was Giuseppe Moro, chief of the communist deputies in the Sicilian parliament. He had known Vittorio in New York, where he had waited a decade for Mussolini to expire. That evening we went to a restaurant with Moro and discovered ourselves two tables away from Luciano, his bodyguard, and the two blond girls. Vittorio had rather boasted—he could not help it—that he had had a long talk with Lucky. Seeing him a few yards away, Vittorio nodded powerfully to him. Moro looked once at Luciano and Luciano at him, and the air froze along their line of vision. Vittorio saw this but went right on telling Moro about our entrapment in the restaurant and later in the hotel. Moro listened sternly. "You were afraid? What were you afraid of?" he said quite loudly, his indignation barely controlled. Vittorio started to back off, explaining that it wasn't really fear but some sort of apprehension, when Moro reached under his arm and slipped out a pistol and laid it on the tablecloth.

"Luciano," he said very loudly—but none of the other guests so much as turned an inch, "is my——!"

He said this in English, but the underlying information was clear enough. Luciano went right on eating.

When we returned to our room to sleep that evening, we had hardly gotten our ties off when there was a knock at our door. The end, evidently, had arrived. The knock was repeated. A few minutes earlier we had been laughing near hysteria at this chain of idiotic adventures. Now neither of us could quite make the move to the door, but one of us did, and a handsome man of perhaps twenty-three stood there in a green-plaid Mackinaw, a good tweed cap, peasant's heavy shoes, and a silk shirt open at the collar. He was smiling. His teeth were incredibly white and even, his Sicilian skin nearly black, and he entered the room smiling and chesty, his brown eyes glancing from Vittorio to me to decide which of us could talk to him.

"I understand," he said, "you want to see the country."

"Yes," said Vittorio and shut the door.

"It is possible," the Sicilian said—much amused, it seemed, for he kept on smiling. He could have been a movie star.

"Sit down," Vittorio said.

The Sicilian sat without removing cap or coat. We sat on the bed facing him. "I believe," he said, "that you will be able to find petrol in the country. There is petrol."

Vittorio asked him his name. He said, "Emmanuel," and his smile widened so that we understood it was not his name and that he was beyond the law. Vittorio asked how he knew about us. He said that he knew the people who rented the few cars there were in Palermo. In fact, he knew almost everyone in Palermo. And Vittorio's sense of the Sicilian's power quickened so openly that the young man, seeing it, could not leave his power undescribed. He had been the poor son of a poor peasant in the hills, and when the Germans had come, he had, like all the peasants, sold vegetables to them. Then he had organized the cabbages, later on the beets, still later the entire vegetable production of the area. So that whoever wanted vegetables called Emmanuel. Finally he had organized the Germans' own gasoline supply by blowing up their trucks in the back country. The Germans at first had retaliated but soon understood the message and simply ordered their own gasoline from Emmanuel, who issued his own printed forms to be pasted on the trucks' windshields for safe passage. It would therefore be no great problem to organize gasoline for us if we wished to tour the island.

He rose to leave. His smile had never for a moment relaxed. His even white teeth seemed to fill the room. Vittorio asked him how much we should pay him. He held up a lordly palm and gave a brief shake of his head. "I welcome you to Sicily," he said. Vittorio offered him a cigarette from a pack. He took the cigarette, and then he took the pack. Vittorio asked if he wanted more, and he nodded. I took out an unbroken carton from my valise and started to tear the cardboard, and he took the carton and put it under his arm. He stood there waiting. Vittorio took a carton from his bag and handed it to him. Then he held out his hand, shook ours, opened the door, and walked out with a rocking, proud, seaman's gait.

A rattling old green car appeared at eight in the morning, and the driver took us all over Sicily; in tiny hamlets he would pull up at the solitary gas pump, a man would come out, fill our tank, hang up the hose, and go into his house with no money passed. Whether this was Luciano's gift or truly Emmanuel's we never knew. And why should Luciano have done this for us? For that matter, why should Emmanuel have done it? The fact, however, was that on mountaintops where there were a dozen slumping peasants' huts, in towns, and along the rivers, wherever our driver stopped before a gas pump a man would appear and without a word fill our tank and hang up the hose and go back to where he had come from.

The outskirts of Rome were surrounding the Fiat now, and the lights of stores bled out the melodrama. I watched the driver carefully. He exuded uncertainty, hunching himself down and forward as though to see better where he was going.

I reviewed. He knew my name. He had been happy to see me. The car was not a taxi. But he did not know di Castello or even where I was going. There was guilt on his face. But not the aspect of the operator. In fact, objectively speaking, he seemed a mild man with no secrecy covering his quick emotions. In other words, he did this kind of thing not with a domineering impulse bur rather pitifully. One was supposed to pity him and thus pay double. None of it hung together. With one overnight bag and traveling alone I was obviously not the usual guilty tourist but more likely a man on business. Would men on business be likely to pay double out of pity? Unlikely. My confusion remained absolute.

The streets were beginning to look familiar. The driver had slowed considerably until we were moving at little more than a walking pace, and he was looking around. *"No conosco Hotel d'Inghilterra?"*

"Sì, sì!" he promised, but it was obvious he was lost. How could a gangster, a professional hijacker of foreigners, not know that hotel? We were now passing what I was almost sure was a street leading to the hotel. Emilio's bordello was not far from here. A young man with my name had walked endlessly in this neighborhood, trying to absorb the new age, the age after Fascism was hung up by the feet, the coming-on time of brotherhood and war's educative end, when the whores moved in pairs, hundreds of them everywhere, and if you turned them down they would look you in the eye and say, "When you gonna make us the forty-nine state, Joe?" I saw a policeman on the corner now and quickly leaned forward and shook the driver's shoulder and pointed at the man.

The driver stopped the car, got out, and slammed the door on his thumb. The door bounced open. It had been a direct hit, a real smash. The blood started running over his palm. He took out his handkerchief and hurried to the policeman, wrapping his finger. By the time he returned the handkerchief was soaked. I pointed to his finger. *"Dottore,* hospital," I said. The wound had gone into my stomach.

"No, no," he said and started the car. I repeated "Hospital, *dottore,*" but he waved me away. The sweat was pouring down his cheeks now. He turned a corner and there was the Hotel d'Inghilterra. I got out, taking my bag, but he was upon me at once, and I let him carry it. I reached into my pocket and realized I had no Italian money. We walked into the hotel as I was assuring him not to fear, I had only to change money. He kept nodding and with his good hand assuring me of his trust, it seemed.

It was the same lobby, tiny and confused. In the center a marble table and carved chairs where no one could possibly sit in the flow of guests. A small booth to one side sheltered the concierge, a tall and stout man in a green tail coat and braid. I went to him and said I had a reservation. He knew my face and smiled a welcome. I asked him what the normal rate was from the airport, knowing I could not pay less than double now, now that the driver was trying to hide his wounded hand behind his good one. His face was pale, the eyes spread open wider by the pain, the pain and some tidal wash of guilt that seemed to immobilize him.

The concierge glanced at the driver and then said to me under his lip, "Pay what you like."

"But what's normal?"

The concierge looked at the driver again, sizing him up but without hostility. They were both Italians in a poor country. "Speak to him," I said, giving up.

He came around the small counter and walked up to the driver and said something. The driver shook his head, again with that deeply negative denial, which was the only thing I had seen him do since we had met. It suddenly seemed as though everybody was saying utterly inappropriate things to him and that his whole life was a series of misunderstandings. He was telling the concierge something now, something more lengthy, occasionally pointing at me. For the first time I saw him smile with a little joy, a little release, an unburdening of his heart, it seemed. And as the concierge nodded and returned to me, the driver waited, watching my face.

"He doesn't want anything. He simply recognized you at the airport and wanted to be of help. He admires your plays."

I looked at the driver. A fan. With a bleeding thumb. A suit wrinkled now by his anxiety. Wet hair from the sweat. I strode over to him, started to offer my hand but feared to hurt his thumb and ended by grasping his arm. "I'm terribly sorry," I said.

The concierge translated.

"I thought you might be one of those drivers who overcharge foreign——" I broke off, realizing that all this was of no interest to him at all, a noise down in the valley far below the mountaintop where he lived with books, dramas, poems, God-knows-what loving concourse with beauty and truth. And my embarrassment seemed not to reach him; he merely went on faintly smiling now, a shy man surely, a small private person I had been mortifying for half an hour with talk of fares, *agenzias,* taxis. He said something, something brief, directly to me.

"He is deeply honored to have met you," the concierge said.

"Tell him that I am honored, too."

The concierge translated. The driver shyly nodded. He turned and walked out the doorway, holding his bloody hand a little higher than his heart, to slow the bleeding, I supposed.

1969

Essays: 1972–1980

Making Crowds

As in Chicago so in Miami—this had to be the Last Convention. So said half-a-dozen newsmen of my acquaintance, and I felt the same myself a good part of the time. There is the shock and charm of the American crowd in all its variety and sheer animal power, but in any real sense the thing simply cannot work. How can the same man "represent" Richard Daley and Bella Abzug? For that matter how could Franklin Roosevelt stand for the principles of Georgia's Governor Talmadge and his red suspenders and simultaneously for the young trade-union movement whose organizers were being crucified in the South?

But this is too rational. Democracy is first of all a state of feeling. A nominee, and later a president, is not a sort of methodical lawyer hired to win a client's claim but an ambiguously symbolic figure upon whom is projected the conflicting desires of an audience. Like the protagonist in a drama he rises to a level of the fictional. As he comes closer to being the nominee he becomes less an ordinary man than a performer who is merely like a man. One proof of this is that we demand a perfection of character of him which would be absurd and childish were he not a nominee but which is somehow reasonable as he approaches that status. For he is now a hero who must act out what we would believe is the best in our own faulted personalities.

So it is inevitable that the Issues dim in a convention quite as they do in a good play whose moral conclusions and thematic point, while necessary to give it form, recede in importance for the mind which is swayed by personalities, color, the surprises and sudden switches of the action itself.

As a Connecticut delegate in '68 I was at first surprised by the relative impotence of the Issues for the Humphrey men who made up the bulk of our delegation. I had assumed that as machine politicians whose very livelihoods depended on winning the election they would be ruled by this consideration, but I could not find one who believed Humphrey had a chance against Nixon. One would assume they would therefore be casting about for an alternative. This would be rational. Nor were they under the illusion that continuing the war would do anything but hurt their cause. Yet they would not hear of any idea to set themselves against Johnson's policy, which had no hope of bringing peace reasonably soon.

It was clear then that it came down to their *belonging* somewhere, the way people belong in a certain neighborhood and are strangers in another in no objective way different than their own. Win or no win, issues or no issues, they belonged with Humphrey and the binding tie was visceral. And when I thought about it later in the calm of total disaster for our side, I found my own case too similar. Had Humphrey by some miracle turned against the war and come out for immediate withdrawal I knew it would be hard for me to go with him. I did not belong with him. Objectively, his record on other issues was as good or better than McCarthy's, yet in his camp I'd have been a stranger and at odds with myself. It is a bit like asking an audience in the last act of *Hamlet* to side with the king. Assume we suddenly learn that the king might well be literally innocent of the murder of Hamlet's father, could it change our nonidentification with him? Hamlet has already said too many things which moved us and carried us with him, and mere facts could never prevail over expended feelings.

It could have been a feeling of déjà vu which made the Miami thing seem so manifestly theatrical an occasion, but there were also striking signs that whatever principles they had come to fight for the delegates were *on;* they had come to symbolize, not merely to transact public business. It was another element in the transformation of the party which had now become contemporary. Nobody vomiting rye or smoking Admirations, no rebel yells from blue-eyed yahoos, and surely the highest IQ level in any convention in history—they actually kept up with most of the parliamentary maneuvering which was lost on the crowd in Chicago. To be sure there was the same air of total disorientation in the first days, like a freshman class at a large university asking where the gym is, but these people bore a double perspective; like actors they related to the reality around them, but at the same time they played it for the home screen.

One could remember when people went shy and reticent before the TV lights and camera, and the old-time delegate caught by a TV interviewer would either puff himself up and try to look like a statesman, or wave to his mother through the lens. These young, suckled on TV, knew that you never look into the lens and that you have to condense the statement of your position or be cut off, and they did both with ease and naturalness. The old guard had been more cagey than this before the camera, suspicious of the interloper, for a convention was an authentic rather than an artistic occasion. The new understood that the camera is the main thing and that nothing could be said to *happen* until it had been filmed.

These shadings are politically instructive. The men of Chicago knew it was all as staged a performance as *The Follies* and that their part in it was to obey instructions while evincing the requisite enthusiasms on cue. They too were acting, but the difference was that they believed in the form itself while the new delegates were ironical toward the very idea of a convention and even the party. After all, McGovern had let slip that if he lost the nomination he would bolt. They were here to win their demands upon society, would use the form as long as it was usable and if the form failed them they were capable of walking off the stage and out of the theater. For the old, the stakes used to be the party and the convention. For the young it was to dominate the age itself, and when the young were tapped by the TV men they played it fully, not strategically and strained as the old men used to. In theater terms, the classic fourth wall of the stage was no more—they were trying to mingle with the audience, but they were playing nonetheless.

It has been said that this convention had much more content than previous ones, but it was not merely that there were so many blacks, and actual girls in jeans rather than the fat ladies led in from hard precinct chairs. It was that—had McGovern not been nominated—they would have burst the form itself, abandoned the convention, and burst through into the streets and real life. No such implicit threat hung over Chicago against the possibility of a Humphrey defeat. So in Chicago and Miami were two levels of art, one more naïve than the other perhaps, but both were performances. And in the mind vague prospects rose of some more authentic means of choosing the most powerful officeholder on the planet.

This performance-orientation, I thought, suppurated the city itself, the people's tone of voice became unreal and emblematic. Unable to park the car I had foolishly rented I reverted to cabs, and I had no sooner sat down in one than the driver in his New York accent announced, "I'm a Republican, been one thirty-five years. Who likes Nixon? You can't like Nixon. But I'm a Republican. Because my father-in-law's a Democrat." He laughed. "I like to get the knife in. It's all shit." I hadn't mentioned I was a writer, but it wasn't necessary—we are a nation of the interviewed.

This outer-directedness took stranger forms than usual in Miami. Flamingo Park, normally a preserve for the arthritic aged, the pensioner, and the babysitter, had by mutual agreement become a corral for the Outraged, the much-feared hippies who now lay about in the shade of dusty palms like the cast of an abandoned show. Some, veterans of the Chicago battles, others new recruits, they sent up dutiful wisps of grass smoke, demonstrating, as it were, their fundamental intelligence rather than the advertised rage. In fact, by the middle of our Passion Week the TV people had already sucked the marrow of their news and had abandoned them to life's ironies, which can be crueler than the clubs of the police. Even the lawn looked tired. I heard through the terrible moist heat the voice of a girl and The Gospel According to Saint Matthew.

At an impromptu pulpit made of a crate over which a faded purple cloth was draped, she stood alone, reading the Bible to Miami, a pretty seventeen-year-old totally ignored by the few strollers from the straight world who had come to see the animals and unheard by her contemporaries who blinked cruddy eyes at the morning sun or stared dead-brained at the old, half-crippled Jews sliding the shuffleboard disks along the baking concrete slabs. The dust, it seemed, had settled again, and America had once more transformed her revolutionaries into screwballs, as in my youth she had hung the hobo's mask on the Depression unemployed who, in their hour, had made a bid to characterize the country and had failed. Then I heard actual Hebrew.

A small drooping pup tent, one of several propped up on these deserted fairgrounds, and before it stood a young Jew with a yarmulke on his head, doing something with a man of sixty-five or so who wore a brown felt hat, a blue vest without a shirt, and had a two-day gray stubble on his cheeks. Amazed and unbelieving, I approached—the young Jew was teaching the old man how to wind phylacteries around his arm! I saw now that under the old guy's hat brim was the single strand of leather attached to which was the leather box containing the Holy Word pressed to his forehead. He was having trouble learning how to wind the leather reins around his fingers, but the young teacher was patiently redoing the procedure. And all the while a few yards away stood another Orthodox, a confederate of nineteen who, as I came near, asked if I wanted to be next.

"Are you proselytizing?" I asked.

"No, we don't proselytize. We're only interested in Jews. Come on, try it."

"I gave that up when I was fourteen."

"Try it. You might like it again."

The confederate's sublime arrogance, irritating as it was, nevertheless contrasted with the surrounding air of cultivated purposelessness and was strangely fitting in this highly political, outer-directed city. But the worst was yet to come—I heard the old pupil *counting*. I went closer to hear what to my atavistic heart seemed an abomination, for when you wind the phylacteries you are talking to God. But he was, he was counting even as he at last had managed to correctly wind the narrow leather rein around his fingers and up his arm.

"One thousand, two thousand, three thousand," he muttered, hardly moving his lips. Why was he counting? And why did not the young Orthodox soul-fisher seem to notice? Was this all a mockery, and the two young Jews acting out some kind of travesty of holy instruction, hoping to kill their parents with heart attacks? But now the old pupil glanced past me and I followed his gaze to another man, a companion his own age, who was standing there photographing his friend's conversion with a home movie camera.

The old pupil, who to the naked eye, or rather to the silent film, was the very picture of the hatted old pious Jew performing one of the most ancient of rituals, now lowered his arm and having rehearsed sufficiently ordered his cameraman to begin shooting; "Count to ten, one thousand, two thousand, up to ten," he instructed him, and then turned back to perform the winding of the phylactery. Meanwhile, the shill never ceased inviting me to join the fun, but the thing that brought me back to my twentieth-century senses was the fact that the two Orthodox, who I have no reason to think were anything less than sincere fishers of men, were also cooperating and knew how to place themselves on each side of the new convert so that their ministrations would show to good effect on film. Meanwhile—and this is the final note on this edifying scene—the convert put on a look of such powerful piety as he performed his newly rediscovered Godly duty that I had to wonder whether this was as faked as it appeared to be. For all I know he would from that day return to the synagogue and the Jewish life, the more so when it has all been filmed, registered, you might say, in God's very eye. Flamingo Park, this whole city in fact, had taken on the air of scenery, the MGM back lot in whose perfect imitations of streets the extras and featured players filled up waiting time with games, naps, and horse-play while the stars and the producers worried out the continuity in closed rooms somewhere up high.

Which reminds me of my shock on first learning that Eisenhower had his makeup man. But what did I expect—a presidential candidate sweating on television and his wrinkles showing? What is this nostalgia for the authentic? Must not Lincoln have had some crowd-related object in mind when he trimmed his beard just so? Still, the idea of Lincoln pausing for his pancake and going over in his mind, "Fourscore and seven years ago . . ."

And were we not set up for this by the Renaissance painters who made the miserable Magdalen so beautiful, Jesus so unearthly? Was it at least part of his motivation in a Roman colony where every official action was surrounded with show business that Jesus knew he must really die to break through with the message? Did the wild men of the '68 Chicago streets understand that they'd be clowns until they bled real blood on a medium where blood was as ketchup theretofore?

It seems that even George Meany was carried away by the pull of the symbolic. One assumed an ideological cleavage behind his and I. W. Abel's refusal to go with the convention's choice, and the cynical would make the stakes even more material—

McGovern was not in debt to labor and so would be independent of its claims on the presidency. But surely Meany knew what later was revealed, that the pro-McGovern unions controlled more campaign money than the unions he and Abel held in their grip, so we are face-to-face again with symbolic gestures. To Meany and such standard types this convention might as well have been a Mayan ritual whose application to himself or anyone he knew was simply not possible. The whole thing just wasn't real, a lot of kids acting out a drama of power politics when they had never even *worked,* owned businesses, met a payroll, or paid homage to the industrial machine in any form. They watched it all like legionnaires at a convention in Sandusky, Ohio, before a performance of *Waiting for Godot* or *The Bald Soprano.* What the hell is this?

You can call it a culture gap, but you'd think that faced with another four Nixon years they would have been able to temper outrage, if only for the sake of the lesser evil. Men acting rationally surely could have done so. But they had been reached where art reaches men—in the hollows of disgust and primordial rage, until they left their famous hardheaded objectivity behind and retreated to a gesture of revolt, which had to be mostly empty since the forces to inflict damage were not theirs to command. And so George Meany for a moment joined the cast, long enough to curse a world he never made and departing a play too spurious for any belief. It was a revulsion of taste, but taste is always a matter of identification, as the history of art makes clear enough.

When I went to Miami Beach it was with the near certainty that the pros would rob George McGovern of the nomination; after a day in the lobbies looking in vain for the Old Boys I was afraid he would win everything but the power that goes with the nomination. It seemed to me then that underneath the conflict of issues and lifestyles and the rest, what we were witnessing, and still are as the election battles shape up, is the most complicated and ambiguous construction man makes—the Crowd.

To put it briefly, a Crowd is not merely a large collection of people but an organism in itself, having its own energies which are aimed at a discharge. The McGovern phenomenon can be seen as the creation of a new Crowd whose existence, in terms of its individual members, was previously known but as a Crowd was unforeseen. The common assumption was that the two parties—that is, the two Crowds—had preempted the field and the most that could happen was perhaps a lowering of the age of the Democratic crowd, which would demand a quicker peace in Vietnam and some changes in the tax and welfare systems. What McGovern demonstrated, surprisingly, was that a new Crowd has in fact secretly been forming itself not only among the previously ignored and dispossessed but also in some undetermined degree among that eight to ten percent of the straight people as well, that mercurial group of the unaligned which may shift to or away from either party and decide an election. By pulling out, the Meanys are signaling their hope and belief that this new construction is merely that—a rather adventitious seizure of party power by a fragment which is not, in fact, a crowd at all but a self-announced facsimile.

A merely random collection of people becomes an operative Crowd at the point when each of its members begins to feel a strong sense of equality with all the others. This must not be mistaken for a virtue or an evil; a Nazi crowd and a Democratic one are subject to the same generic sensations regardless of their opposing ideologies. William L. Shirer once told me that when he attended Hitler's mass meetings as a hostile reporter he often felt the skin crawling on his neck as he realized that something within him was being sucked into the general sweep of the crowd's fused identity. Whatever the crowd's larger social purposes its first purpose is to exist as a crowd, and it achieves its existence when differences have been eradicated among its members. At this moment, like any organism, a crowd tends to expel what is alien to itself, and that is when its Crowd-life begins. The phenomenon is common in the theater where a lot of unrelated people gather and fuse only if and when a common, equal response is ignited in them by what they are seeing. The play which fails, in effect, to make a crowd out of a disparate collection of people has simply left their differences intact. So it is that the politician, like the writer or actor, must make a crowd for himself by providing that locus around which a great many people may transcend their ordinary bounds of feeling and join in the crowd's equality.

What has misled observers of the McGovern phenomenon is that its adherents' viewpoints and class memberships are so various and even conflicting. A great many well-to-do people, for example, have contributed a lot of money even in the face of McGovern's announced intention to raise their taxes; the professional women continue working for him despite a nearly total refusal on his part to adopt their positions; blacks who until very recently swore to support only candidates vowing fealty to their cause have gone for McGovern, who has not. And so on. Contrariwise, the Jews, or a lot of them, have conceived McGovern as lukewarm at best about Israel despite his avowals of continuation of past U.S. policy.

Something more than the sheer consideration of issues is working here, and it is obviously so when Wallaceites can regard McGovern without falling to pieces.

To put it this way is not to make Issues disappear but to set them in their place below the question of symbolic identification. At the least, it is certain that McGovern's Crowd is a real one and not a facsimile and that it has important possibilities for growth. But this is due as much to the openness—you might call it vagueness—of his positions as their sharpness. With some surprise I found, for whatever one man's experience may be worth, that to his own followers McGovern stands for more than his orientation toward Issues, and this may be the basic reason why the Republicans—at least around convention time—had stopped laughing.

Driving to my lodgings in the small hours, I picked up hitchhikers, all of them the McGovern Young. At half-past four one morning my headlights flashed on a girl walking alone along Collins Avenue. She was twenty-one, short-bobbed, wore white slacks with fake stiff lace around the bells, a black jersey, and came all the way from Alaska to this hot place. But she was not even a delegate, just a "worker" for George; she had scraped the fare together and was now stone broke, trying to walk the seven miles way out to her motel in the next town, Hollywood. In fact, she was eating once a day at the canteen in the Convention Hall where the Democratic Party provided fried chicken to just such faithful. I offered to give or loan her money, but she refused, either on some arcane principle or for fear of a sexual approach. In any case, she was placidly resentful that McGovern workers were not being paid as evidently they had been promised. This did not amount to a betrayal in her mind but simply a fact. Like the other Georgeans I came to meet, she was remarkably factual. For example, she had accompanied an Eskimo delegate (there exploded in my mind a furred man in this frightful heat) who also had to surmount barriers in order to get here. "He had to borrow his brother's plane to fly to Nome."

She said this with a certain hurt. I doubt that in all the history of revolutionary gatherings a delegate has been reduced to borrowing his brother's plane, but in surreal Miami I must admit that this piece of information seemed perfectly ordinary. And what, I asked, had moved her toward McGovern? The war? Ecology? The Alaskan pipeline?

"I wouldn't say it was those things," she said, and her tone made "those things" seem distant indeed. "I just wanted to participate."

It was a longer drive to Hollywood than I had booked in my mind when I picked her up, and in the surrounding blackness between the towns our interview gave way to conversation. She was studying biology and lived alone in a cabin heated by a kerosene stove on the outskirts of whatever Alaskan town, eating out of cans. Her parents were divorced. I looked at her more carefully now—she was rather plain, a turned-up nose, round face, straight black hair, pudgy. A lonely girl. One understood the issue. It is not to denigrate it or its political force to make note of it this way. She had felt the pull of her Crowd and had answered it as she never could have by watching it all on the tube.

I had told her I also was for McGovern, and before her motel door she smiled for the first time and offered her hand. In the morning she would awaken hungry and suffer through the day until the Democratic fried chicken in the evening. But, as she said, it was helping her to lose weight. This whole experience had innumerable benefits, and should Nixon solve the war before election time or even make the air pure, she would remain a McGovern worker. And this is strength, not weakness, in a political movement.

In full sunlight another partisan, a boy from Vermont, sat beside me on the way to the Doral Hotel, McGovern's headquarters, but he was not only a delegate; he had been on TV as the youngest delegate in history, eighteen. He seemed extremely tired, with an inner exhaustion known especially to performers who must go on despite everything. Yet he was already a little sick of his notoriety, he said. "I'm not sure I'll go on in politics. I don't feel like it right now."

Had something disillusioned him?

"Not exactly. But I don't think he should have said that to Wall Street."

Said what?

"How they hadn't to worry none about his tax reforms. He had no call saying a thing like that to Wall Street. I mean is he serious?"

Then you've gone sour on him?

"No—no, I'm for him. But I wish he hadn't said those things."

And what had brought him in? The war? Ecology? Unemployment?

He glanced at me. I could, I thought, hear his mind saying, "What war?"—he gave me that kind of blank. But what had brought him out to do political work?

"It was interesting. I met a lot of people, and I enjoy that. I don't know, I just felt I wanted to get into it. But I don't think I'd make it a life's work."

A third was Boston Irish and feverish with all his appointments and the caucuses; red-haired, twenty-three, he was having the time of his life. But he was serious. "I think we can take Massachusetts."

And why was he in it? The war? Ecology? What?

Again that surprised look.

Or maybe, I said, you're Irish and just like the game.

He laughed. "It's not the Irish, but I do, I like the game. I want to do it all my life."

Why? What's there about it?

"I just like it. I like doing it. I think we can take Massachusetts."

There would be an opportunity later to learn about those issues (or the lack of them) and the young, but a conversation over breakfast reminded me of the complications in the hearts of the other Crowd, the one that had stopped growing. Two or three times I had passed these two immense men in the Americana lobby—I would go there to sleep in my room or simply because, as Muskie's headquarters, it was the only place you could park. As in Shakespeare, it was separated from the chief contenders' camps, housing Meany's entourage as well as John Bailey's Connecticut troops. Thus it was the quietest lobby of all, and you could find middle-aged and elderly John of Gaunts bemoaning the partition of this England, this blessed Isle and so forth. I had exchanged waves with these two giants, who, I figured, must know my face, so polite and friendly were they every time our paths crossed. On this morning I found myself at the next table, and since they looked kind of lonely and in need, for some reason, of my company I moved over and joined them over eggs. I discovered they had merely waved to be friendly. Also, to talk with someone who might, hopefully, help them understand what had happened to their kind in Miami.

This was Wednesday, when McGovern had already turned back the California challenge and had the nomination in the bag.

I asked, "You fellas for Humphrey?"

"I am. He's for Muskie," said the black-haired man, relieving his thick wrist by stretching his watch band which was extended near to bursting.

"You delegates?"

"No. Just here. You?"

"No, I'm trying to write about it."

"The papers."

"Magazine. But I'm for McGovern."

"I seen you somewhere."

I knew he wouldn't like what he dimly saw, and I waited, and he finally pointed a finger. "You were with the McCarthy side at the '68 Convention."

"That's it. I'm Miller."

"Oooh ya." Then he turned to his friend. "He's that writer."

"O-o-h ya," the brown-haired man said. Their curiosity overtook their distaste. The black-haired man's eyes flickered at notoriety so close. "Well, he'll never win Connecticut."

"Still, he certainly came up fast for the nomination."

"He got that for one statement. When he said he'd end the war on Inauguration Day."

"That's how Eisenhower beat Stevenson, wasn't it? When he said he'd go to Korea? Stevenson said we'd have to fight on forever."

"That's true." He opened a little, his uncertainty peeked out. "You think he's got a chance?"

"What've you got against him?"

"He's not honest." And the brown-haired friend nodded.

"By the way, where you from?"

"Hartford."

"What do you do?"

"I'm a Sheriff. We both are." The brown-haired man nodded again, and said, "Sheriffs." I could see them both emerging from the squad car, chests immense, holsters shining, Americans in charge.

"How do you mean, not honest?"

"Well, Humphrey … a man goes out and works for him, he takes care of you. McGovern, I'm afraid, is gonna tell you if you don't qualify, get out."

Unhorsed by his unblinking honesty, the whole convention came alive for the first time. "But you could work with him, couldn't you? With his people?"

The brown-haired man spoke; "They've got no use for ethnics. I'm a Ukrainian. You don't see any Ukrainians up there" (on the convention platform).

"Or Poles either. I'm a Pole. Fifteen percent of the delegates are black. Which is all right, but where's the others?"

They looked hurt. Beetle-browed, appealing for justice. "You're right about that. He's going to have to come to you people."

"I don't know what you are, but …"

"I'm Jewish."

"Okay. If Ribicoff was made vice president …"

"He won't take it. I just talked to him."

"Sure he won't take it," the Pole said; "he's not going to sink with a loser."

"I don't think that's it. He's been sponsoring McGovern for years. He just doesn't want any more than he's got. He's a senator and that's what he likes."

"And he's got the scratch," the Pole said.

"Plenty," the Ukrainian added, rubbing two fingers.

"But say he was vice presidential nominee," the Pole said; "that'd be a terrific feather in your cap, now wouldn't it."

"Sure."

"Well that's it."

The point driven home, they both leaned back heavily in their chairs. But they wanted another move; mine. It surprised me.

"Under Roosevelt they had all kinds of Democratic clubs where I come from. Ukrainian, Polish, Irish, Lith …"

"Sure!" the Pole agreed. "Roosevelt *came* to the ethnic people."

"Supposing McGovern came to you people. Is it too late? Could he make a difference now?"

"He won't do it. He comes from that place out there. They got no ethnics out there."

"But if he did, would you accept him?"

"You can't live on 'ifs.' What he likes is these hippies. If it wasn't for them in Chicago, where they made such a bad impression, Humphrey'd have been elected. Those riots destroyed the Democratic Party."

"The war did that."

"Well, naturally the war. Without the war it'd been heaven. Even now, people don't realize there's a lot of boys out there."

"McGovern's trying to bring them home."

"That's right." They both nodded agreement. They believed or disbelieved each separate thing separately. There was no ideology to wrack falsehoods into a straight line. I didn't think they were lost to McGovern at all. If he cared enough, and if he, as native as an Indian, could project himself into the immigrant heart which is torn between shame of the old-country beginnings and resentment of that shame. Their most heartfelt emotion is a piece of the dignity pie which Nixon even more than McGovern cannot ever give them. I have heard deeply anticommunist, Catholic Poles evince pride that Poland is advancing, has stood up to Moscow, and can boast of artists and writers, even if they are Reds. Similarly Italians. McGovern, strange as it sounds, is in the best position to fire these people up. Nobody is more American than he, none could more legitimately show them the recognition that would bring them home. Looking at these men I was mystified that they had been left so far out on a limb. Is it possible McGovern thinks they are lost to him? Or can he really lack the requisite sympathy as they suppose? Or is it that they represent the outer limits of the new Crowd? Surely a Kennedy would have long since visited Hamtramck and Hartford by this time. But the Kennedys are immigrants.

A politician, like a playwright, has to work with his viscera as well as his head or he's no good. Humphrey, Daley, Meany, Muskie cannot feel the changes in the country. Senator Abe Ribicoff at eight-thirty in the morning in the lobby of the Americana. His car was waiting outside the revolving door to take him over to McGovern at the Doral, but he sat down to talk; he has evidently learned how to relax into the moment and not be rushed by time. In Chicago on the worst night of the carnage in the streets, he had stood at the podium of the convention over the heads of the Illinois delegation and, looking directly down at Richard Daley, had been the first official Democrat to flash the facts of life to the grand and doomed machine, declaring his horror that the Chicago police department was using "Gestapo tactics." At which the crevasse opened and the waters of Miami rushed through the dikes, for that was when Daley had drawn a finger over his throat as he glared up at Ribicoff and told him to drop dead. Connecticut had been placed on Illinois' flank so that I was close to Daley's troops, whose size-eighteen necks swelled, it seeming, for a moment, that if Daley gave the signal they would have gladly rushed the platform and torn Abe's head from his shoulders. The parliamentary system is a paraphrase for murder, and Abe could feel the killing waves. I thought I saw his head shake, but he stood and nodded back to Daley's gesture and curse, affirming again what he had declared. If there was a single instant when the new Crowd split from the old and began to form a separate entity it was then, when Ribicoff s heel drew the borders of the old Crowd's growth.

Apart from his courage, and it took a great deal of it in that moment of ignition, I suppose he could be the one to tell the party the time of day, because there is something in him that has had enough of politics. I wanted to know if he would accept the vice presidential nomination, about which there was much talk. "I'm going to tell them that after thirty-nine years in politics I'd prefer to run for local office with McGovern. It's the only enthusiasm I have left for politics. There are other things I want to do with my life." A recent widower, he seemed to see the turmoil through the quietus of mortality. For over two years he has been McGovern's sponsor in the Senate and, from all accounts, foresaw every step of his rise from what at first seemed an impossibly obscure beginning. In fact, he sensed early on the real extent of the new third Crowd— McGovern's—and now showed no surprise that it turned out to be there. But at least until very recently the general opinion of McGovern was that he was too colorless, even mildly professorial, and no leader. "McGovern is a very ambitious man. I asked him two years ago, 'But are you ready to give up everything for this? Your family life, your own peace, every minute of your existence?' He said, 'I want to be president.' He's a very great organizer, and he's tough. I believe he's going to make it."

I thought again of our mythmaking apparatus. For no solid reason I can name I also had had the idea of a professorial McGovern, the first Ph.D. since Wilson to run for high office, but two years ago he had shown up at my neighbor's house at a party for Joe Duffey's campaign for the Senate, and he looked to me then like a beautifully tailored, middle-aged cowboy with that long blue gaze and thick thumbs. Maybe it was his dovish antiwar stance that had characterized him so softly or maybe just the journalistic shorthand which bedevils us all. I could not help thinking of our other great figures of myth, movie stars when there still were stars, and the hilarious misapprehensions of their characters which the public, especially intellectuals, devour. It is a rule never to be broken that the most lasting picture of a star is always created by his or her earliest interviews. The reason is simply that lazy journalists forever after unearth the file and basically rewrite what was written before. The same is true of politicians who are tagged early on. Someone somewhere must have portrayed McGovern as an overcivilized professor, when in fact he is the most direct political descendant of the Kennedy operational technique.

That technique was most spontaneously demonstrated not so much on the podium in Miami but in the lobby of the Doral Hotel when about three hundred hippies, SDS, Progressive Labor Party, and assorted Outraged suddenly filed in and sat down on the floor, demanding to see McGovern, who had to explain himself then and there as to why, the previous evening, he had stated that he would retain the U.S. armed presence in Thailand. The entire hotel was promptly shut down tight, the management cutting off the elevators for fear the invasion would spread through the upper floors. A squad of police soon arrived and were quickly ordered out, for violence in that narrow lobby would have left a lot of red meat lying about. Besides, it is a part of our awareness in post-Chicago times that the young savages are daughters and sons of the middle class and bear a political legitimacy which, as always in every era, is the reward given the violent and the brave. In the bargain, you can see long-haired cops everywhere now, four years after Chicago.

But arriving quite by chance an hour or more after the sit-down had begun it was hard to gauge the beat. Beneath the uproar the kids were clearly disciplined, and when a thin girl of nineteen or so ordered them through a bullhorn to sit, they formed in ranks and sat facing her as in class. Many were shirtless, and all were styled in the latest Army–Navy store bargains. I could not help my mind's resurrection of the continuity here—the last sit-down I had seen was in Flint, Michigan, in 1936, when the auto workers shut down Fisher Body Plant Number 2, and this was a reassurance, for the act of sitting together on signal is political, not temperamental, a call for parley rather than riot. Nevertheless, even to the untutored eye the taunting factions stood out, primarily the Zippies, who clustered—all fifteen of them—in one corner with their own portable p.a. system, holding up a six-by-ten-foot photo of Johnson which they had stolen out of the Convention Hall where it had hung in a line of the Great Democratic Leaders of the past. Over LBJ's forehead they had stuck a McGovern bumper sticker. The echo of their yells and latter-day Dadaist ebullience, rapping against the marble lobby walls combined with the rhythmic chants of the sitters led by the young girl, left all options open. Three TV cameras with their crews were ranged on a platform to one side, but no photo lights were on yet, the opening curtain evidently being delayed, for what cause no one seemed to know. It needs be mentioned that in a more open area nearer the entrance doors a dozen or so straights in conventional clothes were standing around, people with Midwestern eyeglasses and flowered dresses, who looked on with more curiosity than the apprehension which the occasion seemed to deserve; their estimate of the mood turned out to be quite correct, probably because the riots they had seen on TV numerous times had never harmed them.

The sitters, split though they were among their factions, were nevertheless united in one object, to force McGovern down from his suite; understanding the program, the TV men were not wasting light and tape on the preliminaries. "We want McGovern! We want McGovern!" For half an hour the demand repeated itself under the orchestrating arms of the young girl at their head, and now, having achieved the inner organization of a true Crowd, which was their mutual equality and unanimity, a victory or discharge beyond mere chanting had to be found. But nothing of that kind seemed about to happen, so hands were raised quite as in the classroom, their sole previous experience of purposeful action, and from the floor came proposals to climb the stairs to McGovern or to physically force the management to turn an elevator on. Now the TV men stirred but continued smoking and drinking their Cokes. Meanwhile the Zippies, mocking McGovern as well as the political purposefulness implied in the surrounding orderliness, had raised the volume of their p.a. to drown it all. Long since used to the blasts of rock music, the seated majority was immune to interruption. That pall of stalemate descended when anything can happen; they had committed themselves symbolically, and there could be no retreat this side of confrontation or violence. And the sense of timing in headquarters upstairs caught the danger by some telepathic means, for an elevator door opened and Mankiewicz appeared. A roar of curses, applause and yells greeted him. He seemed an even smaller and more fragile man than he is, possibly because by this time the girl leader was sitting on the shoulders of a boy and was bent over looking down at him, while she carefully held her microphone close to her mouth so that her rage would carry throughout the lobby's chaotic acoustics.

Now one camera was trucking into the center of the lobby from the common roost at one side, and the Outraged carefully made way for it. From the ranked PL group came the rhythmic chant, "Fuck McGovern!" but the camera's lights were not yet on, and this soon died away. Now the Zippies, who had been left behind by the moving camera, pressed ahead into the crowd with their immense Johnson photograph, screaming at lung-bursting levels through their p.a. but suddenly going silent to hear the camera crew's advice not to block the entire view. They moved accordingly and, once properly positioned, resumed their particular version of passion, grouped at the right-hand bank of elevators opposite the Progressive Laborites who were standing on the other flank of the sitting majority. So we had the full panoply—against the left wall the PL's program summed up in Fuck McGovern, in the center the bulk of the sitters waiting for orders from the sharp-faced girl perched next to a very serious if not humiliated Mankiewicz, and on the right flank the Zippies carrying on where Tristan Tzara had left off in Zurich, 1924.

I can't vouch for the accuracy of Mankiewicz' dialogue with the girl leader, because his appearance caught me so by surprise. A moment before his arrival I had seen three boxes of a dozen eggs each handed up from the crowd on the floor to the leadership around the girl—food had been brought in for a long sit, if necessary—and even she had involuntarily to register a disclaimer, however humorously, of the purpose these potential missiles would serve. Laughing, she said they were hard-boiled, but there was room for doubt. The vision of McGovern being pelted by three dozen eggs from a crowd of young, usually identified as his most fervent supporters, would on TV have changed even bad odds to none at all. In addition, as these boxes of eggs were moving from hand to hand up to the front, a haggard, bearded fellow in torn cut-off-at-the-knee dungarees came up to me and said he had played in *The Crucible* in college and thought now that he should straighten me out as to what was happening here. Indicating the Progressive Laborites and their Fuck McGovernism, he said, "They're trying to puddle him right here and now. They think the Vietcong are bourgeois and Mao is ready for his Cadillac. You're looking at the stormbirds of American fascism—the worse it gets the quicker the workers will turn against capitalism, you see?" I saw. He looked sickened, in which case what was he doing here at all? "I thought we had to call McGovern on that statement he gave out about keeping forces in Thailand. But this is therapy time, and it's going through the roof. He's out of his head if he comes down now. They'll ruin him right in the living room. It's awful. We're in prime time now."

I caught the end of the Mankiewicz confrontation. The girl, beet red in the face, arching over from her perch on the boy's shoulders, was screaming, "Okay, in fifteen minutes we're either getting an answer or McGovern is coming down. Within fifteen minutes, is that right?"

Mankiewicz kept his eyes down. He had evidently agreed to this already, but she wanted it loud and clear. I thought I could hear his teeth gritting. "That's right."

"Okay, get going!" she dismissed him. He disappeared to the triumphant screams of the mob, and she turned with electric eyes to the whooping audience, a thin-lipped grin gashing her face. A stout girl in a once-white blouse and a skirt stepped up beside her with a pad and pencil and called out, "Okay, cool it. Now let's get the issues!"

As slices of white bread and pieces of cheese were being handed around and the Dadas were going wild with satire of this participatory democracy, the white-bloused girl was having trouble dredging issues from the orderly majority. "Abortion!" finally sounded loud and clear, and she dutifully wrote it down and turning her eyes over the whole assembly for its agreement, said, "Abortion—right?" "Right on!" Then after some more soul searching in which hiatus it was clearer than ever that the issues were being dragged behind them rather than leading them forward, they resurrected the litany of the vanguard. A PL boy cried out, "Socialism now!" but was cut off by his fellows who knew better. They were still seated on the floor but pressing on into history and scrambling for their declarations, their flags, as it were, and the only sure thing in them was their existence now that the perhaps future president of the United States was descending from his sequestered throne room to pay homage to their power. For myself, a mixture of resentment and a hard-to-win confession; they were right in insisting McGovern face the contradiction of his peace position which his previous night's statement clearly implied, perhaps even at the cost of his national humiliation on the tube, for betrayal by politicians has been the brand upon the forehead of this system. But I was flummoxed by their contempt for human dignity, let alone the dignity of their own demand for honesty. Mankiewicz, after all, was still a human being, and the girl had all but urinated on his head to the crowd's apparent appreciation. No country could be led by such contempt, excepting to a very dark place.

Like heavy cannon the two remaining TV cameras lumbered into place amid the crowd, which now got to its feet as the TV lights burst on, illuminating the bottom of a curving stairway to one side of the lobby. My mind was on three dozen eggs secreted somewhere, cradled in pairs of children's hands. McGovern arrived at the bottom of the stairs to find the girl leader swaying over his head with her microphone pressed to her mouth. I cannot recall her lines, but the command in them was filled to bursting with the audience's fantasy of power which had been sucked up from so many sources—the snarling orders of the tough cops on TV, the Chinese students' interrogations of erring professors and landlords, Perry Mason, and their dreams dreamed not long ago in Larchmont bedrooms surrounded by the hated chintz. Surely, an authentic rather than a role-playing voice here could not have sought to demean the one senator who has stood alone for so many years against their hated war. But despite myself I realized now that McGovern had correctly chosen to recognize his duty to answer for his press statement which had trimmed his peace position.

McGovern appeared in the white light at the foot of the stairway, and if an observer had arrived at that very moment he could not have known whether the roar of the crowd was hostile or friendly. For the crowd had already won by this giving-birth, and the sound was the sound of relief after labor, from enemy and friend alike. He spoke right through the din of the Zippies' mockery and the counterincoherence of his supporters, in a voice amazingly the same as it had been in my neighbor's house, without a trace of apology or trepidation and yet not with that false charm designed to kid away the conflict. His references are from within. There was about him not the slightest air of being put upon, no sign of anger, but an even estimation of the trouble he was in, neither more nor less. All three cameras were on now, and he was speaking on prime time to America, but the inevitable tension of performing fused with his being here before this particular group of young. It was the first authentic feeling any of them had heard since the demonstration began.

He came directly to the issue of his previous press statement and overrode it; he would say now precisely what he had been saying all along, that on Inauguration Day the war would end and all American forces would be out of Indochina within ninety days. The inevitable cheer went up and the inevitable digging in of heels—what about abortion, a guaranteed annual wage, legalization of pot, amnesty? He lobbed the ball back—surely they accepted that human beings could not agree on absolutely everything.

This summoning up of their own creed derailed them, for it did not sound strategic or cynical but a genuine aspect of his character. He had still left unexplained his paradoxical statement, but it had fallen away, lost in the discharge of their feelings of common identity which had succeeded in materializing him before them as though they had created him. The sharp-faced girl yelled on in vain, and when he said that they would surely understand he had a lot of things he must do and waved farewell, the applause swept up to the ranks of the PL's who were now mounted on each other's shoulders, middle fingers raised, hands jerking upward in the air, shouting, "Fuck McGovern!" But they had fallen into place, they too were enjoying now, and the fabled Issues had gone by, were merged in the climactic fact that he had come down because they had demanded him, had grown him. Moses smashed the tablets in a fury with the Jews for their failure to rise to the sublime commandments, but despite everything he had forged a tribe of many disparate peoples, for what mattered was not the words but the mime, the fact that they had been present when he went up and when he came down from the Lord, and if few would remember exactly what was said or settled, none would forget the essential—that they had been there when for their sake he had climbed Sinai, they had seen it and had been the cause and were the sinews of a leader and thus transcended.

As they dispersed and the white lights of the cameras flowed out, I walked out into the heat of night and was stopped by another bearded one naked to a pair of murky shorts. "I played in *The Crucible* at Louisiana State. Terrific, wasn't it?" I wasn't so sure, although I was surer than I had been ten minutes earlier. He was an associate professor somewhere. I was curious whether he dressed like this for class. No, of course not— "This is theater," he said with a pleased smile, "you don't go onstage in your ordinary clothes." We both laughed. "Come over to Flamingo Park in the morning. I'll show you our plans to trash the Republicans in August." It was precisely the same tone a director might use toward his next production, that suppressed brag about a coming masterpiece, that basic joyfulness in being an artist at all.

I find I have left the convention itself for last, and it isn't by accident since it was so anticlimactic after the second day. Certainly it signified a renovation of politics, a major party opened at last to the streets, the teacher, the student, the amateur. It showed that a new machine has been born, but the question remains the depth of its reach into the country. The truth is that the legitimitizing weight of the working class was not there to make it the real reflection of America it wanted to be. If only for this absence it can be but a stage along the way. But it is equally true that there never has been a new movement, be it Abolition, the New Deal, or Wilson's New Democracy, which did not first arrive in the heads of intellectuals. Still, there was not yet Power, only an aversion for what is, and these are not the same. So there was a certain surreality, as though a new king had just been crowned but the old one had neither died nor could he be located, he had simply wandered off.

Which probably symbolizes the pervading sense of an inner unrelatedness in the country itself. Ours is a president whose paternality has never settled on him. Patricides, we live now in the shadow of something homogenized, whose leadership consists at best of a benign distrust between the people and itself and at worst of its implicit violence. This vagueness of a ruling personality had to enter the convention where, quite strangely, the enemy Nixon's name was barely mentioned at all. The one moment when an authentic emotion was felt was Teddy Kennedy's evocation of the nostalgia of the past when indeed there had been kings even if you didn't altogether admire them. But otherwise there was nothing handed down, no grail, no flag, no helmet emptied of its immortal knight, and so nothing was quite won, not yet. But something may have created itself if history is kind.

It was literally as though we had no past at all. A man from Mars must surely have wondered if this race was new. Yet we live under the oldest continuous government on earth, and, strangely, the convention could not find one old man loved enough to bless the new leader and send him forth with something memorable and good. Within the bounds of conventioneering there was less a classic conflict with the dying than a sheer assertion of new birth, a dangerously immaculate conception.

But it could turn out yet to have been realer than it seemed. Within America a certain Crowd has certainly lost its old cohesion, and the lines of force no longer hold. The vote is floating. As late as Jack Kennedy's campaign one could still speak of Left and Right, but this time only of a mood. What else than a mood could have found a leader for so city-bred a revolution in a man from the sparsest population in the country? If historical formulations had their classic impress, how could so ministerial a man be leader of an avant-garde whose advertised faith is in smoke, a movement of women clamoring for the right to abort, students for whom the conventional disciplines are laughable?

It may be that in some primordial way there is a reaching back to roots in the raising-up of George McGovern. Even for his enemies his menace is not radicalism but righteousness, that quality which always hovers on the ridiculous but when it stands and holds can smash through all confusion. It could well be that righteousness is all we have left. If Kennedy was of the Left, if only symbolically, he was also as much the author of the Green Berets and the war as any man was, and if Nixon is the Right he has thrown the line to China. Yet few know how to call Kennedy bad, and this country has enormous trouble trying to think of Nixon as good. But it is indeed a word McGovern suggests to the mind despite everything, not that one really knows his character but that he seems to be seriously obsessed with the creativity of the people rather than the manipulability of institutions. If he truly is so, and can make it palpable, anything can happen.

As for conventions themselves, they will surely have to go. Perhaps a national primary is the answer, something at least more straightforward than this travesty which all of us know is but a time-honored means of manipulating symbols. The much-touted finesse of the new machine is a doubtful achievement, finally; it has only proved that amateurs can learn cynicism fast. The nominees will have to make the fight at the supermarket and on film, which brings us back to where we started—to the man on the stump attempting with directness to make his Crowd.

1972

Arthur Miller *vs.* Lincoln Center

I'll say something I've never said before: the Lincoln Center board *never* intended to have a repertory theater—a theater doing several productions at the same time—and they don't intend to now because they cannot and will not supply the money for repertory. When they originally consulted Robert Whitehead about the plans for a theater, he explained that it would have to have a vast area for the storage of scenery and everything else that goes with a repertory theater. His one aim was a repertory theater, but he told them there was no rule which said they had to build a repertory theater and suggested that maybe they should just build a place to put on plays, which would cost much less than a repertory installation.

They told Whitehead, "No, don't bother your head about costs, just build the nicest theater you can imagine." But when the point arrived at which the operational budget began to come up, it turned out that they had never established a budget on how much money would be allotted to the building, and how much was to be reserved for paying salaries for actors, and so forth. It was as simple as that. They were building a twelve-million-dollar monument, period. It's like building a new department store with practically no merchandise or employees.

The smallest repertory company I know of in Europe has about seventy-five people in its company. Lincoln Center originally eked about twenty-three out of its budget. The city of Munich pays $750,000 a year for the salaries and scenery and costumes of one repertory company out of four in that city. When the time came for the Lincoln Center board to bring repertory into being, they had no budget anywhere near to sufficient for it (by the way, the Robert Whitehead-Elia Kazan operation of the ANTA Theater downtown cost some $200,000 *less* than anticipated).

The Vivian Beaumont Theater was ready to open three months earlier than expected, but instead of giving Whitehead and Kazan the extra rehearsal time, the board began secretly dealing with Alexander H. Cohen to bring Rex Harrison to open this theater in a revival of some British comedy instead of opening it with a repertory production. This charade went on for months, mind you; they were on the verge of signing a contract with Cohen. In other words, they wanted a show in there at which you could really *dress*.

The Lincoln Center board's persistent, adamantine refusal to admit the facts continues to the present moment. These great giants of industry, banking, and commerce can't get it through their heads that the more successful a repertory theater is, the more it must cost. It contradicts all business principles.

The only explanation of their behavior I've ever come up with that made any sense was that they see credit to themselves in building monuments but not in paying actors.

In their favor, it can be said that they would like to have had a repertory theater but, once having seen what it would cost, they should not have assumed the responsibility and then refused to make good on it, while at the same time pretending that they were indeed subsidizing such a theater. Except for the few weeks in the 1968–69 season when *King Lear* and *A Cry of Players* alternated, Lincoln Center has never operated as a repertory theater.

It may be as stupid as this: donors like to have their names on the back of a seat. When you pay an actor's salary, your name doesn't get engraved on the back of his head. Who will ever know that Mr. Rockefeller helped develop some great actor? Donors not only want to do good, they want their good to be seen being done.

What was their idea of a solution in the Lincoln Center Repertory situation last fall? Moving concrete. That makes sense to them. They will raise money to break down an existing thing as long as they can see an object being moved from one place to another. But they cannot conceive that the man who acts on the stage has got to get paid, *especially* if some weeks he's not working. Now you run into the ultimate absurdity where they planned to tear down the Forum, the best theater in that mess over there, and eliminate it.

At first, the board was great with Kazan and Whitehead, because Whitehead had a reputation as a tasteful and successful producer, and Kazan—well, Kazan was Kazan. Then the New York City drama critics began to slam these men, and the board decided to get rid of them. When they canned Whitehead, there were fourteen of the best American actors about to sign with Lincoln Center. I don't want to use names now, but in a season or two you would have had a marvelous company that no Broadway show could afford to hire, and they were possibly going to act for salaries close to minimum. As it was, the core of the company was in being. Faye Dunaway, John Phillip Law, Joseph Wiseman, Zohra Lampert, Hal Holbrook, David Wayne, Barbara Loden, Michael Strong and Jason Robards are all first-class talents, and something alive could have begun with them.

I don't know Jules Irving at all, I only met him once, I have no opinion about him one way or another as an administrator. But why did they reach all the way to California for Irving and Herbert Blau to run a New York theater? At the time, I thought it was because of the onslaught by the so-called intellectual critics, and these two fellows were more or less on the academic side. They had run a small provincial repertory company which had gotten good reviews in the local press, and everybody loved them out there. I figured the board looked around and said, "Who is loved?" and found Irving and Blau, poor fellows.

But the answer is simpler, I think now. They'd be *cheaper* than Whitehead, who was not trying to build a San Francisco repertory company but something in America that would vie with the great companies of the world.

When Whitehead was fired, I challenged the board, and I lost. I was the only one to make a statement in *The New York Times*. Nobody else would, and nobody picked mine up. The critics went right on yelling at the actors. If the critics would criticize *them*— the members of the Lincoln Center board—for a change, they might start to get very nervous, and when they get nervous they start to listen to *everybody*. You can't imagine how insecure these guys are. They're afraid of publicity, they want people to at least not notice. As you start to home in on them, I believe something would happen.

The critic has a duty here, because this is a public business. It's not entirely the board's business how Lincoln Center is run, because public money is involved and it's New York City's land, our property, that they're sitting on. It doesn't belong to them. You will *never* have a repertory company so long as that board is in control, and that is where the critics should make their attack, carefully and coolly. The critics must stop regarding Lincoln Center as just another Broadway operation where you hit the producer or director. You can't reach them by criticizing Jules Irving, or the actors, or the scenery design—this just creates a diversion and allows them to sit back and explain, "Well, you see, we didn't get good scenery this time."

Remarkably enough, in this age of anti-establishment feeling, this is one establishment which has never been attacked, and they are at the root of the entire Lincoln Center disaster. Look at them up there, you've got the heads of some of the biggest banks and other institutions in this country—nobody takes a critical shot at them. The critics will beat up the actors, the author, the director, that's easy. But it never occurs to any critic to go after those board fellows. Why not? Because the surrounding sociology of repertory is unknown to us.

All of us are always complaining about the death of the theater, now here's an instance where we can conceivably exercise an influence because we're dealing with a public institution. Now is the time for all of us, including the press, to say to them, "Anything *doesn't* go. You can't have it this way."

Most critics and other Americans don't understand what a repertory theater is, anyway. What does it take to run a repertory theater? Is it possible within the budgets the Lincoln Center board has envisaged? Let's investigate. These aren't mysteries on the moon. There are hundreds of repertory theaters all over the world. A study could be made, we could then lay out some kind of schematic idea of what it really takes to run a repertory theater.

Start with that, and leave artistic matters aside for the moment. Tell them: "All right, gentlemen, this is what is required to run a repertory theater, according to every piece of evidence. Can you supply it? If not, get out and let people in who can and will."

We have to face the economic issue, or else let's stop fooling around and rent the damned building out for whatever it will bring. The present situation is merely perpetuating a demoralizing feeling, as if to say, "Look, repertory doesn't work." We've never *had* anything like real repertory, so the alternative to the commercial Broadway theater has never come to be. The board is only pretending that it can come to be, and is thus preventing it from happening.

When we first started at the ANTA Theater downtown, Laurence Olivier asked me, "What are the critics screaming about? We were in Chichester for seven years before we ever came in to London. Our company was weeded out from hundreds of actors before we ever faced the London critics." He was bowled over by the fact that nobody here understood the rudiments of what goes into making a repertory company. It's an extraordinarily difficult thing to do, but it is worthwhile and so we must be clear about what the difficulties are, what the aims are, what it really takes to do this job, instead of going on saying, "When are we going to have a good show at Lincoln Center?" That is not the way to do it.

Let's look at budgets of repertory companies anywhere. If, indeed, the public or the donors will *not* give the money it takes to run a repertory theater, then let's stop pretending we have anything called the Lincoln Center Repertory Company and get rid of it. Maybe our culture will not support a repertory theater, or maybe some day, when we are all dead, there will be a repertory theater when they make up their minds to have it.

If you go to German theaters, you see facilities that are much larger than ours. Some of them, as in Frankfurt, have two stages, one to rehearse on behind the one they play on, with a movable wall between. So we shouldn't imagine that the Vivian Beaumont is outstandingly elaborate.

It's simply an impossibility to run this kind of an operation anywhere by selling tickets, even though the response of the audience with their subscriptions and admissions at Lincoln Center has been immense, tremendous. Let's clear the air. There could be no Kabuki, No ballet, theater, opera, hospitals or libraries without an act of will. No marketplace ever has or can support such things.

Our cultural life seems to be drying up, we're becoming a utilitarian society in the crudest sense, namely, that which is not bought cannot be art. Whole sections of the New York Public Library, one of the greatest libraries in the world, are closed. Museums have short hours. Even the hospitals have to curtail their services and are threatened with closing because they have no money. We are becoming a second-class cultural power and in theater we are neck and neck with the Congo.

But the Lincoln Center situation may be amenable to improvement, theoretically, because it is not a part of the government. These guys are not elected officials, and they do not have the defense of the elected official, "How many votes do actors have?" The constituency of the Lincoln Center board is public opinion in general, and therefore something might come of our efforts.

All of which presumes that a repertory theater is really wanted here. Objectively speaking, though, maybe we'd do more good trying to raise money for libraries and hospitals, but let that lie for the moment. Maybe repertory theater isn't wanted as yet because it isn't understood. The first thing we have to do is declare our ignorance, and I include the lot of us.

I would also like to mention a mystery, however. Before there was a single production at the ANTA Theater downtown, before an actor had walked onto that stage, the mere announcement of the project set off an incomprehensible eruption of ridicule, cynicism and outright hostility in many theater people and the press. I still am unable to understand why. Maybe something in our culture rejects the idea as some kind of foreign body. We can't seem to connect prestige with repertory as we do with Broadway, God save the mark, while at the same time we are on our knees before the Royal Shakespeare and British National Theatres.

Repertory is certainly no panacea. It often breeds bureaucracy, time-saving lethargy. It always stands or falls on far-seeing, talented and selflessly ambitious artists at its helm, and these are scarce anywhere. But these problems can wait. Right now we don't even have a problem, because we have nothing. So the first order of business now is to get clear in our own minds what such a theater is, what it can do, and what is financially needed to do it. Then if we are convinced of its value, a considered serious attempt must be made to transform Lincoln Center into such a theater.

I think it is time the Lincoln Center board is called to account, just as playwrights, directors, and actors are. The Dramatists Guild and all concerned parties should demand they come forward and explain why they have failed to provide what they implicitly claim to provide. What is their policy? Surely they have a defense; what is it? They must no longer be allowed to fob off their failure on the artists working for them.

I repeat that a real repertory company may be impossible in the social system of New York today. Or it might be possible. We don't have the facts to make a judgment. The first thing to do, I believe, is to go in and challenge those men, to face the realities together, and decide what is to become of a potentially great theater that belongs to all of us.

1972

Arthur Miller on *The Crucible*

I saw the movie of *The Crucible* with some very mixed emotions. I have never thought that a screen adaptation of a play must or even should hew to the details of the play, the film being so different a form. In fact, I don't think it is a good idea as a general rule to try to make movies of plays because the play is based primarily on what words can make true, while the movie is our most directly dream-based art and dreams are mostly mute.

The sheer visualness of *The Crucible* film is its best feature. It was made by the French on the Baltic coast of East Germany at a time when no American film company would touch the story for fear of attack by our righteous Right. The barrenness of the locale and the hardbitten peasantlike crudeness of the townspeople—all Germans—did indeed create the sense of our Puritanical forebears and the hard territory they were trying to transform into the New Jerusalem. In fact, I was later told that when it came time to shoot the hanging of the "witches," the actors and director got some expert advice based on real experience from some of the actors about how a hanging man reacts. (His feet continue to twitch for one thing.)

The actors, especially Simone Signoret as Mrs. Proctor, had enormous authority. Inevitably in a French picture the man-woman relationship took on marvelously tender and complicated shades of resentment. The twisted marital love between Proctor and his wife was not seen as a mere means to a political end, but as something natural and moving in itself, and the Proctors' disaster was a wonderful mixture of personal and social themes. The Abigail, Mylene Demongeot, was truly beautiful and so bursting with real sexuality as to become a generalized force whose effects on the community transcended herself. As I had intended, she personified that force which the society of the time in turn suppressed and worshipped, for witchcraft—whatever else it is—is revolt, the revolt of the blood.

I don't like criticizing the film, primarily because I was grateful that it was made when it had become a symbol of what the ruling American idea could not tolerate. Fundamentally, I thought that it was weakened and made less actual, rather than more pointed, by Sartre's overly Marxist screenplay. Or maybe it is less a Marxist distortion than a European one. It is made very clear, for example, that the hysteria is rather coolly manufactured by a ruling class of big proprietors whose aim is to enslave the poorer farmers and the indigent. The feudal class structure of seventeenth-century French society is the prism through which Massachusetts is viewed, and this works to oversimplify the reality of the time. The fact is that while the Putnam family was wealthy and did indeed spur on the hysteria and in all probability engineered certain aspects of it, the line of battle was not nearly so clear or straight. Some very respectable people, some of them even in the Putnam family's class, were among the victims.

The original play stresses individual conscience as the ultimate defense against a tyrannical authority, but conscience in the screenplay is more an expression of rebellion against a class oppressor than a transcendence of a man over himself. Thus my viewpoint in the play was probably regarded as overly romantic and even bourgeois. In the screenplay this conscience carries the freight, so to speak, of a social-political lesson, but I am not sure it convinced many people of the truth that lesson was supposed to bring out. It didn't convince me because it mechanized the process by which very particular individuals become murderers of their fellow townspeople and others choose to give their lives rather than join the pack. This process may despiritualize the story and make it more politically recognizable, but it also reduces man to a digit in the social dialectic and in the end leaves everything explained but not illuminated. A Marxist interpretation of the Salem witch hunt could well throw light on many still mysterious and incomprehensible social motivations, but this moral puzzle will not give way to it. The victims as well as the persecutors were socially mixed in their backgrounds. This does not mean that an analysis based on socioeconomic forces is useless in analyzing such outbreaks, but it serves no purpose if it cannot penetrate the crazily various—and often decisive—courses which people took because of or despite their economic interests.

But the movie set itself a different task than faced me when I sat down to write *The Crucible*. The movie's intent is to prove that a landholding class in fear of losing its privileges instituted a terror against its social opponents. My play was an investigation into the how and the why of resistance to terror. The French, so far away and so conscious of their own history, transferred their very different sophistication to another place and another time, but not, I think, with sufficient grace of imagination to keep their grasp on the primary historical materials. The play was made more intellectually satisfactory to the Left, perhaps, but moved us further away from that confrontation with that very difficult-to-explain phenomenon of the human spirit refusing to go on living at the price of a terrible lie. This has more to do with faith than bare economics or even politics. I do not mean necessarily a religious faith but a belief, one might call it, in man as a creature transcending his appétites. We are what has made us but we are also something more, which is unpredictable finally. What comes to mind here is the fact that the people who kept their morale best in the German concentration camps were the devout Communists and the Jehovah's Witnesses. Their common denominator is something to think about in times when whole societies are in the process of being degraded.

But despite all this, I found it a stimulating and even gripping picture, which was finally deeply moving and quite beautiful. It is not to me *The Crucible* but a version of it and a strong film in its own right.

                                                                    1972

Miracles

Sometime back in the Fifties, *Life* sent out a questionnaire asking opinions on the new revolution then taking place, allegedly. I sent mine back unanswered, with the note that there was no revolution. It seems to me now that I was right and wrong.

The only moment of near revolution I know about, at least in my lifetime, was in the winter of 1932 when the leading bankers went to Washington and seriously discussed with the Treasury Department the idea of the Government taking over all the banks. That, and a few days in Flint, Michigan, during the sit-down strikes. These events—along with the widespread talk in business circles and among the people, that the system was actually at an end and some form of socialist ownership had to be the next step lest total chaos overwhelm the United States—had the look of the real thing. In the ensuing one hundred days, the Roosevelt Administration devised a flood of legislation that saved capitalism by laying down what essentially were limits to how crooked you were allowed to be, or how rapacious, without going to jail. And direct money payments to desperate people was made public policy. It was a revolutionary moment, and it lasted for perhaps four or five years, primarily, I think, because the Establishment had lost its nerve, did not really have a clue to solving mass unemployment. Inevitably, to stand in the avant-garde meant espousing socialism; it meant being political.

The turmoil of the Fifties and Sixties came to a head in a booming economy, just after the Establishment had retrieved its poise to the point where it had cleaned out—through McCarthyism—the universities, the arts, of the last of the people who had a social, let alone a socialist, vision. If there were one concept that might stand for the Thirties avant-garde, it was the solidarity of humanity, and if the Fifties had an emblem, it was loneliness. The Thirties radical, of whatever stripe, saw a pattern of deliquescence in the American system; the Fifties youth was bereft of any such comfort. When the new struggle came, it was inevitably a personal and not a political one—because American politics had its strength back and was at least working again.

But if the Sixties was not a revolution in any classic sense—a transfer of power between classes—it did partake of the revolutionary process by overturning certain attitudes toward what a human being is and what he might be. More, the latter-day revolt has offered a new pattern, just as the one in the Thirties attempted to do, to account for the human condition, a hidden matrix which guided us all. So, in the psychological sense, there is a continuity between both generations, and there are others too.

It is commonplace to say that the Thirties revolt was one of the mind while the latest is one of the gut, a contrast between rationalism and mysticism. This distinction is too neat to be true. Of course a lot of people, probably the majority who became radical in the Thirties, were inspired by unfilled bellies and narrowed-down chances to make a buck. Which is natural and legitimate. As natural and legitimate as the number of Fifties and Sixties revolutionaries whose new vision was limited to the idea of getting laid without the etiquette of courting and bullshit.

I was about fourteen when the Depression hit, and like a lot of others who were more or less my age, the first sign of a new age was borne into the house by my father. It was a bad time for fathers who were suddenly no longer leaders, confident family heads, but instead men at a loss as to what to do with themselves tomorrow. The money had stopped, and these men were trained by American individualism to take the guilt on themselves for their failures, just as they had taken the credit for their successes. Under the streetlamp at the corner drugstore the talk was suddenly shifting from whether you were going to be a doctor, lawyer, businessman, or scientist, to what the hell you were going to do after the dreaded day you were graduated from high school. There were suicides in the neighborhood. We had all been sailing this proud and powerful ship, and right there in the middle of the ocean it was beached, stuck on some invisible reef.

It seems easy to tell how it was to live in those years, but I have made several attempts to tell it, and when I do try I know I cannot quite touch that mysterious underwater thing. A catastrophe of such magnitude cannot be delivered up by facts, for it was not merely facts whose impact one felt, not merely the changes in family and friends but a sense that we were in the grip of a mystery deeper and broader and more interior than an economic disaster. The image I have of the Depression is of a blazing sun that never sets, burning down on a dazed, parched people, dust hanging over the streets, the furniture, the kitchen table. It wasn't only that so many high-class men, leaders, august personages, were turning out to be empty barrels—or common crooks, like the head of the stock exchange. It was that absolutely nothing one had believed was true, and the entire older generation was a horse's ass.

So I went back to the synagogue—an Orthodox synagogue. And there I found three old men playing pinochle in the entrance corridor of that ugly building. I drew up a chair and sat with them. I had no idea what I wanted there. I could read Hebrew but understand little of what I had been saying. I walked inside and looked at the altar. I thought something would speak to me, but nothing did. I went home and came back a few more times. But the sun stood as still in the heavens as it ever had, and nothing spoke. I even joined the little choir, but still nothing happened to me, nothing moved within me.

The mute threat underlying unemployment is that you will never cease being a child. I was favored—I had gotten a job delivering rolls and bread from four to seven every morning, for four dollars a week. Freezing cats followed my bike from house to house, crying in pain. The summer dawns were lovely over the sleeping one-family houses, but they were spoiled by my fear of time bringing me closer to graduation. A man was not wanted anywhere, and the job ads in *The New York Times* specified "White," or "Christian," although there were never more than a dozen openings, anyway. A man, let alone a boy, wasn't worth anything. There was no way at all to touch the world.

One afternoon on a windy street corner, while I was waiting my turn to play handball against the pharmacist's brick wall, a guy who was already in college started talking about capitalism. I had never heard of capitalism. I didn't know we lived under a system. I thought it had always been this way. He said that the history of the world (what history?) was the history of the class struggle (what is a class?). He was incomprehensible but a hell of a handball player, so I respected him. He was unique, the only one I knew who stayed on the same subject every time I met him. He kept pouring this stuff over my head, but none of it was sticking; what he was saying didn't seem to have anything to do with me. I was listening only for what I wanted to know—how to restore my family. How to be their benefactor. How to bring the good times back. How to fix it so my father would again stand there as the leader, instead of coming home at night exhausted, guilty.

This guy kicked the trip wire one afternoon. We were on the beach at Coney Island. In those days families were living under the boardwalk in scrap-metal or wood-slat shacks. We could smell feces and cooking there in the sun. And this guy said, "You are part of the declassed bourgeoisie."

Life quickened, insane as it sounds, because . . .

My father was no longer to blame. It wasn't he who had failed; it was that we were all in a drama, determined by history, whose plot was the gradual impoverishment of the middle class, the enrichment of the upper, and the joining of the middle with the workers to set up a socialist economy. I had gotten what the synagogue had not given me—the ennobling overview. It was possible again to think that people were important, that a pattern lay hidden beneath the despair and the hysteria of the mothers, that the fathers would again be in their places. Life suddenly had a transcendent purpose, to spread this news, to lift consciousness. For the day would arrive when conflict would end. Things would no longer have value, the machines would provide. We would all live, like people in a park on Sunday, quietly, smiling, dignified. The age of Things was over. All that remained was for people to know it.

They usually call this the experience of materialist religion, but it had little materialism for me. I wasn't looking to it for anything like money or a better job but for a place, literally, in the universe. Through Marxism you extended your affection to the human race. The emptiness of days filled with a maturing purpose—the deepening crisis of capitalism, bursting into the new age, the inexorable approach of nirvana.

It was the last of the forgoing philosophies. The deeds of the present, the moment, had no intrinsic importance, but only counted insofar as they brought closer or held back the coming of the new. Man-as-sacrifice was its essence; heroism was what mattered. We were in the Last Days, all signs pointed to Apocalypse. Self was anathema, a throwback; individual people were dematerialized. A Russian, Ostrovsky, wrote *An Optimistic Tragedy*, and the title signified the mood, I think, wherever Marx's vision had taken root. Joy was coming—no matter what.

The Thirties has never been rendered in literature, because the emotions reported are all coiled around political and economic events, when in truth a religious sweep was central to everything one felt, an utter renewal of mankind, nothing less. The mystic element was usually elided, I imagine, because to share Marx was to feel contempt for all irrationality. It was capitalism that was irrational, religious, obscure in the head, and Hitler was its screaming archangel. Pride lay not in what one felt but what one was capable of analyzing into its class components. The story went around that Wall Street stockbrokers were calling Earl Browder, head of the Communist Party, for his analysis of the economy. A communist *knew*, had glimpsed the inevitable.

Similarly, the movement in the Sixties was hermetic and, like its ancestor, was unable to penetrate the national mind with anything more than its crude, materialist side. To the man on the street, it was merely a generation lying across the road of Progress, crying out F—— Work. And its worst proponents so defined it, too. In the case of both "revolutions," a redemptive thrust, without which such movements are never propelled, could not be transmitted beyond the ranks, and both revolutions appeared to the outsider as contemptuous of man's higher ideals, spirituality, and innate goodness. To most supporters of the Spanish loyalists, their struggle was far more profound than any politics could embrace; the Spanish civil war was a battle of angels as well as the lowly poor against the murderous rich. When the dark spirit won, it was not only a factional victory but the shaking of Inevitability, human future itself had been overwhelmed. While Picasso painted *Guernica*, the State Department, business and religious leaders, and most of the press were oddly hesitant about saying unkind words about Hitler and Mussolini, the law-and-order boys behind Franco. Of the minority of Americans who even knew a war was going on in Spain, probably half were on the side of the Church and fascism. To these people, the republic stood for license, atheism, radicalism, and—yes, even the socialization of women, whatever that meant. So for me the commonly held attitude toward Sixties youth had echoes. The country was fixated on the body of the new revolt while its spirit went either unnoticed or was mangled by the media or the movement's own confused reporters.

The Thirties and Sixties "revolutions," for want of a better word, show certain stylistic similarities and differences. The earlier radical took on a new—for the middle class— proletarian speech, often stopped shaving and wore the worker's brogans and the lumberjack's mackinaw: his tailor, too, was the Army-Navy surplus store. He found black jazz more real than the big band's arranged sentimentality, found Woody Guthrie and Ledbetter and folk music authentic because they were not creations of the merchandiser but a cry of pain. He turned his back, or tried to, on the bounds of family, to embrace instead all humankind, and was compromised—when he found himself lifted up the economic ladder—in his effort to keep his alienation intact. When he married he vowed never to reconstruct the burdensome household he had left behind, the pots and pans, the life of things. The goal was the unillusioned life, the opposite of the American Way in nearly all respects. The people were under a pall of materialism, whipped on unto death in a pursuit of rust. The list of similarities is longer than this, but the differences are the point.

Once nipped by Marx, the Thirties radical felt he was leading a conditional life. He might contribute money, or himself, to help organize a new union, but important as the union was, it paled before its real, its secret, meaning—which was that it taught the worker his strength and was a step toward taking state power away from the capitalist class. If the Thirties radical viewed a work of art or a friend, the measure of value came to be whether socialism was being brought closer or pushed farther away by that art or that friend. And so his life moved into a path of symbols, initially ways to locate himself in history and in society, but ultimately that which ruled his mind while reality escaped.

The Thirties radical soon settled into living for the future, and in this he shared the room of his mind with the bourgeoisie. It could not have been otherwise. Capitalism and socialism are forging systems; and you cannot tend the machine, on which both systems are based, whenever the spirit moves you, but *on time*, even when you would rather be making love or getting drunk. Remember the radical of the Thirties came out of a system that had stopped, and the prime job was to organize new production relations that would start it up again. The Sixties radical opened his eyes to a system pouring its junk over everybody, or nearly everybody, and the problem was to stop just that, to escape being overwhelmed by the mindless, goalless flood that marooned each person on his island of commodities.

The Sixties people would stop time, money time, production time, and its concomitant futurism. Their Marxist ancestors had also wanted man as the measure of all things but sought to center man again by empowering the then-powerless. What came of it was Russia and, at home, the pork-chop trade-union leaders and their cigars. So power itself was now the spook, and the only alternative, if humankind was to show a human face again, was to break the engagement with the future, with even sublimation itself. You lived now, lied now, loved now, died now. And the Thirties people, radical or bourgeois, were horrified and threatened by this reversal because they possessed the same inner relation to the future, the self-abnegating masochism that living for any future entails.

Dope stops time. More accurately, money time and production time and social time. In the head is created a more or less amiable society, with one member—and a religion, with a single believer. The pulsing of your heart is the clock, and the future is measured by prospective trips or interior discoveries yet to come. Kesey, who found his voice in the Sixties, once saw America saved by LSD, the chemical exploding the future forever and opening the mind and heart to the now, to the precious life being traded away for a handful of dust. Which leads to another big difference between the two generations and something that I think informs the antic jokiness in the Sixties radical style.

The Thirties radical never dreamed the world could really explode. In fact, as Clausewitz had said and Marx would have agreed, war was merely politics by other means. If we hated fascism, it too was merely politics, even the clubbing of radicals and Jews. That even fascists could burn up people in ovens was unthinkable. What the Holocaust did was posit a new enemy who indeed was beyond the dialectic, beyond political definition. It was man.

So that Apocalypse, as inherited by the Sixties generation, was not what it used to be, the orderly consequence of a dying system, but an already-visual scene in Hiroshima and Auschwitz whose authors were, in one case, parliamentary politicians. Oppenheimer-like humanists quoting the Upanishads, decent fellows all and, in the other, their tyrant enemies. Political differences and principles guaranteed nothing at all. What had to be projected instead was a human nowness, Leary's turning on and dropping out, lest the whole dark quackery of political side-taking burn us all in our noble motives. The very notion of thinking, conceptualizing, theorizing—the mind itself—went up the flue; and many bourgeois governments, for a little while, backed up in fear not of an ideology but of a lifestyle—a mass refusal to forgo.

For myself, I knew this had no hope and not because it eschewed a political vision but because its idea of man was wrong. Because a man cries "Brother!" doesn't make him one, any more than when his father muttered "Comrade." The struggle with evil doesn't cancel out that easily, as the fate of Marxists had shown. More, from where I sat, the religious accents of Sixties radicalism were not entirely apart from those of Thirties radicalism. Like the Christians, Marx had projected a Judgment Day on the barricades, an Armageddon out of which the last would rise to be first, then to direct the withering away of the state itself once socialism came to pass, the veritable kingdom where conflict is no more and money itself vanished in an abounding surplus of goods. You wanted a car, you just picked one up and left it when you didn't need it any more—a sort of celestial Hertz. If the last thing Jesus or Marx had in mind was a new fatalism, that was nevertheless what most human beings made of the stringent and muscular admonitions these prophets pronounced, and what most of the voyagers into the Age of Aquarius were making, I thought, of the punishing, disciplined yoga that had evolved this new vision. Once you have thought yourself into an alignment with Fate, you are a sort of Saving Remnant for whom mere reality is but an evolution of symbolic events, until finally you are no longer really anything at all except a knower—and thus your deeds cannot be judged by mortal judgment, so anything goes. Differences there are, of course, but Manson, Stalin and that long line of Christian crusaders join hands in this particular dance. How often have I heard survivors of the Thirties astonished that they could have said the things they said, believed what they had believed. A faith had been running underneath that newfound pride in objective social analysis, that sense of merging with the long line into the Inevitable, and a faith exploded is as unrecoverable to the heart in its original intensity as a lost love.

The latter-day Edenism of the Sixties had a sour flavor, for me at least: it was repeating another first act of another disillusioned play. I saw the love-girls, free at last, but what would happen when the babies came?

Most girls with babies are funny. They like to know exactly *where they are*. If only because babies reintroduce linear time and long-term obligation, high-flying anarchy must come to earth.

Kesey's new book *Garage Sale*, a mélange of his own and his friends' writing, is a sort of geologic section of some thirteen years in the wilderness. But his screenplay, which appears in this book, is the real surprise, a hail and farewell to the era. From the height of its final pages you can look down and begin to sense a form at last in the whole insane pageant. For Kesey had not merely taken a dive into his bloodstream and glimpsed, as it were, the interior of his eyes, but emerged into the ring where the Others are, the brothers and sisters toward whom a newfound responsibility flows, and toward the world itself. The time-honored way to make that discovery was the Hebrew-Christian self-torture—the near-dissolution of the body inviting God. Here it is otherwise, the enhancing of the senses and pleasure, the blending of the physicality of Eastern mysticism with the Mosaic injunction to serve the People, whose well-being is the measure of all truth. If responsibility can be reached through pleasure, then something new is on the earth.

Skeptic that I am, I could believe in this. My zodiacal friends tell me that in terms of an individual, the Great Wheel says the human race is now thirty-five years of age, and that's when human beings are most creative, when Jesus gathered together all that he was and died. So Love is coming toward us, the Age of Aquarius. Scorched by an earlier Inevitable, I shy from this one, and I warn whoever will listen that the tension with evil has no end, or, when it does, the man within has died. Nevertheless, when I think back to what life was like in the Thirties and see from that long-ago vantage what is happening now, I stand in the glistening presence of miracles.

Radical or conservative, we worshipped the big and the smoke from the chimney, and the earth was only there to chew up and drill holes in, the air a bottomless garbage pail. Now my ten-year-old daughter turns the key off when I am parked and waiting for someone. How miraculous. We got out of Vietnam because the Army wouldn't fight it any more. That's the simple truth and how miraculous. Nixon—Billy Graham and prayer breakfasts notwithstanding—has revealed himself—and, really, by himself. As though the earth had squeezed up his roots and he rotted where he stood, this lawless man of disorder. How miraculous. The seed of the visionless has spent itself in him. How miraculous. In the early Fifties a Catholic university survey asked me why I thought there were so few of the faith in the arts or in the contentions of social debate. I wrote back that Irish Catholicism and Yankee Puritanism had combined in this country to sink the inquiring mind without a trace. Now? The spectacle of a Catholic priest demonstrating, leading the poor, is miraculous. Reporters stand up and yell at a presidential press officer, accusing him of having told them lies, and this in the White House, with the flag on the platform. How miraculous. The power company wants to run a high-tension line across my countryside and my neighbors, many of them having voted for Nixon, descend on what used to be routine, company-dominated "hearings," and invoke beauty and demand their aesthetic rights as though they were poets. How miraculous. Notre Dame University invites me to read. How miraculous. The stock market drops at rumors of war and soars with signs of peace. Incredible. I speak at West Point. Not believable. And tell them, a week after Nixon's invasion of Cambodia, from where I had just returned, that it is a disaster, a disgrace, and will surely bomb the Cambodians into the communist camp. A sixty-year-old colonel, with a horizontal Guards moustache, ramrod fellow beribboned up to his chin, stands and says he was U.S. Military Attaché in Phnom Penh for nine years and that Mr. Miller has spoken the truth. How miraculous. Only one cadet stands to ask why I choose to undermine their morale, and he is the son of the union chief in Chicago. How miraculous. And afterward, on the porch of an officer's house with a dozen colonels, all Vietnam vets, close-cropped and loose on scotch, they confide their mourning—for the Corps, the country, and a dwindling sense of honor. They talk of resigning, of being ashamed to wear the uniform into New York and, longingly, of Eisenhower's Order of the Day to the legions about to storm the Normandy beaches because that order spoke of mankind, of lifting the yoke of tyranny, and one man exclaims: "Imagine those words in an order any more!" Would they ever know a rightful cause again, in or out of war? They were acolytes in a sullied church, and if these men blamed the politicians for defeat, they were also no longer sure we had deserved to win. That ancient scorn for human circumstances was faltering, even here, in the cannon's heart. Something is changing.

I suppose that in part I have been looking at Sixties radicalism from the Left Bank, from Prague and Red Square, as well as from my own home. It is always disappointing to American radicals to hear that things are worse abroad. Sounds like liberal smuggery. But I don't mean conditions, only the spirit. Especially is this difficult to swallow right now when the tide has played out here, the revolution eddying, and indifference again prevails. Who has gained from it all except MGM Records and the department stores with their new lines of eighty-dollar jeans? What came of the love-ins but fatherless children? And heavier contracts for the stars? And the sharp-eyed managers of perfidious guitars? What comfort that the cop looking for hash under the mattress has curls sticking out behind his helmet? The truth is that the fundamental demand of the French students in the 1968 revolution was that their universities be changed into the utilitarian American kind.

In 1968 I met with some thirty writers and editors and other hairy types in the office of *Listy*, the Prague literary magazine. They wanted someone from outside to know they were about to be jailed by the Russian toadies running the government. They asked me to come because I am an American, and only the Americans *might* respond to their disaster. These fellows had little hope, but it was all they did have. The Vietnam war was raging then, and they could read *The New York Times* and know we were imperialists and racists and lacked anything you could call culture, and yet the hope, what there was of it, pointed toward us. A few of them had been here and knew the score, had seen Harlem and Bedford-Stuyvesant and our wrecked cities—compared to their Prague, barbaric, corrupt, incredibly hard places, and merciless to the unsuccessful. Yet it was as though from this insane country were the impossible help possible—from this armed place that was at the moment killing another struggling people.

Under the Kremlin wall one day I remarked to my Soviet interpreter, a bright chap, that there must have been some fast footwork in that palace.... To my surprise the fellow was offended and said, "It is not our business." And the few who try to make it their business keep a bag packed with clean underwear, for jail. Those few, to my amazement, look to Americans as the free-swinging opposites of what their countrymen are. Not really to the American radical but to what they see as a man-centered idea still alive among us.

One of the owners of a German automobile company, this man naturalized now and based in New York, tells me he had to bring over the company's engineers and make them attend Senate hearings on auto emissions to convince them that they must take seriously the problem of auto pollution—because the Americans meant business, something these engineers had refused to believe because nobody in Europe meant business. A swim in the Mediterranean off Nice, a sail in the Sea of Japan, or a water-ski off the Italian west coast makes Coney Island look as pristine as Thoreau's pond.

But no listing of hopeful improvements can really alter the despair with modern life which is shared everywhere; the difference, if there is one, is a residual eagerness in Americans to believe despair is not life's fixed condition but only another frontier to be crossed. Perhaps only the black man can know the more universal despair—which changes only to remain forever the same—yet he has certainly evolved out of his passivity toward it.

In the central square of Wilmington, North Carolina, in the twilight of a fall 1940 evening, about a thousand blacks spread out along the storefronts and sat down or lounged among their jalopies and busted trucks. I happened to be there, temporarily employed by the Library of Congress to record speech patterns, no less, in that state. Quite accidentally I came upon this strange display. Eerie—for I knew instantly that they were not there to no purpose, and in 1940 you simply did not connect black people with assertion, let alone protest. (Blacks had stood apart from the whole radical

Thirties, except for a handful who had never succeeded in rousing their own people.) I used the excuse of my microphone to find out what was going on, and I collected a crowd of men who were somewhat reassured by the Great Seal of the U.S. painted in gold on my truck—in those days the Federal Government was Roosevelt, whom white racists hated.

They were diffident country people, shy and suspicious, but pieced out for me the fact that they had been recruited from backwoods farms and hamlets to build the new Wilmington shipyard in the swamps nearby, a mucky, mosquito-tormented job. Now that the yard was finished, they had all been summarily fired to make way for white workers to come in and take the clean shipbuilding jobs. Only one of the men so much as raised his voice, a large fellow with powerful arms and a heavy bass voice. He stepped out of the polite shyness and roared, "Captain, we just about tripped! We got *no place to go!*" Then they dispersed. No police came to ride them down. By nine that night these people had all vanished, presumably into the woods from which they came. White Wilmington had barely taken notice of the occupation of the square, and in fact these black people had hardly raised their voices. Next day I interviewed the chief of Bethlehem's operation there and he was bewildered that there could even be an issue. Blacks hired in a shipyard to work alongside *whites?* That level of awareness is not possible any more, even if so many blacks still live as though in an occupied country, a territory the Depression never left.

If only because the good news of Aquarius never touched our racism, it left an uneasiness; but there is another disquiet as well. Like the Thirties, the Sixties did not know quite what to do with evil. In the fever of the newfound Marxism, evil was seen evaporating with the disappearance of the private owner and his exploitation of people, but the snob T. S. Eliot said it better—"They are trying to make a world where no one will have to be good." Now again, by means of drugs or prayer or sex, we'll merge all impulses into a morally undifferentiated receptivity to life, and evil will shrivel once exposed to the sun. It is as though evil were merely fear, fear of what we conceal within, and by letting it all hang out we leap across the categories of good and bad. To both "revolutions," good and bad were inventions of the Establishment, mere social norms, and so it seemed that Stalin was liquidating not people but the dying past. Just as Manson, to many, is an ambiguous villain—the faces of his victims fade beside his victory over self-repression. There was something strangely pure in his massacre, since he did not even know his victims. André Gide wrote this story long ago—of a man who fires his gun in a railroad car and kills a man he never saw before—this in order to spring free of the ultimate repression through a totally gratuitous act, to find the irreducible self. Nihilism may save pride but it leaves its casualties and no fewer than does the moral code it sought to squash. Embittered now and defeated, the Sixties people find themselves no longer trained for nirvana but, yet again, in the United States. Still, they changed it forever, if this is a comfort.

By 1949, a Thirties man would never know there had ever existed, only a few years before, a movement for social justice, loud and pervasive. By 1949 the word "society" had become suspect again. But ten years later, justice was once more the issue. It was simply that the inventions of the Thirties had been absorbed, just as now the nation has both rejected and digested the Sixties idea. And this may be why, in my case anyway, a return from abroad always yields a faintly surprising experience of hope. It does keep changing here, it does go on: the blind, blundering search—which is not the case in more completed places. Evidently we are not fated to be wise, to be still in a contemplation of our cyclical repetitiousness, but must spawn new generations that refuse the past absolutely and set out yet again for that space where evil and conflict are no more.

It will not come—and it is coming.

1973

What's Wrong With This Picture?
Speculations On A Homemade Greeting Card

Here is a New Year's card I recently received many months late. Like couples everywhere, this one decided to celebrate the occasion with a humorous photograph. It could have been taken in any one of a number of countries. It happens to have been made in Czechoslovakia.

The wife is wearing just the right smile for a woman standing hip-deep in water with her clothes on. It is a warm and relaxed smile. The husband, likewise, expresses the occasion with his look of grave responsibility, his walking stick and dark suit, his reassuring hand on Eda, their beloved dog.

The wife's floppy hat and gaily printed dress and the husband's polkadot tie and pocket handkerchief suggest that the couple might have started off for a stroll down a Prague boulevard when, for some reason unstated, they found themselves standing in the water. One sees, in any case, that they are fundamentally law-abiding people who do not make a fuss about temporary inconvenience. Instead, the couple displays almost exhilarating confidence in the way things are.

Actually—although of course it does not show in the picture—the man and woman are within a short drive from the encampments of the Red Army, which entered their country some six years ago to protect it from its enemies, and has never left. This contributes to the calm atmosphere of the photograph, for with the Red Army so close by there is no reason to fear anything beyond the Czech borders, or, for that matter, within them.

One can see, in short, that these people live in a country blessed by peace. True, a certain tension arises from one's not being certain whether the water they are standing in is rising or falling. But, either way, it seems certain these people will know how to behave. Should the water rise to their chins, the man and woman will swim away, without in the least altering the amused resignation that animates them now. They will be accompanied, of course, by their dog, whose life preserver they will continue to grasp.

So we may conclude that here is a couple that has learned how to live without illusions and thus without severe disappointment. He happens to be on a list of 152 Czech writers who are forbidden to publish anything within the borders of the Czechoslovak Socialist Republic or to have their plays produced on a Czech stage. But one does not see the man and his wife thrashing about angrily in the water, as might be expected.

Instead, they stand in the water for their New Year's photograph, not in the least resentful or angry but with the optimistic obedience the present leadership of Czechoslovakia expects of all its citizens. Since it has been decreed that the couple stand in the water, so to speak, then that is where they will stand, and nothing could be simpler. Their dog, of course, is not blacklisted, but she always follows them so closely that they allow her to share their fate.

Considering all this, one might conclude the husband and wife are expressing utter hopelessness, and there is indeed some truth in this interpretation. In its desire for peace, the United States, much as it might wish to, cannot officially raise the issue with the Soviet Union, and this leaves the writer and his wife standing in the water.

On the other hand, the Soviet Union, much as it might wish to, cannot withdraw its military support of the regime it placed in power in 1968. At the same time, however, many Czechs believe the cultural cemetery their country has become is even too extreme for the Russian taste. The problem is that only mediocrities have been willing to take positions in the regime, and of course mediocrities lack the finesse to deal with the country's intellectuals, except to sentence them to an internal exile or force them to emigrate.

When some people, like the writer in this photograph, refuse to emigrate, they are nevertheless described in the controlled press as having left the country. A more bloodless and efficient solution is hard to imagine, but it is another reason why the writer is standing in the water fully dressed. When he and his wife are on dry land, walking down the streets of their neighborhood, they know that the official version is that they are living in another country; therefore, the couple's hold on reality—all that is really left for them—requires some expression, and so they occasionally stand hip deep in a lake or a river.

Yet another reason is that fellow intellectuals abroad, specifically those who espouse socialism or radical reforms in their own capitalist states, often march with placards denouncing tyranny in countries like Greece, Spain, Brazil or Chile, but none of these people seems to have noticed what is happening in Czechoslovakia. This is because Czechoslovakia is already a socialist country. And for this reason too the writer's wife smiles as cutely as she does and the writer himself shows no sign of surprise as the couple stands together in the water. Indeed, there is yet another reason for their expressions—namely, that the writer has for many years been advocating communism.

If the photograph could have been much wider, it would have revealed a veritable crowd of writers, professors, and intellectuals and their families, standing in the water. Not a few of these would be authors whose works come out in France, England, America—other places and other languages. For this these artists are not punished, although the government tries to discourage foreign publishers. Also, royalties are specially taxed so as to leave the artists with next to nothing. Thus they are quite successful in other countries but are forbidden to publish in their own language. And this also helps explain why the writer and his wife do not feel it so extraordinary to be standing hip-deep in water with their clothes on.

In Russia, quite otherwise, writers do not have themselves photographed in this curious way, because the Soviet government simply forbids their publishing abroad without official permission to do so. So Russian writers are photographed on perfectly dry land. The unique situation has therefore arisen whereby Czech writers would be delighted if foreign publishers or foundations would put out their work not only in foreign languages but in *Czech*. So persecuted a national pride is unequaled in any of the other socialist countries!

As matters stand, Czech writers can never read their work in other than strange languages, and this makes some of these writers feel they are instead the authors of translations. This is also why the couple is photographed standing hip deep in water with their clothes on.

The man in the picture has had half a dozen plays produced abroad and receives press notices now and then from Paris, London, Frankfurt or New York, but he does not feel he has ever finished a play, since a play is usually finished inside a theater and he is not allowed inside a theater in Czechoslovakia to work with actors and a production. This is also why he is standing in the water with his clothes on.

At the risk of overelaborating on so simple a picture, it is nevertheless necessary to add that a path, so to speak, lies open before this couple, if they would only take it. It would be the work of half an hour for this playwright to secure for himself a place on dry land. He need only appear before the proper authorities and deliver a confession that he was wrong in 1968 to oppose the Russian invasion, the elimination of human rights, et cetera, ending with praise for the present regime and a confirmation of its correct and humane position. His confession would then be widely published—in Czech, of course—and with it his condemnation of friends who still insist on standing in water, calling upon them to come out against alien, imperialist ideas and to take up their part in the building of a new Czechoslovakia instead of pretending, as they do now, that their consciences are more valuable and right than the wisdom of the present rulers. With a few well-chosen words, the couple and the dog could dry off and become real Czechs.

That the playwright finds himself unable either to accommodate the government in this or to emigrate and write freely in a foreign country indicates a certain stubborn affection for his own land. This is also why his wife smiles as she does and why he seems on the verge of either laughing or crying, it is not clear which.

It is not to be assumed, however, that his seeming imperturbability extends into the depths of his heart, let alone that the scores of other writers who would be visible in a wider picture have left to them the humor which this playwright is still capable of showing. Some, for example, will say that they are writing more purely, more personally, now that they can only write for their circle of friends. But others feel reality is closing down around them, that in their enforced isolation they are losing their grasp on life itself. These last, if photographed, would be shown farther out, in deeper water, with only their noses visible.

If the whole crowd of intellectuals could be shown where they are—in the water, that is, and fully clothed—and if they could be heard announcing their preference as to what sort of system they would want for their country, hardly one would not declare for socialism. But a socialism that is not confused with absolutism. This leaves the government in the awkward position of having to forbid these people to publish in their own language. Awkward because it is doubtful that so total a silence was enforced even by the czars or Hitler himself. Yet the present regime is certainly anti-czarist and violently opposed to Hitlerism.

And so the writer and his wife and their dog wish us all a Happy New Year. Needless to say—but possibly advisable to say to the Czech police—all these interpretations are entirely my own and not those of the subjects in the photograph, who were doubtless moved by their very Czech sense of humor to send out such a New Year's card, whose symbolism, in all fairness, applies to many other countries, and not all of them Eastern or socialist. It's simply that in certain countries at certain times a rather universal condition is more palpable and clear. Where, after all, are the waters not rising? Who does not feel, as he positions himself to speak his mind in public, a certain dampness around his ankles? In the days of his glory, did not the United States president propose to dismantle the television news organizations in order to get himself a still more silent majority? Was he not setting in place a secret police force responsible only to himself?

All this photo does is rather wittily inform us of how infinitely adaptable man is to whatever climatic conditions, firstly; and secondly, that—as the numbers on the life preserver make so terribly clear—the year is 1974 rather than, let's say, 1836, 1709, 1617, or 1237 in, for example, Turkey.

1974

The Limited Hang-Out:
The Dialogues of Richard Nixon as a
Drama of the Antihero

Let us begin with a few meaningless statements. The president is the chief law-enforcement officer of the United States. He also represents what is best in the American people, if not in his every action then certainly in his aims. These assertions were violated by Lyndon Johnson, John Kennedy, Dwight Eisenhower, and Franklin Roosevelt, not once but many times in each case. Johnson fabricated the Tonkin Gulf hysteria. Kennedy set the country on the rails into Vietnam even as he espoused humanistic idealism. Eisenhower lacked the stomach to scuttle Nixon despite his distaste, if not contempt, for Nixon's unprincipled behavior. Roosevelt tried to pack the Supreme Court when it opposed him and stood by watching the destruction of the Spanish republic by fascism because he feared the outrage of the Catholic hierarchy if he supported a sister democracy. And so on and on.

When necessity dictates, our laws are as bendable as licorice to our presidents, and if their private conversations had been taped an awful lot of history would be different now.

Yet Nixon stands alone, for he alone is without a touch of grace. It is gracelessness which gives his mendacity its shine of putrescence, a want of that magnanimity and joy in being alive that animated his predecessors. Reading the presidential transcripts, one is confronted with the decay of a language, of a legal system; in these pages what was possibly the world's best hope is reduced to a vaudeville, a laugh riot. We are in the presence of three gangsters who moralize and a swarming legion of their closely shaved underlings.

Let us, as the saying goes, be clear about it—more than forty appointed cohorts of Richard Nixon are already either in jail, under indictment, or on the threshold of jail for crimes which, as these transcripts demonstrate, the president tried by might and main to keep from being discovered. The chief law-enforcement officer could not find it in his heart to demand the resignation of even one of them for betraying the public trust. Those whom public clamor forced to depart were given sad presidential farewells and called "fine public servants."

This, to me, is the unexpectedly clear news in these transcripts—that, had he had the least civic, not to say moral, instinct, Richard Nixon could have been spared his agony. Had he known how to be forthright and, on discovering that the direction of the Watergate burglary came, in part, from his own official family, stood up and leveled with the public, he would have exalted his partisans and confounded his enemies, and, with a tremendous electoral victory in the offing, he would have held an undisputed national leadership. Nor is this as naïve as it appears; it seems believable that he need not have literally given the order to burgle Ellsberg's psychiatrist, was surprised by it, in fact. If, as also seems likely, he gave the nod to an intelligence operation against the Democrats at some previous meeting, it would not have been the first such strategy in political history, and he could have assumed the responsibility for that while disclaiming the illegal means for carrying it out. The nut of it all is that, even on the basis of self-survival, he marched instinctively down the crooked path.

So we are back with Plutarch, for whom character is fate, and in these transcripts Richard Nixon's character is our history. But to ask why he could not come forward and do his duty as the chief law-enforcement officer is to ask who and what Nixon is, and there is no one we can ask that question. All one can really affirm is that these transcripts show certain attributes which now are evidentiary. Like a good play these dialogues spring from conflict surrounding a paradox: his power as president depends on moral repute, at bottom; therefore, one would expect him to go after any of his associates who compromised him. Instead, something entirely different happens. He sits down with Haldeman and Ehrlichman and proceeds to concoct a double strategy: first, to convince the public that he was totally ignorant of the crimes, which is an intelligent decision; and, second, to make it appear that he is launching an outraged investigation of the facts in order to reveal them, when actually he is using his discoveries to keep his associates' infractions concealed. The latter objective is impossible and therefore stupid, and in short order he finds himself in possession of guilty knowledge, knowledge an honest man would have handed over to the requisite authorities. So the crux is always who and what he is. Another man need not have been swept away by events.

In the face of the sheer number of his appointees and their underlings who turn out to be unprincipled beyond the point of criminality, the issue is no longer whether he literally gave the orders for the burglary and the other crimes. The subordinates of another kind of man would have known that such despicable acts were intolerable to their patron and leader simply by their sense of his nature. That more than forty—thus far—are incriminated or in jail speaks of a consistency of their understanding of what this president was and what he stood for. Many of his staff members he barely knew personally, yet all of them obviously had caught the scent of that decay of standards emanating from the center, and they knew what was allowed and what was expected of them. The transcripts provide the evidence of the leader's nature, specifically his near delusionary notion that because he was "the president" he could not be doing what it was clear enough he was, in fact, doing.

At one point he and Haldeman and Ehrlichman are discussing the question of getting Mitchell to take the entire rap, thus drawing the lightning, but they suddenly remember John Dean's earlier warning that the two high assistants might well be indictable themselves.

Nixon: We did not cover up, though, that's what decides, that's what's [*sic*] decides . . . Dean's case is the question. And I do not consider him guilty . . . Because if he—if that's the case, then half the staff is guilty.

Ehrlichman: That's it. He's guilty of really no more except in degree.

Nixon: That's right. Then [*sic*] others.

Ehrlichman: Then [*sic*] a lot of . . .
Nixon: And frankly then [*sic*] I have been since a week ago, two weeks ago.

And a moment later, Ehrlichman returns to the bad smell:

Ehrlichman: But what's been bothering me is . . .
Nixon: That with knowledge, we're still not doing anything.

So he knew that he was, at a minimum, reaching for the forbidden fruit—obstruction of justice—since he was in possession of knowledge of a crime which he was not revealing to any authority. One has to ask why he did not stop right there. Is it possible that in the tapes he withheld (as of this writing) there was evidence that his surprise at the burglary was feigned? that, in short, he knew all along that he was protecting himself from prosecution? At this point there is no evidence of this, so we must wonder at other reasons for his so jeopardizing his very position, and we are back again with his character, his ideas and feelings.

There is a persistent note of plaintiveness when Nixon compares Watergate with the Democrats' crimes, attributing the press's outcry to liberal hypocrisy. The Democratic Party is primarily corrupt, a bunch of fakers spouting humane slogans while underneath the big city machines like Daley's steal elections, as Kennedy's victory was stolen from him in Chicago. Welfare, gimme-politics, perpetuate the Democratic constituency. The Kennedys especially are immoral, unfaithful to family, and ruthless in pursuit of power. Worse yet, they are the real professionals who *know* how to rule with every dirty trick in the book. A sort of embittered ideology helps lower Nixon into the pit.

For the Republicans, in contrast, are naïve and really amateurs at politics because they are basically decent, hardworking people. This conviction of living in the light is vital if one is to understand the monstrous distortions of ethical ideas in these transcripts. Nixon *is* decency. In fact, he is America; at one point after Dean has turned state's evidence against them, Haldeman even says, "He's not un-American and anti-Nixon." These men stand in a direct line from the Puritans of the first Plymouth Colony who could swindle and kill Indians secure in the knowledge that their cause was holy. Nixon seems to see himself as an outsider, even now, in politics. Underneath he is too good for it. When Dean, before his betrayal, tries to smuggle reality into the Oval Office—by warning that people are not going to believe that "Chapin acted on his own to put his old friend Segretti to be a Dick Tuck on somebody else's campaign. They would have to paint it into something more sinister . . . part of a general [White House] plan"—Nixon observes with a certain mixture of condemnation and plain envy, "Shows you what a master Dick Tuck is."

This ideology, like all ideologies, is a pearl formed around an irritating grain of sand, which, for Nixon, is something he calls the Establishment, meaning Eastern Old Money. "The basic thing," he says, "is the Establishment. The Establishment is dying and so they've got to show that . . . it is just wrong [the Watergate] just because of this." So there is a certain virtue in defending now what the mere duty he swore to uphold requires he root out. In a diabolical sense he seems to see himself clinging to a truth which, only for the moment, appears nearly criminal. But the *real* untruth, the real immorality shows up in his mind very quickly—it is Kennedy, and he is wondering if they can't put out some dirt on Chappaquiddick through an investigator they had working up there. But like every other such counterattack this one falls apart because it could lead back to Kalmbach's paying this investigator with campaign funds, an illegal usage. So the minuet starts up and stops time after time, a thrust blunted by the realization that it can only throw light upon what must be kept in the dark. Yet their conviction of innocent and righteous intentions stands undisturbed by their knowledge of their own vulnerability.

And it helps to explain, this innocence and righteousness, why they so failed to appraise reality, in particular that they were *continuing* to act in obstruction of justice by concealing what they knew and what they knew they knew and what they told one another they knew. It is not dissimilar to Johnson's persistence in Vietnam despite every evidence that the war was unjust and barbarous, for Good People do not commit crimes, and there is simply no way around that.

Yet from time to time Nixon senses that he is floating inside his own psyche. "If we could get a feel," he says, "I just have a horrible feeling that we may react . . ."

Haldeman: Yes. That we are way overdramatizing.

Nixon: That's my view. That's what I don't want to do either. [A moment later] Am I right that we have got to do something to restore the credibility of the Presidency?

And on the verge of reality the ideology looms, and they scuttle back into the hole—Haldeman saying, "Of course you know the credibility gap in the old [Democratic] days." So there they are, comfortably right again, the only problem being how to prove it to the simpletons outside.

Again, like any good play, the transcripts reflect a single situation or paradox appearing in a variety of disguises that gradually peel away the extraneous until the central issue is naked. In earlier pages they are merely worried about bad publicity, then it is the criminal indictment of one or another of the secondary cadres of the administration, until finally the heart of darkness is endangered, Haldeman and Ehrlichman and thus Nixon himself. In other words, the mistake called Watergate, an incident they originally view as uncharacteristic of them, a caper, a worm that fell on their shoulders, turns out to be one of the worms inside them that crawled out.

So the aspects of Nixon which success had once obscured now become painfully parodistic in his disaster. He almost becomes a pathetically moving figure as he lifts his old slogans out of his bag. He knows now that former loyalists are testifying secretly to the grand jury, so he erects the facade of his own "investigation," which is nothing but an attempt to find out what they are testifying to, the better to prepare himself for the next explosion; he reverts time and again to recalling his inquisitorial aptitude in the Hiss case, which made him a national figure. But now he is on the other end of the stick, and, after a string of calculations designed to cripple the Ervin committee, he declaims, "I mean, after all, it is my job and I don't want the Presidency tarnished, but also I am a law-enforcement man," even as he is trying to lay the whole thing off on Mitchell, the very symbol of hard-line law enforcement, the former attorney general himself.

Things degenerate into farce at times, as when he knows the Ervin committee and the grand jury are obviously out of his control and on the way to eating him up, and he speaks of making a "command decision." It is a sheer unconscious dullness of a magnitude worthy of Ring Lardner's baseball heroes. There are scenes, indeed, which no playwright would risk for fear of seeming too mawkishly partisan.

For example, the idea comes to Nixon repeatedly that he must act with candor, simply, persuasively. Now, since John Dean has been up to his neck in the details of the various attempts to first discover and then hide the truth, should Dean be permitted by the president to appear before a grand jury, eminently qualified as he is as the knower of facts? The president proceeds to spitball a public announcement before Ehrlichman's and Ziegler's sharp judgmental minds:

Nixon: Mr. Dean certainly wants the opportunity to defend himself against these charges. He would welcome the opportunity and what we have to do is to work out a procedure which will allow him to do so consistent with his unique position of being a top member of the President's staff but also the Counsel. There is a lawyer, Counsel … [it starts breaking down] not lawyer, Counsel—but the responsibility of the Counsel for confidentiality.

Ziegler: Could you apply that to the grand jury?

Ehrlichman: Absolutely. The grand jury is one of those occasions where a man in his situation can defend himself.

Nixon: Yes. The grand jury. Actually, if called, we are not going to refuse for anybody called before the grand jury to go, are we, John?

Ehrlichman: I can't imagine (unintelligible).

Nixon: Well, if called, he will be cooperative, consistent with his responsibilities as Counsel. How do we say that?

Ehrlichman: He will cooperate.

Nixon: He will fully cooperate.

Ehrlichman: Better check that with Dean. I know he's got certain misgivings on this.

Ziegler: He did this morning.

Nixon: Yeah. Well, then, don't say that.

Refusing himself his tragedy, Nixon ends in farce. After another of many attempts at appearing "forthcoming" and being thwarted yet again by all the culpability in the house, he suddenly exclaims, "What the hell does one disclose that isn't going to blow something?" Thus speaketh the first law-enforcement officer of the United States. Excepting that this government is being morally gutted on every page, it is to laugh. And the humor of their own absurdity is not always lost on the crew, although it is understandably laced with pain. They debate whether John Mitchell might be sent into the Ervin committee but in an executive session barred to the public and TV and under ground rules soft enough to tie up the Old Constitutionalist in crippling legalisms.

Nixon: Do you think we want to go this route now? Let it hang out so to speak?

Dean: Well, it isn't really that …

Haldeman: It's a limited hang-out.
Dean: It is a limited hang-out. It's hot an absolute hang-out.
Nixon: But some of the questions look big hanging out publicly or privately. [Still, he presses the possibility.] If it opens doors, it opens doors ...

As usual it is Haldeman who is left to interpolate the consequences.

Haldeman: John says he is sorry he sent those burglars in there—and that helps a lot.
Nixon: That's right.
Ehrlichman: You are very welcome, sir.

(Laughter), the script reads then, and along with everything else it adds to the puzzle of why Nixon ordered his office bugged in the first place, and especially why he did not turn off the machine once the magnitude of Watergate was clear to him. After all, no one but he and the technicians in the secret service knew the spools were turning.

As a nonsubscriber to the school of psychohistory—having myself served as the screen upon which Norman Mailer, no less, projected the lesions of his own psyche, to which he gave my name—I would disclaim the slightest inside knowledge, if that be necessary, and rest simply on the public importance of this question itself. Watergate aside, it is a very odd thing for a man to bug himself. Perhaps the enormity of it is better felt if one realizes that in a pre-electronic age a live stenographer would have had to sit concealed in Nixon's office as he exchanged affections with a Haldeman, whom he admired and whose fierce loyalty moved him deeply. At a minimum, does it not speak a certain contempt even for those he loved to have subjected his relationship with them to such recorded scrutiny? Can he ever have forgotten that the record was being made as count would show he has more broken speeches by far than anyone in those pages. He is almost never addressed as "Mr. President," or even as "sir," except by Henry Petersen, whose sense of protocol and respect, like—remarkably enough—John Mitchell's, stands in glaring contrast to the locker-room familiarity of his two chief lieutenants. He can hardly ever assert a policy idea without ending with, "Am I right?" or, "You think so?" It is not accidental that both Ehrlichman and Haldeman, like Colson, were so emphatically rough and, in some reports, brutal characters. They were his devils and he their god, but a god because the Good inhabits him while they partake of it but are his mortal side and must sometimes reach into the un-clean.

To turn off the tapes, then, when an elementary sense of survival would seem to dictate their interruption, would be to make an admission which, if it were made, would threaten his very psychic existence and bring on the great dread against which his character was formed—namely, that he is perhaps fraudulent, perhaps a fundamentally fearing man, perhaps not really enlisted in the cause of righteousness but merely in his own aggrandizement of power, and power for the purpose not of creativity and good but of filling the void where spontaneity and love should be. Nixon will not admit his share of evil in himself, and so the tapes must go on turning, for the moment he presses that STOP button he ends the godly illusion and must face his human self. He can record his own open awareness that he and his two bravos are quite possibly committing crime in the sun-filled, pristine White House itself, but as long as the tapes turn, a part of him is intrepidly recording the bald facts, as God does, and thereby bringing the day of judgment closer, the very judgment he has abhorred and dearly wants. For the hope of being justified at the very, very end is a fierce hope, as is the fear of being destroyed for the sins whose revelation and admission will alone crown an evaded, agonized life with meaning. The man aspires to the heroic. No one, not even his worst enemies, can deny his strength, his resiliency. But it is not the strength of the confronter, as is evidenced by his inability to level with John Mitchell, whom he privately wants to throw to the wolves but face to face cannot blame. It is rather the perverse strength of the private hero testing his presumptions about himself against God, storming an entrance into his wished-for nature which never seems to embrace him but is always an arm's length away. Were he alive to a real authority in him, a true weight of his own existing, such a testing would never occur to him. There are leaders who take power because they have found themselves, and there are leaders who take power in search of themselves. A score of times in those pages Nixon refers to "the President" as though he were the president's emissary, a doppelgänger. Excepting in official documents did Roosevelt, Eisenhower, Kennedy, even Truman, so refer to himself? Surely not in private conversation with their closest friends. But to stop those tapes would mean the end of innocence, and in a most cruelly ironic way, an act of true forth-rightness.

If such was his drama, he forged the sword that cut him down. It was a heroic struggle except that it lacked the ultimate courage of self-judgment and the reward of insight. Bereft of the latter, he is unjust to himself and shows the world his worst while his best he buries under his pride and the losing hope that a resurrected public cynicism will rescue his repute. For it is not enough now, the old ideology that the Democrats are even more corrupt. The president is not a Democrat or Republican here, he is as close as we get to God.

And if his struggle was indeed to imprint his best presumptions upon history, and it betrayed him, it is a marvel that it took place now, when America has discovered the rocky terrain where her innocence is no more, where God is simply what happens and what has happened, and if you like being called good you have to do good, if only because other nations are no longer powerlessly inert but looking on with X-ray eyes, and you no longer prevail for the yellow in your silky hair. The most uptight leader we have had, adamantly resisting the age, has backhandedly announced the theme of its essential drama in his struggle—to achieve authenticity without paying authenticity's price—and in his fall. The hang-out—it is a marvel, is unlimited; at long last, after much travail, Richard Nixon is one of us.

1974

Rain in a Strange City

A rainy day out there does it. Paris in rain, Budapest, London. Also Leningrad, Stockholm and Vienna. And Rome, Rome, yes. Oh, and Amsterdam. Yes, Amsterdam especially. Yes, and New York, come to think of it, and Mexico City. And of course Dublin. Oh definitely Dublin, and almost any suburb in this chill but not freezing late morning. Even Moscow. The heads-down people, indrawn and all thinking of shelter, everywhere alive below the incoherent languages, alive to the drizzle and the gray, the plans that must be changed are everywhere the same plans. The oneness of all the countrysides is the same, the dank short grass is always making the same remark, it is all Holland, swept and dripping from the eaves of the sheet metal sheds of the businesses outside Maria Enzersdorf and Meaux and the steelyards north of Philadelphia and outside Ljubljana and Graz, this rain allows these, all these, to gather in a rough circle like men with turned-up collars and soaked shoes around a fire in an oil drum, silent and tolerant of one another. This rain anywhere brings the girl to the curb where calculating the width of the puddle she makes the leap with her pointed galosh describing an arc underneath her as her feet come down splashing the inside of her thigh, and the girl everywhere having had her hair done by appointment when the sun was shining, she is also crossing Mount Street or Knightsbridge or Dorottya Utca behind the dank Pest café, miraculously springing from a taxi on Gorki Street her head huddling in wet fur.

It is perhaps that nothing can be done. Without any thought of remedy all must simply endure, and without a cure for it there can be no manipulating the cure for other purposes. There can be no interference with it in any city, neither a technique nor a refusal of it, but only the same receiving of it everywhere in all cities, the act of being given something, a condition which all must recognize and submit to, the Emperor Rain, soft humiliator who feminizes and gentles, halts the thief in his own doorway turning him back to wait it out, forces the farmer to sit and rest his back and talk, for once, to his thin-faced daughter who has taken a dead wife's place, grounds the plane, turns armies from attack to letter writing and empties slum boulevards whose very windows glisten under the grit of their blind bitterness until all gleams and glistens, even filth and garbage cans.

Things that must be hidden from rain are heavily made-up clowns' faces, mascara and magazines, felt, wool blankets, very small infants, malt, good hay and photographs, bedroom slippers, diplomas, lecturers and violins, poets reading and much more regardless of zone or language area. Things which rain won't harm are naked girls and boys, grass, glass, galoshes and trees, spectacles, nonelectric typewriters, autos and boats, pens and pots and bald heads. For these rain is good or neutral and this is a division true in all cities, two groups of consequences whether in Beirut or New York or Gaza and Prague; wherever rain falls men and women go about blinking the drops off their eyelashes, in all places everywhere thinking of shelter in the wet cities and smelling of damp, in all places, all cities everywhere. Beyond my window now it is raining on the two bare young cherry trees, the crab apple, the pruned branches lying on the ground, and overhead the gray, rainloaded sky stretches away toward the east, the Atlantic, Ireland and England, Norway and Holland, France and Germany and Poland, all in this drizzle, collars turned up, the hiss of taxi tires on all their avenues, the hatless Sorbonne student peering through the fogged café window for his friends on Boul' Mich or Third Avenue, King's Road, Dorottya Utca. Rain. Gray. Nothing whatsoever to be done about it. Can't be helped.

1974

On True Identity

Frances Knight, for a generation in charge of deciding who is worthy enough to receive a United States passport and who not (I was not for several interminable years), has now conceived an awesome idea. She proposes that every American be required to carry a card of identity. It would be issued, inevitably, by the federal government, which "owes every American citizen a true, recorded national identity to protect him from criminal impersonations," Miss Knight says.

That a person might really be identified by a government-issued card is a breathtaking thought whose clear simplicity brings to nought the labors of philosophers and poets from Socrates to Freud and back to Shakespeare who, aside from eating, spent their time doing nothing but trying to identify people. Personally, it would end the waste of a good half of my day during which, it seems to me, I am in one way or another trying to nail down who I am. With Miss Knight's card I shall merely have to pat my wallet and get on with my business. People who presently clog analysts' offices and mental clinics will simply have to stop by long enough to drop their cards off. Having read them, the doctors will merely have to nod and say something like, "Oh."

What baffles me is why nobody ever thought of this before, especially when the procedure has been so stunningly successful in other countries. Under the czars, who, I believe, invented the idea in the first place, and under the Soviets now, the government is so adept at identifying each and every citizen by his card that he hardly dares go downstairs to get the mail in his pajamas. In South Africa, or so I read, no black can enter or leave any area without his passbook, which any policeman is at liberty to require he produce on command. In Nazi Germany the internal passport, which is what an identity card is, took on a positively metaphysical importance. Since you could not get a ration card without it, should the authorities confiscate your card for whatever reason, you lost your identity and your legal right to eat in the bargain.

One assumes, inevitably, that like every other privilege the government distributes to the population, the internal passport will also be revocable or simply canceled. In fact, Miss Knight refused to renew my own passport in the early Fifties, when I wanted to go to Brussels in response to a Belgian invitation to attend the European premiere of *The Crucible*. My trip, it seems, was not then in the country's best interests.

I have searched my mind, and I can see no reason why the government couldn't decide that a man's internal passport could be lifted because traveling from Brooklyn to Jersey City is not in the country's best interests. For there is no law of life more unbreakable than that which decrees the right of the government to take away that which it giveth.

But why stop at limiting travel? There are untold possibilities. With no effort at all I can imagine a card of what might well be called Limited Identity. This might dis-identify anybody once he has crossed the borders of his own neighborhood. Indeed, I can see Green Cards, Yellow Cards and Red Cards (after all, the passport issued me after my four passportless years was limited to six months instead of the customary three or five years).

In truth, Miss Knight told her interviewer for *U.S. News & World Report* that her idea was "loaded with political dynamite" because it "touches on the sensitive issues of personal privacy and a free society." But not necessarily, I think; provided everybody were identified *properly*. For example, the suspension of a sixth of the Bristol, Conn., police department for pilfering from local stores some years ago was made possible by the fact that they were loading the goods into squad cars early in the morning, while in uniform. Now both the cars and the uniforms were manifestly identifiable. But the point, I think, is that their possession of certified identity cards would have revealed only that they were perfectly ordinary policemen.

So we shall have to do more than identify people with these cards. We shall have to characterize them. On such cops' identity cards there would have to be a coded number, or probably a dot, which, translated into Miss Knight's files, would tell her that Officer Blue "Has Tendency to Pilfer."

But who is to make these characterizations? Who, in short, is to supply the new identities—the government or the citizen? Take Richard Nixon. If he were to fill in his card without interference, it would doubtless read, "Pres. of U.S." If "true" identification is to be the standard, however, the government would have to stamp his card "Pardoned Pres. of U.S.," but would that really be fair? In years to come, when Watergate is totally forgotten, ought Mr. Nixon be forced to show his card and to explain to some ignorant postal clerk that he was not pardoned for having been president but for felonies? So, self-identification is bound to lead toward flattery, while if left to the government it is likely to be a constant humiliation; but which is true?

No, I'm afraid that telling us who we are still leaves *what* we are a matter for divination, the psychoanalyst, the insightful clergyman, or the friendly bar buddy. And if these seem inadequate, as they surely are, they can't be any worse than those in the Passport Office—which, according to Miss Knight's interview, has been unable to prevent a rise in passport frauds from 501 in 1970 to 791 in 1974. In fact, Miss Knight gives as a reason for the new cards this very rise in passport frauds. This would seem a small number of fakers in comparison to the hordes of passport-holders, but to Miss Knight it is frighteningly large. In short, because a few have succeeded in evading spouse, police, the tax man—indeed, the government itself—we who have failed must be doubly punished now with yet another mark of identification.

But even on the most practical level the notion needs more work, it seems to me. For example, it is impossible to imagine that a man with nerve enough to rob a bank or rip off an apartment would faint at the idea of forging an identity card. I have the sinking feeling that the honest people, those who have scruples about forgery, would end up being the most controlled. In fact, if I were living under a government which had shown even the very slightest tendency toward repression, this would seem the very heart and soul of the proposal.

So let us pray together that Miss Knight's proposal dies aborning. Oh, I know how shaky things are, and undefined. Surely no earthly pleasure beats that crystalline clarity of mind and soul by whose light the enemy among us is revealed. But the real evil, if one may use a drastic word, is that the urge to "identify" is the urge to freeze and fix forever what in truth is fluid and flowing. Indeed, if a "true identity" is needed in this country it is the government's; every poll shows that the people don't know what it stands for any more, yet it takes more of their substance from them than all the con artists put together. If a "minority" is opposed to an internal passport, only another minority will benefit from it—the manufacturers of wallets.

1975

A Genuine Countryman
(from *In the Country*)

Three hours from New York City in those days and, with superhighways, an hour closer now, the area in the late Forties still had farmers who recalled shoveling a path through snow for miles cross-country, followed by the team and wagon filled with milk cans. In a district settled since the 1700s they lived in houses like the one I live in; without a closet, and in a lifetime had never traveled farther than forty miles from home. I still have the arched-lidded trunks in which generations kept their few good clothes and the linens. One of these people, a fellow named Bob Tracy, was born in that first house I bought, but it was something he never mentioned until we had known each other for two or three years.

In fact, it had as little significance for him as the fact that his family name showed up on deeds of thousands of acres of land, while he lived now on an acre down in a gully where the postmaster, a part-time mason with an enormous wen on the left hinge of his jaw, had built him a cinder-block cabin. "Well," he explained one time, "I had six sisters, don't y'know, and whenever one of 'em wanted a new hat they'd sell twenty acres." Now he did odd jobs for farmers, spelling them with the chores when they were sick or lazy or had to go off to a wedding or funeral, and mowed lawns for the few professional people around the township.

The interior of his cabin smelled, as the saying goes, like a bachelor on Friday, the atmosphere a mixture of kerosene, body sweat, and dog. More than once I had come on him asleep in his cot beside his dozing coonhound, Ella, the last remaining of three that he believed hunters from Waterbury had stolen. Awakened, he would clump out of bed pulling up his suspenders and, pretending the decency of surprise, would yell at the bitch to get out of his bed. She would open one eye and move a leg and go back to sleep and he would shake his head and say for the hundredth time, "Well, they stole my *good* dogs, don't y'know," and glare back at Ella as though it were her fault.

He must have been in his late fifties then, a thin but hard-bodied man with crinkly eyes and a mum mouth that he could press shut when listening with skeptical amusement. He first stopped by on hearing a city man had bought a house, to ask if I had any junk I wanted to discard. Quickly catching on to my penchant for never throwing anything away if I can help it, he conceded, "Well, waste not, want not," and from then on we got along fine, for the profligate habits of the few city people he knew left him confused about their characters, and character for Bob and his kind was something like what television was later to become for millions of people—the most delicious amusement, a source of infinite interest, the chief escape from humdrum existence. Thinking of him now, and of the others of his generation, it seems to me that this sets them apart from those who followed them into a quite altered time. When you came by for a visit they sat back, and with a certain appetite, an eagerness born of much silence and few interruptions, seemed to wait like an audience for the curtain to rise and reveal something wonderful. With none of them did I ever sense that they feared. It had nothing to do with bravery or nobility, but was simply a confidence that the man before them had an existence worth looking into.

Every item in Bob's cabin had either been given to him as junk or rescued from the town dump. Except, of course, for his rifle and three shotguns standing on their butts against a wall, shining and clean. On an upended crate stood a two-burner kerosene stove and an iron frying pan with a deep layer of yellow grease that had probably not been disturbed since the first Roosevelt administration. The longer I knew him, the more likely it seemed that if he were to wake one morning and find himself living at the turn of the eighteenth century, he would have needed less than ten minutes to feel at home, and much more so than he did now, as the 1950s were beginning. For one thing, he could never understand why people discarded cars, refrigerators, furniture, pots and pans that were still perfectly usable, reminder of an age when people spent a large amount of time repairing things. Once, inspecting a new car I had just bought, he turned to me and asked, "How long you going to keep it?" The question was pure, without irony; he was trying to understand what objects meant to people like me, for in his mind we sort of rented what we possessed.

Useless as a carpenter, he would nervously consent to steady one end of a board while I nailed the other. Once when I stood back to admire my work, and asked for his opinion, which I hoped would be positive, he asked, "How long you going to keep this place?" It bewildered him that people bought places, rushed about for two or three years redoing them, planting new trees and shrubs, and suddenly one morning were loading everything into a moving van—divorced, or changing states on orders from their companies. Finally he thought he understood the rationale: "It improves the countryside anyway."

One day early in our acquaintance when he was helping me to set posts for a fence around the new vegetable garden, he said, "I hear you write movies."

"Not movies, plays. For the stage."

Oh! those old-fashioned shows. Where they put them on?"

"New York."

"Well now—I didn't know they still had them."

At the approach of any female he removed his hat and pressed it against his chest, and his face turned pink. He would wash the outsides of windows but not the insides and the cellar stairs only to the top step, past which point he might find himself trapped inside a house with a woman. Anyway, inside a house was "woman's work," which he did not so much disdain as fear he would be criticized for doing badly, and to face a woman criticizing him was as close to dying as a man could come this side of the grave itself.

Through his eyes I saw the countryside emerging from its anonymity. Not far from his cabin, the one-room schoolhouse still stands, surrounded with old lilac bushes, a space twenty by thirty feet where he had gone to school as a boy along with the children of nearly every family for miles around. So they came to know each other's kinks and habits from the beginning and what to expect from them as adults.

"This Donald Price. When he grew up he come to run the general store. Old Donald was always on the lookout for a trick to play on y'. Well, there was this Mrs. Croker used to have him deliver everything, never would carry a bag out of the store herself. This one time he delivered the groceries and she says to him, 'I forgot a spool of white thread, Donald, would you bring it by if you don't mind.' Well, Donald thought about that and says to her, 'You want one spool of white thread delivered?' And she says that is what she wanted.

"So he goes back to his store, and they had this great big wagon for delivering lumber and a team pullin' it. So he hitches up the team, and sets this spool right on the bed and drives over to Mrs. Croker's and knocks on the door and she opens up and he says, 'I have your thread, where do you want it?' And he goes back to the wagon and pulls out these two heavy planks they used to roll down barrels on, and sets them on the tail of the wagon, and doesn't he roll that spool down the planks and picks it up on his shoulder like it weighed two hundred pounds and staggers up to her porch and sets it carefully right next to her feet. And that was that."

The World War II years were the best in his life. If he had a profession, it was hunting red fox, worth a dollar a pelt, if it had not yet been destroyed by rabies. Walking a dirt road he would point to the crotch of a tree where twenty-five years earlier he had rested his gun and gotten three big ones. His mind was filled with pictures of encounters on the roads.

"About midnight once, I's coming down this road looking for fox, and off ahead I hear this sound, *zoo, zoo, zoo,* like somebody sawing. No wind at all, and a full moon you could read your paper by. Well, I stood still listening, and sure enough it sound just like somebody sawing up ahead in the middle of night. So I come around the turn and there's this Pollack—they used to live in your house—and he's sawing this horse's head off right there in the middle of the road. It'd dropped dead there that afternoon and he was taking him apart to feed the pigs. They'd cut a hole in the kitchen floor and'd drop food down to the pigs in the cellar when it was winter. They certainly were peculiar people."

He parted the brush beside a road one day to show the remains of a stone foundation where he claimed an inn once stood, and beside it a blacksmith shop. "All the kids'd come and sit right here and watch the people getting out of the stage from Litchfield. This was the busiest spot around." I doubted a stage was still running in what must have been the nineties, but he insisted. "One time two robbers held them up and ran off with a bag of gold from the bank. They caught them, but they never found the money. It's buried up back on your land if you ever want to go look for it." I said I'd go half with him if he looked for it, and he burst out laughing, but it was still hard to tell how much of a spoof it was. Keeping a straight face was one of life's pleasures, and like his friends he cultivated a talent for Yankee one-liners.

Albert, the local state trooper, had been repeatedly warning Bob that it was illegal for him to be selling junk without a license. The weeds around his cabin were studded with burned-out vacuum cleaners, rusted gears, refrigerators, lawn mowers, and the first thing he did each morning when he came out the door on his way to the brook where he took his bath was to run his eye over his treasures to see if anything had been stolen during the night. Paying the license fee, about ten dollars, was bad, but his real reluctance was to have his name written down on any government register. This was why he refused a job as a grounds keeper at a nearby private school. "They make you put in for that social security, you know, and you got to sign for that. Next thing they'll be after me for the income tax." So he took care to cover whatever he was taking to the junkyard with burlap bags until someone gave him a derelict truck. Piece by piece he transported the vehicle to the junkyard, but at last he was down to the long rear axle housing, which there was no way to conceal—the end of it stuck out several feet from under his trunk lid.

He decided to take the chance, however, and set out with it for Waterbury. On his way he stopped off for bread, and coming out of the store he saw Albert standing behind his car staring down at the protruding axle. Selling auto parts without a license is especially frowned on. "So I knew I was in for it now. Well, I couldn't do much about it and I walk over to him and he looks at me and says, 'Hi, Bob.' And I says, 'Hi, Albert.' And he says, 'Nice day.' And I says, 'It was.'"

His class consciousness was stubborn, a reminder of a long-gone populism very much at odds with the new wisdom of the Fifties, when the intellectual centers were busy announcing the end of ideology and the imminent disappearance of the American poor. The system's only remaining problem, they said, was to save itself and the world from communism, while internally we need only rely on the automatic spreading of infinite riches to everybody. Bob read the only available local newspaper with its prideful Republican slant, never missing the local newscasts on his radio, a Thirties model shaped like a cathedral. He ended up supporting Henry Wallace for President, a candidate favored by the Left who piled up a full one million votes against Truman. "He's the only one I can understand," he would say, but the real reason was that most people hated and feared Wallace as a menace. In his mind these were the same kinds of people who kept pushing for stricter zoning regulations requiring three-acre lots around any new house. "They just don't want the workingman living around here," was his interpretation. From where he sat, the prospect was weird; "You be turning it all into a park." The land, he meant, which had always been a place of work and workingmen.

Through his vision of the land, the picturesque tended to disintegrate into long-forgotten purposes that had once created its aesthetic. The New England landscape is partitioned by patterns of stone walls, lichen-painted and enduring. Originally, they were convenient dumps for the rocks cleared from the fields they enclose that otherwise could not be planted. I was dismantling a section of wall one day when he came by in his bouncing Olds that stalled a few yards away. Its gasoline pump had died a year or so earlier and above the engine he had hung a Mazola can with a rubber tube from an enema bag leading to the carburetor. We got to talking about walls.

"My grandfather built your wall. A man and a team of oxen could do a rod of fence a day. That's the fence that nearly got him in the Civil War."

"How come?"

"Well, he was a real small man, and he's out here building this wall, and this squad of cavalry come riding down the road here conscripting men for the army, and they catch sight of him working here. But my grandmother was out behind the house, and she heard the horses and came running. She was a tremendous woman, and don't she pick up my grandfather and set him on her hip and says, 'You can't take my boy!' That saved him cause they wouldn't take boys helping their mothers."

Talking of war, he was reminded of Ben Fitzer. Fitzer was in his nineties during World War I, a farmer in this secluded valley who rarely even came into town. "But this one time, he come in for some reason, and this fellow come over to him and says, 'Isn't it awful all those men killing each other by the millions?' It was the first beautiful day of spring and old Fitzer says, 'What men you mean killing each other?' And the fellow says, 'Over in Europe, Ben. There's a terrible big war going on over there.' 'Well,' says Fitzer, 'they got a nice day for it.'"

Speaking of isolated people reminded him of the two unmarried brothers who had once lived in my house. "They were real churchgoers, don't y'know, went down there every Sunday. And around about January or so they didn't show up. Then next Sunday come and they're not there either. Finally, after they hadn't been for three Sundays, a committee was appointed to go up and see if there's anything wrong. Well, they come up the house and knock, and the door opens, and there's one of them, and they goes inside and asks why they hadn't been to church all month. And he says his brother'd died and he didn' feel he ought to leave him. 'Ought to leave him! Why? Where is he?' 'In the front room,' he says. And sure enough, they go over to the parlor, and there he's got him laid out on two sawhorses and a board. 'I'm waitin' for the thaw,' he says. That'll give you an idea how cold those houses were."

He would go through seizures of business acumen, especially on hearing how somebody had gotten thousands of dollars for a few acres. In the late Forties when I arrived, land was sold with a wave of the arm indicating the bounds, and it was so cheap, around forty dollars an acre, worth three or four thousand fifteen years later, that the "more or less" on the contract could often leave the purchaser with fifteen acres when he had paid for ten. By the Sixties, when the farms were being transformed into residences, ledgy back pastures that had hardly had a money value were discovered to have a view, and surveyors were popping up in the brushy woods with their transits and stakes, marking off lines as though an inch either way mattered greatly. Bob would suddenly show up in my yard trying to incarnate himself into a canny businessman. "Sell y' my whole place including the house for six thousand dollars," he said one day.

"What the hell would I do with it?"

"Sell it. Make yourself a profit. My cabin's *quiet,* it's *secluded*"—he had picked up the real estate jargon by now but spoke it uncertainly, as if it were some foreign language— "nice running brook, too."

"In August?"

"Well hell, *nothin'* runs in August." I expected the usual mock-innocent spoofing look, but his humor was no longer in his eyes. Instead, he actually seemed to be waiting for me to begin dealing about his miserable house and his damp and weedy gully, and his face showed an avidity I had never seen in him before. It was as though suddenly we were adversaries—he wanted what I had, and I was refusing what he had to offer. Our bantering connection was over with; he was trying to clamber aboard the great American train and resenting me as though I were stamping on his fingers.

We would meet on the road after that but he hardly paused. He sold his place and moved in with a retired bachelor, Dr. Steele, whose estate he tended, a miserly watcher of oil stocks, and they argued a lot, I heard. Years passed. I had forgotten about him entirely, when from my car window I spotted him mowing a lawn in front of the home of Mrs. Tyler, a divorced nurse. He had occasionally worked for her years before when we were still friends, and one time she had left a note for him on her door listing his chores, all of them to be accomplished in the two hours she paid him. "Dear Bob," it read, "please mow the lawn, put up the storm windows, clean out the flower beds, sweep out the garage, and take the garbage to the dump." Bob studied the list, then took out the stub of a pencil from his shirt pocket and carefully inscribed below, "Dear Mrs. Tyler, my ears are not that long, yrs, Bob," and never went back.

I stopped my car and called to him. It was good to see the grin that broke out on his face when he looked up. He stopped the mower, came over, and stood beside the car. It was hot, and his shirt was off, and it was a shock to see hanging flesh on his once tight-skinned body. His Irish blue eyes seemed to be shrouded by an unhealthy gray wetness. The old shyness seemed like shame now. Our paths had been crossing for nearly twenty-five years, and this was the first time in his presence that the thought of failure struck my mind. He was grinning, but his impishness had gone to bitterness in the curl of his mouth. As he came close, I could smell beer. He had never drunk enough to smell in daytime. His swollen-knuckled hands, the fingers arthritically curved, the faint wheezing of breath in his chest all sent me back to the day long ago when, teaching me to scythe, he had grasped the snath, and, trading his weight from leg to leg, his eyes fixed in a pleasurable gaze, he had circled half an acre, leaving behind a swath of smooth lawn, and returned to me hardly winded.

"You working for her again?"

"Well, she's not too bad."

"How's it going with Dr. Steele?"

"Oh, he's dead."

"I hadn't heard. When'd he die?"

"Oh it's over a year now," he said, and then he glanced carefully up and down the empty road and leaned down to me, and lowering his voice, he confided, "Won't be missed."

The mum, mock-proper mouth and the wicked eye were suddenly there again, and we laughed, and for an instant we were back the way it had been before he had learned caution, before all the land had become real estate and when his own kind were still on the farms around him and he was at home and free to savor whatever flew from his mouth.

He died a few months later, alone in a room he had taken over a tavern in town facing the railroad tracks. It was surprising to learn he had reached eighty. Then it was possible that he had sat by the inn as a boy to watch the passengers dismounting from the stage.

1978

The Sin of Power

It is always necessary to ask how old a writer is who is reporting his impressions of a social phenomenon. Like the varying depth of a lens, the mind bends the light passing through it quite differently according to its age. When I first experienced Prague in the late Sixties, the Russians had only just entered with their armies; writers (almost all of them self-proclaimed Marxists if not Party members) were still unsure of their fate under the new occupation, and when some thirty or forty of them gathered in the office of *Listy* to "interview" me, I could smell the apprehension among them. And indeed, many would soon be fleeing abroad, some would be jailed, and others would never again be permitted to publish in their native language. Incredibly, that was almost a decade ago.

But since the first major blow to the equanimity of my mind was the victory of Nazism, first in Germany and later in the rest of Europe, the images I have of repression are inevitably cast in fascist forms. In those times the communist was always the tortured victim, and the Red Army stood as the hope of man, the deliverer. So to put it quite simply, although correctly, I think, the occupation of Czechoslovakia was the physical proof that Marxism was but one more self-delusionary attempt to avoid facing the real nature of power, the primitive corruption by power of those who possess it. In a word, Marxism has turned out to be a form of sentimentalism toward human nature, and this has its funny side. After all, it was initially a probe into the most painful wounds of the capitalist presumptions, it was scientific and analytical. What the Russians have done in Czechoslovakia is, in effect, to prove in a Western cultural environment that what they have called socialism simply cannot tolerate even the most nominal independent scrutiny, let alone an opposition. The critical intelligence itself is not to be borne and in the birthplace of Kafka and of the absurd in its subtlest expression absurdity emanates from the Russian occupation like some sort of gas which makes one both laugh and cry. Shortly after returning home from my first visit to Prague mentioned above, I happened to meet a Soviet political scientist at a high-level conference where he was a participant representing his country and I was invited to speak at one session to present my views of the impediments to better cultural relations between the two nations. Still depressed by my Czech experience, I naturally brought up the invasion of the country as a likely cause for American distrust of the Soviets, as well as the United States aggression in Vietnam from the same détente viewpoint.

That had been in the morning; in the evening at a party for all the conference participants, half of them Americans, I found myself facing this above-mentioned Soviet whose anger was unconcealed. "It is amazing," he said, "that you—especially you as a Jew, should attack our action in Czechoslovakia."

Normally quite alert to almost any reverberations of the Jewish presence in the political life of our time, I found myself in a state of unaccustomed and total confusion at this remark, and I asked the man to explain the connection. "But obviously," he said (and his face had gone quite red and he was quite furious now), "we have gone in there to protect them from the West German fascists."

I admit that I was struck dumb. Imagine!—The marching of all the Warsaw Pact armies in order to protect the few Jews left in Czechoslovakia! It is rare that one really comes face to face with such fantasy so profoundly believed by a person of intelligence. In the face of this kind of expression all culture seems to crack and collapse; there is no longer a frame of reference.

In fact, the closest thing to it that I could recall were my not infrequent arguments with intelligent supporters or apologists for our Vietnamese invasion. But at this point the analogy ends, for it was always possible during the Vietnam war for Americans opposed to it to make their views heard, and, indeed, it was the widespread opposition to the war which finally made it impossible for President Johnson to continue in office. It certainly was not a simple matter to oppose the war in any significant way, and the civilian casualties of protest were by no means few, and some—like the students at the Kent State University protest—paid with their lives. But what one might call the unofficial underground reality, the version of morals and national interest held by those not in power, was ultimately expressed and able to prevail sufficiently to alter high policy. Even so it was the longest war ever fought by Americans.

Any discussion of the American rationales regarding Vietnam must finally confront something which is uncongenial to both Marxist and anti-Marxist viewpoints, and it is the inevitable pressure, by those holding political power, to distort and falsify the structures of reality. The Marxist, by philosophical conviction, and the bourgeois American politician, by practical witness, both believe at bottom that reality is quite simply the arena into which determined men can enter and reshape just about every kind of relationship in it. The conception of an objective reality which is the summing up of all historical circumstances, as well as the idea of human beings as containers or vessels by which that historical experience defends itself and expresses itself through common sense and unconscious drives, are notions which at best are merely temporary nuisances, incidental obstructions to the wished-for remodeling of human nature and the improvements of society which power exists in order to set in place.

The sin of power is to not only distort reality but to convince people that the false is true, and that what is happening is only an invention of enemies. Obviously, the Soviets and their friends in Czechoslovakia are by no means the only ones guilty of this sin, but in other places, especially in the West, it is possible yet for witnesses to reality to come forth and testify to the truth. In Czechoslovakia the whole field is pre-empted by the power itself.

Thus a great many people outside, and among them a great many artists, have felt a deep connection with Czechoslovakia—but precisely because there has been a fear in the West over many generations that the simple right to reply to power is a tenuous thing and is always on the verge of being snipped like a nerve. I have, myself, sat at dinner with a Czech writer and his family in his own home and looked out and seen police sitting in their cars down below, in effect warning my friend that our "meeting" was being observed. I have seen reports in Czech newspapers that a certain writer had emigrated to the West and was no longer willing to live in his own country, when the very same man was sitting across a living room coffee table from me. And I have also been lied about in America by both private and public liars, by the press and the government, but a road—sometimes merely a narrow path—always remained open before my mind, the belief that I might sensibly attempt to influence people to see what was real and so at least to resist the victory of untruth.

I know what it is to be denied the right to travel outside my country, having been denied my passport for some five years by our Department of State. And I know a little about the inviting temptation to simply get out at any cost, to quit my country in disgust and disillusion, as no small number of people did in the McCarthy Fifties and as a long line of Czechs and Slovaks have in these recent years. I also know the empty feeling in the belly at the prospect of trying to learn another nation's secret language, its gestures and body communications without which a writer is only half-seeing and half-hearing. More important, I know the conflict between recognizing the indifference of the people and finally conceding that the salt has indeed lost its savor and that the only sensible attitude toward any people is cynicism.

So that those who have chosen to remain as writers on their native soil despite remorseless pressure to emigrate are, perhaps no less than their oppressors, rather strange and anachronistic figures in this time. After all, it is by no means a heroic epoch now; we in the West as well as in the East understand perfectly well that the political and military spheres—where "heroics" were called for in the past, are now merely expressions of the unmerciful industrial-technological base. As for the very notion of patriotism, it falters before the perfectly obvious interdependence of the nations, as well as the universal prospect of mass obliteration by the atom bomb, the instrument which has doomed us, so to speak, to this lengthy peace between the great powers. That a group of intellectuals should persist in creating a national literature on their own ground is out of tune with our adaptational proficiency which has flowed from these developments. It is hard any more to remember whether one is living in Rome or New York, London or Strasbourg, so homogenized has Western life become. The persistence of these people may be an inspiration to some but a nuisance to others, and not only inside the oppressing apparatus but in the West as well. For these so-called dissidents are apparently upholding values at a time when the first order of business would seem to be the accretion of capital for technological investment.

It need hardly be said that by no means everybody in the West is in favor of human rights, and Western support for Eastern dissidents has more hypocritical self-satisfaction in it than one wants to think too much about. Nevertheless, if one has learned anything at all in the past forty or so years, it is that to struggle for these rights (and without them the accretion of capital is simply the construction of a more modern prison) one has to struggle for them wherever the need arises.

That this struggle *also* has to take place in socialist systems suggests to me that the fundamental procedure which is creating violations of these rights transcends social systems—a thought anathematic to Marxists but possibly true nevertheless. What may be in place now is precisely a need to erect a new capital structure, be it in Latin America or the Far East or underdeveloped parts of Europe, and just as in the nineteenth century in America and England it is a process which always breeds injustice and the flouting of human spiritual demands because it essentially is the sweating of increasing amounts of production and wealth from a labor force surrounded, in effect, by police.

The complaining or reforming voice in that era was not exactly encouraged in the United States or England; by corrupting the press and buying whole legislatures, capitalists effectively controlled their opposition, and the struggle of the trade union movement was often waged against firing rifles.

There is of course a difference now, many differences. At least they are supposed to be differences, particularly, that the armed force is in the hands of a state calling itself socialist and progressive and scientific, no less pridefully than the nineteenth-century capitalisms boasted by their Christian ideology and their devotion to the human dimension of political life as announced by the American Bill of Rights and the French Revolution. But the real difference now is the incomparably deeper and more widespread conviction that man's fate is *not* "realistically" that of the regimented slave. It may be that despite everything, and totally unannounced and unheralded, a healthy skepticism toward the powerful has at last become second nature to the great mass of people almost everywhere. It may be that history, now, is on the side of those who hopelessly hope and cling to their native ground to claim it for their language and ideals.

The oddest request I ever heard in Czechoslovakia—or anywhere else—was to do what I could to help writers publish their works—but not in French, German or English, the normal desire of sequestered writers cut off from the outside. No, these Czech writers were desperate to see their works—in Czech! Somehow this speaks of something far more profound than "dissidence" or any political quantification. There is something like love in it, and in this sense it is a prophetic yearning and demand.

1978

The Pure in Heart Need No Lawyers
(from *Chinese Encounters*)

In Peking only four days, I feel the intense need to talk to someone about the law, a subject in which no one in China seems to have the least interest. (In fact, however, within two weeks of our departure from China there were demands voiced in demonstrations and on wall posters that the leadership adopt a new attitude of respect for legality.) Surely if I were Chinese and did not wish to see my country losing another decade or two to anarchy, and more important, did not wish to be unjustly charged and punished for nonexistent crimes, I would look to the law for at least some reassurance that the past would not return. But China has still not yet passed a legal code. The Party has the power to punish or let pass whatever it deems harmful or helpful to its rule, and worse yet, can change back and forth at will. It is government not by law but by political resolution, something understandable in a revolution's early stages but questionable, to say the least, after nearly thirty years of existence. There is a constitution, of course, but this cannot be more than a guide if beneath it there exists no body of laws designed to make its provisions universally applicable.

Sid Shapiro came to China in the early Forties, has lived here since, and is a Chinese citizen. In his sixties now, he translates from English and is fluent in Chinese. He studied at "the subway law school," St. John's University in Brooklyn, and was raised a few blocks from my family home in the Midwood section. His house, in a quiet part of Peking, is close by an artificial lake, and the neighborhood is rather suburban in its somnolence this midmorning. As is the case in some parts of Brooklyn, it is hard to find a passerby who knows where his street is, though we are only three blocks away, and as our driver squeezes down one narrow lane after another I find myself staring out at the mamas and babies and grandmas and grandpas padding around the neighborhood—carrying a chair or a package or looking for a key on the ground—just being people, and I experience a vain longing for the day when it will be possible, perhaps a thousand years hence, to govern people by leaving them alone.

As Inge talks with his Chinese wife (Shapiro Tai-tai), a former actress and now a drama critic, my fellow Brooklynite corrects my vision of things here. "No, they don't need lawyers," he explains. "At least only very rarely, hardly ever at all." He is a man who is as comfortable with his ideas as he is with his Hopje candy (it has a Chinese name here), reminding me of Brooklyn where this formerly Dutch, coffee-flavored sweet was the dentist's best friend.

"Where the hell'd you get Hopjes?" I ask.

"They don't know they're Hopjes," he confides, "they just make them. But aren't they terrific?"

We sit there chewing away in his rather somber living room. He recently went back to Brooklyn to see his family, but after an absence of thirty years all he found impressive in America was the fear of crime. "They were worried as hell that I was going back to Manhattan on the subway at midnight. I couldn't believe it; imagine being afraid to go out of your house!"

"No fear here?"

"Not for a minute. These people are members of society."

"But don't they *ever* get out of line?"

He settles back and I realize we are into his favorite topic. We both unpeel paper from our Hopjes. I can see him clearly in Depression Brooklyn, cramming his courses, getting good grades, turning his face from a failed economy and feeding his soul on the communist ideal of effortless justice. For injustice is not an inclination of humanity but something imposed by unjust conditions. Man is not only by nature good, he is most often Chinese.

Sid got out of the United States before McCarthyism took over, no doubt because he had analyzed the future and found nothing but American crisis and decline while China was climbing upward and building the world he dreamed of.

"As Mao said, there are two kinds of contradictions: among the people, and between the people and the enemy. The courts don't involve themselves with the first kind of trouble . . ."

"Let's say a kid smashes a window, a guy beats up his wife."

"That kinda stuff never gets into a court."

"What about cops?"

"Rarely get near it. What happens, the neighbors lean on the kid and his parents to straighten him out. The peer pressure can weigh fifty tons."

"Like in Brooklyn."

Shapiro hesitates to agree—there should be nothing in China like anything in America.

"I mean," I continue, "that families were really the main source of discipline in those times."

"Well, in a way," he agrees, politely rather than actually, "but here the pressure is not just sentimental, it's based on political principle."

"To beat your wife is anticommunist." And I suddenly think of a line in a Depression play by Clifford Odets: "A man who beats his wife is the first step to Fascism."

"You could put it that way, sure. But beating a woman is political, since it cuts across the Party's position on women's equality; it's a feudal throwback."

"Gotcha."

"Stuff like that."

We both laugh at the revival in us of our ancient speech. "But what do they do with hard cases?"

"There aren't that many."

"But there have to be some."

"Well, in that case he goes before a judge and two laymen who know the defendant. And they struggle with him to reform his ideas. Crime is basically political, the result of reactionary ideas."

"Give me an example. Take theft."

"Okay. Theft is the attempt to consume goods without working or producing, so it is antisocialist and therefore a political act."

"That's very good." I am impressed.

"So political means are the only ones that can cure it."

"In other words, instead of moral inhibitions . . ."

"Which mostly don't work," he quickly adds.

"Why don't they work?"

"Because under capitalism you've got enormous crowds that don't have anything, while a few have a lot."

"So, in a sense," I say, "it is politically correct to steal under capitalism."

"And even morally correct. They are righting injustice. But," he cautions, "you can't graft the Chinese system onto America because it is based on a just economy. You can blame a man for stealing when he has a job and the chance to eat, but you can't if he's unemployed and starving."

It is the socialist lesson I first learned in Depression Brooklyn days, but Sid clearly delivers it like late news, and I find myself both marveling and irritated at the windless space he occupies, where in truth nothing has penetrated in forty years. "But you really don't feel anyone needs to be defended once he's in trouble?"

There is a certain smidge of defensiveness, though not enough to tip over his rice bowl. "But why? Before anybody's accused, the investigation is absolutely fair and thorough, and it goes on for weeks. Believe me, people who aren't guilty are never accused. The problem is never guilt, it's how to reform a person."

"There can't even have been a case of mistaken identity?"

"Well, maybe one in ten thousand, but that's not a real problem to the point where you'd have to introduce lawyers into the system."

"But, Sid," I say, trying to smooth the anger out of my voice, "from my first minute in this country I have heard nothing but the crimes of the Gang of Four, the thousands jailed without charges, without appeal, unjustly . . ."

"Yes, but that was not the system, it was the *breakdown* of the system! The Gang of Four *disrupted* the system!"

I am surprised that this particular kind of childishness can still start anger flowing into me. But there are millions like him all over the world who have managed to convince themselves that revolution cannot and should not make men freer. Every eighteenth- and nineteenth-century revolution at least declared the rights of the person to be the centerpiece of society and sought to draw a line beyond which the state could not reach into the individual's life. Now only the state has rights and powers, and the person, like his property, belongs to the collective, with no recourse or appeal if fools or factions should decide on his ruin.

With our disagreement in the open, Sid Shapiro does not look contented any longer, but that is life and cannot be helped. What occurs to me, however, is that this moment is emitting the same opaque quality as frequently arises with Chinese when any principle is up for discussion. Shapiro must surely be disturbed, if only remotely, by a society in effect without law, but a revolutionary cannot display his own uncertainties, let alone allow them to be part of a discussion. So it is once again not so much a cultural barrier I feel warding me off in China—Shapiro and I could not be more alike culturally—as a political creed whose fundamentals must not be so much as examined, most especially in the presence of those not of the faith.

As we drive away down the quiet Peking back streets, mazelike and narrow, the thought returns that hardly more than ten percent of Chinese live in cities, and that "out there" is the vast majority, bent to the earth as it has been forever. Is Marxism, with its nearly religious expectation of the human community reborn, the true successor system of capitalism or feudalism? The distance to post-Renaissance parliamentary capitalism is truly vast, but to feudalism it is amazingly close. Feudal man "owed" much to the group; everything, in fact. Under the Chinese kind of socialism he cannot move his residence without higher permission, for he is "part" of his commune, his factory, his social organization, and every single one of the nearly billion Chinese, like the Russians, is a member of what in feudal times was called a guild and here is called a collective—of doctors, dentists, workers, peasants. Looked at this way, there is indeed no place for lawyers, for the very concept of an individual standing apart from the group is no longer possible for the mind to entertain.

And it has happened, too, I recall, in another place and another time. The Puritans also forbade lawyers; I even gave to Judge Danforth in *The Crucible* a response to the very mystery I am now turning around in my head. "The pure in heart need no lawyers," he assures the complainants who come to beg him for lawyers to defend their loved ones against the charge of witchcraft.

And there, as here, it was not mere cynicism that drove intelligent men to embrace and celebrate their own vulnerability before injustice. It was the age-old dream of unity, of sonship and daughterhood, of the trustingness of family transposed into social relations. And all of it by virtue of a high belief in the state's sublimity, in the Society of Saints in Massachusetts and in socialism here in China. One may smile at its naïvetés, but not at the morale it so often imbues its believers with, and the feats in war and construction it rallies them to perform.

The Puritan theocracy lost its monopoly when surpluses of food and goods undermined the earlier need for a near military unity and the justification for the suppression of conflicting ideas. Has the time approached for China when suppression, for analogous reasons, no longer appears as justified as it did when the Japanese army still occupied the country, and a feudal Chiang Kai-shek had yet to be pushed into the sea?

A Sid Shapiro, in a word, persists in his warm bondage to the sublime, the very same condition from which the Chinese are cautiously emerging, for the first time daring to judge their leaders on a human scale.

1979

Essays: 1982–1990

The American Writer: The American Theater

It is quite beyond me to really do justice to this great occasion. The fiftieth anniversary of the Avery Hopwood Awards deserves a thorough historical account of their impact on American literature. I do not mean a mere listing of the notable writers who were first recognized and encouraged by the Awards, but perhaps, as important, the impact of the idea itself of a university that has the nerve not only to teach contemporary writing but, in effect, to act as its sponsor and to administer money prizes for student writing. I am not sure that this was a first, but I am certain that there could not have been many precedents fifty years ago. In fact, a look at the lives of some of our more distinguished writers who were born around the turn of the century and were of college age when universities were far more conventional in their attitudes toward the arts, will show that a large number of them either never bothered to finish college or had no connection as writers with any such institution. The Hopwood Awards, I believe, announced not merely annual winners but an attitude that has since spread through many other universities—that the writer can be just as valuable during his lifetime as he is afterwards.

So rather than attempt some sort of historical appreciation, I think it wiser to stick to my own experience as a beginning writer, a more modest strategy, to be sure, but one that I hope will throw a more certain light on a far larger scene.

I believe I had two reasons for choosing Michigan, apart from its educational repute. The first was that it did not require mathematics. By the time I graduated from high school I was possibly the world's greatest expert on Algebra; having failed it twice, and only been passed a third time because they could not bear to look at me any more, I came to a certain intimacy with every problem in the textbook. All I lacked was the remotest idea of how to solve them. The second attraction was the astounding news of the Hopwood Awards. The idea of a university handing out cold cash to students was, I confess, almost too glorious to contemplate. The money itself was important of course—even on the lowest prize, $250, I would later manage to live for a semester. And, of course, with money so hard to come by in the Depression thirties, giving it away for nothing more than words on a piece of paper had miraculous overtones when I had been working in industry for years for twelve and fifteen dollars a week. But the central attraction was even more mysterious—the fact that money was given out meant that the judges—unlike your mother or your friends—could really tell good writing from bad. Thus, the recognition of an award touched more than the pocket; it might even point the future.

I am forced to wonder whether, if Avery Hopwood had been a novelist and had neglected to give prizes for plays, I would not have tried harder to become a novelist. For the theater meant little to me when I began to write. I had seen only a handful of plays and those had seemed so remote and artificial that I could find no connection with myself at all in them. It must be remembered that in the thirties there was nothing that could be called an Off-Broadway theater. It would have been inconceivable to draw a separation between dramatic art and show business, which were treated as one and the same. I had heard vaguely about a Provincetown Theater, an experimental place where Eugene O'Neill had started out, but he, after all, had headed for Broadway as soon as producers would accept his plays. Later in the thirties, there would be two or three left-wing theater groups, most notably the Group Theater, but they, too, strove to succeed on Broadway, even as they pronounced anathema upon its commercial greed.

Whatever triggered my imagination toward the play form is lost to me now, but it may well have been a production of an early Odets play by the Group Theater. Oddly enough, I cannot recall which play; all I remember was seeing actors who for the first time in my experience were physically vivid, whose faces seemed to have commonplace outlines, palpable noses and eyes that moved, and hands with veins. The *moments,* so to speak, of the play seemed superheated, isolated one from the other so that they counted eloquently, while at the same time—and this was the weird paradox—everything flowed together. More than this, I found myself believing that offstage—and I had never set foot on a stage but could imagine what it must be like back there—offstage was not offstage at all but the city itself, the New York I knew. So that the play was not like a little isolated cell where things went on disconnected from the city around us, but was one cell among the myriad, part of the sound and the anxiety and almost universal frustration of life at that time. Had I been capable, as I was not, of rationalizing the experience, I should have called it an experience of theater as life, as much a part of life as going into the subway or bringing home a bottle of milk or sitting in the back yard and wondering anxiously what was ever going to become of me after failing Algebra three times.

It would be decades before I would see it all from the opposite side of the equation—life, that is, seen as theater. Politics as theater, love as theater, lecturing on Chaucer as theater, psychoanalysis as theater, the church as theater. But perhaps there won't be time to go into all that.

Anyway, having seen that acting was not, as it had seemed till then, the art of speaking with an English accent, and that a play had something to do with sweat and hunger, I was hooked. I am speaking personally, of course, but only to support my generalizations. For example, I am sure that had I come of age in any other time and had seen some other production of high excellence, I would also have been similarly inspired. But one can't really be sure. I can only be sure that it did happen then; and I know it was not only the acting or the crazy poetry of Odets's lines. It was also what he was saying and what this whole way of acting was saying. It is a convenience to call their message Marxist or revolutionary; but for me it was more like being provided with an emotion, an emotion appropriate to the frustrations of living in the early thirties, specifically, the verb, if you will, for protesting the cursed irrationality of our lives. For people were starving then in America, while food was being burned up on the farms for want of a price. Odets seemed to provide a license for outrage, which has to be the first step toward a moral view. To me, as to most of the critics and the media of the time, he was overwhelmingly the clarion playwright. It would be years until I discovered, quite by chance in a conversation with Harold Clurman, who had directed the Group, that Odets's plays themselves—I am not speaking of the royalties, but of his plays—never made any money. Nor, as a matter of fact, did most of O'Neill's, although his made more than Odets's. And I mention this crass subject for reasons that will be alarmingly clear in a moment, but one point needs making right now. The American theater at that time was not about O'Neill or Odets, quite obviously; it was about entertainment of a quite different kind, the kind that offers an escape from life rather than a confrontation with it. I would only add that this is what most theater in most places is about most of the time.

But when I set about writing a play for the first time, I shared a certain illusion of community, which, I think, is implicit in the act of writing for publication or production. I felt alone, of course, and I was scared of making myself ridiculous, and I felt light years away from any suggestion of professionalism, for I was painfully aware that I knew very little about plays and nothing at all about the theater. My only hope was that the other plays being written for the Hopwood contest would be worse. This thought was the only one I had at the time that approached reason. The Awards provided a world small enough to grapple with.

For the real world of theater was quite different than it is today. As I have suggested, it consisted of the commercial Broadway theater and, to all intents and purposes, that was it. How did one achieve the requisite professionalism? It was all a mystery too deep for me. I had by this time dipped into the contemporary Broadway plays, those that had been published, for very few were then, and found little I could relate myself to. For I did not understand about charm in those days. Unawares, I had come to connect plays and the theater with some sort of prophetic function. Again, I was not in the habit of rationalizing such things, but a playwright for me was a man with his own church. Not that it was a question of preaching but rather of being the vessel of a community's need to talk to itself and to the world. It was possibly my Jewish heritage that imposed such a burden, or, if you will, such a challenge. But O'Neill was not Jewish any more than Ibsen was, or Chekhov, Strindberg, or the Greeks. (And, parenthetically, none of those writers could run very long on Broadway either, then or now.) How odd, then, to even imagine them as spokesmen, as prophets, for such they were to me then, and conventionally are still, even though we all know that the vast majority of plays are and always have been rearrangements of trivia.

It had not seemed to me to be too short a time—the five days of spring vacation—to write a three-act play. When it won a Hopwood Award, it was like an artillery shell fired right through the ranks of my opposing army—down went all my old Algebra teachers, for one thing. Then, soon after, another award fell upon the same play, The Bureau of New Plays Prize, administered by the Theater Guild in New York. This was a nationwide contest for college students. Another winner was a Brooklyn student who is surely present today, Norman Rosten. Another was a fellow from St. Louis named Tennessee Williams.

The main thing about this prize was the money—$1,250. I had already earned more with my first play than I had in three years as a shipping clerk. Needless to say, the contrast was not lost to my mind. And if I seem to linger on the subject of money, it is, I assure you, at the center of the great tradition of playwriting. As George Bernard Shaw replied to a businessman who had asked to discuss art with him, "No, I am an artist, not a businessman; businessmen always want to talk about art, but artists only talk about money." But with all the luck I seem to have had with that first play, the idea of actually making a profession of the theater was still quite unreal.

One problem was that I had spilled out into that first play everything I knew or could imagine about life. For I had hardly lived at all. I must invent something, I thought with sinking heart, and for this I supposed one had to have some kind of objectified technique. So, I promptly groped my way into Professor Kenneth T. Rowe's playwriting class. Such were the times—such was our theater, I should say—that one assumed to begin with that a certain technique could be learned that would more or less, if properly utilized, insure success. Again, the Broadway theater loomed in the background, the only theater we had and that indeed, rewarded certain formulas, as theater inevitably does at all times, including the present. That formula had numerous variations, but if it had to have a name it might be the Theater of the Rational. A problem was put in Act I, complicated and brought to a crisis in Act II, and resolved or answered in Act III.

It is hard to define what I took from Professor Rowe's classes. Perhaps it was, above all, his enthusiasm for the catholicity of dramatic literature, the sheer variety of forms that time had developed. And indeed, there was no single overriding style of writing in his class as there would be in the coming decades when fashion, for some reason, has so dominated and, I think, in many cases crushed invention. People then were writing Realism, Impressionism, Expressionism, poetic drama, verse drama, and Bronx comedies. It did not yet seem that there had to be obeisance to a prevailing mode. Perhaps fewer people were reading the Arts section of *The New York Times* then.

I suppose it was somewhat like learning how to draw in order to go on to painting, liberated from the tyranny of line. In any event, I think I came to believe that if the dazzling glory of the masters was finally their poetry, the fundamental poem was the structure. The structure, indeed, *was* the poem, the one element whose removal or disturbance collapsed the whole. One knew how Chekhov or Ibsen or Sophocles felt and *sounded*—now it was necessary to know how they were made. Paradoxically—or maybe it was quite logical—in less than ten years I would arrive on Broadway with a play, *The Man Who Had All the Luck,* that began with a problem and ended not with a solution, but at the door of the mystery of fate—why one person is chosen to win and another to lose, a question unanswerable whatever technique might be applied to it. I might add that the play lasted four nights. There was one encouraging review, but that from an alcoholic critic who was well on his way to the big bottle in the sky.

And speaking of the big bottle, it is time, I think, to talk about the critics. It is futile to criticize critics. It is quite enough to condemn them totally. Suffice it to say, I have never met a playwright who claimed he had learned anything from a review. Perhaps it can all be summed up in a story, which may just possibly be true, told me by the late Jed Harris who was the first director of *The Crucible* and in his best time, the twenties, one of the most creative men in the American theater. When he was directing *Our Town,* the most important critic, as always, was the man who happened to be on the *Times,* Brooks Atkinson, the very dean himself. Harris, concerned that Atkinson would not understand the play, which had certain innovations in staging, asked him to lunch, and there proposed to him that he begin a course of theater training by attending a few rehearsals. "I told him," said Harris, "that he really did not know very much about acting, directing, and scene design, and that I would be glad to teach him. He sat there very sweetly, listening to me and agreeing with me. But he didn't come to rehearsals because he felt it would be unethical and might tilt his opinion of the finished production."

Harris's point was one that everyone would have accepted in the decades before and after World War II—the New York reviewer was not necessarily a man who knew anything, he merely had to react with common sense in a manner representative of his readers. Thus, among the seven or eight main reviewers from the clutch of daily papers that still existed then, one found a remarkable number who arrived at the theater opening night on a tilting sidewalk. Others were unwashed refugees from the sports department, and one or two prided themselves on being professional humorists. The intellectual critics, exemplified perhaps by Joseph Wood Krutch, mattered very little to the box office, having disliked everything since the early Euripides. The reigning intellect of the Broadway scene was George Jean Nathan who, indeed, displayed occasional insights, but whose reviews, it seemed to me, most often consisted of lengthy lists of plays going back into antiquity of which the play at hand reminded him. To read American theater reviewing then and now is to be convinced that the reviewer owns a certain sacred space, which it is his moral duty to prevent the playwright from entering. It is quite as though the entire purpose of the whole theater enterprise, its very *raison d'être*, is to provide a subject for criticism. This might be acceptable if one could recall the name of a single critic who, for example, had wounded Chekhov, Ibsen, Strindberg, or O'Neill by dismissing their works out of hand.

I won a second Hopwood in my Junior year, but I failed to win the big one as a senior. Nevertheless, it seemed possible to hope that I might become a professional playwright. The theater I was trying to enter seemed as always to be dominated by its critics, just as our immortal souls are dominated by our decaying flesh. But there was a certain illusion, shared by everyone involved, that I think helped to form a certain kind of play, and that kind, if I am not mistaken, was in the high tradition of the art. The illusion I speak of was that there was one single audience containing within itself in some mystical fashion the whole variety of America and Americans. The same audience that went to the Ziegfeld Follies one night might flock to O'Neill the next. And so it was not quite as odd as it might seem now that some of the reviewers would have been more at home at a ball game or a prize fight, for the same was true of much of the audience. In actual fact, of course, the audience may have been *emblematic* of American taste, but it was certainly not representative in the absence of blacks and workers in general. Still, there was a certain rough and ready air to its acceptance or rejection of a show.

The consequence to playwriting, however, is what is important here. Facing such an audience, the playwright could not console himself with yearnings for another, more sensitive and cultivated audience. Balcony seats in the thirties cost 55 cents and in them, at least, if not in the orchestra, were the salt of the earth—the student and his teacher, the neighborhood intellectuals of modest means, the housewives, and the more culturally hip of the working class. Downstairs in the orchestra were the business people and the professionals and, for certain shows, the usual sprinkling of cafe society. It may have been a better mix than we have today, but on the whole it never thought it owed anything to anyone, including even a minimal acquaintance with its own historical or literary culture. If a play had an idea, it had to be embodied in action; speeches had to be short, muscular, direct. If you had a message, said the prevailing wisdom, send it by Western Union, for it did not belong in a play. Plays were for fun, for obliterating your troubles, a chance to live other people's lives. It was a pragmatic, fundamentally uneducated audience, and if it simply turned its back on the poetic and the philosophical far more often than it should have, it could also make a quite proper demand upon a play: specifically, that its theme flow effortlessly from its action, and that meaning and viewpoint not be smeared all over it like mustard on a hotdog. It may be because of this kind of confrontation that I would find many years later a tendentiousness in so many absurdist plays that seemed to crudely slant life in favor of the meaningless conclusion, the hero slipping on a banana peel. It is a fact, nevertheless, that in the earlier time there was a dangerous intolerance of the ineffable unless even *it* were made active and packed with emotion, as in *The Glass Menagerie,* for example. That play, I would remind you, was regarded as certain to fail on Broadway because it seemed so delicately inactive, so ineffable and talky, and when it did succeed, it proved yet again that this audience for prize fights and ball games could be stretched and lifted by poetry, if it aimed for the heart rather than the education. In effect, then, the playwright was speaking to his country, and he had no other audience nor was it thought that he should have.

So, he was compelled to find language and theatricality broad enough in its humanity to hold such an audience. He could not rely for support on a clique pre-tuned to his cultural signals. Alienation in itself, in other words, had not yet become synonymous with style, let alone high art. And if it was mostly a theater of extroversion, its desire to make contact with the mass was not really different from that of the New and Old Testaments, the Classical Greek theater, and the best of the Elizabethans. It was a brutal challenge and could be a brutal confrontation, even unfair; but to accept it was to know the difference between grace under pressure and grace before dinner.

Sometime in the mid-fifties the profound shift within the audience as well as in the organization of the Broadway theater changed all these elements forever. In a word, one became aware that the audience was losing even its former superficial unity; it had begun to atomize. In my case, it was at the opening night of *The Crucible* in 1952 that I realized I was no longer precisely among friends. I have written of this elsewhere at greater length; let it be enough to say now that I was obviously not to be a part of what was then extolled as The American Century, a dawning era when the United States was going to be the new imperium abroad while jumping with democratic prosperity at home. What it all looked like to me was fear and anxiety covered over with the same old self-infatuation that had always led us to our disasters.

I have always supposed, however, that it was *Waiting For Godot* that signalled this shift within the audience. Why precisely it should have occurred at that moment must be left to another time; it is sufficient to say now that the absurdities of life moved into the stage as well as into the common wisdom of the time. But if the majority of the audience had no taste for shaggy dog stories and remained loyal to Broadway, most of the young left to support what now became known as the Off-Broadway theater, a theater whose main stock in trade was the absurd. I cannot attempt a sociological explanation for that absurdist vogue, but I can say that until the mid-fifties it would have been impossible to have met an American who could believe that General Motors, Chrysler, and Ford would one day find themselves incapable of building an automobile competitive with, of all things, the Japanese. It would have been equally hard to convince anyone that not only a President but his brother would be gunned down one after the other. The inconceivable, in short, had not yet become commonplace. And so, where before the structures of cause and effect, of fate and character-as-fate had supported the arch of dramatic structure, now it was the inconceivable itself that was raised up and given the kind of obeisance reserved for first principles. And in one sense, it was indeed a kind of naturalistic reportage of how the world was, for the concept of the absurd tended to legitimize the common conviction that absolutely nothing followed necessarily from anything else. One of the doubtful virtues of this philosophy was to liberate some of us from having to understand anything at all, and that included dramatic structure.

There were several reasons why I would find myself somewhat uneasy with this style. In principle, for one thing, it seemed odd that, whether in Paris, London, Berlin, or New York, regardless of the great differences between these societies, precisely the same mode of feeling and writing should have spontaneously arisen. In short, it seemed too obviously a fashion rather than a truth that had taken hold of the Western imagination. Secondly, our American despair is not quite the same as the European variety, for we have never ceased to hope, awkward as that may be to explain to strangers. So, it seemed somehow wrong that you should enter a theater and not be sure what country you were in. And, finally, so long as a writer writes, he hopes; this is what tragic writing assumes to begin with and black humor denies. I suppose what I am saying is that a work ought to acknowledge its premises.

With the atomization of the audience between avant and rear garde, a new breed of critic came on the scene. He or she was far more literary than the roughnecks of the past, far better trained academically, making the new demand for a theater of ideas and, in many instances, the more revolutionary the better. Some were brilliant stylists, others merely wished to be; the best that might be said of them is that their appearance was doubtless inevitable in the evolution of sophistication in American society, and the worst, that on the whole they seemed unwilling or incapable of admitting the contradictions of their own positions. Was it enough, for example, to abandon the majority audience in a democracy, or should playwriting and theater in general persist in trying to find the key to that audience rather than to play reassuringly to enclaves of the washed, the already saved, and the elite?

Nor is it altogether wrong to note that some of these critics were not too revolutionary to resist the call to assume the role of critic for the better paying magazines and even *The New York Times*. But perhaps their most harmful work was done upon the truth of history, for by the sixties they had all but persuaded their public that nothing in American theater was to be discussed in the same breath as the British, French, German—indeed, nearly any other theater. Modernity was European; mere naive sentimentality belonged to us. This was more than misleading nonsense. In fact, it was almost diametrically the opposite of truth.

In the early winter of 1956 I happened to experience a moment of historical change that might throw some light on this question of the American contribution to international theater. I was in London at that time working with Peter Brook on his production of *A View from the Bridge.* At the same time, my wife was starting a film, *The Prince and the Showgirl,* with Laurence Olivier. One evening soon after we arrived, he asked if there was anything in the London theater I wished to see. I glanced down the nearly full page of theatre ads—there were many dozens of shows then—and was at a loss. Not only had I never heard of any of the titles, but they seemed to promise precisely the kind of precious, upper-middle class nursery tales that had relevance, perhaps, to life among the fox hunters, but not very much else. My eye fell at last upon one title that I found intriguing—*Look Back in Anger.* It was not, of course, the looking back but the anger that seemed so un-British then. But Olivier dismissed it as an ugly travesty on English society. This made it even more interesting, and I persisted, and he finally agreed to get me a ticket. When I arrived at the Royal Court Theatre the following evening, I found Olivier in the lobby awaiting me. He had decided to see the play again.

To be brief about it, here was the first English play I had any knowledge of that told me something about actually living in England. And I had a strange *déjà vu* sensation when I realized that it was doing for the English rather precisely what Odets had done in the early thirties for New Yorkers—letting loose a cleansing invective, an unbridled anguish and fury at the hapless decrepitude of the social system, its injustices and its frustrating stupidities.

Whether the author had ever read an Odets play was beside the point; the quite similar style, a certain apt wedding of lyricism and social outrage, had flashed out of the English sky a quarter of a century after it had done the same thing in New York, and doubtless for similar social reasons—namely, because a deadly formalized, polite, and rather bloodless commercial play had dominated in both countries for several decades earlier. Incidentally, after his second viewing, Olivier ended at the bar with the young Osborne who had written the play, and while I talked with George Devine, the director of the Royal Court Theatre, I overheard Olivier asking Osborne whether he could write something for him. Which he promptly did—*The Entertainer.*

I was invited to be one of the speakers at an informal rally a few nights later in the Royal Court Theatre, where hundreds of young actors and writers had jammed the place to discuss the state of their theater. One of the recurrent questions directed to me was what they might do to begin creating plays like the Americans, plays that seemed to them so vital, so alive to current American life. There could simply be no mistaking that for these young men and women it was the American play and the American actor that had grasped the hour and the style of contemporary existence. In a few short years, of course, to listen to some of our own critics, it would be quite as though the American play and the American playwright had two left feet and could barely manage to read the hands of the clock. Indeed, this self-rejection went to such an extreme that nothing would do but an English critic had to be imported to oversee the New York theater for *The New York Times.* Such is the ineluctable power of fashion, I suppose. Indeed, the only English-speaking place left where you could find any real critical understanding and enthusiasm for the American play, its vigor and its poetry, was precisely in Britain, especially among the British actors, authors, and directors.

I have talked far longer than I meant to, but before I finish I must complete the winding of the noose from which American theater currently hangs. I am speaking, of course, of the Broadway theater, the so-called professional theater. If it was once *the* theater in the sense that almost everything original began on Broadway to be imitated by repertory and amateur theaters, it is now quite the opposite. Nothing but musicals now originates on Broadway; what serious work is shown, and it is practically extinct, has been transferred from Off-Broadway or regional theaters across the country. Broadway is hostile to serious work, that is no exaggeration, and so it should be. It is really too much to ask that people should spend twenty-five to forty dollars a seat to watch painful scenes and troubled characters. If it makes any sense at all, which I doubt, it indeed is far more sensible for the entertainment-seeker to spend that kind of money on song and dance shows, and that is just what has happened. The great audiences, which it used to be said great poets required, are no more. The student, the teacher, the man of modest means, the working woman—these will hardly be found in a theater anymore, not at such prices. But, as if this were not enough, we have the monopoly of theatrical criticism exercised by *The New York Times*.

Now the *Times* would doubtless deny this, pointing out that its critic has sometimes praised a play that in short order has closed anyhow. This is true but not particularly heartening. The far more decisive truth is that when the *Times* condemns a play it closes, and this regardless of how many other papers may have praised it. In fact, in 1963, when the *Herald Tribune*, the last of the *Times*'s competitors, shut down, the editors of the *Times*, led by their chief, Clifton Daniel, were sufficiently worried about the monopoly that had befallen them to call a meeting of theater people, at which I was one of the panel of speakers, in order to gather suggestions as to how that monopoly could be mitigated. I suggested that they provide readers with a healthy variety of views, three, four, or more critics to each show, but Mr. Daniel feared that nobody would know *who represented the opinion of The New York Times*. I thought this quite astonishing. It sounded suspiciously like an unacknowledged desire to wield the very power that they denied wishing to possess. But no matter—the absurdity remains, and given the massive domination of the *Times* over the theater, it is by no means an exaggeration to say that if every book published by a major American publisher— poetry, history, fiction, or whatever—were to be judged by a single individual and his word taken as to whether it ought to live or die, it would be an equivalent situation to the one obtaining on Broadway right now. Even in the Soviet Union plays can only be killed by a committee and not one man.

And on the outside chance that some of you may think me biased against the *Times*, let me say that in 1947 my first successful play, *All My Sons*, was recognized almost alone by Brooks Atkinson of the *Times*, his colleagues having been either indifferent or hostile to it. Having said that, I ought to add that the serenity of my confidence in critics is what it is because the same group of negative reviewers turned themselves around by the end of that season and voted *All My Sons* best play of the year. Such is life among the playwrights.

It seems to me that after fifty years of Hopwood Awards a cycle has been closed. I am sure that when Avery Hopwood conceived of financing prizes for young writers it was in some part an act of subversion against the commercial system of theater. I am also sure he wanted to encourage and support writers who would not only entertain but prophesy, and to give them a couple of years to strengthen themselves for a hard life. The

Broadway theater today is, if anything, even more hostile to serious work than it was a half century ago, but all is not by any means lost. Today, unlike in Hopwood's time, there is a truly decentralized system of theaters spread across this country. Much fine work is done in these theaters—indeed, much of their work is stolen by Broadway. If there is any note of lamentation in this speech, it is not for a lost glory—there was never very much of that. But there was a level of professionalism in production, design, and performance that is not easy to find any more. We have it still in the musical theater on Broadway, which is the best of its kind in the world. But the origination of serious theater is a thing of the past. Nor can one imagine how this will soon change; how forty-dollar seats will ever again come down in price, or how the monopoly of the *Times* will be broken, given the ingrained habits of theater-goers who follow the lead of that paper's tastes.

But maybe there is a disguised blessing in all this. A decentralized theater may turn out to be closer to the people than the New York-based one was, and perhaps this closeness will reflect itself in a more mature drama that reflects more of the balance of light and darkness in the country as a whole. I can see but one long-term danger, and it comes down to the problem of subservience. It is something that has cropped up frequently in the American theater since the early nineteenth century when Washington Irving complained that American authors and producers seemed to need the reassurance of foreign models for their works. Except in the musical, our most democratic form in the sense of its being adored and understood by the vast majority of the people, we seem uncertain about both the value of our own works as compared to foreign ones, and, more importantly, what the nature of serious theater really ought to be at this historical moment.

That last, of course, is a subject all by itself Right now, one fundamental point might be made: what is evil in the United States and what is good, what is confused and what is clear, what is progressive and what is retrograde and reactionary, this whole crazy house— apart from this or that judgment upon it—is in the vanguard of history, and continues to create the century in ways that no other civilization can. Whether into the morass or onto the higher altitudes, we do break the ground. Our drama, therefore, has the right if not the obligation to see itself as a vanguard, as confronting human situations as though they had never existed before in quite the same fashion and bearing quite the same significance. I have traveled a great deal and in every kind of extant social system, and whatever may be the local opinion of us, it is from this land that they wait for news, for what's coming up, for word of our state of mind, our hopes, and our despair. Confronted by a professional theater that, between its greed and its irresponsibility, no longer has use for him, the American writer must now write for his own people, for the theaters he finds around him. There is no center anymore, and in this sense the writing of plays is no longer a profession but a calling to be practiced for the love of it or not at all.

I hope that what I have said has some truth in it. But since it is of the theater I have talked, and in a larger sense America herself, whatever is true now probably has been changing as we sit here. All I can hope for is that you will catch her on the wing, willing and ready to fly to wherever in her unpredictable wisdom she decides she wants to go.

1982

After the Spring

I have never understood why we keep a garden and why, thirty-five years ago when I bought my first house in the country, I started digging up a patch for vegetables before doing anything else. When you think how easy and cheap, relatively, it is to buy a bunch of carrots or beets, why raise them? And root crops especially are hard to tell apart, when store-bought, from our own. There is an atavism at work here, a kind of backbreaking make-believe that has no reality. And besides, I don't particularly like eating vegetables. I'd much rather eat something juicy and fat. Like hot dogs.

Now hot dogs and mustard with some warm sauerkraut—if you could raise *them* outside your window—you'd really have something you could justify without a second's hesitation. Or a hot pastrami vine.

As it is, though, I can't deny that come April I find myself going out to lean on the fence and look at that cursed rectangle, resolving with all my rational powers not to plant it again. It's not even economical any more with the price of seed so high now, and if I calculate what I have invested in a tiller and other tools, fertilizer, wire fence, and all the rest, it becomes ludicrous. I don't dare speak of my time and my wife's—which would figure out to be about six or seven thousand dollars per tomato—in good years.

But inevitably a morning arrives when, just as I am awakening, a scent wafts through the window, something like earth-as-air, a scent that seems to come up from the very center of this planet. And the sun means business, suddenly, and has a different, deeper yellow in its beams on the carpet. The birds begin screaming hysterically, thinking what I am thinking—the worms are deliciously worming their way through the melting soil. But it is not only pleasure sending me back to stare at that plot of soil, it is really conflict. The question is the same each year—what method should we use? The last few years we unrolled thirty-six-inch-wide black plastic between the rows and it worked perfectly, keeping the soil moist in dry times and weed-free, and when we go off for a few days it's not hard to find our garden again, as it has been when we used to cultivate.

But, here we go again—black plastic looks so industrial, so unromantic, and probably gives cancer of the fingertips from handling it. And of course some people think it unfair to use black plastic because it does work so efficiently. Like the early opposition to the large tennis rackets. Anything that reduces suffering has to be a little evil. Nevertheless, I have gradually moved over to hay mulch, mostly because we cut a lot of hay and it does improve the soil's tilth as it rots, looks lovely, and comes to us free. But it needs to be very heavily laid on or you will have planted a hayfield, which we did one year, long ago. No less than six inches deep, unless you buy salt hay, but that costs so much you might as well eat salad in a restaurant.

Keeping a garden makes you aware of how delicate, bountiful, and easily ruined the surface of this little planet is. In that fifty-by-seventy-foot patch there must be a dozen different types of soil. Parsley won't grow in one part but loves another and the same goes for the other crops. I suppose if you loaded the soil with chemical fertilizer these differences would cease to affect growth, but I use it sparingly and only in rows right where seeds are planted rather than broadcast over the whole area. I'm not sure why I do this beyond the saving in fertilizer and my unwillingness to aid the weeds between the rows.

I never spray anything principally because insect damage and fungi have never affected more than a scant proportion of plants in this garden. I am not sure why it is spared except that it lies in the midst of a former hayfield where there is heavy grass growth, and maybe insects get enough to eat out there beyond the fence.

The attractions of gardening, I think, at least for a certain number of gardeners, are neurotic and moral. Whenever life seems pointless and difficult to grasp, you can always get out in the garden and *get something done*. Also, your paternal or maternal instincts come into play because helpless living things are depending on you, require training and discipline and encouragement and protection from enemies and bad influences. In some cases, as with squash and some cucumbers, your offspring—as it were—begin to turn upon you in massive numbers, proliferating more and more each morning and threatening to follow you into the house to strangle you in their vines. Zucchini tend to hide their fruits under broad leaves until they have become monster green phallic clubs to mock all men and subvert the women.

Gardening is a moral occupation, as well, because you always start in spring resolved to keep it looking neat this year, just like the pictures in the catalogues and magazines, but by July you once again face the chaos of unthinned carrots, lettuce, and beets. This is when my wife becomes—openly now—mistress of the garden. A consumer of vast quantities of vegetables, she does the thinning and hand-cultivating of the tiny plants. Squatting, she patiently moves down each row selecting which plants shall live and which she will cast aside. Tilling and planting having been completed, I excuse myself from this tedious task, for one thing because the plants have outgrown their grassy look and show signs of being lettuces. (Although on certain days unaccountably I like lettuce.)

At about this time my wife's eighty-five-year-old mother, a botanist, makes her first visit to the garden. She looks about skeptically. Her favorite task is binding the tomato plants to stakes. She is an outspoken, truthful woman, or she was until she learned better. Now, instead of saying, "You have planted the tomatoes in the damp part of the garden," she waits until October when she makes her annual trip to her home in Europe; then she gives me my goodbye kiss and says offhandedly, "Tomatoes in damp soil tend more to get fungi," and toddles away to her plane. But by October nothing in the garden matters, so sure am I that I will never plant it again.

The psychology of gardening, obviously, is quite complicated. In my experience far more educated city people who move to the country bother with gardens than do people born in the country. The latter take immense pleasure in being well enough off *not* to have to work that hard to eat lettuce. City people feel they have to work off their sins, perhaps, or are convinced they are being poisoned by sprays on their vegetables. Country people, being generally more conservatively business-oriented, spray everything in sight, perhaps to show their faith in chemical companies.

I garden, I suppose, because I must. It would be intolerable to have to pass an unplanted fenced garden a few times a day. But if it makes little economic sense to plant it, and a very debatable taste advantage, there are certain compensations and these must be what annually tilt my mind toward all that work. There are few sights quite as gratifyingly beautiful as a vegetable garden glistening in the sun, all dewy and glittering with a dozen shades of green at seven in the morning. Far lovelier, in fact, than rows of hot dogs. In some pocket of the mind there may even be a tendency to metamorphose this vision into a personal reassurance that all this healthy growth, this orderliness and thrusting life must somehow reflect similar movements in one's own spirit. Without a garden to till and plant I would not know what April was for.

As it is, April is for getting irritated all over again at this pointless, time-consuming hobby. I do not understand people who claim to "love" gardening. A garden is an extension of oneself—or selves, and so it has to be an arena where striving does not cease, but continues by other means. As an example: You simply have to face the moment when you must admit that the lettuce was planted too deep or was not watered enough, and *cease hoping* it will show itself tomorrow, and *dig up the row again*. But you will feel better for not standing on your dignity. And that's what gardening is all about—character building. Which is why Adam was a gardener. (And we all know where it got him, too.)

But is it conceivable that the father of us all should have been a mason, weaver, shoemaker, or anything but a gardener? Of course not. Only the gardener is capable of endlessly reviving so much hope that this year, regardless of drought, flood, typhoon, or his own stupidity, this year he is going to do it *right!* Leave it to God to have picked the proper occupation for His only creature capable of such perpetual and unregenerate self-delusion.

I suppose it should be added, for honesty's sake, that the above was written on one of the coldest days in December.

1983

Suspended in Time

I began living on Brooklyn Heights in 1941 in an old apartment house overlooking Montague Street and the bay. That was long before the Promenade cut off the Heights from the waterfront and the life of the piers. You descended Montague on a long steep cobbled grade, and if you turned to the right, you saw the bridge. It seemed, as indeed it was, of the same vintage construction and the same verdigris and silvered patina as the pier structures and the warehouses down there. You were conscious of treading the stones of the nineteenth century and even in some places the eighteenth, for it had not been improved or changed since Whitman's and in some cases Melville's time.

So the bridge, before it was renovated in the Fifties, was ironically less remarkable than it seems now, less an artwork and more a normal element of a venerable neighborhood, conceived by an obsessively caring industrialist-engineer. Now that newer structures line its approaches, and probably also because of a greater awareness of such things in the press, it seems to stand out as a work of art. I must have walked or biked across the bridge a hundred times without once thinking I was passing along a work of art; it was simply the bridge, the most challenging and at the same time tension-relaxing object in my world.

Born in New York, in Harlem, as a matter of fact, I have never been without a certain background apprehension about crime, but before World War II there was not the current air of doom. In good weather one crossed the bridge and found people on the benches on the pedestrian path watching the sunset as though suspended in a park over the glistening river. There was a trolley that took you in both directions for the same nickel. The motorman would get out at either end and push the car around a turntable to start his run again. I don't think I ever saw more than three or four people on that trolley, but they ran it anyway, no differently than it had been run since fourteen years after the bridge was opened. I remember the pink stub they gave you when you bought your ticket, which was good for one day.

It had really not changed since my father as a very young man used to hire a horse and gig and drive from the Lower East Side over the bridge to Coney Island for a Sunday's outing. He fell asleep on the way back and always found himself waking up in the stable on Rivington Street.

To walk the bridge then without thinking of Hart Crane's poem was an impiety, and it came to one's lips the way grace does to the devout at dinner. But unlike grace at dinner, it somehow defined the object being blessed more vividly than even one's own eyes could.

How many dawns, chill from his rippling rest
The seagull's wings shall dip and pivot him,

Shedding white rings of tumult, building high
Over the chained bay waters Liberty—

and

O harp and altar, of the fury fused,
(How could mere toil align thy choiring strings!)
Terrific threshold of the prophet's pledge,
Prayer of pariah, and the lover's cry,—

Through that poem, "To Brooklyn Bridge," your vision rippled under sunbeams broken by the cables and did indeed "descend/ And of the curveship lend a myth to God." The poem by a poet not celebrated, not even widely known, a broken and suffering man who died at thirty-two, seemed to confirm the sublimity of an architecture that alone of all the stoneworks in the city moved the heart as an unaggressive structure made to ease people on their way rather than to exploit or rule them. In the city, which was and is really a bazaar, a market, a place for exchange and a striver's arena, where proofs are given of victory and the self's magnitude, this walk across air and water asked of you only that you breathe in the sea scents and see the sky through those altarlike harp strings—in a word, to enjoy and yet to recall with some surprise that the thing was, above all, useful, a structure born of commercial need.

The more remarkable, then, that it has always been a poet's bridge, a dreamed bridge. Possibly because it seemed to have sprung not so much from the calculations of an engineer but the imagination of a dreamer. And because its feasibility from its inception had been surrounded with so much hardheaded doubt. So entirely the idea of a single man, it came to life not unlike an artwork does, a poem, in fact, which is always launched with bated breath, in fear and with something like a prayer that it will live. It was never a bridge that was ordered, so to speak, for its concept had little precedent. John A. Roebling, after all, was not primarily a bridge builder but a maker of cables. And so it seemed a kind of amateur bridge, a craftsman's oddity with its unheard-of span and almost total steel construction. And indeed, the mistakes made, the accidents, the failures and victories were not unlike the moves and revisions and backtrackings of artists feeling through the confusion of mind to the original image that first evoked the energy of creation. Above all, perhaps, for artists it meant the challenge thrown against the elements and naysaying against the antipoetic sludge of the threatening commercial civilization that seemed unable to aspire, to celebrate the spirit rather than the body alone. The bridge, astonishingly, unified them both.

But like many things of beauty it could be dangerous, and there was a night in the early Fifties when the bridge nearly killed me. In those pre-renovation times, two narrow roadways carried the cars and they were still paved with cobbles made of wooden blocks. Worse yet, they were a car and a half in width, making passing impossible.

At about one o'clock one morning I started across from the Manhattan side and saw the banks of fog rising up from the river. I slowed to a crawl at once, knowing that this much moisture would turn the old wooden, grease-covered blocks into butter. But at that hour, I figured, there would not be many other cars to contend with, and so I mounted the crest and started the ride down to the Brooklyn side in fairly good cheer when far ahead I thought I saw the glow of a pair of taillights. I tested my brakes. The car simply continued moving at a nice five-mile-an-hour clip as though it were sliding down a long hill of mud. Horror began to move into my spine when it became clear that those taillights were not moving; the car was doubtless stalled down there, and I had no possibility of getting around it. Now the final idiocy—I could faintly make out human figures behind the car. They would have to die of their stupidity unless I could stop.

I had an almost new green Studebaker convertible with a beige top, the Raymond Loewy squared-off design that had revolutionized the looks of automobiles, the first of my trophies from the success of *Death of a Salesman*. Gritting teeth, I maneuvered the car to the edge of the roadway and gradually pressed the front left wheel against the stringer, a girder that ran a few inches above the entire length of the road, hoping the friction would slow me down to a stop. But a break in the girder grabbed my tire, and the car spun completely about and came to a stop facing Manhattan. But at least it had stopped, and I could slowly back down to Brooklyn once the other car was gone. I peered through the rear window, and naturally it had now departed and the way was clear.

Then, inevitably, I saw a pair of headlights rising over the crest at the bridge's center and coming down toward me. I knew this driver could no more stop than I had been able to. There had to be a crash, and my momentary sympathy went out to the poor guy facing my headlights. I slid out from behind the wheel (it would have been even worse to get out of the car and be vulnerable to flying debris that might well knock me into the river) and rolled up in a ball on the floor on the driver's side, wedging myself against the seat.

A few seconds, and the crash came. Then silence. I got out and nearly slipped on the cobbles. My headlights were still on, throwing light on a highly polished but wet Ford, both of whose front wheels lay flat on the road, its headlights popped out, its radiator crushed and bleeding. A stout man with a tiny porkpie hat stood facing me with the angry fright of a solid workingman whose dearest possession had been not only wounded but also humiliated.

"What da hell yiz doin'? Yiz're goin' the wrong way!" Only his suspicion that I was drunk or insane held him in place, and I quietly explained how my car had gotten turned around. But once again he repeated, "But yiz're goin' the wrong *way!*"

And there we stood in the drifting fog, the blinded ships below bawling through their horns, the bridge dripping on our heads, while for the tenth time I explained my car's unorthodox position. Exchanging licenses, I saw his name—Rudy Zizzo. It all ended with my driving him around for half an hour searching for a cop—there was supposed to be one cruising the bridge at all times but he was off on some private business. And when finally we did flag down a cruiser, Zizzo, still stunned by the apparition that had confronted him as he had come over the crest of the roadway, almost cried to the cop, "He wuz goin' the wrong *way!* And I just this afternoon got my car out of the shop!"

So along with Hart Crane's lyric, the bike rides across and the walks, the people watching sunsets, the trolley and much else, I have Mr. Zizzo's awestruck face under the glare of headlights and a glistening gauze of fog and my new green Studebaker to remember when I glance at that bridge. Plus one thing more. In the early Fifties there bloomed on walls and the stone buttresses of the bridge, scrawled in white chalk, "Dove Pete Panto?" (Where is Pete Panto?). The rains washed off these words, but they were soon redone by unseen hands. I discovered that Panto, a young longshoreman, had risen from the ranks to challenge the corrupt leadership of the union and that the common idea was that he had been murdered. I would ultimately write a movie about him and the abortive movement he had started, but it would never see the screen for reasons that are another story for another time.

It was also the ironic contrast between its clean and airy span, with the tides of mindless traffic flowing back and forth, and the fury of the life in its shadow below that brought me the title and the angle of vision of *A View from the Bridge*.

What millions of such human connections must be caught in its lacy steel mesh over this century! It is a veritable myth, a kind of speech to the city's endless forgetting.

1983

The Night Ed Murrow Struck Back

Fear, like love, is difficult to explain after it has subsided, probably because it draws away the veils of illusion as it disappears. The illusion of an unstoppable force surrounded Senator Joseph McCarthy of Wisconsin at the height of his influence, in the years from 1950 to 1954. He had paralyzed the State Department, cowed President Eisenhower, and mesmerized almost the entire American press, which would in all seriousness report his most hallucinatory spitballs as hard front-page news. His very name struck terror not only in the hearts of the several million Americans who in the previous decades of the Forties or Thirties had had a brush with any branch or leaf of the Left, but also those who had ever expressed themselves with something less than a violent hatred of the Soviets, Marx, or for that matter cooperatives—or even certain kinds of poetry. At my own hearing before the House Un-American Activities Committee, a flank of the McCarthy movement, a congressman from Cincinnati asked me with wild incredulity, "You mean you believe that a man has the right to write a poem about *anything?*" When I confirmed this opinion, he turned to his fellow committeemen and simply threw up his hands.

How this Vaudeville-like absurdity could have been taken in dead seriousness by vast numbers of Americans is hard to explain in retrospect. The Fifties' Red hunt not only terrified people but drove some few to suicide. It is not easy to conceive of Harry Truman, ex-artilleryman and quintessential small-town American, being labeled a traitor to his country, yet Senator Joe McCarthy and his fellow Republican leaders blithely went about pronouncing Truman's and Roosevelt's administrations "twenty years of treason." Never was this greeted with scorn or laughter. How to explain it?

Of course, an outrageous mixture of viciousness and naïve provincialism is endemic to the political extremes. Stalin awoke one morning and decided that all the Jewish doctors were in a plot to poison the party leadership, and nobody laughed then either. I had known an outlandish tap dancer who in desperation was touring Europe in the Thirties with his little troupe; in Berlin he found himself to his amazement the idol of the newly risen Nazi establishment, and soon of Hitler himself. Tap dancing so delighted Hitler that he spoke of ordaining it the *echt* German dance, which all the *Volk* must begin learning at once—a veritable nation of tap dancers was to spring forth, with my friend to be the head teacher. One morning a uniformed "race expert" showed up at his hotel prepared to measure his cranium, nose, mouth, and the spatial relationships of his face to make sure he was the Aryan type. My friend, a Jew, explained that he had an urgent appointment and took the next train out of the country.

By 1953 it was common talk in Europe that America had at last met her own native dictator in Joe McCarthy; but if a great many Americans agreed, they were in no position to say so safely, especially if they worked in government, or as teachers, or in the larger corporations. Another dreamlike element, moreover, was that McCarthy's Senate investigating subcommittee, whose claimed intent was the rooting out of communists hidden in the government, never seemed to find any actual Reds, let alone one who might be guilty of betraying the United States. To his critics, however, McCarthy would reply, "It isn't the number of communists that is important; it's the general effect on our government," one of his more candid statements.

He rose like a rocket to his power in a matter of weeks once he had stood on a podium waving a piece of paper and declaring, "I hold in my hand the names of . . ." I have since forgotten whether it was sixty-two or thirty-nine "card-carrying communists" inside the State Department, but it hardly matters because in subsequent months he himself kept changing the count and of course could never produce one name of an actual person. Yet his fraudulence, which had perhaps seemed so obvious to me because I had uncles like him who shot off their mouths in argument and said anything that came into their heads, was frighteningly persuasive to a lot of Americans, including some important newsmen. One half understood why the country was still in shock at having "lost" China to Mao, whose revolution had swept into Peking in 1949. How could this mucky peasant horde have won fairly and squarely against a real general like Chiang Kai-shek, whose wife, moreover, was the graduate of an American college and so beautiful besides? It could only be that worming their ways through our State Department were concealed traitors who had "given" the country to the Reds. In the light of Vietnam, we have perhaps come to understand the limits of our power, but in the early Fifties any such concept was unimaginable. Henry Luce, for example, was confidently propagating "the American century," when we would lead the grateful human race into baseball, private enterprise, eight-cylinder Buicks, and, of course, Christianity; and for a fact, the Swiss franc aside, the American dollar was truly the only nonfunny money in the world. Before he had finished, Joe McCarthy would have "named" the revered ex-general of the U.S. Army, George Catlett Marshall, as a communist.

McCarthy had struck gold with the point of a syllogism; since he was totally and furiously against communism, anyone who opposed him had therefore to be in favor of communism, *if only by that much*. This simply numbed the opposition or backed them into futile defensive postures. For example, when Senator Millard Tydings, having investigated McCarthy's charges that the State Department was full of Reds, reported that they were "a fraud and a hoax perpetrated on the Senate of the United States and on the American people," McCarthy, for revenge, then went into Maryland and, charging Tydings with being "soft" on communism, helped defeat him for reelection! His was a power blessed by Cardinal Spellman, a power that the young John F. Kennedy would not bring himself to oppose any more than did Eisenhower until 1954, near the end of McCarthy's career. For myself, I believed McCarthy might well be on his way to the presidency, and if that happened an awful lot of Americans would literally have to take to the boats.

When it was announced in 1953 that Edward R. Murrow would be devoting the entire half hour of his prestigious weekly TV commentary to an analysis of McCarthy, my own joy was great but it was mixed with some skepticism. Murrow had been the brightest star at CBS for more than a decade and remains to this day the patron saint of anchormen for his judiciousness and devotion to the truth. It was during the London blitz that he had seared our minds with the unique sound of his voice, a gravelly baritone that had rolled out to us across the Atlantic each night from the fog and blast of London under bombardment, his quiet toughness a reassurance that the great beleaguered city was still alive.

But all that anti-Nazi wartime gemütlichkeit was long gone now; indeed, CBS in the past couple of years had cooperated with the unacknowledged blacklisting of radio and TV writers, actors, and directors who had or were accused of having too much enthusiasm for the Left by newly sprouted self-appointed guardians of the airwaves like *Red Channels*, a broadsheet listing the names of purported subversives. In true private-enterprise style they were always ready to "clear" you for a fee plus your signed anticommunist declaration, or preferably an ad in *Variety*, which you paid for, with some similarly edifying and spontaneous patriotic locution. Still, it would be fascinating to see how far Murrow and CBS would want to go against the snarling senator from Wisconsin whose totally missing scruples had made him murderously effective as a debater. I was not at all sure it would be far enough.

There was such a widespread feeling of helpless paralysis before the McCarthy movement by this time that one questioned whether any mere journalist, whatever his wit and courage, could stay on his feet with him.

In such apocalyptic gloom, very nearly convinced that my days as an American playwright were numbered even as I was generally thought to be a great success, I adapted Ibsen's *An Enemy of the People* with the hope of illuminating what can happen when a righteous mob starts marching. But despite a brilliant performance by Fredric March as Dr. Stockmann, the critics batted the play right back at my feet. For one thing, it was a post-Odets and pre-Brecht time, when things artistic were supposed to deal with sentiments and aspirations, but never with society.

The failure of that production only deepened the sense of a mass mythic shadow dance, a ritualized, endlessly repeated consent to a primitive anticommunism that could end only with demagogues in power over the country. In the Salem witch hunts of 1692, a story I had known since college, I thought I saw nakedly unveiled something like the immemorial psychic principles of what we were once again living through. There too people had been at odds with a reality that indeed was sawing straight across their conception of themselves and nullifying the omnipotent powers of their society. There too men had been seized with paranoid terrors of dark forces ranged against them. It is hardly accidental that apart from *The Crucible* our theater would mount no other reply to a movement that surely meant to destroy its freedom. So feverish, so angry, so fearful had people become that any mention of the senator's name on a stage, or even an allusion to his antics, would have generated an impacted silence in the majority, and open rage in his partisans.

In *The Crucible* a public hysteria, based upon economic, sexual, and personal frustrations, gathers the folds of the sublime about itself and destroys more than twenty lives in the village of Salem, Massachusetts, in 1692. Between its heroes and villains stands a timeless hunger for mythic solutions to intractable moral and social dilemmas—particularly the myth of a hidden plot by subterranean evil forces to overwhelm the good. But *The Crucible*, too, would fail; either mistrusted as a "false analogy"—there had never been witches but there certainly were Reds, quite as though McCarthy had really uncovered a Soviet plot utilizing highly placed Americans—or regarded as a "cold" play, a charge partially justified by its direction as a disinterred classic. Interestingly, within two years, a new Off-Broadway production would succeed, judged hot stuff now by many of the same critics who theorized that I had more warmly revised the script. But the only revision had been the relaxation of society after McCarthy's quick decline and death—which, I suppose, permitted a longer view of the issues raised in the drama.

Shortly before Murrow's broadcast was announced, I had had my own personal little brush with a McCarthyite State Department. The Belgo-American Association, a business group, had invited me to come over to Brussels for the European premiere of *The Crucible* in the National Theatre, and I applied for a renewal of my outdated passport. A new passport was quickly denied me. "Not in the best interests of the United States," they said. So at the end of the opening performance, the audience, believing I was in the house, the papers having reported I had accepted to attend, began calling for the author, who, of course, was still in Brooklyn. The roar of the audience would not cease—to Europeans *The Crucible* at the time was reassurance that fascism had not yet overwhelmed Americans—and the United States ambassador had finally to stand and take my bow for me, a scandal in the papers the next morning when the imposture was revealed. (But who knows if he had stood up in sympathy for me or in silent protest at his department's stupidity in denying me a passport?)

All in all, by the time of Murrow's broadcast, I had only a small capacity left to believe that he would really do more than remonstratively tap McCarthy's shoulder. The broadcast was coming somewhat late in the game, now that an occasional soft murmuring of common sense was being heard in the press—although that, too, was still in danger of being suppressed once the senator got around to blasting its authors. For me, there was little reason anymore to expect a meaningful resistance to McCarthyism when I knew that, myself not altogether excepted, people were learning to keep a politic silence toward idiocies that a few short years before they'd have derided or laughed at.

An unsettling experience at a cocktail party shortly before the broadcast had stayed with me. I had overheard a TV producer assuring a circle of guests that he was free to hire any actor or produce any script he chose to and that no blacklist ever existed. Since I had friends who had not been hired in over a year despite long careers in TV and radio, and two or three who had suffered mental illness as a result, and I knew of at least two suicides attributable to the despair generated by blacklisting, I walked over to the producer and offered him the television rights to *The Crucible*. He laughed, assuring me and his listeners that he would of course be honored but his budget would never stand for what such rights would doubtless cost. So I offered them to him for a dollar. He went on laughing and I went on persisting, growing aware, however, that our little audience, many of them in television and the theater, was turning against me for a display of bad manners.

Leaving that party, I exchanged glances with people who I was certain shared my knowledge and views but who showed nothing in their faces. It was an experience that would be useful to me in future years when writing about the life of the artist in the

Soviet Union, China, and Eastern Europe, where what might be called a permanent state of McCarthyism reigns, at times more virulently than others, but always warning artists—who, after all, are the eyes and voices of the society—that their souls ultimately belong to Daddy.

Edward R. Murrow appeared on the screen that night of the much-anticipated broadcast, as usual a picture of classy Bogartian straightforwardness, the cigarette between the fingers with the lethal smoke coiling up around the peaked eyebrows and the straight black hair, unsmiling as ever, his voice nasal and direct. I did not yet own a set, so I was watching this at my poet-friend Leroy's house a couple of blocks from my own in Brooklyn Heights. Leroy believed he was blacklisted in TV and radio, but a few producers occasionally gave him scriptwriting work because they loved him. People also gave him old but usable cars, trips to Florida, and more or less shared a mystic belief that Leroy must not die of want, with which Leroy agreed. He had once found a new can of anchovies on the sidewalk and a month later, on a different street, the key. Leroy had even graver doubts than I about what Murrow would be able to do.

Murrow could often affect an airy confidence and even sentimentality, rather like Cronkite talking about Vermont farmers, but not tonight; tonight he had his chin tucked in like a boxer and apprehension tightened the corners of his eyes with the knowledge, no doubt, that if some back talk against McCarthy had squeaked up recently in the press, his partisans were still passionate, religiously devoted to him, and numerous. Watching Murrow appear on the tube we were all aware of those millions out there who must hate him now for spoiling their god, or trying to; and even in that poet's snug and remote living room with its in-laws' cast-off furniture, the American violence charged the air. Tina, Leroy's wide-cheekboned blonde wife, who usually could never see a TV set switched on without turning away and launching a new topic of conversation, now stared in silence at Murrow's familiar face blossoming on the black and white tube.

To her and Leroy this broadcast was of far more than academic or abstract interest. Two of Leroy's closest relatives had gained some fame as American volunteers fighting for the Spanish loyalists against Franco. This, combined with his having the usual Left views of a Thirties survivor, was enough of a taint on Leroy to damage his right to sign his own name on the occasional radio script he was able to sell. On the slim proceeds of such fitful commerce he pressed on with writing his poems. And Tina pressed on with her winsome complaints that Leroy was stubbornly immune to the American Dream of wealth and fame. Thus she stared at Murrow like a woman in love with a fighter climbing into a ring.

I think it only dawned on us as he started to speak that Murrow was the first man to challenge McCarthy out in public rather than into his sleeve, and I think we were scared for him now, although we were still pretty sure that establishment politesse would gentle his confrontation with the senator. And indeed, Murrow's introduction was not at all belligerent. But this was television, not print, and it quickly became clear what his strategy was going to be—McCarthy was going to hang himself before the whole country by reruns of his own filmed performances. And there now unwound pictures of him hectoring witnesses before his Senate subcommittee, railing against a bespectacled author of an obscure college textbook with the accusation that this man was a member of the American Civil Liberties Union, "listed as a front doing the work of the Communist party." But the stinger was the speech before a mass rally during the recent Eisenhower–Adlai Stevenson contention for the presidency.

A cold and windy day, and McCarthy behind the podium, hatless, a burly and handsome man in a saturnine way, quick to laugh through a clamped jaw—more of a tight-assed snicker really, as though not to overly warm his icy ironies. Watching him again in these reruns was even scarier than seeing him the first time, in the previous months, for now somehow he was there to be studied and he was indeed villainous, almost laughably so. Now one saw that his great wish was for a high style, his models might well have been Oscar Wilde or Bernard Shaw, epigrammatists of the cutting Irish persuasion who could lay the opponent low with a jibe impossible ever to erase. Oddly, though, it was hardly ten minutes into the program when one knew it was the end of McCarthy, not altogether for reasons of content but more because he was so obviously handling subjects of great moment with mere quips, empty-sounding jibes, lumpy witticisms; it had not seemed quite as flat and ill-acted before.

At one point, as the applause of his audience died down he gave them his little knowing grin and said, "Strangely, Alger . . . I mean Adlai . . ." and a sweep of appreciative roaring laughter sent him into a helpless giggling spell and redoubled his audience's big-decibeled recognition for this association of Adlai Stevenson with Alger Hiss, an accused communist with whom Stevenson had no connection whatsoever. Now, with the election over and settled and its passions gone, the sheer vileness of this man and his crummy tactic was abstracted from its original moment and there he stood in all his mendacity, appearing joyfully immune to all moral censure or the most minimal claims of decency.

The Murrow broadcast was a deep, if not mortal, wound for McCarthy. At least it seemed so to me at the time. By the end of the half hour all our debt to Murrow came clear and my skepticism toward him had gone. But McCarthy was given his own half-hour rebuttal period three weeks later, and we gathered again to hear what he would have to say. Now live in the studio, a subdued McCarthy seemed to know he had been badly hurt by the Murrow broadcast. A plaintive tenor line lifted his voice into the doubtlessly authentic plaint of a persecuted man. "If there had been no communists in our government, we would not have given China to the communists!" This was one of his standards, but under attack now he knew he had to get more specific, and so maps appeared on the screen, showing how the dark stain of communism had spread from Russia over China, engineered by a tiny secret group of schemers, their agents, and their dupes like—yes, like Edward R. Murrow. In his rebuttal, McCarthy, left to himself, undid himself. Unaccustomed to anyone confronting him with his lies, he seemed unable to use elementary caution. Murrow, he blithely said, was a member of the terrorist organization the Industrial Workers of the World; Harold Laski, "the greatest communist propagandist in England," had dedicated his last book to Murrow. Now snarling, he attempted the ultimate unmasking of Murrow with his by-then familiar horror words: "Edward R. Murrow, the cleverest of the jackal pack which is always found at the throat of anyone who dares to expose individual communists and traitors; Murrow, who served the communist cause as part of the transmission belt from the Russian secret police into the American home." McCarthy's desperate appeal ended something like 'The Communist Party opposes me; Murrow opposes me; Murrow is a transmission belt of communist propaganda." Such was his counterattack.

But Murrow, unlike others, had a network to allow him the last word. And he had easy pickings: the ACLU had never been "listed" by any agency as a front; Murrow had simply never belonged to the IWW; and Laski, a rather confused on-and-off-again Marxist professor, had dedicated his book to Murrow for his valiant broadcasts from bombed London in the late war. As for the communists supporting Murrow, this consisted of a notice in the *Daily Worker* that his upcoming McCarthy telecast was a "Best Bet."

Oddly, one lacked the urge to applaud Murrow at the end. He had been so persuasive because he had said what everyone had always known, that Joe McCarthy had merely been the master of the rhetorical style of lawyer-talk, an actor in love with the sound of his voice and his capacity to hold an audience in astonishment.

What ultimately undid McCarthy was hubris, his attacks on the patriotism of the leadership of the Army, on General George Marshall and Eisenhower himself. He may have gone mad with his power and too much booze. But Murrow's broadcast had cut the bag open and it was empty. How could one applaud our having striven so long after wind? Still, there was no doubt that night that Murrow's was the voice of decency, and if he and CBS had not struck at McCarthy until his decline had begun—if it was less a dragon slaying than a coup de grace—it still demonstrated, and would continue for years to come, the persistence of scruple as a living principle, one that had for so long been defied and doubtless would be again, and yet would live.

Murrow, in his summing up, said, "We are not a nation of fearful men," and one knew that there are things that do have to be repeated as fact even when they are only hopes. But for that kind of hope this nation is in Murrow's eternal debt.

1983

Excerpts from 'Salesman' in Beijing

March 22

Arriving at the rehearsal hall at exactly 9:00 a.m., I find Ying Ruocheng, Liu Housheng, General Secretary of the Chinese Dramatists Association, and an ebullient, strong, laughing woman of fifty whose name is Zhou Baoyou—Joe, for short—who is filled with bursting good health from her forty-five-minute bike ride to her office, which she does every morning, winter and summer.

She is the Mrs. Trouble of China's entertainment industry, solving everybody's transportation problems, health and food difficulties, getting them airport and railroad tickets, and in general making foreigners believe they are safe in the laps of the gods. (As I would learn later, she is the daughter of a banker who decided to cast his and his family's lot with the Revolution; she studied English in a Christian school; her enjoyment of life springs in part from the post-Cultural Revolution liberty, which she loves, and in part from her children's success—her son is studying music in the United States and her daughter studies in China. Above all, she wants, she says, "to contribute something," and feels this production will be the best thing she has ever had a chance to help into life.)

Liu Housheng is her boss, a diffident man with short-cropped gray hair, wearing a particularly much-laundered Mao jacket and a gentle, rather humorous look. I take him to be—from his position—a Communist Party member and probably its representative to me, for he has a certain amount of power, I am sure, at the apex of the Dramatists Association. But at the moment I have no interest in pursuing the submerged world of political controls in my eagerness to have my first readings of the play today.

Joe's news is that we must decide what to do about some twenty-two foreign television and print correspondents—and many more than that from Chinese media— who want to interview me about the production. I have already in hand about a dozen requests routed through the Association. Joe, thank God, has kept my telephone number secret but doesn't know for how long this will be possible. After much back and forth it is clear the Chinese have been caught up in the publicity hunger and want me to honor all the requests—a faint surprise, since I had somehow assumed that media pressure would inflame their phobias about being used. Instead it has amplified mine and pleases them no end. This is a very different China. It is funny to hear them talking Chinese among themselves with "CBS, ABC, NBC" thrown in. I finally decide that I will give the journalists interviews independently provided they're kept short. This is not going to work, of course, but has to be tried, I guess.

By ten we have all assembled, the whole cast seated around an ample room in armchairs, scripts in their hands. There is a moment of dread as Linda says the first line—"Weelee!"—from the bedroom, having heard him enter the house. The first surprise is how easy it is for me to follow the scene in my Penguin paperback. It is a triumph of Ying's translation—even the rhythms seem the same, the flows to the peaks and the slopes toward the silences. In a few minutes it is obvious that Zhu Lin and he will easily seem related, husband and wife, and of this particular class. I cannot believe they have come this far in a few rehearsal days. Ying hardly looks at the script, and she only a little more often. What am I going to do with six weeks of rehearsal time!

Zhu Lin is an actress of awesome experience in classic Chinese as well as modern plays—"a heavyweight," in Ying's words. She already knows she must keep Willy from wandering too close to the edge, affects a happiness with his positive moments, insinuates the truth when he cannot bear hearing it, always reaching a hand out as to a child who cannot walk without falling down. I can detect no trace of the declamatory style in either of them, something I had feared and still do. On the contrary, seated side by side in chairs, they create the Lomans' bedroom. Ying has a kind of absolute control that brings Olivier to mind—he simply does what is called for, easily, directly, effortlessly. But a few of his shifts of temper are repetitious and we shall work on those. The shape of the first scene does not yet exist, but the main thing is almost palpable—the truth of where the Lomans are with each other as a couple. The reading approaches a read performance in that they already possess consistent attitudes and are not merely groping. What gratifies me is the absence of the distance I had supposed would separate them from the feelings in the roles, but whatever is lacking, it is never intimacy with their own feelings. Or so it seems. If they were merely posing, imitating "American," I don't think I could follow every speech as easily as I do.

With the reading over I ask the cast to tell me what, in their roles, if anything, they feel alien to. "What are you called on to do that a Chinese would not do?" There is a silence. Then the actor playing Happy says (in Ying's translation), "I can't imagine a Chinese continuing to talk to his brother once he says, as Biff does, that he is going to sleep."

Ying clarifies: "He is talking not so much about impoliteness as that a Chinese would not feel such pressure to continue talking once his listener has said he is going to sleep."

"Then an American, you mean, feels the need to speak more urgently?"

"Exactly, yes. An American feels he must say what he has to say no matter what. Whereas a Chinese would feel that to continue would be ineffectual."

"Is this politesse?"

"No, not really. It is probably a recognition of the limits. Once the limits are reached, that is all that can be done."

I feel there is some hidden relationship to this analysis in a question the actor playing Charley asks a few minutes later. Today he is wearing a sweater in two shades of gray and looks more elegant. "I don't understand why Charley is so kind to Willy," he says.

"He feels pity for him, perhaps."

"Ah." He nods. I don't think he is really convinced.

"Maybe there are people like this, who feel for others and try to help if they can."

"Yes," he says, still weighing the possibility. I like him—an actor who has to make his information work and asks a solid question.

"They are old friends, you know."

"Yes, I know." There is a pause, and then he says, "I don't think any man would be so good to another in China." The others show no reaction.

This reminds me of the problem we had in casting the part in the original production. Kazan had reached out into what seemed the totally wrong direction for Howard Smith, a shouting comic who had been in vaudeville for years before becoming a minor star in farces, where he played the standard bewildered father of teenage girls. *Dear Ruth* was his big current success. Howard had never been near a serious play and had no desire to be, when comedies ran so much longer. He was a stout, gruff, tall man with sparse blond hair and a loud, rather common baritone voice. He read the play and refused the part, surely the best he had ever been offered in his life. Kazan, Bloomgarden, and friends of his all tried to change his mind but to no avail. "That play is *terrible*," he'd say. "Who's going to want to see something that sad?"

Finally, in desperation, a meeting was fixed with him and me alone in Bloomgarden's office. I had learned from Kazan what his objection was, but pretending ignorance I asked him to tell me why he was so against the play. "The poor man, for God's sake; the rotten things his sons say to him. And his boss. Everybody's so down on him. It's just awful!"

"Except Charley," I said. I could see his eyes change. He stopped moving. "Charley gives Willy good advice, lends him money, always makes time for him during office hours. . . . Charley really tries, Howard."

He sat there staring. Finally he said, "I'll think about it." That night he accepted the role. His instincts were as right for it as his personality: a hardheaded, realistic, decent man; slightly dense, perhaps, but filled with human warmth. A mature actor, he was instantly credible, no matter what he did or said.

We had been rehearsing for more than two weeks, the play was fully blocked, and while Arthur Kennedy, Lee Cobb, Mildred Dunnock, Cameron Mitchell had all had their turns asking Kazan or me what something meant, Howard Smith had never asked a single question. He was especially glorious in the card-game scene, where Willy is beginning to talk both to Charley and to his vision of his brother Ben, who has materialized at his elbow as he plays. Charley is of course totally unaware that Willy is addressing a wraith as well as himself, and from his viewpoint Willy is making less and less sense. Howard Smith managed this mystification with subtlety and discretion, never overdoing his bewilderment, always curious as to what Willy means.

But on this day he surprised everyone. He broke off the scene, and raised his hand up to shade his eyes and look out into the dark theater. "Can I ask a question?" he said. "Gadg? Are you there?"

"I'm right here, Howard," Kazan answered. "What's your question?"

Pointing at the actor playing Ben—Thomas Chalmers, an immense man, formerly an heroic basso with the Metropolitan Opera—he asked with a certain super-intensity that told of a long conflict he had been living through over possibly many days, "Do I see him?"

Kazan kept a straight face. "No, Howard."

"I don't see him at all," Howard Smith confirmed—happily, it seemed.

"Not for a minute, not at all, never. You just don't see him, Howard."

"Good. Okay. That's what I thought."

Apparently Howard had simply been obeying Kazan's instruction never to look at Ben, for what reason he did not really know, and had been puzzling it out for the past days until he could no longer hold back his question. It was a comically embarrassing setback for all the Stanislavski actors in the cast, who, in order to make themselves real, had put all they had into studying the reasons why they did what they did, while the realest one on the stage had not known what he was doing—and it was one of the most difficult feats of acting in the play.

Now, a world away in space and 35 years later, here was an actor being Charley again. How odd, yet fitting, that in this time and this place, after revolution and civil war and cruelties beyond the mind's power to contain, this Charley should be asking not why everyone is so bad to Willy but why Charley is so good to him.

I raise the question with the cast whether this play would have been performed, let's say, in 1977 or 1978, and they quickly reply, as though it were obvious, that it could not have been understood by the audience then. I take this to mean that they would not have understood the unusual form. Under the Gang of Four through the Cultural Revolution, they had only Jiang Qing's "Eight Permissible Plays," demonstrations of problems. But in the past five years a few foreign plays have been performed, and the audience, especially the younger majority, are eager for new forms.

"I read *Salesman* to this company in 1978," says Ying, "but they rejected it, sure that it would be incomprehensible. The elements of American society in it had no preparation in the public mind; nowadays everybody knows foreign films and TV and a great deal about how the West lives. We think even the liquid form of *Salesman* has also been prepared for in their minds now. They will be eager for it."

All this reminds me of how much doubt there was about the play when I wrote it. In fact, Joshua Logan, who had invested a thousand dollars in it sight unseen, withdrew five hundred after he read the script. One day during rehearsal Kazan and I ran into him in the street. He was painfully embarrassed, thinking we knew—which was not the case as yet—of his expression of disbelief in the play, and he urged me to remove Uncle Ben and all the elements of Willy's hallucinatory life because the audience would be hopelessly uncertain whether they were in the past or the present. At that time American theatrical experience also was primarily realistic, in the pictorial sense of the word.

I keep pressing the cast to ask questions, not only for the questions themselves but to help me judge where their minds are in relation to the play and American culture. At last the actress playing the Woman in Boston, who occasionally sleeps with Willy when he is there, asks, "Is she a Bad Woman?" This actress has the right voluptuousness, the round Chinese face and a sexy solidity of flesh. Ying quickly interrupts to explain that to the Chinese a woman has to be "Bad" to be so promiscuous, and I detect no irony in his voice.

Considering how I am to reply, I think that the actress and perhaps Ying as well and maybe the whole cast are hoping that she is *not* Bad—a prostitute—so it is easy to tell them that she is a lonely woman who has a regular office job and is not at all a prostitute, and that she genuinely likes Willy and his line of gab and his pathos, and so she sees him for dinner perhaps twice a month and they talk and "behave like husband and wife for a night." Great relief on all sides. It would have been difficult to add that she might have a similar relation to a couple of other salesmen from time to time and still not be thought of as a prostitute or even Bad. But this would also be hard to explain in parts of the United States.

I am not sure they accept her behavior as truly non-Bad, but I leave it ambiguous in the hope that she will not try to play a Chinese vamp. I don't trust their notions of Western sexuality, even if I have no experience of the Chinese kind; I remember that on our last visit in 1978, couples did not so much as touch hands in public. Amazingly enough, nowadays they have had to clear a small, dense patch of shrubbery not far from the American Embassy because of its attraction for extrabotanical exercises.

Now that the subject of sexuality is opened up, Happy raises his hand to say that the Chinese would probably not understand his character. This actor's personality baffles me; he is rather small and slight, with straight black hair, longer than usual here, that flows down above his left eye, and a thoroughly pleasant but somehow indefinite, even evasive smile. He seems too young for Happy, about twenty-four, and far too passive for that sexually overheated character, but I keep telling myself that maybe these traits will appear different to Chinese and that I must give him his head. Ying's casting was so right in the other parts, it is hard to believe this fellow is as wrong as he seems at this point.

"What do you think they won't understand?"

Ying intervenes. "He means, I believe, that they will understand the workings of his character, but the play seems not to condemn his womanizing. In Chinese society a man talking about women as Happy does—bowling them over and so on—would be a rotter."

"You mean it will leave them uneasy because he is sympathetic?"

"Exactly. The *i*'s have to be dotted here."

Ying translates our little exchange and the cast laughs, but with a certain uneasiness, as though they are not sure themselves about the matter.

I decide to leave it right there, for the time being. Let their anxieties deepen, it will charge them up all the higher. And anyway I am leaving the country two days after we open.

I ask Linda how she feels about her character and whether such women are to be found in Chinese society today.

"Oh, many, many. There are a lot whose lives are wound around their husbands', and who think only of their men and very little about themselves." The cast nods reassuringly to me. The time has not yet come to tell her that this idea of Linda is mistaken. I am better at working in detail than in throwing out broad generalities.

But in an attempt to fill in my sense of the country—rather than to document the character, which I see somewhat differently than the actress does—I ask whether this attitude, even if so prevalent, is not regarded as old-fashioned now. The cast is emphatic—it certainly is old-fashioned. To pin it down, I ask Biff and Happy, who are seated together, if their generation has women in it like Linda, and they are incredulous that I can have imagined such a thing, and set up a cross talk directed at me through Ying.

"The women," he translates, "earn their own livings now and that's the basis of the whole relationship. In fact"—he grins, pursing his mouth comically again and popping his eyes behind his thick lenses—"it's usually the women who throw the men out, not the other way around." Everyone guffaws. They are aware of riding a wave of change that has by no means hit the beach and flattened out yet.

I have been catching a certain tone of condescension toward Willy's character coming from Linda and Willy—from him, especially—from time to time. Perhaps it is unconscious; or possibly I misunderstand. It came at me yesterday and again two or three times today, an indefinable but dangerous attitude that could lead to a satiric interpretation, which would leave Ying Ruocheng unable to sustain the role the whole length of the play. (I am not sure he has yet caught on to how physically difficult this part is going to be.) But most important, I cannot let the play become a satire.

"I want to say a few things about the play and Willy now," I announce. They become silent quickly. It is now clear, incidentally, that they normally discuss a play for days and sometimes weeks before trying to do scenes and, like all actors, would—up to a certain point—much prefer interesting general discussions to hard work. But I am coming to realize that in this type of theater there is no rush to do anything. "You are all aware, I'm sure, that Willy is foolish and even ridiculous sometimes. He tells the most transparent lies, exaggerates mercilessly, and so on. But I want you to see that the impulses behind him are not foolish at all. He cannot bear reality, and since he can't do much to change it, he keeps changing his ideas of it." I am veering close to ideology; I note some agreement here, but it is uneasy. Charley is especially rapt and unable, I believe, to come down on the side of my argument. "But the one thing he is not, is passive. Something in him knows that if he stands still he will be overwhelmed. These lies and evasions of his are his little swords with which he wards off the devils around him. But his activist nature is what leads mankind to progress, doesn't it. It can create disaster, to be sure, but progress also. People who are able to accept their frustrated lives do not change conditions, do they. So my point is that you must look behind his ludicrousness to what he is actually confronting, and that is as serious a business as anyone can imagine. There is a nobility, in fact, in Willy's struggle. Maybe it comes from his refusal ever to relent, to give up."

Silence. It worries me, their never having seen it in this light, the character of this screwball; quite probably they had been moving toward a satiric interpretation, or at least one that would let them off the hook as actors, and the audience as well. I see now why Ying was so insistent that I come and direct; he is especially still, especially open to this apparently novel line on the play, although I have no doubt he has always seen the role as basically a tragic one.

Now Ben has a question. This actor is a short fellow with a certain ferocity in his gaze; the outer corners of his eyes are curled up like those of the Chinese opera villain-masks, especially when he concentrates on what I am saying. Compact and quick-moving, he already has a certain pecky style. Even when he suddenly changes, and bursts out laughing, there is some danger in him—all of this is perfectly subjective, of course; he is doubtless sweet and kind.

"Is Uncle Ben a ghost?" he asks.

"A ghost?"

"Yes."

"I'm not sure what you want to know." I dread misleading him; it will take days to undo some mistaken but—to him—attractive image.

"Chinese plays," he explains, "do not have ghosts."

"Really? I had some idea they did, but it doesn't matter. I realize that you cannot play a 'ghost' but what you should play is Willy's brother."

"Ah!" This seems to please him. "But I am really dead?"

"Oh yes. And you exist in his memory with certain characteristics that are not necessarily realistic. I mean that you must play him as Willy recalls him. He carries tremendous meaning for Willy, and you must learn what that is as time goes by. But for now you can forget the 'ghost' and think of yourself as his elder brother who made a great success in South African diamond mines, okay?"

He has an image and he is happy. A real actor, thank God.

But Ying is not quite satisfied. "What Mr. Miller was trying to say, I believe, is that sometimes Ben has his own character and sometimes he simply voices Willy's thoughts. In other words, he is and is not a real person like the other people in the play."

"That's not a contradiction," I add. "We all remember actual people we once knew but we remember them in a nonobjective way, a way that emphasizes and even parodies some of their qualities. It depends on what they mean to us, doesn't it."

Ying understands, and translates this for Ben, who seems to sop it up, nodding eagerly. So Freud works here, too.

Now Charley is back with another question—I feel good about their being relaxed enough now to leave off raising their hands like students. "He wants to know," Ying says, "whether he and Willy play cards for money."

I had never thought of this before, but actually they would be putting down small bets, and so I ask, "Do Chinese play cards much?"

"Oh, we love cards but never play for money."

Which brings back a walk I took in Yanan five years ago, when I saw a pretty hot card game going on in the middle of a field on the edge of town, with money on the ground and guys yelling with every card played. I had learned then of the state's prohibition on card gambling, a national vice the government was trying to stamp out. Without raising the political issue, I ask, "Could you play for small stakes in that scene?"

"Certainly, if that's called for." (Whether by design or simply because the very complicated mechanics of the scene made it nearly impossible, no money was ever subsequently used. However, it wasn't in the first New York production either, but it is interesting that the political side of the question was not put to me.)

Still drugged by the worst jet lag I have ever experienced I return to the theater at seven o'clock in the evening for the first reading of Act Two. I believe they might well turn out to be quite fine, and allow myself a more or less total silence as the reading proceeds. Inge is in tears at the end.

The weirdest part of this day is that in the car on the way back to our lodgings at the end of the reading, I realize again that I had been able to follow the dialogue almost always without using my English script, staying with the actors line for line. Even the lengths of sentences are nearly the same. It is uncanny. Yet, on questioning Inge I learn that the *content* of the lines is very often quite different, involving as it does the imagistic Chinese vocabulary. For example, Willy reports to his boys on his vastly successful selling trip: "Knocked 'em cold in Providence, slaughtered 'em in Boston." This becomes

"I tumbled them backwards in Providence-ah, and they fell on their faces in Bos-i-ton!" But it had an uncannily similar sound and almost precisely the same beat.

I fall asleep as soon as I contemplate the bed, but wake every few hours, startled. I am still drugged, numbed, but not unhappy. These will be fifteen-hour days for me, rising at seven to have breakfast and drive to the theater, with bedtime only after the ten o'clock finish of rehearsals at night. But I am looking forward.

March 31

On arriving this morning I discover a dozen or so bewigged dummy heads standing in rows on some tables pulled together, the cast trying them on with the fervent advice and aid of four or five women and one man from the theater's own wiggery. These specialists are all, of course, dressed in the standard blue trousers and plain jackets, the man wearing his blue cap as befits wigmakers in a workers' theater. Ying is trying on a scraggly mouse-colored wig with a receding hairline; a hairdo like that would get anybody fired from his job for sheer neglect. To my amazement he is studying himself in a mirror with serious deliberation. Worse yet, I spot two platinum-blonde wigs that are undoubtedly intended for the two women in the restaurant scene whom Happy picks up. In other words, they are intending to "whiten" themselves for the play even though I had stated in my first day's lobotomized speech, without any demurral, the principle of their not trying to imitate Americans but to play as Chinese doing an American work. Admittedly, this places them in a never-never land, ethnically speaking, but at a minimum it is a more beautiful sight to see than Chinese with blonde hair, something that can only convince an audience that the actor is capable of wearing a wig. Of course I am leaving out their conventions, but I am doing so purposely since I cannot honestly judge by a taste I do not share or even understand. In any case I have a gut conviction that Westernizing the cast will vitiate the production.

Ying asks my opinion of the wig and I tell him it is all wrong, and he is easily convinced. In his case a wig is necessary to help age him and that is all. But it must have a pre-Beatles look, unlike the long hair he had been trying on. It has to be reminiscent of the fairly close-cropped businessmen of the 1950s, 1940s, and earlier. If a salesman can be ruined, as Charley says in the Requiem, by a couple of spots on his hat, a scraggly haircut would have sunk him without a trace.

From nowhere—we are now a milling mob of actors, wiggers, technical people with opinions, the sweet and aged doorman with his point of view, and me in the middle with bewigged Ying walking around and looking as if he could frighten bats—a small wigger woman appears with a fat illustrated book of Great Movies, which I open to a picture of Jimmy Steward in *Mr. Deeds Goes to Washington*. Stewart has the standard American haircut of the period. "That's it!" I yell. Whereupon I find myself facing a large, jolly, rather overweight, cherry-cheeked man—a wigger—in his late fifties who is just taking off his blue cap to scratch his head.

"*There's* your hair, Ying!" I call, and at a glance Ying is taken with it: dense, silvery-white hair clipped short all over but in a distinctive, efficient-looking way that is not quite conventional and yet could be. Immediately, of course, all the wiggers object that it is too short for Weelee. It is the old story—if you can make a wig, make a big one, something that *looks* like a wig, or why else bother? And so I must fight off wigs for Biff and Happy, whose own haircuts are perfect, with Biffs rather short cut quite right for an athlete, and Happy's about the style of Adolphe Menjou, very black, carefully shaped, and natty. My suggestion that Biff shorten the length of his sideburns, which are halfway down to his jaw, arouses his instant defensive indignation—"My jaws are so wide I must have these sideburns to make my face narrower!"—and I give up quickly without argument. And he does, I admit, tend to bulge toward the jaw hinges in rather a pear or punching-bag shape.

Speaking of which, as we finally settle down to begin running a scene, and everyone is getting back to his tea or taking position on stage, the tall doors to the outer corridor open and a monstrous shape begins moving into the room, its gait shuffling, its progress a few inches with each shove from the rear. The entire cast turn, as I do, transfixed by this apparition. It appears to be brown leather, about six feet in height, and as big around as a large culvert, with great brass grommets set around its open top through which a veritable hawser could have been threaded before it was separated from whatever might have been its normal abode. It is with sinking heart that I slowly realize that this is supposed to be the punching bag that Willy bought for his boys in Boston and brought home as a surprise in the trunk of his little Chevrolet.

The thing now ceases to shuffle into the room, and around from its rear appears a small man in the usual blue, his cap and shoulder whitened with the dust of the bag that he has, incredibly, been pushing single-handed, God knows from what distance and over what boulevards and even mountains. "I think that's the punching bag," Ying says with typical Manchu understatement, staring up at me with his thick lenses, doubtless aware—at the least—of a slight awkwardness in my coming attempts to stage the moment when Happy will rush onstage carrying this object in one hand. The man now comes forward, I suppose to claim his credit from the great star and the Foreign Expert for having accomplished the impossible. I refuse even to imagine what they must have gone through even to locate this thing in Beijing. An ordinary punching bag, of course, is about the size of a lengthened basketball, and a sandbag is about four feet in height and perhaps a foot in diameter. This thing could only have been fabricated in prerevolutionary times, probably from a description of one seen in a New York or London gymnasium by a Chinese businessman who was extremely small.

But I know that Chinese are tough in the face of discouragement—how else could they have endured their history of suffering? "That is not the right punching bag," I tell the man, as quietly and forthrightly as possible, and draw him a picture of a light bag suspended from a round board. The stage manager suddenly recognizes this and explains it to the moving man, who, looking stunned, nods vaguely as he is led out of the hall into the corridor. Another day another dollar, as my father would say.

1984

The Will to Live:
Interview by Steven R. Centola

Centola: I've always been fascinated by your ability to maintain a singleness of vision in plays remarkably different from each other in form, style, mood, theme, characterization, plot, and even at times in language. Would you agree that this underlying continuity in your work derives from a vision of the human condition that can be described as a kind of existential humanism—a vision that emphasizes self-determinism and social responsibility and that is optimistic and affirms life by acknowledging man's possibilities in the face of his limitations and even sometimes in the dramatization of his failures?

Miller: That's very good. I would agree with that. That's a fair summary of what I feel about it—my own views about it.

Centola: The one play that seems to provide the clearest revelation of your vision is *After the Fall.*

Miller: Just about, yes.

Centola: Not many people see it that way.

Miller: Well, I think they were, to be quite frank—I've said this before; it's no news—but I think that they were blinded by the gossip and the easy way out. But it's not just in my work. I think people go for tags for any writer; you don't have to think about what he's doing any longer, especially if he's around a long time. But then simply you know what you think you want to expect. It may or may not have much to do with what he's doing. But they find whatever in the work fits that expectation, and the other is simply not dealt with or is rejected. This is an old story here that we all know.

Centola: Your vision, what I've called your existential humanism, seems to have a lot in common with Jean-Paul Sartre's existentialist philosophy.

Miller: You know that Sartre did the screenplay for *The Crucible,* and we were on the verge of meeting three or four times and never managed to because he was out of France when I was there. There was always a mix-up, and I always thought that there was more time than there actually turned out to be. But I think there was a relationship which was not programmatic in any way. It just means people leaning in the same kind of direction.

Centola: So you wouldn't say it was a matter of influence?

Miller: No, no.

Centola: Would you feel as though I were going for a tag if I pointed out some of the similarities between your vision and Sartre's existentialism?

Miller: Well, I don't think that's a danger because he certainly was always attractive to me in a vague way. But I'll tell you, I'm not a methodical, philosophical writer; I don't spring out of that kind of tradition. I work out of instinct. And so whatever similarities that there turn out to be, somebody's always related to something.

Centola: Do you think an identification of these Sartrean correspondences in your plays could bring out the metaphysical issues in your work and help to put to rest the notion that you're merely a social realist, the tag which you seem to have been stuck with for some time now?

Miller: The social realist thing is what they were doing with Ibsen all his life. He was supposed to be interested in sewers because of *An Enemy of the People,* or in syphilis because of *Ghosts,* or in women's rights or something like that because of *A Doll's House,* and all the rest of it. Of course, what is inevitable is that these are all, in a certain sense, metaphors, and had the writer merely been interested in sewers, violence, women's rights, and the rest of it, we would have long since lost track of his name. These are metaphorical situations of the human race as it goes on forever.

Centola: The great writer gets at the universal through the particular.

Miller: Sure. If you don't, you end up with a kind of blatantly philosophical dialogue of some sort that nobody really is interested in. It isn't the way these obtrude into experience. That's as simple as it can be.

Centola: I read some of your unpublished works that I was able to get through the Humanities Research Center at the University of Texas. One of these was a letter you wrote called "Willy and the Helpless Giant," and in that letter you suggest that tragedy results when one tries to attain honor by putting on a mask and performing for the public instead of being what one really is and does best. In many ways, that idea parallels Sartre's distinction between being-for-itself and being-for-others. I'm wondering if that conflict isn't part of the tragedy of modern existence: individuals feel obligated to adopt poses or wear masks in order to make themselves feel significant or honorable?

Miller: That's true. But the question is how old a procedure that is, how old that process is. Because the more class-structured a society is (for example, a royal society like, let's say, the eighteenth-century or seventeenth-century French society), people had to fit into a mold that was given them by the class that they felt they belonged to. And all costume, dress, manners, habits, and the mores were predetermined, in effect, so that sincerity was hardly a value at all. It's just that it wasn't necessarily cynical. It was simply that the society and sincerity could not comfortably coexist. So that for the sake of good order, one had to adopt some kind of persona, which is not necessarily the one that one really has. Now, for us, I think this is an old thing in the United States. Alexis de Tocqueville mentions the fact that we don't want to be set aside from the mob. That means people will adopt a mask in order to be like everybody else. And maybe it's implicit in that statement that Americans don't want to be separated from the mask.

Centola: That's an interesting way of establishing a connection with others.

Miller: But there's also a price to pay for that. And the price, obviously, is the loss of something. Society makes such a heavy demand upon the individual that he has to give up his individuality (and we do have a high percentage of mental breakdowns and neuroses and the rest of it). So, maybe it goes along with democracy, oddly enough.

Centola: That's interesting.

Miller: I think that the British, for example, are far more able and willing to endure characters than we are. (What would you call characters? People who don't necessarily abide by the rules.) We're much less tolerant. We won't lend them money; we won't see them through school sometimes. We impose a discipline on them because they are different, and so on.

Centola: So we place a greater emphasis on conformity?

Miller: Conformity is a terrific power here. To jump to another sector of this, I think it lay behind the power of the Un-American Activities Committee, because, after all, what they were threatening most people with was not jail, and it certainly wasn't shooting; it was being disgraced—social disgrace.

Centola: What I was getting at in that question is whether tragedy could be considered as a fundamental condition of being. Take Hamlet as an example. Here's an individual who is obsessed with living up to the image expected of him by others. It's the same with Othello and Oedipus. It seems that all these characters find themselves torn between....

Miller: Mask and reality. You ought to look into the whole question of the fact that the Greek plays were played in masks. I'm not sure where that fits here, but it just occurred to me. Well, of course, I have been very conscious of this as a writer, that is, of the conflict, the friction, the opposition between the individual and his social obligations, his social mask, his social self. And it always seemed to me that the perfect society would be one in which that gap, the friction, would be able to be minimized, but people don't seem to be driven crazy about it. It isn't that totally American kind of a thing, though, obviously. It's everywhere; it just takes different shapes. I suspect it's in tribal Africa. You see, there are social duties and social fears that can create a tragic event.

Centola: That's why I mentioned Sartre; he's dealing with the fundamental condition of being human: being self-conscious.

Miller: It's certainly in the center of it.

Centola: Well, it seems that the tragedy of displacement, which you have discussed in your essays, is really a type of existential crisis that results when one has to make a conscious choice between his public self and his private one. You say that displacement results from a character's violation of his nature through compromises or mistakes. And then his effort to regain his sense of identity against overwhelming obstacles makes the play take on a tragic dimension.

Miller: I think in the plays of mine that I felt were of tragic dimensions, the characters are obsessed with retrieving a lost identity, meaning that they were displaced by the social pressure, the social mask, and no longer could find themselves, or are on the verge of not being able to. There in the private man is the real one.

Centola: In your introduction to your *Collected Plays,* Volume I, you say that the one unseen goal toward which almost all of your plays strive is the "discovery and its proof—that we are made and yet are more than what made us." That statement seems to pinpoint the central tension underlying all of your plays, a tension created by the antagonistic forces of fate and free will acting upon each other.

Miller: Right. Did you ever read my first play on Broadway, which failed, called *The Man Who Had All the Luck?* In the line of this kind of discussion, that really was a very important play for me, because while the play failed, I learned in that play where I was positioned in the world, so to speak. And the play taught me something which I wasn't even aware of at the moment. But looking back—just this kind of a question is raised. He wants to know where he begins and the world begins; where he leaves off, the world begins. He's trying really to separate himself and to control his destiny.

Centola: Or to make himself aware that he has been controlling it, and that he's not just a pawn of the forces around him.

Miller: Yes, right. So, it goes right back to the beginning in the most vague part of my career.

Centola: That play didn't get the justice it deserved because the critics misunderstood it. If I'm not mistaken, a major complaint at the time was that the play displayed "jumbled philosophies" because you didn't choose to advocate either fate or free will. But why should you choose one and not see the interplay?

Miller: The interplay was the point! Well, you see, this was where they couldn't run with a tag. That's exactly what I started out by saying today. Had I been very clever and sophisticated about it, I would have thrown out a tag that they could run with and feel that they had it in their pocket. But I let the tension run on right through the end, instead of resolving it for them the way it never is in life.

Centola: So you would say that dialectic exists also in your other plays?

Miller: Oh, yeah. No question about it. It goes right on now.

Centola: Like Sartre, you often seem to concern yourself with the alienation of the individual in your plays. Frequently, alienation has something to do with the individual's recognition of (and reluctance to accept) his separateness. Such alienation is perhaps most apparent in *After the Fall,* but it is also evident in your other plays. Willy Loman and other characters also cannot accept the fact that they are separate beings.

Miller: That's right. You know, I have a line somewhere—oh, I think it's in an introduction I wrote to *A View from the Bridge* or one of the editions of *A View from the Bridge,* but I could be wrong about this because it's now twenty years or more—to the effect that the underlying tension is that man is looking for a home. In other words, he's looking for an unalienated existence, and this can be terribly attractive and seductive and is the root of a lot of mystery. See, one of the greatest appeals of

Christianity as well as of Communism is that it promises to end alienation. If I want to subjugate man, I can declare alienation a sin, and anybody who is alienated or causes anybody else to be alienated should be punished. See, this is what the Puritans did among themselves. This is what the Communist party does in Russia. And this is what the loyal extreme patriots in every country do. They're always against aliens, just as simple as that. It's the root of antiforeignism; it's the root of this philistinism that we're always confronting. And everybody does it! The function of a group is to define itself, and its definition is: "We are us, and you are you." You see?

Centola: Isn't that a type of psychological projection? Couldn't people who create these groups of others, or outsiders, just as easily say: "We are good, and you are evil?"

Miller: Absolutely. "We are us."

Centola: And they project everything they don't like about themselves onto others?

Miller: Absolutely. That's what it's all about. It's a form of psychological warfare. My view from the beginning has more or less been (it has shifted with each play to a certain degree) to find a form, in effect, for the condition of tension, rather than resolution of this particular dichotomy through consciousness, through being aware that indeed I am alienated. I'm not you, but that doesn't mean because I'm not you that I can't sympathize with you. Well, to maintain that kind of tension in all of the thing, especially in political and social existence, we're without and refuse to resolve it. You might be able to, but the solution is always false. That's the difficulty. And in a play, it's very aggravating for the audience.

Centola: Not for the dramatist?

Miller: No. It's a condition of existence. In fact, you could almost say that the tragic view is that it is tragic because of the fact that it's unresolvable. We wish so for a pillow to lay our head upon, and it's a stone.

Centola: So man is always alienated, and yet he is constantly striving to get beyond his condition.

Miller: Right.

Centola: There's something dignified in his effort though.

Miller: I was just about to say that the whole point of it is that the aspiration is holy. See, the Biblical prophets are terrific because they refused to compromise. They maintained the tension through people like Ezekiel or Isaiah. Isaiah will project the plowshares and the peacemakers will be blessed and all the rest of it, but that's the aspiration. The implicit fact is that they're not around yet, these blessed people.

Centola: So what makes the characters tragic is partially the fact that only a few people, perhaps, ever attain that kind of self-recognition, or get to the point where they try to transcend their condition?

Miller: Right.

Centola: So the great mass of people aren't moved this way, or at least aren't aware of it?

Miller: The great mass of people are in the chorus. They perceive perfectly well what's happening, or very often. But, for whatever reason, they are bereft of the power or the lust for the power or the sacrificial nature that is required to go seeking. You know, the other day with that case, the Hinckley case, is a very good example of something like this. Now this was a jury, I think, of almost all black people, and they gave this perfectly horrible (to most people) verdict. And then people said, "Well, that's because they're so dumb, you know; they aren't educated people." Well, they interviewed them on television, and they were remarkably sophisticated. And they dug it very, very well. They were really on a knife-edge, and they reacted in a very sharp and profound way: they blamed the code. And they said: "That's the code, and that is all the choice we had by that code." Well, that's terrific. See, now there's an instance of people who perforce were put in a position of having to make moral decisions, which normally in ordinary life they wouldn't be required to do, not in a public way certainly. My point is that you don't have to be a "noble" creature. This is changing the subject slightly, but since you raised the question of most people, this is certainly most people. These were blacks in Washington, D.C. They dug it; they understood it perfectly.

Centola: So, it's just that most people usually aren't placed in that position, or they prefer not to be?

Miller: Or they prefer not to be!

Centola: But everyone could experience this same fate, this same tragic existence?

Miller: Sure. Absolutely everyone as far as social rank is concerned.

Centola: In an interview a few years ago, you said that Americans seem to have a "primordial fear of falling." I was wondering if you thought Americans, more than anyone else, have that feeling because it goes with the territory?

Miller: I think that that is more American than any other country, yeah, in my observation. I think we are more afraid of losing caste, losing our hard-won place in the middle class. People will kill for that. I think that that causes more racial hatred and hostility and fear than anything else. Incidentally, I regard racism as a class phenomenon. I was born in Harlem, and I saw it happen in Harlem—I think I did, anyway. That's been my reason for it: that blacks are not acceptable more for the fact that they are working-class or poor than because they are black. If in a short period of time by some miracle there were hundreds and hundreds of thousands of black professionals, middle-class people, the thing would begin to fade. We're seeing it now with the Arabs, the sheiks, the wealthy Arab who was formerly a creature of ridicule. Well, now he can come in and buy up a whole city. With a new class identity he starts to take on a new kind of persona, a new kind of dignity. It isn't so jokey any more to see somebody walking around in those funny clothes which might conceal millions.

Centola: So most people chase their American dreams because they know that success determines how much they are accepted by others.

Miller: No question about it.

Centola: In *Incident at Vichy,* Leduc tells the others as they await examination that they have been trained to die, to be willing victims for their persecutors. I'm wondering if he implies in that statement that death is often preferable to life for those who would have to live without illusions. And, once again, isn't such self-deception a peculiarly American trait? Haven't we been trained to see the world through rose-tinted glasses? Aren't we essentially a nation of people incapable of coping with reality?

Miller: Yes. I think that tremendous power does that to people, incidentally. The British did it for two centuries as their power got tremendous. They were able to enforce their wishes upon the world. So they wished more than they observed. I think they were primarily that way, and I think the Germans were able to do this once where they had the power to do it. It goes with power; it goes with the territory.

Centola: I'm going to take a different direction here. Some critics have complained about Charley's speech in the Requiem in *Death of a Salesman,* saying that it's out of character for a realist like Charley to be making sentimental speeches about dreams.

Miller: It's not even sentimental. You know that speech is almost a handbook of what you've got to think if you're going to be a salesman. Under the circumstances, of course, it is said over a grave, so naturally it is full of feeling and mourning. But it is objective information, so to speak; it is absolutely real. Those are the visionary qualities that make salesmen tick.

Centola: Aren't you also doing in this play what Fitzgerald does with Nick in his portrayal of Gatsby? In other words, you have a character who is fairly objective throughout the work make that statement over the grave because it can carry more weight coming from him, a realist.

Miller: You're right! That speech is the obverse of the early speech that Charley makes in the play to Willy when he says: "Why must everybody like you? Who liked J. P. Morgan?" Which is an absolutely dead-on, existentialist kind of way of looking at salesmanship. This is the obverse of it. He knows damn well what Willy was feeling; that's why he can make that speech to him. This is now said as the obverse of the other, but it's complementary. These are two halves of the same thing.

Centola: In an interview with Ronald Hayman some years ago, you defined fate as "high probability" and said that it is what happens "when a man starts out to do what he intends to do ... [and] creates forces which he never bargained for, but whose contradictions nevertheless spring directly from the force of his thrust." Would you say that this is the kind of fate that's in the background of plays like *All My Sons, Death of a Salesman,* and *The Price?*

Miller: Yes.

Centola: Many of the characters in these plays seem to believe that they have no free will. But don't they have free will and just fail to consider all the consequences when they commit themselves to certain courses of action?

Miller: Right. And I would add that it's all but impossible to take into consideration most of the time.

Centola: We can't be that farsighted?

Miller: No, because the possibilities are too complex, too complicated, too infinite.

Centola: But, eventually, we have to accept what we do; we can't say we are excused from responsibility because the consequence was beyond our realm of control.

Miller: Right. You started it. For me, the typical case of our time is the Oppenheimer thing. I use him as the symbol of the scientists who put together this ferocious world-ending trick hat. And what they were exercising was technical curiosity, a time-honored civilizing trait of mankind. And then it goes off, and as Oppenheimer says, he starts to quote Hindu scripture: "I've taken the shape of death. I started the dance and I end it by killing everyone."

Centola: I'm going to shift directions again. In *The Price,* Solomon says he would not know what to say to his daughter if she were to return from the grave. Isn't Solomon essentially saying that no one can transcend the bounds of human subjectivity?

Miller: That's a good way to put it.

Centola: Doesn't he imply that because each individual is totally and irremediably separated from the other, only each individual can take responsibility for what he is in life?

Miller: That's a very good way to put it. Yes. He accepts something there, doesn't he? He says, in effect: "I was the way I am; she is the way she was; and what happened was the inevitable result of that. So what could have changed it?"

Centola: "And if she comes back, I still can't change it. So just accept it as it is."

Miller: Right. There's a kind of a cosmic acceptance of the situation.

Centola: That kind of acceptance seems to occur in your plays where characters like Quentin, Leduc, Von Berg, or Solomon decide that they must accept what is and not try to mold reality to fit their perceptions of it.

Miller: Exactly. And from that comes not passivity but strength.

Centola: That sounds again very much like Sartre. Like you, he was also accused of being a pessimist, and he responded to the charge by saying: "I'm not a pessimist; I merely believe in optimistic toughness." Isn't that also what you're saying?

Miller: Right.

Centola: In *After the Fall* both Rose and Elsie seem to betray the men they love because they want to deny their complicity in their husbands' problems in order to maintain their own innocence, a counterfeit innocence that helps them see themselves as victims.

Miller: Those particular women feel that they did not participate in the decision making (if you want to objectify the whole thing), so they are not going to submit to the victimization. And that separation takes place, in effect saying: "You made your bed, now lie in it; I'm not going to get in there with you." It's a reassertion of separateness, incidentally.

Centola: With that kind of separateness, though, isn't there also some kind of betrayal?

Miller: Sure. It's inevitable because the implicit, although largely unannounced, larceny behind their relationship is that they were irrevocably joined. Right? And it turns out, they're not. It turns out that when the interests change, the arrangement has to change. This isn't cynicism, though, to me. It's just the way it is.

Centola: I see Maggie in that play as a perfect illustration of the individual who counterfeits her innocence to appear as the helpless victim of others. I know you have spoken about this in some of your essays.

Miller: Yeah, right.

Centola: Would you say that Maggie is guilty of bad faith, of lying to herself or of trying to see only the illusions, more or less?

Miller: Sure. In a way she's dying of the lie, as Quentin says to her. It's the only time in the play that he's absolutely right. She's a slave to the idea of being victimized. Oddly enough, it's a paradox that the awareness of being enslaved becomes the principle of the person. Instead of a key to freedom, it's a lock on the door. I guess it all comes down to a pact of nonrecognition with all human nature, which is what enslaves us all. And all these philosophical attempts are really, in one way or another, attempts toward a confrontation with the dialectic of how we operate.

Centola: So what she does is self-destructive because she makes herself be what she really doesn't want to be?

Miller: It's conformity to a perverse image. In one way or another, we're all involved with that, but for some people it's terminal.

Centola: In *After the Fall* you seem to suggest that the original Fall, the Biblical Fall, is perpetually reenacted with each individual's fall into consciousness, his conflict with others, his struggle with his egotism, and his fundamental choice between good and evil, or as you have called it, his choice between Cain's and Abel's alternatives. Do you think that with the fall into consciousness comes the dilemma of choosing to live either for oneself or for others?

Miller: Well, people are threatened with freedom; it's the reaction to the threat of freedom. The fall is the fall from the arms of God, the right to live, to eat, to be conscious that there exists all the world. It's the fall from nonconscious existence and from the pleasant and unconscious slavery of childhood and so on. The fall is the threat of freedom, of having to make choices, instead of having them made for you.

Centola: In a few different places, you say that man is in the society and society is in the man, just as the fish is in the water and the water is in the fish. That statement reminds me of Jung, and I was wondering if you believe his theory about the individual carrying around with him in the collective unconscious, deep within his psyche, the cargo of his ancestral past?

Miller: Yeah. I've often been tempted to believe that, although, of course, it's unprovable. And in my own case, I think, for example, I was never really a religious person in any conventional sense. I didn't even make sense out of the Bible until fairly recent years, if you can make sense out of the Bible. Yet, all of the ideas that we are talking about now are stemming from the Old Testament. The more I live, the more I think that somewhere down the line it poured into my ear, and I don't even know when or how. But I'm reading it again now, and I'm amazed at how embedded it is in me, even though, as I say, I never dealt with it objectively before.

Centola: Do you think that we also contain racial instincts?

Miller: Yeah, I think so. I think that they're not racial instincts; that's kind of a gross way, a gross measure of it, calling it a racial instinct. There is a culture that is in gestures, in speech, in temperament, and in the reactions of one to another, which is certainly so basic that it is the first thing probably a kid, I think, is taught. And it goes right into the irrational of the unconscious before the child even gets asleep. We call this some kind of an ethnic or a racial inheritance. It doesn't matter, but I don't see how either one is saying that.

Centola: That's interesting in light of recent studies which seem to prove that a very young child is extremely sensitive to his surroundings.

Miller: Oh, I have no doubt about that, no doubt about it. See, it's an ingenuous example of schizophrenic people, of mothers especially who tend to have those traits even though they might not break down. They look in the bloodstream for it, and maybe sometimes it is there. But there is a certain schizophrenic reaction to life which the child is subjected to or lives with. They're going to have a schizophrenic frame of reference. I don't see how you can avoid that. That's how that damn thing, I think, gets carried on from generation to generation. For a part of them there is a question about the blood and how the blood can be a problem suddenly. But there is a predisposition as soon as that—excuse the term—mother starts to infect each child or reality. How is it avoided? Well, we can't avoid that.

Centola: Is that why Quentin says something to the effect that the sins of the father are handed down to the sons?

Miller: Yeah. There's a truth in it. It's true. The older one gets, the more of one's parents one recognizes in oneself. You'd think it would be the opposite; it isn't. The more purified it becomes, the more obvious it becomes.

Centola: In a lot of your works, you deal with guilt and seem to suggest that guilt can become a type of bad faith if it provides an individual with an excuse for not acting or taking his life into his own hands.

Miller: Yeah, it's a cop-out—guilt—in one sense if it doesn't mean anything underneath to that person. Guilt is not guilt if it is conscious. It is then something even more sinister. But I suppose the way I perceive it is that guilt is a sense of unusable responsibility; it's a responsibility that can't be expressed, that can't be utilized for one reason or another. On the other hand, it is a way of self-paralysis. It's a many-faceted thing. It's self-love, but I don't want to go on with a list of what it is. But it may be the most complicated phenomenon that a society embeds in its citizens. It's the consent that one gives to superior power. It's the way that we police ourselves in the name of the greater power. I could go on and on and on about what it consists of.

Centola: Would you say that at the end of *After the Fall*, Quentin transforms his guilt into responsibility?

Miller: He at least sees the need and feels the strength to attempt to do that, yeah.

Centola: The fact that he accepts Holga's love and then their movement off the stage together certainly seem to symbolize that transformation.

Miller: Yeah, right. See, I think, too, what is resented in that play is that he refuses to settle with being guilty. This is where most people stop, because if you don't stop there then you've got to act. It would have been far more palatable if he shot himself or jumped into the river with her. I would add that *After the Fall*, the title, is probably—I didn't think of it then, but I was very moved years earlier by *The Fall* by Camus. In Camus's *The Fall* the man is guilty for not having acted to save a woman he never even saw or knew. And that's his fall. He recognizes all kinds of culpability, a species of responsibility, you might say, that was unacknowledged by his actions. And he's given up judging people, etc. The question in my play is what happens if you do go to the rescue. Does this absolve? Does this prevent the fall? Supposing he had run over to the bridge where he thought he heard someone fall in and had become involved with her and found out that she had an inexorable lust for destruction, at what point and when would he see wisdom?

Centola: The point at which one says to himself: "Self-determinism—everyone has to be responsible for himself."

Miller: Exactly!

Centola: I saw the connection between these two works, but I never saw it in these terms before.

Miller: That's why it's *After the Fall*.

Centola: In *Incident at Vichy*, do you choose to have the prisoners face their interrogations alone to underscore, through their physical separation from each other, the fact that man must ultimately confront absurdity alone?

Miller: I hadn't thought of it in those terms. Actually, it was—what you say is true—but it is constructed that way because that's the way it was done in France.

Centola: The play has a symbolic movement.

Miller: Well, a lot of these things turn out to be symbolic—these symbolic bureaucratic processes that they invent. They do it instinctively; they're the great instinctive behavioral psychologists.

Centola: Do the white feathers that escape from the Old Jew's bag in *Incident at Vichy* symbolize ineffectual religions and value systems that make one take a passive or resigned posture in the face of his persecution?

Miller: I'll tell you that I didn't know myself what was in the bag, and that when I suddenly saw that they were feathers, it was totally out of some subconscious pocket in my mind. Then sometime later I saw a film, *The Shop on Main Street,* which is a Czech film, about a little town in Bohemia where all the Jews are rounded up. And they're told to bring a few things; they don't know where they're going, but they're going to their deaths, of course. They're loaded on the trucks, and the whole town in devastated; that is, it is emptied out of all the Jews that live in this town. And there's a shot of the town square where a little while ago we saw this crowd of people assembled and thrown into the vehicles. And what's blowing around on the square is the feathers. And this was a kind of race memory of mine, quite frankly, because nothing like that ever happened in my family. My mother was born in this country; my father was brought over here at the age of six. But feathers—you see, you carry your bedding. It's the refugees' only possible property. It's light, it's warm, it's something he might sell if he had to, it's a touch of home, x, x, x; it has all kinds of uses. And also it's the plumage of birds that are blown about. They're weak things—it does have an aspect of weakness, but also of domesticity, an uprooted domesticity. Then once they're released, you can't capture them any more. And there's a pathetic quality to that: the fact that the old guy's clutching what to our minds would be a practically valueless bag of nothing, of air. It's his identity, though. There's a lot of feed into that symbol.

Centola: I identified it with religious systems because he just sits there praying instead of doing anything actively to try to change his situation.

Miller: He's transcended it; he's got one foot in heaven. He knows that this is the ancient persecutor, the face of hell, that comes in every generation, and this is his turn with him. And it's been happening forever, and probably will go on happening forever. And he's praying against it. With one eye or the other, he's got his eye on God, who's reaching out His hands to him.

Centola: But is that an effective way of dealing with that type of crisis?

Miller: It's not effective; it's the last gasp of his limited range of possibilities.

Centola: You present a lot of different characters in that play who have their own ways of coping with that crisis.

Miller: That's right.

Centola: But only Von Berg, after being enlightened by Leduc, takes the action that turns things around and gives him a momentary triumph over his oppressors.

Miller: Yeah, right.

Centola: Doesn't a similar triumph occur in *Playing for Time,* when Fania Fenelon refuses to play in the orchestra unless her friend is allowed to join her?

Miller: Right. Well, she's pressing it to the limit there.

Centola: Isn't her survival itself another expression of her resistance to her persecutors?

Miller: Yeah, well I guess that story is the story of the survival of one who has a picked identity of herself. This is the survival of an alienated woman who knows she is alienated and has a vision of an unalienated world.

Centola: How about one last question? Would you agree that affirmation in your plays stems from the fact that the individual has the potential for the kind of self-determinism that is found in Proctor's resistance in *The Crucible* and Von Berg's actions in *Incident at Vichy*?

Miller: Absolutely! Yes. I think, incidentally, that what you choose to call optimism is interesting. See, it's interesting, isn't it, that I'm generally thought of as a pessimist, and I've always denied it, even though most of the time I feel pessimistic, personally. But I find that the more I investigate my own feelings, the less capable I am of conceding that in truth there is no hope to the extent that one logically should lie down and let evil triumph, because there is too much evidence that I see of the will to live. It's everywhere. Maybe it's because I've lived for 25 years out here where if you look around, life is just overwhelming. It is simply overwhelming. It's also in my relationship with children; one sees that struggle in the child, his wish to be taught. If the lesson of life was that we are hopeless, we should have to teach children to breathe, and to struggle for hunger, to teach them to be hungry, to teach them to multiply; in other words, to awaken them to that tropism until death. But it's on the contrary. So you can see from that why I still have hope.

Centola: Thank you, Mr. Miller.

1984

Tennessee Williams's Legacy: An Eloquence and Amplitude of Feeling

So long as there are actors at work in the world, the plays of Tennessee Williams will live on. The autocratic power of fickle taste will not matter in his case; his texture, his characters, his dramatic personality are unique and are as permanent in the theatrical vision of this century as the stars in the sky.

It is usually forgotten what a revolution his first great success meant to the New York theater. *The Glass Menagerie* in one stroke lifted lyricism to its highest level in our theater's history, but it broke new ground in another way. What was new in Tennessee Williams was his rhapsodic insistence that form serve his utterance rather than dominating and cramping it. In him the American theater found, perhaps for the first time, an eloquence and an amplitude of feeling. And driving on this newly discovered lyrical line was a kind of emotional heroism; he wanted not to approve or disapprove but to touch the germ of life and to celebrate it with verbal beauty.

His theme is perhaps the most pervasive in American literature, where people lose greatly in the very shadow of the mountain from whose peak they might have had a clear view of God. It is the romance of the lost yet sacred misfits, who exist in order to remind us of our trampled instincts, our forsaken tenderness, the holiness of the spirit of man.

Despite great fame, Williams never settled into a comfortable corner of the literary kitchen. It could only have been the pride born of courage that kept him at playwriting after the professional theater to which he had loaned so much dignity, so much aspiration, could find no place for his plays. But he never lost his humor and a phenomenal generosity toward other artists. A few months before his death, I had a letter from him about a play of mine that had had some of the most uncomprehending reviews of my career. I had not seen Tennessee in years, but out of darkness came this clasp of a hand, this sadly laughing voice telling me that we had both lived to witness a chaos of spirit, a deafness of ear and a blindness of eye, and that one carried on anyway.

His audience remained enormous, worldwide. Hundreds of productions of his plays have gone on each year—but not on the Broadway that his presence had glorified. He would end as he had begun, on the outside looking in—as he once put it, scratching on the glass. But of course, past the suffering the work remains, the work for which alone he lived his life, the gift he made to his actors, his country, and the world.

1984

The Face in the Mirror:
Anti-Semitism Then and Now

Some part of the genesis of this novel, *Focus*, must lie in the Brooklyn Navy Yard where I worked the night shift in the shipfitting department during World War II, one of some 60,000 men and a few women from every ethnic group in New York. It is no longer possible to decide whether it was my own Hitler-begotten sensitivity or the anti-Semitism itself that so often made me wonder whether, when peace came, we were to be launched into a raw politics of race and religion, and not in the South, but in New York. In any case, whatever the actual level of hostility to Jews that I was witnessing, it was vastly exacerbated in my mind by the threatening existence of Nazism and the near absence among the men I worked with fourteen hours a day of any comprehension of what Nazism meant—we were fighting Germany essentially because she had allied herself with the Japanese who had attacked us at Pearl Harbor.

Moreover, it was by no means an uncommon remark that we had been maneuvered into this war by powerful Jews who secretly controlled the federal government. Not until Allied troops had broken into the German concentration camps and the newspapers published photographs of the mounds of emaciated and sometimes partially burned bodies was Nazism really disgraced among decent people and our own casualties justified. (It is a fiction, in my opinion, that national unity around the war reached very deep in a great many people in those times.)

I cannot glance through this novel without once again feeling the sense of emergency that surrounded the writing of it. As far as I knew at the time, anti-Semitism in America was a closed if not forbidden topic for fiction—certainly no novel had taken it as a main theme, let alone the existence within the Catholic priesthood of certain militants whose duty and pleasure was to stoke up Jew-hate. When one is tempted to say that everything in the world has gotten worse, here is one shining exception.

I was reminded of this only recently when, quite by chance, I happened to tune in on a local Connecticut radio station and heard a Catholic priest trying to reason with an obviously anti-Semitic man who was laying the blame for several bombings of Jewish homes and synagogues in the Hartford area on the Jews themselves. There was a widespread search going on for the perpetrators, so the man had called in to the priest's talk program to offer his ideas as to who might have been responsible. He had no doubt it was somebody whom a Jew had mistreated, either one of his employees, or somebody who had bought some defective item from him, or someone he had bilked out of money. Or maybe it was the work of the client of a Jewish lawyer outraged at having been defrauded. There were, he thought, all sorts of interesting possibilities since the Jews, as everyone knew, have a habit of defrauding and exploiting their workers, and in general have no respect for right and wrong and feel responsible only to one another. (The arsonist was caught some weeks later—a mentally disturbed young Jew.)

I had not heard this litany since the 1930s and early '40s. But here it was again, as though freshly minted, brand new discoveries which the caller was supremely confident everyone knew perfectly well but thought it bad manners to talk about in public. And such was the confidence of his manner that he soon had the poor priest on the ropes, and could assert with utmost self-assurance that he was simply being factual and not anti-Semitic.

The differences now, of course, are that no Hitler stands at the head of the greatest armed force in the world vowing the destruction of the Jewish people, and there is an Israel which, notwithstanding all the futility of much of its present vision, is still capable of defending the right of Jews to exist. *Focus,* in short, was written when a sensible person could wonder if such a right had reality at all.

It is inevitable that one should wonder whether anything like the situation in this novel could recur, and it is a question no one can answer. In the Fifties and Sixties I might have persuaded myself that its recrudescence was not likely, and I would have based such reasoning on what had begun to seem a truly profound shift in the world's conception of the Jew. For one thing, anti-Semitism, linked as it was to totalitarianism, was being viewed as one of the keys to the dismantling of democracy and at least in its political forms was no longer an option for people who, whatever their private grievance against Jews, were still committed to the liberal state. By the end of World War II, anti-Semitism was no longer a purely personal matter.

But there was also the shift, however paradoxical, in the perception of the Jew as a consequence of the first successful decades of Israel's life as a state. In a word, the Jew was no longer a shadowy, ghettoized mystery, but a farmer, a pilot, a worker. Throwing off the role of victim, he stood up and was suddenly comprehensible as one of the world's dangerous peoples—dangerous in the conventional military and characterological sense. He was like everybody else now and for a time it would be difficult to imagine the traditional anti-Semitic attitudes feeding themselves on warriors rather than passive victims. For a time, Israeli technical and military missions were spread across Africa and her example seemed about to become an inspiration for any poor country attempting to enter this century.

This exemplary condition was not to last. By an irony so gigantic as to sweep the mind into the explications of mysticism, Israel has turned in the world's perception from a land settled by pastoral socialists and internationalist soldier-farmers into a bellicose armed camp whose adamant tribal defensiveness has inevitably hardened against neighboring peoples to the point of fanaticism. Jewish aloneness is back, but now it is armed. One more impersonation has been added to the long historic list that supplied so many contradictory images; Einstein and Freud and/or Meyer Lansky or another gangster; Karl Marx and/or Rothschild; the Prague communist chief Slansky running Czechoslovakia for Stalin and/or the Jew Slansky hanging by the neck as tribute to Stalin's paranoid anti-Semitism.

Focus is much involved with impersonations. Its central image is the turning lens of the mind of an anti-Semitic man forced by his circumstances to see anew his own relationships to the Jew. To a certain degree, it seems to me that Newman's step toward his human identification with some part of the Jewish situation has indeed occurred, at least in sectors of the democratic world, since the mid-Forties, and so the projection of such a change as occurs in this story was not altogether romantic and unlikely.

But in the four decades since I wrote *Focus,* new perspectives on the Jewish situation have opened up from surprising angles. In particular, the attitudes of some Asian peoples toward certain successful strangers settled in their midst, for example the Chinese in Thailand and the Vietnamese in the Cambodia of Sihanouk before the Vietnamese occupation of that country. It used to amuse me to hear descriptions in Bangkok of the local Chinese which were so exactly similar to what people used to say about Jews, and doubtless still do in the West: "The Chinese really have only one loyalty, to one another. They are very clever, study harder in school, always try to be first in their studies. There are lots of Chinese bankers in Thailand, too many; in fact, it was a real mistake to give Chinese Thai citizenship, because they have secretly taken control of the banking system. Besides, they are spies for China, or would be in time of war. Actually, what they are after is a revolution in Thailand (despite their being bankers and capitalists), so that we would end up as dependents of China."

Many of the same contradictory things were said about Vietnamese who had been settled in Cambodia for generations. The similarities in these two instances were striking—the Chinese in Thailand and the Vietnamese in Cambodia were very frequently visible as merchants, landlords of stores and small houses, peddlers, and an inordinate number of them were teachers and lawyers and intellectuals, enviable in a peasant country. They, so to speak, visibly administered the injustices of life as far as the average Thai or Cambodian could see, since it was to them that one paid the rent or the limitlessly inflated prices of food and other necessities of life, and one could see with one's own eyes how soft a life they led as intellectuals.

It is important also that the host people characterized themselves as somehow more naïve than these strangers, less interested in moneymaking, and more "natural"—that is, less likely to become intellectuals. In the Soviet Union, and the lands ruled by her arms and culture in Eastern Europe, the same sort of accusations are made openly or implicitly. *Focus* is a view of anti-Semitism that is deeply social in this particular sense: the Jew is seen by the anti-Semitic mind as the carrier of that same alienation the indigenous people resent and fear, the same conniving exploitation. I would only add that they fear it because it is an alienation they feel in themselves, a not-belonging, a helplessly antisocial individualism that belies fervent desires to be a serving part of the mythic whole, the sublime national essence. They fear the Jew as they fear the real, it often seems. And perhaps this is why it is too much to expect a true end to anti-Semitic feelings. In the mirror of reality, of the unbeautiful world, it is hardly reassuring and requires much strength of character to look and see oneself.

1984

Thoughts on a Burned House

In the weeks that followed, I would be surprised at the dimness of my reaction when our daughter called us in China to say that the house had burned. "But a lot of it is okay. My room is pretty much gone, but yours is only sort of half. And the dining room is just smoked up, and the front parlor. But the living room is pretty much sort of disappeared, but the kitchen's okay. . . ." None of this registered; it simply dropped into my velvet-lined shock pocket.

Some ten days later, driving up to the house with my wife, I still wondered at the way I had so quickly canceled the place out of my heart, so it seemed, a place I had lived in for nearly thirty years, a home full of our living and our junk. How strange; all the second- and third-floor windows nailed shut with plywood sheets, and long smoke stains on the white paint above them. The house looked blinded, the victim of an attack by a wild maniac who had thrown everything out the windows. Piles of bedding, window frames, doors, broken glass, lay vomited out on the front lawn. The garage was stuffed with burned couches, chairs, cushions, trunks; piled high with boxes, which turned out to be filled with books, an old pipe rack hung from a lawnmower handle, a couple of partially burned dolls, steel file drawers with their contents obscenely displayed. The fire department had done a fine job saving paintings and anything else that could be quickly moved outside, but my mind said to forget it all, truck the whole mess to the dump.

Inside, the silence of death in the black stench of ashes and the damp of water-soaked leather and woolen carpet. The back veranda, with its view of endless hills, was buried under mounds of our scorched clothes, silk scarves, brocaded jackets, evening gowns, shoes curled by water. From the edge of the vast hole in the living room floor, I looked down at the dark cellar where it had all started—in a failed oil burner cut-off valve. Overhead, the great ceiling beams were cooked, charred black. The floor varnish, according to the firemen, had bubbled in 1800-degree heat. The hi-fi had melted; I looked at its littered insides, thinking of all the music that had come out of it, and thought of the word *garble*. It had been a fine-sounding set, bought in the Sixties. The TV cabinet had imploded into a Daliesque hourglass with a square dead eye. How silly to treasure things. I had no link to this charred ruin of a room; the house I had known had swiftly receded into memory.

It was black dark on the second floor, with all the windows covered by plywood, and the water smell was stronger, ashen. Our bed stood on edge, spring coils melted, the fibers all gone. My flashlight caught flecks of our life here. The wrath of fire had simply eaten up my wife's closetful of clothes, leaving nothing but a few wire hangers and shreds of the shoulders of garments, soles of shoes. In one of the side tables, though, I found amid the trash a leather box in which I had kept a gift, a gold watch thin as a quarter. Surprisingly, the box opened, and there was the watch, and I wound it and it ticked. Leather and wood, it turned out, protect better than steel, which conducts heat.

The house would have to be gutted back to the frame itself, the timbers sandblasted to remove the char, and a special paint sprayed on the inside of the clapboards to kill off the smoke smell. Now, each day, two masked men with crowbars and sledges smashed the place apart and threw it out the windows. Trim installed two hundred years ago groaned as it was pulled apart, panes of old glass with rainbow bubbles were ground underfoot, chestnut flooring screeched against the old square-cut nails as it was yanked up. In less than two weeks, two centuries had been dropped onto the lawn; an anonymous skeleton was left. Yet it was interesting to inspect the immensely weighty framing, which, by custom in those early days, was probably joined together on the ground, tenon into mortise, then raised in a single day by family and neighbors. Washington was still fighting the French then, at the borders of the Great Lakes. In some walls were corncobs for insulation; horsehairs stuck out of the plaster. How much labor has been bombed to pieces in this century! Slowly, over days, the mortal wounds of the house and its resurrection, rather than thoughts of our possessions, began to move within me.

I was unprepared for the shock I felt when the architect builder, in his offhand way, implied we ought to think about building a new modern house instead of restoring this one. The impulse to fill this frame with life again was more powerful than I would have imagined, especially when we really did not need so large a house any more. Then it occurred to me, for the first time, that in some hidden sense we had been borrowing a history here and had unknowingly enlisted in its continuation. And it was not a question of sentiment, I thought, but of something else. Absurd as it sounded to me, I only now thought of the fact that I had spent more than a quarter of my life here. Still, I could not say precisely why I could not think of abandoning what now was little more than a framework of three boxes, set one on top of the other under a roof, with an immense chimney in the center supporting the whole thing.

The bachelor farmer I had bought the place from was the last of his long line stretching back to Washington's army. For some years I had lived down the road and envied the cool breeze that always seemed to blow through the line of grand maples in front of this house at the top of the rise. When the farmer's mother died, at the age of ninety-three, he wanted to sell right away and start enjoying life at sixty-four, and he immediately took off with my purchase money to Florida, to die of lung cancer six months later.

I began to wonder whether there were many left who would recall him any more. Or the barn, so neglected and filthy, where I had discovered a faded slip of pink paper nailed up over the Monel milk tank, a typed note from the county inspector: "Your milk temperature is still too high. Floor has not been hosed down. Cobwebs still everywhere. What do you intend to do about this?" Underneath, scrawled with a blunt pencil, the reply, "Stick it up your ass." Ah, tradition! Up in the dark windowless attic I would find a wooden stool beside a large spinning wheel, and a great loom with a five-foot span, at which the women must have worked through the winters in a windowless darkness and freezing cold, unless the original chimney had had an opening up there. And then there was the shoebox full of postcards that turned up in the cellar.

They were posted by the farmer during World War I from his army camp in California. "Have just come back from Los Angeles. Pie 15 cents bread five per loaf milk five per qt. Yrson Lewis," said one. Another read: "Been to Los Angeles again. Yrson Lewis." Another: "Have been to nearby town. Very pleasant. Pie 10 cents milk ten" (up five from Los Angeles) "nice grapes cheap. Swam. Yrson Lewis." Another: "Am feeling fine now. Out of quarantine." (Quarantine? Had he been to Los Angeles once too often?) "Say we'll be home by November or thereabouts. Yrson Lewis." Not a bad war.

One day we had to choose the new windows, and the most efficient for insulation and letting in light were the single-pane type. But they would undo the authentic colonial look of the house. And so I found myself recalling the house when I'd bought it. The great old baking oven-fireplace had been removed after World War I, when labor-saving kerosene heaters were the rage; a steep stairway had been plunked into the living room for access to the second floor, where the brother and his wife had an apartment—electric kitchen and all—while the bachelor lived below with Mother. A concrete front porch was stuck out the end of the house nearest the road, so that Mother could sit and watch the one or two cars and wagons passing each day, and indeed a whole kitchen wing had been added in 1881—I found the date in chalk on a beam exposed by our rebuilding nearly thirty years ago.

What exactly was the continuity in this so-American place? In my first weeks here I discovered, under a pile of old hay, four enormous gilt-framed family portraits, photographs of two stern, heavily bearded farmers and two Victorian, high-busted women, and I offered them to the farmer's elder brother, who lived in the next village. Stopping by one day, he looked at them and said, "Oh yes, there's Grandpa and Grandma, and Father and Mother. Yes, indeed." It did my heart good to see the warmth of recognition in his seventy-odd-year-old face, but when I offered to load them into the car for him, he gave me a look of surprise that was close to shock, and soon drove off, and I no longer recall exactly what I did with them.

I suppose what is continuous is change. At least in this instance, the only tradition is the memory of it. This place has gone through one more revision of many, and it is, I think, more beautiful than it ever was—certainly it is more efficient, which is a form of beauty. Nevertheless, nothing prevents one from imagining the unknown, unknowable generations who watched the same march of night across these hills and heard the same wind whispering under the eaves.

1984

Dinner with the Ambassador

In March, Harold Pinter and I went to Turkey for a week on behalf of the International PEN Club. We made the visit not primarily to conduct an investigation of human rights—an impossibility in so short a stay—but to demonstrate to the country's writers and artists and to its political prisoners that the outside world cares about what is happening to them. It was to be an act of moral solidarity by the members of International PEN, and we hoped it might also have an effect on the country's military government.

We had wanted to talk to people of all political views, including Prime Minister Turgut Ozal and the martial law commander of Istanbul, Gen. Necit Torumtay. The prime minister was in Saudi Arabia, however, and the commander declined to see us, saying that the government is now controlled by Parliament—nonsense, since the military runs the country. We did meet with publishers and editors of conservative newspapers, who more or less support the regime. All of them, however, said that under censorship the truth about touchy issues could not be printed. We also attended the trial of a lawyer who had defended the Turkish Peace Association, a banned group which used to lobby for nuclear disarmament and détente, and we spoke with people who have been jailed and tortured without being accused of any act. We went to a dinner in my honor at the American ambassador's residence. Apart from the government-imposed news blackout on our press conference at the end of the trip, that dinner turned out to be the climax of the week.

It is important to understand that the 1980 military coup in Turkey was preceded by two years of terrorism, which had piled up some five thousand dead. At times, as many as twenty people a day were killed, and by all accounts the country appeared to be on the verge of civil war. Justification for the military takeover rests on this fact, which no one seems to deny. But some observers, including Suleyman Demirel, the prime minister at the time of the coup, find it suspicious that although seemingly helpless to curb the violence for two years, the military brought an amazing peace within a matter of weeks after taking power. In Demirel's view, the generals deliberately allowed the chaos to expand until their intervention would be gratefully accepted. Support for the military government is still based on fears that the violence will return.

A former high-level government official told us that there are currently about two thousand political prisoners in Turkey. In addition, seven thousand people are said to have been arrested as terrorists; most of them are under the age of twenty-four, and some are as young as sixteen. Many of these young people were picked up on the street for scrawling slogans on walls or arrested for harboring others in their homes. It is generally believed that about forty-eight "terrorists" have been hanged and that seventy more are awaiting execution.

The Turkish Constitution permits the police under martial law to detain a citizen for forty-five days without notifying his family or lawyers, and most instances of torture take place during that time. We met a respected Turkish publisher who had been arrested with his brother and had seen him beaten to death. In spite of his anguish as he related the details, he insisted on conveying the horror to us step by step. He told how he and his brother had been put in a van and, on their way to the prison, had been struck repeatedly by four guards. He believed he had survived because he had been handcuffed with his arms in front of him, allowing him to use them to protect his head. His brother's hands were cuffed behind his back, so he was helpless. When they arrived at the jail, the guards pulled them out and kicked his brother as he lay on the ground until he stopped moving.

Because of his prestige, the publisher was able to sue the police for assault. He won the case, but the four guards were sentenced to a few years in jail. Their superiors, who had ordered the arrests, were not mentioned in the proceedings.

We had looked forward to meeting U.S. ambassador Robert Strausz-Hupe, if only to hear the official U.S. view on the situation in Turkey. The dinner took place the day after we spent a deeply moving evening with the fiancée of Aly Taygun, a young director whose innovative work had created much excitement at Yale University's drama school a couple of years ago, and the young wife of a painter who, like Taygun, is serving an eight-year jail sentence for his membership in the Turkish Peace Association. The second woman's hope that we might help her husband in some way prompted her to show us several sepia drawings he had handed her during the five-minute visits she is permitted every two weeks. The drawings, mostly portraits of her, were packed with an almost palpable sensuous power.

When I found myself momentarily alone with the ambassador, I immediately began telling him about the imprisoned artist and his wife. To my surprise and pleasure, he was at once caught up in the story. He wanted to know their names, implying he would inquire about them. It seemed a good beginning. The ambassador, a spry, diminutive man in his eighties, is famous for his absolute deference to the Turkish military, with whom he has completely identified American interests. All I knew about him was that he had worked as a campaign adviser to Barry Goldwater. I learned later that he had been a professor at the University of Pennsylvania and has been considered a leading thinker of the far right.

That night he displayed a cultivated, literary air, not at all the image of a fiercely militant right-winger. He is an Austrian, naturalized in 1938; his rosy complexion and full head of silver hair, his blue baggy eyes with their soft drooping lids, his natty gray suit and sharp intelligence all suggested Vienna and civilized coffeehouse discussions. As we moved toward the dinner table, he confided to me that there might well be a declaration of amnesty in Turkey in the near future, giving the impression of cautious liberalism. "We can't push them too far," he said of the military. "We don't want to lose them."

Taking my seat across the table from the ambassador and to the right of his wife, I thought how functional the elegance of the table was, as though to protect power by enforcing good manners and empty conversations. The image of the imprisoned painter would not go away, but could such an unpleasant thought be introduced at a dinner given by my country's ambassador in my honor?

Harold Pinter was seated on the same side of the table as I was, half a dozen places down. The soup had hardly been served when I heard his strong baritone above the general babble and caught in it the flow of a quickened mind. On my left, Mayrose Strausz-Hupe, a beautiful woman who looks less than half her husband's age (the daughter, she volunteered, of a Ceylonese Ford dealer), was drawing a map of her country on the tablecloth with her fingernail, showing the demarcations between the religious factions that had been tearing the country apart in the years since the British left.

As the roast veal was served, Pinter's voice rose higher, his British diction sprouting angry ratchets. I could hear that he was engaged in a cross-table discussion with Nazli Ilicak, a widely read columnist whom we had met at the offices of her husband's newspaper, *Tercuman,* some days earlier, and Frank Trinka, the American deputy chief of mission, an unsmiling, tight-bodied man, with tinted glasses and a knife-like self-assurance. I could not make out what Pinter was saying, but I could hear Ilicak and the deputy chief replying, "That's your viewpoint. We have to see it in the round. You are only seeing part of it ...". The ambassador, forking his veal, did not even glance in Pinter's direction as the playwright's voice reached the volume of an M.P. in the House of Commons. Madame Ambassador continued with her geographical drawing, maintaining an admirable aplomb. Her husband was trying to engage his neighbor in conversation, when Pinter, with open rage, shouted across the table at Ilicak, "That is an insult and was meant as an insult and I throw it back in your face!" As I learned later, she had told Pinter that although the Turks would have to remain and face the realities of their country, he could go home and put it all into a profitable play.

The ambassador quickly tapped his crystal water glass with a silver spoon and brought silence. "I wish to welcome Mr. Miller as our honored guest," he said, and went on to extol my work in the theater. He ended with a glance around the table which came to rest only for a moment on Pinter. "This demonstrates that all viewpoints are welcome here," he said. And then, pointing to the floor of his residence, his voice thick with emotion: "Here is democracy. Right here, and we are proud of it. Imagine this happening in a communist country!" Whereupon he thanked me for coming.

I understood that it was up to me to respond to the toast. Protocol must be observed, and the ambassador had been an engaging host. But as we sat there in the brightly lit room, an image popped into my mind: the painter's wife staring at an empty pillow; her husband lying on his mattress hardly a mile away, with six more years of prison ahead of him, all for an offense that, had I been a Turk, I surely would have committed myself.

I began by quietly thanking the ambassador for the dinner and the welcome, at which he looked relieved. "Whatever our political differences," I said, "we share the same faith in democracy." The ambassador nodded appreciatively. I went on:

As democracy enhances candor, my speech being without fear, it is impossible for us to ignore what we have witnessed in Turkey. We are playwrights, and playwrights are different from poets or novelists or perhaps any other kind of writer. We deal in the concrete.... An actor has to be moved from point A to point B, and so you cannot act in general, only in particular. We do not know what the situation in Turkey was last year, so perhaps it is better now, as is claimed. We don't know what it will be in the future. We do know concretely what we have seen, and what we have seen has no tangency with any democratic system in Western Europe or the United States. I wrote in *The Crucible* about people who were jailed and executed not for their actions but for what they were alleged to be thinking. So it is here; you have hundreds in jail for their alleged thoughts. We are told that Turkey is moving closer and closer to democracy, and that may turn out to be so, no one can say, but what it is now is a military dictatorship with certain merciless and brutal features. We are helping Turkey, and I am not saying we should not; but the real strength of a state in the last analysis is the support of her people, and the question is whether the United States is inadvertently helping to alienate the people by siding so completely with those who have deprived them of their elementary rights. Not a single action is alleged against the hundreds of Peace Association people in prison.

As I continued, I thought I saw the eyes of the ambassador glaze with astonishment or horror. But at the same time, he seemed to be listening to a kind of news: not political news, for he knew better than I did the state of affairs there, but news of an emotion, an outrage. After twenty minutes I ended my speech:

There isn't a Western lawyer who could come to this country and see what is happening in these military courts who would not groan with despair. The American part here ought to be the holding up of democratic norms, if only as a goal, instead of justifying their destruction as the only defense against chaos.

The ambassador turned, gazed at the faces around the silent table and asked Erdal Inonu, son of a former president and prime minister and head of a political party, if he would respond to my remarks. Inonu, sixty, balding and squinting, a man with a gentle face and long hands which he softly clasped above the table, said that in general he could not help agreeing with my views and wanted to add his welcome to that of the ambassador. I could hardly believe this apparent victory. The ambassador gestured toward Ilicak; she simply shook her head, her eyes rounded in shock. A bearded journalist was then invited to comment; he chose simply to rub his hands together, smile and welcome me to Turkey (though Pinter later revealed that this man had exchanged approving glances with him while I was speaking). And so, with no more takers, we all rose, as the ambassador said something to the effect that it had been a fascinating dinner. Before I could stop myself, I added, "This is one you won't forget soon," to which the ambassador responded with an uncertain smile.

The company adjourned to the sitting room for coffee, and I sought out the deputy chief, sensing that he occupied the center of power in the place. But I had hardly sat down when once again I heard the awesome baritone of Harold Pinter. Near the entry hall, Pinter was just turning away from the ambassador, who, half his size, was shouting something and walking abruptly toward an astonished guest. Pinter came directly to me and said proudly, "I have insulted your ambassador and have been asked to go."

Forced to be practical by Pinter's visible emotion, I wondered about transportation and found a guest whom we had met at a gathering of Peace Association supporters. He was happy to share his car, but the French ambassador intervened, at the risk of offending Strausz-Hupe, his colleague and friend, and offered to drive us to his residence. On the way out to the black Peugeot, Pinter explained that the ambassador had remarked that there can always be a lot of opinions about anything, and he had replied, "Not if you've got an electric wire hooked to your genitals." The ambassador had stiffened and snapped, "Sir, you are a guest in my house!" Whereupon Pinter had concluded he had been thrown out. Pinter was brimming with admiration for my peroration, as I was for his righteous indignation, without which I could not have launched my twenty-minute speech. We decided we ought to form a team that would visit American embassies around the world.

Throughout our stay we had declined interviews, promising instead to hold a press conference on our last day. It took place in the building of the Journalists' Association in Istanbul, and was attended by twenty-five or thirty men and women and a television crew from United Press International. What we said at the press conference was more or less what we had said at the ambassador's dinner. We understood that Turkish journalists would be forbidden to print more than scraps of such opinions, but we felt we had to speak candidly. The next day, in London, we learned that reporting about the press conference had been banned by the government and that an investigation was to be launched into the whole visit. But news of it has nevertheless penetrated the prisons, as we have indirectly learned, and has brought some hope that the world has not forgotten these people. Unhappily, Prime Minister Ozal could stand before the Washington Press Club a few weeks ago and declare there are no political prisoners in Turkey without causing a ripple in his audience. There is nothing farther away from Washington than the entire world.

1985

The Mad Inventor of Modern Drama

It wouldn't have been very difficult to dislike August Strindberg, even to hate him. As a friend he was insupportable, inevitably turning with deadly suspicion on those who helped him; as a lover he was lethal; as a husband and father unpredictable, to say the least. Olof Lagercrantz does not stoop to sparing his subject and perhaps that is why, by the last chapters of his absorbing and profound biography of the great nineteenth-century Swedish author, the question of admiration or condemnation simply ceases to exist. In his life's struggles Strindberg regarded himself as paradigmatic, mankind's leading edge cutting into the future, and he is one of the rare instances of a man with such a conviction who turned out to be right.

The impact of his dramatic method, reflected in his many plays, most notably *The Father* (1887), *Miss Julie* (1888), and *The Dance of Death* (1900), is probably greater and less acknowledged than that of any other modern writer. If his plays are much less frequently produced than Ibsen's, his playwriting personality, his way of approaching reality, is evidenced far more deeply and more frequently in our contemporary theater. Strindberg struck strongly into O'Neill, is quite directly mirrored in Beckett and Pinter, in Tennessee Williams and Edward Albee. Writing before Freud was published, he wanted to offer, in Mr. Lagercrantz's words, "the pure naked truth." And this meant his entering into the world of the subconscious, where the sexual encounter especially was a fight to the death, a world where the mother did not nurture but suffocated and destroyed her offspring, a world where domination (usually female) was the key to life. And, of course, it is this digging the unconscious for its terrors, its lawless desires, and its ultimately creative thrusts that has provided the fodder of literature in this century. If Ibsen was the revolutionary, seeking new, refurbished social institutions to order mankind, Strindberg was the rebel for whom no order would ever be true enough.

Married three times—each time disastrously—involved with women who would appear fairly undisguised as figures in his plays, Strindberg was a walking scandal from his first burst onto the literary scene with *The Red Room* (1879), his autobiographical novel, to his death in 1912 at the age of 63. It is no mean feat to encompass, as Mr. Lagercrantz has done, the life of an author as busy as Strindberg must have been with his train of personal catastrophes—a manifestly mad man and yet the author of over fifty volumes of plays, poetry, histories, political and cultural commentary, scientific and pseudoscientific monographs and speculations on the occult. One of the great virtues of this fascinating biography is its level-headed acceptance of Strindberg's impossibly paradoxical nature. He was certainly insane for long spells, actually striking with a knife at invisible enemies behind his back, lying perfectly still "in state" as though dead, a paranoid given to great swings of mood from exultation to the contemplation of suicide in the space of a few hours.

Mr. Lagercrantz, a Swedish poet, critic, and editor, in effect considers insanity not quite as aberration but as integral to the insights of the man's art and of his invention of so much that has come to seem modern in the theater. He shows Strindberg both split by his madness and simultaneously observing his own delusions. He was a triumphantly unhappy man, often unsure when he was living in life or in one of his plays, and part of his modernism springs quite probably from his awareness that he was dipping his pen directly into his unconscious where truth is of a kind that is unarguable. His emotional nakedness is modern, his blatantly confessional and autobiographical style, his having obviously witnessed what he was trying to express. Part of the persuasiveness of his plays is that their truths seemed to be driving him crazy.

Thus his dramatic method is obsessive, an endlessly repeated drumming on a kind of monomaniac and fearsome vision. If O'Neill did not consciously imitate this feature, he paralleled it, but at far vaster length, Strindberg's major plays being quite short and for many mercifully so. For even in his own time, when the perverse news he brought was fresh and new, audiences often laughed in the wrong places because he was carrying things much too far. Nor, with the possible exception of *Miss Julie,* was he able to leaven the spectral unreality of his dialogue with a depth of characterization. In any meaningful sense there are no characters in his plays; there are lethal relationships, concatenations that illuminate the whole inside of Strindberg's head, if nothing else, a head that was filled with the fear and hatred of womankind.

In any other man without the physique of a horse and nerves of piano wires, it would have been a fear that might have perhaps left us with a play or two or a brilliant essay followed by the mourning silence of a brain sick to death. But, as Mr. Lagercrantz repeatedly demonstrates, the fecund Strindberg not only suffered what by most definitions would be madness, but managed it like a conductor managing an orchestra. It makes his suffering no less real and painful to say that it was always being turned over and over by the bloody fingers of his mind, unceasingly searching out the artistic possibilities inside his explosions.

Yet Mr. Lagercrantz sees the playwright's unbalanced mental state as something less than a self-contained phenomenon. Strindberg, the third of six children born to a Stockholm steamship merchant and his wife, matured into a Sweden that was tearing up its roots in the past and becoming increasingly "developed," to use a modern term, which is to say that people were becoming more and more anonymous and the solaces of religion less useful. Reason and progress, as elsewhere, were the lures to self-completion and happiness, and it was Strindberg's intellectual as well as temperamental choice to strike out at what he thought of as the prison of the rational. Nietzsche would then be his brother-in-arms, supporting his claims to lead the anti-bourgeois revolution to come.

Strindberg apparently hated Ibsen, especially for his elevating women to heroic stature but also, one suspects, as a competing prophet. Yet Ibsen, the feminist, kept Strindberg's picture hanging over his desk, and it is possible to imagine why. Both men were truth-seekers in a world perpetually chained by hypocrisy and by denial of the perverse in nature and, with it, a denial of the human potential. Strindberg took his role as social critic with intense seriousness, seeing himself in one of his poems as the fireman coming to save the burning house. But "you prefer to die in your burning house to being roused by one who does not belong to the brigade." It may be, I think, that Strindberg's paranoia was also his weapon against social resistance to his ideas, for he was in fact quite alone against the self-satisfaction and inertia of the Swedish society of his time.

Inevitably, his social context having vastly changed with time, he has come to seem a merely visceral playwright and a self-confronter, but he thought of himself as a social prophet and a healer, a brother to the Paris Commune of 1871. George Bernard Shaw perceived him that way too, and until 1886 Strindberg thought of himself as a socialist. His later development, not unlike O'Neill's, was toward the occult, the Swedenborgian mysticism that would support work like *The Ghost Sonata* and the other so-called Chamber Plays written for small audiences of adventurers into the unknown. One wonders, indeed, whether Strindberg was not right in claiming himself as the first of the modern writers if only because he came to destroy the linear-thinking drama of cause and effect, the story moving from point to provable point. His drama is the conflict of essences, not characters, and it lives where the sun hardly rises and a perpetual twilight reigns. Indeed, his longing for an ultimate, superhuman world of causation lends his work a tragic grandeur at times, quite as though it were an effort to scale human limits.

Of Mr. Lagercrantz's book it must be said that a certain telegraphic style may make the opening chapter too factually dense for the non-specialist, but the writing soon relaxes and one finally feels in the presence of the ultimate Strindberg biography. Maybe more important than any other of its qualities is its refusal to regard the writer's novels, poems, essays, and plays as "nothing but" some kind of barely disguised reportage of his life experiences. This would be a powerful temptation in a biography of a writer like Strindberg who lived in a panic of libel and self-incrimination. Everyone knew who his characters "really were," but the gossip is gone and his art, in the end, is what endures.

And it has endured, quite probably, because the hallucinatory world Strindberg saw seems much closer now to being real. We really walk the moon, and with the press of a button can really crack the planet, and if we have mastered the physics of this magical power, the morals of it all are, if anything, farther from us than from Strindberg who, mad as he was, believed that his labors were essentially moral and in God's service. Or at least should be. He could be vile, hypocritical, opportunistic, violent, but one cannot avoid the hopefulness in him, of which his boundless creativity was the manifestation. Mr. Lagercrantz, rather than turning this mass of paradox into a monument, has brought him alive. His is a wonderful biography, worthy of a maddeningly foolish, wrong, and presciently wise writer who was one of the prime inventors of our theater and our time.

1985

An Interview with Arthur Miller: Interview by Matthew Roudané

The Interview took place on November 7, 1983 in the playwright's New York City apartment near Central Park. Throughout our conversation Miller spoke patiently and frankly about his work and modern drama in general. Eager to speak, Miller never stopped the conversation, not even while in the bathroom washing up, dressing for the evening, or walking the crowded streets later that evening.

Roudané: Reflecting back upon five decades of playwriting, which plays hold the fondest memories for you?

Miller: Each play comes out of a quite different situation. Sometimes I feel proudest of *The Crucible,* because I made something lasting out of a violent but brief turmoil, and I think it will go on for a while yet, throwing some light. It also happens to be my most produced play, incidentally. I also get a big kick out of *The Price,* especially the old man in that play. I still enjoy him, and that I created him.

Roudané: Few American plays have exerted as much influence as *Death of a Salesman.* In terms of characterization, language, story, plot, and dramatic action, why do you think this play continues to engage audiences on a national as well as international level?

Miller: Maybe because it's a well-told, paradoxical story. It seems to catch the paradoxes of being alive in a technological civilization. In one way or another, different kinds of people, different classes of people apparently feel that they're in the play. Why that is I don't really know. But it seems to have more or less the same effect everywhere there is a dominating technology, although it's also popular in places where life is far more pretechnological. Maybe it involves some of the most rudimentary elements in the civilizing process: family cohesion, death and dying, parricide, rebirth, and so on. The elements, I guess, are rather fundamental. People *feel* these themes no matter where they are.

Roudané: So you think that the plight of Willy and his family is as valid today as it was immediately after production?

Miller: Who knows? People tell me that *Death of a Salesman* is more pertinent now than then. The suppression of the individual by placing him below the imperious needs of the society or technology seems to have manufactured more Willys in the world. But again, it is also far more primitive than that. Like many myths and classical dramas, it is a story about violence within a family.

Roudané: If *Death of a Salesman* is primitive in a Sophoclean sense, would you call it a tragedy?

Miller: I think it does engender tragic feelings, at least in a lot of people. Let's say it's one kind of tragedy. I'm not particularly eager to call it a tragedy or anything else; the label doesn't matter to me. But when Aristotle was writing, there were various kinds of tragedy. He was trying to make definitions that would include most of them. There are tremendous differences between an *Ajax, Oedipus,* the *Theban Women*; they're all different and don't meet Aristotle's definition of tragedy in the same way. I suppose he was defining what he felt should be the ideal case.

Roudané: Throughout much of your theater you seem concerned with the notion of the American Dream, with its successes and failures. Could you discuss the influence of this Dream on your artistry?

Miller: The American Dream is the largely unacknowledged screen in front of which all American writing plays itself out—the screen of the perfectibility of man. Whoever is writing in the United States is using the American Dream as an ironical pole of his story. Early on we all drink up certain claims to self-perfection that are absent in a large part of the world. People elsewhere tend to accept, to a far greater degree anyway, that the conditions of life are hostile to man's pretensions. The American idea is different in the sense that we think that if we could only touch it, and live by it, there's a natural order in favor of us; and that the object of a good life is to get connected with that live and abundant order. And this forms a context of irony for the kind of stories we generally tell each other. After all, the stories of most significant literary works are of one or another kind of failure. And it's a failure in *relation to* that screen, that backdrop. I think it pervades American writing, including my own. It's there in *The Crucible,* in *All My Sons,* in *After the Fall*—an aspiration to an innocence that when defeated or frustrated can turn quite murderous, and we don't know what to do with this perversity; it never seems to "fit" us.

Roudané: What is the relationship of form to content, and how have you arrived at the forms you've used in several of your plays which have a very inventive form— *Death of a Salesman, After the Fall,* which is almost cinematic, and the use of the narrator in *A View from the Bridge.* Did the form of these works come from the material or substance, or did the form come first? How does the creative process work for you?

Miller: I think there is a dialectic at work. There are forces working in two directions. The central reality in my plays is the lead character. In one or two of them it would be the leading characters, like *Incident at Vichy* where, while there is one most important character, many others are on almost an equal rank. But basically the story is carried forward by one individual wrestling with his dilemma. I'm not sure I understand what element it is in the dilemma that moves me toward one form or another. *All My Sons* was actually an exception to a dozen or so plays that I had written in previous years which most people don't know about. Those were poetic plays; one or two were in verse; expressionist plays. Starting out I was never interested in being a "realistic" writer. I discovered the engine of the story at a certain point and *All My Sons* seemed a form that would best express it; and even though it was an unusual form for me to use, it best expressed what I was after, which was an ordinariness of the environment from which this extraordinary disaster was going to spring. The amoral nature of that environment; that is, people involved in cutting the lawn and painting the house and keeping the oil burner running; the petty business of life in the suburbs. So once I had that feeling about it, the form began to create itself. No, I am not really interested in "realism." I never was. What I'm very much interested in is *reality*. This is something that can be quite different. Realism can conceal reality, perhaps a little easier than any other form, in fact. But what I am interested in is the poetic, the confluence of various forces in a surprising way; the reversals of man's plans for himself; the role of fate, of myth, in his life; his beliefs in false things; his determination to tell the truth until it hurts, but not afterwards, and so on.

In an early play like *All My Sons* it was realism as we know realism; but I hope all my plays are realistic in the sense that the view of life is on the whole a useful, not a trivial, one. The form of *Death of a Salesman* was an attempt, as much as anything else, to convey the bending of time. There are two or three sorts of time in that play. One is social time; one is psychic time, the way we remember things; and the third one is the sense of time created by the play and shared by the audience. When I directed *Salesman* in China, which was the first time I had attempted to direct it from scratch, I became aware all over again that that play is taking place in the Greek unity of 24 hours; and yet, it is dealing with material that goes back probably 25 years. And it almost goes forward through Ben, who is dead. So *time* was an obsession for me at the moment, and I wanted a way of presenting it so that it became the *fiber* of the play, rather than being something that somebody comments about. In fact, there is very little comment verbally in *Salesman* about time. I also wanted a form that could sustain in itself the way we deal with crises, which is not to deal with them. After all, there is a lot of comedy in *Salesman*; people forget it because it is so dark by the end of the play. But if you stand behind the audience you hear a lot of laughter. It's a deadly ironical laughter most of the time, but it *is* a species of comedy. The comedy is really a way for Willy and others to put off the evil day, which is the thing we all do. I wanted that to *happen* and not be something talked *about*. I wanted the feeling to come across rather than a set of speeches about how we delay dealing with issues. I wanted a play, that is, that had almost a biological life of its own. It would be as incontrovertible as the musculature of the human body. Everything connecting with everything else, all of it working according to plan. No excesses. Nothing explaining itself; all of it simply inevitable, as one structure, as one corpus. All those feelings of a society falling to pieces which I had, still have, of being unable to deal with it, which we all know now. All of this, however, presented not with speeches in *Salesman*, but by putting together pieces of Willy's life, so that what we were deducing about it was the speech; what we were making of it was the moral of it; what it was doing to us rather than a romantic speech about facing death and living a fruitless life. All of these elements and many more went into the form of *Death of a Salesman*. All this could never have been contained in the form of *All My Sons*. For the story of *Salesman* is absurdly simple! It's about a salesman and it's his last day on the earth. There's very little ongoing narrative. It's all relationships. I wanted plenty of space in the play for people to confront each other with their feelings, rather than for people to advance the plot. So it became a very open form, and I believe a real invention. I initially titled it "The Inside of His Head" and had a set in mind, which I abandoned, of the inside of Willy's skull in which he would be crawling around, playing these scenes inside of himself. Maybe that throws some light on the kind of play I wanted it to be.

In *The Crucible* we see the fate of the society from a religious, moral point of view; its merged sublime and political powers forcing the transmission of a man's conscience to others, and then of the man's final immortal need to take it back. In the area of morals and society it had to be a more explicit and "hard" play, hence its form. You know we adopt styles when we speak. When you're speaking to your mother, you speak in a different tone of voice from when you're speaking to your class; you use different gestures when you speak to a friend and to the public; or to a policeman, or judge, or possibly a professor. So it's the kind of address that the play is going to make that also creates its form. The address in *The Crucible* was an insistence, hardly concealed in the play, that if the events we see in that play are not understood it can mean the end of social life—which is based primarily on a certain amount of shared trust. And when the government goes into the business of destroying trust, it goes into the business of destroying itself So, saying this in *The Crucible,* what I believed at the time—the story of the Salem witch-hunt in 1692—was indeed saying it wanted that form. An aseptic form; it's less sensuous than *Salesman. The Crucible* is more pitiless, probably because power is at the bottom of it and because so much of the witch-hunt took place in a theocratic court. The witch-hunt was fundamentally a business of prosecutors and lawyers, witnesses, testimony. Literally the town of Salem did nothing anymore but attend court sessions in the church. It just about destroyed the town within the lifetime of those people.

In each of my plays the central creating force is the character, be it John Proctor or Willy Loman or Mr. Kelly or whoever. If I haven't got that, I haven't got anything. And the form comes as a result of the texture of what I feel about that person. I felt about Willy Loman that he talked endlessly, and in the play he talks endlessly. He had to seem to ramble, and yet be accumulating an explosive force, which is what happens when someone's talking a lot to himself and suddenly shoots himself. In *After the Fall* I wanted to confront somebody with his history, and rather than talk about it in a room in the third person, I wanted him to re-enact it. Maybe I can throw some light on *After the Fall* by saying this; it was done in India and the director came to see me and said that it had required no adaptation for the Indian theater. Now that was kind of a shock to me. He said, "In the old Indian plays the god comes forth and re-enacts his incarnations." And that's, formally speaking, what happens in *After the Fall*: the various paths circle around the same issues, which evolve into the person we finally see on the stage, striving toward a purer awareness of himself and the people in his life. To arrive at that it was necessary to break down some more walls of realistic theater.

I've paid probably an inordinate amount of attention to form because if it's not right, nothing works, no matter what. Form is literally the body that holds the soul of the play. And if that body doesn't maneuver and operate, you have an effusion of dialogue, a tickling of the piano keys, improvisation, perhaps, but you don't have music.

Roudané: How much revision do you go through when composing a play?

Miller: Before I am finished with a play, I have normally written about a thousand to three thousand pages. I suspect that in the case of *After the Fall* it may have been more. So obviously I'm searching around all over the place for what the play wants to be. I have a feeling that a play, if it truly exists, makes an *a priori* demand that it be born with certain shapes and certain features. Sculptors know that feeling: that within the rock is the sculpture, and what they're doing is knocking off the excess stone to find the ordained shape. What I do is go up one dead end after another, picking up a little bit here and a little bit there until I discover where I ought to be and what it ought to look like. But, of course, the form depends a great deal upon how the play's going to end. If it's going to end in death, that has a tremendous effect on the way the play's going to be structured. It tends to draw it up tight because it limits time automatically. Form is a way of expressing the tempo on the stage. If we could sit for 25 hours, which some of our playwrights would like us to do, we would hardly need any form at all. You would just go on and on and on, letting the audience pick what they wished out of the scrambled eggs. I've often said that the best naturalism you could achieve would be to put a tape recorder on the corner of 42nd Street and Broadway and just leave it open! You would get a perfect absurd play, which would be interesting. I would contest that it isn't a play, but that's an academic point. It's not to my taste. Form is a choice, a selection of incident and feeling dictated by thematic considerations. That sounds like a definition! Maybe I better write that down!

Roudané: *A View from the Bridge* was first written as a one-act play, then a two-act play, but in the process the role of the narrator/chorus shifted. That's an unusual shift for you. Could you comment on this form-shift?

Miller: This shift had to do with the circumstances of the play. That was a one-act play, in a time, incidentally, when you couldn't get a one-act play produced in New York. There wasn't an audience for one-act plays, so one wrote very few of them. But a friend of mine was in a Clifford Odets play—*The Flowering Peach*—which was failing on Broadway. He is Martin Ritt who later became a fine movie director. He called me one day and asked if I had any one-act plays because he had a cast of very good actors, and the producer was willing to let them use the theater on Sunday evenings to put on one-act plays. I didn't have any, but I wasn't doing anything and I thought, well, there *was* a story I'd known and loved for years but I could never figure out how to do a full-length play of it. So I said I'd try to do something, and I wrote *A View from the Bridge* in a week or two. That's how it started out; it had always seemed to me to be a one-act play. The form was also influenced by my own curiosity as to whether we could in a contemporary theater deal with life in some way like the Greeks did. Meaning that, unlike *Salesman*, it would not suck tons of water like a whale; everything that is said in the Greek classic play is going to advance the order, the theme, in manifest ways. There is no time for the character to reveal himself apart from thematic considerations. The Greeks never thought that art could be a crap-shoot. They thought art is form; a conscious but at the same time an inspired act. But anybody could be inspired; it was only the artist who had a conscious awareness of form, and this set him apart as the cultic, social voice. When I heard this story the first time—I never knew the man—it struck me even then how Greek it was. You knew from the first minute that it would be a disaster. Everybody around him of any intelligence would have told Eddie that it would be a disaster if he didn't give up his obsession. But it's the nature of the obsession that it can't be given up. The obsession becomes more powerful than the individual that it inhabits, like a force from another world. That to me was interesting. So I began *A View from the Bridge* in its first version with the feeling that I would make one single constantly rising trajectory, until its fall, rather like an arrow shot from a bow; and this form would declare rather than conceal itself. I wanted to reveal the method nakedly to everybody so that from the beginning of the play we are to know that this man can't make it, and yet might reveal himself somehow in his struggle. I must say the play was not cast in the best way; it had very good actors who didn't belong; some actors couldn't really handle the localized language, didn't have the timbre or feeling for it. It failed. Peter Brook saw it and thought that I might have been too relentless in the sense that some of the life of the family, the neighborhood, had been squeezed out. So as soon as I started to let that life back in, especially the dilemma as seen by the wife, it began to expand itself and become a two-act play. It was done in England as such for the first time. That change, however, came from internal considerations. It came because I could see on the stage that I could give those actors more meat, and let the structure take care of itself a little bit. I relaxed the play in the sense of allowing it to have its colors.

Roudané: Do you consider yourself a dramatic innovator?

Miller: I can only confess that the most completely achieved form that I know about is that of *Death of a Salesman*. This is to accommodate the full flow of inner and outer forces that are sucking this man. I daresay I made it all seem so natural that people have accepted it as real. But it's the actors who understand the crush of condensation; they are, sometimes, at three places at the same time. The melting together of social time, personal time, and psychic time in *Death of a Salesman* is, for me, its unique power. I just directed it in China and it struck me all over again. I've always paid a great deal of attention to forms. I've never really written in the same form twice. The only mode that I haven't done much with, although a little of that too, is the absurd. But I did two one-act plays last year—*Elegy for a Lady* and *Some Kind of Love Story*—which are of a different form than I've ever tried before. *Elegy for a Lady* takes place in the space between the mind and what it imagines, and sort of turns itself inside out. *Some Kind of Love Story* concerns the question of how we believe truth, how one is forced by circumstance to believe what you are only sure is not too easily demonstrated as false. They were great fun to do, and were destroyed by the critics, but that doesn't matter—they'll be back one day.

Roudané: Several of your plays have been done at one time and received one way, and done at a later period and received quite differently; I'm thinking especially of *The Crucible, The Price, After the Fall.* How do you account for the changes in the audience's perception of the spectacle?

Miller: We have to remember that, maybe more than any other art, the play lacks independence as an artifact. It is a set of relationships. There really are no characters in plays; there are *relationships*. Where there are only characters and no relationships, we have an unsatisfactory play. A work has to be supported by its time. It's an old story. A work can appear and the audience might not quite know what to make of it. They don't get the clues the work is sending them. It's a sociological and anthropological manifestation. The plays are not accessible to the audience. They haven't tuned into it yet by virtue of their own experiences. Time goes by, and a thousand social developments, and they see differently; they see the same thing now, but with different eyes. When *The Crucible* opened, we were at the height of the McCarthy period. There was simply a lot of fear and suspicion in the audience. This has been said a thousand times; you know the story, I'm sure. It was in many ways a disembodied theater. There was a fear of fear. Once they caught on to what *The Crucible* was about, a coat of ice formed over the audience because they felt they were being called upon to believe something which the reigning powers at the time told them they were not to believe. They would have to disobey very important social commands in order to believe in this play. Consequently the critics, who are merely registering their moment and, with few honorable exceptions, have no real independence from it, thought of *The Crucible* as a cold play. Now anyone who's seen *The Crucible* can level criticism, but that surely isn't a legitimate one anymore. It's that *they* felt cold; they were refrigerated by the social climate of that moment. I stood in the back of that theater after opening night and I saw people come by me whom I'd known for years—and wouldn't say hello to me. They were in dread that they would be identified with *me*. Because what I was saying in the play was that a species of hysteria had overtaken the United States and would end up killing people if it weren't recognized. Two years passed, Senator McCarthy died, the pendulum swung, and people began to recognize that he had been a malevolent influence. Some felt a little bit of shame, some felt angry that they had been taken, and others felt he was right—even though he was wrong. In any case, the heat was off. And the play was done again off-Broadway in a production that in many ways really wasn't as good as the original: the original had really fine, accomplished actors, and in the later one there was a much younger and more inexperienced cast. But the critics were overwhelmed with the play. That's because they allowed the play into themselves, whereas before they were afraid to. They suspected it of being propaganda that they had to defend their virgin minds against.

That was the most frightening change I have ever seen in the reception of a play, but of course there have been many other authors with similar fates. A play has to make an instantaneous connection with an audience made up of all sorts of people—some of them a little dumber than others. Some are smarter but less astute about the feelings they have. It's a mixed audience. That they should all be brought to the same feeling by looking at one play is really remarkable. It's almost too much to ask, but it happens all the time. A play's an arrangement by which the author speaks for himself and for his audience at the same moment. And for that to happen obviously takes a *lot* of luck—and a certain small amount of skill and talent.

Roudané: Reflecting upon Kate Keller in *All My Sons*, Elizabeth Procter in *The Crucible*, and, say, Linda Loman in *Death of a Salesman*, could you discuss the roles the women play in your drama?

Miller: A production of *All My Sons* was on in England two years ago and was directed by Michael Blakemore, a very fine director, who had never seen it here. He saw

Kate (Rosemary Harris) as a woman using the truth as a weapon against the man who had harmed their son. Kate Keller is pretty damn sure when the play begins that, in the widest sense of the word, Joe was "responsible" for the deaths of the Air Force men. She's both warning him not to go down the road that his older son is beckoning him to go, and rather ambiguously destroying him with her knowledge of his crime. She sees the horror most clearly because she was a partner to it without having committed it. There's a sinister side to her, in short. This actress caught it beautifully. The production was "dark" because of her performance of the mother who is usually regarded as ancillary, which she is not.

Roudané: Perhaps, then, there's more complexity to your female characters than critics have generally recognized.

Miller: Critics generally see them as far more passive than they are. When I directed *Salesman* in China, I had Linda "in action." She's not just sitting around. She's the one who knows from the beginning of the play that Willy's trying to kill himself. She's got the vital information all the time. Linda sustains the illusion because that's the only way Willy can be sustained. At the same time any cure or change is impossible in Willy. Ironically she's helping to guarantee that Willy will never recover from his illusion. She has to support it; she has no alternative, given his nature and hers.

Roudané: So, in this context, Linda is supporting what Ibsen would call a "vital lie."

Miller: That's right. The women characters in my plays are very complex. They've been played somewhat sentimentally, but that isn't the way they were intended. There is a more sinister side to the women characters in my plays. These women are of necessity auxiliaries to the action, which is carried by the male characters. But they both receive the benefits of the male's mistakes and protect his mistakes in crazy ways. They are forced to do that. So the females are victims as well.

Roudané: Do you try to get members of the audience to confront themselves and others about key issues?

Miller: I am not a teacher in the theater, despite what you may have read. In the sense that a lesson is arranged on the stage that will give us a certain moral. The play is really an attempt to order life. Now I'm more than happy when people do arrange themselves on one side or the other of the argument of the play. And I think it may do their brain some good to move away from the anguish of daily chaos. But the theater is not an educational institution, certainly not primarily. If a play makes them feel more alive, it is more than enough.

Roudané: Regarding your adaptation of Ibsen's *An Enemy of the People*, in the preface you discuss some of the reasons for producing another version of Ibsen's work in terms of style, language, and so on. In light of the politics as well as the aesthetics of that play, can you discuss the different nature of "your" play—especially since it's so different a production for you personally.

Miller: Let me tell you how it started. Early in 1951 Frederic March and Robert Lewis came to me—they wanted me to do *An Enemy of the People*. The versions that existed in English were very stiff, ungainly, and they didn't think they could do them. This might throw a little light on our theater history: at this time there was no off-Broadway theater. You had to do this on Broadway, complete with the usual Broadway merchandise. What they were interested in was some response to the crucifying of left-wingers. March and his wife were in the midst of a lawsuit against someone who had accused them of being pro-Communist. He was looking for some play which would clarify the principle behind his stand, and he found it in *An Enemy of the People.* I had never seen the play acted. Reading it again, I thought it would be a hell of a thing to do; the backer was a very wealthy young Norwegian who had a lot of love for the United States and was worried that it was turning fascist. He offered to supply me with a careful, word-for-word translation of Ibsen's original manuscript, done by him. It would simply set each word next to each word; there would be no attempt to write English, and, as you know, any foreign language translated that way is really not a language but a set of disconnected wooden blocks. So with that I wrote a version of the play, trying to generate some contemporary feeling. It was not to be a museum piece. It was to threaten us! The play was a very threatening play in its time. I had to reproduce that feeling of threat. You couldn't do it with the other language. It was basically a question of language. Also, the play is monstrously repetitive. Ibsen, in his later years, couldn't remember having written it! He had done it very quickly—in a few months—in response to violent criticism of him for *Ghosts.* He was portrayed as a pornographer, a dreadful antisocial mechanic. He wrote this as a self-defense, based on the idea fundamental to the play, as I saw it: that before many people can know something, one man has to know it. The majority in that sense is always wrong, always trailing behind that one man.

So do I feel the play's "mine"? Not really. Perhaps some of its humor, and a certain quickened throb not in the original. In any case before I did it, it was hardly ever produced here except by academic circles. Afterwards, it was put on fairly often, and still is, because I made the play more accessible, I believe, to a contemporary audience. The original, for example, had long arid debates about Darwinian questions which have been settled and nobody's particularly interested in any more. Some of Ibsen's ideas seemed crackpot even then, however. He had in fact to go around explaining, especially to trade union meetings where he made speeches, that he hadn't intended to say that he believed in the superiority of an aristocracy. The play could lend itself to supporting the idea that an elite should be running the world because the average guy is rather an idiot—as he often is. But he was talking about the aristocracy of the intellect and the spirit, meaning those people who are prepared to disinterestedly venture into the future. They have to sacrifice for it, and they should be somehow protected so that they're not lost to society. But *An Enemy of the People* doesn't quite say that. In the original version it often sounds merely contemptuous of the ordinary citizen. But, on the other hand, maybe Ibsen really was.

Roudané: Earlier you commented that the central character often helps give shape or form to your play; but have you ever written a piece that was generated from a compelling thematic issue?

Miller: *Incident at Vichy* is the closest I've ever come to that. The action originated from an actual event involving a group of men in Vichy, France. Incidentally, there's a man who's recently been arrested, Klaus Barbie, who ran the Gestapo in France; it was he who was running the program that I depicted in *Incident at Vichy*: the Germans hunting down Jewish people in the Vichy zone who were masquerading as French in order to escape the concentration camps. Barbie invented a lot of procedures. I'm very happy to say that in the play, written sometime in the sixties, one of the characters says, "These aren't the Germans, these are the French Police." And that's exactly where things are now. That is, yes, a thematic play. There's another element in *Incident at Vichy*, without which I wouldn't have written the play: that is, the time comes when somebody has to decide to sacrifice himself, and the act of sacrifice was interesting to me. And really the play comes down to that, the step from guilt to responsibility and action.

Roudané: When working with a director on a play, do you make many changes in the rehearsal procedure?

Miller: I have, and most of the time to the detriment to the play. I'll tell you what happens. I've worked on Broadway where there's a very limited amount of time: three-and-a-half weeks and you're on. And we're dealing with a lot of overdone commercialization. And it costs a lot of money per day, so naturally you limit the day. The result? The power that now moves from the playwright to the director is inevitable because he's got to bring that curtain up. Sometimes, if I have a particularly sensitive and able director, this doesn't happen. But when you have a less than capable man, you have to make it possible for him to put that play on. So the playwright starts making up for his weaknesses. The playwright also has to consider what to do about actors who can't really sing on the pitch in which you wrote the music. The alternative is to let it stand there and know that they don't have a prayer: they can't hit certain notes and you've got to change the register. We have a very poor theater now, I'm afraid. It's poor in time: our theater doesn't have sufficient time to really stop and work on a difficult passage. Instead, the playwright is thrown the job of making the actor's or director's job pleasant, while at the same time protecting and defending his own work, as much as he can. Sometimes these things are contradictory and you don't always succeed. I've had that happen; there's hardly a playwright who hasn't from the beginning of time.

Roudané: Given all the economic, social, thematic, political, and aesthetic considerations that go into our theater today, and given all the problems our theater is facing today, what should or could or can theater be, and what in an ideal world should our theater try to accomplish?

Miller: Well, that's a pretty big order. I think that a theater with the most vitality is a theater that confronts an audience made up of the whole people. We don't have anything like that. This is not merely a sentimentally democratic statement. When you break up society, as our theater audience largely does, into a very tiny fragment of the most well-to-do, it can only react in a certain way. I know when I go to Minneapolis or Dayton, there's a different atmosphere between the play and the people, because it costs next to nothing to get in—at least when compared to New York prices. A much wider group of people is in the theater, and I find this very stimulating. You see, Shakespeare had to address nobility, along with people who couldn't read and write; the whole gamut of society was in the theater, and that supported and invited the tremendous variety in his plays. As social and political revolutions took place in England after his passing, the audience got a more and more narrowly bourgeois ideological slant; it couldn't open itself to contradictions of its ideology. So the more you narrow your audience, the more you narrow the plays that serve it. The mechanics of it are quite obvious; if you hand a producer a piece that offends a significant portion of the Broadway audience, not to speak of the critics, he'll think two or three times before putting it on. You are in that way bound to one level of consciousness. It's not a new thing; my argument with our theater on that level is that it's constricted to a degree greater than I have ever known in my lifetime. It is very important that people not have to pay $40 to get into the theater, because if they pay $40, they're probably not going to want what I am writing.

Another element in a great theater is that it tried to place aesthetics at the service of its civic function. See how the plays that we call great have made us somehow more civilized. The great Greek plays taught the western mind the law. They taught the western mind how to settle tribal conflicts without murdering each other. The great Shakespearean plays set up structures of order which became parts of our mental equipment. In the immense love stories, the wonderful comedies, there's all sorts of color. But back of these great plays is a civic function. The author was really a poet-philosopher. A $40 ticket brooks no philosophies, tends toward triviality. I believe that if we had some means of expanding our audience it would take a while but playwrights would respond to that challenge. They'd smell *blood* out there!

The biggest reason playwriting is in such dire straits is because the audience is gone; it's not there any more. We've been talking about this for thirty years. Back in the early fifties I even got the Dramatists Guild to convene a meeting of playwrights, unions, and producers to try to reduce our take and lower our costs. That was over thirty years ago, when it was $10 or $8, something like that, for a ticket. But I saw it happening. I saw friends of mine who could no longer go to the theater, people who loved the theater. They didn't have the money. There are places in the world where this problem, if not solved, has been dealt with, steps have been taken. One of them is England. The National Theatre; the Arts Council in England. That's one of the reasons there have been so many English plays around. There's an English audience for those plays. A writer might not be able to make a good living at it, but he could feed himself on a play that was written, not for the West End, not for Broadway, but for those three or four weeks of performances that he might get with very good actors. This is not amateur theater. Some of the best people in England are involved in this. So my great theater would be a poetic theater. It would have to be because once you're confronted with the Great Unwashed, well, the only image I have is when you go to a prize fight, a ball game, or a political rally. I was a delegate to the 1968 Democratic convention, and *there* was the American people. That's the audience I wish I had. You know: real ugly toughs from Chicago, professors from Massachusetts, southern crackers from Georgia, Alabama. I could talk to those people. But I can't get 'em! They're not in my theater. And if they ever got into the theater, you would have something! You would have fever!

1985

Excerpt from *Timebends: A Life*

Memory inevitably romanticizes, pressing reality to recede like pain. When the escaping Hebrews saw the waters rushing in to cover the God-dried seabed, drowning the pursuing Egyptian army, they sat down on the shore to catch their breaths and promptly forgot all their previous years of miserable argufying and internecine spitefulness.

Now, with only the serene blue sea before them, they were soon telling their children how wonderful life used to be, even under the Egyptians, when at least they were never allowed to forget they were all Jews and therefore had to help one another and be human. Not like now, when everybody's out for himself, etc. . . . The brain heals the past like an injury, things were always better than they are now.

Already in the sixties I was surprised by the common tendency to think of the late forties and early fifties as some sort of renaissance in the New York theater. If that was so, I was unaware of it. I thought the theater a temple being rotted out with commercialized junk, where mostly by accident an occasional good piece of work appeared, usually under some disguise of popular cultural coloration such as a movie star in a leading role.

That said, it now needs correction; it was also a time when the audience was basically the same for musicals and light entertainment as for the ambitious stuff and had not yet been atomized, as it would be by the mid-fifties, into young and old, hip and square, or even political left and middle and right. So the playwright's challenge was to please not a small sensitized supporting clique but an audience representing, more or less, all of America. With ticket prices within reason, this meant that an author was writing for his peers, and if such was really not the case statistically, it was sufficiently so to support an illusion that had a basis in reality. After all, it was not thought particularly daring to present T. S. Eliot's *The Cocktail Party* on Broadway, or Laurence Olivier in a Greek tragedy, or Giraudoux's *The Madwoman of Chaillot,* or any number of other ambitious works. To be sure, such shows had much shorter lives than the trash, but that was to be expected, for most people would much rather laugh than cry, rather watch an actor being hit on the head by a pig bladder than by some painful truth.

The net of it all was that serious writers could reasonably assume they were addressing the whole American mix, and so their plays, whether successfully or not, stretched toward a wholeness of experience that would not require specialists or a coterie to be understood. As alienated a spirit as he was, O'Neill tried for the big audience, and Clifford Odets no less so, along with every other writer longing to prophesy to America, from Whitman and Melville to Dreiser and Hemingway and on.

For Europe's playwrights the situation was profoundly different, with society already split beyond healing between the working class and its allies, who were committed to a socialist destiny, and the bourgeois mentality that sought an art of reassurance and the pleasures of forgetting what was happening in the streets. (The first American plays I saw left me wondering where the characters came from. The people I knew were fanatics about surviving, but onstage everyone seemed to have mysteriously guaranteed incomes, and though every play had to have something about "love," there was nothing about sex, which was all there was in Brooklyn, at least that I ever noticed.) An American avant-garde, therefore, if only because the domination of society by the middle class was profoundly unchallenged, could not simply steal from Brecht or even Shaw and expect its voice to reach beyond the small alienated minority that had arrived in their seats already converted to its aims. That was not the way to change the world.

For a play to do that it had to reach precisely those who accepted everything as it was; great drama is great questions or it is nothing but technique. I could not imagine a theater worth my time that did not want to change the world, any more than a creative scientist could wish to prove the validity of everything that is already known. I knew only one other writer with the same approach, even if he surrounded his work with a far different aura. This was Tennessee Williams.

If only because he came up at a time when homosexuality was absolutely unacknowledgeable in a public figure, Williams had to belong to a minority culture and understood in his bones what a brutal menace the majority could be if aroused against him. I lived with much the same sense of alienation, albeit for other reasons. Certainly I never regarded him as the sealed-off aesthete he was thought to be. There is a radical politics of the soul as well as of the ballot box and the picket line. If he was not an activist, it was not for lack of a desire for justice, nor did he consider a theater profoundly involved in society and politics, the venerable tradition reaching back to the Greeks, somehow unaesthetic or beyond his interest.

The real theater—as opposed to the sequestered academic one—is always straining at the inbuilt inertia of a society that always wants to deny change and the pain it necessarily involves. But it is in this effort that the musculature of important work is developed. In a different age, perhaps even only fifteen years later, in the sixties, Williams might have had a more comfortably alienated audience to deal with, one that would have relieved the pressure upon him to extend himself beyond a supportive cult environment, and I think this might well have narrowed the breadth of his work and its intensity. In short, there was no renaissance in the American forties, but there was a certain balance within the audience—a balance, one might call it, between the alienated and the conformists—that gave sufficient support to the naked cry of the heart and, simultaneously, enough resistance to force it into a rhetoric that at one stroke could be broadly understandable and yet faithful to the pain that had pressed the author to speak.

When Kazan invited me up to New Haven to see the new Williams play, *A Streetcar Named Desire*—it seemed to me a rather too garishly attention-getting title—I was already feeling a certain amount of envious curiosity since I was still unable to commit myself to the salesman play, around which I kept suspiciously circling and sniffing. But at the same time I hoped that *Streetcar* would be good; it was not that I was high-minded but simply that I shared the common assumption of the time that the greater the number of exciting plays there were on Broadway the better for each of us. At least in our minds there was still something approximating a theater culture to which we more or less pridefully belonged, and the higher its achievement the greater the glory we all shared. The playwright then was king of the hill, not the star actor or director, and certainly not the producer or theater owner, as would later be the case. (At a recently televised Tony Awards ceremony, recognizing achievement in the theater, not a single playwright was presented to the public, while two lawyers who operated a chain of theaters were showered with the gratitude of all. It reminded me of Caligula making his horse a senator.)

Streetcar—especially when it was still so fresh and the actors almost as amazed as the audience at the vitality of this theatrical experience—opened one specific door for me. Not the story or characters or the direction, but the words and their liberation, the joy of the writer in writing them, the radiant eloquence of its composition, moved me more than all its pathos. It formed a bridge to Europe for me, to Jouvet's performance in *Ondine,* to the whole tradition of unashamed word-joy that, with the exception of Odets, we had either turned our backs on or, as with Maxwell Anderson, only used archaically, as though eloquence could only be justified by cloaking it in sentimental romanticism.

Returning to New York, I felt speeded up, in motion now. With *Streetcar,* Tennessee had printed a license to speak at full throat, and it helped strengthen me as I turned to Willy Loman, a salesman always full of words, and better yet, a man who could never cease trying, like Adam, to name himself and the world's wonders. I had known all along that this play could not be encompassed by conventional realism, and for one integral reason: in Willy the past was as alive as what was happening at the moment, sometimes even crashing in to completely overwhelm his mind. I wanted precisely the same fluidity in the form, and now it was clear to me that this must be primarily verbal. The language would of course have to be recognizably his to begin with, but it seemed possible now to infiltrate it with a kind of superconsciousness. The play, after all, involved the attempts of his sons and his wife and Willy himself to understand what was killing him. And to understand meant to lift the experience into emergency speech of an unashamedly open kind rather than to proceed by the crabbed dramatic hints and pretexts of the "natural." If the structure had to mirror the psychology as directly as could be done, it was still a psychology hammered into its strange shape by society, the business life Willy had lived and believed in. The play could reflect what I had always sensed as the unbroken tissue that was man and society, a single unit rather than two.

By April of 1948 I felt I could find such a form, but it would have to be done, I thought, in a single sitting, in a night or a day, I did not know why. I stopped making my notes in our Grace Court house in Brooklyn Heights and drove up alone one morning to the country house we had bought the previous year. We had spent one summer there in that old farmhouse, which had been modernized by its former owner, a greeting card manufacturer named Philip Jaffe, who as a sideline published a thin magazine for China specialists called *Amerasia.* Mary worked as one of his secretaries and so had the first news that he wanted to sell the place. In a year or two he would be on trial for publishing without authorization State Department reports from John Stewart Service, among a number of other China experts who recognized a Mao victory as inevitable and warned of the futility of America continuing to back her favorite, Chiang Kai-Shek. *Amerasia* had been a vanity publication, in part born of Jaffe's desire for a place in history, but it nevertheless braved the mounting fury of the China lobby against any opinion questioning the virtues of the Chiang forces. At his trial the government produced texts of conversations that Jaffe claimed could only have been picked up by long-range microphone as he and his friends walked the isolated backcountry roads near this house. Service was one of many who were purged from the State Department, leaving it blinded to Chinese reality but ideologically pure.

But all that was far from my mind this day; what I was looking for on my land was a spot for a little shack I wanted to build, where I could block out the world and bring into focus what was still stuck in the corners of my eyes. I found a knoll in the nearby woods and returned to the city, where instead of working on the play I drew plans for the framing, of which I really had very vague knowledge and no experience. A pair of carpenters could have put up this ten-by-twelve-foot cabin in two days at most, but for reasons I still do not understand it had to be my own hands that gave it form, on this ground, with a floor that I had made, upon which to sit to begin the risky expedition into myself In reality, all I had was the first two lines and a death—"Willy!" and "It's all right. I came back." Further than that I dared not, would not, venture until I could sit in the completed studio, four walls, two windows, a floor, a roof, and a door.

"It's all right. I came back" rolled over and over in my head as I tried to figure out how to join the roof rafters in air unaided, until I finally put them together on the ground and swung them into position all nailed together. When I closed in the roof, it was a miracle, as though I had mastered the rain and cooled the sun. And all the while afraid I would never be able to penetrate past those two first lines. I started writing one morning—the tiny studio was still unpainted and smelled of raw wood and sawdust, and the bags of nails were still stashed in a corner with my tools. The sun of April had found my windows to pour through, and the apple buds were moving on the wild trees, showing their first pale blue petals. I wrote all day until dark, and then I had dinner and went back and wrote until some hour in the darkness between midnight and four. I had skipped a few areas that I knew would give me no trouble in the writing and gone for the parts that had to be muscled into position. By the next morning I had done the first half, the first act of two. When I lay down to sleep, I realized I had been weeping—my eyes still burned and my throat was sore from talking it all out and shouting and laughing. I would be stiff when I woke, aching as if I had played four hours of football or tennis and now had to face the start of another game. It would take some six more weeks to complete Act II.

My laughter during the writing came mostly at Willy's contradicting himself so arrantly, and out of the laughter the title came one afternoon. *Death Comes for the Archbishop*, the *Death and the Maiden* Quartet—always austere and elevated was death in titles. Now it would be claimed by a joker, a bleeding mass of contradictions, a clown, and there was something funny about that, something like a thumb in the eye, too. Yes, and in some far corner of my mind possibly something political; there was the smell in the air of a new American Empire in the making, if only because, as I had witnessed, Europe was dying or dead, and I wanted to set before the new captains and the so smugly confident kings the corpse of a believer. On the play's opening night a woman who shall not be named was outraged, calling it "a time bomb under American capitalism"; I hoped it was, or at least under the bullshit of capitalism, this pseudo life that thought to touch the clouds by standing on top of a refrigerator, waving a paid-up mortgage at the moon, victorious at last.

But some 35 years later, the Chinese reaction to my Beijing production of *Salesman* would confirm what had become more and more obvious over the decades in the play's hundreds of productions throughout the world: Willy was representative everywhere, in every kind of system, of ourselves in this time. The Chinese might disapprove of his lies and his self-deluding exaggerations as well as his immorality with women, but they certainly saw themselves in him. And it was not simply as a type but because of what he wanted, which was to excel, to win out over anonymity and meaninglessness, to love and be loved, and above all, perhaps, to *count*. When he roared out, "I am not a dime a dozen! *I am Willy Loman, and you are Biff Loman!*" it came as a nearly revolutionary declaration after what was now 34 years of leveling. (The play was the same age as the Chinese revolution.) I did not know in 1948 in Connecticut that I was sending a message of resurgent individualism to the China of 1983—especially when the revolution had signified, it seemed at the time, the long-awaited rule of reason and the historic ending of chaotic egocentricity and selfish aggrandizement. Ah, yes. I had not reckoned on a young Chinese student saying to a CBS interviewer in the theater lobby, "We are moved by it because we also want to be number one, and to be rich and successful." What else is this but human unpredictability, which goes, on escaping the nets of unfreedom?

I did not move far from the phone for two days after sending the script to Kazan. By the end of the second silent day I would have accepted his calling to tell me that it was a scrambled egg, an impenetrable, unstageable piece of wreckage. And his tone when he finally did call was alarmingly somber.

"I've read your play." He sounded at a loss as to how to give me the bad news. "My God, it's so sad."

"It's supposed to be."

"I just put it down. I don't know what to say. My father . . ." He broke off, the first of a great many men—and women—who would tell me that Willy was their father. I still thought he was letting me down easy. "It's a great play, Artie. I want to do it in the fall or winter. I'll start thinking about casting." He was talking as though someone we both knew had just died, and it filled me with happiness. Such is art.

For the first time in months, as I hung up the phone, I could see my family clearly again. As was her way, Mary accepted the great news with a quiet pride, as though something more expressive would spoil me, but I too thought I should remain an ordinary citizen, even an anonymous one (although I did have a look at the new Studebaker convertible, the Raymond Lowey design that was the most beautiful American car of the time, and bought one as soon as the play opened). But Mary's mother, who was staying the week with us, was astonished. *"Another* play?" she said, as though the success of *All My Sons* had been enough for one lifetime. She had unknowingly triggered that play when she gossiped about a young girl somewhere in Central Ohio who had turned her father in to the FBI for having manufactured faulty aircraft parts during the war.

But who should produce *Salesman?* Kazan and I walked down Broadway from the park where we had been strolling and talking about the kind of style the production would need. Kazan's partnership with Harold Clurman had recently broken up, and I had no idea about a producer. He mentioned Cheryl Crawford, whom I hardly knew, and then Kermit Bloomgarden, an accountant turned producer, whom I had last seen poring over Herman Shumlin's account books a couple of years before when Shumlin turned down *All My Sons*. I had never seen Bloomgarden smile, but he had worked for the Group Theater and Kazan knew him, and as much because we happened to have come to a halt a few yards from his office building as for any other reason, he said, "Well, let's go up and say hello." When we stood across the desk from him and Kazan said he had a play of mine for him to read, Bloomgarden squeezed up his morose version of a smile, or at least a suggestion of one he planned to have next week.

This whimsical transforming of another person's life reminds me of a similar walk with Kazan uptown from a garage on Twenty-sixth Street where he had left his old Pontiac to be repaired. He began wondering aloud whom he should ask to head a new acting school to be called the Actors Studio, which he and Clurman and Robert Lewis and Cheryl Crawford were organizing. None of these founders was prepared to run the place, Kazan, Clurman, and Lewis being too busy with their flourishing directing careers, and Crawford with her work as a producer. "Lee Strasberg is probably the best guy for it. He'd certainly be able to put in the time." In due course Strasberg became not only the head of the Actors Studio but also its heart and soul, and for the general public its organizer. So his work there was made possible by his having been unemployable at the right moment. But that, come to think of it, is as good a way as any to be catapulted into world fame.

Willy had to be small, I thought, but we soon realized that Roman Bohnen and Ernest Truex and a few other very good actors seemed to lack the size of the character even if they fit the body. The script had been sent to Lee Cobb, an actor I remembered mainly as a mountainous hulk covered with a towel in a Turkish bath in an Irwin Shaw play, with the hilarious *oy vey* delivery of a forever persecuted businessman. Having flown himself across the country in his own two-engine airplane, he sat facing me in Bloomgarden's office and announced, "This is my part. Nobody else can play this part. I know this man." And he did indeed seem to be the man when a bit later in a coffee shop downstairs he looked up at the young waitress and smiled winsomely as though he had to win her loving embrace before she could be seduced into bringing him his turkey sandwich and coffee—ahead of all the other men's orders, and only after bestowing on his unique slice of pickle her longing kiss.

But while I trusted his and Kazan's experience, I lacked any conviction of my own about him until one evening in our Grace Court living room Lee looked down at my son, Bob, on the floor and I heard him laugh at something funny the child had said. The sorrow in his laughter flew out at me, touched me; it was deeply depressed and at the same time joyous, all flowing through a baritone voice that was gorgeously reedy. So large and handsome a man pretending to be thoroughly at ease in a world where he obviously did not fit could be moving.

"You know—or do you?—," Lee said to me one day in Bloomgarden's office a week or so before rehearsals were to begin, "that this play is a watershed. The American theater will never be the same." I could only gulp and nod in silence at his portentousness—which I feared might augur a stately performance—and hope that he would make Willy come alive anyway.

But as rehearsals proceeded in the small, periodically abandoned theater on the ratty roof of the New Amsterdam on Forty-second Street, where Ziegfeld in the twenties had staged some intimate revues, Lee seemed to move about in a buffalo's stupefied trance, muttering his lines, plodding with deathly slowness from position to position, and behaving like a man who had been punched in the head. "He's just learning it," Kazan shakily reassured me after three or four days. I waited as a week went by, and then ten days, and all that was emerging from Lee Cobb's throat was a bumpy hum. The other actors were nearing performance levels, but when they had to get a response from Lee all their rhythms slowed to near collapse. Kazan was no longer so sure and kept huddling with Lee, trying to pump him up. Nor did Lee offer any explanation, and I wondered whether he thought to actually play the part like a man with a foot in the grave. Between us, Kazan and I began referring to him as "the Walrus."

On about the twelfth day, in the afternoon, with Eddie Kook, our lighting supplier, and Jimmy Proctor, our pressman, and Kazan and myself in the seats, Lee stood up as usual from the bedroom chair and turned to Mildred Dunnock and bawled, "No, there's more people now. . . . There's more people!" and, gesturing toward the empty upstage where the window was supposed to be, caused a block of apartment houses to spring up in my brain, and the air became sour with the smell of kitchens where once there had been only the odors of earth, and he began to move frighteningly, with such ominous reality that my chest felt pressed down by an immense weight. After the scene had gone on for a few minutes, I glanced around to see if the others had my reaction. Jim Proctor had his head bent into his hands and was weeping, Eddie Kook was looking shocked, almost appalled, and tears were pouring over his cheeks, and Kazan behind me was grinning like a fiend, gripping his temples with both hands, and we knew we had it—there was an unmistakable wave of life moving across the air of the empty theater, a wave of Willy's pain and protest. I began to weep myself at some point that was not particularly sad, but it was as much, I think, out of pride in our art, in Lee's magical capacity to imagine, to collect within himself every mote of life since Genesis and to let it pour forth. He stood up there like a giant moving the Rocky Mountains into position.

At the end of the act, Del Hughes, our sweet but hardheaded, absolutely devoted, competent stage manager, came out from a wing and looked out at us. His stunned eyes started us all laughing. I ran up and kissed Lee, who pretended to be surprised. "But what did you expect, Arthur?" he said, his eyes full of his playful vanity. My God, I thought—he really *is* Willy! On the subway going home to Brooklyn I felt once again the aching pain in my muscles that the performance had tensed up so tightly, just as in the writing time. And when I thought of it later, it seemed as though Lee's sniffing around the role for so long recapitulated what I had done in the months before daring to begin to write.

The whole production was, I think, unusual for the openness with which every artist involved sought out his truths. It was all a daily, almost moment-to-moment testing of ideas. There was much about the play that had never been done before, and this gave an uncustomary excitement to our discussions about what would or would not be understood by an audience. The setting I had envisioned was three bare platforms and only the minimum necessary furniture for a kitchen and two bedrooms, with the

Boston hotel room as well as Howard's office to be played in open space. Jo Mielziner took those platforms and designed an environment around them that was romantic and dreamlike yet at the same time lower-middle-class. His set, in a word, was an emblem of Willy's intense longing for the promises of the past, with which indeed the present state of his mind is always conflicting, and it was thus both a lyrical design and a dramatic one. The only notable mistake in his early concept was to put the gas hot-water heater in the middle of the kitchen, a symbol of menace that I thought obvious and Kazan finally eliminated as a hazard to his staging. But by balancing on the edges of the ordinary bounds of verisimilitude, Jo was stretching reality in parallel with the script, just as Kazan did by syncopating the speech rhythms of the actors. He made Mildred Dunnock deliver her long first-act speeches to the boys at double her normal speed, then he doubled that, and finally she—until recently a speech teacher—was standing there drumming out words as fast as her very capable tongue could manage. Gradually he slacked her off, but the drill straightened her spine, and her Linda filled up with outrage and protest rather than self-pity and mere perplexity. Similarly, to express the play's inner life, the speech rate in some scenes or sections was unnaturally speeded or slowed.

My one scary hour came with the climactic restaurant fight between Willy and the boys, when it all threatened to come apart. I had written a scene in which Biff resolves to tell Willy that the former boss from whom Biff had planned to borrow money to start a business has refused to so much as see him and does not even remember his working for the firm years ago. But on meeting his brother and father in the restaurant, he realizes that Willy's psychological stress will not permit the whole catastrophic truth to be told, and he begins to trim the bad news. From moment to moment the scene as originally written had so many shadings of veracity that Arthur Kennedy, a very intelligent citizen indeed, had trouble shifting from a truth to a half-truth to a fragment of truth and back to the whole truth, all of it expressed in quickly delivered, very short lines. The three actors, with Kazan standing beside them, must have repeated the scene through a whole working day, and it still wobbled. "I don't see how we can make it happen," Kazan said as we left the theatre that evening. "Maybe you ought to try simplifying it for them." I went home and worked through the night and brought in a new scene, which played much better and became the scene as finally performed.

The other changes were very small and a pleasure to make because they involved adding lines rather than cutting or rewriting. In Act I, Willy is alone in the kitchen muttering to himself, and as his memories overtake him the lighting brightens, the exterior of the house becomes covered with leaf shadows as of old, and in a moment the boys are calling to him in their youthful voices, entering the stage as they were in their teens. There was not sufficient time, however, for them to descend from their beds in the dark on the specially designed elevators and finish stripping out of their pajamas into sweaters and trouses and sneakers, so I had to add time to Willy's monologue. But that was easy since he loved talking to himself about his boys and his vision of them.

The moving in and out of the present had to be not simply indicative but a tactile transformation that the audience could feel as well as comprehend, and indeed come to dread as returning memory threatens to bring Willy closer to his end. Lighting was thus decisively important, and Mielziner, who also lit the show, with Eddie Kook by his side, once worked an entire afternoon lighting a chair.

Willy, in his boss's office, has exploded once too often, and Howard has gone out, leaving him alone. He turns to the office chair, which in the old days was occupied by Frank, Howard's father, who had promised Willy shares in the firm as a reward for all his good work, and as he does so the chair must become alive, quite as though his old boss were in it as he addresses him: "Frank, Frank, don't you remember what you told me? . . ." Rather than being lit, the chair subtly seemed to begin emanating light. But this was not merely an exercise in theatrical magic; it confirmed that we had moved inside Willy's system of loss, that we were seeing the world as he saw it even as we kept a critical distance and saw it for ourselves.

To set the chair off and make the light change work, all surrounding lights had to dim imperceptibly. That was when Eddie Kook, who had become so addicted to the work on this play that his office at his Century Lighting Company had all but ceased operations, turned to me and said, "You've been asking why we need so many lights. [We were using more than most musicals.] The reason is right there in front of you—it takes more lights to make it dark." With fewer lights each one would have to be dimmed more noticeably than if there were many, each only fractionally reduced in intensity to create the change without apparent source or contrivance.

Salesman had its first public performance at the Locust Street Theater in Philadelphia. Across the street the Philadelphia Orchestra was playing Beethoven's Seventh Symphony that afternoon, and Kazan thought Cobb ought to hear some of it, wanting, I suppose, to prime the great hulk on whom all our hopes depended. The three of us were in a conspiracy to make absolutely every moment of every scene cohere to what preceded and followed it; we were now aware that Willy's part was among the longest in dramatic literature, and Lee was showing signs of wearying. We sat on either side of him in a box, inviting him, as it were, to drink of the heroism of that music, to fling himself into his role tonight without holding back. We thought of ourselves, still, as a kind of continuation of a long and undying past.

As sometimes happened later on during the run, there was no applause at the final curtain of the first performance. Strange things began to go on in the audience. With the curtain down, some people stood to put their coats on and then sat again, some, especially men, were bent forward covering their faces, and others were openly weeping. People crossed the theater to stand quietly talking with one another. It seemed forever before someone remembered to applaud, and then there was no end to it. I was standing at the back and saw a distinguished-looking elderly man being led up the aisle; he was talking excitedly into the ear of what seemed to be his male secretary or assistant. This, I learned, was Bernard Gimbel, head of the department store chain, who that night gave an order that no one in his stores was to be fired for being overage.

Now began the parade of the visiting New York theater people to see for themselves, and I remember best Kurt Weill and his wife, Lotte Lenya, who had come with Maxwell Anderson's wife, Mab. We had coffee in a little shop, and Weill kept shaking his head and staring at me, and Mab said, "It's the best play ever written," which I dare repeat because it would be said often in the next months and would begin to change my life.

Of the opening night in New York two things stick to memory. At the back of the lovely Morosco, since destroyed by the greed of real estate men and the city's indifference, Kazan and I were sitting on the stairs leading up to the balcony as Lee was saying, "And by the way he died the death of a salesman . . ." Everything had gone beautifully, but I was near exhaustion since I acted all the parts internally as I watched, and suddenly I heard, ". . . in the smoker of the New York, New Hahven and Hayven." Surely the audience would burst out laughing—but nobody did. And the end created the same spell as it had in Philadelphia, and backstage was the same high euphoria that I had now come to expect. A mob of well-wishers packed the corridors to the dressing rooms. For the first time at a play of mine the movie stars had come out, but my face was still unknown and I could stand in a corner watching them unobserved—Lucille Ball and Desi Arnaz, Fredric and Florence March, and faces and names I have long forgotten, putting me on notice that I was now deep in show business, a paradoxically uncomfortable feeling indeed, for it was too material and real to have much to do with something that was air and whispers.

Finally, edging my way onto the stage, where I hoped to find a place to sit and rest, I saw as in a glorious dream of reward and high success three waiters in rich crimson Louis Sherry jackets arranging plates and silver on an extraordinarily long banquet table stretching almost the entire stage width. On its white linen table-cloth were great silver tureens and platters of beef, fowl, and seafood along with ice-filled buckets of champagne. Whose idea could this have been? What a glorious climax to the triumphant evening! Anticipating the heady shock of cold champagne, I reached for a gleaming glass, when one of the waiters approached me and with polite firmness informed me that the dinner had been ordered by Mr. Dowling for a private party. Robert Dowling, whose City Investing Company owned the Morosco along with other Broadway theaters, was a jovial fellow turning sixty who had swum around Manhattan Island, a feat he seemed to memorialize by standing straight with his chest expanded. I liked his childishness and his enthusiasms. I said that Mr. Dowling would surely not begrudge the play's author a well-earned glass of wine in advance of the celebration, but the waiter, obviously on orders, was adamant. I was dumbfounded, it must be somebody's joke, but a bit later, as Mary and I were leaving with the cast and their friends, we all stopped for a moment at the back of the theater to watch with half-hysterical incredulity as this rather decorous celebratory dinner proceeded literally inside Willy Loman's dun-colored Brooklyn house, the ladies in elaborate evening gowns, the men in dinner jackets, the waiters moving back and forth with the food under a polite hum of conversation suitable for the Pierre Hotel dining room, and the diners of course totally oblivious to the crowd of us looking on, laughing, and cracking jokes. It reminded me of scenes from Soviet movies of the last insensible days of the czarist court. Dowling, an otherwise generous fellow, was simply exercising the charming insensitivity of the proprietor, something Broadway would begin to see more and more of, but never perhaps on so grandly elegant and absurd a scale.

Secretly, of course, I was outraged, but sufficient praise was on the way to put offense to sleep. An hour or so later, at the opening-night party, Jim Proctor grabbed my arm and pulled me to a phone. On the other end was the whispered voice of Sam Zolotow, that generation's theatrical inside dopester and a reporter for the *Times,* who was actually reading our review directly off Brooks Atkinson's typewriter as the critic wrote it—I could hear the clacking of the typewriter on the phone. In his Noo Yawk voice he excitedly whispered word after word as Atkinson composed it under his nose—"Arthur Miller has written a superb drama. From every point of view, it is rich and memorable ...."—and as one encomium was laid upon another Sam's voice grew more and more amazed and warm and he seemed to reach out and give me his embrace. The conspiracy that had begun with me and spread to Kazan, the cast, Mielziner, and all the others now extended to Zolotow and Atkinson and the *Times,* until for a moment a community seemed to have formed of people who cared very much that their common sense of life in their time had found expression.

Driving homeward down lower Broadway at three in the morning, Mary and I were both silent. The radio had just finished an extraordinary program, readings of the play's overwhelmingly glowing reviews in the morning papers. My name repeated again and again seemed to drift away from me and land on someone else, perhaps my ghost. It was all a letdown now that the arrow had been fired and the bow, so long held taut, was slackening again. I had striven all my life to win this night, and it was here, and I was this celebrated man who had amazingly little to do with me, or I with him.

In truth, I would have sworn I had not changed, only the public perception of me had, but this is merely fame's first illusion. The fact, as it took much more time to appreciate, is that such an order of recognition imprints its touch of arrogance, quite as though one has control of a new power, a power to make real everything one is capable of imagining. And it can open a voraciousness for life and an impatience with old friends who persist in remaining ineffectual. An artist blindly follows his nose with hands outstretched, and only after he has struck the rock and brought forth the form hidden within it does he theorize and explain what is forever inexplicable, but I had a rationalist tradition behind me and felt I had to account to it for my rise.

I came to wish I had had the sense to say that I had learned what I could from books and study but that I did not know how to do what I had apparently done and that the whole thing might as well have been a form of prayer for all I understood about it. Simply, there is a sense for the dramatic form or there is not, there is stageworthy dialogue and literary dialogue and no one quite knows why one is not the other, why a dramatic line *lands* in an audience and a literary one sails over its head. Instead, there were weighty interviews and even pronouncements, and worst of all, a newly won rank to defend against the inevitable snipers. The crab who manages to climb up out of the bucket causes a lot of the other crabs to try to pull him back down where he belongs. That's what crabs do.

The fear once more was in me that I would not write again. And as Mary and I drove home, I sensed in our silence some discomfort in my wife and friend over these struggling years. It never occurred to me that she might have felt anxious at being swamped by this rush of my fame, in need of reassurance. I had always thought her clearer and more resolved than I. Some happiness was not with us that I wanted now, I had no idea what it might be, only knew the absence of it, its lack—so soon. In fact, the aphrodisiac of celebrity, still nameless, came and sat between us in the car.

And so inevitably there was a desire to flee from it all, to be blessedly unknown again, and a fear that I had stumbled into a dangerous artillery range. It was all an unnaturalness;

fame is the other side of loneliness, of impossible-to-resolve contradictions—to be anonymous and at the same time not lose one's renown, in brief, to be two people who might occasionally visit together and perhaps make a necessary joint public appearance but who would normally live separate lives, the public fellow wasting his time gadding about while the writer stayed at his desk, as morose and anxious as ever, and at work. I did not want the power I wanted. It wasn't "real." What was?

Outlandish as it seemed, the Dowling party in the Lomans' living room came to symbolize one part of the dilemma; the pain and love and protest in my play could be transformed into mere champagne. My dreams of many years had simply become too damned real, and the reality was less than the dream and lacked all dedication.

1987

Fabulous Appetite for Greatness

To begin with, these letters are essential to any understanding of Eugene O'Neill, if only because they demystify him, It is not merely the ordinary details of living that move him off his pedestal—income tax troubles and marital troubles and frustrations with productions of his plays. Far more powerfully, it is the sustained intensity of his feelings that brings him close, even though that may seem strange in a time of cool and campy fragmentation and disillusion. O'Neill's lifelong naked anger with the American notion of a "Showshop" theater, for example, could be taken as a comment on the theater today—if anyone cared that much now.

"I stand for the playwright's side of it in this theatre," he wrote to the producer Kenneth Macgowan in 1926. "What's the use of my trying to get ahead with new stuff until some theatre can give that stuff the care and opportunity it must have in order to register its new significance? . . . It makes me feel hopeless about writing except for my own satisfaction in a book."

Selected Letters of Eugene O'Neill, edited by Travis Bogard and Jackson R. Bryer, who previously edited the letters of O'Neill to Macgowan (Mr. Bogard is also the editor of the *Complete Plays* of Eugene O'Neill in the Library of America series), is a collection of nearly 600 of his letters, many published for the first time. The volume could once again make his life and work instructive to a generation that needs the example of his integrity and grit, his vision and undying belief in what he called an art theater (something his Provincetown Playhouse ceased to be after a time).

His alienation from Broadway was total even at the height of his success. When he received the Nobel Prize in Literature in 1936, he wrote to Russel Crouse: "I have rec'd congratulations from all over the world . . . Hauptmann, Pirandello, Lenormand, etc. but none from home front playwrights with the exception of Ned Sheldon, Sam Behrman, George Middleton and your esteemed self." Then he applied an unprintable obscenity to his "U.S. colleagues" in general. (Actually, Sidney Howard wrote him a bit later.)

Journalists had him pegged as either a remote mystic or a drunken bum, but in this mass of correspondence he is an entirely different sort—several other sorts, in fact. Passionately involved in his time, a worried father, a canny theater agent for his own plays, an overwhelmed husband, a property owner, and a lifelong anarchist who in 1944 expressed "contempt for [Franklin D. Roosevelt's] sly hypocritical politician's tricks" (he favored the Socialist Norman Thomas), he was sufficiently conformist to advise Eugene Jr. at Yale "to have one fine, perfectly-fitting expensive suit of clothes where others will have three maybe but each minus the distinction."

O'Neill was the anarchist radical to the end. In June 1942 he wrote to his son Eugene: "It is like acid always burning in my brain that the stupid butchering of the last war taught men nothing at all, that they sank back listlessly on the warm manure pile of the dead and went to sleep, indifferently bestowing custody of their future, their fate, into the hands of State departments, whose members are trained to be conspirators, card sharps, double-crossers and secret betrayers of their own people; into the hands of greedy capitalist ruling classes so stupid they could not even see when their own greed began devouring itself; into the hands of that most debased type of pimp, the politician, and that most craven of all lice and job-worshippers, the bureaucrats."

But no other country, he felt, could match America for its spiritual possibilities. In the early 1920s he was not among the wave of disgusted American artists who fled from a mindless materialism to France. He wrote to the journalist Malcolm Mollan in 1921: "One critic . . . has said tragedy is not native to our soil, has no reason for being as American drama. . . . If it were true, it would be the most damning commentary on our spiritual barrenness. Perhaps it was true a decade ago but America is now in the throes of a spiritual awakening. . . . A soul is being born, and where a soul enters, tragedy enters with it. Supposing someday we should suddenly see with the clear eyes of a soul the true valuation of all our triumphant, brass band materialism, see the *cost*. . . . Why, we *are* tragedy the most appalling yet written or unwritten!" And from these letters his life seems, indeed, the work of creating a soul.

But in the end his grandiose, uncompleted cycle of plays about American history from its beginning would go to demonstrate "the bitter assertion," as the editors of this volume put it, that "to gain the world, the United States had sold its soul." He was a man divided, as he himself often said, and pointed to *The Great God Brown* as proof, between despair at a cynical materialism triumphant and his ever-renewing commitment to an ennobled human spirit. But he would never fuse the two conflicting sides excepting in his art, particularly in two of his final plays, *The Iceman Cometh* and *Long Day's Journey into Night*.

There are remarks in these letters that one cannot read without a sort of forlorn delight in the unchangingness of the torture that a playwriting life affords. To the critic George Jean Nathan about H. L. Mencken's criticism of his play *Welded*, O'Neill wrote: "I must confess the greater part of his comment seems irrelevant as criticism of my play. To point out its weakness as realism (in the usual sense of that word) is to confuse what is obviously part of my deliberate intention. Damn that word, 'realism!' When I first spoke to you of the play as a 'last word in realism,' I meant something 'really real,' in the sense of being spiritually true, not meticulously life-like." And finally the inevitable leaning on the last hope: "Well, just wait until you see it played! (if it's done right)."

His contempt for most critics is par for the course—"me that was born on Times Square . . . and have heard dramatic critics called sons of bitches . . . ever since I was old enough to recognize the Count of Monte Cristo's voice!" And "every paper ought to fire from their Drama Department anyone who has written a play. The boys look in the mirror and get bilious with envy." But what is unusual, to say the least, are his friendships with two or three critics—Joseph Wood Krutch, George Jean Nathan, Brooks Atkinson, the heavy hitters to whom he sometimes gave scripts before production so he could confute their opinions or sometimes follow their suggestions. Apparently critics were not always virgins of objectivity whose purity could not withstand the proximity of actual artists and their struggles to create life on the stage.

Belying the usual characterization of him as a total loner is the large number of letters to and about his children. And there is no more painful irony to contemplate in all the events of his life than the way his own "cursed" family evolved. In 1927 he wrote to his second wife, Agnes Boulton O'Neill, from their house at Spithead in Bermuda: "Our Home. *Our Home!* I feel that very much about Spithead, don't you? That this place is in some strange symbolical fashion our reward, that it is the permanent seat of our family—like some old English family estate. I already feel like entailing it in my will so that it must always be background for our children!" Two of those children would end in suicide and one he would in fury disown. And finally, beloved Agnes herself he would call the "idiot mother" of his children, a drunk and a "bigamist."

These letters confound a number of orthodox attitudes toward O'Neill's so-called unsophistication. In fact, he read widely, he knew Chinese and German philosophy, he began a serious study of ancient Greek, and he was far from being an inept writer of prose. Nor did he keep disdainfully apart from his peers—among them Padraic Colum and James Joyce, Sinclair Lewis and Sherwood Anderson, and his left-wing friends Mike Gold and Sean O'Casey, to whom he would exclaim, "I wish to God I could write like that!" He knew his work tended toward garrulousness but dreaded "leaving anything out"—his scenarios for three plays ran to 25,000 words each.

* * *

Despite the fifty-year period that these letters cover, a unity in O'Neill's life strikes the reader; from the beginning he had a fabulous appetite for greatness, and despite many personal and artistic lapses—of which he was helplessly aware—a noble quest emerges. As always, it is the spectacle of great courage that, in spite of his failings, merits a salute. "If we had Gods or a God, if we had a Faith, if we had some healing subterfuge by which to conquer Death, then the Aristotelian criterion might apply in part to our Tragedy," he wrote to Brooks Atkinson. "But our tragedy is just that we have only ourselves, that there is nothing to be purged into except a belief in the guts of man, good or evil, who faces unflinchingly the black mystery of his own soul!"

Toward the end, with his two greatest masterpieces in hand—*The Iceman Cometh* and *Long Day's Journey into Night*—in which at last he had fused character and theme, style and substance, he refused at first to let them be produced in the commercial Broadway theater. He wrote to Macgowan: "I dread the idea of production because I know it will be done by people who have really only one standard left, that of Broadway success.... The big fact is that any production must be made on a plane, and in an atmosphere to which neither I nor my work belongs in spirit, nor want to belong: that it is ... the Old Game, the game we used to defy in the P[rovincetown] P[layhouse] but which it is impossible for me to defy now, except in my writing, because there is no longer a theatre of true integrity and courage and high purpose and enthusiasm.... To have an ideal now, except as a slogan in which neither you nor anyone else believes but which you use out of old habit to conceal a sordid aim, is to confess oneself a fool who cannot face the High Destiny of Man!"

With his great and awesome hammer O'Neill kept striking the mountain to the bitter end, and this book is worthy of his struggle.

1988

Ibsen's Warning

I don't suppose anything has given me more gratification than the success of *An Enemy of the People* in its recent Young Vic production. I have made no secret of my early love for Ibsen's work, and now to have been in some way responsible, along with some very fine young actors and a passionately perceptive director, for a new appreciation of one of his most central ideas, is something that puts a satisfying warmth in my belly.

It is a terrible thing to have to say, but the story of *Enemy* is far more applicable to our nature-despoiling societies than to even turn-of-the-century capitalism, untrammeled and raw as Ibsen knew it to be. The churning up of pristine forests, valleys and fields for minerals and the rights of way of the expanding rail systems is child's play compared to some of our vast depredations, our atomic contamination and oil spills, to say nothing of the tainting of our food supply by carcinogenic chemicals.

It must be remembered, however, that for Ibsen the poisoning of the public water supply by mendacious and greedy interests was only the occasion of *An Enemy of the People* and is not, strictly speaking, its theme. That, of course, concerns the crushing of the dissenting spirit by the majority, and the right and obligation of such a spirit to exist at all. That he thought to link this moral struggle with the preservation of nature is perhaps not accidental. After all, he may well have found enough examples of moral cowardice and selfish antisocial behavior in other areas such as business, science, the ministry, the arts or where you will.

It is many years now since I looked into an Ibsen biography but I seem to recall that the genesis of *Enemy* was usually thought to be a news report of the poisoning of the water supply at a Hungarian spa. If there was a Dr. Stockmann prototype who vainly protested against keeping the public ignorant of the truth, I cannot recall it. But whether or not this was the overt stimulus behind the play the question still remains why Ibsen should have seized upon it so avidly—he wrote this play in a remarkably short time, a few weeks.

Thinking about his choice throws me back to Henry David Thoreau who likewise found in nature's ruin the metaphor of man's self-betrayal. And Thoreau, I think, stood within an intellectual tradition of distrust of progress, one that goes back to the Roman poets, and the concomitant age-old view of the city as inevitably decadent and the unspoiled country as noble. Where it comes to nature even radical artists are likely to be very conservative and suspicious of change; perhaps nature takes on even more of a pure moral value where religion itself has vanished into skepticism. The sky may be empty but to look out on untouched forest or a pristine lake is to see if not God or the gods, then at least their abandoned abode. Ibsen needed an absolute good for evil to work against, an unarguably worthy brightness for dark mendacity to threaten, and perhaps nature alone could offer him that. And, of course, this is even more effective in our time when people have to go to the supermarket to buy clean water.

I am sure that few in the first New York audience of the early Fifties were terribly convinced by the play's warnings of danger to the environment. The anticommunist gale was blowing hard and it was the metaphor that stood in the foreground; moreover, in that time of blind belief in rational, responsible science, any suggestion that, for example, we might be building atomic generating plants that were actually unsafe would have simply been dismissed as dangerous obscurantist nonsense. And given my own identification with the Left, the metaphor was widely suspect as a mere ploy, an attempt to link the Reds, then under heavy attack, with Ibsen's truth-bearer. So neither the story nor the metaphor could carry the credibility that they do now when both have been revalued as alarmingly prophetic instinctual conceptions—it often does indeed take moral courage to stand against commercial and governmental bureaucracies that care nothing for the survival of the real world outside their offices. It is but one more evidence that the artist's powerful desire to penetrate life's chaos, to make it meaningfully cohere, has literally created a truth as substantial as a sword for later generations to wield against their own oppression.

1989

Again They Drink from the Cup of Suspicion

I did not write *The Crucible* simply to propagandize against McCarthyism, although if justification were needed that would have been enough. There was something else involved. I'll try to explain.

A writer friend was recently telling me about a Moscow theater producer who is interested in putting on a play about the Vietnam War. Why Vietnam? It turns out that what he would really like to illuminate is the Russian defeat in Afghanistan, but with feelings about Afghanistan still running so high he felt he needed a metaphor that would go to the dilemmas underlying such a war, rather than attempting an outright confrontation with the thickets of feeling surrounding Afghanistan itself.

That approach reminded me of my decision to write about the 1692 Salem witch trials, rather than trying to take on Joseph McCarthy and his cohorts directly. In the early fifties McCarthyism, so-called, began as a conservative Republican cavalry charge that in the name of anti-Communism helped scatter the left-liberal coalitions of Democrats and union people who had held together the only recently faded New Deal. But this was no ordinary political campaign. This time the enemy was not merely "The Democrat Party," as McCarthy sneeringly renamed it, but the hidden foreign plot which, naively but often knowingly, it shielded. Thus a certain sublime gloss—national security—was varnished over a very traditional grab for domestic political power.

With amazing speed McCarthy was convincing a lot of not unintelligent people that the incredible was really true, and that, say, General of the Army George Catlett Marshall was a Communist sympathizer, or that Senator Millard E. Tydings of Maryland was a buddy of Earl Browder, head of the American Communist Party. (A photo of both of them standing happily together would only much later be proved to have been a fake manufactured by Roy Cohn, McCarthy's right-hand bandido.)

For a time it began to seem that Senator Joe was heading straight for the White House, the more so when the sheer incredibility of his claims appeared to be part proof that they were real; if the Communists were indeed hidden everywhere, it followed that they would certainly be found where common sense indicated they could not conceivably be.

The case being circular, it was finally all but unarguable. Worse yet, you could not rely on the too-trusting police, the naively legalistic courts, or even the slow-moving F.B.I. to root out the conspiracy. As for the press, it was all but sold to Moscow, secretly, of course. Who then was absolutely reliable? McCarthy, naturally, and those who had his blessing.

This was colorful and fascinating stuff for the stage, but a play takes a year to write and months to see through production, and I could not imagine spending so much time on what seemed to me so obvious a tale. But as the anti-Communist crusade settled in, and showed signs of becoming the permanent derangement of the American psyche, a kind of mystery began to emerge from its melodramas and comedies. We were all behaving differently than we used to; we had drunk from the cup of suspicion of one another; people inevitably were afraid of too close an association with someone who might one day fall afoul of some committee. Even certain words vibrated perilously, words like organize, social, militant, movement, capitalism—it didn't do to be on too familiar terms with such language. We had entered a mysterious pall from which there seemed no exit.

Returning around that time to my alma mater, the University of Michigan, to do a story for *Holiday* magazine, I discovered that students were avoiding living in the co-op rooming houses because the very idea of a nonprofit organization was suspiciously pro-left. The F.B.I. was paying students at Michigan to report secretly on teachers' political remarks, and teachers to report on students.

Why was there so little real opposition to this madness? Of course there was the fear of reprisals, of losing jobs, or perhaps only bad publicity, but there was also guilt, and this seemed to me the main crippler, the internalized cop.

No doubt instinctually, McCarthy and Roy Cohn were handing around full plates of guilt which were promptly licked clean by people who in one way or another had brushed the sleeve of the Communist movement in the thirties—some by joining the party or supporting one of its front organizations, a left-wing union or professional guild, or in whatever manner had at some point in their lives turned to the left. Of course such people were used to being guilty—why else would they have bothered to worry about the poor, the blacks, the lynch victims, the Spanish Republicans, and so on when real Americans were only remotely aware of such inequities around them?

It was a charm, a kind of spell. McCarthy could call the Roosevelt New Deal "20 years of treason" with hardly a rejoinder from the vast multitude of Americans for whom New Deal measures, hardly more than a decade before, had meant the difference between living on the street or in their own homes, between hunger and real starvation. It was a sort of benighted miracle that just about anything that flew out of his mouth, no matter how outrageously and obviously idiotic, could be made to land in an audience and stir people's terrors of being taken over by Communists, their very religion in danger.

I had known the Salem story since college, over a decade earlier, but what kept assaulting my brain now was not the hunt for witches itself; it was the paralysis that had led to more than twenty public hangings of very respectable farmers by their neighbors. There was something "wonderful" in this spectacle, a kind of perverse, malign poetry that had simply swamped the imaginations of these people. I thought I saw something like it around me in the early fifties.

The truth is that the more I worked at this dilemma the less it had to do with Communists and McCarthy and the more it concerned something very fundamental in the human animal: the fear of the unknown, and particularly the dread of social isolation.

Political movements are always trying to position themselves as shields against the unknown—vote for me and you're safe. The difference during witch-hunts is that you are being made safe from a malign, debauched, evil, irreligious, wife-swapping, deceitful, immoral, stinking conspiracy stemming from the very bowels of hell. In Wisconsin in the early fifties a reporter went door to door asking residents if they agreed with certain propositions, ten in number, and discovered that very few people did, and that most thought the first ten amendments to the United States Constitution, unnamed of course in the inquiry, were Communistic. To propose that we should be free to express any idea at all was frightening to a lot of people.

The Colonial government in the 1690s saw itself as protecting Christianity (while unknowingly propagating a thrilling counter-religion of Satan worship) by seizing on the ravings of a klatch of repressed pubescent girls who, fearing punishment for their implicitly sexual revolt, began convincing themselves that they had been perverted by Satan. There were economic and social pressures at work, but the nub of it all as it appeared to the locals at the moment was that the Archfiend had been sneaked into the spotless town by an alien who, even better, was black, the Barbadian slave of the Lord's very own man, the church minister himself. Authority quickly converted the poor girls back to the true religion and made them celebrities for their agonizing bravery in pointing out likely adherents of the Devil.

But were there not really Communists, whereas there never were any witches? Of course. And there are also paranoids who are really being followed. There was a very real military face-off in the fifties between America and the Soviet Union, and we had only recently "lost" China, but were these grounds for blacklisting actors and writers in Hollywood, or destroying professionals in many other fields, and for turning the country into a whispering gallery? What research showed me, and what I hoped the play would show the country and the world, was the continuity through time of human delusion, and the only safeguard, fragile though it may be, against it—namely, the law and the courageous few whose sacrifice illuminates delusion.

In the 35 years since the play was written it has become my most produced work by far. I doubt a week has gone by when it has not been on some stage somewhere in the world. It seems to be produced, especially in Latin America, when a dictatorship is in the offing, or when one has just been overthrown.

There is so often a telltale social sidelight connected to its production. Years ago in South Africa, black Tituba had to be played by a white woman in blackface, but the director, Barney Simon, terrified though he was of attack, wanted the white audience to contemplate the story. Last year I happened to meet Nien Cheng, the seventy-year-old author of *Life and Death in Shanghai*, an account of her six-year imprisonment during the Cultural Revolution. Tears formed in her eyes when she shook my hand, tears, as it surprisingly turned out, of gratitude.

Released from prison, she had spent months recuperating when a director friend, Huang Tsolin, invited her to see his production of *The Crucible* in a Shanghai theater. She said she was astounded: "I could not believe the play was not written by a Chinese because the questions of the court were exactly the same ones the Cultural Revolutionaries had put to me!"

I saw the play in Tbilisi, Soviet Georgia, where John Proctor wore seventeenth-century Turkish pantaloons and a gorgeous wide moustache and was chased through a forest by a crowd waving scimitars. At Olivier's fabulous 1965 National Theatre production, with Colin Blakely and Joyce Redman, I overheard a young woman in front of me whispering to her escort, "Didn't this have something to do with that American Senator—what was his name?" I have to admit that it felt marvelous that McCarthy was what's-his-name while *The Crucible* was *The Crucible* still.

Simone Signoret and Yves Montand did a stirring French film, a version of their Paris stage performance, with a screenplay by Jean-Paul Sartre in which the New England farmers were, inexplicably, Roman Catholic. The Long Wharf Theater in New Haven is about to open it under Arvin Brown's direction—it was Long Wharf's first production 25 years ago—and the Roundabout Theater will be doing it later this season. An HBO film of it is to be made this winter for both television and theatrical distribution. In Glasgow recently two productions were running at the same time, one by a young Soviet company. The Schiller Theater in Berlin will have it on in a few months.

I have wondered if one of the reasons the play continues like this is its symbolic unleashing of the specter of order's fragility. When certainties evaporate with each dawn, the unknowable is always around the corner. We know how much depends on mere trust and good faith and a certain respect for the human person, and how easily breached these are. And we know as well how close to the edge we live and how weak we really are and how quickly swept by fear the mass of us can become when our panic button is pushed. It is also, I suppose, that the play reaffirms the ultimate power of courage and clarity of mind whose ultimate fruit is liberty.

1989

Introduction to *The Golden Years* and *The Man Who Had All the Luck*

Both of these plays came out of the years leading up to World War II, between 1938, my college graduation year, and 1944 when the fighting was raging. For me they are a kind of unadulterated evidence of my reactions to that time and it strikes me oddly that, as up to my neck as I was in the feverish anti-Fascism that swept my generation, the plays I chose to write were so metaphorical. This is especially strange when the only tradition in American theater of which I was aware was realism. I can't imagine what I thought I was doing.

Or, rather, I thought I knew that I was writing against the grain of the Broadway theater of the time, the only theater we had, which as usual was happily wallowing in its traditional sidewalk realism. My primary argument with this form was that I could not connect aspiration with it—it was too much like uninterpreted life. *The Golden Years* looked toward a non-existent poetic theater inspired by the Elizabethan models. Its lavish use of actors was no doubt encouraged by the fact that in the early months of its writing I was on the payroll, at $22.77 a week, of the expiring Playwriting Project of the WPA Theater, and at least in theory could call upon any number of actors for my cast. Unfortunately, before the play was finished, Congress had wiped out the WPA Theater and the play, like any play calling for several immense sets and a cast so large, was doomed as a possible commercial enterprise. It was never produced until the BBC did a radio production in 1987.

Excepting for a revision of three pages at the end of *The Man Who Had All the Luck,* and some mild pruning of both plays, I have left them as they were. *The Man Who Had All the Luck* was given a regular Broadway production and lasted less than a full week after the critics, with one or two interested but puzzled exceptions, could make absolutely nothing of it. I recall at the time being unable to find the slightest connection between the production and the play I imagined I had written, and after watching but one bewildering performance fled back to my desk and began a novel, resolved never to write for the theater again. It was 45 years later, in 1988, that I began to understand the reason for my alienation from my own play, as well, very possibly, for the total incomprehension of the critics.

A staged reading of the play under the direction of Ralph Bell, an old friend who had always had a soft spot in his heart for this play, quickly revealed that it is, indeed, a fable with no relation to realistic theater. A fable, of course, is based on an obsessive grip of a single idea bordering on the supernatural and it is the idea that stands in the forefront, rather than the characters and the verisimilitudes of the tale. The coincidences are arrantly unapologetic in this play and so they should be played, rather than attempts made to rationalize them and dim them down.

I recall the original production lit in reassuring pink and rose, a small-town genre comedy. Given the threatening elements in the story, this atmosphere must indeed have been puzzling. The play is after all attacking the evaluation of people by their success or failure and worse yet, denying the efficacy of property as a shield against psychological catastrophe.

From a distance of half a century I am struck by a certain optimistic undercurrent in both plays, despite one being a tragedy and the other veering pretty close. I must say that, at the time, life at best seemed headed for a bloody showdown with Fascism, or at worst a hapless surrender to it, but while there is plenty of worry in these plays, there is no real despair or defeat of the spirit. This will strike some as perhaps a reflection of a callow Leftism, but in truth it was the way most Americans felt even after a very long decade of Depression. By the late thirties and early forties we had, of course, known much social violence and all kinds of vileness, but not yet a Holocaust, not yet the bursting of the banks of evil. I can still recall my incredulity at the daylight bombing of Guernica in the Spanish Civil War. As bombings go, it wasn't a very big one. The big ones were still on the way. But I simply could not believe that a European flying low in an airplane on a sunny day over an undefended town, could, whatever his politics, drop live bombs on women out shopping with their baby carriages, on old men sitting before their doorways, on young lovers strolling across the ancient square! It was hard to sleep for weeks afterwards. It was still possible to be shocked. At least within one's mind the lines of some sort of order of permissible human behavior still held.

In the West since the War of 1914–18 every period has known its main menace, some single force threatening life on the planet. For a long time now it has been Communism, and as this menace disintegrates, there are signs that ecological catastrophe is developing into a worldwide substitute. From the mid-thirties to the outbreak of war with the Axis powers it was the Fascist threat—and for some its promise—that pervaded every discussion. An important source of the energy in these plays was my fear that in one form or another Fascism, with its intensely organized energies, might well overwhelm the wayward and self-fixated Democracies. A reader today may find it strange that two such very different works could spring from the same source, or even, perhaps, that they are at all related to contemporaneous political events.

The telltale mark of this preoccupation, as I now see quite clearly, is much the same in both plays, even if one is a tragedy about the Cortes invasion of Montezuma's Mexico in 1522 and the other the tale of a very successful young man in a pastoral Ohio village. They are both struggling against passive acceptance of fate or even of defeat in life, and urge action to control one's future; both see evil as irrational and aggressive, the good as rational, if inactive and benign. Plainly, I was hounded at the time by what seemed the debility of Americans' grasp of democratic values or their awareness of them. And I must recall—to fill out this picture—that these plays were written after a decade of Depression, which had by no means lifted with any certainty as yet, and that the Depression had humbled us, shown us up as helpless before the persistent, ineradicable plague of mass unemployment. Reason had lost a lot of her credentials between 1930 and 1940.

If as the decade ended, the devaluation of the individual—the main lesson of the Depression—was still spiked to the common consciousness, these plays are somewhat surprising testimony to me that I had not lost the belief in the centrality of the individual and the importance of what he thought and did. On this evidence I suppose I might even have been called an individualist—there is nothing like writing a play for unveiling one's illusions! *The Man Who Had All the Luck* tells me that in the midst of the collectivist thirties I believed it decisive what an individual thinks and does about his life, regardless of overwhelming social forces. And likewise, in *The Golden Years,* the fate of all Mexico hung on what an individual—Montezuma—believed about himself and his role in the universe. Indeed, if these plays are to be credited, there is no force so powerful, politically as well as personally, as a man's self-conceptions.

Hearing *The Man Who Had All the Luck* read after four decades, it only then occurred to me that I had written the obverse of the Book of Job. The story of a man who cannot come to terms with the total destruction of his property and all his hopes, when he has done nothing to earn such treatment from God or fate, is very much the same as that of a man who can't seem to make a mistake and whose every move turns out to be profitable and good. What had Job done to deserve such disasters? David Beeves has much the same question in mind, oppressed by his invariably good luck in everything he attempts. And he projects an imminent disaster that will even things up between himself and the rest of humanity. For both these characters the menace is much the same—anarchy in the high command of the universe, a yawning breach between effect and conceivable causation, and they are both an argument with God.

There is mitigation in the Book of Job, of course, since we are shown a purpose behind Job's catastrophe. God starts all the trouble by wagering with the Devil that nothing he can do will shake good Job's faith in Himself. So it is clearly the Evil One who strips Job of his good life in order to destroy his belief in God's justice. And indeed, it turns out that after much twisting and backsliding Job, despite everything, clings to God—and he is promptly rewarded with the return of all his wordly goods plus God's personal gratitude for his having kept the faith. Of course this won't do in our time if only because most of God's argument with Job consists of reminding the poor man of the incomprehensibility of his obscure powers—"Can you draw out the Leviathan with a fishook?" and so on. This sort of humiliation is less impressive now when we can press a trigger and destroy whales and might even lift them up with helicopters, and the atom in our hands has the power of a sun. It is the question of justice that we haven't come any closer to clearing up, and indeed the goal of achieving it may be moving further away, so perhaps there is still a little room for *The Man Who Had All the Luck.*

As for the ending of this play—which I am sure I have rewritten twenty times over the past half century, it is as satisfactory as it is possible to be, as complete, let's say, as Job's, which also doesn't quite come down on both feet. The simple fact is that, as moving and imperative as our questioning of our fates may be, there is no possibility of answering the main question—why am I as I am and my life as it is? The more answers one supplies the more new questions arise. David Beeves in this play arrives as close as he can at a workable, conditional faith in the neutrality of the world's intentions toward him. I would emphasize the conditional side of it, but it is better than shooting out your brains in sheer terror of what may happen tomorrow.

The Golden Years, its purplish passages notwithstanding, is a harder if earlier look at passivity and its risks, but here the society as well as an individual is at stake. Montezuma, like the Democracies facing Hitler, was as though hypnotized. Weakened by self-doubt, he looks to Cortes, manifestly a brute and a conqueror, as one who may nevertheless bear within him the seed of the future. Something has ended for Montezuma before Cortés ever arrived in Mexico, the heart-lifting glamor of what men call the future is gone out of his life and he can foresee only deadly and meaningless repetition. There was a metaphorical poetry in this in the late thirties when perfectly intelligent, respectable, even heroic folk like the great flier Charles Lindbergh and his wife Anne could return from a visit to Nazi Germany and call it "The Wave of the Future." I recall feeling myself surrounded in those times by a kind of drifting into cultural suicide and a self-blinded acceptance of murder in high places, and this play was written in alarm. A few years later I did believe that had the Japanese not been deluded enough to attack Pearl Harbor there might well have been sufficient isolationist sentiment in the American people to simply let Hitler have his way with a defeated England and Europe. In a word, our passivity seemed in reality a drift toward an unacknowledged arrangement with Fascism. So—perhaps despite appearances—these are two anti-Fascist plays that were written quite close to the abyss. But perhaps more importantly, they were one very young writer's wrestling with enormous themes.

1989

Conditions of Freedom: Two Plays of the Seventies—*The Archbishop's Ceiling* and *The American Clock*

I

It is pointless any longer to speak of a period as being one of transition—what period isn't?—but the seventies, when both these plays were written, seemed to resist any definition even at the time. *The Archbishop's Ceiling* in some part was a response to this indefinition I sensed around me. Early in the decade the Kent State massacre took place, and while the anti-Vietnam War movement could still mobilize tens of thousands, the freshness had gone out of the wonderful sixties mixture of idealism and bitterness that had sought to project a new unaggressive society based on human connection rather than the values of the market economy. There was a common awareness of exhaustion, to the point where politics and social thought themselves seemed ludicrously out of date and naively ineffectual except as subjects of black comedy. Power everywhere seemed to have transformed itself from a forbidding line of troops into an ectoplasmic lump that simply swallowed up the righteous sword as it struck. Power was also doing its own, often surprising thing.

At least as an atmosphere, there was a not dissimilar disillusion in Eastern Europe and, for different reasons, in France too. As president of International P.E.N, I had the opportunity to move about in Eastern Europe, as well as in the Soviet Union, and I felt that local differences aside, intellectual life in the whole developed world had been stunned by a common failure to penetrate Power with a more humane and rational point of view. It may have been that the immense sense of relief and the high expectations that rushed in with the defeat of Hitler and Mussolini's fascism had to end in a letdown, but whatever the causes, by the seventies the rational seemed bankrupt as an ultimate sanction, a bar to which to appeal. And with it went a sense of history, even of the evolution of ideas and attitudes.

The ups and downs of disillusionment varied with time and place, however. It was possible to sit with Hungarian writers, for example, while they talked of a new liberalizing trend in their country, at the very moment that in Prague the depths of a merciless repression were being plumbed. There, with the Soviet ousting of Dubček and the crushing of all hope for an egalitarian socialist economy wedded to liberal freedoms of speech and artistic expression, the crash of expectations was especially terrible, for it was in Prague that this novel fusion seemed actually to have begun to function.

The seventies was also the era of the listening device, government's hidden bugs set in place to police the private conversations of its citizens—and not in Soviet areas alone.

The White House was bugged, businesses were bugging competitors to defeat their strategies, and Watergate and the publication of the Pentagon Papers (which polls showed a majority of Americans disapproved) demonstrated that the Soviets had little to teach American presidents about domestic espionage. The burgling of psychiatrists' offices to spy out a government official's private life, the widespread bugging by political parties of each other's offices, all testified to the fact that the visible motions of political life were too often merely distractions, while the reality was what was happening in the dark.

Thus, when I found myself in Eastern European living rooms where it was all but absolutely certain that the walls or ceilings were bugged by the regime, it was not, disturbingly enough, an absolutely unfamiliar sensation for me. Of course there were very important differences—basically that an Eastern writer accused of seditious thoughts would have no appeal from his government's decision to hound him into silence, or worse. But the more I reflected on my experiences under bugged ceilings, the more the real issue changed from a purely political one to the question of what effect this surveillance was having on the minds of people who had to live under such ceilings, on whichever side of the Cold War line they happened to be.

Vaclav Havel, the Czech playwright who was later to serve a long term in prison, one day discovered a bug in his chandelier when house painters lowered it to paint the ceiling; deciding to deliver it to the local police, he said that it was government property that he did not think rightfully belonged to a private person. But the joke was as unappreciated as the eavesdropping itself was undenied. Very recently, in the home of a star Soviet writer, I began to convey the best wishes of a mutual friend, an émigré Russian novelist living in Europe, and the star motioned to me not to continue. Once outside, I asked if he wasn't depressed by having to live in a tapped house. He thought a moment, then shrugged—"I really don't know how I feel. I guess we figure the thing doesn't work!"—and burst out laughing at this jibe at Soviet inefficiency. Was he really all that unaffected by the presence of the unbidden guest? Perhaps so, but even if he had come to accept or at least abide it fatalistically, the bug's presence had changed him nonetheless. In my view it had perhaps dulled some resistance in him to Power's fingers ransacking his pockets every now and then. One learns to *include the bug* in the baggage of one's mind, in the calculus of one's plans and expectations, and this is not without effect.

The occasion, then, of *The Archbishop's Ceiling* is the bug and how people live with it, but the theme is something different. There are a number of adaptations to such a life: one man rails furiously at the ceiling, another questions that a bug is even up there, a third has changes of opinion from day to day; but man is so adaptable—and anyway the bug doesn't seem to be reacting much of the time and may simply be one more nuisance—that resistance to its presence is finally worn down to nothing. And that is when things become interesting, for something like the naked soul begins to loom, some essence in man that is simply unadaptable, ultimate, immutable as the horizon.

What, for instance, becomes of the idea of sincerity, the unmitigated expression of one's feelings and views, when one knows that Power's car is most probably overhead? Is sincerity shaken by the sheer fact that one has so much as *taken the bug into consideration?* Under such pressure who can resist trying to some degree, however discreet and slight, to characterize himself for the benefit of the ceiling, whether as obedient conformist or even as resistant? And what, in that case, has been done to one's very identity? Does this process not overturn the very notion of an "I" in this kind of world? It would seem that "I" must be singular, not plural, but the art of bureaucracy is to change the "I" of its subjects to "we" at every moment of conscious life. What happens, in short, when people know that they are—at least most probably, if not certainly—at all times talking to Power, whether through a bug or a friend who is really an informer? Is it not something akin to accounting for oneself to a god? After all, most ideas of God see him as omnipresent, invisible, and condign in his judgments; the bug lacks only mercy and love to qualify, it is conscience shorn of moral distinctions.

In this play the most unreconcilable of the writers is clearly the most talented. Sigmund really has no permanent allegiance except to the love of creating art. Sigmund is also the most difficult to get along with, and has perhaps more than his share of cynicism and bitterness, narcissism and contempt for others. He is also choking with rage and love. In short, he is most alive, something that by itself would fuel his refusal— or constitutional incapacity—to accept the state's arrogant treatment. But with all his vitality, even he in the end must desperately call up a sanction, a sublime force beyond his ego, to sustain him in his opposition to that arrogance; for him it is the sublimity of art, in whose life-giving, creative essence he partakes and shares with other artists whose works he bows to, and in the act transcends the tyranny.

In a sense *Archbishop* begs the question of the existence of the sacred in the political life of man. But it begins to seem now that some kind of charmed circle has to be drawn around each person, across which the state may intrude only at its very real economic and political peril.

Glasnost, which did not exist in the seventies, is to the point here, for it is at bottom a Soviet attempt, born of economic crisis, to break up the perfection of its own social controls in order to open the channels of expression through which the creativity, the initiatives, and the improvisations of individual people may begin to flow and enrich the country. The problem, of course, is how to make this happen in a one-party state that in principle illegalizes opposition. But the wish is as plain as the desperate need of the economy itself, indeed of the regime, for the wisdom of the many and the release of their energies. Finally, the question arises whether, after so many generations of training in submission, the habits of open-minded inquiry and independence can be evoked in a sufficient number of people to make such a policy work.

Late in 1986, when glasnost was a brand-new idea scarcely taken seriously as the main thrust of the new administration, a Russian writer expressing the pre-glasnost view said to me, "What you people in the West don't understand is that we are not a competitive society and we don't wish to be. We want the government to protect us, that is what the government is for. When two Western writers meet, one of them most likely asks the other what he is writing now. Our writers never ask such a question. They are not competing. You have been in our Writers Union and seen those hundreds of writers going in and out, having their lunches, reading newspapers, writing letters, and so on. A big number of those people haven't written anything in years! Some perhaps wrote a few short stories or a novel some years ago—and that was it! They were made members of the Union, got the apartment and the vacation in the south, and it is not so different in any other field. But this is not such a terrible thing to us!"

But, I countered, there were surely some highly talented people who produced a good deal of work.

"Of course! But most are not so talented, so it's just as well they don't write too much anyway. But is it right that they should be thrown out in the streets to starve because they are not talented? We don't think so!"

What he had chosen to omit, of course, was that the mediocrities, of which he was all but admittedly one, usually run things in the Writers Union, something the gifted writers are usually too prickly and independent to be trusted to do. And so the system practically polices itself, stifling creativity and unpalatable truth-telling, and extolling the mediocre. But its main object, to contain any real attempts at change, is effectively secured. The only problem is that unless the system moves faster it may be permanently consigned to an inferior rank among the competing societies.

And so it may well have come to pass that the sanctity of the individual, his right to express his unique sense of reality freely and in public, has become an economic necessity and not alone a political or aesthetic or moral question. If that turns out to be the case, we will have been saved by a kind of economic morality based on necessity, the safest morality of all.

II

The American Clock was begun in the early seventies and did not reach final form until its production at the Mark Taper Forum in Los Angeles in 1984, a version that in turn was movingly and sometimes hilariously interpreted in the Peter Wood production two years later at the British National Theatre. The seemingly endless changes it went through reflected my own search for something like a dramatic resolution to what, after all, was one of the vaster social calamities in history—the Great Depression of the thirties. I have no hesitation in saying that as it now stands, the work is simply as close to such a resolution as I am able to bring it, just as the experience itself remains only partially resolved in the hands of historians. For the humiliating truth about any "period" is its essential chaos, about which any generalization can be no more than just that, a statement to which many exceptions may be taken.

With all its variety, however, there were certain features of the Depression era that set it apart, for they had not existed before in such force and over such a long time. One of the most important of these to me, both as a person living through those years and as a writer contemplating them three decades afterwards, was the introduction into the American psyche of a certain unprecedented *suspense*. Through the twenties the country, for me—and I believe I was typical—floated in a reassuring state of nature that merged boundlessly with the sea and the sky; I had never thought of it as even having a system. But the Crash forced us all to enter history willy-nilly, and everyone soon understood that there were other ways of conducting the nation's business—there simply had to be, because the one we had was so persistently not working. It was not only the radicals who were looking at the historical clock and asking how long our system could last, but people of every viewpoint. After all, they were hardly radicals who went to Washington to ask the newly inaugurated President Roosevelt to nationalize the banks, but bankers themselves who had finally confessed their inability to control their own system. The objective situation, in a word, had surfaced; people had taken on a new consciousness that had been rare in more prosperous times, and the alternatives of fascism or socialism were suddenly in the air.

Looking back at it all from the vantage of the early seventies, we seemed to have reinserted the old tabula rasa, the empty slate, into our heads again. Once more we were in a state of nature where no alternatives existed and nothing had grown out of anything else. Conservatism was still damning the liberal New Deal, yearning to dismantle its remaining prestige, but at the same time the Social Security system, unemployment and bank insurance, the regulatory agencies in the stock market—the whole web of rational protections that the nation relied on—were products of the New Deal. We seemed to have lost awareness of community, of what we rightfully owe each other and what we owe ourselves. There seemed a want of any historical sense. America seems constantly in flight to the future; and it is a future made much like the past, a primeval paradise with really no government at all, in which the pioneer heads alone into the unknown forest to carve out his career. The suddenness of the '29 Crash and the chaos that followed offered a pure instance of the impotence of individualist solutions to so vast a crisis. As a society we learned all over again that we are in fact dependent and vulnerable, and that mass social organization does not necessarily weaken moral fiber but may set the stage for great displays of heroism and self-sacrifice and endurance. It may also unleash, as it did in the thirties, a flood of humor and optimism that was far less apparent in seemingly happier years.

When Studs Terkel's *Hard Times* appeared in 1970, the American economy was booming, and it would be another seventeen years before the stock market collapsed to anything like the degree it had in 1929. In any case, in considering his collection of interviews with survivors of the Depression as a partial basis for a play (I would mix my own memories into it as well), I had no prophecy of doom in mind, although in sheer principle it seemed impossible that the market could keep on rising indefinitely. At bottom, quite simply, I wanted to try to show how it was and where we had come from. I wanted to give some sense of life as we lived it when the clock was ticking every day.

The idea was not, strictly speaking, my invention but a common notion of the thirties. And it was a concept that also extended outward to Europe and the Far East; Hitler was clearly preparing to destroy parliamentary governments as soon as he organized his armies, just as Franco had destroyed the Spanish Republic, and Japan was manifestly creating a new empire that must one day collide with the interests of Britain and the United States. The clock was ticking everywhere.

Difficulties with the play had to do almost totally with finding a balance between the epic elements and the intimate psychological lives of individuals and families like the Baums. My impulse is usually toward integration of meaning through significant individual action, but the striking new fact of life in the Depression era—unlike the self-sufficient, prosperous seventies—was the swift rise in the common consciousness of the social system. Uncharacteristically, Americans were looking for answers far beyond the bedroom and purely personal relationships, and so the very form of the play should ideally reflect this wider awareness. But how to unify the two elements, objective and subjective, epic and psychological? The sudden and novel impact of the

Depression made people in the cities, for example, painfully conscious that thousands of farm families were being forced off their lands in the West by a combination of a collapsed market for farm goods and the unprecedented drought and dust storms. The farmers who remained operating were aware—and openly resentful—that in the cities people could not afford to buy the milk for which they could not get commercially viable prices. The social paradoxes of the collapse were so glaring that it would be false to the era to try to convey its spirit through the life of any one family. Nevertheless the feeling of a unified theatrical event evaded me until the revision for the 1984 Mark Taper production, which I believe came close to striking the balance. But it was in the British National Theatre production two years later that the play's theatrical life was finally achieved. The secret was vaudeville.

Of course the period had much tragedy and was fundamentally a trial and a frustration for those who lived through it, but no time ever created so many comedians and upbeat songs. Jack Benny, Fred Allen, W. C. Fields, Jimmy Durante, Eddie Cantor, Burns and Allen, and Ed Wynn were some of the headliners who came up in that time, and the song lyrics were most often exhilaratingly optimistic: "Love Is Sweeping the Country," "Life Is Just a Bowl of Cherries," "April in Paris," "I'm Getting Sentimental over You," "Who's Afraid of the Big Bad Wolf?" It was, in the pop culture, a romantic time and not at all realistically harsh. The serious writers were putting out books like Nathanael West's *Miss Lonelyhearts,* Erskine Caldwell's *God's Little Acre,* Jack Conroy's *The Disinherited,* André Malraux's *Man's Fate,* Hemingway's *Winner Take Nothing,* and Steinbeck's *In Dubious Battle,* and Edward Hopper was brooding over his stark street scenes, and Reginald Marsh was painting vagrants asleep in the subways, but Broadway had O'Neill's first comedy, *Ah, Wilderness!,* and another comical version of the hard life, *Tobacco Road,* Noel Coward's *Design for Living,* the Gershwins' *Let 'Em Eat Cake,* and some of the best American farces ever written—*Room Service, Three Men on a Horse,* and *Brother Rat* among them.

In the Mark Taper production I found myself allowing the material to move through me as it wished—I had dozens of scenes by this time and was shifting them about in search of their hidden emotional as well as ideational linkages. At one point the experience brought to mind a sort of vaudeville where the contiguity of sublime and ridiculous is perfectly acceptable; in vaudeville an imitation of Lincoln doing the Gettysburg Address could easily be followed by Chinese acrobats. So when subsequently Peter Wood asked for my feeling about the style, I could call the play a vaudeville with an assurance born of over a decade of experimentation. He took the hint and ran with it, tossing up the last shreds of a realistic approach, announcing from the opening image that the performance was to be epic and declarative.

Out of darkness, in a brash music hall spotlight, a baseball pitcher appears and tosses a ball from hand to glove as he gets ready on the mound. The other characters saunter on singing snatches of songs of the thirties, and from somewhere in the balcony a man in a boater and striped shirt, bow tie and gartered sleeves—Ted Quinn—whistles "I Found a Million-Dollar Baby in a Five-and-Ten-Cent Store." At one side of the open stage, a five-piece jazz band plays in full view of the audience (impossible in the penurious New York theater), and the sheer festivity of the occasion is already established.

The most startling, and I think wonderful, invention of all was the treatment of the character of Theodore K. Quinn. This was the actual name of a neighbor of mine, son of a Chicago railroad labor organizer, who had worked himself up from a poor Chicago law student to the vice-presidency of General Electric. The president of GE, Quinn's boss through most of the twenties, was Gerard Swope, a world-famous capitalist and much quoted social thinker, who decided as the thirties dawned that Quinn was to succeed him on his retirement. Quinn, in charge of the consumer products division of the company, had frequently bought up promising smaller manufacturers for Swope, incorporating their plants into the GE giant, but had developed a great fear that this process of cartelization must end in the destruction of democracy itself. Over the years his rationalization had been that he was only taking orders—although in fact it was on his judgment that Swope depended as to which companies to pick up. Then the excuses were threatened by his elevation to the presidency, an office with dictatorial powers at the time. As he would tell me, "Above the president of General Electric stood only God."

The real Ted Quinn had actually been president of GE for a single day, at the end of which he put in his resignation. "I just couldn't stand being the Lord High Executioner himself," he once said to me. He went on to open an advisory service for small businesses and made a good fortune at it. During World War II he was a dollar-a-year head of the Small Business Administration in Washington, seeing to it that the giant concerns did not gobble up all the available steel. Particularly close to his heart was the Amana company, a cooperative.

Quinn also published several books, including *Giant Business, Threat to Democracy,* and *Unconscious Public Enemies,* his case against GE-type monopolies. These, along with his anti-monopoly testimony before congressional committees, got him obliterated from the roster of former GE executives, and the company actually denied—to journalist Matthew Josephson, who at my behest made an inquiry in 1972—that he had ever so much as worked for GE. However, in the course of time a film director friend of mine who loved to browse in flea markets and old bookstores came on a leather-covered daily diary put out by GE as a gift for its distributors, circa 1930, in which the company directors are listed, and Theodore K. Quinn is right there as vice-president for consumer sales. The fact is that it was he who, among a number of other innovations, conceived of the compact electric refrigerator as a common consumer product, at a time when electric refrigeration was regarded as a purely commercial item, the behemoth used in restaurants, hotels, and the kitchens of wealthy estates.

From the big business viewpoint Quinn's central heresy was that democracy basically depended on a large class of independent entrepreneurs who would keep the market competitive. His fear was that monopoly, which he saw spreading in the American economy despite superficial appearances of competition, would end by crippling the system's former ingenuity and its capacity to produce high-quality goods at reasonable prices. A monopoly has little need to improve its product when it has little need to compete. (First Communist China and then Gorbachev's Russia would be grappling with a very similar dilemma in the years to come.) He loved to reel off a long list of inventions, from the jet engine to the zipper, that were devised by independent inventors rather than corporations and their much advertised laboratories: "The basic things we use and are famous for were conceived in the back of a garage." I knew him in the fifties, when his populist vision was totally out of fashion, and maybe, I feared, an out-of-date relic of a bygone America. But I would hear it again in the seventies and even more loudly in the eighties as a muscle-bound American industrial machine, wallowing for generations in a continental market beyond the reach of foreign competition, was caught flat-footed by German and Japanese competitors. Quinn was a successful businessman interested in money and production, but his vision transcended the market to embrace the nature of the democratic system for which he had a passion, and which he thought doomed if Americans did not understand the real threats to it. He put it starkly once: "It may be all over, I don't know—but I don't want to have to choose between fascism and socialism, because neither one can match a really free, competitive economy and the political liberties it makes possible. If I do have to choose, it'll be socialism, because it harms the people less. But neither one is the way I'd want to go."

Perhaps it was because the style of the National Theatre production was so unashamed in its presentational declarativeness that the Ted Quinn role was given to David Schofield, a tap dancer with a brash Irish mug, for Quinn was forever bragging about—and mocking—his mad love of soft-shoe dancing. And so we had long speeches about the dire consequences of business monopoly delivered by a dancer uncorking a most ebullient soft-shoe all over the stage, supported by some witty jazz played openly before our eyes by a deft band. As Quinn agonizes over whether to accept the presidency of GE, a phone rings at the edge of the stage; plainly, it is as the new president that he must answer it. He taps his way over to it, lifts the receiver, and simply places it gently on the floor and dances joyously away.

It was in the National Theatre that I at last heard the right kind of straightforward epic expressiveness, joyful and celebratory rather than abashed and veiled, as economic and political—which is to say epic—subjects were in the mouths of the characters. In this antic yet thematically precise spirit, accompanied by some forty songs out of the period, the show managed to convey the *seriousness* of the disaster that the Great Depression was, and at the same time its human heart.

There was one more invention that I particularly prized. Alone in her Brooklyn house, Rose Baum sits at the piano, bewildered and discouraged by the endless Depression, and plays some of the popular ballads of the day, breaking off now and then to muse to herself about the neighborhood, the country, her family, her fading hopes. The actress sat at a piano whose keyboard faced the audience, and simply held her hands suspended over the keys while the band pianist a few yards away played the romantic thirties tunes. Gradually a triple reality formed such as I have rarely witnessed in the theater: first, the objective stage reality of the band pianist playing, but somehow magically directed by Rose's motionless hands over her keyboard; and simultaneously, *the play's memory* of this lost past that we are now discovering again; and finally, the middle-aged actress herself seeming, by virtue of her motionless hands suspended over the keys, to be recalling this moment from her very own life. The style, in short, had fused emotion and conscious awareness, overt intention and subjective feeling—the aim in view from the beginning, more than a decade before.

1989

Uneasy About the Germans: After the Wall

Do Germans accept responsibility for the crimes of the Nazi era? Is their repentance such that they can be trusted never to repeat the past? When people worry about the unification of Germany, these are the usual questions. But for me there is a deeper mystery, and it concerns the idea of nationhood itself in the German mind.

Three attempts to create a successful state have been smashed to bits in the mere seventy-two years since Germany's defeat in 1918. And although we are now in the presence of a great victory of a democratic system over a one-party dictatorship, it is not a democratic system of German invention. The nation about to be born is one that never before existed. And in apprehension over what this may mean, the Jews are by no means alone. The British are concerned and so are the French, not to speak of the Russians and numerous others whose lives were ruined by German aggression.

I have more than the usual contact with Germans and German-speaking people. My wife, Austrian by birth, spent the war years in Germany, and her family is involved in German industry; I have German journalist friends, as well as colleagues in the German theater and the film and publishing industries. If I were to announce that I am not too worried about unification and have confidence in the democratic commitments of the younger generation, my friends would doubtless be happy to hear it—and proceed to worry privately on their own.

No one can hope to predict what course any country will take. I believe that for Germans, including those who are eager for unification, the future of German democracy is as much of an enigma as it is for the rest of us. They simply don't know. More precisely, they are almost sure it will turn out all right. But that's a big almost.

Several weeks ago in West Berlin, one of my wife's high school friends, a woman in her late sixties who never left Germany through the rise of Nazism, the war and reconstruction, had some conflicted, if not dark, things to say about the question. "In Germany it will always be the same," she said. "We go up very high, but in the end we come down. We are winning and winning and winning, and then we lose. And when we are in trouble we turn to authority; orders and work make us happiest."

She is using a cane these days, after a fall on the ice. She has a broad-beamed peasant air, thinning hennaed hair, ruddy cheeks. A survivor of a battered generation, she seems to refer to her own observations rather than to things she has read. "We must go slowly with unification," she said. "It is all darkness in front of us." And if the future is murky to West Germans, she wondered: "What is in the minds of the East Germans? We don't know. For us it was bad enough. We had twelve years of dictatorship, but after that we have had nearly fifty years of democracy. They have had nothing but dictatorship since 1933. To become democratic, is it enough to want a good job and a car and to hate the left?"

She has come to visit, despite her injury, because in her circle it is hard to find an open-minded conversation. "I fear it is all very artificial," she said. "It is the same old story, in one sense. We are not like the French, the British, the Americans. We never created our own democracy, or even our own regime, like the Russians; ours was handed to us by the Allies, and we are handing it to the DDR people. But we had a memory of democracy before Hitler. Even their fathers have no such memory now. Who will influence whom—we over them or they over us?"

She talks about the Republicans, a far-right extremist party that won ninety thousand votes in the last West Berlin election after only a few months of existence. "People say they are nonsensical, a tiny minority," she said. "I remember the other tiny nonsensical minority and how fast it took over. And mind you, we are prosperous now. What happens if we run into hard times and unemployment?"

That conversation could be repeated as many times as you like in Germany. But it is entirely possible that two-thirds of the Germans—those under 50, who can barely recollect Nazism—have only the remotest connection with the woman's sentiments and underlying worry. So hostile are they to any government intrusion in their lives that some of them made it nearly impossible to conduct a national census a few years ago because the questions being asked seemed to threaten them with regimentation from on high. Questions had to be altered, and some census takers were even accompanied by inspectors to make sure more personal questions than those prescribed were not asked.

Nevertheless, the Berlin woman's apprehensions do leave a nagging suspicion. Does the Federal Republic of Germany arouse lofty democratic feelings in its citizens' minds, or is it a system that is simply a matter of historical convenience invented by foreigners? To be sure, this system has helped the nation to prosper as never before, but the issue is how deep the commitment is to its democratic precepts, how sacred they are, and if they will hold in hard times.

I have often sensed something factitious about German society in the minds of Germans, regardless of viewpoint. Discounting the zephyrs—or clouds—of guilt and resentment that obscure conversations with foreigners, especially Jewish liberals like me, it seems that the very reality of the German state is still not quite settled in their minds. I have never, for example, felt that Germans have very transcendent feelings toward the Federal Republic; it does not seem to have imbued them with sublime sensations, even among those who regard it as a triumph of German civic consciousness risen from the ruins of war.

Nothing, at least in my experience, approaches the French emotions toward their republic, the British toward their confusing monarchy, the Swiss toward their multilingual democracy, or Americans' feelings toward their country (which at least once every quarter century is pronounced imminently dead from depression, war, racial conflict or corruption, and therefore requires the loudest avowals of patriotic fervor on the face of the earth).

In a word, the German ship, in the German mind, increasingly powerful and promising though it may be, seems to float slightly above the surface without displacing water. Again, I may get this impression because of the tendency of Germans to apologize for themselves implicitly, which in some is a form of secret boasting, given the incredible success of the German economy.

The Berlin woman's sense of the system as having been conferred on Germans rather than created by them—a routine enough idea in Germany—nevertheless expresses the insubstantiality or, as she put it, the artificiality of the society that is now being merely multiplied by unification. It has sometimes seemed to me in Germany that there is a feeling of walking on Astroturf rather than natural sod. Or maybe it is simply a feeling that the other shoe has not yet dropped.

But when one recalls the polities they did unquestionably create on their own—Frederick the Great's Prussia, Bismarck's state and Hitler's—they were all dictatorial or at least heavily authoritarian and in their time remarkably successful. This is also what my wife's Berlin friend was trying to say to me, namely that as a German she does not quite trust her compatriots' civic instinct when it comes to constructing a free society. And I wonder whether, unspoken, this is the source of the distrust a great many people feel in and out of West Germany, especially now that its territory is to be reunited with the East.

Of course, for the foreigner, Germany's civic failure is most perfectly expressed by the Holocaust and military aggressions of Hitler. But I have wondered whether, foreigners and their accusing attitudes on these counts apart, a different and less obvious historical experience is not more active in creating an uneasiness in them, an experience uniquely German.

It has often been said that Germans alone among the major peoples have never won a revolution. Instead, Germany's intense inner integration of social services, economy and culture was conceived and handed down by kings, princes and great chancellors like Count Bismarck (who though elected was kingly and sternly paternalistic), then a ferocious dictator and, since 1945, by her wartime victors. It is as though George Washington had accepted the widespread demand that he be crowned king, and proceeded to carve out a new society with little or no contribution or interference by elected legislatures. America might well have emerged with a fine well-ordered society in which the rules were very clear and life deeply organized from cradle to grave.

Instead, the state's decisions became the American citizen's rightful business, a conception that destroyed the time-honored relationship in which he was merely the subject of the state's attentions and efforts. The image of himself as citizen was thus vastly different from that in other post-feudal societies of the time—and from that of most people of our time.

Besides a lack of revolutionary past, the Federal Republic is unique among the great powers in another way: it came to life without a drop of blood being shed in its birth. No German soldier can say, "I fought for democracy." It was not given him by history to do so. West Germany is the creation not of arms, but work. The Japanese system, also practically America's creation, is a quite different case, in that the monarchy and government were never destroyed as such; indeed, MacArthur took great pains to make its continuity with the past obvious to all.

The German break with Hitlerism, the last German-made system, had to be total and condign. And German society had to be started almost literally from a pile of bricks under which the shameful past was to be buried, put out of mind, deeply discredited.

If these observations are in fact operative, and I cannot imagine how they can be proved or disproved as such, then what Germans lack now is the consecration by blood of their democratic state. The torrent of German blood that has flowed in this era in the Hitler-launched wars was, in fact, to prevent any such state from coming into existence.

For me, this is what keeps sucking the life out of German protestations of a democratic faith and casts suspicion on the country's reassurances that its economic power is no menace to the world. The fact is, West German civic practice has been as democratic as any other society's for more than forty years and is less repressive and all-controlling than, for example, that of France, whose bureaucracy is positively strangulating by comparison.

I know Germans who are as certain as it is possible to be that democracy will hold; I know other Germans who do not believe that at all. The world, it seems to me, has no choice but to support the positive side of the split and to extend its hand to a democratic Germany. By giving it the recognition it deserves, German democracy can only be strengthened, but meeting it with endless suspicion may finally wither its hopes. A recent New York Times/CBS News poll shows a large majority of Americans in favor of reunification, a vote of confidence with which I agree. At the same time, no German should take umbrage at the reminder that his nation in a previous incarnation showed that it had aggressive impulses that brought death to forty million people. This memory should not vanish: it is part of democratic Germany's defense against the temptation to gather around some new extreme nationalism in the future.

It does not really do any good to remind Germans of those horrendous statistics if the purpose is simply to gratify an impulse to punish. But it is necessary never to forget what nationalistic blood lust can come to, so that it will never happen again.

Likewise, German resentment at such reminders has to be understood. No one can live in a perpetual state of repentance without resentment. In the scale and profundity of its degradation Nazism has no equal in modern time, but each country has had some level of experience with contrition, some taste of it, as a repayment for oppression of other people. What if every nation guilty of persecution were to own up? Are we really prepared to believe in their remorse? And while penitence in the persecutors may be a moral necessity for those who survived victimization, it will not bring back the dead. So is it not infinitely more important that the descendants of persecutors demonstrate something more than contrition, namely political responsibility?

What do I care if a Nazi says he's sorry? I want to know what the constitution and educational system of Germany are doing to defend democracy under possibly difficult future circumstances. That is important to me and to my children. It is equally important that democracy live not only in institutions but in the German heart. But in all candor how are we ever to know that it does, except as crises are faced in a democratic spirit?

The world has a right—its World War II dead have earned it the right—to reproach and criticize and make demands of Germans if and when they seem to revert to bad habits. For a long time to come, the Germans are going to have to face the legacy of their last attempt to dominate other nations.

But there is another Germany—the Germany of high aspirations. It does truly exist, and it must be welcomed wholeheartedly in the hope that one day its permanent dominion over the country will be unquestioned by any fair-minded person. In short, the time has come to look the worst in the eye but to hope for the best.

A German journalist in her mid-forties, typical of many of her generation despite an upper-class Black Forest origin, has struggled with her country's past all her life and by turns is in despair and hopeful. "The problem," she says, "or part of it, is that the world is still thinking of Germany as it was in the Nazi time or shortly after. But a lot has happened in Germany in the last forty years!" As her voice rises, I am struck by an odd resemblance to the attitude of the Berlin woman. They both seem to doubt that they are *registering*; it is as if events were wild horses flying past with no one really pondering how to tame them. "For example," she goes on, "the impact of the 1968 French students' rebellion. It overturned Germany's educational system and for the first time made it possible for German workers to go to universities, the way it happens in America. Until then, we had a very narrow elite system. In fact, ours is now far more democratic than the French or the English, and we are now paying people to go to university, eight hundred marks a month if their parents together earn less than fifteen hundred a month. University education is free. This has had good and bad results—a lowering of standards, actually—but socially it has broken the class system."

Slim, elegantly dressed and a stubbornly heavy smoker, she is unable to come psychologically to rest. "This generation cannot be confused with the stupid, lumpen people who flocked to Hitler," she said. "Moreover, there is an immense amount of travel by this generation. They are not the parochial, isolated mass that Hitler poisoned so easily with antiforeign propaganda. This is not in any sense the pre-Hitler German people."

Then, hardly a moment later: "The problem with the German, the one great weakness of his character, is his worship of loyalty. Loyalty! Loyalty! It's the supreme virtue, the chain around his heart. . . ." And she is quite suddenly angry, and, for a few minutes, blue and uncertain and perhaps fearful.

In short, the uneasiness about national character is subjective, difficult to catch in the nets of rationality, but it may turn out to be more decisive than any other.

The anxiety shown by the journalist and my wife's Berlin friend transcends political viewpoints, I believe. Nor is it purely a product of the catastrophic last war and the Holocaust. I know some liberal Germans, a couple of radicals and some very conservative business types, and from all of them I have felt a similar emanation of uncertainty as to what, in effect, the German is—and consequently what kind of society fits him, expresses his so contradictory nature. And this is what I think the perplexity comes down to.

The Federal Republic is not a nation like others, born of self-determining revolution. Paradoxically, perhaps, West Germany is the first great society born of peace; if it is to achieve a deep sense of identity it will have to be real, not slyly apologetic, an identity reflecting the evil past and the present resurrection together.

If Germany remains implicitly on trial for a long time to come, release must come through good works and a demonstrated devotion to democratic ideals and practice. The past cannot be changed, but the future of democracy is in the nation's hands. Perhaps Germany can one day even stand as an example to other new societies of how to win a place in the world by work and the intelligent use of science rather than arms.

There is now a generation that cannot remember the war or Nazism, and in fact finds it difficult to understand them, especially what to it is the incredible degree of

Nazi regimentation to which Germans submitted. Maybe it is time for Germans to take a look at how and why their society began, not for the sake of cosmetizing an image, but to make themselves more real in their own eyes. If I may quote *Incident at Vichy,* when the Jewish psychoanalyst confronts the self-blaming Austrian prince, "It's not your guilt I want, it's your responsibility." That is to say, to relinquish denial and take to heart the donations of history to one's character and the character of one's people, the most painful but rewarding job a people can undertake.

1990

A Conversation with Arthur Miller: Interview by Janet Balakian

The following conversation took place on Tuesday, June 27, 1989 in Manhattan.

Balakian: In some ways you seem to have begun a new phase in your career with plays like *The Creation of the World and Other Business, Some Kind of Love Story, An Elegy for a Lady, Danger: Memory!, The American Clock, The Archbishop's Ceiling*, and now your new screenplay, *Everybody Wins*. How would you compare these works to your earlier writing? Do you see them as different ventures from the earlier plays?

Miller: I suppose that these last plays, with the big exception of the short play *Clara*, have a different view of life which is not an overtly tragic view. *The Creation of the World*, of course, is really the first tragedy in our religious mythology, a fratricide, but I treated it comedically, as man's groping his way to his own human nature with no instructions. The attempt underneath was to illuminate a kind of biological morality; that is, for the species to survive there had to be negatives in the world, there had to be prohibitions, there had to be a form, in short, because the race would destroy itself through narcissism and competitiveness. You can see it crudely in a litter of puppies where they're all fighting to get fed. The fluctuating moral consequences of a given human nature are really what all my plays are about in a way, but this was an attempt to come closer to its most primitive, naked, and uncomplicated givens. So it's both continuous with the other plays and it's different.

Balakian: The difference being?

Miller: One difference I think is in tone; man is thrashing around blindly, yet, in a kind of a touching and moving way, toward some tolerable civilized form for his alienated feelings, which, he instinctively senses, are murderous. Parenthetically, it's interesting that the first story in the Hebrew Bible, and later in the Christian Bible, is of a murder, and I think what the old rabbis were after with this story was to show why the Bible was necessary.

A play like *Some Kind of Love Story*, which I very roughly based my new film on, is an offshoot in the sense that I present the appearance of reality, namely a woman who knows something about a murder; but she is soon revealed to be a fantasist. But the investigator has a sense that her fantasies don't necessarily negate her facts. Worse yet, he falls in love with her, further warping his hold on reality. So the question of what is real, how you measure the real, becomes the issue when the evidence seems outrageous.

Balakian: Do you see the question of illusion and reality as something that concerns you more now than it did in your earlier plays?

Miller: I always thought of the play as a lifting of the veil, as far back as *All My Sons.* That play took great pains to create a veritable backyard, and people sitting around having very ordinary conversations—the well-known norms of suburbia. And then the screen begins to tip over and we see what's behind it. So, it was always there: I begin with an equilibrium and something tips that equilibrium and interprets it as a result.

Balakian: How the birds come home to roost.

Miller: Right. The past reaches into the present, usually destructively, but leaving some illumination behind. I was thinking of that the other day in relation to China. These awful recent events are really China reasserting herself; it's that 6000-year history of feudalism catching up with this short-lived movement to enter a democratic civilization, and it's just [*Miller punches the palm of his hand with his fist, and makes the sound of an airplane crashing.*] The past is really the stubbornest problem of mankind. This is interesting to me, because a lot of our contemporary drama deals with characters who have no past. It's probably the nature of the film form, which after all is the single great cultural invention of this civilization. And you don't need a past in movies. The movie image is so overwhelming that it's convincing in itself; the person is *there,* simply by being photographed. The movie is eminently the art of the present tense. As soon as it slows down to give you the past you feel the urgency leaking out. It's true all over the West, not just here—this farewell to the past. I even wonder sometimes whether the theater as a form isn't in trouble, because it isn't sufficiently in the present tense and has to build up its effects by painfully accreting information through words. The Absurd drama made an attempt to escape all of that, but it left behind the psychological dialectic and created archetypes or cartoons, emphasizing situations rather than characters.

Balakian: But *The Creation of the World* is an archetypal story. You're less interested in character in the conventional sense. Yet at the same time it's a play completely about the past.

Miller: The play is set in the past, but the First Man and Woman and their sons, of course, have no past; they are all simply the essential human traits being assembled for the first disaster.

Balakian: Would you say that you're becoming less naturalistic and more symbolic in your writing? You have said that if you live long enough that's the way it ends up.

Miller: The time arrives when everything that happens has a certain backward-flowing echo, and little seems to be happening for the first time. You get carried off by the echo, and you see that life is cyclical, that human beings do repeat fundamental reactions. But that certain changes are made as a result of this repetition; it's a repetition and it's also an adventure, motion along a locus. For example, the whole sixties period. Having gone through the thirties, one couldn't help but notice the similarities and the differences. In the thirties it also came down to matters of style, the dress, the counterbourgeois clothing styles. This had all happened before. No Group Theater actor, for example, would be caught dead wearing a suit in a theater where everybody had always dressed like a British, Shakespearean star—conventionally. If you went up for a part to a producer, you dressed as though you were going to a bank. So the first thing that these rebels did was to dress like workers and, along with respect for the establishment, discard all of that clothing. Well, the same thing happened in the sixties *vis à vis* the fifties, and I found a certain futility in the repetition. Nevertheless, when it happened I was all for it—the rebellion—but I made a speech at Michigan telling the students that, while it's absolutely necessary that they do this, it's also a good idea to remember that somewhere down the line they were going to be held accountable for it, either by the F.B.I. spy who may be in the next seat, or simply by life. In other words, they were creating their past which they might have to face one day. Anyway, concerning your question about whether or not I've become less naturalistic and more symbolic. . . . I never really was the former. It's true that I wanted to make the characters as documented as was feasible, as parts of the social scene, but I wasn't interested in simply photographing types, that was only the beginning—the end in view was wonder. Maybe as a result people don't feel these plays belong to a different age; they can relate to these characters as not quite time-bound.

Balakian: Do you see these later plays as being more metaphysical than the early ones, or can't you separate the metaphysical from the social?

Miller: I have never been able to separate them. It's all one piece, one dream, sometimes real-looking, sometimes surreal. Back in 1949 I met Thomas Mann who had seen *Death of a Salesman* here in New York. He said that if a European had written the play, there would have been a discussion of the theme by the characters. And I think he was slightly disappointed about that. He felt the Lomans were like aborigines. I said, that's the greatest compliment I've had yet, although I'm not sure he meant it as a compliment. You see, I was not trying to create a work for academics to discuss. It's a very European idea, also an academic one, that if the characters don't directly discuss the theme, it hasn't got one. The point is that I hope the livingness of what I've written is there, and I let the audience make up its mind what this whole thing is about.

Balakian: You seem to be more interested in myth than in psychology in these later plays, and it reminds me of your character Marcus in *The Archbishop's Ceiling* who says, "I'm not sure I believe in psychology anymore. That anything we think really determines what we're going to do or what we feel." Do you feel this way now?

Miller: I do feel that way very often. Most decisions are made because it's five o'clock. After all, what is psychology? It is the depth to which we can presently reach into ourselves, and that may not turn out to be all that deep finally. [*We laugh.*] Freud started out as a neurologist more than a psychologist, as a "pure" scientist. He said it was all going to end with pharmacology and neurology. In other words, back to the chemistry. That's interesting. In other words, we may be in an intermediate stage between the sidewalk and the stars.

Balakian: Doesn't Leo say in *I Can't Remember Anything* that he's just going to end up as a bunch of chemicals?

Miller: Right. Of course he is taunting mysticism and religion.

Balakian: Are there concerns that you have now at age 74 in 1989 as a playwright that you didn't have when you were launching your career?

Miller: Of course. I'm working on a play that I started eleven years ago, one that I've tried to shake loose from at least 25 times! Formally speaking it's very free flowing, a little bit like *Salesman* was. But this one spills in all directions; time is rather plastic. While the story is moving forward, it's also moving sideways and out. That's probably one reason why it has taken me eleven years to find it and what it seems to be telling me.

Balakian: When I was asking what concerns you have now that you didn't have when you began writing, is it connected to this new play in the sense of time that you're speaking about?

Miller: It's viewing people from a tragic distance again, but with a certain forbearance, even a comic despair. But the play is still asserting that, while we are weak, the rules of life are powerful, and they exist. And that's a tragic view, and therefore hopeful.

Balakian: You have voiced that view throughout your plays.

Miller: Now it's funnier maybe. [*We laugh.*] I'm not sure whether this will end up a tragedy or a comedy. . . . I mean the theatrical impression it will make.

Balakian: So your tragic perspective is becoming more humorous with time?

Miller: Yes. Although what I think is funny has a tendency to make people cry.

Balakian: Do you have a title for your play in progress?

Miller: It's called *The Ride Down Mount Morgan*. But I can't begin to talk about it yet, beyond what I've just told you, because it's in the making.

Balakian: You've said that the older you get the more you'd feel at home in Periclean Athens or Dickens' London. Would you elaborate on that statement?

Miller: The Athens reference . . . if one can judge from the few plays we have, which are a fraction of the ones that were written, it seems as though the main business of life was to illuminate some coherent meaning to the whole human career. And for the plays to be involved so consistently in that kind of quest must indicate that the audience was also. At the same time we know that they were nuts about athletics, human beauty, a sensuous life. In other words, we're not dealing with a monastery. There was a wholeness of spirit that is enviable. We've got here now in New York and in America an enormous variety of experience, but there is also a pervading sense that it's all cornflakes, that it's all collapsing meaninglessly around our ears. I could be wrong about that, because there are millions of people who go to churches, but probably for ritualistic reassurance rather than philosophy; it seems to me that life is perceived as being just one thing after another until it stops.

Balakian: Is this why you never felt at home in the mode of the Absurdists—Ionesco, Beckett, Pinter—to some extent? Their plays aren't trying to illuminate significance but rather confirming the fact that life is a chaotic mess.

Miller: Yes. I think Beckett is different in the sense that, especially in later life, he's emphasizing a challenge that he implicitly hopes we can meet, the challenge of confronting the void without despairing of life. But it's true that I was rather uncomfortable with them. When people tend to celebrate the meaningless, it ends up with fascism. When they get too comfortable with the inevitable defeat of human hope, with man as a creature who is doomed to slip on a banana peel, I smell dictatorship around the corner; probably because I was born into the era when it was not an exaggeration to think that the hopeless could maybe turn out the lights on everything and kill you for being a Jew or a skeptic.

Balakian: The bending of time has interested you since *Salesman* and continues to do so in *Danger: Memory!,* in *The American Clock,* and in your autobiography, *Timebends.* Would you discuss your interest in time and memory, in getting inside the head, as you have always been interested in doing, and the forms that best help you in this exploration?

Miller: I think that a playwright, more than any other kind of artist, excepting possibly dance people, but in a very different way, is, by the nature of the art, involved with intense condensation. So, time is of the essence in everything he does.

Balakian: You're using the word condensation. A poem is certainly condensed, but you're talking about physical movement.

Miller: Theater is a dynamic form; it's going by you in a way that painting isn't but music is. In poetry, technically speaking, you can start and go back and keep combing the poem. To be sure, you can study a play endlessly, too, but for the audience it's in motion going past so that whatever has to be said through the play, has to be said in time. These days they've stretched the limits of performances beyond measure, going on six, seven, eight hours, but those aren't really dramas; they're performance pieces, like Robert Wilson's which are really set design displays, or special works like Peter Brooks's with *The Ik,* which I think of as a form of spiritual naturalism. He's trying to give you the feeling of what has happened by making you sit for a very long, eventless time. (This was an experimental work based on a book about a tribe in Africa called the Ik. It's fascinating, because it's a tribe whose social ties have been so destroyed that the people no longer have even a familial sense; they're so weakened that they can't do what we consider the fundamental actions of civilized people.)

Anyway, apart from these special events, you still have to work within some kind of time limit. So, consequently, time becomes an obsessive thing. It has become more mysterious with me over the years, possibly because I'm getting older, and as I said earlier, echoes of the past are loud in the present so that the idea of time as a circular motion becomes more and more realistic. For example, (my examples are political because we're all conscious of that) I think that ironically enough Ronald Reagan's master image was Franklin Roosevelt. He even went to the extreme of imitating his radio chats. In a time of television he did a weekly *radio* speech. This was literal miming of his father, because Reagan was growing up when this godlike leader was in power. In fact, he became a travesty of the original, favoring the rich over the poor. Now if you weren't aware of Roosevelt, I don't think you could see that dimension. So you need time or history, which is time-as-story.

Balakian: So you need time to have it bend.

Miller: I have become more and more obsessed with time. It's hard to avoid. If I walk down a street in New York, where I was born, I pass new buildings going up and I stand there and try to remember what was there before. In several cases the building they just tore down is the second one torn down on that lot in my memory.

Balakian: That brings me to the question of memory, which is the subject of *Danger: Memory!*.

Miller: And of A Memory of Two Mondays [written in 1955].

Balakian: You've said that's the play closest to your heart!

Miller: I tell in my book how I went back to that warehouse a few years later, but they didn't recognize me. But I recognized them! I knew all of them but when they looked at me, they saw nothing they recalled. That's a wonderful mystery.

Balakian: It is. Although you liken your recent play *Danger: Memory!* to *Salesman* in the sense that the past spills into the present, these characters cannot remember.

Miller: That's interesting. I hadn't thought of that. The past for her is obliterated.

Balakian: Could you talk a little bit about that play? I'm intrigued by it because it seems like a new Arthur Miller phenomenon that I haven't encountered before in your work. It's certainly not a play that deals with social issues. What were you after in that play?

Miller: I guess the play is looking at the phenomenon of time dying. All she's got left are immediate sensations. She sees deer, trees, things that evoke a sense of beauty in her. She wants to see beautiful things. But Leo does not accept the idea that time can die. He even doubts that she's forgetting all of this. He keeps prodding her to remember. Memory is time. He's a life force in a sense. You can interpret it in a lot of ways. One of the actors said that what she is really saying is that sex for her has ended. And he's saying, "It hasn't! You have just suppressed it all."

Balakian: Right. Her husband has died, and Leo is trying to tell her "why don't you go on a trip, why don't you take up piano again!" Is it true that you rewrote the *Clara* play, which follows *I Can't Remember Anything,* for the London production?

Miller: In my original version the adult murdered daughter comes in as a young girl and later as a young woman. Gregory Mosher, the director of the Lincoln Center production, convinced me that we couldn't do it that way here. So, in that version the father talks to her, but she isn't there. I never felt that succeeded, so I put it back the way it was: an actual young girl comes in. We had a very young girl of twelve or so in the New York production. In the London production they had an actress of twenty, but she was also able to be a very young child when required.

Balakian: Would you talk more about your notion of time in this play?

Miller: I guess what fascinated me about it was the idea of dropping out of time.

Balakian: Dropping out of time is something Willy Loman does, but in a completely different way.

Miller: Different. He's trying to get into his life, not out.

Balakian: Leonora is dropping out of time, but Leo isn't.

Miller: He's a direct contrast with her. He thinks the world is real. She was brought up in the New England tradition: life is earnest and has a purpose. And he's saying, "Look, I'm an engineer."

Balakian: I noticed that in both of those plays you use bridge building as a kind of motif.

Miller: I never thought of that. Many years ago I started a play I never finished called *The Half Bridge,* the dominant image being a bridge half finished, because it doesn't connect to the other side.

Balakian: When you wrote *A Memory of Two Mondays,* was the way you dealt with time very different from your use of time in *Danger: Memory!?*

Miller: The significant thing about *A Memory of Two Mondays* for me is that the people are being observed and are not aware that they're in time; only the observer knows.

Balakian: It's like they're in purgatory.

Miller: Yeah. It's the young boy, Bert, who knows they're in time. He's observing time as a pathetic user-up of people. He aches for them. He says there should be a statue in the park for these people to celebrate them, because they're being swept away by the clock. They don't know that they're in time, but he does. That's the pathos. They're involved in repetition; they do the same thing all the time, forever.

Balakian: I know that the Greeks, Shakespeare, and Ibsen have been your models. Are there any contemporary or other novelists, playwrights, or poets whom you revere? I know that you keep very few books in the cabin where you write, one of which is the Bible. What else do you keep in there? Where do you go for fuel?

Miller: There are some books I've found that fed me, but it's unsystematic. As far as plays are concerned, there's a very gorgeous play rarely done in this country, and I don't think it's done much anywhere else, called *The Playboy of the Western World* by Synge.

Balakian: It was done here in New York during the winter.

Miller: I didn't see it. I dread to see it, because I have such wonderful images of it. I don't know why I never mentioned it. When I was in college, that was an inspiration. It was a really lyrical conception. I love O'Casey, *Juno and The Paycock.*

Balakian: I saw it last summer when it was here.

Miller: I didn't like that production. They came over from Ireland. They went for the laughs too much, and it bothered me. I saw the original with Barry Fitzgerald and Sara

Allgood, which was simply a masterpiece. These people were not in that league. [*Pause*] O'Casey has a defect—the integration of events is sometimes a little weak. But the lyricism makes up for everything. And the characters. There are important lapses in these plays, but his spirit meant a lot to me. I'm trying to think whether I'm still feeding off other works. I go back to Sophocles rather regularly; *Hamlet* and *Lear*—but it all vanishes by the time I sit down. In other words, I'm feeding off myself. There were books that simply fascinated me at one time when I was in school, a very formative time. *The Education of Henry Adams*. I remember writing in the flyleaf of that book after I finished it, "Read this book again after twenty years."

Balakian: Did you?

Miller: I did because I didn't understand a lot of it. *Moby Dick* had an impact on me too. And the Russians. The Russians meant a great deal to me.

Balakian: Is it really true that you hadn't been a serious reader until after high school?

Miller: Yes. My mother was a reader, one of those people who read everything. You'd give her the Sears Roebuck catalogue and she'd read the whole thing. Whatever was in the house.

Balakian: In *The American Clock* she's reading all over the place. You have her reading *Coronet*.

Miller: [*Laughs.*] She was totally naive but at the same time she had a discriminatory sense of what was high, low, or so-so.

Balakian: Doesn't she say, "It's supposed to be literature but it's great anyway!"

Miller: "But it's very interesting."

Balakian: Would you discuss how the writers whom you mentioned have informed your work?

Miller: The Russians were the most important of all. The mixture of enormous psychological and physical detail in Tolstoy, Gogol, Dostoevsky, with that realistic detail making everything palpable so that you could practically smell these people, with the metaphysical preoccupation—that's what I took from them. In other words, if you could find a way to penetrate the particles of matter, you can find the spirit.

Balakian: That reminds me of your essay, "The Shadow of the Gods."

Miller: You don't find the spirit by looking for the spirit; you find the spirit by looking at the way matter is organized, by the way experience asserts principles. In other words, hope to find what things mean by what they are.

Balakian: It sounds scientific.

Miller: In a way it is. My ambition used to be, and I guess it still is, that one could write so that the work would transcend science, so that any physicist with some sense of life, or psychiatrist, would stand before these works and realize that drama is presenting the original evidence and that analysis and criticism follow. It's a way of reasserting the primacy of the created work, the imagined architecture.

Balakian: Organizing experience through language as opposed to the way scientists do it. Was Dostoevsky especially important to you?

Miller: Yes. Well, that's a hard race. Tolstoy and Dostoevsky occupy different sides of the brain. I wouldn't put one above the other. I've got to simply worship both of them.

Balakian: Do you still read them from time to time?

Miller: Oh yeah. I read *Karamazov* only three or four years ago. It's simply like eating bread. I had an interesting discussion many years ago with a poet friend of mine, because I was talking the way I'm talking to you now about the primacy of matter, and we were also talking about Dostoevsky at the moment. He said, "You're carrying it too far, because Dostoevsky has long arias about the spirit." I said, "You try to think up a scene that has always stuck in your mind as poetic, spiritual, and we'll get the book out and see how it's constructed." He cited the scene in *Karamazov* where Alyosha is walking down the street of the village and is inspired by the "itness" of everything, the sheer existence of everything, which is a transcendent idea, that somehow it was created by God and shimmers in this space. We found the passage which, of course, was totally circumstantial. With that passage in your hand, if you were an invading army, you would know every street along that route, what each house and picket fence looked like. It's unbelievable. And that's what I'm thinking.

Balakian: You've said that you don't consider yourself a realistic, naturalistic writer.

Miller: Any more than Dostoevsky was.

Balakian: In other words, you're not connecting naturalistic detail, like that window outside, with—

Miller: It's just the opposite of Naturalism. Naturalism thinks that it's going to create reality by repeating reality. And that's impossible. It's the opposite of what I think I'm after, which is the interpretation of whatever I've seen, and the spirit in it, to use a religious notion. The means by which one gets to the spirit is through appearances. Appearances are the beginning of the quest, not the end of it.

Balakian: This makes me think of *The Price*. That play is built on concrete detail, but at the same time that old furniture is the means to transcend itself. Critics call Arthur Miller a realistic writer when you aren't. Labels are terrible, but what could I call your writing? Maybe it's not necessary to call it anything.

Miller: I don't know of a traditional label. The idea is to transcend. Very often in the contemporary theater and in novels too, there's the kind of dialogue, or in a novel, description, which is very stylish, namely, based on a mood, usually of a semi-disguised despair, and some smart remarks about it. When I watch this, very often I think, oddly enough, it's a form of Naturalism. The people aren't interpreting the despair; they're simply delivering it up again.

Balakian: Like a Mamet play. That's naturalism. He is mimetically reproducing sleazy insurance salesmen. And you're after interpreting reality, and you use any form that works for you. You've said, "Fitting means to matter is the name of the game" for you.

Miller: Right. How can you put a play like *Clara* anywhere near naturalism? How can you take *An Elegy for a Lady* … actually, how can you take *Incident at Vichy* as naturalistic? Because they all have stories? So does the Book of Job. I do present the surfaces of life, man in society. There's a whole other school that never wants to get near the surface of life and sometimes they are very successful doing it. Beckett is.

Balakian: Although you and Beckett are using different means, your end is the same.

Miller: The same. Maybe the question is whether a work simply exploits chaos or strives to resist it for survival's sake.

Balakian: If you had to say what it is that you're after, what it is that you want to convey, or that you want to happen in your plays, what would you say? Is there an underlying thrust in your writing?

Miller: It's to achieve a coherency out of the chaos, and, of course, the deeper the chaos, the more difficult it is to symbolize in a coherent, integrated symbol. It's a question of how deep the resistance to chaos is even as it is a pleasurable necessity to embrace it.

Balakian: If I asked you what a play should do, could it be the same answer you would have given when you began writing?

Miller: Maybe. It's really illumination. It's the light. We strike it in life rarely. There's endless talk, and then suddenly somebody says something or does something and that's all that has to be said. It's to arrive at that point of illumination.

Miller said he had not slept much the night before because he had his new play in his head, and he graciously offered to continue our conversation in Roxbury. Then he told me that there will be productions of The Crucible *at the Longwharf Theater and at the Roundabout Theater this year. In Budapest* The Archbishop's Ceiling, The American Clock *and* Salesman *are playing: "There are 52 productions going on in Germany this year. Michael Blakemore is directing* After the Fall *at The National Theater in April. And* The Price *will be at The Young Vic in London," he remarked.*

I asked him about his trip to Turkey with Harold Pinter to free imprisoned writers. "I'm told they freed some sixteen hundred after we left," he said.

I noticed a book of Havel's letters in his bookcase and asked him about the Czech playwright. "I have great admiration for Havel," he remarked emphatically.

As we were walking out together, I saw an Italian poster for The American Clock, *which he says is being done all over Europe, and a beautiful poster of a briefcase on a trunk. "That's from the Flemish production of* Salesman," *he said. We discussed the fact that Europe is much more receptive to his work than New York. "I just don't know what's with New York. But I guess I shouldn't complain, because there will soon be two productions of* The Crucible *in the area."*

We walked outside into one of those hot, humid Manhattan days. A tall, Lincolnesque Arthur Miller climbed into my Chevy whose ceiling isn't high enough for him. He tried to fix my air conditioner for me. Looking at those strong, large hands, I asked, "Do you still build furniture?"

"Just started a table yesterday."

"How's your daughter Rebecca?"

"She's great. She just acted in a film in Germany, and she wrote a wonderful screenplay."

I dropped him off on 57th and 6th where he was meeting someone for dinner and then going to a Terrence McNally play. And there was Arthur Miller walking along Sixth Avenue in a crowd of New Yorkers, waving good-bye.

1990

Arthur Miller—An Interview: Interview by Christopher Bigsby

Bigsby: *Death of a Salesman* is a contrast in a number of ways. It seems to me the most lyrical of your plays.

Miller: That's true, yes. Well, I had always done that. Most of the plays I had written before had been reaching toward it. I was trying to find a poetic voice in the theater while at the same time making the scenes and the characters believable. Then I was also interested in time. We don't stop when we remember something; we go right on talking or doing whatever we're doing. Meanwhile, in another compartment of the brain the past is working. That was what I was trying for with that play. That was the form.

Bigsby: Do you ever feel, in looking back, that there is a kind of rift in *Death of a Salesman,* in that our dramatic attention is on Willy Loman, but the play's moral resolution really turns on Biff's self-realization? Is that why some people thought of the play as pessimistic, because they were looking in the wrong place?

Miller: Well, I'm sure that's why. There is a rift in it in that sense. You know, Thomas Mann saw that play, and he said, "You know, the thing about the play is that it is a lyric play, but you never tell them what to think. It is simply an experience that they can't escape." Now of course this is part of the reason that there's all this debate about the play. You see, I never allowed them to go beyond their intellectual and emotional capacity. There is no line in there that goes beyond what they could possibly have realized. The consequence is that, unlike standard tragedy, where you have the right, so to speak, formally speaking, to make self-aware statements where the character is aware of the play he is in, I never let them become aware of the play they are in. All that was driven out, ruthlessly, because at that time I resolved that I was going to make that audience never escape, even at the risk of losing objectivity, if I could do it. Because, I believed in squeezing out all the self-consciousness in the play. Every scene in that play begins late. There are no transitions in the play. It starts with a man who is tired. He doesn't get tired. He's tired in the first second of the play. You can tell from the way he enters the play. On the first line she says, "What happened?" Nothing happened but he's exhausted. You know you're somewhere. The same is true of every scene in that play. I completely drove out the usual transitional material from the play. That's the form of the play, that I never allowed into it the self-conscious statements, which Mann wisely recognized. Now, he thought of it as a pessimistic play, but he loved the fact that the younger generation did not. You know, when I was writing that, there wasn't a younger generation. I was the age of Biff. I wasn't Willy's age. You don't regard yourself as the younger generation. But the key is in the requiem at the end, which everybody wanted me to cut out. They said the audience were never going to stay there because Willy Loman is dead; there's nothing more to say. Of course, they did want to stay there, just as you do want to go to a funeral. And what is the point of a funeral? You want to think over the life of the departed and it's in there, really, that it's nailed down; he won't accept this life.

Bigsby: He had all the wrong dreams. But that's the dilemma, isn't it? Most of our attention has been focused on the man who has now gone and the moral resolution naturally comes from the character Biff, who's been less central.

Miller: I think what is missing, if you want to look at it that way, is what is missing in *Lear,* which a lot of nineteenth-century commentators didn't like for the same reason. It's unalleviated, setting aside the beauty of the poetry which relieves us of the gloom. Lear is unredeemed; he really goes down in a sack, in a coal chute. *Hamlet* has relief, moral relief so to speak; there is a structure remaining.

Bigsby: But you did say that there is a force that is in a race for Willy's soul, which is love. I am not quite sure what you mean by that, Linda's or Biff's, but do you in any way regret not giving Linda more resources to make the battle a bit more equal?

Miller: I regretted it at the time but I couldn't honestly give her what I didn't think she would ever have. You see, if that woman were more articulate in terms of her ability to handle it, probably they would have broken apart earlier on; she couldn't have stood it. You know, he's a cruel son of a bitch, that guy; everybody is charmed by him, but if you objectively face some of those scenes in the bedroom, he just wipes the floor with her from time to time. You see, a woman who was thinking of herself more would simply not have been there one morning, or else she would have put up such a fight as to crush him because he would never be able to accept any independence around him. This is part of the disease.

Bigsby: Is there something of a risk that in emphasizing the state of Willy's mind—and he is getting into a kind of deranged state, in which past and present are indistinguishable—the play might become a pathological case study?

Miller: It depends how you do it. You see, they made a movie of it which did just that. I hated that movie. Let's talk about it for a minute, because it applies to some of the things we have been talking about. I wrote that play in 1948 and it was produced in 1949. It ran for years. They bought the film rights, let's say in 1950. The right wing had not yet taken over in the culture so they would buy a play of mine. They made the film, but as they were making it the country was swinging far over to the right. What did they do? They made Willy crazier and crazier. Interesting. Now I happen to have been a very good friend of Freddy March, who played Willy. We nearly cast him in the original play. He was a marvellous actor. Freddy was a real actor in the best sense; he was an animal and he knew that there was something wrong with making him so crazy. He knew that. I certainly didn't tell him. Of course, these people making the film had to make him crazy or they couldn't make the film. The social and moral dimensions of the picture had to be resolved in this pathological side. By this time I was being attacked left and right as a red and here they were stuck with this *x* million dollars that they had sunk into the film. They were threatened with boycotts from the American Legion, the Catholic war veterans, and all those yahoos. They came to me and said, "Would you make a statement to these people to placate them?" I said, "I'll placate nobody. You bought the picture, fellas, you're stuck with it."

You know what they did? Columbia Pictures had another film made, which they filmed at City College, New York City, the Business School of City College, about the life of a salesman. It was a short, like fifteen minutes, in which they interviewed professors of business administration and heads of corporations and other such people who were experts in this field who said that Willy Loman was absolutely an atypical American. Really! Well, they were using my title in and out of the film and they got nervous about a law suit, so they called me in. Now my picture had not been released yet and they said, "We'd like you to see this." So I saw it and I said, "Why did you do this? You've just destroyed the film you've made, because if this is true then my film must be some aberration of an idiot." "Well, we didn't think it would be bad." And I said, "Well, look, I'll sue you." They wanted to play it with my picture and I had a financial interest in my picture, I suppose, although I doubted if I could make it stick in court. But as far as I was concerned they were injuring my property rights and apparently they were worried about this too or they wouldn't have even consulted me. I convinced them that they would be laughed out of existence, which I doubt would have happened at that moment since nobody was laughing about anything. Anyway, productions of *Salesman* shouldn't be about pathology but it can happen if you play Willy like a real mad fellow, yes. But it would be bad acting and it would be a stupid way to do the show. However, I think that this is a real danger whenever you get into a highly charged personality like Lear. You can make *Lear* an absolutely meaningless play. In fact, you can do it easier than you can with Willy, because what kind of an idiot is it who cannot glimpse what we all see, the fact that he has a good daughter who he thinks is the bad daughter. Well, he's for the looney bin. The audience knew what *Salesman* was about. They knew he wasn't crazy. They were right up with him. See, let me not underestimate it, I was ironically stating all the things that they always state seriously. A man can get anywhere in this country on the basis of being liked. Now this is serious advice, and that audience is sitting there almost about to smile but the tears are coming out of their eyes because they know that that is what they believe. This man is obviously going down the chute and he's telling them exactly what they believe. So I don't have to make a speech that this is wrong. The irony of the whole situation is what is making it work.

Bigsby: But it's not a play which only works in an American context.

Miller: No. Let me put it this way. That play was a great success in Western Europe, Eastern Europe, Japan, it hardly mattered where it was done. You see all countries have people with reveries of how they're going to conquer life. It's just that in this particular situation he is a salesman.

Bigsby: Incidentally, how far is Willy's brother, Ben, intended to be simply a product of Willy's mind and how far an independent character?

Miller: He's a real brother but Willy has invested him already with the whole mythos of that vast brutal success which is larger than life. Nobody can be that successful. Ben is an expressionist figure; every time he opens his mouth he is talking about diamonds, or wealth, or the land, or exploitation of some kind, and that's the way it would be for Willy. Willy wouldn't think of him excepting as the one who won, the victor. *The Crucible* is built on what I would call autonomous characters, who bring on their personalities encased in their social roles as we do in real life: one is poor, one is rich, or whatever. *Death of a Salesman* was conceived literally on two dimensions at the same time. On one level there are autonomous characters while on another there are characters who exist as symbols for Willy Loman.

Bigsby: You mean that Happy and Biff together are aspects of Willy's mind.

Miller: Exactly. It was done up in Minneapolis by Guthrie and I sat with him and he said, "You know, I was never aware before but this is a lyric; this is a long poem by Willy." It is, you know. John Proctor's voice is not all the voices but in a certain sense Willy is all the voices.

Bigsby: Is that why the play was originally to be called *The Inside of His Head?*

Miller: Yes. I conceived it as taking place inside his head and that's why it is different from any other play.

Bigsby: So, the gulf that I was suggesting existed between the physical attention on Willy and the moral resolution through Biff would not have occurred in the original because they would all have been aspects of Willy's mind.

Miller: Yes, that's right. But at that point when he dies, his consciousness vanishes and there is a space between the requiem and the play. It takes place on the earth, so to speak. We've left Willy's head now; we're on the earth.

Bigsby: You've seen, obviously, a lot of Willy Lomans over the years? What have the principal actors brought to that part that was different?

Miller: Well, there have been three chief players, as far as I am concerned. One was Warren Mitchell, who played it marvellously in London. I didn't know Warren and I just saw him in the play and we chatted for a while but his Willy and Dustin Hoffman's are related. They are both small men, feisty fellows. They've got a large world that's trying to kill them and a small man reacts with a kind of nervosity. That is in the part. It is obvious that Willy is leaping from one contradictory attitude to another very rapidly, sometimes with hardly a line in between, and to me that also was the characteristic of a little man, a physically small man. And I wrote it for a small man, if I wrote it for anybody. Lee Cobb, who did the original, was a giant, he was six feet whatever and he weighed a lot and he looked like he was in mourning for his life. He had always been a sad sack and he had what we conventionally think of as a tragic air because he was so damn sad. When he laughed, you wept. He had a dark air about him. Dustin is of another order. First of all, because he is so diminutive, he has to create people, literally create them. I don't know how he gets into the skin of Tootsie or of Kramer or of any of the other parts he's done but he has a true actor's imagination. You see, Warren was playing closer to Lee Cobb Dustin had to make Willy Loman happen as far as he was concerned and what I get from

Dustin's Willy is tragic in a completely different sense. It isn't the tragedy of the portrait but of the idea. Probably Dustin's is the most lucid of all the Willys that I am aware of. I have been so closely involved with the production, maybe it seems so because I know what he is doing and how he arrived there, but he is a fantastically intelligent actor. That's a rare thing in anybody. Actors being feeling people, first of all, we don't normally think of them as being very intellectual. He's by no means intellectual and he doesn't want to be, thank God, but he's very bright and he can analyze his own feelings and know what part of himself he needs to use in order to become Willy.

Bigsby: Have audiences changed, the audiences to *Death of a Salesman?* Do they respond to the same things?

Miller: I tell you, I was just talking about that the other day. I don't see any change whatsoever, in 35 years. Everybody, including me, has been saying that that kind of a play isn't possible any more, purely and simply because nobody's going to sit there that long with that degree of attention. The television has destroyed them. They can only listen for ten minutes and then they start shifting around. Well, it's nonsense. They are doing exactly what they did, in my memory, in the beginning, and what they do in China and what they'd done in Germany and anywhere else I've seen the thing. I think their potential hasn't been used in some years.

Bigsby: Willy Loman is a person who comes out of a different kind of time. He has a different sensibility. He wants to work with his hands. He looks back to the time before the city when things were simpler, relationships were simpler. I wonder if his nostalgia and Biff's nostalgia isn't also partly yours in that play?

Miller: I am very sceptical about that, quite frankly, and I am one of the ones who does not think that in the Depression time people were better. You know, there's a whole romance going on about the Depression that because everybody was broke they were kinder to one another, because they understood that everybody was broke. Well, all I can remember was that I wanted to go to school outside New York because I thought that we were cutting each other's throats and that it would be nicer in a small town where I could breathe easier. I think the Depression time was a ferociously competitive period. There was idealism. There was radicalism, which gave a loftiness to some of the sentiments, but underneath it was murder.

Bigsby: I don't think I was meaning quite so much the thirties as a period for which he was nostalgic, as the nineteenth century.

Miller: That, of course, I share. But I have to say that one of our best writers was Thoreau and he trembled at the sound of the railroad. He thought that this was going to be the end of everything. Maybe it was. But intellectuals are always afraid of change. They are really the most conservative psychological types. They don't want it to change and they want to look back at some better era and what they're doing, of course, what I do, what I think everybody does, is look back to when you were young and you were so dumb and ignorant that you thought the world was full of hope.

Bigsby: Doesn't the logic of that play almost confirm that nostalgia in that, at the end, we are left with Biff Loman who's come to an understanding of who he is and is presumably about to return to a farm in Texas, to light out for territory like Huck Finn. But the territory isn't, for the most part, there any more, is it?

Miller: No, it isn't. But it would be wrong to say that it isn't. You see, there is a different life in certain parts of the United States still, as compared to the New York, Chicago, Los Angeles life. Life can be much more pleasant in a smaller place and Biff wants not to be an integer, a simple little factor, in this gigantic business and industrial operation that the United States is and like most other countries are. And there is an escape in that, of course, a desire to assert different values. He is a precursor of the hippy movement in a way. Vermont, the most remote northern part of the United States, is full of people, young people, very competent, professional people sometimes, who have simply given it all up and have gone up to these places to live a human life. That's really what he's doing. But I had no cultural tools at the time. Biff was not part of any movement.

Bigsby: I wonder, though, if there isn't a sense of doubt on your part when you move on to *The Misfits* in which you have a person who is working with horses . . .

Miller: And you see what it comes to.

Bigsby: And you see what's happened.

Miller: Oh yes, no doubt, it's directly connected with *Salesman*. Sure it is.

Bigsby: Were you aware of that when you were . . .

Miller: No. One of my failings is that I have a very short vision. When I am writing, I think that I am inventing it for the first time. I guess if I didn't, I wouldn't write it. But that's true, though. *The Misfits* is what happens when you are in the great outdoors. You are killing horses for dog food.

Bigsby: I wonder also if there isn't a sense in which you yourself at this stage were feeling a misfit?

Miller: Yes. Well, I've always felt a misfit. I've always identified with those fellows, even down in the middle of New York. I didn't have to go out to Reno, Nevada to feel that way. Yes. Sure. And not only identification with them but identification with the problem, which is to assert value apart from the society, to assert some kind of a human life apart from the society. That's pretty tough because it's got its own contradictions and its own paradoxes. I don't know whether you really can do it.

1990

Introduction to *Plays: Three*

Obviously there are two distinct kinds of theater in our time, the Majority one and the Other. The Majority includes the musicals, light comedies, melodramas of reassurance, and farces—anything that takes peoples' minds off their troubles. The Other, in contrast, is devoted to generating anxiety rather than reassurance, or escape through hermetically circular ironies. Other comedy tends toward snarling parody of love or any similar implication of pure human intentions, and has far more prestige in academic circles. Other theater is most eager to become part of the future; the Majority is perfectly content with immediate acceptance at the highest possible ticket prices. Few seriously discuss the Majority theater; the Other gets written about in articles and books and its authors are treated as seers and philosophers. The Majority theater has only practitioners, no seers. In fact, the Majority theater practitioner who visibly aspires to become a seer is quickly thrown out of both camps and ends in poverty unless he has saved money in his pre-seer period.

How to tell a Majority work from the Other kind is often a tricky problem. A show is Majority when it runs a long time, although some can close in a week or less (in New York). However, the Other kind may also run a long time but almost always in small theaters. One can only theorize that their audiences must abhor large crowds while Majority people like it best when surrounded by thousands in big halls or stadiums. Television they find most enjoyable of all, probably because they know they are watching along with millions of others, a fact which in itself is likely to raise suspicions of fraudulence in the Other audience.

There are differences as well in the receptivity of both audiences. The Majority expects to be reached by a play and to be able to understand what is taking place more or less when it is happening. The Other audience seems to prefer not to understand what is going on, at least not too precisely, probably in order to exercise their own imaginations, much as they have to in real life where most things people do are unanticipated, if not incomprehensible. It follows that the Other audience, disregarding its antipathy for naturalism, harbors an unacknowledged taste for it while the Majority audience prefers a theater based on the archaically formalized relationship to real-life behavior. (One need only stand listening to snatches of conversation on a subway platform to realize the passengers are unknowingly performing what amounts to a real-life Other play.)

In general, life is a mystery to the Other no less than to the Majority theater, the difference being that the latter claims to have cleared it up in two hours. The very idea of clearing anything up is anathema to the Other theater; indeed, if in the course of time and repeated productions an Other play seems to have become clarified to the point of easy comprehensibility, it is gradually absorbed into the Majority repertoire and its author correspondingly becomes richer and richer until, slowly but surely, he is despised.

Many ordinary people—people who never stop to analyze anything, are apt to wonder what the point is of having the Other theater when it is attended by so ludicrously few people, and when even those who do show up cannot often agree on what it was they saw. But these people overlook a fundamental point about Other art— that its object is to analyze *them,* the Majority, in particular their middle-class stupidities, Puritanical or materialistic illusions about money, sex, and war, and general bourgeois dimness. So naturally the Majority is unlikely to catch on that it is, for example, a Rhinoceros, or that despite appearances of immense activity it is really standing around awaiting the non-arrival of the Lord, or that its idealistic patriotism is simply a clever means of enriching the ruling class through warfare. Those are some of the basic proposals of Other theater, and should one ask why, if Other theater is truly attempting to heal the Majority with its wisdom, it does not search out some way, difficult though this might be, to make itself Majority-comprehensible, one is likely to run into a philosophical conundrum; for if the Majority were ever convinced that it is a dangerous conformist Rhinoceros, or that all its worldly strivings, fanatical shopping, money-lust, automobile-fixations, etc., are futile attempts to escape the true and pointless conditions of existence, then—converted to the truth of these radical propositions—the Majority would cease to exist as such and would turn into the Other. In which case, one might ask, would the old Other separate itself from this new Other, detesting it as a *nouveau* or *faux* Other, while turning its back on the original Other theater as outmoded and passé, or historically exhausted, declaring that they, the original Others, are *not* Rhinoceroses and are *not* waiting around for a god who never shows up, thereby moving over inadvertently into former Majority positions? In other words, does the fundamental question finally come down to whether it is preferable to sit in a small theater with few people or a large theater with many?

The issue is complicated in addition by whether the definition of Other theater is or is not linked with immediate comprehensibility. There is—or was—no more Majority text than the Holy Bible whose stories have been drummed into immense mobs of people for close to two millennia. Indeed, whole wars have been launched against people who refused to accept it as God's truth, wars that mobilized hundreds of thousands of passionate Bible readers—or hearers—since most have been illiterate. Yet there is probably no book in whose narratives so much remains inexplicable. Why did Cain have to kill Abel? There is no straightforward explanation, it just happens. Where did Noah learn to build a veritable *Queen Mary,* especially having lived on a desert, no less? And if Adam and Eve were the first and only humans, with what people was Cain sent to live in exile in the land East of Eden so that they could curse him? Where did they come from? This is Other literature if there ever was any; indeed, the entire creation of the world takes less linear space than a cooking recipe, surely an example of Other condensation and elypsis. Yet most Other audiences are sure to consider it fit only for the Majority mentality and its lusting after clear and simple situations.

The possibility of some gross error would seem to open before us, a confusion of matter with manner, of the merely customary with the decrepit. In New York—to step aside from theater for illustration—a new architectural style has set Greek pediments and columns on top of fifty-story buildings in revolt, we are told, against the boring Bauhaus form-follows-function shibboleth. Instead, we are apparently to have form-tops-function since the working interiors of these immense buildings devoted to money-making and therefore impervious to useless add-ons, remain exactly the same as all other skyscraper designs of the past. One has to wonder whether the problem is not so much architecture as simple boredom. Since in other periods a large new building was a rare event, and in pre-industrial times one that took years and even generations to complete, perhaps we are so accustomed to immense new structures suddenly springing up that the sight of them is unlikely to inspire the effort to look up from the street, and so the architect's job, especially the Other architect, is to entertain and draw attention to his performance as much as to make something intrinsically unified and beautiful. In short, art now is an assault on the boredom of excess and the unnecessary with which life overflows, at least for the favored, in this, one of the longest periods of peace between the great-powers in all history.

Perhaps something similar is at work in theater where boredom, of course, has always been the cardinal sin. In Majority theater an event once strove above all for credibility, and to this end was carefully prepared for in advance, impressing the audience with the wonderful, or menacing, inviolability of cause-and-effect. In Other theater, in contrast, nothing is as valued as the unanticipated, the event which, if at all possible, violates every imaginable system of logic to the point of total arbitrariness. It is striking how this mode of perception more and more reflects like qualities that now glare forth from life. For example, the Soviet system, thought to be set in concrete, breaks up without foreign intervention, causing the implosion of vast edifices of Western armed war preparation without a shot being fired. The whole anti-Communist soufflé has simply slid down to the bottom of the pot just like the pro-Communist one. The Other style reflects the elevation to his country's Presidency of a playwright—of all things—who a few short months earlier had been jailed for his views. Other theater, the theater of the unanticipated, would seem to have its roots in the common, blatant world after all, would seem—ironically enough—not to have been as pure a flight of imaginative liberation as it would like to have seemed, but one quite as influenced, if not determined, by social and political circumstances as the Majority theater, with its boring enslavement to the logic of psychological-social-political realities. Other theater is hitched to a different cart, but it is hitched.

What does it all come to? The same old thing, of course—those radiating images, compact imitations of people that inflame the imagination with intimations of completeness; images of the self-defrauded Lear and Oedipus, of the abandoned Estragon, of fatuous Tartuffe, the infinite Alice, pining Bovary, God-hungry Ahab—the qualities of earthly existence, each bearing its self-contained interior system of logical inevitability. In such super-informing images the Majority and the Other merge, fall apart, in fact, into a mutuality of understanding that transcends the size of their theaters, the hipness of their audiences, or the modes they use to get themselves created—in short, despite everything. In the end, the long run, the informing human image—by whatever means it is brought to life—is. The rest is gossip.

1990

Essays: 1991–2000

The Measure of the Man

What struck me strongly about Nelson Mandela in his American public appearances, as well as our Soweto interview for BBC TV, was the absence in him of any sign of bitterness. After twenty-seven and a half years with his nose against the bars he seemed uninterested in cursing out the whites who had put him there for the crime of demanding the vote in a country where his people outnumber their rulers by about six to one.

I suppose his rather majestic poise, unmarred by rancor, lowered white defensiveness to the point where reactionaries could join with liberals in applauding his speech to Congress. But such unanimous appreciation is bound to be suspect when an honest man can hardly please everyone with his views; after all, with all his charm and civility he was still the man who had organized the African National Congress's guerrilla force, for one thing.

Watching from a distance I had found him extraordinarily straightforward in his persistent refusal to pulverize his history to suit current American tastes, crediting communists for being the first whites to befriend his movement, sometimes at the risk of their lives. Likewise, he criticized Israel and in the same breath reminded us that the overwhelming majority of his earliest supporters had been Jews.

In short, he allows himself to remain complicated; with a grandson named Gadafi (which was not his idea, however), he has written that the highest expression of democracy is the British House of Commons and the best legal system the American, with its written Bill of Rights. To me in our interview he would say that he had never joined the Communist Party. He did not add that he had never been a Marxist, but whether or not he thought he had been, I judge that he sees people in all their variety of character and deed in the foreground of events, rather than as shadowy creatures manipulated by forces, as a Marxist usually must.

I agreed to a conversation with Mandela after much hesitation, lasting a couple of weeks. The whole thing had begun with a London phone call from one Beverly Marcus, through whose South African English I discerned that she had proposed to the BBC that they film Mandela and me talking about life rather than politics, and that Mandela was receptive to the idea because he had called a halt to any more interviews in which the same simple-minded questions would inevitably be asked.

Lacking a reporter's killer instinct or investigative techniques I was simply very curious about the roots of this man's unusual character. How does one manage to emerge from nearly three decades in prison with such hopefulness, such inner calm?

But my main impulse came out of my background in New York, a racially splintered city with more than 2,000 people murdered last year. It has next to no inspiring black leadership, and so Mandela's success or failure seemed far from an academic question for me. If he can lead his riven country into a multiracial democracy the ripples could rock New York, Chicago, Detroit—and London and Europe and Israel, where the most explosive social problem is ethnicity and its unmet, often incoherent demands.

South Africa was full of surprises, the first being the fact that Beverly Marcus's younger sister, Gill, is Nelson Mandela's veritable right hand and a spokesperson for the ANC, and that their father was his accountant. I suppose I should have felt my integrity put at risk by this news, but I had never had any intention of drawing and quartering Mandela. I sought only a pathway into his nature and that of his movement. Gill, with her inside knowledge of the movement and unabashed admissions of its amateurish failings, as well as of the constantly shifting so-called tribal conflict, turned out, in fact, to be of great help in my grasping this situation.

Cape Town and the Cape area, which Beverly suggested my wife, Inge Morath, and I visit for a few days to unwind from the fourteen-hour plane trip, is an unlikely place to begin preparing for a talk with a revolutionary leader, since it is as close to Beverly Hills and the California littoral as you can get without tripping over a movie studio. Balmy air, a lazy Atlantic surf lapping white beaches, swimming pools and very good fish restaurants—I felt myself beginning to sink into its lovely lethargy.

But then one climbs a dune a hundred yards across a beach road in Hought Bay that fronts some extremely lavish homes and their tennis courts—and from the dune's ridge one looks down into a squatter town of hundreds of cardboard and tin shacks thrown one against the other right up to the edge of the sea. Don't the rich who live nearby object? Not all do—some happily sell drinking water to the blacks here who have no supply of their own. But of course this shantytown will have to go, for the view of the sea is superb here and the sand as white as sugar, a piece of prime real estate that will not be denied its promise forever.

One can drive around the Cape and Cape Town and indeed South Africa end to end without the slightest awareness that this sanitized prosperity involves only five million of its thirty million inhabitants. The famous South African schizophrenia is not hard to understand. To be sure, the back pages of the papers display ads for razor wire with which to surround one's home, and the walls surrounding most whites' homes show a metal sign reading "Instant Armed Response," and in many areas you are instructed not to stop at red lights at night lest your car be hijacked. But you quickly get used to this palpable fear, just as we have in New York, where as a child in Harlem I always carried my belongings with me to the blackboard or they'd be gone when I got back to my seat.

But South Africa is unique; it has state socialism for the whites—until very recent privitizations, sixty percent of all jobs were in state enterprises—and fascism for the blacks. Still, by the time we got back to Johannesburg after five days in the country I felt the place strange but comprehensible as merely one more kingdom of denial, unusual mainly for the immense proportion of its majority ghettoized and stripped of all civil rights.

Mandela's new house in the middle of Soweto has been criticized by some as one of Winnie Mandela's ostentations, standing as it does in the midst of the Soweto slum. Actually, donations built it. And there is a scattering of other quite good middle-class homes in the midst of the squalor, since the few successful middle-class blacks have been barred from white areas along with the poor. It is all part of a hopeless muddle of a modern technological state trying to sustain the most primitive, chest-pounding, Nazi master-race dogmas. So surrealism looms at every turn—a BMW dealership, black-owned, stands at the center of Soweto, a glass cube showroom exploding beams of white light toward houses yards away that have neither water nor sewers and whose occupants are no doubt unemployed and probably illiterate.

From the outside the Mandela house seems less elaborate than odd, a large chesty configuration of obliquely angular brick walls, an impromptu sort of construction until one is inside and realizes that it is a kind of fortress, its vulnerable dining and living rooms with their glass doors protected by a deep brick veranda extending outward some thirty feet. One drives into a receiving yard surrounded, as with so many other homes in this scared country, by a high wall with a steel, electronically controlled sliding door. And the doors of the main rooms are double-hinged to support a steel inner gate painted a discreet ivory to match the walls. Presumably these are barriers to an invading force.

Mandela's daughter, Zindzi, came into the living room pursuing her three-year-old son, both of them handsome, round-faced and no doubt accustomed to crowds of strangers in the place. Our crew was stringing its cables out; Gill Marcus was already on the phone; the floors and walls seemed covered with gifts, trophies and bric-a-brac; and now Winnie was here, explaining that she would not be eating with us because Nelson kept watching her calories and she liked to eat what she liked. Whereupon Mandela appeared, making a round gesture with both hands referring to her weight and saying "Africa!," both of them laughing while she bent to lift her rampaging grandson, whom she handed to a nurse. Even in his quick glances at her one saw his overwhelming love for his still-young wife, and she clearly basked in it. But her indictment in a murder case and impending trial seemed to hang in the air despite her tired jocularity.

Mandela was not wearing one of his formal London suits but a collarless short-sleeved African blouse with a gold-embroidered yoke—a chief's blouse, it looked to me. Gill hoped he would relax with me, and after a while he did come quite close. But he is by nature a formal, conservative man who in a peaceful country would have been chief justice of its Supreme Court or perhaps the head of a large law firm. My first question to him—after we had walked out on his veranda and looked down at Soweto, the dumping ground for human beings—was how he had been raised.

At first he sat pressed against the back of his couch, somewhat on guard, having been cornered by interviewers who find it impossible to believe that he simply means what he says. He was the son of a chief, and one could see how serious it was to be a chief's son; he had been taught early on that he would have the responsibilities of governing and judging. Even now he straightened a bit as he told with pride how, when he was ten and his father died, an uncle had taken over his education and his life. "My father occupied a position equivalent to that of prime minister in the tribe.... To me as a child the Transkei was the center of the entire world.... The missionaries tried to destroy the belief in custom and they created the perception that we have no history or culture." And with an amused grin: "When the 1939 war began we felt we were loyal subjects of the British monarch. That was the atmosphere in which we were brought up."

"And what went on inside you when the missionaries told you you had no history?"

"I'm not so sure I knew that I had a history." And later, "I must confess that Africa remained a dark continent in that I knew very little about it and I knew better about Europe, especially Britain."

This meticulous specificity, and his staid, almost Victorian structure of speech and demeanor suddenly had a root and expressed an innate authority which no doubt helped to keep him together through his prison decades. Mandela, to put it simply, *is* a chief.

And this may help explain why it has been so difficult for him to deign to confer with Mangosuthu Buthelezi of the Zulus, who have recently been on the attack against the ANC Xhosa people. Buthelezi, it is felt, helped to justify apartheid by accepting the headship of a concocted homeland where his people were dumped. It is the equivalent of a French maquisard guerrilla accepting political equality with a Vichy collaborator; there is not only a moral issue but his pride. Nevertheless, when Mandela did appear at a recent press conference with Buthelezi, the latter's people so threatened him that he was forced to leave the area.

The tribe, he insists, is basically an extended family. And in modern times there is no "natural" conflict between tribes, which are largely urbanized now, living side by side and intermarrying, joining the same unions and attending the same schools. It was the British and then the apartheid government that had always tried to tribalize Africa, pitting one against the other, setting up so-called homelands, newly founded territories that had never existed before. "There is one Africa and there will be one," Mandela said, creating a ball with his two hands.

The present conflict is "simply a conflict between two political organizations," a conflict that has failed to make headway in Soweto, as one example, because Soweto is more politically sophisticated rather than because the people are mainly Xhosa. "But when Zulus attack they never ask whether you are Zulu or something else, like the recent attack on people in the train, who do not sit according to tribes. They attack anyone."

And who would be interested in orchestrating these attacks?

He pauses before his answer, which goes to the heart of his hopes. "My belief is that Mr. de Klerk wants South Africa to take a new direction, and it is therefore difficult . . . to say that the government itself is orchestrating this violence."

De Klerk still has Mandela's confidence, it seems, but the miasma remains dense and impenetrable where some of his government's lower officials are concerned. Last July Mandela's people had gotten information that an Inkatha (Buthelezi's political organization) attack on a township was being planned and had notified the police and higher officials. The attack came off, thirty were murdered, and the police did nothing to prevent it. "I immediately went to see de Klerk. . . . Why were they allowed to enter the township when we told you beforehand that this attack was coming? . . . Mr. de Klerk is a very smart man, a strong leader. He was unable to give me an answer." However, on the day of Mandela's visit to the scene of the slaughter de Klerk personally sent four helicopters and five hundred police to protect him. And besides, "When you discuss with Mr. de Klerk he seems to have a genuine sense of shock, unlike others."

And finally, "They have either lost control over certain elements of their security forces or those elements are doing precisely what the government wants. . . . They want to negotiate with a weakened ANC. . . . You are not dealing with tribal people from the countryside but people who are sophisticated in the use of weapons, who know how to move very swiftly with military precision. . . . There are efforts now to start the Renamo movement in South Africa." (Renamo was the Rhodesian-organized mercenary outfit that murdered thousands in Mozambique.)

I turned to a discussion of his prison time. He and his comrades had originally been assured by a prison officer that they'd be out in five years because the world was so outraged by their life sentences. But five years came and went. Winnie could visit only twice a year; his children were growing up with no father. Here his face showed pain at his inability to protect his family—the helplessness desecrated his chiefly role.

Government harassment of Winnie was driving her out of one job after another until "there were certain moments when I wondered whether I had taken the correct decision of getting committed to the struggle. But at the end of these hesitations with myself I would feel that I had taken the right decision. . . . The certainty of our final victory was always there. Of course I sometimes became very angry when I thought about the persecution of my wife and that I could not give her the support she needed. I felt powerless. And also my children were hounded out of one school after another."

His vulnerability was plain here, but over it his hardness flared. This was as close as he was able to come to acknowledging what must have been the loss of hope for release before he died; instead he preferred to find something positive to emphasize. When the world began to forget him and all black movements were suppressed, the government restated that a life sentence meant life, "but in the English universities they came all-out to oppose these harsh measures. . . . People tend to forget the contribution that was made by the National Union of South African Students, which was a white organization."

This was not an opportune, upbeat recollection but his ultimate vision of a nonracial South Africa. I am convinced it is more than a tactic to recognize the absolute future need for whites who have advanced education and business prowess. It was striking how he never seemed to categorize people by race or even class, and that he spontaneously tended to cite good men even among the enemy.

"That came from my prison experience. It gets very cold on Robben Island and we had no underwear. Some warders went strictly by regulations—you were allowed two blankets. But another warder would slip you an extra one. I made some good friends among the warders; some of them visit me now."

In fact, toward the end of his imprisonment he ran "Mandela University" on Robben Island, and white warders were among his pupils. But there wasn't time to talk about this. We'd scheduled two sessions and at the last minute had to settle for one because he had to rush off to deal with the murders going on all over the place and the government's inability—or unwillingness—to keep order.

On the way back to Johannesburg that night, Gill Marcus pressed the driver on no account to stop at red lights and to drive as fast as possible through the darkness.

1991

Get It Right: Privatize Executions

The time has come to consider the privatization of executions.

There can no longer be any doubt that government—society itself—is incapable of doing anything right, and this certainly applies to the executions of convicted criminals.

At present, the thing is a total loss, to the convicted person, to his family and to society. It need not be so.

People can be executed in places like Shea Stadium before immense paying audiences. The income from the spectacle could be distributed to the prison that fed and housed him or to a trust fund for prisoner rehabilitation and his own family and/or girlfriend, as he himself chose.

The condemned would of course get a percentage of the gate, to be negotiated by his agent or a promoter, if he so desired.

The take would, without question, be sizable, considering the immense number of Americans in favor of capital punishment. A $200 to $300 ringside seat would not be excessive, with bleachers going for, say, $25.

As with all sports events, a certain ritual would seem inevitable and would quickly become an expected part of the occasion. The electric chair would be set on a platform, like a boxing ring without the rope, around second base.

Once the audience was seated, a soprano would come forward and sing "The Star-Spangled Banner." When she stepped down, the governor, holding a microphone, would appear and describe the condemned man's crimes in detail, plus his many failed appeals.

Then the governor would step aside and a phalanx of police officers or possibly National Guard or Army troops would mount the platform and surround the condemned. This climactic entrance might be accompanied by a trumpet fanfare or other musical number by the police or Army band, unless it was thought to offend good taste.

Next, a minister or priest would appear and offer a benediction, asking God's blessing on the execution.

The condemned, should he desire, could make a short statement and even a plea of innocence. This would only add to the pathos of the occasion and would of course not be legally binding. He would then be strapped into the chair.

Finally, the executioner, hooded to protect himself from retaliation, would proceed to the platform. He would walk to a console where, on a solemn signal from the governor, he would pull the switch.

The condemned man would instantly surge upward against his bindings, with smoke emitting from his flesh. This by itself would provide a most powerful lesson for anyone contemplating murder. For those not contemplating murder, it would be a reminder of how lucky they are to have been straight and honest in America.

For the state, this would mean additional income; for the audience, an intense and educational experience—people might, for example, wish to bring their children.

And for the condemned, it would have its achievement aspect, because he would know that he had not lived his life for nothing.

Some might object that such proceedings are so fundamentally attractive that it is not too much to imagine certain individuals contemplating murder in order to star in the program. But no solution to any profound social problem is perfect.

Finally, and perhaps most important, it is entirely possible that after witnessing a few dozen privatized executions, the public might grow tired of the spectacle—just as it seizes on all kinds of entertainment only to lose interest once their repetitiousness becomes too tiresomely apparent.

Then perhaps we might be willing to consider the fact that in executing prisoners we merely add to the number of untimely dead without diminishing the number of murders committed.

At that point, the point of boredom, we might begin asking why it is that Americans commit murder more often than any other people. At the moment, we are not bored enough with executions to ask this question; instead, we are apparently going to demand more and more of them, most probably because we never get to witness any in person.

My proposal would lead us more quickly to boredom and away from our current gratifying excitement—and ultimately perhaps to a wiser use of alternating current.

1992

Lost Horizon

I must confess that I am not a proper estimator of theater in America because I see too few productions. But I have my own experience as reference as well as reports I get from writer, actor and director friends.

It seems clear, now in 1992, that we are at the end of something. Without indulging in overblown praise for theater in the Forties and Fifties, I do think that on the whole theater had far greater importance than it does now, not least for actors. Television held much less promise then of either fame, steady work or income for actors. And the movies, while always attractive to them for obvious reasons, did not gobble them up as they have since.

Judging from my own experience and that of several very active director and writer friends, theater now is a minor adjunct of the film media. It is basically a training ground for movies and television, the ultimate evidence of success. The people eager to play in theater are for one reason or another not wanted in TV or the movies. This doesn't mean they are lesser talents necessarily, merely that as types they do not attract roles in film or TV. To be blunt about it, the mature actors, people who have learned the trade and in other eras would be ready for the great roles, are not interested in theater. The money is ludicrously low compared to the film media, the work is much harder, and the chances of being blasted out of the water by critics immeasurably higher. What is the point?

When a well-known actor, not to speak of a "star," accepts a stage role now it is almost always for a limited time, three months or perhaps four or five, at most. And when a young actor who was previously unknown makes an impression in a play and is offered TV or film work, he is gone before he has practically learned all his lines. A director I know, who is probably a typical example, had a big Off-Broadway (really near-Broadway) hit recently in which the cast was replaced three times in a matter of months. The man kept directing the same play for a quarter of a year, and he does this all the time.

Can you blame the actors? I used to years ago, when, for instance, after a few months on Broadway, Lee Cobb quit the part of Willy Loman to gallop off as a movie sheriff. That cannon of an actor was using himself as a peashooter when he had a talent that could have developed into a major force in world theater. Of course he never did.

The waste of people is what bothers me. That and my own inconvenience, of course, when it is so bloody hard to find mature people for my own plays, old and new. Theater is the fifth wheel of a wagon that only really needs four.

This is not only an American dilemma, of course. Actors in London are not eager to tie themselves up for the run of play on the West End, for fear they will lose a TV series or a great film role. But what they have in London, and we don't have here, is a subsidized group of theaters which keeps alive—and sparkling so—both the old repertoire and new plays that need big and mature acting. As for France, Germany and Italy, commercial theater is barely extant, the main work being done by either tiny Off-Broadway–type theaters or the main subsidized houses.

I daren't look too far ahead for fear I will see only a downward slope for us. I think it a miracle even now when something really first-class is done, and there are a very few such productions still. It seems to me our level of work is barely acceptable most of the time, and lower than that too much of the time. And how could it be otherwise with the kind of insecurity, cynicism and haphazardness we live with? I could be wrong, but I think this country is bursting with talent—and it is being wasted like so much else that is human among us, when it is not brought up at its first youthful bloom, and then is too often tossed aside. It seems to me we don't have an American theater but only the shards of one, some of the broken pieces reflecting lights, others covered with the dust where they have fallen.

Theater is not an end only because so many people want desperately to act and write and direct and design. "Always the young strangers," as Carl Sandburg wrote. But our system is simply kicking them in the teeth most of the time. It's a pity. The vision of a prideful theater, with art rather than cynical greed at its center, is still beyond the horizon.

1992

The Good Old American Apple Pie

What a strange irony it is that at the very moment when all over Europe and Latin America repressive regimes have been driven out of power and with them their censors from office, that we Americans should be increasingly discovering the uses of censorship over our own writers and artists. The devil, as was once said, has many disguises; defeated in one place he pops up somewhere else.

Evidently there are many Americans who still do not understand why censorship and democracy cannot live happily together. What so many seem to forget is that a censor does not merely take something out, he puts something in, something of his own in a work that does not belong to him. His very purpose is to change a work to his own tastes and preconceptions.

Many forget that when they read a work that has passed through censorship, they are putting themselves in the hands of an anonymous person whose name appears nowhere and cannot be held responsible for what is published.

Perhaps we can appreciate what censorship really means by looking at a strange story that took place in Britain at the end of the eighteenth century.

A teenager named William Henry Ireland, illegitimate son of a wealthy London antique dealer, desperate to get into his father's good graces, came home one day claiming to have been given various papers in Shakespeare's hand, as well as a lock of hair of Shakespeare's wife, by a stranger whose carriage had nearly run him down on the street. Following the near accident, he and this stranger had become friends, according to young William, and as a token of the man's regard for him he had been given these invaluable papers and the lock of hair.

The elder Ireland immediately had the handwriting on the papers checked by the authorities who pronounced it Shakespeare's, and the ink and paper were without question of the Elizabethan period, nearly two centuries old. All London was agog, and the boy and his father became overnight sensations. Naturally, young Ireland, until now utterly ignored by everyone, got enthusiastic and announced that his new friend had a whole trunkful of Shakespeare's original manuscripts which he promised he might let the boy have one day.

After producing various forged snippets of Shakespeare's love notes, and a few of the Bard's "lost" verses, young Ireland (would-be poet and idolizer of the late Thomas Chatterton, another young forger-poet) proclaimed that his benefactor had decided to give him nothing less than the original manuscript of *King Lear*, but only in due time. And sure enough, after some weeks young Ireland showed up with that very manuscript. A gathering was instantly convoked in the Ireland living room where the new discovery was read to a dozen of the most authoritative literary critics, noble patrons of the arts, and cultural leaders of the time.

At the end, James Boswell, the famous biographer of Samuel Johnson, fell to his knees before the manuscript to thank God that at long last the true Shakespeare had been revealed to the world, a Shakespeare who was positive and cheerful rather than brooding and dark and defeatist, a Shakespeare who scorned foul language and never brought up sex or bodily functions, a Shakespeare who was clearly a true Christian gentleman rather than the barbaric, foul-mouthed rotter whose works had always embarrassed decent people with their obscenities and blood-covered view of mankind and the English nation.

Of course what young Ireland had done was to clean up *King Lear* to suit the narrow middle-class tastes of his time. It was a time when revolution was gathering in France, threatening to British stability, if not the idea of monarchy itself. Ireland's major fix was to brighten up the end so that the aged king, rather than raving on the heath, swamped in his madness and abandoned by the world, was reunited with his daughters in a comforting sentimental scene of mutual Christian forgiveness, whereupon they all lived happily ever after. The paper on which this version was written was indeed authentic, the young forger having snipped off sheets of it from the blank ends of Elizabethan wills and deeds in the files of the London law office where he worked as a clerk. The antique ink he had produced himself after months of lonely experiment.

Only one critic, Edmund Malone, saw through the forgery, but he did not expose the fraud by analyzing ink or paper but rather the mawkishness of the "newly discovered" alterations, the shallow naïveté behind their versification. But as important as any technical doubts was his conviction that the spirit behind this "new-found authentic *King Lear*" was pawky, narrow-minded, fearful of sexuality and the lustiness of the English tongue, and fearful too of the play's awesome image of human judgment's frailty, and the collapse of the very foundations in reason of government itself. The real *King Lear* reduces man to his elemental nature, stripping him of rank and money and his protective morality, in order to present a vision of the essence of humankind with no ameliorating illusions. In place of these challenges the "newly discovered" play was a story of reassurance fit for family entertainment, one that offers comfort by turning a far-ranging tragedy into a story of misunderstandings which are pleasantly cleared up at the end.

In a word, young William Ireland did what censorship always attempts to do—force a work to conform to what *some* people want life to look like even if it means destroying the truth the work is written to convey.

Had the Ireland forgery been left uncontested, we can be sure that *King Lear* as a play would never have survived the hour. Many critics then and since have thought it a nasty work with an improbably black estimate of humanity, but succeeding generations have come to treasure it precisely for its truthfulness to life's worst as well as its best.

What Ireland did was erase the doubts about life that were in the original play and were so discomforting to the upper class of Britain at the time.

Censorship is as old as America. The Puritans forbade the reading of novels—or, indeed, anything but scripture—as one of the condemned "vain pursuits." A reader nowadays would find it impossible to recognize in those novels what could possibly have aroused the Puritan fathers to such fury against them. But closer to our time, there is hardly a master writer who has not felt the censor's lash, from James Joyce to Gustave

Flaubert to D. H. Lawrence to Hemingway and Fitzgerald, to William Faulkner and a long, long list that just about comprises the roster of world literature. Someone somewhere could doubtless find reasons for moral outrage in a McDonald's menu or a phone book.

Of course there is no denying that there are people who misuse freedom to appeal to the sinister in us, our brutality, scorn for justice, or concealed violence and lust. By exploiting our suppressed feelings people with no interest in anything but making an illicit buck can prosper, for example, by exploiting human sexual curiosity even if it victimizes children.

But the problem, clearly, is that when we legitimize censorship of what we agree is antisocial art we come very close to legitimizing it for real art. For example, right now some three hundred and fifty lines of *Romeo and Juliet* are customarily removed from American school textbooks because they are about sex. There is a similar emasculation of the two other most commonly taught Shakespeare plays, *Julius Caesar* and *Macbeth*. In other words, lines of very high poetry are forbidden American students who, it is assumed, will think that much less often about sex. Of course this is ridiculous; all this censoring does is deprive them of realizing that there is something sublime and beautiful in sex and that it is not merely dirty. It throws them entirely to the mercies of suggestive videos and rock lyrics and really raw pornography which apparently nothing will stop, and will certainly not be slowed by censoring *Romeo and Juliet*.

The purported aim of censorship is always to preserve public morality but we ought not forget that for those who advocate censorship pornography is by no means necessarily the only kind of immoral communication. If it becomes established policy that blotting out certain sexual images in art is acceptable, then there is nothing in principle to stop the censoring of other "immoral" expression.

I have had some experience with "moral" censorship myself. In 1947, my play *All My Sons* was about to open in the Colonial Theatre, Boston, for its first performances before coming to Broadway. The Catholic Church at that time exercised censorship over the Boston theaters and threatened to issue a condemnation of the play unless a certain line were eliminated from it. I should add that the raunchiest burlesque shows in America were playing on the Boston "Strip" at the time, but these apparently were not bothersome to the moral authorities. What troubled them terribly was the line, "A man can't be a Jesus in this world!" spoken by Joe Keller, a character who has knowingly shipped defective engine parts to the Air Force resulting in twenty-odd fighter planes crashing and who is now pleading for his son's forgiveness. The name of Jesus was forbidden utterance on the Boston stage, no matter that in this case it was used to indicate Jesus' high moral standard. I refused to change the line, as much because I could not think of a substitute as anything else, but the hypocrisy of the complaint was painful to contemplate, given the level of entertainment of the Boston "Strip" a few blocks from my theater.

In 1962, when my film *The Misfits* was previewed by religious censors, the gravest displeasure was expressed with a scene in which Marilyn Monroe, in a mood of despair and frustration—fully clothed, it should be said—walks out of a house and embraces a tree trunk. In all seriousness this scene was declared to be masturbation, and unless it was cut the picture would be classified as condemned and a large part of the audience barred from seeing it. Once again it was necessary to refuse to oblige a censor, but I would not have had that privilege had I lived in a different kind of country. Experiences like these have helped me to stand against censorship.

Life is not reassuring; if it were we would not need the consolations of religion, for one thing. Literature and art are not required to reassure when in reality there is no reassurance, or to serve up "clean and wholesome" stories in all times and all places. Those who wish such art are welcome to have it, but those who wish art to symbolize how life really is, in order to understand it and perhaps themselves, also have a right to their kind of art.

I would propose to censors and their supporters that they write the stories and paint or shoot the pictures they approve of, and let them offer them to the public in open competition with the stories and pictures of those whose works they want to suppress.

Let them write a new *Romeo and Juliet* that is wholesome and unoffending and put it on a stage and invite the public to come and enjoy it as millions have enjoyed Shakespeare's play for three hundred years. Who knows?—maybe they will win out.

But of course they cannot accept this challenge; censorship is an attack on healthy competition. It comes down to a refusal to enter the arena and instead to wipe out the competitor by sanctions of suppressive writs and the police power.

I write this as one who is often disgusted by certain displays that call themselves art and are really raids on the public's limitless sexual curiosity, purely for the purpose of making money. As an artist I sometimes wonder at my having to compete with this easy and specious way of attracting attention and gaining a public following. And I will not deny my belief that there may ultimately be a debasement of public taste as the result of the incessant waves of sexual exploitation in films and other media.

But bad as this is, it is not as bad as censorship, because the censor is given a police power no individual ought to have in a democracy—the power not only to keep bad art from the public, but good art, too; the power not only to protect people from lies but from uncomfortable truths. That way lies not wholesomeness, not community values, but the domination of the many by the few acting in the name of the many. Nobody said it was easy to be a free people, but censorship not only makes it harder, it makes it in the end impossible.

Probably because we in general enjoy freedom to express ourselves we are unaware of not only the power that a censor takes but the hypocrisy that inevitably accompanies it. In the winter of 1965 I interviewed a lady in her Moscow offices, one Madame Elena Furtseva, then head of all culture of the Soviet Union. In theory and often in practice this woman and the committee she headed had the power to shut down any play before or during its run in a theater, or to cancel a film or suppress a novel or book of poems or whatever. She could also promote certain books if she so pleased. She had been Khrushchev's special friend and when he was ousted she cut her wrists but was saved and restored to her job.

Behind her chair was a long table piled high with at least a hundred books lying on their sides. Each volume had a few slips of paper sticking out of its pages which I deduced marked passages of censorable writing which her assistants were submitting to her to decide upon.

She looked quite exhausted and I remarked sympathetically on this. "Well I have so much I must read, you see," she said, and gestured toward the possibly offending books behind her.

With nothing to lose—my U.S. passport snug in my pocket, I ventured: "You know, I have never met writers anywhere who are as patriotic as your Russian writers. Whatever their criticisms, they have a deep love of country. Why don't you make an experiment; don't tell anybody but let's say for one month just don't read anything. See what happens. Maybe nothing will happen. Then you won't have to be reading all this stuff every day."

She tried hard for a sophisticated smile but it came out looking hard and painful. And then she said something interesting: "The Soviet worker cannot be asked to pay for the paper and ink to print ideas that go counter to his interests and his moral ideas of right and wrong."

I can't help thinking of that statement when I hear people saying that the American taxpayers ought not be asked to pay for artworks that offend their tastes or their ideas of right and wrong. The fundamental fallacy in such a statement is quite simple and inexorable; how did Madame Furtseva know what the Soviet worker thought was right and wrong, moral or immoral? How *could* she know when no one but her and her assistants were allowed to read possibly offending works?

Indeed, for nearly three-quarters of a century Soviet writing has been kept remarkably chaste, with very strict rules about depicting sex, while at the same time the Soviet abortion rate was rising to the highest in the world. It was also very strict about barring negative pictures of Soviet conditions in all the media and forbade any genuine attack on the system. After three-quarters of a century of such censorship the Soviet system appears to have collapsed. Why? Because reality does not go away when a censor draws a line through a sentence or tears a page out of *Romeo and Juliet*.

If there is a way to curb pornography, if there is any possibility of preventing people from lathering after obscene material, it can only be the result of changing their tastes. If they don't want the stuff it won't be profitable and it will vanish. I doubt that day will ever come, no matter what, but surely cursing the darkness never brought light. Through education raising the intelligence level of the population, sensitizing people to real rather than cosmetic feeling, enhancing mutual respect between the sexes and between races—these are the paths to decency, not calling in the cops to drive out the bad guys.

There is an analogy here to the narcotics problem. We spend tens of millions on planes to spot smugglers, more millions to wipe out Peruvian coca crops, more millions on narcotics police; but of course the narcotics keep coming in because Americans want dope. Meantime, an addict who wants to get rid of the habit has to wait as long as a couple of years to get placed in a rehabilitation clinic because these are underfunded.

Censoring Shakespeare won't make us good and may possibly make us a little more stupid, a little more ignorant about ourselves, a little further from the angels. The day must come when we will stop being so foolish. Why not now?

1993

We're Probably in an Art That Is—Not Dying

It happens to be a very bad historical moment for playwriting, because the theater is getting more and more difficult to find actors for, since television pays so much and the movies even more than that. If you're young, you'll probably be writing about young people, and that's easier—you can find young actors—but you can't readily find mature actors. They've either gone to the movies or weren't very successful, so they didn't stick with it. It's an extremely difficult thing in this country right now. It's never been worse.

That and the demise of the Broadway theater are probably part of a whole cultural shift. In New York, of course, it's a question of real estate and the costs of production. In a few weeks there will be only a couple of straight commercial plays on Broadway, and nineteen dark Broadway theaters. The theater culture in this city has been dispersed. It's been going on for about 25 years now, and I think it has almost completed its devolution.

People don't feel excited at the idea of going to the Broadway theater, even though occasionally a very good thing comes on. They've deserted it. They feel it's not for them. It's not up to date. It doesn't have any news to give them. And this was quite different some years ago. It was the most exciting thing in New York.

It's partly the price of the ticket. It's hard to get happy when you're going to lay out $100 to sit down for two hours with your friend—or even your wife. People are willing to do it for a musical with a big orchestra and a lot of sets, but they're not so willing to do it for a straight play. Especially when some critic has said it's pretty good but not a masterpiece. Today the critic's power varies according to the price of the ticket. When the ticket is cheap, the critic's power is low. When the ticket is very expensive, the power of the critic is high. So we're probably in an art that is—not dying. I don't think it is ever going to die because it's so simple: all you need is a board and a man standing on it and a woman saying something interesting. You don't need machines. But it is going to have to develop a different way of production. The problem is not that people can't write plays any more, the problem is that the audience's relationship to the theater has simply dribbled away. And the playwright is nothing without his audience. He is one of the audience who happens to know how to speak. We are a kind of church. And if the parishioners are no longer interested in that church, you know what happens. It becomes a garage or a grocery store.

It's different in other countries, especially with public subsidy. I just directed *Death of a Salesman* in Stockholm. They have many theaters, but in the main one, the Royal Dramatic Theater, they have six stages and ninety actors under permanent contract. In my case they had chosen a cast. There was one actor who I thought wasn't quite right for the role of Happy, and I told him. "It's all right," he said. "I'm playing Hamlet at the moment three times a week." So I asked the director of the theater if there were any other people at that age and general type. And he said, "We have some." The next afternoon we had *six* sitting in the room, all actors who were working in different plays in that building.

The Swedes, however, don't originate much drama. I don't know why, with all that encouragement. We do generate more plays in this hurly-burly, self-defeating system. Still, there's no comparison. They've got a couple of million people, and we're this mammoth society.

The problem for us is not that the plays are not there or that the playwrights are not there; it's that the audience is not in those Broadway seats. What the solution is, given the tremendous investment in real estate, I don't know. Maybe there is none, the way it stands. Maybe we're just going to have to have a theater of the United States, where the work goes on in smaller places and occasionally is brought in to the city—which is what we do now.

The great excuse for commercial theater in America for a hundred years was that it was the only theater that *originated* anything. The theater outside New York City didn't originate very much, it copied what was here. Well, what they do now is bring in stuff from outside and therefore our Broadway theater is a cripple looking for a crutch. But nothing is going to change until this is recognized as a crisis that could turn out to be terminal for what we used to call professional theater in America.

1993

The Parable of the Stripper

The Yugoslav catastrophe raises, for me, an especially terrible and comical memory. In the 1960s I presided over the congress of International PEN that was held in Bled, a beautiful resort town built around a crystal-clear lake high in the lovely mountains of Slovenia. Bled had been the watering hole for generations of Europeans, a fairy-tale place. And it was already more than a decade since Tito had broken with Moscow.

Marxist intellectuals in Yugoslavia were remarkably open in their criticisms of the economy and politics of the country. That the system needed deep changes was taken for granted, and new concepts were being floated that would free individual initiative while retaining the social gains of the communist system. Worker ownership of factories was being tried, and identical consumer products, such as radios, were given different names in order to spur competition between factories, in the hope of raising quality and lowering prices. Yugoslavia was prodding the limits of socialism; and to come there from the dictatorships of Hungary, Czechoslovakia, East Germany, not to mention Russia, was to experience the shock of fresh air. In the Sixties Yugoslavia the place seemed filled with enormous energy. These were the proudest, friendliest people I had met in Europe, and the most frank and open.

There was one taboo, unmentioned but obvious: the ethnic nationalism that Tito had ruthlessly suppressed. I knew, of course, that Slovenians, Bosnians, Serbs, Croatians, Montenegrins and other nationalities made up the Yugoslav delegation to the PEN congress, but to me they all looked alike and conversed in a mutually understood language, so their differences might be no more flammable than those separating the Welsh and the English, or maybe even Texans and Minnesotans. And when I asked an individual, out of curiosity, if he was Croatian or Slovenian or whatever, and the question caused a slight uneasiness, it seemed minimal enough to be dismissed as more or less irrelevant in this rapidly modernizing country.

Then one evening a group of four writers, one of them a Serb journalist friend called Bogdan, invited me out for a drink after dinner. Two of my companions were poets, a Croatian and a Montenegrin, and one a Slovenian professor. We walked down the road to the local nightclub that usually catered to tourists. The room was very large, like a ballroom. There were maybe fifty bare, plastic-covered tables, only a few of them occupied by stolid, square-headed Alpine types. The cold night air was not noticeably heated. The place had the feeling of a big Pittsburgh cafeteria between meals.

Then a three-piece band took places on a platform up front and began tootling American jazz standards, and a woman materialized and stood unsmilingly facing the audience. Small and compact, she wore a matching brown skirt and jacket and a shiny white rayon blouse. In a businesslike way, she began undressing, in what I was informed was to be a delightful striptease. The scattered audience of men and their chunky women silently gulped beer and sipped slivovitz as the dancer removed her suit jacket, her shoes, her blouse and her skirt, until she stood looking out upon us in her pink rayon slip and bra. It was all done rather antiseptically, as if preparing for a medical examination. Each garment was tidily laid out and patted down on the piano bench, there being no pianist.

Then she stepped out of her slip, and in her panties did a few routine steps in approximate time to the music. She had very good legs. Things were heating up. From somewhere she picked up a heavy blue terry cloth robe and, wrapped in it, she slipped off her bra and flashed one breast. My fellow writers broke off their dying conversation. I don't know what got into me, but I asked a fatal question: "Can you tell from looking at her what her nationality is?"

My Serb friend Bogdan, depressed by his wife's absence in Belgrade, since it had left him for an entire week to the mercies of his melancholy mistress, glanced across the room at the stripper, and gave his morose opinion: "I would say she could be Croatian."

"Impossible!" the Croatian poet laughed. And with a sharpened eye and a surprising undertone of moral indignation, he added, "She could never be Croatian. Maybe Russian, or Slovenian, but not Croatian."

"Slovenian!" The mocking shout came from the Slovenian literature professor, a tall, thin fellow with shoulder-length hair. "Never! She has absolutely nothing Slovenian about her. Look how dark she is! I would say from the South, maybe Montenegrin."

The dark-skinned Montenegrin poet sitting beside me simply exploded in a challenging "Ha!" Just a few minutes earlier, he had been ethnically relaxed enough to tell a joke on his own people. Montenegrins are apparently famous for their admirably lethargic natures. One of them, said the poet, was walking down a street when he suddenly whipped out his revolver and, swiveling about, shot a snail on the sidewalk behind him. His energetic Serbian friend asked what the hell he had done that for. The Montenegrin explained, "He's been following me all day!"

When it came to the stripper, however, humor had noticeably evaporated, as each of the men kept handing her over to somebody else. And in the middle of this warming discussion of ethnic types, I noticed that the dancer had left the platform in her thick terry cloth robe, with her clothes cradled neatly in her arms. She was just about to pass us when I stuck out my arm and stopped her. "May I ask where you come from?" With a wan, polite smile, she replied "Düsseldorf," and continued on her way.

None of the writers allowed himself to laugh, though I thought one or two blushed at the irony of the situation. A bit tense, struggling awkwardly to reconstruct the earlier atmosphere of comradely warmth, we strolled through the dark Balkan night, the president and four distinguished delegates of the writers' organization established after World War I by H. G. Wells, George Bernard Shaw, Henri Barbusse and other war-weary writers as an attempt to apply the universalist tradition of literature to the melting down of those geographical and psychological barriers of nationalism for whose perpetuation humanity has always spent its noblest courage, and its most ferocious savagery.

1994

Let's Privatize Congress

It is great news, this idea of selling a House office building now that the Republicans are dissolving so many committees and firing their staffs. But I wouldn't be surprised if this is only the opening wedge for a campaign to privatize Congress. Yes, let the free market openly raise its magnificent head in the most sacred precincts of the Welfare State.

The compelling reasons for privatizing Congress are perfectly evident. Everybody hates it, only slightly less than they hate the president. Everybody, that is, who talks on the radio, plus millions of the silent who only listen and hate in private.

Congress has brought on this hatred, mainly by hypocrisy. For example, members are covered by complete government-run health insurance—while the same kind of coverage for the voters was defeated, with the voters' consent and support, no less.

The voters, relieved that they are no longer menaced by inexpensive health insurance administered by the hated government, must nevertheless be confused about not getting what polls show they wanted.

The important point is that even though they are happy at being denied what they say they want, they also know that the campaign to defeat health insurance was financed by the big private health insurance companies to the tune of millions of dollars paid to congressional campaigns. The net result is that with all their happiness, the voters are also aware of a lingering sense of congressional hypocrisy.

Health care is only one of many similar issues—auto safety, the environment, education, the use of public lands, etc. The way each issue is decided affects the finances of one or another business, industry or profession, and these groups naturally tend to butter the bread of members of Congress.

We can do away with this hypocrisy by making Congress a private enterprise. Let each representative and senator openly represent, and have his salary paid by, whatever business group wishes to buy his vote. Then, with no excuses, we will really have the best representative system money can buy. No longer will absurdly expensive election campaigns be necessary. Anyone wanting the job of congressional representative of, say, the drug industry could make an appointment with the council of that industry and make his pitch.

The question arises whether we would need bother to go through the whole election procedure. But I think we must continue to ask the public to participate lest people become even more alienated than they are now, with only thirty-nine percent of the eligible voters going to the polls in November.

A privatized Congress might well attract a much higher percentage of voters than the present outmoded one does because the pall of hypocrisy would have been stripped away and a novel bracing honesty would attract voters to choose whichever representative of the auto or real estate industries or the date growers they feel most sympathy for.

Once Congress is privatized, the time would have come to do the same to the Supreme Court and the Justice Department. If each justice were openly hired by a sector of the economy to protect its interests, a simple bargaining process could settle everything. The Auto Industry justice, wishing to throw out a suit against General Motors or Ford, could agree to vote his support for the Agribusiness justice, who wanted to quash a suit by workers claiming to have been poisoned while picking cabbages.

Some will object that such a system of what might be called legalized corruption would leave out the public and its interests. But this is no longer a problem when you realize that there is no public and therefore no public interest in the old sense. As Margaret Thatcher once said, "There is no society," meaning that the public consists of individuals, all of whom have private interests that to some degree are hostile to the interests of other individuals.

Possible objections: the abstract idea of justice would disappear under a system that takes only private economic interests into account. Secondly, the corporate state, which this resembles, was Mussolini's concept and resulted in the looting of the public by private interests empowered by the state.

Objections to the objections: we already have a corporate state. All privatization would do would be to recognize it as a fact.

Conclusion: we are in bad trouble.

1995

On Mark Twain's *Chapters from My Autobiography*

One of the books that as a teenager tore me from the football field to the library was *A Connecticut Yankee in King Arthur's Court*. It may be a flawed book, but it made a friend of Mark Twain for life, and if in later years I came to question the innate superiority of a scientific civilization over one based on supernatural faith, I must in the end bow before the undeniable—it is better to be vaccinated against cholera than to land in India with one's blood in its virginal purity.

I am not at all sure that every one of his sentences is golden, not to speak of his paragraphs, but he somehow managed—despite a steady underlying seriousness few writers have matched—to step around the pit of self-importance and to keep his membership in the ordinary human race in the front of his mind and his writing. His wit notwithstanding, he found the ways to let his feelings show, even his sentiments. In this he is not modern, incidentally, when so much of the late century's writing is one or another version of camp, our preferred tonality above all others. One cannot, for example, read his anguished record of his daughter Susy's death and its effects upon him without admiring not only his stoicism in being able to write at all on so painful a subject, but his maintaining so fine a balance between a flow of genuine feeling and the restraint of a man trying to stay lucid after a mortal blow to his sanity. But one must beware of ascribing too definite a purpose in Mark Twain's writing; he wrote, or affected to, for a living, but in reality because he had to, in the way water has to boil when it is heated.

He seems always to have been an observer of himself, albeit an often mystified one, as well as of the world. "I was born reserved as to endearments of speech and caresses, and hers [his young wife's] broke upon me as the summer waves break upon Gibraltar. I was reared in that atmosphere of reserve. . . . I never knew a member of my father's family to kiss another member of it except once, and that at a death-bed." And indeed, it was only to ask to be allowed to die that the kiss was given by the dying man.

He is cool but without the duplicity of camp, which after all is a strategy of indicating feeling in place of feeling very much, thus escaping any commitment which might make embarrassingly visible the heart on the sleeve, or worse yet the absence of any heart at all. Twain's style is different. He admits to his feelings, and in full-throatedly saying so he often moves us just before he makes sure to mock himself. But what supports this acerbic distancing is his announced role as a lifelong witness to his experience rather than a participant. I suppose what also keeps his sentiment from overflowing is his incredible truthfulness. One never feels one is being worked over, pumped for sympathy or anything else. He seems to be saying, quite simply, Here are the facts of myself on this occasion. And of course he manages to express this distancing through what might be called his confessional laughter. Speaking of the large prices paid at auction for some of his old letters, and comparing them to the lower prices brought by General Grant's: "I can't rise to General Grant's lofty place in the estimation of this nation, but it is a deep happiness to me to know that when it comes to epistolary literature he can't sit in the front seat along with me." He has not only beaten Grant out but is enjoying it, and that's funny because its truth threatens our defenses against admitting the pleasure of besting someone we respect.

Clemens, as this autobiography reminds us again and again, was an alienated man, but with the difference that he admits to sharing the absurdities himself which he has observed and often ruthlessly criticizes in others. He seems to have seen his role, and probably the role of literature in general, differently than most cultural observers presently see theirs. He is not using his alienation from the public illusions of his hour in order to reject the country implicitly as though he could live without it, but manifestly in order to correct it. The notion of a lost generation, for instance, something which recrudesces with almost every generation from the expatriates of the Twenties to the Beats and onward, would be beyond his imagining; he is very much part of what needs changing. But by the onset of the twentieth century the human race had not yet crossed over the line at which its insanities could no longer be easily forgiven. I can think of two possible reasons that he stops short of giving up on the whole race, including its corrupted politics; first, because doomsday thinking was not yet the style which would come on after the two world wars, plus the fascist and communist depredations and the dawning awareness among the civilized of the physical and psychic damage of racism; and second, because Clemens wrote much more like a father than a son. He doesn't seem to be sitting in class taunting the teacher but standing at the head of it challenging his students to acknowledge their own humanity, that is, their immemorial attraction to the untrue. Nor does he spare himself, except indirectly by virtue of bringing up, time and again and in a host of disguises, the whole matter of lying. If you peel off some of its hilarity, his book is a litany of treachery, deceit, mendacity unmasked—odd if you think of him as the American Homer, the writer *sui generis*, more than any other the surveyor who marked the boundaries of American literature.

He can't stop his boasting, especially now in his old age, quickly following up by puncturing whatever balloon he has just inflated. Tracing his lineage, whose distinction in Britain he has just been bragging about, he quickly comes down to earth with "But I am forgetting the first Clemens—the one that stands furthest back toward the original *first* Clemens, which was Adam."

Clemens, a second son, writes as though he were the eldest. His older brother, Orion, was a touchingly inept man who flew from perch to perch all his life and never found one where he felt comfortable, and Henry, two years younger, was apparently a rather dull fellow whose role in the family was to bore their mother with his tedious goodness until she turned for relief to Sam and his pranks, wisecracks and unexpectedness. Looking back over his seventy years, Clemens seems to see himself as the preferred child, and maybe this helps account for the air of confident, abundant love which lies just below the surface of these recollections. If a more skeptical author would be hard to find—"Carlyle said 'a lie cannot live.' It shows that he did not know how to tell them"—he can speak in almost the same breath of his daughter's death in some of the most nakedly painful prose imaginable: "It is one of the mysteries of our nature that a man, all unprepared, can receive a thunder-stroke like that and live." His hard-edged, hard-eyed contempt seems not to have interfered with admissions of grief, empathy, limitless affection and weakness. Perhaps this accounts for the devotion he seems never to have lost among his countrymen. In the end readers love love.

Apart from his never completing it, I am not sure—not that it matters—that this is an autobiography in any proper sense. It is rather a string of riffs on themes that rise and fall out of consciousness. That it was not written but dictated, talked out, no doubt helps explain the lack of formal structure. But this looseness tends to lend the text more credence as a spontaneous record of the author's own contradictions as well as those of his time. It is interesting to note what he apparently felt were the limits that a prudish churchgoing America would expect him to observe. The Clemens childrens' fifteen-year-old German nanny was "a clear-souled little maiden and without offense, notwithstanding her profanities, and she was loaded to the eyebrows with them. . . . She was always scattering her profanities around, and they were such a satisfaction to me that I never dreamed of such a thing as modifying her." Yet revealing his admiration for a cussing young woman was one thing, quoting her in plain English was another. One day, finishing with the tedious job of braiding the girls' hair, the nanny exploded to heaven, "Gott sei Dank ich bin fertig mit'm Gott verdammtes Haar!" To which Clemens added, "I believe I am not brave enough to translate it." If the nanny's expostulation—"Thank God I am finished with this goddamned hair"—really breached the propriety of the time, I wonder whether some of Clemens's popularity reflected a near-scandalous titillation with the shock of his candor. Through most or all of his writing life, after all, nothing of a respectable woman's body could be seen outside her bedroom except her hands and face, and there was hardly a household furnishing, from a lamp to a window shade to a drape to a chair seat, whose modesty was not suggested by a discreet fringe.

Mark Twain could not have existed anywhere but in America not only because the very web of his work is woven out of our geography, our spaces, rivers, mountains; it is also because there are no sexually alive women in his writings. His women are ideals, vapors, mothers and aunts who are almost always wise protectors of hearth and home, or virginal girls who are never pursued or are not old enough to be married. It is not a question of hostility toward women on his part; they seem never to threaten him at all. It is more likely the simple blindness of the culture toward the feminine, which, as with practically every other American trait, he exemplified.

American prudery, needless to say, is still alive just beneath the surface, awaiting the hypocrite's rousing touch. But nowadays it takes other forms, some of them of political importance. Early in Bill Clinton's presidency he was nearly brought down by charges of having had sex some years ago with a lady of doubtful morals. Had the real and pretended feelings of moral outrage evoked by this charge been permitted to skew the images of our former chief executives, we should have been without the services of—let's see now—Washington, Jefferson, probably Jackson, Cleveland, Harding, Roosevelt, Eisenhower, and Kennedy, among others, which would have left us to the characterological flavorings of Chester Arthur, Calvin Coolidge, Herbert Hoover and

Richard Nixon. Admittedly, we might pepper the pot with Harry Truman, but what improvement a president's marital fidelity or lack of it bestows upon his official service it is not possible to speculate. All we can be sure of is that since some time around the Kennedy administration, the American press, obedient as ever to the zeitgeist, has done what it could not have done in Clemens's time—stationed itself at the keyholes of politicians' bedroom doors and reported the findings. That the public weal is benefited is doubtful; what is clear is that stoking suspicion of hanky-panky makes it easier to kid the public that a villain who never cheats on his wife (Nixon, for instance) is thereby to be granted high moral grades as public servant—an invitation to calamity.

Who was Mark Twain writing for? The question becomes important when one realizes that he is still selling in the millions and certainly sold in the hundreds of thousands during his lifetime. To be sure, he is plain-spoken, but there is an elegance here and an irony whose appreciation requires an uncustomary patience in a contemporary reader. As universally popular as he was, he vigorously disdained the major political parties of his time and their leaders. Was there more tolerance in America then, or simply greater self-certainty? Clemens's eagerness for popularity notwithstanding, he declared himself a mugwump, in effect a political independent of a kind some would have condemned for an aristocratic contempt of rank-and-file party adherents, i.e., the very people themselves. Manifestly he refused to pander to the loyalists of any party, to the point where almost every reference to a party is touched with ridicule. Yet he was clearly passionate about the need for honest men in government in an age when corruption was rife, and there was no surrender, at least none that is obvious, to cynicism and despair, for he was always quick to note the honest citizen who deserved his compliment.

It has been noted before that the final years of a century are often touched with foreboding of the millennial judgment approaching, the last days. This was the case as the century turned in America. The democratic promise was being overwhelmed by the greed of unprincipled, socially irresponsible forces, the moneygrubbers, the little foxes who spoil the vineyards, uncontrolled capitalism. "The Gilded Age" was an enduring title invented by Mark Twain much earlier, and his last books are indeed darkened by forebodings of the ruin of the country's early promise. In this autobiography is probably his most unmitigated prophecy of approaching doom.

> Human nature being what it is, I suppose we must expect to drift into monarchy by and by. It is a saddening thought, but we cannot change our nature; we are all alike, we human beings; and in our blood and bone we carry the seeds out of which monarchies and aristocracies are grown: worship of gauds, titles, distinctions, power. We have to worship these things and their possessors, we are all born so, and we cannot help it. We have to be despised by somebody whom we regard as above us, or we are not happy; we have to have somebody to worship and envy, or we cannot be content.... Like all other nations, we worship money and the possessors of it—they being our aristocracy, and we have to have one. We like to read about rich people in the papers.... "Rich Woman Fell Down Cellar—Not Hurt." The falling down the cellar is of no interest to us when the woman is not rich.

The republic, he continues, is inexorably heading for monarchy, "but I believe that if we obstruct these encroachments and steadily resist them the monarchy can be postponed for a good while yet." His political awareness was of course acute, and for all his scoffing at any direct influence of his own on public events, it seems implicit that he hoped his work would be useful in the struggle to maintain a democracy. But what did his audience make of this commitment? Or did they simply skip over it to enjoy his humor and tales? After all, some of his heartiest admirers were the great millionaire capitalists of the time as well as the leading politicians, men whose like manned the legislatures which, as the common saying went, were the best that money could buy.

Clemens was always the artist first and foremost, and the artist is a liar who, in Harold Clurman's phrase, tells lies that are like truth. Here as elsewhere in Clemens's canon there are a number of charming, innocuous-seeming stories which, intentionally or not, are metaphors of the artist's moral situation. There is his story of the mesmerist who performed in Hannibal when he was a boy of fourteen and wanted to stand before the town dripping with glamour. The mesmerist would select members of the audience, put them in trances, and control their actions by his commands. The young Clemens eagerly submitted himself, but unlike others, he could never manage to escape his stubborn consciousness. Finally, in order to astound the credulous audience, he faked a hypnotic state, pretending to carry out the mesmerist's orders. So convincing was his spirited acting that he quickly became a favorite subject for the mesmerist, who obviously knew a good thing when he saw it. But not everyone in the audience was convinced. A clutch of elderly men thought he was faking until in one of his trances he began recalling the details of a long-forgotten theater fire which he had once overhead them talking about, unbeknownst to them. Amazed by his "vision" of an event which only they were old enough to have witnessed, they rallied to his side and helped lift him triumphantly over any doubters in the audience.

But having hit once, he had to repeat. One evening, spotting a local bully who had been making his life miserable, he fell into his usual trance and then suddenly grabbed a rusty revolver off a prop table, leaped from the stage and took out after his persecutor, who fled in terror. Uproar! But the mesmerist assured the frightened audience that the Clemens boy could not possibly have done any damage because he had been under mesmeric control the whole time and would have been stopped by the great mind-pilot before he could shoot anybody. Clemens had now become a veritable star in the mesmerized-performer business, walking proof of the power of hypnosis. "It is curious," he writes. "When the magician's engagement closed there was but one person in the village who did not believe in mesmerism, and I was the one." And here speaks the artist surrounded by his trunks filled with stringed puppets, his technique, and his bag of tricks which sweep the public imagination as mere fact never can. Again, the human mind loves the lie which ironically can be made beautiful in the shape of art.

It needs no special psychiatric sensibility to note that his first subject after this public triumph of his boyhood is his mother, and how he entertained her with his lies. Visiting the lady thirty-five years after these "evil exploits of mine"—and after an unexplained hiatus of more than ten years during which he failed to visit her—he is filled with remorse, not only for having ignored her but for having convinced her, his own mother, with the lie that he was so famously mesmerized so long ago. He resolves to confess himself. The consequence is typical Clemens, and a bit strange.

By this time he had long felt revulsion at his ill-earned fame in Hannibal, based on fraud as it indeed had been. It is very odd, the depth of this self-revulsion at what would seem a boyish prank, and stranger still that he sustained the sensation for nearly four decades. "How easy it is to make people believe a lie, and how hard it is to undo that work again!" Only after much anguish can he bring himself to tell her the truth, in dread "of the sorrow that would rise in her face and the shame that would look out of her eyes," but "after long and troubled reflection" he makes his confession.

Naturally, being Clemens's mother, she rejects the confession, calmly insisting that after so many years he can't possibly remember accurately what happened, and that as a witness to his victory she is sure he earned it honestly and was certainly under the mesmerist's control. Her turning his guilt away alarms him. He protests that he had no "vision" at all of the theater fire as he pretended, but merely overheard the men talking about it some time earlier. And more, the mesmerist's trick of pushing needles into his arm while he showed no pain was also a fraud, for he was in fact in agony, just as he would be now if she stuck pins into his flesh.

But she is tranquilly adamant in her belief in him. "I was nettled, to have my costly truthfulness flung out of the market in this placid and confident way when I was expecting to get a profit out of it." In short, she denies him absolution in favor of his artistic triumph, his power and fame which she loves, and far more than she loves his picky purity. In effect, she rejects the real him and the bared soul he has offered her. And here is the artist's complicated disgust with his art, the disgust mixed with equal amounts of pride plus the feeling of control over the imaginations of other people and his guilt at having planted images in their minds which he alone knows are hot air molded to beautiful and sometimes meaningful forms. It is all a lie, a lie like truth. Again, there is a certain indefinable sadness an inch beneath Mark Twain's happy art, like a painful longing for some elusive reconciliation which lends it an indefinable depth. There is hardly a story in this autobiography which does not pose the lie against the truth; and the victory of the lie leaves everyone basking contentedly in life's normative stasis. The victory of untruth and illusion simply doesn't matter one way or the other in the long scheme of things, and yet it is important to Clemens that there be honest people in the world.

Reading along, one becomes aware of being spoken to by this book, that it is really a chat, something that in our day could easily be turned into half a dozen tapes to be played in the car. It is wonderfully visual, full of recollected pictures, the best kind of listening. You can just about hear him laughing, or his voice growing husky in the sad parts. Clearly there are long rambles with no particular thematic relevance beyond the simple pleasure of the telling, like rummaging through cabinets and closets and trying on discarded shoes, old gloves and a half-remembered jacket or two.

He thinks he once remembered his brother Henry walking into a fire when he was six months old; it took years for him to realize that walking is impossible at that age. But memory, he believes, has no morals and no rules. "When I was younger I could remember anything, whether it had happened or not; but my faculties are decaying now, and soon I shall be so I cannot remember any but the things that happened." But of course there are more rules to memory than his pre-Freudian time suspects. At another point in his ramble he has the remarkable experience of dreaming yet again of Henry's death and of his lying in a metal coffin and being covered with white flowers, with a red rose in the center. This is followed by Clemens's great relief at realizing, within the dream, that it is only a dream. But a short time later the dream turns out to have been prophetic. His brother has indeed died, possibly as a result of the ineptitude of a young physician, and is laid out, with no help from Clemens but precisely as in his dream, in a metal coffin, with white flowers covering him and a red rose in their center.

In view of recent objections to Clemens's attitudes toward slavery and black people, it comes as a surprise to read his apparently spontaneous words about them, written, as far as I am aware, not in any defensive spirit but simply as memorable fact no different from other recollections in his mind at the moment, the turn of the century. Of the slave after whom he modeled Jim as well as other of his black characters, a man whom life has badly used, and who "has endured ... with the patience and friendliness and loyalty which were his birthright," Clemens says, "It was [from him] that I got my strong liking for his race and my appreciation of certain of its fine qualities. This feeling and this estimate have stood the test of sixty years and more and have suffered no impairment. The black face is as welcome to me now as it was then." One can't help sensing a subconscious agenda behind such remarks (there are others like it), a personal affirmation before the majority of Americans, who by the turn of the century—a time when American black life was as hopelessly oppressive as South Africa's would later be—were light-years away from so warm and positive an opinion.

In essence, the book is a valediction. There is overall a tone of farewell, of a life's work done. Naturally, Clemens can't sustain this idea too long and is soon back to his old habit of making things up out of half-remembered fragments of his life and writing. And the book is at the same time a confession, unique in his works, of the superstitious streak that accompanied his lifelong skepticism.

> I think that in *Tom Sawyer* I starved Injun Joe to death in a cave. But that may have been to meet the exigencies of romantic literature. I can't remember now whether the real Injun Joe died in the cave or out of it, but I do remember that the news of his death reached me at a most unhappy time—that is to say, just at bedtime on a summer night when a prodigious storm of thunder and lightning accompanied by a deluging rain that turned the streets and lanes into rivers, caused me to repent and resolve to lead a better life. ... By my teachings I perfectly well knew what all that wild riot was for—Satan had come to get Injun Joe. ... With every glare of lightning I shrivelled and shrunk together in mortal terror, and in the interval of black darkness that followed I poured out my lamentings over my lost condition, and my supplications for just one more chance, with an energy and feeling and sincerity quite foreign to my nature.

> But in the morning I saw that it was a false alarm and concluded to resume business at the old stand and wait for another reminder.

The prophetic dreams in this book—I believe he mentions three that come to mind in this connection—all concern death, and each precedes the actual death of the person dreamed of, and in precisely the dream situation. Mark Twain at seventy was gathering his powers unto himself; the same man who went through deep depressions that may well have tempted him with suicide was demonstrating for his own benefit and for the world's his mastery over his life, including a touch of the prophetic gift—a tour through all that he had created, all that he had dreamed. There were sins he dared not speak of even now, but I doubt any other major writer has ever allowed the world so close a look at his own insides and the experiences which he acknowledges having used and transformed into his fiction.

The effect of this opening up of the secret files, so to speak, is in no way a weakening of the force of his art. Or so it seems to me. "Tom Sawyer" is still "Tom Sawyer" even after we know the real character's name without quotation marks.

Mark Twain was a performer, obviously, a man drawn happily toward center stage. Almost from the start of his career he moved about the country from one lecture platform to another, telling his stories, cracking his jokes. It was years before he was taken seriously—or took himself seriously—as an artist, let alone a major one who would be looked to for insights into America's always uncertain moral life and its shifting but everlasting hypocrisies. One has to wonder what would have become of him in our television age, when he may well have found fame as essentially a comedian, like Will Rogers, or a character with his own program, perhaps like Jack Benny or Bob Hope. Sam Clemens did not disdain money, not at all, and TV could have made him very rich, could have addicted him to the compromises that come and must come with that territory, could have fed his appetite for soft celebrity rather than the hard bed of art. He would have been pressured to round the edges of his satire so as to emphasize uplift for the folks, perhaps to spare some fraudulent politician his lash whose subcommittee might make trouble for the broadcasting industry. Or even simpler, he would have been told in very clear tones, as I and doubtless other writers have been told by a network producer, that American television does not want "art." (They pronounce the quotation marks.) And that he must eliminate diversions from the main drive of his stories and simplify his syntax lest the audience lose track of a too-lengthy sentence. One way or another he would surely have ended in a head-on crash on the information superhighway, there can be no doubt of that.

It isn't easy to say how strong his resistance would have been to the suborning of his talent by his own declared wish to capture the big audience rather than settling for a far easier triumph with a narrower and more elegant supportive clique that already agreed with him. That big audience today is facing the TV screen, not the book or the lecture platform. My own inclination is in his favor; I think he would certainly have fallen for the power and emoluments of national TV celebrity, but would have found his way home again. Because he was an artist, and one who fed upon his own soul as much as on what he observed, and the call of the soul was the most powerful emotion he knew.

Of course this estimate may be wrong. Orson Welles, another man of brilliance and also a performer, was basically neutered by the American entertainment business, and spent most of his creative powers at poolside thrilling other artists with his culture, his knowledge and the spectacle of a greatness that was always on the verge of retaking the stage but could not be reborn, at least in my opinion, because it had no spiritual support in a country where few people knew enough to want what he could give. All that is certain is that the country by and by would have tired of listening to the *Mark Twain Weekly Hour;* and if he wanted to remain a national prime-time asset, the bubbling up of his genuine material would have slowed in due time and he would have had to begin clawing at himself, scouring his memories to feed into the television maw, and would have ended in a wealthy, self-contemptuous defeat.

We had Mark Twain when it was still possible to have him as an artist intent on addressing the whole country without having to pay the price of celebrity and the inevitable desiccation of his talent. We had Mark Twain when it was still possible to have him as the celebrity he was and the respected artist at the same time; the culture would support such a phenomenon still. That he might have survived intact the crush of the bottom line of mass communications—which in theory would have attracted him—is not easy to imagine. So the treasure is intact, and our American luck, at least in this case, has held.

1996

Clinton in Salem

A number of commentators have seen a resemblance between the extravaganza around President Clinton and the witchcraft hysteria in Salem three hundred years ago. There are some similarities and some important differences.

The tone of iron vituperation and the gut-shuddering hatred are reminiscent of the fury of the Salem ministers roaring down on the Devil as though they would grind their heels into his face. Though there were never any witches while there certainly is a Bill Clinton, the underlying emotions are not all that different—the evident wish is to end the Evil One's very existence.

In both cases there is a kind of sublime relief in the unearthing of the culprit's hidden crimes. The Salem church, which effectively controlled the village, had been so fractious that minister after minister had fled the pulpit or been dismissed. But with the discovery of Satan in town, the people understood in a flash what the source of their troubles had been, and a new era of social peace opened before them—provided they could root out the diabolically corrupt. Suddenly paranoia ruled and all were suspect and no one was safe.

What is very different now is the public reaction. Rarely does just about every newspaper and television commentator agree so thoroughly. Be it *The New York Times, The Washington Post*, or the television and print tabloids whose normal business is reporting news of the gutter, media outlets all became highly moral in a single stroke, as though an electric charge had passed through iron filings, instantly pointing them all in the same direction. Not often does one sinner raise so many so quickly out of their moral slumber.

But what is strange and interesting is how the public, that great stallion that is so often led to water, this time dipped its head but refused to drink, perhaps scenting the stale smell of political manipulation.

It may also be that with so many American marriages ending in divorce, and most of those surely involving a mate in the wrong bed, an unspoken self-identification with this kind of marital misery has restrained people from losing all sympathy for their leader, disappointed as they might be in his behavior.

Despite the lashings of almost all the press and the mullahs of the religious right, the people seem largely to have withheld their righteous anger. This did not happen in Salem, where the members of the clergy, who were also the leaders of the community, were strangers to mercy and indeed to common sense, and helped drive the public into a lethal panic.

There is, I think, a parallel in the sexual element underlying each phenomenon. Witch-hunts are always spooked by women's horrifying sexuality awakened by the superstud Devil. In Europe, where tens of thousands perished in the hunts, broadsides showed the Devil with two phalluses, one above the other. And of course mankind's original downfall came about when the Filthy One corrupted the mother of mankind.

In Salem, witch-hunting ministers had the solemn duty to examine women's bodies for signs of the "Devil's Marks"—a suggestion of webbing, perhaps, between the toes, a mole behind an ear or between the legs, or a bite mark somewhere. I thought of this wonderfully holy exercise when Congress went pawing through Kenneth Starr's fiercely exact report on the president's intimate meetings with Monica Lewinsky. I guess nothing changes all that much.

In any case, those who think it trivial that Mr. Clinton lied about a mere affair are missing the point: it is precisely his imperious need of the female that has unnerved a lot of men, the mullahs especially, just as it has through the ages. This may also help to account for the support he still gets from women. He may be a bit kinky, but at least he's not the usual suit for whom the woman is a vase, decorative and unused.

Then there is the color element. Mr. Clinton, according to Toni Morrison, the Nobel Prize–winning novelist, is our first black president, the first to come from the broken home, the alcoholic mother, the under-the-bridge shadows of our ranking systems. He is also the most relaxed and unaffected with black people, whose company and culture he clearly enjoys.

His closeness to blacks may, in fact, have contributed to the relative racial harmony we have been enjoying these past few years. But it may also be part of the reason for his estrangement from his peers, and it may have helped uncork the sewer of contempt upon his head, the Starr report.

The Devil in Salem was white, but two of the few black people in the village were his first suspected consorts, John Indian and Tituba. Both were slaves. Tituba was tortured into naming women she had seen with the Devil, thus starting the hunt on its way. The conflation of female sexuality and blackness in a white world is an old story, and here it had lethal results.

In Mr. Clinton's case, there comes an overflowing of rage reminiscent of that earlier explosion. If he lied under oath he of course broke the law, but it seems impossible that the Founding Fathers would have required Congress, as a part of his punishment, to study what parts of a woman's body the president had touched. Except for this hatred of Mr. Clinton, which sometimes seems to mount to a hellish fear of him as unclean, a supernatural contaminator, it would surely have sufficed for Mr. Starr to report that he had had an affair and falsely denied it under oath.

The Salem paroxysm left the town ravaged, accursed and almost deserted, a place where no one would buy land or farm or build for one hundred years. Salem's citizens had acted out the mythology of their dark subconscious and had eaten their own— all in the name of God and good morals. It was a volcanic explosion of repressed steam that gave people license to speak openly in court of what formerly would have been shamefully caged in their hearts—for example, the woman who testified that her neighbor flew in through her window one balmy night and lay upon her and had his way. Suddenly this was godly testimony, and the work of heaven was to kill the neighbor.

Salem purified itself nearly to death, but in the end some good may have come of it. I am not historian enough to assert this as fact, but I have often wondered if the witch-hunt may have helped spawn, one hundred years later, the Bill of Rights, particularly the Fifth Amendment, which prohibits forcing a person to testify against himself—something that would have stopped the witch-hunt in its tracks. It may also have contributed to the wall of separation between church and state in America, for in Salem theocratic government had its last hurrah. Or so one may hope.

1998

Salesman at Fifty

As far as I know, nobody has figured out time. Not chronological time, of course—that's merely what the calendar tells—but real time, the kind that baffles the human mind when it confronts, as mine does now, the apparent number of months, weeks, and years that have elapsed since 1948, when I sat down to write a play about a salesman. I say "apparent" because I cannot find a means of absorbing the idea of half a century rolling away beneath my feet. Half a century is a very long time, yet I must already have been grown up way back then, indeed I must have been a few years past thirty, if my calculations are correct, and this fact I find indigestible.

A few words about the theatrical era that *Death of a Salesman* emerged from. The only theater available to a playwright in the late Forties was Broadway, the most ruthlessly commercialized theater in the world, with the Off-Broadway evolution still a decade away. That theater had one single audience, not two or three, as is the case today, catering to very different levels of age, culture, education, and intellectual sophistication. Its critics were more than likely to be ex–sports reporters or general journalists rather than scholars or specialists university-trained in criticism. So a play worked or it didn't, made them laugh or cry or left them bored. (It really isn't all that different today except that the reasoning is perhaps more elevated.) That unified audience was the same for musicals, farces, O'Neill's tragedies, or some imported British, French, or Middle European lament. Whatever its limitations, it was an audience that loved theater, and many of its members thought theatergoing not quite a luxury but an absolute necessity for a civilized life.

For playwriting, what I believe was important about that unified audience was that a writer with ambitions reaching beyond realistic, made-for-entertainment plays could not expect the support of a coterie of like-minded folk who would overlook his artistic lapses so long as his philosophical agenda tended to justify their own. That unified audience had come in from the rain to be entertained, and even instructed, if need be, provided the instruction was entertaining. But the writer had to keep in mind that his proofs, so to speak, had to be accessible both to the lawyers in the audience and to the plumbers, to the doctors and the housewives, to the college students and the kids at the Saturday matinee. One result of this mix was the ideal, if not the frequent fulfillment, of a kind of play that would be complete rather than fragmentary, an emotional rather than an intellectual experience, a play basically of heart with its ulterior moral gesture integrated with action rather than rhetoric. In fact, it was a Shakespearean ideal, a theater for anyone with an understanding of English and perhaps some common sense.

Some of the initial readers of the *Death of a Salesman* script were not at all sure that the audience of 1949 was going to follow its manipulations of time, for one thing. Josh Logan, a leading stage and film director of numerous hits, *Mister Roberts* and *South*

Pacific among them, had greeted *All My Sons* two years earlier with great warmth, and invested a thousand dollars in *Salesman*, but when he read the script he apologetically withdrew five hundred. No audience, he felt, would follow the story, and no one would ever be sure whether Willy was imagining or really living through one or another scene in the play. Some thirty years later I would hear the same kind of reaction from the theater people in the Beijing People's Art Theater, where I had been invited to stage the play, which, in the view of many there, was not a play at all but a poem. It was only when they saw it played that its real dramatic nature came through.

In the 1949 Broadway audience there was more to worry about than their following the story. In one of his letters O'Neill had referred to that theater as a "showshop," a crude place where a very uncultivated, materialistic public cut off from its own spirituality gathered for a laugh or a tear. Clifford Odets, with his first successes surely the most hotly acclaimed playwright in Broadway history, would also end in bitter alienation from the whole system of Broadway production. The problem, in a word, was seriousness. There wasn't very much of it in the audience, and it was resented when it threatened to appear on the stage.

So it seemed. But *All My Sons* had all but convinced me that if one totally integrated a play's conceptual life with its emotional one so that there was no perceptible dividing line between the two, such a play could reach such an audience. In short, the play had to move forward not by following a narrow, discrete line, but as a phalanx, all of its elements moving together simultaneously. There was no model I could adapt for this play, no past history for the kind of work I felt it could become. What I had before me was the way the mind—at least my mind—actually worked. One asks a policeman for directions; as one listens, the hairs sticking out of his nose become important, reminding one of a father, brother, son with the same feature, and one's conflicts with him or one's friendship come to mind, and all this over a period of seconds while objectively taking note of how to get to where one wants to go. Initially based, as I explained in *Timebends*, my autobiography, on an uncle of mine, Willy rapidly took over my imagination and became something that has never existed before, a salesman with his feet on the subway stairs and his head in the stars.

His language and that of the Loman family were liberative from any enslavement to "the way people speak." There are some people who simply don't speak the way people speak. The Lomans, like their models in life, are not content with who and what they are, but want to be other, wealthier, more cultivated perhaps, closer to power. "I've been remiss," Biff says to Linda about his neglect of his father, and there would be many who seized on this usage as proof of the playwright's tin ear or of some inauthenticity in the play. But it is in Biffs mouth precisely because it is indeed an echo, a slightly misunderstood signal from above, from the more serious and cultivated part of society, a signal indicating that he is now to be taken with utmost seriousness, even remorseful of his past neglect. "Be liked and you will never want" is also not quite from Brooklyn, but Willy needs aphoristic authority at this point, and again, there is an echo of a—for want of a better word—Victorian authority to back him up. These folk are the innocent receivers of what they imagine as a more elegant past, a time "finer" than theirs. As Jews light-years away from religion or a community that might have fostered Jewish identity, they exist in a spot that probably most Americans feel they inhabit—on the sidewalk side of the glass looking in at a well-lighted place.

As it has turned out, this play seems to have shown that most of the world shares something similar to that condition. Having seen it in five or six countries, and directed it in China and Sweden, neither of whose languages I know, it was both mystifying and gratifying to note that people everywhere react pretty much the same in the same places of the play. When I arrived in China to begin rehearsals the people in the American embassy, with two exceptions, were sure the Chinese were too culturally remote from the play to ever understand it. The American ambassador and the political officer thought otherwise, the first because he had been born and raised in China, and the second, I supposed, because it was his job to understand how Chinese thought about life. And what they were thinking turned out to be more or less what they were thinking in New York or London or Paris, namely that being human—a father, mother, son—is something most of us fail at most of the time, and a little mercy is eminently in order given the societies we live in, which purport to be stable and sound as mountains when in fact they are all trembling in a fast wind blowing mindlessly around the earth.

1999

The Crucible in History

It would probably never have occurred to me to write a play about the Salem witch trials of 1692 had I not seen some astonishing correspondences with that calamity in the America of the late Forties and early Fifties. There were other enticements for me in the Salem period, however; most especially the chance it offered to write in what was for me a practically new language, one that would require new muscles.

I was never a scholar or an historian, of course; my basic need was somehow to respond to a phenomenon which, with only small exaggeration, one could say was paralyzing a whole generation and in an amazingly short time was drying up the habits of trust and toleration in public discourse. I refer, of course, to the anticommunist rage that threatened to reach hysterical proportions and sometimes did. I can't remember anyone calling it an ideological war, but I think now that that is what it amounted to. Looking back at the period, I suppose we very rapidly passed over anything like a discussion or debate and into something quite different, a hunt not alone for subversive people but ideas and even a suspect language. The object, a shock at the time, was to destroy the least credibility of any and all ideas associated with socialism and communism, whose proponents had to be either knowing or unwitting agents of Soviet subversion. An ideological war is like guerrilla war, since the enemy is first of all an idea whose proponents are not in uniform but are disguised as ordinary citizens, a situation that can scare a lot of people to death.

I am not really equipped to deliver a history of Cold War America, which like any other period is packed with passionately held illusions and ideas distorted on all sides by fear. Suffice to say it was a time of great, no doubt unprecedented fear, but fear, like love, is mostly incommunicable once it has passed. So I shall try to limit myself, as far as possible, to speak of events as they struck me personally, for those are what finally created *The Crucible*.

One knew that congressional investigations of subversion had been going on since the Thirties. The Dies committee, beginning with Nazi subversion in America, ended up with a neverending and often silly investigation of communists. But the country in the Thirties was not under external threat, and nobody seemed to take seriously any menace from an American Communist Party that could hardly elect a dogcatcher. From my perspective, what changed everything was the victory of the Chinese communists in 1949. Inevitably, the Chinese Reds were seen as all but an arm of the expansionist post–World War II Soviet machine, and a look at the map would indeed show that an enormous new part of the planet had turned red.

"Who Lost China!" almost instantly became the Republican mantra. Who were the traitors inside the Democratic administrations, going back to Roosevelt, that had sold out our favorite Chinese, Chiang Kai-Shek? This, I think, was the first notable injection of the idea of treason and foreign agents into domestic political discourse. To me the simplicity of it all was breathtaking. There had to be left-wing traitors in government, otherwise how could the Chinese—who, as everyone knew, loved Americans more than anybody—have turned against the pro-American Chiang Kai-Shek in favor of a Soviet agent like Mao Tse-tung?

All I knew about China in 1949 was what I had read by Edgar Snow and Jack Belden and Teddy White and other American reporters. What it amounted to was that the Nationalist regime was feudal and thoroughly corrupt and that the Reds were basically a miserably exploited peasantry that at long last had risen up and thrown their exploiters into the sea. I thought it was a great idea. In any event, the idea of our "losing" China seemed the equivalent of a flea losing an elephant. Nevertheless, there was a growing uproar in and out of Congress. One read that the China Lobby, a wealthy support group backing Chiang Kai-Shek's hopes to return to Beijing from Taiwan, was reportedly paying a lot of the bills and that Senator McCarthy was one of their most effective champions. The partisan political manipulation of a real issue was so patent that President Truman could dismiss the Republican scare as a "red herring." But it is an indication of its impact on the public mind that he soon had to retreat and institute a loyalty board of his own to investigate the allegiance of government employees.

To call the ensuing atmosphere paranoid is not to say that there was nothing real in the American–Soviet standoff. To be sure, I am far more willing than I was then, due to some experiences of my own with both sides, to credit both the American and Soviet leadership with enough ignorance of each other to have ignited a third world war. But there was something of the inauthentic, the spurious, and the invented in the conflict, if only because of the swiftness with which all values were being forced in a matter of months to literally reverse themselves. I recall some examples.

Death of a Salesman opened in February of 1949 and was hailed by nearly every newspaper and magazine; parenthetically, I should add that two exceptions come to mind, one Marxist, the other ex-Marxist. The Marxist was the *Daily Worker*, which found the play defeatist and lacking militant protest; the ex-Marxist, Mary McCarthy, who seemed outraged by the idea of elevating it to the status of tragedy and just hated it in general, particularly, I thought, because it was so popular. Real tragedy would have to close in two weeks. Anyway, several movie studios wanted it, and it was finally Columbia Pictures that bought it and engaged a great star, Fredric March, to play Willy.

In something like two years or less, as I recall, with the picture finished, I was asked by a terrified Columbia to sign an anticommunist declaration in order to ward off picket lines which apparently the American Legion was threatening to throw across the entrances of theaters showing the film. In the numerous phone calls that followed, the air of terror was heavy. It was the first intimation of what would soon follow. I declined to make any such statement, which, frankly, I found demeaning; what right had any organization to demand anyone's pledge of loyalty? I was sure the whole thing would soon go away, it was just too outrageous.

But instead of disappearing, the studio, it now developed, had actually made another film, a short which was to be shown with *Salesman*. This was called *The Life of a Salesman* and consisted of several lectures by City College School of Business professors. What they boiled down to was that selling was basically a joy, one of the most gratifying and useful of professions, and that Willy was simply a nut. Never in show business history has a studio spent so much good money to prove that its feature film was pointless. I threatened to sue (on what basis I had no idea), but of course the short could not be shown lest it bore the audience blind. But in less than two years *Death of a Salesman* had gone from a masterpiece to a pariah that was basically fraudulent.

In 1948, '49, '50, '51, I had the sensation of being trapped inside a perverse work of art, one of those Escher constructs in which it is impossible to know whether a stairway is going up or down. Practically everyone I knew, all survivors of the Great Depression of course as well as World War II, was somewhere within the conventions of the political left of center; one or two were Communist Party members, some were sort of fellow travelers, as I suppose I was, and most had had one or another brush with Marxist ideas or organizations. I have never been able to believe in the reality of these people being actual or putative traitors any more than I could be, yet others like them were being fired from teaching or other jobs in government or large corporations. The unreality of it all never left me. We were living in an art form, a metaphor that had no long history but, incredibly enough, suddenly gripped the country. So I suppose that in one sense *The Crucible* was an attempt to make life real again, palpable and structured—a work of art created in order to interpret an anterior work of art that was called reality but was not.

Again—it was the very swiftness of the change that lent it this unreality. Only three or four years earlier an American movie audience, on seeing a newsreel of—let's say—a Russian soldier or even Stalin saluting the Red Army, would have applauded, for that army had taken the brunt of the Nazi onslaught, as most people were aware. Now they would have looked on with fear or at least bewilderment, for the Russians had become the enemy of mankind, a menace to all that was good. It was the Germans who, with amazing rapidity, were turning good. Could this be real? And how to mentally deal with, for example, American authorities removing from German schoolbooks all mention of the Hitler decade?

In the unions, communists and their allies, who had been known as intrepid organizers, were now to be shorn of union membership and turned out as seditious, in effect. Harry Bridges, for example, the idol of West Coast longshoremen, whom he had all but single-handedly organized, would be subjected to court trial after court trial to drive him out of the country and back to his native Australia as an unadmitted communist. Academics, some of them prominent in their fields, were especially targeted, many forced to retire or simply fired for disloyalty; some of them communists, some fellow travelers, and inevitably, a certain number who were simply unaffiliated liberals who refused to sign one of the dozens of anticommunist pledges being required by college administrations.

The sweep went not only very wide but deep. By 1950 or thereabouts there were subjects one would do better to avoid and even words that were best left unspoken. The Spanish Civil War, for example, had quickly become a hot button. That war, as some of you may not recall, resulted from an attack in 1936 by the Spanish army upon the democratically elected Spanish government. After almost three years of terrible fighting, in which Nazi air force planes and Mussolini's troops helped him, the fascist

Generalissimo Franco took power. Spain would become the very symbol of the struggle against fascism; but more and more one heard, after about 1950, that Franco's victory was actually a not unworthy triumph of anticommunists. This despite the common belief through the Thirties and Forties that had Franco been thrown back, opening Hitler's Atlantic flank to hostile democrats rather than allied fascists, his war against Europe might well have had to be postponed if not aborted.

Again, it was the swiftness of this change that made it so fictional to me. Occasionally these quick changes were rather comical, which didn't help one's sense of reality.

One day in 1950 or thereabouts a stranger called, asking to come and see me about some matter he would prefer not to talk about on the phone and dropping as one of his bona fides that he had fought in Spain. I figured he was in trouble politically and must be really desperate if he imagined that I could help him. (A few ill-informed people still imagined I had some clout of this kind.) He arrived at my Brooklyn Heights house, a bright, youngish fellow carrying a briefcase. We chatted for a few minutes and then got down to business. Opening his briefcase, he took out a large map of a Texas oil field, rolled it out on my desk, and pointing at various black dots explained that these were oil wells in which he was selling stock. When I confessed surprise that an idealistic antifascist fighter should be ending up as an oil stock salesman, he asked, "Why not?" and with a touch of noble sincerity added, "Once the workers take over they're going to need oil!" This was a harbinger of the wondrous rationalizations that I would have cause to recall as our future arrived.

I should add that my uneasy fictional view of things turned out not to be entirely unwarranted; some six or seven years later, I would be cited for contempt of Congress for refusing to identify writers I had met at one of the two communist writers' meetings I had attended many years before. Normally, these citations resulted in a trial in federal court that took half an hour to lead to inevitable convictions. But my lawyer, Joseph Rauh Jr., brought in a former senator, Harry M. Cain, who had been head of the loyalty board under Eisenhower, to testify as an expert witness that my plays showed no signs of having been written under communist discipline. Cain had a curious history; a decorated Korean War veteran and fierce anti-communist, he had been a sidekick of McCarthy's and a weekly poker partner of his. But disillusionment had worn him down when, as head of the loyalty board, he had had to deal with the hundreds of letters a week from people suspecting neighbors, friends, and relatives of communist sympathies. The idea of the whole country spying on itself began to depress him, and he came to feel that from his Washington window he was looking out at a terrified nation and worse—some substantial fraction of it was quite literally crazed. The climax for him came with a series of relentlessly persistent letters from a Baltimore postman complaining of having been fired for disloyalty. What bothered him was the handwriting, which was barely literate. Communists were bad people, but they were rarely illiterate. Finally Cain invited the man to his office and realized that the accusations were not credible; this led him to wonder about the hundreds of other accusations he had with little or no examination been regularly forwarding to the FBI. At last he went directly to Eisenhower and told him he was convinced that the loyalty board itself was incompatible with political liberty. The next morning he found that he himself had been fired.

But that was still six or seven years on. My brushes with the fictional world in which I lived went back to 1947, when *All My Sons*, as the result of protests by the Catholic War Veterans, was removed from the Army's theatrical repertoire in Europe as a threat to soldiers' morale—since it told the story of a manufacturer selling defective parts to the Air Force. In a few years a former officer in that theatrical troop wrote to inform me that not only had *All My Sons* been banned but an order was given that no other play written by me was to be produced by the Army. As far as the Army was concerned, I had simply disappeared as an American writer. But this would be a useful experience when, in the late Sixties, as president of International PEN, I would find myself commiserating with Soviet writers and those in other communist countries who had seen their names obliterated from the rosters of living authors.

But it is impossible, certainly not in this short time, to properly convey the fears that mark the period. Nobody was being shot, to be sure, although some were going to jail, where at least one, a man named William Remington, was murdered, by an inmate hoping to shorten his sentence for having killed a communist. Rather than physical fear it was the sense of impotence, which seemed to deepen with each passing week, of being unable to speak simply and accurately of the very recent past when being Left in America, and for that matter in Europe, was simply to be alive to the dilemmas of the day. To be sure, I had counted myself a radical since my years in college and had tried and failed to read *Das Kapital*; but the Marxist formulations had certainly given shape to my views of politics— which in fact meant that to understand a political phenomenon you had to look for the money. It also meant that you believed capitalism was quite possibly doomed, but between 1929 and around 1936 there were moments when *not* to believe that would put you in a political minority. I may have dreamed of a socialism where people no longer lived off another's labor, but I had never met a spy. As for the very idea of willingly subjecting my work not only to some party's discipline but to anyone's control, my repugnance was such that as a very young and indigent writer I had turned down fairly lucrative offers to work for Hollywood studios because of a helpless revulsion at the thought of someone other than myself literally owning the paper I was typing on. It would not be long, perhaps four or five years, before the fraudulence of Soviet cultural claims was as clear to me as they should have been earlier, but I would never find it believable, either in the Fifties or later, that with their thuggish self-righteousness and callous contempt for artists' freedoms, the unabashed Soviet way of controlling culture could be successfully exported to America, except, perhaps, in Madison Avenue advertising agencies. In any case, to believe in that danger I would have to share a bed with the Republican Right.

Which is not to say that there was not much sincerity in the fears people felt in the Fifties, and, as in most things human, much cynicism as well, if not corruption. The moral high ground, as in most things human, was wreathed in fog. But the fact remained that some greatly talented people were being driven out of the country to live and work in England, screenwriters like Carl Foreman and Donald Ogden Stewart, actors like Charlie Chaplin and Sam Wanamaker (who, incidentally, in his last years, led the campaign to build a copy of Shakespeare's theater on the Thames). I no longer recall the number of our political exiles, but there were more than too many.

My subpoena before the House committee came some four years after *The Crucible* was produced, but I had been shot at more than once as a result of that play. Shortly after its production, the renewal of my outdated passport had been denied when I applied in order to go to Belgium, at the invitation of the Belgo-American Association, to attend the first European performance of the play. The stated grounds for confiscating my passport were that my presence abroad was not in the best interests of the United States. A rather farcical situation soon developed—and I should say that farce was always a step away from all the tragedies of the period. Since the play was the first and practically the only artistic evidence Europe had of resistance to what was considered a fascistic McCarthyism, the applause at the final curtain was intense and insistent, and since the newspapers had announced that I had accepted the invitation to be present, there were calls for the author. These went on and on until the American ambassador felt compelled to stand and take a bow. A species of insanity was spreading everywhere. Here was the ambassador, an officer of the State Department, acknowledging the applause for someone deemed by that department too dangerous to be present. It must surely have struck some of the audience as strange, however, that an author would be wearing a wide diplomatic sash diagonally across his chest; and the next morning's papers had loads of fun with the scene, which, of course, could hardly have advanced the best interests of the United States.

I should explain what I meant by the cynicism and corruption of the Red hunt. By 1956, when HUAC subpoenaed me, the tide was going out, and the committee was finding it difficult to make the front pages any more. However, the news of my forthcoming marriage to Marilyn Monroe was too tempting to be passed up. That it had some connections with my being subpoenaed was confirmed when Chairman Walter of HUAC sent word to Joseph Rauh, my lawyer, that he would be inclined to cancel my hearing altogether if Miss Monroe would consent to have a picture taken with him. The offer having been declined, the good chairman, as my hearing came to an end, proceeded to entreat me to write less tragically about our country. This lecture cost me some $40,000 in lawyer's fees, a year's suspended sentence for contempt of Congress, and a five-hundred-dollar fine. Not to mention about a year of inanition in my creative life.

But back to the late Forties and early Fifties; my fictional view of the period, my sense of its unreality was, like any impotence, a psychologically painful experience. A very similar paralysis at a certain point descended on Salem.

A new cautionary diction was swiftly ensconced in our way of talking to one another. In a country that a bit more than a quarter of a century earlier had given three million votes to Eugene Debs, the Socialist presidential candidate, the very word "socialism" was all but taboo. Words had gotten fearsome. As I would learn directly from students and faculty in Ann Arbor on a 1953 reporting visit for *Holiday* magazine, students were actually avoiding renting rooms in the houses run by the housing cooperative for fear of being labeled communist, so darkly suggestive was the word "cooperative." On hearing this, even I was amazed. But there was more—the head of orientation at the university told me that the FBI had enlisted professors to report on students voicing left-wing opinions and—some more comedy—they had also engaged students to report on professors with the same views. When I published these facts in *Holiday*, the Pontiac division of General Motors threatened to withdraw all advertising from the magazine if I ever appeared in it again; Ted Patrick, its editor, promptly badgered me for another piece, but I didn't know the reason why for some years.

It was a time—as I would learn only decades later from my FBI record, obtained under the Freedom of Information Act—when the FBI shadowed a guest of mine from a dinner party in my Brooklyn Heights house. The guest's name was blacked out, and I have been puzzling ever since about his identity. The point is that reading my FBI record in the Seventies I was not really surprised to learn this. In the Fifties everybody over forty believed that his phone was being tapped by the FBI, and they were probably right.

What is important here is that none of this was secret; everybody had a good idea of what was happening but, like me, felt helpless to reverse it. And to this moment I don't think I can adequately communicate the sheer density of the atmosphere of the time, for the outrageous had so suddenly become the accepted norm.

In the early Fifties, for example, with Elia Kazan, who had directed *All My Sons* and *Death of a Salesman*, I submitted a film script to Harry Cohn, the head of Columbia Pictures. It described the murderous corruption in the gangster-ridden Brooklyn longshoremen's union, whose leadership a group of rebel workers was trying to overthrow. Cohn read the script and called us to Hollywood, where he simply and casually informed us that, incredibly enough, he had first had the script vetted by the FBI and that they had seen nothing subversive in it; on the other hand, however, the head of the AFL motion picture unions in Hollywood, Roy Brewer, had condemned it outright as totally untrue communist propaganda, since, quite simply, there were no gangsters on the Brooklyn waterfront. Cohn, no stranger to the ways of gangsterism, having survived an upbringing in the tough, famously crime-ridden Five Points area of Manhattan, opined that Brewer was quite naturally only trying to protect Joe Ryan, his brother AFL union leader, the head of the AFL Brooklyn longshoremen. Brewer also threatened to call a strike of projectionists in any theater daring to show the film, no idle threat since he controlled *their* union. (Ryan, incidentally, would shortly go to Sing Sing prison for gangsterism. But that was not yet.) Meanwhile Cohn offered his solution to our problem with Brewer; he would produce the film if I would agree to make one simple change—the gangsters in the union were to be changed to communists. This would not be easy; for one thing, I knew all the communists on the waterfront; there was a total of two of them (both of whom, incidentally, in the following decade became millionaire businessmen).

And so I had to withdraw the script, which prompted an indignant telegram from Cohn: "As soon as we try to make the script pro-American you pull out." One understood not only the threat in those words but the cynicism; he certainly knew that it was the Mafia that controlled waterfront labor. Nevertheless, had I been a screenwriter in Hollywood, my career would have ended with this refusal to perform this patriotic idiocy. I have to say that there were days when I wondered if we would end in an unacknowledged, perhaps even comfortable American fascism.

But the theater had no such complications, no blacklist, not yet anyway; and I longed to respond to this climate of fear if only to protect my sanity. But where to find a transcendent concept? As I saw it, the difficulty was that we had grown so detached from any hard reality I knew about. It had become a world of signals, gestures, loaded symbolic words, and of rites and rituals. After all, the accusations of Party membership of film writers, actors, and directors never mentioned treasonous acts of any sort; what was in their brains was the question, and this created a kind of gestural phantom land. I did not yet think of it this way at the time, but looking back I think we had entered an ideological war, as I have said, and in such wars it was ideas and not necessarily actions that arouse anger and fear. And this was the heart of the darkness—that it had come rather quickly to be believed that a massive, profoundly organized conspiracy was in place and being carried forward mainly by a concealed phalanx of intellectuals, including labor people, teachers, professionals of all sorts, sworn to undermine the American government. And it was precisely the invisibility of ideas that was helping to frighten so many people. How could a play deal with this mirage world?

There was a fundamental absurdity in the Salem witch-hunt, of course, since witches don't exist, but this only helped relate it more to what we were going through. I can't recall the date any more, but to one of the Un-American Activities Committee hearings, several Hollywood writers brought piles of their film scripts for the committee to parse for any sign of Marxist propaganda. Of course there would hardly be anything that provocative in a Hollywood movie of the time, but in any case the committee refused to read the scripts, which I imagined was a further humiliation for the writers. But what a cruel irony, that these terribly serious Party members or sympathizers, in the attempt to prove themselves patriotic Americans, should feel compelled to demonstrate that their work was totally innocuous!

Paranoia breeds paranoia, of course, but below paranoia there lies a bristling, unwelcome truth, a truth so repugnant as to produce fantasies of persecution in order to conceal its existence. For example, the unwelcome truth denied by the Right was that the Hollywood writers accused of subversion were not a menace to the country or even the bearers of meaningful change. They wrote not propaganda but entertainment, some of it of a mildly liberal cast, to be sure, but most of it mindless; or when it was political, as with Preston Sturges or Frank Capra, entirely un-Marxist. In any real assessment, the worst they could do was contribute some money to Party coffers. But most Hollywood writers were only occasionally employed, and one doubted that their contributions could have made any difference to a party so completely disregarded by the American public and, in the bargain, so thoroughly impregnated by the FBI. Yet they had to be portrayed as an imminent danger to the republic.

As for the Left, its unacknowledged truth was more important for me. If nobody was being shot in our ideological war but merely vivisected by a headline or two, it struck me as odd, if understandable, that the accused were largely unable to passionately cry out their faith in the ideals of socialism. Attacks on the committees' right to demand that a citizen reveal his political beliefs, yes; but as for the idealistic canon of their own convictions, the accused were largely mute. It was a silence, incidentally, that in the public mind probably tended to confirm the committees' characterization of them as conspirators wrapping themselves in darkness. In their defense, the committees instantly shut down as irrelevant any attempts to explicate their ideas, any idealistic displays; but even outside, in public statements beyond the hearings, they relied almost wholly on legalistic defenses rather than the articles of the faith in which they unquestionably believed. The rare exception, like Paul Robeson's forthright declaration of faith in socialism as a cure for racism, was a rocket that momentarily lit up the sky, but even this, it must be said, was dimmed by his adamant refusal to recognize, at least publicly, what he knew to be the murder of two Soviet Jewish artists, his good friends, under Stalin's anti-Semitic decrees. It was one of the cruel twists of the time that while he would not in Washington display his outrage at the murders of his friends, he could in Moscow choose to sing a song in Yiddish that the whole public knew was his protest against Soviet anti-Semitism.

In a word, the disciplined avoidances of the Left bespoke a guilt that the Right found a way to exploit. A similar guilt seems to reside in all sorts of American dissidents, from Jehovah's Witnesses to homosexuals, no doubt because there is indeed an unacknowledged hostility in them toward the majority for whose cherished norms they feel contempt. It may be that guilt, perhaps, helped to account to some degree for the absence in our theater of plays that in any meaningful way confronted the deepening hysteria, which after all was the main event in our culture. Here was a significant part of a whole generation being forced to the wall, with hardly a word about it written for the stage. But it may simply have been the difficulty of finding a dramatic locution, a working symbolization that might illuminate the complex fog of the unspoken in which we were living.

To put it differently, stuffed in the pockets of both sides was a hidden agenda. On the Right it was, quite simply, their zeal to finally disgrace and wipe out what remained of New Deal attitudes, particularly that dreadful tendency in Americans to use government to help the helpless and to set limits around the more flagrant excesses of unbridled capitalism. Instead, their advertised goal was the defense of liberty against communism.

What the Left was not saying was that they were in truth dedicated to replacing capitalism with a society based on Marxist principles, and this could well mean the suppression of non-Marxists for the good of mankind. Instead, they were simply espousing constitutional protections against self-incrimination. Thus the fresh wind of a debate of any real content was not blowing through these hearings or these terrible years. The result was miasma, and on the Left, the guilt of the wholly or partially insincere. The Right, of course, convinced as it always is of its persecution, is certain that it represents the incoherent and stifled but genuine wishes of the majority and is thus a stranger to guilt.

How to express all this, and much more, on a stage? I began to despair of my own paralysis. I was a fisherman without a hook, a seaman without a sail.

On a lucky afternoon I happened upon a book, *The Devil in Massachusetts*, by Marion Starkey, a narrative of the Salem witch-hunt of 1692. I knew this story from my college reading more than a decade earlier, but now in this changed and darkened America it turned a wholly new aspect toward me, namely, the poetry of the hunt. Poetry may seem an odd word for a witch-hunt, but I saw now that there was something of the marvelous in the spectacle of a whole village, if not an entire province, whose imagination was literally captured by a vision of something that wasn't there.

In time to come the very notion of equating the Red hunt with the witch-hunt would be condemned by some as a deception. There certainly were communists, and there never were witches. But the deeper I moved into the 1690s, the further away drifted the America of the 1950s, and rather than the appeal of analogy I found something somewhat different to draw my curiosity and excitement.

First of all, anyone standing up in the Salem of 1692 who denied that witches existed would have faced immediate arrest, the hardest interrogation, and quite possibly the rope. Every authority—the church in New England, the kings of England and Europe, legal scholars like Lord Coke—not only confirmed their existence but never questioned the necessity of executing them when discovered. And of course, there was the authority of the Bible itself [Exodus 22:18]: "Thou shalt not suffer a witch to live." To deny witches was to deny the existence of the Devil's age-old war against God, and this, in effect, left God without an opposite and stripped him of his first purpose—which was to protect the Christian religion and good order in the world. Without evil, what need was there for the good? Without the Devil's ceaseless plotting, who needed God? The existence of witches actually went to prove the existence of God's war with evil. Indeed, it became obvious that to dismiss witchcraft was to forgo any understanding of how it came to pass that tens of thousands had been murdered as witches in Europe, from Scandinavia across to England, down through France and Spain. And to dismiss any relation to the hunt for subversives was to shut down an insight into not only the remarkably similar emotions but literally the numerous identical practices, both by officials and victims, in both outbreaks.

Of course there were witches, if not to most of us then certainly to everyone in Salem; and of course there were communists, but what was the content of their menace? That to me became the issue. Having been deeply influenced as a student by a Marxist approach to society (if less so as I grew older) and having known any number of Marxists and numerous sympathizers, I could simply not accept that these people were spies or even prepared to do the will of the Soviets in some future crisis. That such people had thought to find some hope of a higher ethic in the Soviets was not simply an American but a worldwide irony of catastrophic moral proportions, for their like could be found all over Europe and Asia. But as the Fifties dawned, they were stuck with the past they had chosen or been led into. Part of the unreality of the great anti-Left sweep of the Fifties was that it picked up a lot of people to expose and disgrace who had already in their hearts turned away from a pro-Soviet past but had no stomach for naming others who had merely shared their illusions. In short, then, the whole business for me remained what Truman had initially called it, not a moral crusade but a political red herring.

Nevertheless, the hunt captured some significant part of the American imagination, and its power demanded respect. And turning to Salem was like looking into a petri dish, a sort of embalmed stasis with its principal moving forces caught in stillness. One had to wonder what the human imagination fed on that could inspire neighbors and old friends to suddenly emerge overnight as hell's own furies secretly bent on the torture and destruction of Christians. More than a political metaphor, more than a moral tale, *The Crucible*, as it developed for me over the period of more than a year, became the awesome evidence of the power of the inflamed human imagination, the poetry of suggestion, and finally the tragedy of heroic resistance to a society possessed to the point of ruin.

As I stood in the stillness of the Salem courthouse, surrounded by the miasmic swirl of the images of the 1950s but with my head in 1692, what the two eras had in common was gradually gaining definition. In both was the menace of concealed plots, but most startling were the similarities in the rituals of defense and the investigative routines. Three hundred years apart, both prosecutions were alleging membership in a secret, disloyal group; should the accused confess, his honesty could be proved only in precisely the same way—by naming former confederates, nothing less. Thus the informer became the very proof of the plot and the investigation's necessity.

Finally, in both eras, since the enemy was first and foremost an idea, normal evidentiary proof of disloyal actions was either deemphasized, left in limbo, or not required at all; and indeed, actions finally became completely irrelevant; in the end, the charge itself, suspicion itself, all but became the evidence of disloyalty.

And, most interestingly, in the absence of provable disloyal actions both societies reached for very similar remedies. Something called the Attorney General's List was promulgated, a list of communist-front organizations, membership in which was declared not so much illegal as reason to suspect subversive conduct or intentions. If membership in an organization could not be called illegal, it could at least be made disgusting enough to lose you your job and reputation.

One might wonder whether many spies would be likely to be joining communist fronts, but liberals very possibly might and indeed had done so at various turns in the road, frequently making common cause with the Left and with communists during the New Deal period a decade earlier. The witch-hunt in 1692 had a not dissimilar evidentiary problem but a far more poetic solution. Most suspected people named by others as members of the Devil's conspiracy had not been shown to have actually *done* anything—not poisoning wells, setting barns on fire, sickening cattle, aborting babies or calves, nor somehow undermining the virtue of wives (the Devil having a double, phenomenally active penis, as everybody knew). Rather than acts, these suspect folk needed only to have had the bad luck to have been "seen" by witnesses consorting with the Devil. The witnesses might be dismally addled hysterics, but they might also be sober citizens who'd somehow gotten themselves suspected of practicing witchcraft and could clear themselves only by confessing and naming coconspirators. But, as in the Fifties, there was a supply of nonhysterical lawyers in and around the witch-hunt, as well as Harvard-educated ministers, and as accusations piled up one obvious fact was more and more irritating to them; as they well knew, the normal fulcrum of any criminal prosecution, namely, acts, deeds, crimes, and witnesses thereto, was simply missing. As for ordinary people, as devout as they might be and strictly literal about Biblical injunctions, they still clung to the old habit of expecting some sort of proof that an accused was guilty, in this case, of being an accomplice of the Devil.

To the rescue came not an Attorney General's List but a piece of poetry smacking of both legalistic and religious validity; it was called "spectral evidence." Spectral evidence, in normal jurisprudence, had been carefully winnowed out of the prosecutorial armory by judges and lawyers as being too manifestly open to fabrication. But now, with society under this hellish attack, the fateful decision was made to bring it back in, and the effect was like the bursting of a dam. Suddenly all the prosecution needed do was produce a witness who claimed to have seen not an accused person but what was called his familiar spirit, his living ghost, as it were, in the act of poisoning a pig or throwing a burning brand into a barn full of hay. You could be at home asleep in your bed, but your spirit could be crawling through your neighbor's bedroom window to feel up his wife.

The owner of that wandering spirit was thereupon obliged to account to the court for its crime. With the entrance of spectral evidence, the air was quickly filled with the malign spirits of those identified by good Christians as confederates of the Beast, and with this, of course, the Devil himself really did dance happily into Salem village and proceeded to take the place apart.

And in no time at all, people in Salem began *looking* at each other with new eyes and *hearing* sounds from neighbors' throats that they had never heard before and *thinking* about each other with new insights far deeper than their former blind innocence toward one another could have given them. And now, naturally, a lot of things that had been bewildering before suddenly made sense. Why, for instance, had London annulled all property deeds, causing everybody to be fighting with everybody else over boundary lines? Why was the congregation forever turning in on itself in fierce doctrinal fights and bitter arguments with ministers who one after another had had to flee the contentiousness of Salemites? Clearly, it was the Devil who had been muddling people's brains to set them against each other. But now, now at last, with the Lord's help, they had the gift of sight; the afflicted children had opened up their eyes to the plot in which, unknowingly, like innocent birds in a net, they were all caught. Now, with the admission of spectral evidence, they could turn to the traitors among them and run them to their deaths.

I spent some ten days in the Salem courthouse reading the crudely recorded trials of the 1692 outbreak, and it was striking how totally absent was the least sense of irony, let alone humor. I can't recall whether it was the provincial governor's nephew or son who with a college friend had come from Boston to watch the strange proceedings; at one point both boys burst out laughing at some absurd testimony. They were promptly jailed and were saved only by friends galloping down from Boston with a bribe for a guard, who let them escape from a very possible hanging.

Irony and humor were not exactly at a premium in the Fifties either. I was in my lawyer's office one afternoon to sign some contract, and a lawyer in the next office was asked to come in and notarize my signature. While this man was stamping the pages, I continued a discussion with my lawyer about the Broadway theater, which at one point I said was corrupt, that the art of theater had been totally displaced by the bottom line, that being all that really mattered any more. Looking up at me, the notarizing lawyer said, "That's a communist position, you know." I started to laugh until I saw the constraint in my lawyer's face, and despite myself I quickly sobered up.

I am glad, of course, that I managed to write *The Crucible*, but looking back I have often wished I'd had the temperament to have done an absurd comedy, since that is what the situation often deserved. There is something funny in the two sophisticated young Bostonians deciding to trot down to Salem to look in on the uproar among the provincials, failing to realize that they had entered a new age, a new kind of consciousness. I made a not dissimilar mistake as the Fifties dawned, and I continued to make it. A young film producer I didn't know asked me to write a script for a film about what was then called juvenile delinquency. A mystifying, unprecedented outbreak of gang violence had exploded all over New York. The city, in return for a good percentage of the profits, had contracted with this producer to open police stations, schools, and so on to his camera. I spent the summer of 1955 on Brooklyn streets, wrote an outline, which, incidentally, was much praised by the Catholic Youth Organization's leadership, and was ready to proceed with the script when an attack on me as a disloyal leftist was opened in the *New York World-Telegram and Sun*. The cry went up that so long as I was the screenwriter the city must cancel its contract with the producer. A hearing was arranged, attended by some twenty-two city commissioners, including those of the police, fire, welfare, and not least the sanitation departments, as well as two judges. At the long conference table there also sat a lady in sneakers and a sweater who produced a thick folder of petitions and statements I had signed, going back to my college years, provided to her, she said, by the House Un-American Activities Committee. I defended myself; I thought I was making some sense when the lady began literally screaming that I was killing the boys in Korea. She meant that I *personally* was doing it, as I could tell from the froth at the corners of her mouth, the fury in her eyes, and her finger pointing straight into my face. The vote was taken and came up one short of continuing the city's collaboration, and the film was killed that afternoon. As we were filing out, the two judges came up and offered their sympathy. I always wondered whether the crucial vote against me came from the sanitation department. But it was not a total loss; it would soon help with the writing of *The Crucible*, the suffocating sensation of helplessness before the spectacle of the impossible coming to pass.

Since you, or some of you, are historians, I have emphasized history in these remarks, but I doubt if I'd have written the play had the question of language not so powerfully drawn me on. The trial record in the Salem courthouse, of which I was allowed to borrow a photocopy, was written by ministers in a primitive shorthand. This condensation gave emphasis to a gnarled, densely packed language that suggested the country accents of a hard people. (A few years on, when Laurence Olivier staged his London production, he used the gruff Northumberland accent.) In any event, to lose oneself day after day in that record of human delusion was to know a fear, not perhaps for one's safety precisely but of the spectacle of perfectly intelligent people giving themselves over to a rapture of such murderous credulity. It was as though the absence of real evidence was itself a release from the burdens of this world; in love with the invisible, they moved behind their priests closer to that mystical communion that is anarchy and is called God. Evidence, in contrast, is effort; leaping to conclusions is a wonderful pleasure; and for a while there was a highly charged joy in Salem, for now that they could see through everything to the frightful plot being daily laid bare in court sessions, their days, formerly so eventless and long, were swallowed up in hourly revelations, news, surprises. *The Crucible*, I think, is less a polemic than it might have been had it not been filled with wonder at the protean imagination of man.

As a commercial entertainment, the play failed, of course. To start with, the title: Nobody knew what a crucible was. Most of the critics, as sometimes does happen, never caught on to the play's ironical substructure, and the ones who did were nervous about validating a work that was so unkind to the same basic principles as underlay the current hunt for Reds, sanctified as it was. On opening night, old acquaintances shunned me in the theater lobby, and even without air-conditioning the house was noticeably cool. But the problem was also with the temperature of the production. The director, a great name in the theater of the Twenties, Thirties, and into the Forties, had decided that the play, which he believed a classic, should be staged like what he called a Dutch painting. In Dutch paintings of groups, everyone is always looking front. We knew this from the picture on the wooden boxes of Dutch Masters cigars. Unfortunately, on a stage such rigidity only propels an audience to the exits. It would be several years before a gang of young actors, setting up chairs in the ballroom of the McAlpin Hotel, set fire to the audience and convinced the critics; and the play at last took off and soon found its place in the world. There were cheering critics this time, but now of course McCarthy was dead, and the fever on whose waves of heat he had spread his wings had cooled, and more and more people found it possible to face the dying embers and read the terrible message in them.

It is said that no one would buy land in Salem for a hundred years. The very ground was accursed. Salem's people, in the language of the time, had broke charity with one another.

But the Devil, as he usually does after such paroxysms, had the last laugh. Salem refuses to fade into history. A few years ago the foundation of an old colonial-era church in a town near Salem began to sag. The contractor engaged to make repairs dug out some of the loose stones and crawled underneath to inspect matters. There he discovered what looked like barely buried human skeletons. Harvard scientists were called in and confirmed that the remains of some twenty-two people were under the church. Now no one has ever known exactly where in Salem the gibbet was located, but the bodies of the twenty-two people hanged there for practicing witchcraft had never been found. Moreover, according to one legend, as their ultimate punishment they were denied Christian burial.

The scientists wanted to remove the skeletons and try to identify them. But some quite aged parishioners, descendants not only of the witchcraft victims but no doubt of their persecutors as well, were adamantly opposed. The younger church members were all for it but decided to wait until the elders had passed away rather than start a ruckus about the matter. In short, even after three centuries, the thing, it seems, cannot find its serene, uncomplicated end.

And, indeed, something very similar occurred in Salem three hundred years ago. After the hunt had blown itself out, after Cotton Mather, having whipped up the hysteria to and beyond the point of murder, finally conceded that demanding the admission of spectral evidence had been his dreadful mistake, the legislature awarded to some, though not all, of the victims' families a few pounds' damages along with a mild apology: "Sorry we hanged your mother," and so forth. But in the true Salem style of solemn bewilderment, this gesture apparently lacked a certain requisite disorder, so they also included reparations to some informers whose false accusations had hanged people. Victims and victimizers, it was all the same in the end. I suppose it was just the good old American habit of trying to keep everybody happy.

The Crucible is my most-produced play, here and abroad. It seems to be one of the few shards of the so-called McCarthy period that survives. And it is part of the play's history, I think, that to people in so many parts of the world its story seems so like their own. I think it was in the mid-Seventies—dates at my age take on the viscosity of poached eggs—but in any case, I happened to be at my publishers when another Grove Press author came in. Her eyes filled with tears at our introduction, and she hastened to explain: She was Yuen Cheng, author of *Life and Death in Shanghai*, the story of her six-year solitary confinement during the Cultural Revolution. It seems that on her release, an old friend, a theater director, took her to see a new production of his in Shanghai, *The Crucible*, a play and author she had never heard of. As she listened to it, the interrogations sounded so precisely the same as the ones she and others had been subject to by the Cultural Revolutionaries that she couldn't believe a non-Chinese had written it. And picking up the English text, she was amazed, she said, not least by the publication date, which of course was more than a decade before the Cultural Revolution. A highly educated woman, she had been living with the conviction that such a perversion of just procedure could happen only in the China of a debauched revolution! I have had similar reactions from Russians, South Africans, Latin Americans and others who have endured dictatorships, so universal is the methodology of terror portrayed in *The Crucible*. In fact, I used to think, half seriously—although it was not far from the truth—that you could tell when a dictator was about to take power in a Latin American country or when one had just been overthrown, by whether *The Crucible* was suddenly being produced there.

The net of it all, I suppose, is that I have come, rather reluctantly, to respect delusion, not least of all my own. There are no passions quite as hot and pleasurable as those of the deluded. Compared with the bliss of delusion—its vivid colors, blazing lights, explosions, whistles, and sheer liberating joys—the dull search for evidence is a deadly bore. In *Timebends*, my autobiography, I have written at some length about my dealings with Soviet cultural controllers and writers when as president of International PEN I would attempt to impress its democratic values upon them in their treatment of writers. Moving about there and in East Germany, Hungary, and Czechoslovakia in communist times, it was only by main force that I could dredge up memories of my old idealism, which I had attached to what in reality had turned out to be little more than a half-feudal society led by an unelected elite. How could this possibly be? I can only think that a man in a rushing river will grasp at any floating thing passing by. History, or whatever piece of its debris one happens to connect with, is a great part of the answer. For me it was my particular relation to the collapse of key institutions in the Great Depression, the sometimes scary anti-Semitism I kept running into and the Left's thankful condemnation of it, the Spanish Civil War and the all-but-declared pro-fascist sympathies of the British, and Roosevelt's unacknowledged collaboration with their arms blockade of the republic (the so-called Non-Intervention Policy). Indeed, on Franco's victory, Roosevelt told Secretary of the Interior Harold Ickes, according to Ickes's autobiography, that his Spanish policy was "the worst mistake I ever made." In a word, out of the Great Crash of 1929, America and the world seemed to awaken to a new sense of social responsibility, something which to the young seemed very much like love. My heart was with the Left if only because the Right hated me enough to want to kill me, as the Germans amply proved. And now, of course, the most blatant and foulest anti-Semitism is in Russia, leaving people like me filled not so much with surprise as a kind of wonder at the incredible amount of hope there once was and how it disappeared and whether in time it will ever come again, attached to some new illusion.

And so there is hardly a week that passes when I don't ask the unanswerable—what am I now convinced of that will turn out to be ridiculous? And yet one can't forever stand on the shore; at some point, even if filled with indecision, skepticism, reservation and doubt, you either jump in or concede that life is forever elsewhere.

Which I daresay was one of the major impulses behind the decision to attempt *The Crucible*. Salem village, that pious, devout settlement at the very edge of white civilization, had taught me—three centuries before the Russo–American rivalry and the issues it raised—that a kind of built-in pestilence was nestled in the human mind, a fatality forever awaiting the right conditions for its always unique, forever unprecedented outbreak of alarm, suspicion, and murder. And to people wherever the play is performed, on any of the six continents, there is always a certain amazement that the same terror that had happened to them had happened before to others. It is all very strange. On the other hand, the Devil is known to lure people into forgetting precisely what it is vital for them to remember—how else could his endless reappearances always come with such marvelous surprise?

1999

The Price—The Power of the Past

The sources of a play are both obvious and mysterious. *The Price* is first of all about a group of people recollected, as it were, in tranquility. The central figures, the New York cop Victor Franz and his elder brother, Walter, are not precise portraits of people I knew long, long ago but close enough, and Gregory Solomon, the old furniture dealer, is as close as I could get to reproducing a dealer's Russian-Yiddish accent that still tickles me whenever I hear it in memory.

First, the bare bones of the play's story: the Great Crash of 1929 left Victor and Walter to care for their widowed father, who had been ruined in the stock market collapse and was helpless to cope with life. While Victor, loyal to the father, dropped out of college to earn a living for them both and ended up on the police force, Walter went on to become a wealthy surgeon.

The play begins decades later on the attic floor of the decrepit brown-stone where the cop and his father had lived, surrounded by piles of furniture from their old apartment that the father had clung to. Now the building, owned by the father's brother, is to be torn down, so the furniture must be sold.

The conflict of how to divide the proceeds cuts open the long-buried lives of both men, as well as that of Victor's wife, Esther, and reveals the choices each has made and the price each has paid. Through it all weaves the antic ninety-year-old furniture dealer Gregory Solomon, who is yards ahead of them as he tries to shepherd them away from the abyss toward which he knows they are heading.

Behind the play—almost any play—are more or less secret responses to other works of the time, and these may emerge as disguised imitation or as outright rejection of the dominating forms of the hour. *The Price* was written in 1967, and since nobody is going to care any more, it may as well be admitted that in some part it was a reaction to two big events that had come to overshadow all others in that decade. One was the seemingly permanent and morally agonizing Vietnam War, the other a surge of avant-garde plays that to one or another degree fit the absurd styles. I was moved to write a play that might confront and confound both.

I enjoyed watching some of the absurd plays—my first theater experiences were with vaudeville in the Twenties, after all, and absurdist comics like Bert Williams and Willie Howard, with their delicious proto–shaggydog stories and skits, were favorites. More, for a while in the Thirties our own William Saroyan, who with all his failings was an authentic American inventor of a domestic absurdist attitude, had held the stage. One would not soon forget his *Time* magazine subscription salesman reading—not without passion— the entire page-long list of names of *Time*'s reporters, editors, subeditors, fact checkers, department heads and dozens of lesser employees, to a pair of Ozark hillbillies dressed in their rags, seated on their rotting porch and listening with rapt incomprehension.

But the Sixties was a time when a play with recognizable characters, a beginning, middle and end was routinely condemned as "well made" or ludicrously old-fashioned. (That plays with no characters, beginning or end were not called "badly made" was inevitable when the detonation of despised rules in all things was a requisite for recognition as modern. That beginnings, middles, and ends might not be mere rules but a replication of the rise and fall of human life did not frequently come up.)

Often against my will, however, I found myself enjoying the new abstract theater; for one thing, it was moving us closer to a state of dream, and for dreams I had nothing but respect. But as the dying continued in Vietnam with no adequate resistance to it in the country, the theater, so it seemed to me, risked trivialization by failing to confront the bleeding, at least in a way that could reach most people. In its way, *Hair* had done so by offering a laid-back lifestyle opposed to the aggressive military-corporate one. But one had to feel the absence—not only in theater but everywhere—of any interest in what had surely given birth to Vietnam, namely, its roots in the past.

Indeed, the very idea of an operating continuity between past and present in any human behavior was démodé and close to a laughably old-fashioned irrelevancy. My impression, in fact, was that playwrights were either uninterested in or incapable of presenting antecedent material altogether. Like the movies, plays seemed to exist entirely in the now; characters had either no past or none that could somehow be directing present actions. It was as though the culture had decreed amnesia as the ultimate mark of reality.

As the corpses piled up, it became cruelly impolite if not unpatriotic to suggest the obvious, that we were fighting the past; our rigid anticommunist theology, born of another time two decades earlier, made it a sin to consider Vietnamese Reds as nationalists rather than Moscow's and Beijing's yapping dogs. We were fighting in a state of forgetfulness, quite as though we had not aborted a national election in Vietnam and divided the country into separate halves when it became clear that Ho Chi Minh would be the overwhelming favorite for the presidency. This was the reality on the ground, but unfortunately it had to be recalled in order to matter. And so fifty thousand Americans, not to mention millions of Vietnamese, paid with their lives to support a myth and a bellicose denial.

As always, it was the young who paid. I was fifty-three in 1968, and if the war would cost me nothing materially, it wore away at the confidence that in the end Reason had to return lest all be lost. I was not sure of that any more. Reason itself had become unaesthetic, something art must at any cost avoid.

The Price grew out of a need to reconfirm the power of the past, the seedbed of current reality, and the way to possibly reaffirm cause and effect in an insane world. It seemed to me that if, through the mists of denial, the bow of the ancient ship of reality could emerge, the spectacle might once again hold some beauty for an audience. If the play does not utter the word Vietnam, it speaks to a spirit of unearthing the real that seemed to have very nearly gone from our lives.

Which is not to deny that the primary force driving *The Price* was a tangle of memories of people. Still, these things move together, idea feeding characters and characters deepening idea.

Nineteen sixty-eight, when the play is set, was already nearly forty years since the Great Crash, the onset of the transformed America of the Depression decade. It was then that the people in this play had made the choices whose consequences they had now to confront. The Thirties had been a time when we learned the fear of doom and had stopped being kids for a while; the time, in short, when, as I once noted about the era, the birds came home to roost and the past became present. And that Depression cataclysm, incidentally, seemed to teach that life indeed had beginnings, middles and a consequential end.

Plays leave a wake behind them as they pass into history, with odd objects bobbing about in it. Many of these, in the case of *The Price*, are oddly funny for such a serious work. I had just finished writing it and with my wife, Inge Morath, went to the Caribbean for a week's vacation. Hurrying onto the beach in our first hour there, we noticed a man standing ankle-deep in the water, dressed in shorts and a wide-brimmed plantation hat, who looked a lot like Mel Brooks. In fact, he *was* Mel Brooks. After a few minutes' chat I asked if there was any fishing here. "Oh, God, yes," he said, "yesterday there was one came in right there," and he pointed a yard away in the shallow water. "Must have been three feet long. He was dead. But he may be over there today," he added, pointing down the beach.

He wanted to know if I was writing, and I said we were casting a new play called *The Price*, and he asked what it was about. "Well," I said, "there are these two brothers . . ."

"Stop, I'm crying!" he yelled, frightening all the Protestants lying on the beach.

Then there was the letter from the Turkish translator, who assured me that he had made only one change in the text. At the very end, he wrote, after the two brothers nearly come to blows and part forever, unreconciled and angry, there follows a quiet, rather elegiac moment with the old furniture dealer, the cop, and his wife.

Just as they are leaving the stage, the translator explained, he had to bring back the elder brother, Walter, to fall tearfully into the cop's arms. This, because the audience would fear that *the actors themselves* would have had to have a vendetta that could only end in a killing if they parted as unreconciled as the script required. And so, out of the depths, rose the Turkish past . . .

1999

Subsidized Theater

The commercial system of theatrical production in New York is some two centuries old. In contrast, theater has been carried on in various parts of the West for a couple of thousand years but under very different production circumstances. The New York system is thus a sport, something created to reflect a vibrant capitalism with its joy in risk-taking and the excitement of the win-all-or-lose-all rodeo. We have arrived—in New York—at the expiration time of that theatrical way of life as far as straight plays are concerned. The system no longer works for non-musical theater and hasn't in years. The time has come to consider alternatives.

I have sometimes wondered if there ever was what one could call a "healthy" theatrical circumstance. The classical Greek situation, turning out one masterpiece after another, usually appears to us as serene, like some great ship cruising stormy seas unperturbed by the tons of water crashing down on its decks. But then one recalls stories of the *choreaqi,* the men of wealth chosen for the honor of paying the bills for the chorus, who tried as best they could to duck the distinction. And to read almost any twenty pages of Aristophanes is to sense the backbiting and posturing and nastiness surrounding Greek theater. Much the same mess seems to have prevailed in Elizabethan times, and Molière's, Strindberg's, Chekhov's, Shaw's, O'Casey's, just as in our own.

Theater production these days is a problem with not even an acceptable definition let alone a solution. The theater owner will tell you that it is simply that costs are too high even as he takes fifty-two percent of the gross. Nor is the stagehand or author or actor likely to look to himself for the source of the difficulty. All one can say is that the play that cost less than forty thousand to produce a generation ago now comes in at a million and a half or even two million and rising, the price of a ticket soaring from four or six dollars to seventy-five and up. It is a system which has almost literally eaten its own body alive.

In the belly of the beast, as always, is the money and the conflicts it breeds. Where the state finances production, as it partially does in England and other parts of the world, its built-in urge to censor has to be curbed; where private investment does so, it is greed that must be bridled lest it lead down into the swamp of theatrical triviality where the great mass of the public is alleged to live and hence the promise of the biggest returns. Theater is born to trouble as the sparks fly upward, but we are in more than trouble now and an altogether new spirit will have to infuse those interested in changing—perhaps saving is the word—the production of plays on a professional level.

Amid the gratitude, which I share, for the annual arrival of fine British plays on and off Broadway, it is useful to remember that every one of them, practically with no exceptions, came out of subsidized theaters. It is not possible to imagine that a Pinter, a Stoppard, a Hare, a Frayn, would have been nurtured in London's commercial West

End. They are all too chancey and their audiences admittedly too limited to warrant investment-for-profit. The British public, in short, has been financing a significant part of New York's theater for a long time now.

The minds of probably most American politicians—and even some critics and editorialists—seem to curdle at the idea of subsidizing any art, least of all theater. To them, subsidized theater seems to imply a crutch to help hold erect failed artists who can't make it in the tough, Darwinian for-profit arena. After all, a good number of people have gotten rich on doing theater work, why can't these mendicants? And besides, isn't theater attendance on Broadway higher than ever? And if almost all the increase has gone to musicals, then so be it—the public has decided it doesn't want straight plays. The system operates like any other market and if one can't manage on its terms maybe he ought to give up and go into another line of work.

With the richest theater in America unable to produce a single new straight play season after season, leaving only a very occasional revival on the boards in that category, one is given the reason as being the failure of playwrights who somehow have forgotten how to do the job. That hundreds, thousands of plays are written in this country every year, without a single one good enough for professional production in our greatest entertainment city, is nothing short of a statistical marvel. So extreme is the situation that one is driven to drastic explanations; is it possible, one wonders, that this generation of New York producers, who will travel to England or even Australia to sign up a new hit play, are not competent to read and judge a script but only its reviews, or by having sat in the midst of a laughing or weeping audience to decide to reach for their contracts? I find this illiteracy far more likely than the idea that the playwriting art has simply gone to earth forever in a United States of two hundred and fifty million souls.

For reasons I can't pretend to understand, there are never more than a handful of playwrights in any age. Poets, novelists, essayists show up in numbers, but playwrights come in two's and three's. We presently have many more than this handful but the most commercialized theater in the world has no place for them. Can it be that the commercial organization of professional theater is, in fact, preventing the flowering of theater, most especially in New York, where theater is so important to the economy as well as the spirit of the place?

But why bother even to complain about the Broadway theater when it is clearly so artistically bankrupt where production of original straight plays is concerned? There are good reasons for caring, most of them forgotten. In the two- or three-hundred seat off-Broadway theater, whatever its charm, it is next to impossible to produce plays with casts larger than half a dozen, not to mention those requiring multiple sets. Thus, the esthetic of playwriting itself is affected by this total commercialization, and playwriting becomes of necessity a constricted technique. I do not believe that, for example, most of my own plays would have found production on today's Broadway, and what would one do with *The Crucible* on a shoebox stage with its twenty-one characters and several sets? I don't think *Salesman* would have been produced by the present breed of Broadway producers because it is too sad—and in fact even in 1949 there was pressure to find a more upbeat title, the producer actually paying to poll theater audiences asking if they'd like to see a play called *Death of a Salesman*. Practically none, quite naturally, said they would. Off-Broadway has its uses but creating plays of breadth and physical size is not one of them. Broadway theaters, on the other hand, once welcomed plays of size, which of course is not to deny that in any age the producer's dream is a very funny play with a cast of two in one set.

As things stand now, it is almost impossible to imagine an actor making a lifelong career acting in the theater. The off-Broadway theater is basically subsidized by people without families to support, its young underpaid actors whose eye is really on television or films, not theater. Much is made of the great British actors, but almost without exception the Oliviers, Richardsons, Gielguds, Gambons, Guinnesses came out of subsidized theaters where they developed their craft in great roles in classic plays. There is no play in New York where anything like this kind of muscle building is possible. We have wonderfully talented actors who do incredible things in the three- or four-week rehearsal period normally allowed them, but if a bottom-line theater, which is what we have, cannot afford longer rehearsals it doesn't justify making a virtue of our deprivation.

If we have theaters, we don't have Theater, which is not real estate but a collection of people of talent whose main interest and devotion is the creation of something beautiful. This is difficult to discuss because it is basically about an atmosphere. Playwrights as different as Clifford Odets and Eugene O'Neill have hated the absolute commercialization of New York theater, and it is hard to think of any artist who has loved it, including some who have made fortunes out of it. My own impression is that the atmosphere has in some ways degenerated even further than when the earlier generation complained of it. Perhaps it is the immensity of the investment required now, but where there was once a certain comity between producer and artist, a certain collaborative equality between people with different but complimentary functions, it seems now like merely one more employer-employee relationship. A real power shift seems to be taking place. Producers speak now of having "given" a production to an author, quite as though profit-making were not at all involved in driving the deal but the generosity and largesse of one who is not only the holder of a lease on a theater building but the proprietor of the art itself. There is some dangerous, if superficial, logic in this; the businessman is always around but the author, director, and actors vanish sometimes for years before they show up again with a new play and new roles. So that the illusion can easily grow that the business of theater is business, and the art rather incidental. Indeed, the pressure is actually on now by certain producers to junk the traditional royalty arrangements with authors, who of course have for several generations retained ownership and control of their scripts, and to replace it with the producer's taking over if not actual ownership then the right to make any script changes he desires. Some think we are moving into the Hollywood system, where the producer buys or commissions scripts and the author moves down to the bottom of the totem pole, without control or contractual rights once he is paid. Indeed, the Hollywood system sprang from the old Broadway practice of producers buying plays and even attaching their names to them as authors, as the famed John Golden did for many a year before the Dramatists Guild was organized to protect writers.

Broadway has been pronounced dead too many times for me to do so again, but one thing is new—its impotence before the challenge to produce new plays. It is now a secondhand merchandiser of plays from abroad or, on occasion, one of the off-Broadway theaters. That there is an audience there can be no question—the success of revivals of famous, proven works over the past decade has shown that a sizable number of people want to see straight plays on Broadway. It is the production system that has broken. It needs replacement by a new, broader vision, a rededication to essentials—the writer, the director, the actor, the audience. Whoever can bring these elements together deserves praise and gratitude, but excepting for occasional flukes, the risks have clearly grown too great now for private capital alone to manage any more. Something not particularly novel, of course, but rather as old as theater itself awaits us—at least partial subsidization of production by either private or public funds or a mixture of both.

Having worked in two great state-subsidized theaters—in China and Sweden, where I directed *Death of a Salesman*—I can testify to some of their failings as well as their virtues. Inevitably, their worst problem, I think, is bureaucracy. People nestle into state jobs and can't be blasted out of them regardless of competency or even sobriety. (In Stockholm I had two drunks operating a hidden platform on my *Salesman* set, and on their cue to lower a bed they were found in the basement playing a bleary, oblivious card game. As union men they could not be fired, but one of them felt he had so humiliated himself that he resigned his position.) It is hard to see any ready solution to this dilemma. But friction arises with anything that moves, and these theaters are nevertheless often capable of work far beyond what any New York theater can presently contemplate. Ingmar Bergman's *Peer Gynt* and the *Teahouse* of the Beijing People's Art Theater, which I happened to see, were of a conceptual grandeur, a lyricism and exactitude of acting that simply cannot be achieved in our hit-and-run, semi-hysterical production process. They were reminders once again that every play of the European masters of the nineteenth and twentieth centuries has come out of subsidized theaters. From Brecht to Strindberg and Ibsen and reaching back to Shakespeare and the Greeks, there was a partial or complete state subsidy or, as in Elizabethan times, a noble patronage supporting the art.

But there may not necessarily be one single solution to the problem. It has to be said that in our hazardous, high-stakes gambling house called Broadway the thrill of the dice throw can be exhilarating, and in times past when productions did not yet bear killing costs the flow of new American plays was greatly admired by theater folk in other countries. But that was then and this is now.

My own experience indicates that the best system is most probably a mixed one, with the private commercial theater coexisting with the subsidized one. Their functions may often overlap but in general the private theater would most likely offer entertainment while the other would be free to pursue its more difficult theatrical dreams.

The subsidized theater can indeed settle into an institutionalized stupor if allowed to drift that way, but the British, for one, have shown that it need not, or at least not for long. In any case, if there are other alternatives than I have named to the present system, let them be heard and debated.

Theater is not going to die. To paraphrase Carl Sandburg, there will always be the young strangers, people desperate to act, to interpret what they have seen, and now and again a writer gathering stray beams of light into a flaming focal point. Most of these now dream of the filmic media, but some of that attraction is due to the present theater system which ignores or repels the young rather than working to open itself to them. Whole generations have passed now which have gone through the taste-forming years of youth without having seen a play, but only film. Would people want music who have never heard music? A responsible subsidized theater would, as it does elsewhere, open the world of plays to students. If it was always at bottom an entertainment machine devised to make money and fame for a few, commercial production nevertheless did keep open a certain space for writers, directors, and actors with serious intentions and visions of a world they passionately wished to make real. No more. That whole developmental function has simply been passed along to off-Broadway and academia while commercial Broadway waits to skim off some floating drops of cream.

2000

Index